Cavalryman of the Lost Cause

A BIOGRAPHY OF J. E. B. STUART

Jeffry D. Wert

SIMON & SCHUSTER

New York London Toronto Sydney

Simon & Schuster
1230 Avenue of the Americas
New York, NY 10020

Copyright © 2008 by Jeffry D. Wert

Designed by Paul Dippolito

Maps by George Skoch

Manufactured in the United States of America

ISBN-13: 978-0-7432-7819-5

Book Club Edition

To Jason, Kathy, Rachel, Gabriel, Natalie, and Grant,
with love

Contents

Preface and Acknowledgments

Gettysburg has defined, like an indelible stain, James Ewell Brown "Jeb" Stuart's place in Confederate history. Within days of the campaign's conclusion, his famous "ride" brought forth a chorus of criticism that has not been stilled since. In the search for the reasons for the defeat at Gettysburg—the haunting "if" of the Southern past—Stuart remains a primary culprit. His performance and that of others, notably James Longstreet, have elicited uncounted pages of historical inquiry. The controversy will not likely end soon.

There was, however, much more to Jeb Stuart the man and the soldier than those eight days between June 25 and July 2, 1863. He was a complex and fascinating man, a loving husband and father, a devoted Confederate, and one of America's finest horse soldiers. At the time of his death, his renown among the Southern populace rivaled that of Robert E. Lee and Stonewall Jackson. In their struggle for independence, Southerners required a knight, a cavalier who embodied their image of bygone days, and Stuart fulfilled that need.

These reasons and more drew me as a historian to Stuart. My book is the first full-scale biography of him to appear in more than two decades. In those intervening years additional manuscript collections have become available and modern scholarship has opened new paths for study. I have integrated primary sources with the finest recent works. My biography is replete with the words of Stuart and of those who knew him well and fought beside him from the frontier West to the campaigns and battles of the Civil War.

Central to my narrative are Stuart's relationships with his wife, Flora Cooke Stuart, his superior officers, and his subordinates. Not only the soldier, but the man intrigued me. Behind the image of a knight in plumed hat and cape was a deeply religious person, an unbending believer in the justness of the Confederate cause, a student of warfare, a firm disciplinarian, and a man whose ambition and craving for public acclaim burned intensely.

My judgments and conclusions will not silence the debate about Stuart. Nor should they. The craft of history teems with disagreement. Like historians and biographers before me, I have examined closely Stuart's "ride" to Gettysburg. Whether justly or not, it has framed historical judgments about him and has been a central tenet of the Lost Cause interpretation of Confederate defeat. It is this controversy and the man himself that drew me to undertake this biography.

A work of history arises from the collective efforts of individuals. To them, I extend my deepest appreciation and gratitude. Their knowledge, assistance, and insight have made this a better book. All errors of omission and commission are solely mine, however.

I wish to thank the librarians and archivists at the institutions cited in the Bibliography for their unflagging patience and understanding.

Other individuals merit my particular gratitude and recognition:

Dr. Richard Sommers, Head of Patron Services, and his superb staff at the United States Army Military History Institute; E. Lee Shepard, Director of Manuscripts and Archives, and Frances S. Pollard, Director of Library Services, Virginia Historical Society; Dr. Ervin L. Jordan, Jr., Records Manager and Research Archivist, Special Collections, University of Virginia; Julie Holcomb, Archivist, Pearce Civil War Collection, Navarro College; John Coski, Historian and Library Director, and Ruth Ann Coski, Librarian, the Museum of the Confederacy; interlibrary loan staff, Centre County (Pennsylvania) Library.

Joseph Pierro, historian and author, for sharing unpublished material.

Michael Musick, historian and retired Civil War authority at the National Archives, for guiding me through the untapped collections at this national treasure.

Robert K. Krick, historian, author, unmatched authority on the Army of Northern Virginia, and valued friend, for providing me access to his files on the army.

Robert E. L. Krick, historian with the National Park Service and author, for sharing with me material on Stuart's June 1862 ride and Yellow Tavern.

Ted Alexander, chief historian, Antietam National Battlefield, and good friend, for reading several of my chapters and offering his comments.

Horace Mewborn, historian, author, authority on Confederate cavalry, and good friend, for reading the entire manuscript, correcting my errors, and challenging my conclusions.

Tom Perry, an authority on the Stuart family and prime mover behind the salvation of Laurel Hill, the Stuart family homesite, for reading the majority of the manuscript, offering insight into the Stuart family, and correcting my errors.

Nicholas Picerno, Sr., a noted Civil War collector and longtime family friend, for his encouragement.

Daniel Laney, Civil War historian and preservationist and dear family friend, for reading chapters, offering astute criticism, and valued support.

Robert Gottlieb, president, Trident Media Group, and my agent, for his advice and his unwavering support.

Bob Bender, my editor, for his skillful editing, wise counsel, and friendship; Johanna Li, associate editor, for her unfailing patience, kindness, and assistance; and Fred Chase, copy editor, for his skillful work.

Our son, Jason Wert, our daughter-in-law, Kathy Wert, our grandchildren, Rachel and Gabriel Wert; our daughter, Natalie Wert Corman, and our son-in-law, Grant Corman, for their cherished love and for blessings too numerous to count. For all that they mean to Gloria and me, this book is dedicated to them.

My wife, Gloria, who has been by my side throughout all these years of work. Without her skills, patience, and love, none of this would be possible or worth the journey.

Jeffry D. Wert
Centre Hall, Pennsylvania
October 2, 2007

Chapter One

Son of Virginia

R UMORS HUNG OVER the camps of Confederate cavalrymen on June 24, 1863. Throughout the day their regiments had gathered, riding toward the village of Salem in the Virginia Piedmont. Officers had ordered them to unsaddle their horses for the first time in ten days and to rest. But as one of them informed his family in a letter, "it is the opinion of a good many that we will cross the Potomac in a few days."[1]

To the west, across the Blue Ridge Mountains, strings of Southern infantry, artillery, and wagons filled the roads in the Shenandoah Valley, angling toward the Potomac River and Maryland. Farther north, the vanguard of General Robert E. Lee's Army of Northern Virginia was spreading across southern Pennsylvania, heralding a major Confederate thrust into the Keystone State. A pair of cavalry brigades sealed the gaps of the Blue Ridge, protecting the final elements of Lee's army as they marched north through the Valley. At Salem, meanwhile, the cavalrymen—numbering nearly 5,500 in three brigades—rested and awaited orders.[2]

As many of them had speculated, their halt at Salem was to be brief. They had been brought together by their commander, Major General James Ewell Brown "Jeb" Stuart. Lee had issued orders to Stuart to join the army in Pennsylvania, either by passing around the Union Army of the Potomac or by following Lee's infantry and artillery units on their march through the Shenandoah Valley toward Pennsylvania. If Stuart chose to move east and around the Federals, Lee cautioned him only to do so "without hindrance." The instructions were vague and discretionary, but given to an officer Lee trusted.[3]

At thirty years of age, Stuart was the youngest of Lee's senior officers. Devoted to the cause of Southern independence, Stuart was one of the Confederacy's most renowned soldiers. He relished the pageantry of warfare, carefully crafting and guarding his reputation. His and his men's exploits had inspired Southerners and buttressed their morale. Beneath the veneer of a cavalier's trappings of a plumed hat and gold-braided uniform was a gifted cavalryman with the soul of a warrior. He had organized his command, drilled horses and men regularly, enforced discipline, and led them with unquestioned personal courage.

Under Stuart's leadership, the Confederate horsemen had dominated mounted operations in the East for two years. They had fought with skill and élan. Recently, however, Union cavalrymen had carried the fight to the Southerners, meeting them saber to saber. After the Yankees attacked Stuart's men at Brandy Station on June 9, igniting a day-long engagement, Southern newspapers editorialized that Stuart had been surprised and nearly defeated. He knew of the criticism and believed it to be unjust.

Now, as he rode toward Salem to join his command, an opportunity lay ahead of him, not to the west but to the east. Not long into the morning of June 25, shielded by the night, Stuart led his veteran troopers on a road familiar not for its landmarks but for where it led. Within hours he would face a fateful decision. The course he chose shaped events in a campaign that climaxed at Gettysburg. His choice has become central to history's judgment of him as a man and as a soldier.

JAMES EWELL BROWN Stuart was born at Laurel Hill, Patrick County, Virginia, at 11:30 P.M., Wednesday, February 6, 1833, the fourth son and eighth child of Archibald and Elizabeth Pannill Stuart. The parents named their new son for Judge James Ewell Brown, the husband of Archibald's sister, Anne Dabney Stuart Brown. Family members and childhood friends called the boy James, Jim, or Jimmy.[4]

The Stuarts were Scotch-Irish and had lived in Virginia for nearly a century at the time of James's birth. His great-great-grandfather and his father's namesake, Archibald Stuart, had emigrated from Londonderry to Pennsylvania in 1726. A Presbyterian, Archibald had helped in fomenting a rebellion against authorities who were persecuting members of the church. Charged with treason, he left his wife, Janet, and two children and fled to America. Janet and the children joined him several years later, and in 1738, the family settled in Augusta County, Virginia. The couple had two more children, including a second son, Alexander, born in 1733 or 1734.[5]

Alexander Stuart, James's great-grandfather, lived his entire life in the Shenandoah Valley of Virginia. During the American Revolution, Stuart served as a major in a militia regiment, commanded by Colonel Samuel McDowell. At Guilford Court House, North Carolina, on March 15, 1781, Stuart led the regiment in the fighting, fell wounded, and was captured. Released after six months in captivity, he returned to Augusta County in the Valley.[6]

Major Stuart was married three times, widowed twice. His second wife, Mary Moore Paxton, bore him a son and namesake, Alexander, born on May 11, 1770. According to a letter written by Flora Cooke Stuart, James's future wife, it was this third generation of Stuarts in America who changed the spelling of their surname from Stewart to Stuart. Her statement has not been verified by other accounts.[7]

The second Alexander Stuart, James's grandfather, had a distinguished career in the law and politics as a federal and state jurist in Illinois and Missouri. Like his father, Judge Stuart was widowed twice and had three wives. His first wife was Nancy Anne Dabney, whose kinfolk included Thomas Jefferson, John Marshall, and the Lee family. Alexander and Nancy had two children—Archibald, born December 2, 1795, and Anne Dabney, born in 1798. Nancy Stuart probably died from complications in the birth of her daughter—a common occurrence in that era—as Alexander remarried in June 1800. While on a visit to Virginia, he died in Staunton, on December 9, 1832, less than two months before the birth of his famous grandson.[8]

It would appear that the judge's two children remained in Virginia with a stepmother or relatives when he moved to the West. Archibald Stuart, James's father, followed his father in the legal profession and politics. After serving in an artillery unit in the War of 1812, Archibald studied law and opened a practice in Campbell County. Described by local folks as a "hell of a fellow," Arch, as he was known, enjoyed the conviviality of company and alcoholic drink. Gifted with a ringing voice, he regaled listeners with rousing tales and songs. His personality drew people to him, and in 1819, the citizens of Campbell County elected him to the House of Delegates. It was only the beginning of a career that combined law and politics for Arch Stuart.[9]

By the time Arch Stuart served in the state legislature he was married with two daughters. He had met and courted Elizabeth Letcher Pannill of Pittsylvania County. They were married on June 17, 1817, and lived on the family farm outside Lynchburg. Like her husband's family, Elizabeth's had been in Virginia decades before the American Revolution. Her maternal grandparents, William and Elizabeth Letcher, settled in southwestern Henry County—present-day Patrick County—on the Virginia–North Carolina boundary in 1778. It was at their new home where Elizabeth Stuart's mother, Bethenia Letcher, was born on March 21, 1780.[10]

During the Revolution, the region along the Virginia–North Carolina border was bitterly divided between Patriots and Loyalists. William Letcher enlisted in a local militia company that supported independence. On August 2, 1780, a Loyalist shot and killed him, an act that enraged Letcher's fellow Patriots and resulted in a mass hanging of local Tories. Five months later, his widow married George Hairston, and together they had twelve children. Bethenia Letcher grew to adulthood in the Hairston household. When Hairston died in 1827, he was one of Virginia's wealthiest men, owning plantations in the state and in Mississippi.[11]

Bethenia Letcher was eighteen years old when she married David Pannill. His family had settled along the Rappahannock and Rapidan rivers in central Virginia. More than a year later, on January 4, 1801, Bethenia gave birth to Elizabeth. A son, William, followed two years later. David Pannill died in November 1803, and at some later time, Bethenia and her children were living in Pittsylvania County, just south of Campbell County. When Archibald Stuart and Elizabeth Letcher Pannill married, a vast network of relatives became intertwined because of second and third marriages. This extended family of uncles, aunts, and cousins would be important in the life of their son James.[12]

The wedding of Archibald Stuart and Elizabeth Pannill united two disparate individuals. While he was described as charming and witty, "the center of attraction at every social gathering," she was reserved, religiously pious, a woman "of no special patience with nonsense." When they moved finally to Patrick County, she attended regularly Episcopal services in the Methodist Episcopal church in Mount Airy, North Carolina, a few miles south of their home. She instilled devotion to the church into her children.[13]

Their marriage underwent difficult times, and their relationship became strained. Archibald's law practice and political career prospered throughout their years together. "A powerful orator and advocate," according to one account, "he charmed the multitude on the hustings, and convinced juries and courts." He was a delegate to the Virginia constitutional conventions in 1829 and 1850, was a commonwealth attorney for Floyd County, and served terms as a Democrat in the United States House of Representatives and in the Virginia Senate. He built a home, provided for a wife and ten children, and owned slaves. He was, however, a spendthrift, amassing debts that plagued the family even after his death.[14]

The sources of his financial difficulties have been attributed to his lack of business acumen, indulgent spending, and a gambling habit. While he appears to be have been an able and respected lawyer, the legal field did not ensure monetary reward during this era. A fellow Virginia attorney stated that the profession was "not always and, in fact, not generally, the road to wealth. The practice of Law is one of the most uncertain and precarious of all pursuits." If Archibald gambled frequently, he only worsened the family's financial straits. At one point he admitted in a letter: "I know I have been improvident and wasteful to a criminal extent but if I know myself I can safely say I shall be so no more. I have been punished sufficiently by the horrors of being in debt to teach me caution in future. You will probably say that I have made these resolutions before and they have not been followed up." It was a pledge he could not keep.[15]

In 1828, Archibald Stuart apparently traded the farm in Campbell County that he had received from his father to his brother-in-law, William Pannill. In turn, Pannill gave his share of the land in Patrick County given to him and Elizabeth Stuart by their mother. Part of the acreage came from the grandparent Letchers' original claim. The Stuarts' landholdings amounted to about 1,500 acres, with additional acres bought and sold as time passed. The Stuarts moved to Patrick County, building a house at Laurel Hill in 1831.[16]

Patrick County was overwhelmingly rural in the 1820s and 1830s. The county seat of Taylorsville—present-day Stuart—consisted of fewer than sixty residences and businesses. The largest town in the region was Mount Airy, North Carolina, just south of the state line. The Blue Ridge Mountains loomed over Patrick County to the west, and Bull Mountain, running east to west, divided it. The Ararat River and tributaries of the Dan River, with such names as Goblin Town Creek and Roaring Creek, drained the rich bottomlands. Farmers raised livestock, corn, and tobacco on the fertile ground. The ridges and uplands were rocky, with deposits of iron ore. African-American slaves, comprising about a quarter of the population, worked the fields and in the tobacco warehouses for the slaveholding families.[17]

It was into this "rural isolation" in the family home at Laurel Hill that James E. B. Stuart was born. Although no known painting or illustration of the house exists, it was probably two-story, built of logs and clapboard. The house sat near the crest of Laurel Hill, amid a grove of oak trees. James's mother brightened the landscape with an extensive flower garden. A separate kitchen, other outbuildings, and slave quarters completed the Stuart homestead. The number of black servants at Laurel Hill varied through the years, from approximately twenty to twenty-eight, the majority being women and children.[18]

From what can be gathered, James had a happy childhood. In a letter he wrote years later, he recalled the "blazing hearth" with all the family members around it. He noted the "old garden," with hollyhocks and hummingbirds hovering over the roses. "I can call no other place home," he told a sister, "but that of my youth and happy dreams."[19]

The Stuart household brimmed with the laughter and pranks of ten children. Seven brothers and sisters—Nancy Anne Dabney, born 1818; Bethenia Pannill, 1819; Mary Tucker, 1821; David Pannill, 1823; William Alexander, 1826; John Dabney, 1828; and Columbia Lafayette, 1830—preceded James. An unnamed brother, who lived three months (1834), Virginia Josephine (1836), and Victoria Augusta (1838) followed. Virginia Josephine died in 1842, at the age of six.[20]

James formed his closest bonds with his brother William Alexander, whom the family called Alex or Alick, and with his sister Columbia Lafayette, known affectionately as Lummie. He wrote of Lummie later that her "nature once chimed so with my own & who always was all love and affection towards me." When she died in childbirth in 1857, he said, "I never received intelligence of the death of one so near & dear to me with less grief."[21]

A childhood friend remembered that James "was full of life and fun; loved to be outdoors, and to romp and play." He fished in nearby streams and hunted for game, becoming an exceptional marksman. Like other boys of the times, he learned to ride a horse. His friend asserted that he was "a fearless rider, the wilder and more spirited the horse, the more enjoyment for him." Restless and physically strong for his age, he never seemed to tire and "could undergo any amount of bodily strain and fatigue."[22]

James appeared to be unwilling to or incapable of backing down. On one occasion he and Alex discovered a hornet's nest. When the bees swarmed out, Alex fled. James stood, however, enduring the stings until he had knocked down the nest. This combativeness led him into numerous scrapes and fights with other boys. While away at school at the age of thirteen, he wrote a revealing letter to a cousin. "Contrary to the expectations of all," he stated, "I have been so fortunate as not to have a single fight since I have been going to school. . . . Not from cowardice either (for I know you will immediately suspect that as being the reason)."[23]

David French Boyd, a schoolmate and friend, attributed James's pugnacious nature to his "rather quixotic" ways. He had an "over-sensitiveness" that led him "to take offense at real or supposed injustice or slight." Boyd added, "Stuart never liked to be checked or contradicted, never liked to be thwarted or opposed; it excited him; it made him mad and *stronger*." He disliked losing at games and became particularly incensed when beaten at marbles. Although good friends, he and Boyd clashed a number of times. James was, admitted Boyd, "a dangerous boy to tackle."[24]

In a memoir, Boyd recounted that Stuart had a "florid complexion, light hair and blue eyes, with strong features; a pleasant, smiling face; above medium size, and somewhat inclined to be corpulent." During the three years they spent together, Stuart "grew rapidly; was loose-jointed, gawky; still of great activity and strength." Boyd confessed, however, that his friend "was rather an ugly boy."[25]

The two schoolmates met in the fall of 1845, when Stuart left Laurel Hill for schooling to Wytheville, Virginia. Elizabeth Stuart had taught the children, but she and her husband decided to further their sons' education with private tutors. Archibald's sister Anne and her husband, Judge James Ewell Brown, had a home, Cobbler's Spring, a few miles east of Wytheville. Their nearby presence probably contributed to the Stuarts' decision to send their sons across the Blue Ridge Mountains. Alex Stuart had moved to Wytheville, and the two brothers lived together during James's first year in school.[26]

When James departed from Laurel Hill, he would return only periodically during breaks from school and leaves from the army. He studied under private tutors from 1845 until 1848. The teachers charged a tuition and had boys and girls as students. The curriculum consisted of history, basic mathematics, algebra, Latin, and Greek. David Boyd remembered that the teachers were "wielders of the rod of correction and enlightment." When he attended college, Stuart wrote to one of his former instructors about his Latin lessons, "I am trying to stick to the old principles of reading which you instilled into me partly by mouth and partly by the *rod*."[27]

Young Stuart studied under Richard T. Mathews, Peregrine Buckingham, a Mr. Buchanan, and at J. B. Wise's music school in Wytheville. Buckingham, whom Boyd described as "a queer specimen of humanity," and Stuart clashed. "Both were high-tempered," wrote Boyd, "and occasionally there was a row, with Buckingham getting the best of it." Stuart also spent one term with George W. Painter, who held classes in a log building behind his brick home, located twelve miles southwest of Pulaski. Painter, who "wore his hair long and fastened up in the back with a tuck comb," farmed, taught school, and preached.[28]

Stuart strove to be a fine student, even putting a Bible in his desk for divine assistance on examinations. Boyd claimed that his friend had a mind that was "clear, strong and quick—attentive and retentive, of great power of concentration." He burned with a desire to "outrank" all of his schoolmates. "He wanted no one to excel him," wrote Boyd. He contracted mumps, measles, and typhoid fever at different times, which affected his studies. Months after he had recovered from typhoid fever, he stated, "even at this time my head is as bald as an eagle and I am very much laughed at by the gals."[29]

"The gals" intrigued and perplexed him. "I have gotten out with the girls," Stuart asserted in a letter. "I believe they were just made for man's troubles." Nevertheless, according to Boyd, "he was fond of the Society of ladies; and especially did he enjoy the company of the more intelligent and refined ladies beyond his own age. They had a great charm for him; he loved to talk with them freely." They appealed to him; he, to them. He was engaging, witty, sincere, frank, courteous, and honorable, attributes that drew girls and later women to him.[30]

Homesickness for his family at Laurel Hill, however, gnawed at him. Weeks before Christmas in 1846, he implored his mother in a letter: "I can't tell why you don't write to me, for you have no idea how acceptable a letter from home is of any sort, especially to me away off at boarding school where I never hear from home or anywhere else. I have no doubt that you have all experienced this, and for that reason it appears still most astonishing why you do not have mercy on a poor little insignificant whelp away from his mammy. I hope you will not defer writing any longer, but WRITE! WRITE! WRITE!"[31]

Unable to travel home for the holiday because of snow in the mountains, Stuart spent Christmas with his uncle and aunt James and Anne Brown at Cobbler's Spring. Stuart visited with relatives whenever circumstances allowed for the remainder of his life. Like other antebellum Virginia families, the Stuarts developed close relationships with their many kinfolk. Cousins were regarded as intimate family members. Marriages between male and female cousins were not uncommon. Stuart's network of Letchers, Hairstons, Dabneys, Prices, and others formed an important part of his career and life.[32]

Stuart returned to Laurel Hill the following spring, spending the summer with his family. He recrossed the Blue Ridge to Wytheville in the fall of 1847 for his final year of boarding school. Sometime during the winter, the Stuart home at Laurel Hill burned. Stuart described it as a "sad disaster" for the family. His father and brother John stayed behind, living in the kitchen. Where his mother and younger children moved to is uncertain. Stuart wrote, "We have not decided whether we will build again or not." The family never rebuilt the house.[33]

Stuart remained in Wytheville during the summer of 1848, working in the county clerk's office. Wanting to attend college, he had decided upon the recommendation of his cousin Alexander Stuart Brown to attend Emory and Henry College in Washington County, ten miles from Abingdon, Virginia. He entered the college with the freshman class that fall as "an irregular student," deficient in some of the college's requirements for admission.[34]

Founded by the Holston Conference of the Methodist Church in 1838, Emory and Henry had begun as an institution that combined learning with manual labor. The students had been required to attend classes and to work in the college's fields. The experiment ended after three years, but some students continued to perform various chores to help pay their tuition. The college was the first institution of higher learning in southwestern Virginia, established to serve students from that region of the state.[35]

When Stuart enrolled, a four-story brick building, "utterly devoid of architectural beauty," dominated the college grounds, holding classrooms and student quarters. A three-story hall lay to the east, housing a kitchen and additional student rooms. Residences for the president and faculty, barns, stables, a brick springhouse, toolsheds, and a grammar school for children of faculty members completed the college's structures. A Maine-born minister, Charles Collins, served as its president.[36]

A classmate of Stuart at the college described him as "generous to a fault, genial and vivacious in spirit." Stuart rectified his deficiencies during his freshman year, earning good grades in mathematics and science and immersing himself in Latin and Greek classics. He joined the Hermesian Literary Society, and at the annual celebration of the college's societies, he spoke on "The Triumph of True Principles." To his embarrassment, he fell off the stage during the address.[37]

During the 1848–1849 school year, a religious revival swept the college, and Stuart formally joined the Methodist Church. As he wrote later, he possessed "the evidence of a Savior's pardoning love . . . and prayed God to guide me in the right way and teach me to walk as a

Christian should." His faith, kindled initially by his mother, defined a central aspect of his character.[38]

In the winter of 1850, Stuart applied for appointment to the United States Military Academy at West Point, New York. In a letter of recommendation, President Collins stated that Stuart had maintained "an irreproachably moral and social character and by his superior diligence and devotion to his studies had acquired a high rank as a scholar." Months after he had departed from the college, Stuart wrote: "I look back to the time I spent at Emory with fond delight. . . . My heart is wedded to Emory, and long will it be before I return to its hallowed hills."[39]

When Stuart decided upon a military career is uncertain. During the summer of 1848, he had tried to enlist in the Regular Army but was rejected because of his youthful age. Ironically, he secured the appointment from Representative Thomas Hamlet Averett, a Whig who had defeated Archibald Stuart for the seat in the 1848 election. Tradition maintains that Stuart's appointment was Averett's first act as a congressman.[40]

Secretary of War George W. Crawford informed Stuart of his "conditional appointment" in a letter dated April 5, 1850. Stuart replied with "my acceptance of the same." Archibald Stuart endorsed his son's letter, granting his permission to bind James to eight years of service in the army. The formal appointment, signed by President Zachary Taylor, was dated June 30, 1850. All that was left now for the seventeen-year-old were preparations for the journey to West Point.[41]

From the accounts of those who had known James Ewell Brown Stuart he possessed endearing qualities of a generous nature and compelling personality. But ambition burned within him, and combativeness smoldered beneath a ready smile. He was physically strong, restless, self-reliant, and self-confident. From his mother came his religious convictions, his serious work habits, and his vow never to drink alcohol. From his father came a love of music, a sense of humor, and a zest for life. From home—"the dear old hills of Patrick," as he called it—came an attachment to Virginia that had seeped into his soul. He wrote later, during the midst of the Civil War, that he hoped "to spend the rest of my days there." So as he readied himself to leave the state for the first time, this son of Virginia, in a sense, never departed. It would count for much as he began a soldier's journey.[42]

Chapter Two

West Point and Texas

I AM GREEN AS a gourd vine yet," admitted James Ewell Brown Stuart as he walked the streets of Washington, D.C., on June 3, 1850. He had arrived in the city the day before, visited the grounds of the White House, and passed President Zachary Taylor on a street. "He is a plain looking old fellow with a slight squat as he walks," Stuart wrote of the president. He attended sessions of Congress, listening to senators Daniel Webster, Henry Clay, Jefferson Davis, and Sam Houston. He thought Webster was "the finest looking man in the Senate," Davis, the most effective speaker, and Houston "appears better with his mouth shut than open." The House of Representatives "was a rowdy place compared with the Senate."[1]

The capital was a brief, two-day stop on his trip from Laurel Hill to West Point. Before he arrived in Washington, Stuart had passed through Wytheville, Lynchburg, and Charlottesville, staying with relatives. In Charlottesville, he visited the University of Virginia and Monticello, which he called "truly a romantic place." He walked down the slope from the house, chipped a piece from Thomas Jefferson's gravestone, and took two roses as souvenirs. He lost a badge, pinned to his coat while on a stagecoach, and in his letter written in Washington, he joked, "I would not have been worthy of the name Stuart had I arrived here safely and without losing or forgetting something." From the capital, he traveled by train to Baltimore, where he boarded a steamer to New York City, and then up the Hudson River to West Point.[2]

He arrived there during the second week of June. Located on a towering bluff above the Hudson River, thirty-seven miles north of New York City, the academy was built of stone, brick, and mortar, and already underpinned by tradition. President Thomas Jefferson had created a Corps of Engineers in 1802, designating West Point as the site for an academy, with the army's chief engineer serving as superintendent. When the War of 1812 demonstrated a need for a trained officer corps, Sylvanus Thayer, an engineer and former instructor at the school, was appointed superintendent in 1817 to implement an overhaul of the curriculum and to oversee the construction of new buildings.[3]

Thayer transformed the institution, improving the standards of instruction and instituting a strict code of conduct for cadets. West Point authorities regimented daily cadet life and regulated cadet conduct with a system of demerits. A cadet could receive demerits for a host of offenses—tardiness or absence at roll calls, unkempt quarters and equipment, unshaven faces and uncut hair, visiting with fellow cadets after taps, altercations or fights, insubordinate behavior toward cadet and academy officers, and other various misdeeds. If a cadet amassed two hundred demerits in a year, he faced expulsion.[4]

Rigid rules and classroom demands governed cadet life, while routine marked the passage of time. "At West Point all is monotony," grumbled a cadet of the era. "What is said of one day will answer for it almost years after." Academic success depended less on intelligence than on "untiring energy and resolution not to fail," in the estimation of graduate William T. Sherman. "A habit of close study and application," argued Sherman, "is worth an actual knowledge of half the students at the Academy." Cadets who "at first sailed along with flying colors, presuming upon knowledge previously acquired, . . . in the end were far outstripped by plodding students."[5]

At the end of each term, in January and in June, cadets underwent examinations. Failure meant dismissal. Mathematics—algebra, geometry, trigonometry, descriptive and analytical geometry, and calculus—constituted the majority of the course work. A cadet, probably expressing a shared complaint, scribbled in a calculus book: "God damn all mathematics to the lowest depts. of hell!! May it be capable of bodily suffering & undergo such torments that the veriest fiend in hell shall shrink in horror at the sight."[6]

When a new cadet or plebe, like Stuart, arrived at West Point, he saw a large plain, framed by the academy's buildings. The cadet barracks, containing 172 rooms and built of granite, dominated the grounds. A chapel, library, observatory, laboratories, mess hall, and a riding hall in "dangerous dilapidation" comprised the core of the academy. A new stone mess hall, under construction, was finished in 1851. Nearby, a row of wooden residences housed the superintendent, commandant, professors, and instructors. It was within these confines that a cadet's life was measured for four years.[7]

An incoming class of cadets was introduced to academy life with a two-month summer encampment. Officers and upper classmen conducted daily infantry and artillery drills. They learned to march with a distinct stride. "I think the most difficult thing for each of us," stated Oliver Otis Howard, a fellow plebe with Stuart, "was to so walk as to strike the ball of the foot first. To point the toe and do this were required, and it gave a cadet a peculiar gait." Each day concluded with a parade, attended frequently by politicians, civilians, and army officers.[8]

During the encampment, Stuart wrote to a cousin about the academy, "it is a great place in every respect—great for the facilities for education—as studying human nature, learning the ways of the world and for straightening the form." Weeks later, he stated in another letter: "I am pleased with my new situation. So far I know of no profession more desirable than that of a soldier; indeed every thing connected with the Academy has far surpassed my most sanguine expectations."[9]

September marked the beginning of the academic year, with the cadets moving into the barracks. A barracks room measured twenty-two feet by fourteen feet and contained four iron beds and four tables. Three or four cadets roomed together. Stuart's roommates during his first year were Judson D. Bingham of Indiana and a fellow Virginian, Charles C. Rogers. Stuart said Bingham and Rogers were "both very studious and clever fellows."[10]

At some time, perhaps soon after his arrival at the academy, Stuart's fellow cadets began calling him "Beauty." The nickname stuck, at least among those who were with him at West Point. Stuart had probably reached or soon would attain his adult height of five feet, nine or ten inches. He had blue-gray eyes and auburn brown hair. But he possessed a chin "so short and retiring as positively to disfigure his otherwise fine countenance." In time, while serving with the army in the West, Stuart grew a beard to conceal this facial weakness. A fellow officer remarked that Stuart was "the only man he ever saw that [a] beard improved."[11]

While at West Point, Stuart had confrontations or scrapes with other cadets. His pugnacity and prickly sense of honor, evident as a boy, caused his combative responses to perceived slights. Twice in letters, his father cautioned him to "avoid getting into difficulties in which such maintenance [of honor] may be demanded at your hands." Archibald Stuart understood his son's conduct because "an insult should be resented under all circumstances." Cadet Stuart apparently refused, however, to fight another cadet over the affections of a young woman.[12]

Despite his contentious reputation, Stuart was a popular cadet. His genial and generous nature, wit, and liveliness attracted other cadets to him. Among the plebes in the Class of 1854, he counted among his friends future Confederate generals George Washington Custis Lee and John Pegram of Virginia, William Dorsey Pender of North Carolina, and Stephen D. Lee of South Carolina. Others in his class who attained rank or distinction in the Civil War included Confederates James Deshler and Archibald Gracie, while future Union generals included Oliver Otis Howard, Thomas H. Ruger, and Benjamin F. Davis. Among the Class of 1853 were Northerners James B. McPherson, John M. Schofield, and Philip H. Sheridan, and Southerners John B. Hood and John R. Chambliss, Jr. When the Class of 1855 entered the academy a year later, three members—David McM. Gregg, Alfred T. A. Torbert, and William W. Averell—were destined to command mounted units against Stuart's cavalry.[13]

Stuart wrote after his graduation, "I sometimes think that the taste of classmates for each other's society particularly West Pointers is unequalled by the strangest attachment and what is more remarkable, it becomes more and more intense as time continues." During his four years at the academy, his closest friends were Custis Lee, John Pegram, and Otis Howard. Lee was, he said, "the most intimate friend I had in my class." In turn, Howard described Stuart as "my best friend." Years later, Howard stated, "I never can forget the manliness of J. E. B. Stuart, of Virginia. . . . He spoke to me, he visited me, and we became warm friends, often, on Saturday afternoons, visiting the young ladies of the post together."[14]

The Howard-Stuart friendship was rather remarkable. While both men were deeply religious, they shared few other views. Howard was from Maine, and an outspoken abolitionist. Stuart was "imbibed," in Howard's word, with the idea of state supremacy and opposed to abolitionism. When a group of Southern cadets, probably including Lee and Pegram, ostracized Howard, Stuart sided with the Maine Yankee. It was a courageous act in that closed society, rooted in his sense of justice and honor.[15]

Friendships were often established and deepened during long hours of study "by the same candle." "For one to succeed here," Stuart argued, "all that is required is an ordinary mind and application, the latter is by far the most important and desirable of the two." His letters contained such phrases as "we have studied hard"; "'hard study' has been our constant watchward"; and "I turned into studying pretty hard." He told a friend from Emory and Henry, "I am resolved on graduating if I can."[16]

The reckoning for cadets came with the end-of-term examinations in January and June. Stuart explained them to a friend: "There is one respect in which West Point differs from all other Institutions of learning, which is this; Here every man's grade, or 'standing,' as it is here called, is definitely established at every Examination, it is not made out in decimals or by any complicated process of calculation, but simply his *relative* standing in his class and this is published everywhere in a Register to the world. So that if a man is fool every body knows it, and if he is head every body who wants to can know it."[17]

Stuart achieved a commendable academic record and class standing during his first two years. After the January 1851 examinations, he stood sixth in mathematics and fifteenth in English, with an overall rank of eighth out of ninety-three in the class. Twenty-two members of the class failed and were dismissed. In June, he ranked eighth in mathematics, twelfth in English, and fifteenth in French, maintaining his overall rank. By the completion of the June 1852 examinations, Stuart stood seventh in a class of sixty. He had joined the Dialectic Society, a debate group, and had been promoted to the cadet rank of first sergeant, responsible for preparing bimonthly company muster rolls.[18]

During these first two years, Stuart amassed a total of eighty-five demerits—forty-three, the first year; forty-two, the second. The violations included being late for reveille, roll call, or class; visiting a fellow cadet in his room during the morning; leaving his gun outdoors; appearing in ranks without gloves; failing to salute an officer; and visiting with others while on sentinel duty. The infractions were minor and typical for a cadet.[19]

Academy policy granted summer furloughs to cadets who had completed two years at West Point. "There is no period in a man's life cherished dearer and *wished nearer* than a cadet's furlough," Stuart declared in a letter. His father sent him $40 for the trip home. Each cadet received $24 a month, but most of the money went for the cost of rations and uniforms. Like most cadets, Stuart had incurred debts and had borrowed money. He had brought with him to the academy a "Private accounts" book into which he listed purchases, debts, loans, and in time, income and investments. He maintained entries in the book until he left the army in 1861.[20]

When Stuart returned from leave in August, a new superintendent, Major Robert E. Lee, had been appointed. An 1829 academy graduate, Lee was one of the army's most distinguished engineer officers. He had served on the staff of General Winfield Scott during the Mexican War, earning three brevets or temporary promotions for gallantry and distinguished conduct. Prior to his appointment to West Point, Lee had overseen the construction of Fort Carroll in Baltimore. A forty-five-year-old Virginian, Lee shared Dabney kinfolk with Stuart.[21]

Lee improved the curriculum and classroom instruction and tightened discipline. He worked with the faculty, which included two of his former professors, William H. C. Bartlett and Albert E. Church. Bartlett was a renowned astronomer, while Church taught mathematics. Church, whom a cadet called "an old mathematical cipher, bereft of all natural feeling," failed more cadets than any instructor. But the academy's most noted and influential professor was Dennis Hart Mahan, who taught engineering and tactics. An 1824 graduate, Mahan joined the academic board in 1830. His lectures on military science and the art of war were heard by a generation of future Civil War officers. Stuart described Mahan's course on civil engineering as "the most interesting study I have ever pursued."[22]

Discipline had been lax under Lee's predecessor, Captain Henry Brewerton. While Lee enforced the rules, he acted fairly and with understanding. He opened his office each morning for an hour to listen to the young men's concerns and their explanations for misbehavior. On Saturday afternoons, he invited a few cadets at a time to his residence for a visit and for dinner.[23]

Custis Lee, the superintendent's son, stopped by nearly every Saturday. Stuart often accompanied his close friend to the quarters. After having dinner with the Lees on one occasion, Stuart informed a cousin, "I have formed a high regard for the family." Lee's wife, Mary Custis Lee, wrote years later that Stuart "has ever been to me as one of my own family & I felt that we had no where a truer friend." Of Mrs. Lee, Stuart stated, "She has always treated me as kindly as if I were her own Son."[24]

The course work increased for cadets during their third year at West Point. Stuart and his classmates studied philosophy, chemistry, and drawing. Stuart struggled with the latter subject: "I can safely say that I have always exerted myself to take a high stand. Drawing has been a great obstacle and will still be one for it is very necessary in Engineering." After the June 1853 examinations, he ranked higher in drawing, thirteenth, than he did in chemistry, twenty-first. He had earned forty-four demerits, with his worst violation being for "Insubordinate and Disrespectful conduct, to his instructor" in philosophy class. His overall rank was eleventh in a class that now numbered fifty-four. His friend Custis Lee stood first.[25]

Stuart's overall class rank and conduct record earned him promotion to second captain. Lee served as cadet adjutant; John Pegram, as quartermaster. Later, Stuart was appointed a cavalry officer with seven fellow cadets, "solely upon merit in riding." The position, he explained, "is the most desirable one in the corps as the officers are granted choice of horses and many other privileges."[26]

First classmen or cadets in their final year at West Point participated in the summer encampment. "The Encampment so far fully meets my expectations," Stuart wrote during its early days, "that for which I most wished being granted in abundance that is—*rest*." Members of the Dialectic Society selected him to read the Declaration of Independence at the Fourth of July festivities. Three times a week cotillion parties brought together cadets and young women. "I must say that amid all the array of love-seekers and heart-breakers by whom we have been surrounded, I have escaped unscathed," asserted Stuart. His mother, sister Columbia, and a cousin traveled from Virginia for a visit. They stayed only three days, moving Stuart to write, "I was too much gratified to see them, to think of complaining."[27]

With the resumption of classes in September, Stuart studied ethics, engineering, mineralogy, and geology. According to Stuart family tradition, he eased up on his classwork, not wanting a high class rank that might place him in the engineers. Although his acceptance to the academy committed him to eight years of service, he could, like all officers, resign his commission and pursue a civilian career. He wrote in October, however, that he planned to remain in the army: "It has attractions which to one who has seen a little of the 'elephant' [combat] are overpowering. There is something in 'the pride and pomp and circumstances of glorious war.'" He preferred to be "a bold Dragoon" rather than "a petty-fogger lawyer."[28]

In December, Stuart lay in the post hospital with bruises and a black eye. As a cadet captain, he had reported William P. Sanders, Class of 1856, for shouting against orders after an evening parade. Stuart vowed that as an officer he would *do my duty to the letter*." When Sanders learned that Stuart had turned him in, he challenged him to a fight. In Stuart's words, Sanders "was a strapping big Mississippian."[29]

The encounter had the semblance of a duel, with each man having a second who arranged the time and place. "We had no fears being caught," Stuart informed his father afterward, "for it was a colder morning than you ever felt in Virginia and it was too early for officers to frequent such a secluded spot." Charles Rogers acted as Stuart's second and suggested that his friend use a club because of the disparity in size and weight between the two men. Stuart refused, saying, "it was a matter of little consequence whether I *whipped* or *was whipped*, and I would not have the appearance of seeking an advantage for the sake of a victory."[30]

Stuart had the best of it early, but Sanders's strength prevailed in the end. The fight ceased with both men exhausted and Stuart admitting that he had been whipped. Stuart went to the hospital with a badly swollen eye, which he attributed to the fact that "my flesh puffs up like a bladder from the slightest bruise." The surgeon did not notify authorities of the incident as he regarded "such things as professional secrets." He told his father that his fellow cadets were "said to be in my favor, but the majority condemn my consenting to fight him *even-handed.*"[31]

Stuart's final term at the academy passed without any major incident. He wrote a letter to a United States senator endorsing the application of William Henry Fitzhugh Lee to West Point. Known as "Rooney," Lee was Custis's younger brother. In the letter, Stuart stated, "I have without his knowledge determined to write to you, in hopes that you will if practicable use your influence in his behalf." He continued, "The only possible objection that can be urged is the fact that he had a *brother* educated here, but that regulation is so dead a letter that the President has repeatedly disregarded it and if there ever was a case which ought to remove far more serious objections, *this is one.*" Rooney Lee's application was denied, and he enrolled at Harvard. Stuart's letter indicated the attachment he felt toward the Lee family.[32]

When examinations concluded in June 1854, Stuart ranked thirteenth in a class of forty-six, from its original ninety-three members. Custis Lee stood first; Otis Howard, fourth; John Pegram, tenth; and his roommate, Charles Rogers, eleventh. Stuart ranked his best, seventh, in English and French, and his worst, twenty-ninth, in engineering. His parents gave him a gold class ring with a green stone for graduation. Inscribed beneath the stone was,

JAS. E. B. STUART
JUNE 1854

He was now a brevet second lieutenant in the Regular Army.[33]

WEST POINT HAD fulfilled Stuart's youthful ambitions. He had received a coveted education, with a commendable academic record, from one of the country's finest institutions. He had formed friendships that would be critical to him in the years ahead. Like many others, he cherished the memories of the place. While a cadet, he had written that if West Point were in Virginia, "I would consider it a paradise." Now, it was time to return to Virginia and a welcome leave.[34]

The academy graduate spent the summer and early fall months with his family and with relatives and friends in the state and in North Carolina. Throughout the weeks, he awaited orders from the War Department. They arrived in September, dated August 14, assigning him to the Regiment of Mounted Rifles in Texas. He traveled to Washington, where he learned that his leave had been extended until October 15. From there he went to New York to equip "myself fully for Texas." He evidently purchased the items on borrowed money.[35]

Stuart described his assignment to the regiment as a "consummation of my wishes . . . which my taste, fondness for riding, and desire to serve my country in some acceptable manner led me to select above all the rest." He had "but one aim," he told a cousin, "and that is to do some service to my country in return for what she has done for me." He could have sought a post in the East, instead of on the frontier, "but when there are hard knocks to be felt, and hard blows to be dealt, a man *really desirous* to serve his country will not hesitate a moment to declare for the latter."[36]

While still at home, Stuart composed a prayer, writing it in the back of a prayer book:

> O God where'er my footsteps stray
> On prairies far or battles dim
> Still keep them in thy holy way.
> And cleanse my soul from ev'ry sin.
>
> Lord! When the hour of death shall come
> And from this clay my soul release
> O grant that I may have a home
> In thy abode of endless peace.[37]

The trip to Texas lasted more than two months. From Wheeling, Virginia, Stuart traveled by steamboat down the Ohio and Mississippi Rivers to St. Louis, where he was forced to stop because of a yellow fever epidemic in New Orleans. Although he enjoyed St. Louis, visiting with relatives, attending a wedding, and meeting the Missouri politician Edward Bates, he chafed at the delay. "The longer I am detained from the field of action," he asserted in a November 28 letter, "the more anxious I become to reach it. I am burning with all the enthusiasm of youthful ambition to show my prowess in a fight. What the result will be I cannot tell but I hope and pray to be always prepared for the worst."[38]

Stuart left St. Louis the next day, passed through New Orleans, and into the Gulf of Mexico. A violent storm tossed the steamer about, making him *"dreadfully seasick."* From Galveston, Texas, he took a mail boat to Corpus Christi, where he secured a horse and rode to Fort McIntosh in Laredo, arriving on December 28. Assigned an escort, he continued north, through the region between the Rio Grande and Nueces rivers, which he said, was "infested" with bands of Comanche. It was not until January 28, 1855, that he arrived at Fort Davis, an outpost on the San Antonio–El Paso Road, after a journey of roughly 450 miles.[39]

The Regiment of Mounted Rifles had been authorized in 1841 and assigned to duty on the frontier. Like the 1st and 2nd Dragoons, the command served as mounted infantrymen. In Texas, the federal government had established a string of forts—Davis, Clark, Duncan, and McIntosh—that served as a loosely knotted cordon of protection for the state's settlements, which lay approximately 150 miles to the east. Two companies, or about one hundred or so men, occupied each post. Members of the Mounted Rifles wore uniforms with green trim, but casual attire prevailed on the frontier. Food and living conditions were abominable. There was little pomp and less glory in the vast remoteness of Texas.[40]

The Mounted Rifles' primary duty consisted of preventing Indian raids into the settlements. If a band of warriors attacked ranches and villages, the soldiers pursued, frequently spending days and weeks on a scout across rugged terrain. Rarely did the riflemen overtake and engage the elusive foe, which was usually Comanche. When Stuart finally joined his unit, Company G, it was fifty miles beyond Fort Davis, marching west as part of a force under the command of Major John S. Simonson.[41]

For the next three months, Stuart participated with his company in a number of scouts. It was bone-numbing duty, with marches that could cover fifty miles in a day. They rode through narrow ravines edged by precipitous cliffs, scaled mountains, were drenched by rain and hail storms, narrowly escaped a prairie fire, and lived on scant rations. At one point, the command was, as he noted, in "deplorable condition" and was forced to return to a camp. Stuart seemed to endure the arduous duty well, being blessed with remarkable stamina and a tirelessness. He had begun growing his beard, which he wore for the remainder of his life.[42]

"We have threaded every trail," he informed a relative about one scout, "clambered every precipice and penetrated every ravine for hundreds of miles round we have not been able to find Mr Camanche." On one march, Stuart succeeded, with the aid of twenty men, to lower a cannon, using lariat ropes, down a mountainside. Major Simonson, believing that it could not be accomplished, praised Stuart's determination.[43]

While on the scouts, Stuart noted the abundant wildlife and the country's beauty. Quail, prairie dogs, and panthers fascinated him. After the riflemen crossed the Sierra Guadalupe, he informed a newspaper at home, "I was raised in the Blue Mountains of Virginia, but never have I beheld anything to compare with the grandeur of the scenery from that Comanche pass." His only regret after three months in the field was that he had not been tested in a fight with the Indians.[44]

In Washington, meanwhile, Congress had authorized the creation of two new mounted regiments, the 1st and 2nd Cavalry. The War Department selected Stuart for one of the lieutenancies in the 1st Cavalry. He learned of the appointment when he read a list of the officers printed in the Washington *Union* newspaper. He said later, "It was very gratifying to me to be thus selected from so large a number of meritorious applicants, for I had no prestige of former brilliant services to back me." He attributed his appointment to the influence of his congressman, Thomas S. Bocock.[45]

Before Stuart left to join his new regiment, Major Simonson wrote to him:

> During your service with Company "G," your duties have, at times, been necessarily arduous; and it has afforded me pleasure to notice that, under these circumstances, you have not omitted to display that cheerfulness and zeal in their performance which if preserved, will not fail to be appreciated by those with whom you may serve, and to secure you a favorable reputation as an officer.
>
> A regret for the loss of your services in the Regiment is therefore mingled with the pleasure with which I offer my congratulations on your promotion, and my best wishes for your future success and happiness.[46]

Chapter Three

"I Go with Virginia"

F ORT LEAVENWORTH, KANSAS Territory, symbolized a nation's stride. Established in 1827, the post stood on a bluff above the Missouri River, roughly five hundred miles upstream from the river's confluence with the Mississippi. The fort's stone, brick, and frame buildings gave it a permanence, a guardian for America's continental quest. Farther west, forts Riley, Kearny, and Laramie extended the army's reach toward the Rocky Mountains.[1]

The military installations had been constructed to protect white settlers as they trekked westward on the Santa Fe and Oregon-California trails. The routes, appearing like rutted scars upon the vast landscape, brought thousands of emigrants. With the passage of each successive mile, the creaking wheels of covered wagons rolled deeper into the homelands and hunting grounds of Native American plains tribes. Inevitably, clashes occurred as the Indians resisted a darkening future.[2]

The domain of the plains Indians encompassed hundreds of thousands of square miles, from the Dakotas to Texas. Sioux, Cheyenne, Arapaho, Kiowa, and Comanche comprised the major tribal groups. Nomadic people, the tribes followed buffalo herds, roaming across the endless grasslands. They were superb horsemen and fierce warriors. Their societies honored individual deeds of courage in warfare. Treaties had been signed between some tribes and the distant government in Washington. By the mid-1850s, however, tribal resistance mounted as more settlers came and the military surveyed new roads through Indian lands.[3]

Congress reacted to violence along the trails by creating the two new light cavalry regiments, the 1st and 2nd Cavalry, on March 3, 1855. The new units were to be deployed on the plains, reinforcing the dragoon and mounted rifle companies that were scattered at outposts. While the dragoons and mounted rifles acted as infantrymen on horseback, the light cavalrymen, with uniforms trimmed in yellow braid, could operate with more mobility. Armed with a saber, a .36-caliber Colt Navy revolver, and a .54- or .58-caliber carbine, they could engage Indians either on horseback or on foot.[4]

It was to Fort Leavenworth, then, that the officers and enlisted men of the 1st Cavalry came during June 1855. The War Department appointed Colonel Edwin V. Sumner as regimental commander. A soldier for nearly four decades, Sumner had served during the Mexican War and most recently with the 1st Dragoons. Known as "Bull," either for his booming voice or for the story that a musket ball had been deflected by his thick skull, Sumner could be stubborn and direct, but he had earned the respect of officers and men who had served with him. Lieutenant Colonel Joseph E. Johnston and Major John Sedgwick served as the regiment's senior subordinates.[5]

Second Lieutenant James E. B. Stuart arrived at Fort Leavenworth on June 23. Before long, Sumner appointed him regimental quartermaster and commissary officer. "It is a very responsible office and for so young an officer a distinction," wrote Stuart. "I will endeavor to give the Colonel no cause to regret what he has done." He also acted as temporary commander of Company H, whose captain was on leave. He roomed with Sedgwick and Lieutenant Robert Ransom, Jr., the regiment's acting adjutant. The living arrangements fostered friendships among the three men.[6]

Since his days in college when writing letters primarily to nonfamily members, Stuart had signed them "J.E.B. Stuart." His use of the three initials in his signature undoubtedly earned him the famous nickname of "Jeb." According to the memoir of his boyhood friend David French

Boyd, to distinguish him from Captain George H. Steuart of the 1st Cavalry, fellow officers called him Jeb and the name stuck. Flora Cooke Stuart, who had read the manuscript, offered a few comments and corrections to the memoir but did not question or change Boyd's account of the nickname. To fellow West Point classmates and friends, however, he remained "Beauty."[7]

Family tradition holds that Jeb Stuart first saw Flora Cooke at a regimental review in July. She had come to Fort Leavenworth to be with her family for the summer. During the review her horse became excited, and she skillfully controlled the animal. Impressed by her horsemanship, Stuart later asked her if she would join him for afternoon rides. A courtship ensued. Before long, he confided to a cousin, "If you don't hurry I will beat you getting married."[8]

Nineteen-year-old Flora Cooke was the daughter of Lieutenant Colonel Philip St. George Cooke of the 2nd Dragoons and Rachel Hertzog. The Cookes were Virginians; the Hertzogs, Pennsylvanians. The Cookes had three daughters—Flora, Maria, and Julia—and a son, John Rogers. Flora had recently finished at a private school in Detroit, Michigan. Her parents planned to have her make a societal debut in Philadelphia, her mother's hometown, but she insisted on joining them on the plains.[9]

Flora was not a particularly beautiful young woman, but she was slender and athletic, with blue eyes and a fine complexion. She possessed a charming, if not lively, personality, enjoyed singing and playing a guitar, could ride a horse as well as a man could, and could shoot a gun, qualities that attracted Stuart to her. Being the daughter of a career army officer, whose family roots were Virginian, must have further enhanced her appeal to him. For those reasons and others veiled by time, they came together in a burst of romance.[10]

The opposite sex had been alluring to Stuart since he was twelve or thirteen years old. As a cadet, he had escorted and flirted with many young women. Mary Lee, Robert E. Lee's daughter, had entranced him in particular. In March 1854, he affirmed to his cousin Alexander Stuart Brown that marriage was "the most sacred of earthly ties." The bond between a husband and wife must be fused by love, "a *passion* which will rise intuitively in the breast whenever it is brought under the influence

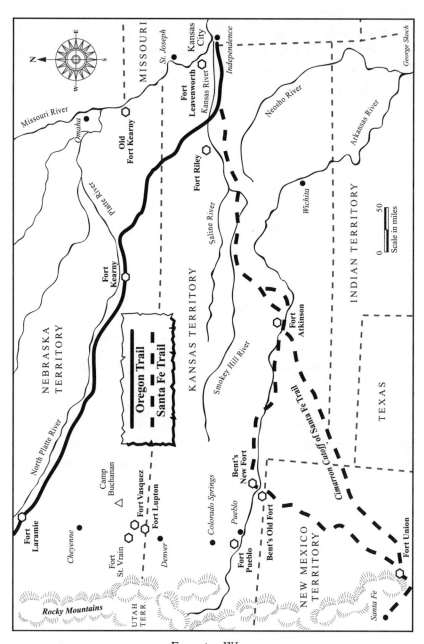

Frontier West

of its corresponding object in the other sex." Unlike any other woman, Flora had inflamed that passion in him.[11]

Within weeks he proposed, and she accepted. Her parents approved, although her father stated later that the prospect of Flora's marriage had occurred "rather suddenly." He described Stuart after the wedding as "a remarkably fine, promising, pure young man, and has had so far an extraordinary promotion." Many years later, Flora wrote of her husband, "He was *noble* & true, but his inner life was one of the purest, & most exalted, I have ever known." Stuart described the whirlwind courtship and engagement in Latin to a friend, "*Veni, vidi victus sum,*" or "I came, I saw, I was conquered."[12]

The couple set the wedding for a day in November. The exact date remained uncertain as seven companies of the 1st Cavalry prepared to leave Fort Leavenworth on a so-called Sioux Expedition. In August, a force of infantry, artillery, and cavalry, the latter led by Flora's father, had marched west to punish a band of Sioux implicated in the killing of thirty soldiers and an interpreter in 1854. This column had moved toward Fort Laramie, Wyoming Territory, with the companies of the 1st Cavalry, under Major Sedgwick, to follow on a roving patrol. As quartermaster and commissary officer, Stuart was responsible for the expedition's supplies.[13]

Sedgwick's command spent several weeks following the Oregon-California Trail past Fort Kearny on the Platte River toward Fort Laramie. In all, the horse soldiers covered more than eight hundred miles, without encountering any Indian bands. On October 27, while riding with an advance party on the return march, Stuart received a letter from Flora. She informed him that Archibald Stuart had died. He had passed away on September 20, with Elizabeth by his side. A few days earlier, Stuart had received a letter from "my own dear father," who said that he was in "perfect health." "Those dispensations of an all wise providence must be experienced by all," Stuart wrote of the sad news. "*His* will *not* mine be done."[14]

Upon his return to Fort Leavenworth, Stuart and Flora set the wedding for November 14, at Fort Riley, where her father was now stationed. "It will, however, be rather private—only a few special friends being present," he wrote to Alexander Brown, asking his cousin to join them from Virginia and to be "my attendant." Before he had gone on the patrol, he sent Brown $150 to purchase a silver set, with "'Stuart' cut on the handles." He requested a sixty-day leave so he and Flora could visit family in the East.[15]

Jeb Stuart and Flora Cooke were married Wednesday evening, November 14, 1855. An army chaplain, a Reverend Clarkson of the Episcopal church, performed the ceremony. When Stuart had served with the Mounted Rifles, he switched church affiliation from Methodist to Episcopalian. The Cookes belonged to the latter church. Flora wore the white dress that she had worn at her school graduation. Two men and two women served as attendants for the bride and groom. A day or two later, the couple traveled to Fort Leavenworth, where they resided for more than a month.[16]

On December 20, Stuart was promoted to first lieutenant. Since his graduation from West Point, he had risen from brevet second lieutenant to the present rank. As his father-in-law had noted, he had received an "extraordinary promotion" in a peacetime army. Like many, if not most, officers, Stuart was sensitive to matters of rank. In June 1855, he had written to the adjutant general's office, complaining about the appointment of two lieutenants to the 1st Cavalry. Both of them were placed above him although each man was a brevet second lieutenant, Stuart a permanent second lieutenant. "I respectfully request your early attention to this matter," he ended the letter, "as it is *one of very great interest to myself.*"[17]

A week later, on December 27, Stuart and Flora departed Fort Leavenworth for their trip east. He informed the War Department that his temporary address would be "at the residence of my deceased father" in Wytheville, Virginia. It must have been a joyful return for Stuart, introducing Flora to his mother, brothers, sisters, and other family members. He requested and secured a thirty-day extension to the leave. It was not until March 1856 that the couple returned to Kansas, and he resumed his duties at Fort Leavenworth.[18]

By the time of Stuart's return to the fort, Kansas boiled with violence between anti-slavery and pro-slavery settlers. The passage of the Kansas-Nebraska Act in May 1854 had triggered a national firestorm. The law repealed the Missouri Compromise of 1820, opening the Louisiana Purchase lands north of Missouri's southern border to the possible introduction of slavery. The idea behind the measure was popular sovereignty or allowing the settlers to decide if a territory should be free or slave. In the North, opposition groups coalesced into the Republican Party, which wanted no additional slave states. The issue became a clarion call for both Northerners and Southerners as residents from both regions moved to Kansas, making it a battleground over the extension of slavery. The intense feelings ignited killings, pushing the territory into civil war and pulling the country into a more terrible abyss.[19]

The killing and maiming increased during the fall and winter of 1855–1856. Fraudulent elections inflamed passions. On May 21, 1856, a pro-slavery force attacked the free soil town of Lawrence, ransacking two newspaper offices. Three nights later, a fervidly religious abolitionist named John Brown led six cohorts, including four of his sons, to Pottawatomie Creek, where they hacked to death with broadswords five Southerners. Less than ten days later, on June 2, at Black Jack, Brown and free soilers captured a band of Missouri state militiamen led by Captain Henry Clay Pate.[20]

The army soon learned of the capture of the Missourians. On June 5, Colonel Edwin Sumner and a detachment of the 1st Cavalry arrived at Black Jack. Sumner announced to Brown that the army had orders to disband armed groups, and he had the prisoners released. Although a murder warrant had been issued for Brown for the Pottawatomie slayings, Sumner did not arrest the abolitionist, perhaps because of the colonel's anti-slavery views.[21]

Stuart accompanied Sumner's column. It would not be his last encounter with John Brown. It would be the same with Pate, a fellow Virginian. Pate's conduct—he had surrendered at gunpoint and signed a treaty with Brown—prejudiced Stuart against him. Stuart forgot neither man.[22]

Unlike Sumner, Stuart held staunch pro-slavery views. It could hardly have been otherwise. He had grown up in a slaveholding family and seemed never to question the social, political, and economic basis of the Southern way of life. At this time, he and Flora owned two slaves—a woman named Bettie and a man named Ben. One of the servants, most likely Ben, he had inherited from his father's estate; the other he had purchased. But he would own neither one by the fall of 1859.[23]

Stuart blamed the bloodshed in Kansas on abolitionists like Brown and their supporters. It had been them and "Black Republicans" who had been responsible, as he wrote to his sister Mary, for "lighting the torch of civil war in our midst." Months later after the fall elections in some states, Stuart rejoiced over Democratic victories, telling her, "It is a matter of congratulation to all true Patriots that the Abolitionists have met with such a signal overthrow at the ballot-box and such a frustration of their nefarious schemes against the peace of Kansas and the perpetuity of the Union."[24]

In the letter to his sister, Stuart noted, "Flora and I are getting along happily." Not long before, however, Flora had given birth to a daughter, but the baby died a short time later. "It was a great disappointment to lose our little daughter," Stuart confided to Mary, "but it is better to lose it thus than in maturer years." He added that he seldom heard from his mother or other family members.[25]

Except for the loss of their child, the Stuarts spent a quiet autumn and winter of 1857. Harsh winter weather prevailed across Kansas and the southern plains. His duties as quartermaster and commissary officer at Fort Leavenworth meant much paperwork. During these periods of inactivity, officers at army posts entertained themselves with dances and formal dinners. Officers and enlisted men gambled and drank whiskey, but Stuart indulged in neither. He once told an acquaintance "that if he were to drink any strong liquors at all, he is sure he should be too fond of it, and therefore prefers total abstinence." He preferred lemonade.[26]

Activity quickened at Fort Leavenworth during May 1857, with preparations for a campaign in the field. Sumner had been ordered by Secretary of War Jefferson Davis to march against the Cheyenne the previous fall, but the turmoil in Kansas had postponed the movement. The cavalry would now advance in two columns—Sumner and two companies would follow the Oregon-California Trail, adding dragoon and infantry companies at forts Kearny and Laramie, while Sedgwick and four companies would take the southern route along the Santa Fe Trail. Sumner planned to unite the two forces in the region between the Platte and Arkansas rivers in western Kansas and eastern Colorado.

A third command of four companies, led by Joseph E. Johnston, was assigned to survey the southern border of Kansas and to observe the Kiowa.[27]

The proposed rendezvous of the two wings lay in the homeland of the southern Cheyenne, who shared the hunting grounds with their fellow Algonquin-speaking Arapaho. The Cheyenne numbered fewer than 4,500 men, women, and children in the spring of 1857 as cholera had ravaged their camps less than a decade ago. The Cheyenne were, historian William Y. Chalfant has written, "a true warrior society," which "emphasized military virtue beyond nearly all else." They had raided emigrant trains along the Oregon-California Trail, attacks that had brought Davis's order to the 1st Cavalry. The winter stopped movement along the trail and ceased Cheyenne forays. They called themselves Tsistsistas or "the people," and they were formidable foes.[28]

Sedgwick's column departed Fort Leavenworth on May 18; Sumner's, May 20. Stuart accompanied Sumner as quartermaster and commissary officer. Stuart had been confined to a bed with a fever in the days before the regiment marched. A surgeon described his condition as "very critical," and he needed a cane to walk. He oversaw the preparation and signed the receipts from his bed, relying upon the wagonmaster and quartermaster sergeant for accurate tally of supplies. On the morning of May 20, "although sick weak and emaciated," Stuart supervised the final details, riding in a buggy around the post.[29]

As he performed the work, Stuart received an order from Sumner that appointed him temporary ordnance officer. Stuart went to headquarters and objected to the assignment, stating that he had been unable to take an accounting of ammunition and arms beforehand. He cited regulations that assigned the duty to Sumner. A heated exchange ensued between Stuart and Sumner, with the colonel declaring, "I'll give you this order and you can obey it or not as you like." Stuart agreed to comply but said that he would file an appeal to the War Department.[30]

The dispute worsened once the column was on the march. Stuart informed Sumner that he was submitting his resignation as quartermaster and commissary officer. Before he could write the letter, however, Sumner relieved him on May 31. The next day, Stuart wrote a nine-page letter to the adjutant general in Washington. He detailed the circumstances and then asserted, "I am convinced that Col. Sumner's course toward me, to say the least is calculated to injure one seriously in the estimation of all not cognizant of the *facts*." He requested an investigation, arguing that he had been relieved not for his performance but for his appeal of the orders. He was particularly incensed by Sumner's claim that it had been "necessary and just" to remove Stuart from the duty. He was submitting this letter "for the sake of justice to *me*."[31]

Ironically, Sumner reassigned Stuart to commissary and quartermaster duties months later. Stuart, however, never forgave the colonel for what he regarded as a stain upon his record. Stuart remained with Sumner's wing as it marched west to Fort Laramie, which it reached on June 22, having covered more than three hundred miles. Sumner's column and Sedgwick's united on July 7 on the north bank of the South Platte River at Camp Buchanan. Stuart resumed command of Company G under Sedgwick.[32]

The hunt for the Cheyenne continued on July 13, when the combined force marched east into the Sand Hills region between the South Platte and Republican rivers. Stuart noted in a diary that the country was "finely watered with numerous small creeks." They passed a deserted village site, and Pawnee scouts "found fresh Indian pony tracks." On the morning of July 29, the horse soldiers and infantrymen came upon about 350 Cheyenne warriors aligned for battle along the south fork of the Solomon River. The Cheyenne "had their shields and all their warlike utensils flying [and] they came up very boldly," stated an officer. Sumner deployed the infantry in the center and wheeled six companies of the 1st Cavalry into line. The Cheyenne closed to within a hundred yards.[33]

The cavalrymen drew sabers, and Sumner ordered a charge. With a "terrific yell," the troopers surged ahead under a wave of Indian arrows. The Cheyenne scattered, and a chase ensued. Stuart and lieutenants Lunsford L. Lomax, James McIntyre, and David S. Stanley rode together after the fleeing Indians. Stuart was, claimed a trooper, "sternly anti-Indian." The four men overran a warrior on foot. Stuart fired his revolver, striking the Indian in the thigh. As he swung his saber at him, the Cheyenne discharged "an old fashioned self-cocking 6 shooter" at Stuart. The bullet hit Stuart in the chest, piercing the skin near his left nipple. McIntyre killed the Indian.[34]

Lomax placed Stuart on the ground and shaded him with a blanket tied to upright sabers. The bullet had not penetrated deeply into his chest. Sumner came and spoke to him before troopers carried him in a blanket to the rear. Surgeon Charles Brewer, who would marry Flora's sister Maria, attended to the wound. Within the next few days, Stuart and other wounded men were taken to a recently built field fortification designated Fort Floyd. While Sumner and the command pursued the Cheyenne, an escort and the wounded stayed at the fort until August 8, when the party started for Fort Kearny. Stuart had written in a diary two days earlier, "I am still rapidly improving."[35]

While en route to Fort Kearny, the Pawnee guides deserted. Captain Rennselaer W. Foote, who commanded the detachment, was uncertain about the direction to the post. Having fairly recovered from the wound, Stuart volunteered to ride ahead with a small party to the fort. Foote gave him Lieutenant John McCleary, three enlisted men, and a Mexican guide, whom Stuart described as "cowardly [and] worthless." Ben, Stuart's servant, had accompanied him on the campaign and now went with him. The party rode out on August 15.[36]

A man who served with Stuart in Kansas later declared that he was "worth a dozen ordinary men . . . always prolific of expedients for working his way out of difficult or embarrassing situations." During the first night a thunderstorm roared in. "If I live 100 years," Stuart recorded in the diary, "I never expected to pass such a night." The creek by which they had camped suddenly rose from the downpour, nearly trapping the horses and mules. The men led the animals to higher ground. The next morning, McCleary suggested that they dry saddles and clothing before they resumed the search. "I told him," Stuart recounted, "that under such circumstances we ought to endure anything rather than delay when our speedy arrival at Kearny was of such importance to the command."[37]

They continued, spending much of the day, in Stuart's estimation, "going in a circle." He was convinced that Kearny lay to the north and east. Clouds, however, masked the sun. At night, he wrote, "I prayed God to be my guide & felt an abiding hope that all would be well with us." August 17 dawned clear, and they rode north, struggling across a flooded stream, and finally came upon the mail train from Kearny at noon. The teamsters gave each man a piece of hardtack, "the most deli-cious morsel I ever tasted," said Stuart. They rode into the fort that afternoon, having covered fifty-five miles during the day. Within hours, Stuart led an escort and two wagons, "loaded with hardbread & all sorts of luxuries," back toward Foote's group.[38]

Stuart returned to Fort Leavenworth and a reunion with Flora dur-ing the second week of September. Two months later at 4:20 P.M. on November 14, the second anniversary of their wedding, Flora gave birth to a daughter, whom the parents named Flora. There are no known let-ters written by Stuart at this time that convey his reaction to what must have been a joyous event for both of them.[39]

Weeks after daughter Flora's birth, Stuart commanded a mail escort along the Santa Fe Trail to its crossing of the Arkansas River. He was away for twenty days and rode 250 miles. Upon his return, he was trans-ferred to Fort Riley, resuming command of Company G. Fort Riley lay roughly 150 miles southwest of Fort Leavenworth on the north bank of the Kansas River. Established in 1852, the fort was another of what Indi-ans called "soldier towns." By January 1858, the post consisted of stone and frame officers' quarters, enlisted men's barracks, a hospital, guard-house, and storehouse. Outside the fort, the prairie teemed with game, and steamboats could reach the fort three months out of the year. Fort Riley would be home to the Stuart family for the next three years.[40]

The Stuarts settled into the routine of garrison life during the winter of 1858. A fellow officer remembered Stuart at Fort Riley: "The only thing I can now call to mind of him was his having a favorite horse which would follow him about like a dog, whenever he dismounted. Stuart was whiskered to the eyes like a Cossack, and had a great thick head of hair besides, to complete the resemblance."[41]

Since his arrival in Kansas, Stuart had seen the prospects for invest-ing in land. He told a cousin in 1857, "I am now entirely convinced from personal knowledge, that with a little, and attention I could in a short time make a handsome fortune, by investments in real estate." He borrowed money to purchase property, securing loans that amounted to nearly $5,000. In the spring of 1858, he hired a banking company in Washington, D.C., to sell two lots for him in the town of Leavenworth and forty acres outside of the village.[42]

At the end of May 1858, Major John Sedgwick led six companies from Fort Riley toward Utah Territory. Mormon settlers had attacked wagon trains along the Oregon-California Trail. The army had dispatched a force to quell the violence, and the cavalrymen were being sent as support. Sedgwick, whom Flora disliked and called "a coarse man," appointed Stuart as quartermaster for the command. They spent three months in the field, reaching the Sweetwater River in Colorado Territory before receiving word that a peace settlement had been negotiated between the Mormons and federal authorities. The horsemen arrived back at Fort Riley on August 29.[43]

Upon his return from Utah, Stuart sought a transfer out of the 1st Cavalry. He approached Major William H. Emory of the regiment. In turn, Emory wrote to Major William J. Hardee, commandant of cadets at the military academy: "Lt. Stuart is anxious to go to West Point as asst Instructor of Cav Tactics and I know of no one better qualified in personal deportment or skill as a drill officer of horse than Stuart. If an opportunity presents itself to get him ordered to West Point, I think you will have every reason to congratulate yourself upon the acquisition of a zealous and able assistant."[44]

Stuart's desire went unfulfilled, and he, Flora, and "Little Flora" remained at Fort Riley. They celebrated their wedding anniversary and their child's birth, "two incidents," he noted, "to which I owe what little earthly happiness I possess." In March 1859, Stuart applied for and was granted a six-month leave. When spring blossomed across the plains, the Stuarts embarked for the East. Once again, Wytheville, Virginia, served as a temporary home.[45]

The family appeared to have spent the summer months with kinfolk and friends. Stuart attended as a lay member the Episcopal General Convention in Richmond, and traveled to Washington, to see Lunsford Lomax's family. After he left his friend's home, Mrs. Elizabeth Lomax recorded in her diary: "I never met a more interesting and charming young man. He is very musical and sang many songs with Virginia and Vic." At some point, Stuart returned to Emory and Henry College, where he addressed fellow members of the Hermesian Society. In his speech, he averred: "Ours is a glorious country. I love it but like Mr. [John C.] Calhoun, while I love the Union I love *Virginia more*, and if one attachment ever becomes incompatible with the other I scruple not to say 'Virginia shall command my poor services.'"[46]

Stuart had been at work on a saber hook, or as he termed it, an "improved method of attaching sabers to belts." He secured a patent for it, No. 25,684, on October 4. In his description, he stated, "The nature of my invention consists in having the saber so attached to the belt as to enable the wearer to detach it at pleasure in an instant, so that when mounted troops are called upon to dismount and fight for the time being as infantry they can by this method leave the saber hanging to the pommel of the saddle, and when they remount by the same easy method they can attach the saber again to the belt."[47]

The government purchased the "right to use" his invention for $5,000. Stuart contracted with Knorr, Nece and Company of Philadelphia to manufacture the attachment. The company agreed that every saber belt it produced would have the hook on it and be stamped, "Stuart's patent 1859." For each one sold at $6, Stuart would receive $2. Stuart bound himself and his heirs to refund $2 for each unsold belt. After some hooks had been manufactured, he recommended that they be made of "spring brass instead of spring steel." The money he received from the government he deposited, at 10 percent interest, in the Bank of the State of Missouri in St. Louis.[48]

Patent business and promotion brought Stuart to Washington by mid-October. Earlier in the month, he had applied for an appointment into the quartermaster department. While he was in the city, he visited with Robert E. Lee and family at their Arlington home, across the Potomac River from the capital. Lee invited the former cadet and Custis Lee's close friend to spend the night of October 16–17 with them. The next morning Stuart went to the War Department to negotiate the terms of his contract for his saber attachment and possibly to pursue further his request for promotion.[49]

At the building at Pennsylvania Avenue and 17th Street, Stuart overheard a report from the president of the Baltimore & Ohio Railroad that the arsenal at Harper's Ferry, Virginia, had been seized by an armed force. A rumor estimated the mob at more than three thousand. "It was pretty generally surmised," Stuart wrote later, "that it was a servile insurrection." He volunteered his services to Secretary of War John B. Floyd, who gave Stuart an order to carry to Lee at Arlington. He recrossed the river, handed the message to Lee, and together they hurried to the War Department.[50]

Floyd, Lee, and Stuart walked to the White House to discuss the situation with President James Buchanan. Despite the uncertainty and extent of the uprising, they fashioned a plan, and Lee was given command. Floyd ordered a company of marines from the Washington Navy Yard and four companies of Maryland militiamen to the scene. Stuart volunteered to act as Lee's aide. Being on leave, both Lee and Stuart were dressed in civilian clothes. Stuart, however, managed to borrow a uniform coat and sword.[51]

The two men boarded a train for Relay House and the direct rail line from Baltimore to Harper's Ferry. Lee expected to join the marines at the station, but they had passed through earlier. While Lee and Stuart waited for a locomotive, Lee wired ahead to have the marines wait for them at Sandy Hook, Maryland, across the Potomac from Harper's Ferry. Lee and Stuart joined the marines and militiamen at 10:00 P.M. on October 17. From there, they continued on to the town, arriving before midnight. Lee ascertained from local citizens that early reports had vastly exaggerated the number of raiders. Those who had not been shot were trapped in the armory's engine house with hostages.[52]

The band of nineteen raiders had crossed the Potomac from Maryland twenty-four hours earlier. Ironically, the first man they killed was a free black railroad baggage handler. Abolitionist John Brown from the bloody Kansas strife led the group. Calling himself Smith to shield his identity, Brown had plotted for weeks to seize the armory's weapons and use them in leading slaves in an armed rebellion against whites. It was a far-fetched, if not quixotic, scheme.[53]

Once in Harper's Ferry, however, Brown acted indecisively, dooming the enterprise. The raiders, including two of Brown's sons, rounded up more than thirty hostages, whites and black slaves. Initially, townsfolk reacted in disbelief until the reality became clear. Word spread rapidly, bringing hundreds of armed local men and militia companies from Virginia and Maryland. A gun battle ensued, lasting throughout the day and into the night. Brown tried to negotiate with local leaders an exchange of hostages for passage out of town. It was refused. Finally, after leaving two men with most of the hostages in the armory, Brown led most of his men and eleven white prisoners to the brick engine house.[54]

When Lee arrived and assessed the situation, he replaced the militiamen on the armory grounds with the marines. Fearing for the safety of the hostages with an attack on the engine house in the darkness, Lee decided to wait until daylight and then to demand the surrender of the raiders. Expecting a refusal of his surrender offer, Lee readied an assault party, led by Lieutenant Israel Green, commander of the marines. Stuart wrote afterward of Lee, "I presume no one but myself will ever *know* the *immense* but quiet, service he rendered the state and the country" on this day.[55]

At 7:00 A.M., October 18, Stuart approached the engine house, carrying a flag of truce and Lee's surrender note. He stopped before one of the three heavy oak doors, which was opened a few inches. "When Smith came to the door," recounted Stuart, "I immediately recognized Old Ossawattomie Brown." The abolitionist had been given that nickname while in Kansas. Stuart read the note's terms to the anti-slavery warrior. Brown refused to surrender unless he and his men were granted a safe passage to Maryland. Minutes passed as Brown bartered for new terms, which Stuart repeatedly refused. Finally, Stuart stepped away from the door and waved his hat, the signal for the assault.[56]

Green and two dozen marines raced toward the engine house. Brown and his men opened fire. Using a ladder, the marines battered open a hole in one of the doors, and Green and his men crawled through it. Inside, Green pummeled Brown to the floor with his sword. The marines killed two raiders, and three more were either dead or dying from the previous day's fighting. Two of them were Brown's sons. The marines took into custody Brown and four raiders. Within days, two more of the group were captured in Pennsylvania and sent back to Virginia. The hostages were safe.[57]

The marines carried Brown outside and lay him on the grass. Stuart knelt down beside the wounded man and took a bowie knife from him as a souvenir. A local citizen claimed in a memoir that Stuart joined with others in questioning Brown. When a man asked the abolitionist what wages he had paid his followers, Stuart remarked, "The wages of sin is death." Brown replied, "Young man, had you been *my* prisoner and wounded, I would not have insulted you." Lee, Stuart, and Green's marines stayed in Harper's Ferry until October 20.[58]

Virginia authorities incarcerated the prisoners in the county jail in Charlestown. They charged the raiders with treason, murder, and inciting slaves to rebellion. From his cell, Brown conducted interviews, justifying his actions and saying, "I think I cannot better the cause [of black freedom] I love so much than to die for it; and in my death I may do more than in my life." Found guilty in a trial, he was hanged on December 2, surrounded by a throng of eyewitnesses and hundreds of militiamen.[59]

The events at Harper's Ferry reverberated across the country like a tocsin in the night. Most Northerners condemned the raid while a few voices hailed Brown as a martyr. Southern politicians and newspapers reacted with outrage, blaming Black Republicans and warning Northerners of the dangers to the Union of such attempted slave insurrections. Stuart wrote to Governor Henry Wise and urged him to press the legislature to strengthen militia companies "in view of the exposed position of Virginia to attack from the North." While on leave during the past summer, he had "done all in my power to encourage and help organize military companies." Virginia and other Southern states began purchasing more arms and organizing additional companies.[60]

Less than a month after Harper's Ferry, the Stuarts began the return trip to Fort Riley. They wanted to reach the fort before the Missouri River froze over. The family left Wytheville on November 11, traveling by railroad to Louisville and then by steamboat to St. Louis. They stayed with the Edward Bates family for several days, and Stuart was confirmed in the Episcopal church by a Bishop Hawkes. From St. Louis, the Stuarts and twenty recruits for the regiment traveled by steamboat to Utica, Missouri, where ice closed the river. A train and stagecoaches brought them to Fort Riley by mid-December.[61]

"As for myself & mine," Stuart told his friend Custis Lee as they spent their fourth winter on the plains, "we are very comfortably quartered here, with every luxury that a region abounding in deer, turkey, prairie chickens & poultry of every kind, can afford. Our Garrison society is pretty good. . . . This kind of life agrees with me first rate." In a letter to his mother, he bragged about their daughter, using his affectionate nickname for her, "La Petite." The child was "remarkably robust and hearty, and is learning rapidly to talk. We still think she is a wonder of a baby." He left unsaid in his correspondence that Flora was pregnant with another child, due later in the spring.[62]

Stuart served as temporary commander of Company G during the winter months. "A better company never strode their horses," he declared. Drills and preparations for a spring expedition marked the days. In his letter to Lee, Stuart stated: "We expect very stirring times next summer among the Indians. A campaign of about 5 months duration. The Kiowas & Comanches are the particular objects of vengeance, and all our dispositions and arrangements are made with a view to such a campaign though no order has yet been received, relative thereto."[63]

By May, the orders had been issued and the arrangements completed. The campaign's purpose was, noted a captain, to punish the two tribes "for their murderous depredations during the past winter." On May 15, Sedgwick and companies F, G, H, and K rode out of Fort Riley. Stuart went with Company G, leaving Flora, who was in the final weeks of her pregnancy.[64]

The four companies of the 1st Cavalry spent the next three months in the field, marching more than 1,400 miles, following part of the Santa Fe Trail, searching for the tribes along the Arkansas and Smoky Hill rivers, and crossing into Colorado Territory before turning back for Fort Riley. The only action with Indians occurred on July 11, when Stuart and a twenty-man detachment pursued some Kiowa for more than twenty miles, overtook a small party, and killed two warriors. The cavalrymen failed to locate their main foe, Chief Santaka's band of Kiowa. Stuart thought that the campaign "was unusually arduous."[65]

Throughout it Stuart kept a personal diary and the command's official journal. He wrote few personal comments. When he received letters and a package from Flora, however, he confided: "Bless her heart. Who with my experience could live with a wife, heightening every joy, lightening every sorrow." In the journal, he recorded meticulously, the date, hour of march, weather, distance, drawing of route, and remarks. In the latter column, under June 4, was a typical entry: "Crossed Arkansas River, fording it without difficulty & marched fm south bank at 7:30 a.m., due south 3½ miles touch mulberry creek,—high banks. Good wood and water, Tributary to Arkansas. Crossed ½ mile above there. Dry bed. Continuing southward over barren and monotonous prairie, intersected by many ravines, reach tributary to crooked creek. Water milky hue, but good. Well timbered. Grass scarce and poor." Stuart's experience and attention to detail were evident in the journal.[66]

Upon his return to Fort Riley, Flora welcomed him with a newborn son. Philip St. George Cooke Stuart had been born on the afternoon of June 26. Named for Flora's father, the infant was baptized in the Episcopal church by a Reverend Preston on August 19. Stuart remained united with his family until October, when he left for Fort Wise. Flora and the children stayed behind at Fort Riley, joined by her mother and sisters. The couple would be separated for five months.[67]

Stuart had been ordered to Fort Wise to assist in the construction of the post. The army had selected the site during the summer campaign against the Kiowa and Comanche. It lay on the upper Arkansas River, nearly four hundred miles west of Fort Riley, at "Big Timbers," an extensive span of cottonwoods, "in the heart of Indian country." When Stuart arrived in early October, the officers and men of six companies of cavalry and infantry lived in tents. Work on the quarters and stables had been slow due to "the rudest tools and very scant materials." By November 1, most of the buildings had been erected.[68]

Stuart termed his stay at Fort Wise as "my exile in this wilderness." Flora wrote a letter every week, but it took a month for the mail to arrive. In this isolation, he and the others waited expectantly for news about the presidential election and the reaction of Southern states. As a result of the electoral victory by Republican Abraham Lincoln, South Carolinians voted for secession on December 20. By February 1, 1861, six more Southern states had left the Union. Without knowing of South Carolina's action, Stuart wrote on the date of its decision, "I believe the north will yield what the south demands and thereby avert disunion. *I go with Virginia.*"[69]

Eventually, word came in newspapers to Fort Wise of the nation's descent into disunion and possible civil war. In January 1861, Stuart wrote to a fellow officer stationed at West Point, "Of course, every true patriot deplores even the possibility of disunion, yet let its blessings not be purchased at too great a price." It was a matter of "constitutional rights without which the Union is a mere mockery. . . . For my part, I have no hesitancy from the first that, right or wrong, *alone* or otherwise, *I go with Virginia.*" A week later, he told his brother Alex, "Events are transpiring so rapidly that furnish no little hope of perpetuating the Union." He wanted to raise a legion of cavalry or an artillery battery for Virginia. "I could soon drill and discipline such a corps—and with such material I would feel sure of making 'Stuart's legion' as formidable as 'Lee's legion of the Revolution.'" About the same time, he asked former Mississippi senator Jefferson Davis for a position in the "Army of the South."[70]

On February 2, Stuart was granted a sixty-day leave of absence. He requested it "for the purpose of removing my family to this station." While he completed his duties at Fort Wise, delegates from the seven seceded states met in Montgomery, Alabama, formed the Confederate States of America, wrote a constitution, and chose Jefferson Davis as president and Alexander Stephens of Georgia as vice president. Stuart's wilderness exile ended on March 5, as he traveled east toward Fort Riley and his family. He arrived eight days later.[71]

"I found all well," he wrote of his reunion with his family. "The glowing description of my children were I find no exaggerations. St. George is I think much like Pa. They say here he is very much like me." Like many others, uncertainty clouded his and Flora's future. He informed Alex on March 14: "I will 'quietly and calmy await the march of events.' I do not think Virginia will long hesitate about her final course, and the moment she passes the ordinance of secession I will set out immediately for Richmond and report in person to Governor [John] Letcher unless I ascertain that my services would be more needed at some other point in the state." If there were no conflict, he might still resign from the army and practice law in Memphis, Tennessee. He had passed a legal examination during the previous year.[72]

Several days after his letter to his brother, Stuart wrote to a friend in Richmond. Virginia would determine his fate, but he blamed Lincoln for the crisis. He accused General-in-Chief Winfield Scott, a fellow Virginian, of conducting "a secret inquisition through the army to know whom he can trust with his diabolical designs." He warned his friend that if war came to Virginia, the Tredegar Iron Works in Richmond would be of vital importance to the South and must be secured.

Recalling Colonel Edwin Sumner's treatment of him in 1857, Stuart commented: "If we have war I want to be vis a vis Sumner so as to *teach* him some cavalry evolutions, & take him prisoner. It would be '*sweet revenge.*'" He stated, however, if Virginia did not secede by April 15, he expected to rejoin his regiment.[73]

"The march of events," as Stuart described it, had been moving relentlessly, it seemed, toward an irrevocable confrontation. It came on April 12, at Fort Sumter in the harbor of Charleston, South Carolina, when Southern gunners opened fire on the installation. The garrison surrendered two days later, followed by Lincoln's request for 75,000 volunteers to suppress the rebellion. On April 17, a convention of Virginians voted for secession. From his jail cell before his execution, John Brown had warned Americans, "the crimes of this *guilty, land: will* never be purged *away*; but with Blood."[74]

When Stuart learned of Virginia's action, he and Flora packed for the journey to the East and away from the life they had known together for more than five years. Although he had not resigned his commission, officers and men at Fort Riley understood where the journey would end. John Sedgwick spoke to him before they departed. Stuart valued no superior officer's friendship more than Sedgwick's. There was a quiet reserve to Sedgwick, an almost expressionless countenance to him, but when they met for a final time, tears streaked his face. "Stuart," he said, "you are wrong in the step you are taking, but I cannot blame you for going to the defence of your native state. I am a Northern man and will be true to my own section."[75]

The Stuarts were not alone. His friend Lunsford Lomax went with Virginia, telling George D. Bayard, a fellow officer who remained loyal to the Union: "I feel that I must go. I regret it very much and realize that the whole thing is suicidal." For Flora Stuart, the choice was particularly painful, dividing the Cooke family. Her father refused to leave the army and to side with their native state. Flora's mother and sister Julia joined her father, while her brother, John Rogers, and sister Maria headed south. Like Flora's, Julia's and Maria's allegiance had been determined by their husbands'. Although Stuart was, in his word, "devoted" to Philip St. George Cooke, he never forgave his father-in-law for forsaking Virginia.[76]

The Stuarts traveled a familiar route—from Fort Riley to Fort Leavenworth, down the Missouri and Mississippi rivers to St. Louis, on to Memphis, and then to Cairo, Illinois. In this Northern town on May 3, 1861, Stuart wrote to the War Department in Washington, "From a sense of duty to my native state of Virginia, I hereby resign my position as an officer in the Army of the United States." That same day, he offered his services to Confederate authorities in Montgomery, Alabama, stating that he had resigned "to unite my destinies to Virginia." "My preference is Cavalry, Light Artillery and Light Infantry in the order named," he said, "but I would prefer a position as asst adjt Genl or Topo Engr. if such a position would give me a greater rank." All correspondence to him should be addressed to Governor John Letcher in Richmond.[77]

It could not have been otherwise for Jeb Stuart. While uncertainty gnawed at him for months, a certainty controlled his destiny. He had said repeatedly, "I go with Virginia." He belonged to a generation of Virginians, mostly college-educated, who believed that their state and the South must restore their former preeminence in the nation. When their institutions came under attack by "an aggressive abolitionist-led North," they supported secession. Stuart, historian Peter Carmichael has written, possessed a "sacred regard for Virginia." When Virginia summoned her sons, he answered with devotion few could match.[78]

His five years on the plains had readied him for what lay ahead. He had gained administrative and organizational experience, witnessed the value of scouts and guides, understood the importance of discipline and training, and demonstrated personal bravery at Solomon's Fork and unbending determination in the search for Fort Kearny. Duty on the frontier had been bereft of pageantry, yet he seemingly adhered to the war's romantic nature. Ambition fired him, defense of home impelled him. Virginia had a knight.

Chapter Four

"A Rare Man"

I HAVE A HERCULEAN task before me," Jeb Stuart informed Flora
from Harper's Ferry, Virginia, on May 13, 1861. He had arrived
three days earlier, and the irony of his role in the events of October
1859 could hardly have escaped him. Harper's Ferry lay in the bottom
of a natural bowl, rimmed by three heights, at the confluence of the
Shenandoah and Potomac rivers. Within days of the Old Dominion's
secession, militia companies occupied the town, seizing the armory
buildings, arms, and gun-making machinery.[1]

It had been a scant ten days since Stuart had submitted his resignation from the army in Cairo, Illinois. He and his family had continued
on to Wytheville, where Flora and the children stayed. The parting
between them was difficult. Flora wept and told him that he must love
his country more than his wife. Fearing for his life, she thought that she
would never forgive him. He said that her anguish over his safety hung
about her "like a harbinger of evil."[2]

Stuart hurried to Richmond, reaching it on May 9. Governor John
Letcher, a kinsman, appointed him a lieutenant colonel of infantry in
the state's forces. From his meeting with the governor, he went to the
office of Robert E. Lee, who was now a major general and commander
of Virginia's forces. "General Lee is very much harassed by the trifling

duties he has to perform," Stuart wrote. Lee ordered him to "proceed without delay" to Harper's Ferry and report to Colonel Thomas J. Jackson. That night, Stuart told his wife, "I have received an intimation that I will be in the Cavalry of Va."[3]

Stuart entrained for Harper's Ferry at six o'clock the next morning. Accompanying him were a body servant, named Jo, and Peter W. Hairston. The bondsman had been given to him by his mother. Elizabeth Stuart had been living in the city for a year, and he was able to visit with her before he left for Harper's Ferry. Hairston was Stuart's cousin and had been married to his late sister, Columbia. At Stuart's request, the forty-one-year-old Hairston agreed to serve as a volunteer aide-de-camp.[4]

The trip took most of the day. When Stuart arrived at Harper's Ferry, there were roughly six thousand to seven thousand poorly trained, ill-armed, and ill-equipped volunteers at the place. In the words of their commander, however, "a fierce spirit animates" them. "Strict military discipline prevails," contended a militia captain. Drill was constant, moving a volunteer to grumble, "Days and nights were all full of work and unrest."[5]

The regimen of discipline and training had been instituted by the commander, Colonel Thomas Jonathan Jackson. The thirty-seven-year-old Jackson had been graduated from West Point in 1846, and served in the Mexican War, earning brevets of captain and major. He had resigned from the army in 1852 and joined the faculty of the Virginia Military Institute in Lexington. Assigned to command at Harper's Ferry, he had arrived wearing the blue uniform of a VMI instructor. When cadets at the institute had celebrated the firing on Fort Sumter, he admonished them, "The time for war has not yet come, but it will come and that soon, and when it does come, my advice is to draw the sword and throw away the scabbard."[6]

Jackson stood nearly six feet tall, weighed about 175 pounds, with brown hair and beard and blue eyes. There was a fervency to the man that few others possessed, kindled by a deep religious piety and a strict adherence to duty. A former student of his at VMI declared: "His nature was intense in everything. He was an *intense* Presbyterian. He was an *intense disciplinarian*." A staff officer, writing from Harper's Ferry, called him "one of the most conscientious men I know, pious, determined and brave." At least one soldier thought Jackson eccentric. "He seems to be cut off from his fellow men and to commune with his spirit only."[7]

Jackson was, said future aide Henry Kyd Douglas, "essentially a silent man, not morose, but quiet. He smiled often, rarely laughed." When he spoke, argued an officer, "his words were few and to the point, the voice distinct but rather low." Douglas believed that words "seemed to embarrass him." Those who came to know him well saw the politeness, kindness, even gentleness of the man. He could be abrupt with individuals, however, when at work. In the estimation of a fellow Virginian, Jackson might have been "a gentle-man in peace," but "he was a *warrior* in war."[8]

As an entire country would come to bear witness, warfare touched something deep within this profoundly devout man. Jackson saw the Lord's handiwork in all of mankind's affairs and prayed constantly to discern God's will. Months later he affirmed to his wife that he wanted to forge "an army of the living God as well as of its country." But it was to be his will that he imposed upon his troops. Unbending in his commitment to a soldier's obligations, Jackson "measured other men by his own standard," averred a fellow officer, "and required them to come to his own ideas of duty to be performed." This servant of the Lord would be, before long, a formidable adversary.[9]

This then was Thomas Jackson to whom Stuart reported at his headquarters in the home of the armory's superintendent. They had not met before. To be sure, they possessed disparate personalities. Stuart reveled in life; Jackson saw it as a testing. Stuart could be playful, if not joyous; Jackson, reserved and taciturn. Beneath the outward differences, however, were shared values that defined each man—unshakable Christian faith, fierce attachment to Virginia, firm adherence to duty, and steadfast devotion to the Confederate cause. Like Jackson, Stuart forsook tobacco and alcohol and did not curse.[10]

In time, a friendship deepened between them unlike any other among the senior officers in the army. "Jackson unbent to Stuart more perhaps than any one else in the army," contended Stuart's friend David Boyd, "and Stuart, more than any one else was free and easy with him." One of Jackson's staff officers stated that Jackson's "fondness for General J. E. B. Stuart was very great, and the humor and frolic of that genial and splendid cavalryman was a source of unbounded delight." A biographer of Jackson, James I. Robertson, Jr., has written, "Stuart was the only man in the Confederacy who could make Jackson laugh—and who dared to do so."[11]

But their friendship awaited subsequent days. For the present, as Stuart said, "a Herculean task" confronted both of them. Jackson had instituted a daily routine of formations, guard duty, training, and a dress parade. He assigned VMI cadets as drillmasters. Many of the volunteers belonged to antebellum militia companies, but as a Georgian recounted, prewar drill "closely resembled that of the music at Mr. Bob Sawyer's party, where each guest sang the chorus to the tune he knew best." Stuart told Flora, "the material is however good."[12]

Stuart assumed command of several cavalry companies, mainly from the Shenandoah Valley, which became the 1st Virginia.* He established his headquarters on Bolivar Heights, west of the town, and began "a stirring drill twice every day." Dressed in his blue Regular Army uniform and forage cap, he instructed officers and men in mounted and dismounted tactics, picketing, and conducting patrols. After one day of drill, he allegedly remarked: "They're pretty good officers now. They'll be good soldiers after a while. All they need is reducing to the ranks."[13]

A critical duty assigned to the cavalry was picketing the fords along the Potomac River east and west of Harper's Ferry. Stuart rotated the companies from the river crossings to training at Bolivar Heights. The morale of the officers and men pleased him. "The greatest enthusiasm prevails," he exclaimed, "and the determination to do or die is impressed on every man's features."[14]

On May 23, Brigadier General Joseph E. Johnston arrived at Harper's Ferry and assumed command of the forces. A Virginian and West Point classmate of Robert E. Lee, the fifty-four-year-old had been lieutenant colonel of the 1st Cavalry, serving with Stuart on the frontier. E. Porter Alexander, a future member of the general's staff, said of him: "I think Gen. Jos. E. Johnston was more the soldier in looks, carriage

---

* The term "Cavalry" will not be used with Civil War mounted units. The terms "Infantry" and "Artillery" will be used when applicable and to designate the difference in commands.

& manner than any of our other generals. . . . His whole aspect was to me military discipline idealized & personified." He was, Alexander noted, of "medium stature but of most extraordinary strength, vigor, & quickness."[15]

Johnston found the situation at Harper's Ferry dismaying. Despite Jackson's efforts at discipline and drill and the troops' attitude, the force needed arms, cannon, clothing, equipment of all kinds, and artillery horses. Thousands of men lay ill with measles and mumps in make-shift hospitals, which an inspector described as "very deficient in every respect." As for Stuart's mounted companies, an inspector reported: "The cavalry, under Lieut. Col. J. E. B. Stuart, is in very good condition, and quite effective. Their arms are the small-sized revolver and a saber; no carbines. The horses are good, and all the men ride well. They are made exceedingly useful in the duties of scouts and vedettes, covering a considerable extent of country to the front."[16]

As Johnston worked to alleviate the shortages, Stuart moved his headquarters to Bunker Hill, southwest of Harper's Ferry in the Shenan-doah Valley. "Here all looked like business," according to Lieutenant William W. Blackford of the cavalry. Blackford described Stuart at this time, "He was a little above medium height, broad shouldered and pow-erfully built, ruddy complexion and blue-gray eyes." Stuart had long arms and legs, but on horseback, his short torso made him appear "mas-sive and nearly square," in the words of historian Douglas Southall Free-man. His reddish brown beard and mustache framed and nearly filled his face. He still wore his old blue army uniform.[17]

Stuart spent little time at his headquarters. "Stuart was closely attentive to his business and a hard worker," recalled Blackford. He was constantly in the saddle, riding Skylark, a Maryland-bred sorrel horse. For weeks a Federal army, commanded by Major General Robert Pat-terson, had been forming in southern Pennsylvania, with its pickets and horsemen edging south toward the Potomac River. Occasionally, Yan-kee detachments crossed the stream, clashing with Stuart's troopers. He stayed near the front, alternating pickets every other night. A member of the 1st Virginia, writing in early June, stated, "we are stationed at a very dangerous place for the northerners are trying to get around us in every direction." In Stuart's words, "The ball is open up here."[18]

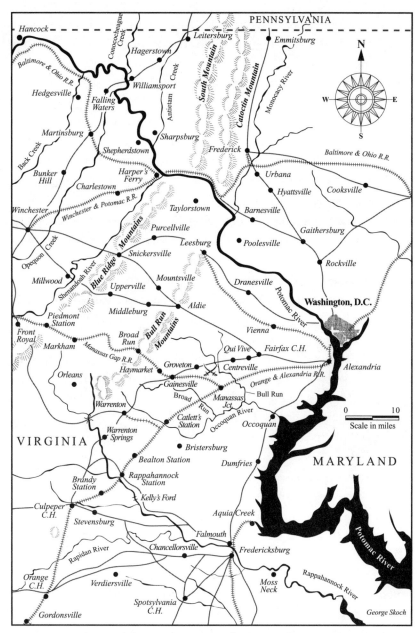

Area of Operations, North-Central Virginia

"Every moment I have," Stuart professed to his wife, "is in requisition for active service in some shape—arresting spies, blowing up bridges, patrolling &c." His presence was not without benefits, however. Women in the area brought him strawberries, flowers, and "other nice things." "The young men of the regiment wonder why it is that I am the recipient of so much favor," he added. "They forget that rank will tell."[19]

Since he had arrived at Harper's Ferry, he had written to Flora as often as he could, numbering each letter. He began most of them with "My Darling Wife" or "Darling One." He reassured her of his love—"I think of you Dear one every day & hour. . . . I want to see you, to hold you in my arms with your head resting on this breast as I always hold it but duty & fate has otherwise ordered it." He wrote about the children, telling her, "Kiss our dear ones a thousand times and keep them in mind of their Pa."[20]

He addressed other matters in the correspondence. He needed a saddle, camp equipment, and a flag for the regiment. He learned that President Lincoln had accepted his resignation from the army on May 14. He admitted being "extremely anxious" about her father and brother. "How can they serve Lincoln's diabolical government?" In fact, John Rogers Cooke had already resigned his commission and joined the Confederacy. Philip St. George Cooke was still in the West and loyal to the Union. "Principle, interest and affection demand his immediate resignation and return to his native state," Stuart declared about his father-in-law.[21]

He kept her apprised about the military situation. "It may become absolutely necessary for this command [Johnston's army] to fall back in order not to be cut off from supplies—but every inch of our retreat will be marked with the blood of the invader." In mid-June, he stated: "Things are hastening to a crisis, every day, sometimes twice a day, I hear of the enemy's drawing a little closer. He has not yet reached the Potomac. Gen'l. Johnston writes himself to me every day, and I have little doubt that the moment the enemy is near he will march out near me and meet him, instead of waiting to be attacked at Harpers Ferry."[22]

As he predicted, the Confederate Army of the Shenandoah began its withdrawal from Harper's Ferry on June 15. Johnston had not liked the vulnerability of the position since his arrival. If the enemy occupied Maryland Heights across the Potomac and advanced south, up the Shenandoah Valley, his army could be trapped. Robert E. Lee and Confederate authorities in Richmond, where the nation's capital had been relocated from Montgomery, regarded the possession of the town as indispensable to the defense of Virginia's borders. After weeks of correspondence, the government acquiesced to Johnston's arguments. Before they retreated, the Southerners removed the armory machinery, burned the buildings, and destroyed the railroad bridge across the Potomac. They retired to Winchester.[23]

Stuart's and Captain Turner Ashby's cavalrymen screened the retreat. Ashby had been with the first body of troops who entered Harper's Ferry in April. Ashby was a small, darkly complexioned man, with a long, flowing beard and intense black eyes. A superb horseman, he commanded the mounted companies until Stuart arrived. To avoid a possible clash between them, Jackson assigned Ashby to two companies of scouts and gave Stuart the other units, which formed the 1st Virginia. Like Stuart, Ashby was as "fearless as a lion." But unlike Stuart, he either could not or would not instill discipline in his command.[24]

With the Confederate retreat from Harper's Ferry, Ashby's companies guarded the fords downriver from the town, while Stuart's horsemen covered the approaches into the Shenandoah Valley. A small vanguard of Patterson's Union army entered the Valley on June 16, remained a few days, and then recrossed the river. Stuart reported their presence to Johnston, who instructed him to feint an attack on the enemy. He led his men to the river opposite Williamsport, Maryland, which was occupied by "a large force" of Federal infantry. "I flew around," Stuart boasted to Flora, and the Yankees fired upon his troopers. He sent a message to Johnston, proposing a crossing of the Potomac with cavalry and infantry to attack the enemy's rear. "We are too distant to avail ourselves to it," replied Johnston. "Look well to your flanks. I write it knowing it to be superfluous to do so."[25]

Johnston's chief engineer reported that Stuart's cavalry was "under that very active and vigilant officer" who "gave almost hourly information of every movement of the enemy." The vigilance was necessary, but Stuart acted with a calculated boldness. He wanted to infuse his men with an élan in combat. He explained his thinking: "I realize that if we oppose force to force we cannot win, for their resources are greater than ours. We must make up in quality what we lack in numbers. We must substitute *esprit* for numbers. Therefore, I strive to inculcate in my men the spirit of the chase."[26]

At first, his daring convinced his men that he was a "hare-brained fellow" and a "reckless colonel." His training exercises, which he led them as close as he could to the Federals, they called "madcap expeditions." When they went into action, Stuart did not use army commands but shouted, "Come on, boys, let's go!" When he wanted them at a gallop, he used "go a-kiting." But he won them over because, as one of them claimed, "he led almost everything." He worked ceaselessly—"Perpetual activity was a necessity of his existence," added the trooper. He possessed a boyishness that the men identified with, and he remembered their faces and names. "Stuart's was one of those magnetic natures," concluded a Virginian, "which always impress their own likeness upon others."[27]

Stuart reveled in the chase. Although his men continued to lack adequate arms, it did not deter him from the "madcap expeditions." Johnston described him as "indefatigable," with the "habit . . . of leaving the protection of the infantry" to harass the enemy and to put outposts far in advance. His aide, Peter Hairston, believed, "Lt. Col. is one of the bravest & noblest men I have ever seen & a fine officer." "We have amusing times around our camp fires at night talking the adventures of the day and cracking jokes."[28]

At this time, Stuart heard a rumor that a senior officer might be assigned to the army to command the cavalry. He inquired of Johnston whether there was any truth to it. The army commander responded: "I should regard the assignment of any other officer than yourself to the command of the cavalry as a misfortune, & of course, therefore, will do what I can to keep you in the position. I have not moved in the matter because it has seemed to me impossible that any one could be put over you."[29]

By the end of June, activity along the Potomac River increased. Johnston sent Jackson, a brigadier general now, and his brigade of five Virginia infantry regiments to Martinsburg. Jackson's men burned the

shops, engines, and cars of the Baltimore & Ohio Railroad, before establishing a camp four miles north of town. Beyond the river, Patterson
and 11,000 troops closed on Williamsport, Maryland. Stuart's videttes
dotted the southern bank, watching the fords.[30]

"Our troops are anxious for an engagement," wrote Jackson. At 7:30
A.M., on July 2, he received a message from Stuart, who reported that
a contingent of Federals had crossed the river and was marching south
on Valley Pike. Jackson hurried forward the 5th Virginia Infantry and
an artillery battery, bringing up two more regiments in support. Stuart,
meanwhile, gathered three companies—"Col Stuart instantly had us
in the saddle," stated a trooper—and rode to delay the Yankees. Two
mounted companies covered Jackson's advance, while Stuart and Company E circled west against the enemy's right flank. The opponents met
at Falling Waters, a bend in the river.[31]

While Jackson's Confederates engaged the enemy in a fitful action,
Stuart led Company E toward the Union flank. Stopping his men in
a stand of trees, Stuart saw a company of enemy infantry halted in a
road, which lay west of the pike. When a small detachment of Yankees
marched forward, Stuart sent a party of troopers to intercept it. Wearing
his blue army uniform, he rode ahead alone, halted at a fence along the
road, and ordered the Federals to open a section of it for cavalry. Believing him to be an officer in their army, the infantrymen complied. Stuart
spurred through, and drawing a revolver, said, "Throw down your arms
or you are dead men!"[32]

The stunned Yankees, members of Company I, 15th Pennsylvania
Infantry, obeyed and lay facedown in the roadbed. Stuart's men rushed
forward from the woods, lifted the prisoners onto their horses, and hastened away. Stuart's audacity had bagged about fifty Pennsylvanians.
"Colonel Stuart and his command merit high praise," reported Jackson,
"and I may here remark that he has exhibited those qualities which are
calculated to make him eminent in his arm of the service."[33]

Jackson withdrew toward Winchester after the Falling Waters
engagement, followed by Patterson's army, which halted initially at
Martinsburg. On July 4, Stuart predicted to Flora, "Look out for stirring events here." For the next two weeks, his horsemen were "as
usual, detecting every movement and harassing their pickets by con-

tinual activity," stated Johnston's chief engineer. Johnston augmented Stuart's command, adding four companies to the regiment. The army commander wired the Confederate War Department: "I become more convinced daily of the great value of cavalry, compared to infantry, for service on this frontier. . . . If you can send companies enough to make up another regiment under such an officer as Colonel Stuart, you will add vastly to the strength of this force."[34]

A private in the 1st Virginia boasted about the men's prowess, "it is hard to trap us but we trap the boys regular our Boys have had such good luck that they become fond of it we go and take their pickets off their post and catch others while out hunting something to eat they are as afraid of us as they need be." An infantryman thought that Stuart's men brought in prisoners every day. Staff officer Hairston claimed, "The first regiment of Cavalry is getting so popular that every one wishes to join it."[35]

Stuart issued a general order to the regiment, commending them for the "accomplishment of the arduous and dangerous, as well honorable duties, which of late devolved upon it." He went on, "The Col takes this occasion to impress upon the gallant men of the 1st Cavalry that vigilance and cheerful obedience to orders are the highest attributes of the soldier, and that the cause in which our sabers are drawn, deserves the best efforts, and demands every sacrifice of the true patriot."[36]

On July 16, Patterson's army resumed its march south toward Johnston's 11,000 men at Winchester. Stuart's horsemen blocked the roads with felled trees and gnawed at the edges of the Union columns. Patterson halted at Bunker Hill, and then retreated. On this day to the east, beyond the Blue Ridge, a 35,000-man Federal army, under Brigadier General Irvin McDowell, lumbered out of Washington toward Manassas Junction. If Patterson could hold Johnston's forces in the Valley, McDowell would face only 22,000 Confederate troops under Brigadier General P. G. T. Beauregard.[37]

Such a Union movement had been expected for weeks. The Manassas Gap Railroad, coming from the Shenandoah Valley, connected with the Orange & Alexandria Railroad at Manassas Junction. If a Union army planned an overland advance on Richmond, defense of the junction was vital to the Confederates. After Virginia's secession, Robert E.

Lee directed units there. As more regiments arrived, Beauregard organized them into brigades, readying them for a probable battle. With Northern newspapers clamoring, "Forward to Richmond! Forward to Richmond!," the Lincoln administration ordered an advance by McDowell.[38]

About 1:00 A.M. on July 18, Johnston received a telegram from Richmond, requesting, "if practicable," to join Beauregard at Manassas Junction. He stated afterward that he believed the "best service" he could do with his army "was to prevent the defeat" of Beauregard's forces. Leaving some militia companies behind to guard Winchester, Johnston started his army east in the afternoon, with Jackson's brigade in the lead. To the north, Stuart's cavalrymen screened the movement, aggressively moving toward Patterson's lines. There were no clashes, he informed Flora, and "we feel disappointed, but all things are for the best." He withdrew toward Winchester for the night, and followed the infantry and artillery across the Blue Ridge the next morning. An officer with Patterson recorded in his journal, "In my opinion Patterson could not have prevented this."[39]

The 1st Virginia arrived at Piedmont Station on the Manassas Gap Railroad late at night on July 19 and bivouacked. At the station for most of the day, Johnston's infantry had been piling into railroad cars for the eight-hour, thirty-five-mile ride to Manassas Junction. Not until July 21 would all of Johnston's units join Beauregard's troops.[40]

A hard rain fell as Stuart resumed the march at three o'clock the next morning. While en route east, a company of Maryland volunteers joined the regiment and Stuart appointed Lieutenant William Blackford to his staff as adjutant. Riding near Stuart as he had for nearly two months was Private George W. Freed, his bugler, who would remain with him until May 1864. Whether Stuart learned of it or not, he had been promoted to colonel in the Confederate army, to date from July 16. The cavalrymen reached the junction at sundown.[41]

Beauregard had deployed his brigades along Bull Run to cover the numerous crossing sites. When the vanguard of the Union army neared on July 18, a minor clash had occurred at Blackburn's Ford. Beauregard considered an offensive strike, but it was McDowell who prepared an attack for July 21. His plan, too complicated for inexperienced officers and men, required a flanking movement around the Confederate left. When this column had driven back the Rebels and cleared fords and a bridge, more Federal units would cross the stream and assail the enemy position. On the night of July 20, a Union sergeant recorded in his journal, "I pray that I may have the strength & courage to carry me safely through or to die decently in a manner becoming an American soldier." His plea was likely repeated on both sides of Bull Run.[42]

Sunday, July 21, 1861, was a Sabbath unlike any in the collective memory of Americans. By sundown, the country had lost some of its innocence, and young men who had answered a clarion call had witnessed the terribleness hidden behind the cheering crowds, the patriotic oratory, the playing bands, and the unfurled flags. Tragically, it was only a disturbing dream in an unfolding nightmare.

The reckoning developed slowly as jammed roads and the men's fatigue delayed the Union attacks until past 9:30 A.M., hours behind schedule. The Federals charged up Matthews Hill, wrenching it from the defenders, who fled rearward to Henry House Hill. On the second rise stood Jackson's brigade of five Virginia infantry regiments and the re-formed ranks of other units. It was after noon when the Yankees ascended the slope into a cauldron of rifle and cannon fire. Union commanders sent the regiments, upward of twenty of them, in piecemeal. Two batteries rolled on to the hill, bracing the attackers. On this day Jackson and his Virginians earned the nickname "Stonewall" for their fierce defense. The combat ebbed and flowed with charges and countercharges. A Wisconsin captain called it "dreadful," while a Virginian swore to his wife, "I never expected to see you again."[43]

Adjutant William Blackford recalled that Stuart spent much of the morning "uneasy for fear that he would not be called into action." The 1st Virginia and Colonel Richard C. W. Radford's six companies of cavalrymen had been instructed by Beauregard "to be held in hand, subject to future orders and ready for employment." While he waited and the fighting increased to the front, Stuart sent couriers to headquarters, requesting instructions to advance. Although the accounts conflict, Johnston and/or Jackson directed him before noon to cover the army's left flank west of Henry House Hill. Stuart divided the regiment into two wings, holding one in reserve and personally leading five companies at a "fast trot" toward "the heaviest fire." Radford's companies moved toward the right and rear of Jackson's line.[44]

Stuart halted his five companies in a woodlot near Manassas–Sudley Road. To the front, the struggle for Henry House Hill raged. Directly ahead, perhaps seventy-five to one hundred yards away, an enemy regiment, "dressed in red," was fleeing rearward. The Federal unit was the 11th New York Infantry or Fire Zouaves. Their uniforms were fashioned after French soldiers, with blue jackets and baggy red pants. They had charged Jackson's line with the 1st Minnesota Infantry and 14th Brooklyn Infantry. In the words of their brigade commander, they were "swept back as by a tornado" by the Confederate fire. Now, the Fire Zouaves were "bewildered and broken" and streaming away from the carnage.[45]

At first Stuart mistook them for Confederates, shouting to them, "Don't run, boys; we are here." "They paid very little attention to this appeal." Stuart rode forward, clearing the treeline into a field, with companies H and D behind him. When he saw the New Yorkers' national flag, he ordered the two companies to charge. Within minutes, the cavalrymen were among the Fire Zouaves. "We slew them at a great rate with pistols," claimed Blackford.[46]

The momentum of the attack carried the Virginians through the splintered ranks. Wheeling around, they surged back toward the woods. Two companies of the Fire Zouaves had been held in reserve, and according to a lieutenant with Stuart, "rose from the ground in mass, and fired a terrible volley at my men." Horses and riders plunged to the ground. Blackford said the wounded animals were "floundering like chickens when their heads are cut off." Stuart rallied his men among the trees, prepared to charge again, but decided against it as other Union regiments entered the field and woods to his right. The cavalrymen retired to the west. Losses amounted to nine men killed or mortally wounded, sixteen wounded, and eighteen horses slain.[47]

Before long the contest for Henry House Hill climaxed when Johnston's final brigades arrived on the battlefield and unhinged the Union right flank. The Yankees had fought valiantly, but their retreat spiraled rapidly into a rout. Several factors contributed to the panic that degenerated into a frenzied mob of men. Stuart's and Radford's horsemen pursued, seizing captives and discarded weapons and equipment. "For

twelve miles," wrote a member of the 1st Virginia, "the road was literally strewn with every description of Baggage, Wagons, Ambulances,
Barrels of sugar, Crackers, Ground Coffee & thousands of Axes, Spades,
Shovels picks Arms by the thousands." Another trooper proclaimed
that so much of the captured items, from tents to ambulances to wagons, "were branded in large letters U.S. you would have thought to see
the camp we were U.S. troops." Stuart admitted that his pursuit was
slowed by the number of prisoners gathered.[48]

The Battle of First Manassas or First Bull Run exacted more than
five thousand casualties, a bloodletting that would pale in numbers with
what lay ahead. The stand on Henry House Hill and the arrival of reinforcements from the Shenandoah Valley gave the Confederates a decisive victory. But it would require time, training, and experience before
these good men became good soldiers.[49]

Stuart's performance earned him commendation. Johnston cited
him among others in his report, and as Stuart informed Flora, "Gen'l
Johnston speaks in the highest terms of my conduct." Beauregard stated:
"Col. J. E. B. Stuart likewise deserves mention for his enterprise and
ability as a cavalry commander. Through his judicious reconnaissance
of the country on our left flank he acquired information, both of topographical features and the positions of the enemy, of the utmost importance in the subsequent and closing movements of the day on that flank,
and his services in pursuit were highly effective."[50]

Rain fell on July 22, as Stuart led his men east through the debris of
the Union retreat. He described the flight as "utter disorder." He halted
at Fairfax Court House, sending out scouts toward the enemy works at
Alexandria. He reported the next morning that a civilian stated that
Major General George B. McClellan would relieve Irvin McDowell as
commander of the Federal army and that Robert Patterson was to be
relieved. The information was quite timely as the War Department in
Washington had wired McClellan to report to the capital on July 22.[51]

Confederate presence at Fairfax Court House, a dozen miles west
of Alexandria on Little River Turnpike, brought the conflict to within
the shadow of the Federal capital. During the next two months, the
Rebels moved closer to their opponents' works, occupying key heights
in the vicinity of Falls Church on Leesburg–Alexandria Turnpike, and

Annandale, seven miles east of Fairfax Court House on Little River Turnpike. They erected signal stations on Munson's Hill, two miles east of Falls Church, and Mason's Hill, two miles northeast of Annandale. From these hills, the Southerners could view the Capitol dome and church spires across the Potomac. Pickets rimmed the edge of the advanced line, with reserves in support.[52]

The bulk of picket duty and reconnaissance fell to Stuart and his cavalry. He established his headquarters on Munson's Hill, spending nearly every night there, sleeping under a pine tree. Writing from the hill, he stated: "I believe this is a fine line of defense; I mean the line passing through this and Mason's Hill. Every inch of the road is visible from here to Bailey's Cross-Roads." Wearing his "old blue undress [army] coat," brown velveteen pantaloons, and a cap with a white havelock, Stuart was on horseback each day, checking on outposts or joining his scouts as they prowled close to Union lines.[53]

Stuart impressed upon his men the seriousness and importance of the duty. A trooper remarked that their colonel "was very strict in his methods." While on picket duty, each man was required to remain mounted. Toward dusk, he and his staff rode to each post, making sure they were complying with orders. After he and his staff had staged a mock raid on the picket line, he told them, in words of one of them, "his object was to teach us to be on the alert all the time; that as cavalry, we were the eyes and ears of the army and that upon our vigilance depended the safety of the army."[54]

Stuart forbade his men from fraternizing or communicating with their Union counterparts unless exchanges "comply with the usages of war." When a cavalryman complained to him about duty at the front, he replied, "Nonsense . . . you don't want to go back to camp I know; it's stupid there and all the fun is out here." He enjoyed having cannon fired at enemy balloons, having drummers beat the long roll near Federal works, and shouting for volunteers to charge, again within hearing distance of the Yankees.[55]

There were grumblings about Stuart in the 1st Virginia. A private lamented, "Stuart has treated us very badly he is a real tyrant to his men!" A captain held a similar view: "He is in my opinion, a man destitute of any humanity. He treats the men just as if we were Savages, And the officers not much better." On one occasion, the colonel of the 18th Virginia Infantry refused to join him in an attack of an enemy outpost. A soldier explained the reason, "Some of the company officers seemed to think it was useless expense, the only end of which would be to magnify J. E. B. as an active, enterprising officer, and opposed it."[56]

The dissent voiced by some of the Virginians resulted evidently from the demands of the duty and Stuart's discipline. When at Camp Cooper, their bivouac area in the rear, officers drilled the men. Disease stalked the camp, affecting more. "The soldiers are dying around me like flies," wrote a private in the regiment. At times, Stuart might have appeared as "destitute of any humanity," but he affirmed to Flora, "I have a reputation of being very fond of saying, 'no,' but I have had but one rule of action from the first and that was duty."[57]

Officers and men in other regiments in the army praised Stuart. An infantryman declared, "Stuart is a terror to the enemy," while a captain in the 4th Virginia Infantry of Jackson's brigade proclaimed to his wife, "Colonel Stuart, you must understand, flaunts his colors in their [the enemy's] faces, all the time." Another member of the brigade worried that Stuart's exploits would "bring on a general engagement." Colonel William Dorsey Pender of the 6th North Carolina said of his West Point classmate and friend: "Beaut Stuart who commands in advance has gained probably more reputation than any young man in the Army. It was talked in Richmond that he was to be made a General. Every one speaks [of Stuart] in the highest terms."[58]

Johnston called him in his memoirs "matchless as commander of outpost." In a letter to President Jefferson Davis, written in August, the army commander inquired about more cavalry regiments and placing Stuart in command: "He is a rare man, wonderfully endowed by nature with the qualities necessary for an officer of light cavalry. . . . Calm, firm, acute, active, and enterprising, I know no one more competent than he to estimate the occurrences before him at their true value. If you add to this army a real brigade of cavalry, you can find no better brigadier-general to command it."[59]

Later in the month Brigadier General James Longstreet was appointed commander of the so-called Advance Forces. A West Pointer, the forty-year-old Georgian had been wounded in Mexico and served on the Texas frontier in the antebellum army. His brigade had resisted the Union reconnaissance at Blackburn's Ford on July 18, but had not been seriously engaged during the Battle of First Manassas. Physically strong, he stood about six feet, two inches and weighed about two hundred pounds. Like Stuart, he never seemed to tire. Once after a long day in the field, a staff officer said he must be exhausted. "No," replied Longstreet, "I have never felt fatigue in my life."[60]

An acquaintance of Longstreet described him as "a particularly taciturn man." When Stuart's adjutant, Lieutenant Blackford, first met the general at Fairfax Court House, he thought that Longstreet was "a man of limited capacity who acquired reputation for wisdom by never saying anything—the old story of the owl." Weeks later, however, after serving under Longstreet on temporary duty, Blackford admitted, "He has been very kind to me and has shown me much attention." Echoing Blackford's words, a member of his staff asserted: "Genl. Longstreet is one of the kindest, best hearted men I ever knew. Those not well acquainted with him think him short and crabbed." When conducting official business, Longstreet could be blunt.[61]

Longstreet enjoyed the camaraderie of soldier life, and old friends and former comrades frequented his headquarters for good food and conviviality. It is not surprising that Stuart, with his zest for life, took meals with Longstreet. The general liked the younger man from the outset. Beauregard had sent Longstreet and his brigade forward "to prevent a *coup de main*" or surprise attack by the enemy. The duty required Longstreet and Stuart to work closely together. Before long, Longstreet wrote to army headquarters that the cavalry officer "has been most untiring in the discharge of his duties. . . . Colonel Stuart has, I think, fairly won his claim to brigadier, and I hope the commanding generals will unite with me in recommending him for that promotion."[62]

Twice, on August 28 at Bailey's Crossroads, and on September 11 at Lewinsville, Stuart engaged Union troops, relying primarily on artillery. In the latter action, a pair of cannon from the Washington Artillery of New Orleans scattered two Federal regiments and exchanged fire with enemy guns. The conduct of Lieutenant Thomas L. Rosser, commanding the Confederate section of artillery, impressed Stuart. Longstreet termed Lewinsville a "handsome affair" and assured the army's chief of staff that when Stuart "has lost a man, he has brought in at least two of the enemy—dead or alive."[63]

After the action at Lewinsville, Stuart received a note, passed through the lines, from academy friend Orlando M. Poe, now a lieutenant and engineer in the Union army. Poe had not recognized Stuart during the fighting but wanted to invite him to dinner at Willard's Hotel in Washington. "I have the honor to report," responded Stuart to his friend, "that 'circumstances were such' that they could have seen me if they had stopped to look behind—and I answered both at the cannons mouth." He declined the dinner invitation.[64]

Although Beauregard and Johnston praised Stuart's performance in the affairs, they worried about his "free use" of artillery. To them, the cavalryman's aggressiveness placed the guns too close to Union lines and their possible capture. Longstreet defended his subordinate, telling Stuart, "without asking authority I took it upon myself to deny the report of imprudence, attributed to you." He reassured him: "you should remember that when there is so much at stake the authorities are of the opinion that too much caution cannot be had. Besides Politics are a little mixed with our cause, and actions. So we cannot be too guarded. Don't give yourself any uneasiness about the matter, however, for you have been entirely successful."[65]

On the day Longstreet wrote to Stuart, September 14, Johnston submitted a significant proposal to the War Department. He, Beauregard, and Longstreet recommended the "forming of a cavalry brigade and putting Colonel Stuart at its head. A new organization of the cavalry arm of our service is greatly needed and greater strength as well as an effective organization. Our numbers in cavalry are by no means in due proportion to our infantry and artillery, yet without cavalry in proper proportion victory is comparatively barren of results; defeat is less prejudicial; retreat is usually safe."[66]

The generals' recommendation led to the creation of an independent mounted command, which gave the Confederates a decided edge in future operations. In contrast, it would be months before the Union government adopted a similar organization. As commander of the now christened Army of the Potomac, however, George McClellan would misuse his cavalry regiments, parceling them out among infantry corps.

Against an opponent unified under a commander with Stuart's talent, the Federals were to be dominated in this arm of the service for a long time. The foresight of the Confederate generals and officials allowed Southern horsemen to undertake raids and to screen the army's movements without much interference from their mounted foes.[67]

Ten days after Johnston forwarded his letter, the War Department rewarded Stuart with promotion to brigadier general. Nearly two months before, he had confided to Flora, "You need not be surprised to see your hubbie a Brigadier. I have been in one real battle now & feel sure that I can command better than many I saw." Arguably, no colonel's performance merited promotion more than Stuart's. As Johnston exclaimed, he was "a rare man" and a matchless cavalry officer in the army. Writing of his friend, Dorsey Pender had it right when he attested, "He has risen from Lt. Colonel by hard work."[68]

Chapter Five

"I Will Not Leave the Van of Our Army"

WAR'S BLIGHT ENVELOPED the land around Centreville, Virginia. The peaceful antebellum countryside had been transformed by scars of dug earth and the voracious appetite of an occupying army. "Such desolation you can't imagine," exclaimed a North Carolina soldier. "The whole country seems laid waste. But such is the desolation of war."[1]

Since the early days of October 1861, the Confederates had been consolidating their lines around Centreville and settling into camps before the onslaught of winter weather. They had abandoned their advanced outposts on Mason's and Munson's hills and at Fall's Church. The infantry and artillery camps sprawled in an arc from north to south, east of the town. Warehouses were under construction at Manassas Junction for the storage of supplies. A Rebel described army life at this time as one of "monotony and miserable inactivity, measles and typhoid fever."[2]

The army underwent a reorganization as it concentrated its lines around Centreville. On October 22, the War Department created the Department of Northern Virginia, assigning General Joseph E. Johnston to command it. The order established three military districts—

Potomac, Aquia, and Valley—and authorized the consolidation of infantry brigades into four divisions. The cavalry brigade retained its separate organization, operating under the direct authority of Johnston. Centreville, described as "a sort of dilapidated place" by a Rebel, served as headquarters for the army.[3]

Jeb Stuart established his headquarters three miles outside Centreville, naming it Camp Qui Vive, or "Who Goes There?" The appointment of Johnston as department commander pleased him. "Johnston is in capacity head and shoulders above every other general in the Southern Confederacy," wrote Stuart. He called the general "the dearest friend I have on earth." When Stuart learned of Robert E. Lee's failed campaign in the western Virginia mountains, he noted, "with profound personal regards for General Lee, he has disappointed me as a general."[4]

The organization and training of the cavalry regiments consumed much of Stuart's days. When Flora suggested joining him in camp, he warned her, "I can't promise that you will see much of your husband when you come & you musn't say it is cruel in me to leave you at short notice for the imperative calls of duty." The number of officers and men in the brigade increased from more than 1,600 present for duty in October to nearly 2,400 in December.[5]

When Johnston had proposed the formation of a cavalry brigade and Stuart's promotion to brigadier, he recommended Captain William E. Jones, with the rank of colonel, as commander of the 1st Virginia and Captain Fitzhugh Lee as the regiment's lieutenant colonel. Johnston wrote that Jones "now commands the strongest troop in the regiment and one which is not surpassed in discipline or spirit by any in the army." He "is skillful, brave, and zealous in a very high degree. It is enough to say that he is worthy to succeed J. E. B. Stuart."[6]

A Virginian, the thirty-seven-year-old Jones had attended Emory and Henry College and was an 1848 graduate of West Point. Like Stuart, he had served in the Mounted Rifles. While en route to join the regiment in Texas, Jones and his bride, Eliza M. Dunn, were passengers on a boat lashed by a violent storm in the Gulf of Mexico. When the wind and waves wrecked the boat at Pass Caballo near Matagorda, Eliza was torn from Jones's grasp and killed. A biographer of Jones has written that he "was changed forever." Resigning his commission in 1857, Jones returned to his home in southwestern Virginia. Elected captain of a militia company, Washington Mounted Rifles, Jones led it to war upon the secession of the Old Dominion. In time, the unit became Company D of the 1st Virginia.[7]

Jones was known universally as "Grumble" for his acidic disposition. A cavalryman claimed that he "was an eccentric officer, who seemed to take pleasure in self-torture, as if doing penance." A member of the regiment recounted, "He was thought by some, to be very austere, as he was very strict; but I thought he was very humane." His men came to call him "*Old pap Jones*." Physically small, Jones dressed plainly, moving one trooper to swear that he looked "like a tramp on horseback." Jones detested any semblance of showmanship and frivolity. In a number of ways, he was the antithesis of Stuart, and a clash between them was probably inevitable.[8]

In their postwar memoirs two of Stuart's closest aides, Henry B. McClellan and William Blackford, alleged that difficulties between Jones and Stuart arose during the autumn of 1861. McClellan claimed, "there was an unfortunate interruption of their personal relations, after which kind cooperation between two such positive natures was hardly possible." Blackford maintained that Jones's "intense jealousy" of Stuart caused the rupture. Jones's feelings "ripened afterwards into as genuine hatred as I ever remember to have seen in my experience in life."[9]

Contemporary evidence indicates, however, that the rupture between them did not occur during the initial weeks of the fall. Jones attended dinners at Stuart's headquarters, and the general wrote that Jones was among a group of subordinates who "give me no trouble at all." Problems might have arisen later in the fall or during the winter that resulted in a breach between them. More likely, the serious rift originated in the spring of 1862. When it happened, it was marked by acrimony and bitterness.[10]

Stuart's relationship with Jones's lieutenant colonel, Fitzhugh Lee, was entirely different. He had wanted Lee, the nephew of Robert E. Lee, appointed colonel of the regiment. In his recommendation for Lee, Johnston wrote: "He belongs to a family in which military genius seems an heirloom. He is an officer of rare merit, capacity, and courage." Another West Pointer, Class of 1856, Lee had served with the 2nd

Cavalry before joining the Confederacy. He was a member of Brigadier General Richard S. Ewell's staff at the time of his assignment to the 1st Virginia.[11]

Lee was, remembered a cavalryman, "a handsome little officer." He stood perhaps five feet, four or five inches tall. A tall aide, who served on his staff after Lee became a brigadier, insisted, "I can sit down & eat soup off the General's head" while Lee stood. He enjoyed good food, and in historian Douglas Southall Freeman's estimation, he was "already too fat." A sculptor who had Lee pose for him after the war described the old soldier as "a large, burly man" with "a cold, assertive, far-gazing, large round blue eyes, a bold eagle nose."[12]

In Lee, Stuart had a kindred spirit in temperament. While a cadet, Lee amassed his share of demerits for pranks and other violations. He and Stuart shared an exuberance for good times, for reveling and joking in camp or on the march. When they rode together, laughter seemed to encircle them. Most important, Lee measured up to Stuart's demands of his officers. The twenty-five-year-old Virginian "at once became very popular in the regiment," recalled a captain. He "was a fine drill officer and drilled us all the time, and I learned more about it than I had ever done before."[13]

The 2nd, 4th, and 6th Virginia, 1st North Carolina, and Jeff Davis Legion joined the 1st Virginia to comprise the brigade. The 2nd Virginia was organized from Colonel Richard Radford's companies at Manassas and additional companies. Colonel Beverly H. Robertson commanded the 4th Virginia. He and Stuart had been warm friends in Kansas. Shortly after the regiment joined the brigade, however, Stuart complained, "I find Bev Robertson by far the most troublesome man I have to deal with." A native Kentuckian and West Pointer, Colonel Charles W. Field, led the 6th Virginia. The arrival of the 1st North Carolina reunited Stuart with his roommate at Fort Leavenworth, Robert Ransom, Jr., who was now colonel of the regiment. Lieutenant Colonel William "Will" T. Martin, a lawyer, led the Jeff Davis Legion, which was composed of six companies from Mississippi, Alabama, and Georgia.[14]

The new regiments had several fine, promising field officers, who were to have prominent roles in future cavalry operations—the 2nd

Virginia's Lieutenant Colonel Thomas T. Munford; the 4th Virginia's Lieutenant Colonel Williams C. Wickham and Major William H. F. Payne; and the 1st North Carolina's Lieutenant Colonel Laurence S. Baker and Major James B. Gordon. Munford and Payne were graduates of VMI, while Wickham had been an attorney, and Gordon a planter and state legislator. Like Stuart, Baker was a West Point graduate and had served in the Mounted Rifles.[15]

While Stuart assembled his brigade, he and Johnston advocated the creation of a horse artillery battery to be attached to the mounted unit. "I need a commander very much to organize the battery forthwith," Stuart wrote Flora on November 24. He preferred Lieutenant James Breathed of the 1st Virginia as the battery commander. On November 29, Johnston assigned Lieutenant John Pelham to the post, recommending his promotion to captain. Stuart had no objection to the twenty-three-year-old Alabamian, who soon became one of the general's most trusted and closest subordinates.[16]

John Pelham impressed everyone who knew him. Contemporaries uniformly wrote of his intelligence, frankness, modesty, gentleness, courage, and passion for the cause. He was a strikingly handsome man, tall, blond, blue-eyed, and athletic. At West Point, where fellow cadets called him "Sally," he had excelled at fencing, boxing, and horsemanship. He roomed with Thomas Rosser, and both of them resigned from the academy on April 22, 1861, weeks before their graduation. Assigned to a battery as a drillmaster, Pelham fought with the unit at Manassas.[17]

After his initial experience in combat, Pelham confessed to his father: "War is *not* glorious as novelists would have us believe. It is only when we are in the heat and flush of battle that it is fascinating and interesting. It is only then that we enjoy it. When we forget ourselves and revel in the destruction we are dealing around us. I am now ashamed of the feelings I had in those hours of danger." But, he added: "We are battling for our rights and our homes. Ours is a just war, a holy cause."[18]

It took Pelham months to recruit volunteers and to obtain cannon, ordnance, horses, and equipment for the battery. He possessed initiative and a talent for organization. By the spring of 1862, with Breathed as his subordinate, they had filled the ranks, secured eight cannon, and completed the battery. The unit adopted the name "Stuart Horse Artillery." Pelham's finest gift, the management of artillery in combat, would have to await an opportunity.[19]

With the promotion to brigadier, Stuart required a larger staff. Peter Hairston and William Blackford left him—the former temporarily left the army; the latter, back to the 1st Virginia as a company commander with the rank of captain. Stuart compared the selection of men for his staff to choosing a wife, for better or for worse. Like other commanders, he needed aides with administrative talent, an ability to deal with mounds of paperwork, and the stamina to endure long hours at headquarters or on horseback. Stuart demanded unquestioned loyalty and personal courage from his staff members. With his reservoir of seemingly inexhaustible energy—"The man was a war-machine which never flagged," contended an aide—Stuart put onerous burdens upon them. He could be an unremitting taskmaster.[20]

But Stuart's boyishness nature never lay far beneath the surface. "With his staff officers," professed one of them, "Stuart was perfectly familiar." He discarded ceremony between him and them and ignored their rank when dealing with them. He delighted in jokes and pranks at both his and their expense. He wanted them to have "a handsome, soldierly appearance," with "cocked felt hats, long black plumes, top boots, and polished accoutrements." Blackford described his relationship with staff members "like that of a brother," while admitting that Stuart "was liable to form sudden fancies for those who courted his good will, and in this way he put on his staff sometimes men who were not at all suitable."[21]

Visitors to his headquarters marveled at how Stuart could be jesting and laughing at one moment and then be "deeply immersed in business, writing rapidly, and turning over the scattered papers before him, or with a book of military tactics in his hand deeply engaged." A newspaper correspondent who spent time with him outside Centreville reported: "An inferior may approach him with ease, as he displays none of that hauteur which some officers assume. He dispatches business promptly, and at the same time converses with his visitors in a social and friendly style that at once secures confidence and commands respect."[22]

During these autumn weeks, Stuart appointed several members to his staff. A Marylander, Captain Luke T. Brien, joined him as assistant adjutant general or chief of staff. Brien had been a civilian volunteer with the 1st Virginia at Manassas. The regiment's chaplain, Major Dabney Ball, became the brigade's commissary officer. Stuart selected two kinsmen—Chiswell Dabney and William E. Towles—as aides-de-camp. Corporal William H. Hagan of the 1st Virginia acted as chief of couriers. One of the most colorful individuals to join Stuart was a native Irishman, Redmond Burke, who served as a scout until being appointed an aide-de-camp. Stuart said that Burke "has a wonderful set of yarns to tell."[23]

Stuart and his staff confronted a myriad of details in the arming and equipping of a cavalry brigade. Each Confederate cavalryman rode to war on a personal mount, not a government-issued animal. Each trooper brought with him the equipage for his horse, but the rigors of service wore out items. The Confederate Congress had enacted a law in August requiring full equipment for volunteer cavalry companies. Shortages persisted, and in November, the War Department ceased accepting companies into service unless men and mounts were properly equipped. The department relied initially on private companies to try to meet the demands.[24]

A completely outfitted cavalryman and his horse needed a saber, revolver, carbine, saddle, bridle, stirrups, blanket, bit, saddlebags, nose feed bags, halters, curry comb, girth, and horseshoes. A shortage of proper arms for the men plagued mounted units for a long time. Some of the early volunteers carried either swords that dated to the Revolutionary War or homemade knives. Pistols ranged from single-shot percussions to the six-shot revolvers. They carried an assortment of rifles and carbines that required a variety of ammunition. Constant supply and forage problems absorbed the efforts of Stuart, his staff, and regimental officers.[25]

The demands of the service during these months wore away horseflesh. Stuart had command of the army's outposts, which stretched for twenty miles. Men and mounts were exposed to inclement weather for days. Horses became crippled and their backs sore from many of the old, poorly constructed saddles brought from home by the troopers. Stuart established "Camp Cripple" in the rear to restore the animals' health. One night a group of men entered the camp seeking their comrades. One of them shouted, "Where is Company Q?" When he heard of the incident, Stuart adopted the name, Company Q, for his remount camp.[26]

Picket duty, reconnaissance patrols, escort duty, and training kept the officers and men active. For details assigned to outpost duty, Stuart instructed them, "As the enemy will probably advance by several columns, the very soul of our success depends upon our early ascertaining the route taken by his *main* column." He kept scouts to the front. He advised them and pickets to establish trustworthy relationships with local women, who could obtain "correct information of what may pass their doors." The War Department gave him money for use "in the secret service," and these funds could be paid to civilian informants. Wherever duty placed Stuart, he relied upon citizens, a string of scouts, and personal reconnaissance to gather timely information. He exploited these resources from the beginning.[27]

When not assigned to outposts, officers and men drilled. They dismantled fences to create an expanse for the maneuvers. Stuart held reviews of his regiments for generals, government officials, and civilians. Reviews were a common practice during the conflict, allowing commanders to demonstrate the soldiers' prowess in drills and to stage a pageantry for onlookers. Few Civil War generals enjoyed reviews more than Stuart. They harked back to earlier times, with unfurled banners, martial music, and serried ranks, touching Stuart's romantic ideas about warfare. After one review, he boasted to Flora: "I was congratulated on my performance—putting them through as no Cavalry was ever put through before. I had 8 full squadrons present. They drilled admirably."[28]

Stuart's constant quest for information about Federal movements sparked encounters between the opposing forces. In one action with Union infantrymen, Fitz Lee had a horse killed from under him. In another, the Yankees ran "like frightened hares." Captain J. Fred Waring led twenty-three officers and men of the 6th Virginia, without permission, on a nighttime scout. In the darkness the Virginians stumbled into an ambush by the 3rd New Jersey Infantry. Waring rallied his men after the initial gunfire, scattering the New Jerseymen, but lost three wounded and eight missing. When Stuart learned of the affair, he declared: "Captain Waring's conduct . . . without authority . . . is so inexcusable as not to be counterbalanced by the extraordinary escape of his command. The field for enterprise and personal daring is wide enough in the legitimate sphere of duty, and I trust that this lesson will curb the thirst of adventure so as not to presume too far upon the irresolution and want of enterprise of the enemy."[29]

On December 20, Stuart led a 1,600-man force of cavalry, infantry, and artillery to Dranesville, Virginia, roughly fifteen miles northwest of Washington. A train of two hundred wagons was in the area, gathering forage for the army, and needed protection. Marching at daylight, Stuart's command arrived about ten o'clock in the morning. Stuart posted his 150 cavalrymen to cover two roads that entered the town from the east. About noon, the horsemen reported the advance of a Union infantry brigade and artillery. Stuart decided to attack the Federals, giving the wagon train time to escape. The Yankees belonged to Brigadier General E. O. C. Ord's brigade of Pennsylvania Reserves, numbering about 3,400.[30]

Four cannon of the Sumter Flying Artillery opened the fighting for the Confederates. Ord's guns replied from a ridge, and Stuart advanced the 10th Alabama Infantry against the Pennsylvanians. The Northerners' artillery fire and musketry stopped the Alabamians, whose colonel and lieutenant colonel fell wounded. Stuart ordered in the 6th South Carolina Infantry and 1st Kentucky Infantry on the Alabamians' left flank. While the pair of regiments were marching through a dense woodlot, confusion ensued, and the South Carolinians and Kentuckians mistakenly fired a volley into each other's ranks. The two regiments broke to the rear as Federal gun crews pounded the Southern line.[31]

"I thought our battery was gone," recalled a member of the Sumter Flying Artillery. Crews wheeled a pair of cannon to cover their left flank. "Just in the nick of time, and not a moment too soon," contended the artillerist, "Gen. S. rallied them [the infantry] and turned them 'right about face.'" With the wagons safely away, Stuart ordered a retreat, with the 11th Virginia Infantry covering the rear. The two hours of combat had cost him forty-three killed or mortally wounded, 143 wounded, and eight missing. Ord's losses amounted to seven killed and sixty-one wounded. Stuart returned with cavalry and infantry to Dranesville the next day to collect his dead and wounded. While the men gathered the casualties, he chatted with "several very pretty young ladies."[32]

In a letter to his wife written December 23, Stuart vastly exaggerated the number of the enemy and their losses. He assured her, "I am perfectly satisfied that my conduct was right, and I have the satisfaction to know that it meets the approval of General Johnston, & all others who know the facts, and my reputation has no doubt been the gainer." Although he knew that Flora worried constantly about his safety, he exclaimed, "I was never in greater personal danger & men & horses fell around me like ten-pins." He claimed that there "is a good deal of envy in this army" among several officers, "but I assure you I let it trouble me precious little." "Tell all our friends," he suggested in closing, "the correct version of the battle as they will get it mixed up in the paper."[33]

The quartermaster officer of the 11th Virginia Infantry viewed Dranesville differently: "Stuart's comb is cut. . . . If these useless forays he is so fond of getting up and which Johnston shows him such partiality in authorizing, are made less frequent by this partial disaster, it may be the means of preventing something worse hereafter." The officer alleged that when the Southerners retreated, Stuart failed to notify the colonel of the 11th Virginia Infantry, leaving the regiment isolated for thirty minutes. In Stuart's defense, he could have handled the units more skillfully, but his aggressive tactics against a numerically superior foe secured the wagon train, the primary purpose of his mission.[34]

Less than a week after he wrote his letter to Flora, she and the children joined him. They had not seen each other for three months. When she had suggested that he take a brief leave and join them in the capital, he replied: "As for my going to Richmond—I don't care what other Generals do, all I have to say is that while this war lasts I will not *leave* the *van* of our army unless *compelled* to. Let that answer put to rest any hope of seeing me in Richmond."[35]

While they had been separated, Stuart continued to express his love for her, writing typically, "I would like to be with you Dearest this dreary winter's night, Do you think of your old stove these cold nights." When she heard of him kissing ladies' hands and questioned him about it, he responded: "My darling if you could know—(and I think you ought) how true I am to you & how centered in you is my every hope—& dream of earthly bliss, you would never listen to the idle twaddle." He wished that he could be with her "to kiss away the petty troubles."[36]

Flora's letters to him evidently do not survive, but his replies to her indicate that her fears about his death in battle could not be stilled. "How much better," he professed in one letter, "to have your husband in his grave after a career true to every duty and every responsibility to you, his country, and his God, than inglorious existence—a living shame to you and to his children." In another he reassured her, "I have no idea of sacrificing myself rashly but I hope to do my duty with a firm reliance on Divine Aid to uphold me." In November, however, he prepared a will, bequeathing his entire estate to her, or in the event of her death, to their children. The document could not have assuaged her darkest thoughts or the dreams that must have haunted her sleep.[37]

Stuart informed her that the Washington *Star* had announced the appointment of her father, Philip St. George Cooke, to brigadier general in the Union army. Although her father's allegiance to the Federal government had been evident for months, the news upset Flora, who probably realized that the estrangement from her parents might be permanent. Stuart classified his father-in-law with Winfield Scott and George Thomas as Virginians who had betrayed their homes and families. He tried to comfort her, "be consoled in what you rightly regard as very distressing, by the reflection that your husband & brothers will atone for the father's conduct."[38]

To Stuart, Cooke's decision was unforgivable; the breach, irreparable. Despite Flora's misgivings, he changed their son's name from Philip St. George Cooke for his grandfather to James Ewell Brown Stuart, Jr. While he and Flora corresponded over the issue in early December, with Stuart suggesting various names for their son, he had already entered the boy's name in his will as "J. E. B. Stuart, Jr." The parents began calling him Jimmie. Stuart assured Flora, "You will find that very few will ever know that his name was ever other than *Jimmie*."[39]

At this time, Stuart learned through a network of spies or the "underground R.R." that Flora's mother was boarding at Brown's Hotel in Washington, and had been inquiring about her daughter. If Flora wrote "a small letter" to her mother, Stuart said he could "have it put under your Ma's breakfast plate . . . & she will never know who brought it." Whether Flora contacted her through this web is not known.[40]

Flora and the children's holiday visit with Stuart was brief, perhaps a week or two. He and she exchanged gifts before Christmas—fifteen yards of silk smuggled through Union lines for her; a golden sash and a set of general's shoulder straps, made by women in Warrenton, Virginia, for him. When she returned to Richmond, he wrote: "we do *enjoy* each other so much when we do meet that it seems somewhat to make amends for the weeks of absence. While away we can look forward to the joy of meeting again. When met we can abandon ourselves to the sweets of each others society as a fresh luxury."[41]

During his family's visit, Stuart probably had his band serenade Flora and the children. Upon his promotion to brigadier general, Stuart assigned three members of the 2nd Virginia—Samson D. "Sam" Sweeney, and his brother Robert M. "Bob" Sweeney, and cousin Charles Sweeney—to his headquarters. Sam Sweeney had been a renowned banjo player in minstrel shows. Bob Sweeney used a violin; Charles Sweeney, a guitar. Stuart's servant, Bob, joined in on bones. "Negro melodies were the favorites," according to William Blackford. The Sweeneys shared meals with Stuart's couriers and were a constant presence in camp and on the march, indulging Stuart's love of music and adding to a public image deliberately crafted by him.[42]

Shortly after Flora and the children left for Richmond, Stuart moved his headquarters to a house in Centreville, with his office in a room across the hall from Joseph E. Johnston's. According to a captain who had been to headquarters on business, both generals were "when at leisure very pleasant gentlemen but on duty as short and snappish as possible." Another visitor, Major John Cheves Haskell, left a perceptive portrait of Stuart: "He was a remarkable mixture of a green, boyish, undeveloped man, and a shrewd man of business and a strong leader. To hear him talk no one would think that he could ever be anything more than a dashing leader of a very small command, with no dignity and most boastful vanity. But with all he was a shrewd, gallant commander." Physically, thought Haskell, Stuart "was a good looking man, coarse in feature and figure, but powerful and enduring, of immense energy, and as coolly brave an individual as ever lived."[43]

Stuart's embrace of the cause was unbending. When he learned of the Federal captures of forts Henry and Donelson in Tennessee in February 1862, he wrote a revealing letter to Flora. As for the North, he had an "inextinguishable hatred." Then he declared, "I *for one*—though I stood alone in the Confederacy, without countenance or aid would uphold the banner of Southern Independence as long as I had a hand left to grasp the staff—and then die before submitting."

He wanted Flora, "when I am gone," to tell their son "how I felt and wrote and tell him never to do anything which his father would be ashamed of—never to forget the principles for which his father struggled. We are *sure to win*, what the sacrifices are to be we can not tell, but if the enemy held every town and hill top—Southern subjugation would be no nearer its consummation than now."[44]

In other letters written to Flora during January and February 1862, he discussed primarily personal matters. The deaths of three of James Longstreet's children from scarlet fever within an eight-day span worried him deeply about the health of "La Pet" and Jimmie. He asked his wife to begin a scrapbook, filling it with "everything of interest to you & me" as "a pretty good history of the war." He informed her that members of the Washington Artillery had presented him with "a pretty red cape." Most of all, he expressed his longing for her, to be with her, "to restore you to my arms." "I don't think I ever wanted to see you quite as bad as I now do," he wrote on February 26.[45]

Stuart's love for and devotion to Flora were undeniable. Nevertheless, he had become entranced with a local woman, a twenty-five-year-old dark-eyed brunette named Laura Ratcliffe. The unmarried Ratcliffe lived with her mother and two sisters near Frying Pan. Stuart met her when she came to Camp Qui Vive to assist with the sick and wounded in the hospital. He was attracted to her and during the next several months corresponded with her; thought about having Christmas dinner at her home near Federal lines; wrote four poems to her; and gave her a gold chain with a gold coin and a leather-bound album in which he inscribed, "Presented to Miss Laura Ratcliffe by her soldier-friend as a token of his high appreciation of her patriotism, admiration of her virtues and pledge of his lasting esteem." He wore a lock of her hair in his hatband.[46]

The nature of their relationship intrigues. A friend of Laura, Antonia Ford, was another local beauty who had warned the Confederates of the advance of the Union army from Washington in July 1861. Stuart came to know her and presented her with a commission as "my honorary aide-de-camp." But nothing uncovered in his acquaintance with Antonia Ford compares with the letters and gifts that he gave to Ratcliffe. In March 1862, for instance, he wrote to Ratcliffe of "that *never to be forgotten good-bye*" in the moonlight. He went on, "That whatever betide me in this eventful year you will in the corner of that heart so full of noble impulses find a place in which to stow away from worldly view the '*Young Brigadier.*'"[47]

Either Stuart had spoken of both women to Flora, or his wife had met them during a visit. In a February 1862 letter to Flora, he mentioned that they "always inquire anxiously after you & the Dear Little ones." Henry B. McClellan, who would become Stuart's chief of staff, maintained in a postwar account that Stuart's "devotion to the society of ladies was one of the noblest and purest instincts of his nature. Towards them he was as *naïve* and unsuspecting as a child, and as pure in thought and action."[48]

But it was more than that. Stuart seemingly needed the flattery of women, particularly young pretty ones, to affirm his fame and reputation. Their attention to him probably kindled the chivalry in his soul. But Laura Ratcliffe was unusual as she touched something within him. In the end, it was almost certainly nothing more.[49]

About this time, March 1862, the army marched away from its winter encampment at Centreville. For weeks Johnston had viewed the position at Centreville vulnerable if George McClellan's more than 100,000-man Union army advanced on it. On February 19, the Confederate commander had traveled to Richmond, meeting with President Davis and the cabinet. Davis conceded that a retreat should be at Johnston's discretion, but implemented only under the reality of a Federal offensive. Johnston, however, left the meeting believing that he could withdraw as soon as practicable.[50]

Upon his return to the army, Johnston ordered the removal of millions of pounds of supplies stockpiled in the warehouses at Manassas Junction. On March 5, Stuart's videttes reported increased activity along the enemy's lines. Convinced that a Federal advance was imminent, Johnston started units south on March 8. The main army followed the next day, abandoning more than a million pounds of supplies, which

Stuart's men burned after local civilians and troops seized what they could carry away. A detail destroyed the Stone Bridge over Bull Run. By March 12, the Confederates had crossed the Rappahannock River in central Virginia, and within another week filed into lines south of the Rapidan River, a tributary of the Rappahannock.[51]

Johnston did not inform the administration of the movement until March 13. The destruction of the valuable supplies incensed Davis. At the War Department, located in the former brick Mechanics Institute building at Ninth and Franklin streets in Richmond, an official recorded in his diary that Johnston "never treats the Government with confidence, hardly with respect." He described the general's correspondence to the department as "ice tempered."[52]

Stuart's cavalrymen screened the army's retreat. Before the withdrawal began, he issued a five-page appeal to the brigade, reminding the members of "further sacrifices to be made." The Federals entered Centreville behind the Southerners, but McClellan did not press the enemy rear except with a few detachments of cavalry. A member of the 4th Virginia noted in a letter home, "we are beginning to realize now what war is." Stuart confessed to Flora during the retreat, "I am enduring the Saddest Sorest trials of the soldier to see this beautiful country abandoned to the enemy." Stuart's West Point friend Oliver Otis Howard, now a Union brigadier, reported that dead horses lined the route of Stuart's march.[53]

A Georgia infantry captain saw Stuart during the movement and recalled: "never have I seen such a magnificent looking soldier. Faultlessly dressed, grandly mounted, with long, silky, auburn locks curling beneath his plumed hat." When the horsemen reached the Rappahannock, Johnston instructed Stuart to gather supplies and to give the Yankees the impression that the entire army manned the line. Union cavalry and artillery appeared north of the river and engaged the Rebels for a brief time. A newspaper correspondent witnessed the action with the Confederates and stated that Stuart "was always in front, and five shells burst very near him, but he bore himself most gallantly and escaped uninjured."[54]

By the end of March, the strategic situation in Virginia had shifted dramatically. Transports, piled full with the manpower and material might of the Union Army of the Potomac, were steaming south down the Potomac River and Chesapeake Bay to Fort Monroe at the eastern tip of the Peninsula. A British observer with the Federals called it "the stride of a giant." After weeks of cajoling and prodding from Abraham Lincoln, McClellan decided to transfer his host of more than 100,000 troops to the Peninsula, framed by the York and James rivers, for an advance on Richmond. McClellan arrived on April 2. To his army's front lay barely 11,000 Confederates under Major General John Bankhead Magruder, aligned behind fortifications along the Warwick River. Magruder's lines extended from historic Yorktown to the James River.[55]

The presence of McClellan's army roughly sixty miles from the Confederate capital forced Davis to act. He directed Johnston to march his army to Richmond. Leaving General Richard Ewell's eight-thousand-man division behind in central Virginia "to deceive the enemy as to the position of the army," Johnston started his remaining three infantry divisions, artillery batteries, and Stuart's cavalry toward the city. The horsemen rode overland as the infantrymen and artillerists crowded onto railroad cars. A private with Stuart remembered: "The march was a most intensely disagreeable one. The roads were in horrible condition." When Stuart reached the city, he paraded his troopers down Franklin Street to Capitol Square and then onto Broad Street. Crowds lined the route, cheering the horsemen, who wore yellow daffodils in their slouch hats.[56]

The cavalry passed through the capital, continuing east down the Peninsula. Davis, Robert E. Lee, the president's military advisor, Johnston, Longstreet, and Major General Gustavus Smith had conferred in Richmond, deciding to augment Magruder's force with Johnston's units. Johnston argued for bringing reinforcements from Georgia and South Carolina to Virginia, and pulling Magruder up the Peninsula. When McClellan pursued, stated Johnston, the combined Southern commands could pounce upon the Federals. Lee objected, questioning whether the defenses in the two states would be secure if troops were withdrawn. Johnston complied with Davis's order, although convinced that it was only a matter of time before the Confederates retired closer to Richmond.[57]

Stuart and the cavalry arrived at Yorktown on the morning of April 18. A Texas infantryman watched the horsemen pass them on the march and wrote that Stuart rode in front with "old Sweeney" by his side. The mounted brigade numbered 1,289 effectives. Stuart had lost two regiments—the 2nd Virginia detached with Ewell; the 1st North Carolina transferred to North Carolina because of a Federal army in the state. Before long, however, the 3rd and 10th Virginia were assigned to his command. Three days after he reached Yorktown, he contended to his wife, "Cavalry will not participate much in it [a battle] owing to the nature of the ground."[58]

During the preceding weeks, the personnel on Stuart's staff changed and new commanders led the regiments. Kinsmen from Mississippi, brothers James T. W. and Samuel H. Hairston, joined the staff. Captain James Hairston served as acting assistant adjutant general, and Sergeant Samuel Hairston as a volunteer aide-de-camp until promoted to major and quartermaster in June. A third new member was Major Philip H. Powers, who acted as quartermaster for three months until he resigned because of ill health. Stuart's chief of staff, Captain Luke Brien, remained although he had been elected lieutenant colonel of the 1st Virginia.[59]

Brien's election to the post resulted from legislation enacted by the Confederate Congress on April 16. The measure authorized for the first time in American history a national conscription or draft, embracing, with some exceptions, all white males aged eighteen to thirty-five. If a man volunteered, he could select his unit. The law also granted enlisted men the right to elect their company and regimental officers.[60]

Stuart admitted that Brien's election "took him greatly by surprise." It was not the case with the regiment's choice of colonel, Fitz Lee. Although the details are imprecise, Stuart managed to have Lee selected over Grumble Jones, the regiment's commander. Stuart conducted the election for company officers in only six of the companies on April 22. When the enlisted men voted in their company officers, Stuart had the company officers elect the colonel, lieutenant colonel, and major for the regiment. Lee was one of his favorites, Jones was not. Stuart and Jones's professional relationship had deteriorated over the winter for unclear reasons. Jones could be "ugly [and] surly," and Stuart wanted him removed.[61]

The election's outcome enraged Jones. He wrote a blistering letter to Secretary of War George W. Randolph on April 28. After describing how Stuart held the vote, he declared: "This election at war with equity and in violation of law deprives me of my command but could I feel the proceeding free of malice I would willingly abide the result. However being fully aware of my inability to repair the mischief done by the stupidity and wickedness of my superior officer I hereby relieve the department of all embarrassment by tendering my resignation to take effect on the 30th inst." He believed "that in law and equity my office is not yet vacated," but "my presence in the Regiment could not now erase the mischief already done." He offered his services "when and where in your opinion they can be useful."[62]

The War Department transferred Jones to the 7th Virginia until his election as colonel of the 11th Virginia on July 2. Stuart had rid himself of one of the cavalry's finest officers. In time, Jones would be placed again under Stuart's authority. Neither man bent; neither forgot. If John Esten Cooke, who joined the staff in May and had his own troubles with Stuart, is to be believed, Stuart "never forgave" those who opposed him personally or professionally. Cooke described him as "a thoroughly good hater." "His prejudices were strong," asserted Cooke, "and when once he had made up his mind deliberately, nothing would change him. He was immovable and implacable; and against these offenders he threw the whole weight of his powerful will and his high position, determined to crush him."[63]

Chapter Six

"Our Exploit Is All the Talk Here"

WILLIAMSBURG, VIRGINIA, HAD aged gracefully since its days as the colonial capital. Few vestiges of that past remained as fire had consumed the Governor's Palace and the abandoned capitol building. The College of William and Mary stood on the town's western edge, and the Eastern Lunatic Asylum held 250 patients. Attorneys argued cases in the James City County courthouse, and nearby farmers hauled grain through its streets. Sturdy brick homes harked back to the earlier times when the elite of Virginia had served in the legislature or studied at the college. The past hung on, but it was the present that concerned Williamsburg's 1,600 residents, white and black, on May 5, 1862.[1]

For a day or more the townsfolk had watched the passage of an army, mud-splattered men in gray uniforms, cannon, and wagons. Women and children wept, knowing that their defenders were marching away toward Richmond, the state and now national capital. As rain fell in torrents, however, some of the Confederate units halted in the town or manned Fort Magruder, an earthen bastion, redoubts, and rifle pits two miles to the east across the Yorktown–Williamsburg Road. If there were to be a fight as May 5 dawned overcast, it would be there.[2]

The landing of the 100,000-man Union Army of the Potomac on the Peninsula in late March and early April had portended this day. It had taken a month because of Major General George McClellan's caution, his unwillingness to assault the enemy's works. Instead, "Little Mac," as his men called him, conducted siege operations, relying upon large-caliber guns to pummel the Confederate line. Inexorably, the Federals moved the cannon into range as sharpshooters on both sides exacted a toll. On April 27, General Joseph E. Johnston notified Richmond, "we must abandon the Peninsula soon." Three days later blue-jacketed gunners lobbed shells into Yorktown. "We are engaged in a species of warfare at which we can never win," wrote Johnston in a dispatch. Lead elements of the Rebel army started up the Peninsula on the night of May 2–3; the main army followed the next night.[3]

The Southerners inched away through sloughs of mud, with infantrymen shouldering wagons and cannon out of the mire. "And so it went on all night," recounted an officer, "march or wade two minutes and halt ten or longer." The retreat proceeded all day on May 4. To the rear, Union bands played music and the troops cheered at the sight of the abandoned works. Mounted units rode forth in pursuit.[4]

Jeb Stuart and his cavalrymen prowled along the rear of the retreating columns, establishing a line along Skiff Creek. The 1st and 4th Virginia and two new units—3rd Virginia and Wise Legion—covered the roads. Along with other cavalry regiments, the 3rd Virginia had undergone its initial training at an instruction camp established at the Ashland Race Course, seventeen miles northwest of Richmond. Since then it had served on the Peninsula. A member of the regiment recalled the first time he saw Stuart: "Being of good stature, he was one of most imposing officers I have ever seen. A real cavalryman, mounted on his chestnut charger, his grey uniform with yellow markings fitting him like a glove."[5]

The heaviest fighting occurred on Telegraph Road, where the 4th Virginia engaged the 1st and 6th United States. Stuart was with the 3rd Virginia farther south, but his father-in-law, Brigadier General Philip St. George Cooke, led the Union cavalrymen. In the action, the 4th Virginia's Lieutenant Colonel Williams C. Wickham fell wounded. By nightfall, Stuart's horsemen had retired to the Confederate works at Fort Magruder.[6]

It was "a terrible morning for a fight," grumbled a Union private as rain poured down, turning the ground into "pudding" on May 5. Before six o'clock, a Federal infantry division, backed by artillery, closed on the Confederate lines at Fort Magruder. Major General James Longstreet commanded the Southern rear guard with orders to stall the enemy until the wagon train had passed safely to the west. Once the Battle of Williamsburg began, it became a day-long struggle in the rain and soggy terrain. The Northern attacks centered upon the fort. Longstreet stayed in town most of the day, directing additional brigades into the combat.[7]

"I have only to say that if you had seen your husband," Stuart told Flora afterward, "you would have been proud of him. I was not out of fire the whole day." He directed artillery from a redoubt and ordered in Captain John Pelham and three guns of the Stuart Horse Artillery. When infantry brigades arrived, he directed them into position. At one point, when the musketry blazed, Stuart rode up to the 4th Virginia and joked, "Boys, don't mind them," referring to the minié balls splattering the ground. "They are spent bullets and won't hurt you." Moments later, a ball smashed into the face of Major William Payne, fracturing his jaw and severing his tongue. More than a month after the battle, Payne asserted, "I fear my jaw will never unite & my tongue gives me great trouble."[8]

Late in the action, Stuart shifted his brigade to the right flank, searching for an opportunity to attack the Federals. When a chance came, he sent forward the 10th Virginia, another regiment added recently to his command. The Virginians had been spared from combat until then, and one of them remembered, "I had no idea what it meant till we made that charge." They went in with a shout only to be repulsed. Darkness ended the engagement, which cost the opponents more than four thousand casualties. The Confederates withdrew during the night, leaving their wounded behind in the homes of Williamsburg residents.[9]

Longstreet commended Stuart in his report, "I am under many obligations to Brig. Gen. J. E. B. Stuart, who, while waiting for an opportunity to use his cavalry, was exceedingly active and zealous in conducting the different columns to their proper destinations and in assisting them to get properly into action." Williamsburg marked for Stuart a different responsibility—he assisted in the tactical deployment of infantry units in an engagement for the first time.[10]

In his report Stuart praised various regimental officers and staff members. In particular, he cited the performance of Captain William D. Farley, a new appointee to the staff as a volunteer aide-de-camp. Farley was a twenty-six-year-old South Carolinian who had been recently exchanged as a prisoner of war. Stuart wrote that he "has always exhibited such admirable coolness, undaunted courage, and intelligent comprehension of military matters that he would be of invaluable service as a commanding officer assigned to outpost service." In a letter to Johnston's chief of staff, Stuart swore that Farley "manages to get into every fight."[11]

A woman who met Farley thought that he possessed "a very pleasant manner but with a touch of conceit which is not quite becoming." Fellow staff members described him of "medium stature," "sinewy," with long hair, blue eyes, and a "soft voice." There was a "reckless courage" to him, and he preferred going alone "upon the most dangerous scouting expeditions." Farley claimed later that he had killed personally more than thirty Yankees. He became invaluable to Stuart.[12]

Farley and his comrades in the cavalry continued to protect the army's rear as its retreat resumed after Williamsburg. Skirmishes occurred daily with the pursuing Union horsemen. The duty was onerous and deadly. "Our horses are never suffered to be unsaddled more than an hour or two," wrote a Confederate officer, "and to be unbridled only when eating." A trooper with the 6th Pennsylvania, seeing a batch of prisoners, fumed: "I had a fine view of them and such a set of mean uncombed unwashed lousy-looking and destitute set of humans I never saw. . . . I felt as though I could take the heart-blood out of everyone of them." He heard a rumor that the Rebels were torturing and killing Union captives.[13]

Major Philip Powers of Stuart's staff detailed the burdens upon the cavalry and the conflict's hardening nature in a letter to his wife: "Our Cavalry service has got to be *odious*. Continually in the rear of our Army we have to subsist by plundering and stealing, and many a home has been made desolate by the approach of Stuart's Cavalry. The standing order is *impress* everything that may fall into the Enemy's hands. And thus we march, with the wailing of women and children constantly ringing in our ears. Oh God! When will the end of these things be?"[14]

The army crossed the Chickahominy River, the final natural barrier between Richmond and the Yankees, on May 15. Two days later
the Confederates filed into fieldworks, erected a year before, and
halted, three miles from the capital. Stuart was instructed to maintain
"a close watch" on the approaching enemy, whose advanced elements
reached the stream the same day. Union engineers began rebuilding
bridges destroyed by the Southerners and erecting new spans across the
Chickahominy. The recent rains had flooded the bottomlands along
the stream. On May 24, McClellan's Fourth Corps, trailed by the Third
Corps, crossed to the south bank of the river, pushing on to a crossroads
known as Seven Pines and the nearby Fair Oaks Station on the York
River Railroad. The Second, Fifth, and Sixth corps remained north of
the river.[15]

"Our soldiers feel the great responsibility resting upon them more
than ever," wrote a Georgia captain at the time. They were not alone.
Jefferson Davis had reacted with disbelief at the news that Johnston's
army was on Richmond's outskirts. The cabinet discussed a possible
evacuation of the city. When a cabinet member inquired where the
army could retreat if necessary, Robert E. Lee exclaimed with fervor,
"Richmond must not be given up; it shall not be given up!"[16]

In the Shenandoah Valley, meanwhile, Major General Stonewall
Jackson was executing a plan that he and Lee had fashioned. Lee had
seen the possibilities of using the Valley and Jackson for an offensive
strike in the region. If Jackson succeeded, he might prevent a junction of
McClellan's army on the Peninsula and another Union force at Fredericksburg, fifty miles north of Richmond. By the final week of May, then,
Jackson had routed a Federal command in the Valley, pushing toward
the Potomac River. While McClellan correctly assessed Jackson's operation as a diversion, the administration in Washington temporarily
halted the movement from Fredericksburg. The wings of McClellan's
army still remained dangerously divided by the Chickahominy.[17]

Stuart brought the information to Johnston that the Yankees at
Fredericksburg were retiring, not advancing. Nevertheless, time was
running out for Johnston. Davis believed that the general was unwilling to risk a battle with the enemy. At last, however, Johnston decided
to strike the pair of isolated Union corps in the Seven Pines–Fair Oaks

area, south of the river. He assigned Longstreet to command of the attack, amassing thirty thousand troops for the operation. The Confederates were to advance on three roads that converged on the Union position. The army's chief of ordnance, Porter Alexander, wrote in his memoirs, "It was an excellent & well devised scheme and apparently as simple as any plan could be." Johnston designated May 31 for the offensive. After nightfall on May 30, however, a spring thunderstorm blew in with a deluge of rain, churning roads into troughs of mud and reflooding the lowlands.[18]

It might have been "as simple as any plan could be," but it unraveled from the outset. Despite spending the previous day with Johnston, hearing "every word and thought expressed," Longstreet somehow misunderstood the instructions. His division took the wrong road, causing a logjam and delaying the attack. When Major General D. H. Hill's division finally advanced at 1:00 P.M., five hours behind schedule, the Confederates achieved initial successes. But as the afternoon lengthened in the wooded terrain, Federal reserves stabilized the line. Each side seemed to grip the combat with a ferocity, unwilling to release its hold. A Rebel confessed that it was a "miracle" that he had not been hit as "every body else was falling around us." Nothing before, either First Manassas or Williamsburg, compared to the deadliness of this fighting.[19]

Late in the day Johnston rode forward to assess the situation. Although he had learned of the disruption of his plans at mid-morning, the army commander remained at his headquarters, unwilling apparently to intervene and to rectify the difficulties. Instead, he waited until twilight to go to the front. In the darkening woods, rifles and cannon still flashed. Before long, a bullet struck his shoulder. Within seconds, an artillery shell exploded above him, its shards ripping into his chest and fracturing ribs. He was carried to the rear by aides, and Gustavus Smith assumed temporary command of the army.[20]

Stuart had predicted three days earlier, "I am *sanguine* of victory." The nature of the offensive and the terrain precluded a role for cavalry. He spent most of the day with Longstreet, who said the cavalryman "was of material service by his presence with me on the field." Stuart related to Flora, "I was determined to be individually useful. . . . I exercised command at various times during the day." During the night of May

31–June 1, he went to army headquarters, and in the words of Smith, "rendered me very important assistance."[21]

The battle resumed on the morning of June 1. A Union officer claimed that the opposing lines "seemed to have become one continuous blaze of musketry." Neither side gained much ground. Instead, the combat was measured in the blood of men. Before midday the Confederates withdrew, and the Battle of Seven Pines or Fair Oaks ended. Southern casualties amounted to more than 6,100; Northern losses to more than 5,000. Stuart described Johnston's wounding as a "severe blow" to the cause. It would be months before the general recovered.[22]

The fighting had subsided on June 1 when Robert E. Lee came to Smith's headquarters. Davis had assigned Lee to temporary command of the army. During the past few months, the two men had established a mutual respect and trust, unlike Davis's contentious relationship with Johnston. The general's fall, however, left the president with few options. No senior general with the army seemed capable of replacing Johnston, so Davis turned to his military advisor. The decision altered the course of the war in the East.[23]

The fifty-five-year-old Lee had been preparing for this responsibility for nearly four decades. The son of Henry "Light Horse Harry" Lee of Revolutionary War renown, Lee had devoted his entire professional career to the army. With the firing on Fort Sumter, the Lincoln administration offered him command of the Union army. Instead, he tendered his resignation, saying, "I have not been able to make up my mind to raise my hand against my relatives, my children, my home." He directed Virginia's mobilization and led a failed campaign in western Virginia. In this operation he could not overcome feuding subordinates, ill-trained and ill-equipped troops, and the rugged Allegheny Mountains. He oversaw the construction of coastal defenses in South Carolina and Georgia before Davis selected him as his military advisor.[24]

When Lee assumed command of the army, which was soon designated as the Army of Northern Virginia, Confederate fortunes appeared bleak. In the words of historian Gary W. Gallagher, the South's "armies had been losing ground in every quarter . . . as a cancer eating at southern morale and will." In Tennessee, the captures of forts Henry and Donelson resulted in the fall of Nashville, and Union forces had won another victory, amid terrible slaughter, at Shiloh. Federal army and naval forces had made inroads along the Atlantic coast and seized New Orleans. Finally, McClellan's army lay only a handful of miles from Richmond, with the Yankees able to hear church bells toll in the city.[25]

Lee believed that if Southerners were to redirect the Union tide and to achieve independence they had to act aggressively. In an exchange at the time, Porter Alexander inquired of Captain Joseph C. Ives of Davis's staff if Lee were audacious enough. Ives answered: "Alexander, if there is one man in either army, Federal and Confederate, who is, head & shoulders, far above every other one in either army in audacity that man is Gen. Lee, and you will very soon have lived to see it. Lee is audacity personified. His name is audacity, and you need not to be afraid of not seeing all of it that you will want to see."[26]

Lee's audacity or boldness was, however, calculated. Lee reasoned that with its limited resources the Confederacy could not sustain a prolonged conflict. In turn, Lee wanted, wrote an aide, to "encourage the belief [among Northerners] that the war would be of indefinite length." If they became convinced that the struggle was not worth the casualties and sacrifices, the Confederacy could achieve its independence. To accomplish this, Confederate armies had to win a series of battlefield victories, which required taking risks against a foe with vast resources. The burden rested primarily with the army Lee inherited.[27]

No Confederate general possessed the attributes of Lee. He had a superior intellect of both breadth and depth, and a temperament and character that elicited respect. He had a commanding physical presence, a bearing that evoked confidence. While passions seethed within, Lee had "remarkable self-control," according to a staff officer. An astute judge of men, he exploited the skills of subordinates. A gifted administrator, he worked assiduously to provide for the welfare of the men in the ranks. Concern for them was always with him, and in time, it bound them to him.[28]

Lee could visualize with clarity a strategic and tactical landscape in which others saw only as a vague outline. He could do so because he excelled in the interpretation of information. "In nothing was he more successful, as an analyst of intelligence reports," concluded his greatest biographer, Douglas Southall Freeman, "than in weighing probabilities, discarding the irrelevant, and adding bit to bit to the first essential fact until his conclusion was sure." He could not divine enemy movements; he required accurate reports from the front. Consequently, Stuart's talent for scouting and reconnaissance was of inestimable worth to Lee.[29]

From the outset, then, Lee readied the army for a possible offensive strike against the Federals. He instructed his division and brigade commanders "to have their commands in readiness at all times for immediate action." He had his chief engineer examine the army's lines and ordered the troops to strengthen them. He conferred with his senior officers soliciting their views. Finally, he sent a dispatch to Stonewall Jackson, inquiring if his command could leave the Shenandoah Valley and unite with Lee's army at Richmond.[30]

Stuart, meanwhile, offered his assessment of the situation to Lee. He must have believed that Lee would give his proposal consideration because of their prior relationship. He was submitting his views based upon "convictions derived from a close observation of the enemy movements for months past, his system of war, and his conduct in battle as well as our own." The enemy would not advance until he had perfected his works. Then McClellan would bring his heavy artillery to bear on the Confederate lines before attacking. To prevent this, Stuart asked that should not Lee's army "move down with a crushing force upon our front and right flank, thwart his designs, and deliver our capital."

"We have an army far better adapted to attack, than defend," continued Stuart. He went on: "It may seem presumption in me to give these views, but I have not thus far mistaken the policy & practice of the enemy. At any rate, I would rather incur the charge of presumption than fold my arms in silence and indifference to the momentous crisis at hand." He would support, however, whatever course of action Lee selected.[31]

A few days after Stuart had written to Lee, John Singleton Mosby came to cavalry headquarters. Mosby had been adjutant of the 1st Virginia under Grumble Jones, an officer he admired. When Fitz Lee was elected colonel of the regiment, Mosby resigned his post. Neither he nor Lee could abide each other. With the reputation as a fearless scout, Mosby joined Stuart's group of scouts. Mosby rivaled William Farley in prowess and daring behind enemy lines or on outpost duty.[32]

A lawyer in southwestern Virginia, Mosby had been a reluctant soldier. He had opposed secession, but with his native state's decision, he joined Jones's militia company. A restless man, he adapted quickly to picket duty and scouting missions. Physically small, standing five feet, seven or eight inches tall and weighing less than 130 pounds, he possessed a keen intellect. His blue eyes, it was said, could penetrate into a man's soul. There was a contrariness to him, a willingness, if not need, to face countervailing winds. He was, admitted an acquaintance, "a disturbing companion." In a way he had not anticipated, war suited him.[33]

When Mosby reported to headquarters at a farmhouse owned by a Mr. Waddle on Charles City Road outside Richmond, Stuart asked him to conduct a reconnaissance toward the Union right flank. Stuart wanted to know if the Federals had erected fieldworks along Totopotomoy Creek, a tributary of the Pamunkey River. Whether Lee had requested such a mission or Stuart acted on his own volition is unclear. Instead of Stuart's proposal to strike McClellan's left flank, Lee had been considering an offensive north of the Chickahominy and the opposite end of the enemy lines. This possibility had moved Lee to write to Jackson about coming from the Valley.[34]

With four men, Mosby went, as he put it, "down among the Yankees." He discovered that they had not fortified the flank and that a cavalry force could penetrate into the Union rear to the York River Railroad, the army's supply line. When he returned and informed Stuart that a raid behind Federal lines "was practicable," the general directed him to prepare a written statement on the reconnaissance. On June 10, with Mosby's report in hand, Stuart rode to Lee's headquarters on Nine Mile Road at High Meadows, the home of Mrs. Mary Dabbs, the widow of Josiah Dabbs.[35]

Lee and Stuart conferred, with Lee explaining that he wanted to bring Jackson "down upon the enemy's right flank and rear." Mosby's report indicated that an opportunity might exist. Lee instructed Stuart to examine the country as to the "practicability of such a move." The next day, Lee issued the orders, marked "Confidential." He directed Stuart "to make a secret movement to the rear of the enemy . . . with a view of gaining intelligence of his operations, Communications & of driving in his foraging parties & Securing Such grain Cattle &." Lee cautioned

Stuart to use only reliable scouts and to take with him only horses and men who "can stand the expedition." Do not take risks, he stated, "be content to accomplish all the good you can without feeling it necessary to obtain all that might be desired." "Remember," the order read, "that one of the chief objects of your expedition is to gain intelligence for the guidance of future operations."[36]

Stuart returned to his headquarters and readied his command. Since Seven Pines, he had imposed a strict discipline upon the officers and men. "Tis almost impossible to get out of camp even for one hour," complained a trooper on June 8. "We have to work very hard are on duty nearly all the time. Some of the men try & see how contrary & muleish they can be." The nearly constant rain only made for more grumbling.[37]

Stuart gleaned from the ranks the officers and men he wanted for the daring enterprise. He selected Colonel Fitz Lee and the 1st Virginia; Colonel William H. F. "Rooney" Lee, the army commander's second oldest son, and the 9th Virginia; eight companies from the 4th Virginia, divided equally and assigned to the other two regiments; two squadrons of the Jeff Davis Legion, under Lieutenant Colonel Will Martin; and two cannon from the horse artillery, under Lieutenant James Breathed. In all, 1,200 troopers, a figure suggested by Robert E. Lee. Mosby, Farley, and Redmond Burke acted as the primary scouts and guides. "The force was quietly concentrated," in Stuart's words, at the farm of a Mrs. Mordecai near Kilby's Station on the Richmond, Fredericksburg, and Potomac Railroad. He confided to no one, even his staff and senior officers, the mission's purpose and destination.[38]

Stuart aroused his staff at two o'clock on the morning of June 12. He was dressed for the occasion, wearing a double-breasted gray shell jacket, with rows of buttons and laced with braid; a tasseled yellow sash, recently sent to him by a woman from Baltimore; a gray cape with scarlet lining, made by Flora; a "fawn colored hat," looped on the right with a gold star and adorned with a black ostrich plume; and long buckskin gauntlets. He carried a light French saber and a revolver. The uniform befitted a man around whom an aura of chivalry and knighthood seemed to hang.[39]

The day dawned bright and pleasant, but with the feel of summer heat. Stuart and the staff joined the command at Mrs. Mordecai's farm, and then started north. The men carried three days' rations. "I have never seen so many troopers at once," a 9th Virginia cavalryman recorded in his journal, "we must make a grand sight." Scouts rimmed the column to the east toward the Federal lines. Up Brock Road to Yellow Tavern, on to Mountain Road through Goodall's Tavern, and then along the South Anna River, they rode. "I purposely directed my first day's march toward Louisa [Court House]," reported Stuart, "so as to favor the idea of re-enforcing Jackson." The men heard a rumor that they were heading to the Shenandoah Valley. Stuart halted them for the night on a farm owned by a Winston, near Elliott's Crossing of the railroad over the river. They had ridden twenty miles.[40]

About midnight Stuart accompanied Rooney Lee on a five-mile ride to Hickory Hill, the home of Lee's father-in-law, Henry Wickham. Lee wanted to visit his wife, Charlotte, while Stuart wished to see her brother, Colonel Williams Wickham of the 4th Virginia. Wickham was recovering from the wound he had sustained in the rearguard clash on May 4. Tradition holds that Stuart spent much of the time at Hickory Hill asleep in a chair. He and Lee returned to the command before daylight on June 13.[41]

"Our noiseless bivouac was broken early the next morning," wrote Stuart, "and without flag or bugle sound we resumed our march." He informed his regimental commanders of the expedition's mission "as to secure an intelligent action and co-operation in whatever might occur." The column rode east toward Hanover Court House, where two squadrons of the 6th United States had entered the town on a patrol. When Stuart learned of their presence, he tried to trap them, but the Yankee horsemen escaped. From Hanover Court House, the Rebels angled southeast past Taliaferro's Mill and Enon Church, where they turned east toward Haw's Shop. The weather was, according to a Union diarist, "Hot, Hotter, Hottest."[42]

About 2:00 P.M. at Old Church, Captain William B. Royall of the 5th United States received a message of the approach of Confederate cavalry. Royall was a native Virginian who had served with Stuart in the 1st Cavalry in Kansas. He and four companies had been sent to Old Church on May 31 to picket the roads toward Hanover Court House. That morning Royall had ordered Lieutenant Edward H. Lieb and Company H on patrol toward Haw's Shop. Lieb reported the appearance of the enemy.[43]

Rooney Lee's 9th Virginia led Stuart's column. After passing through Haw's Shop, Lee's vanguard encountered Lieb's Federals. The Virginians charged, and the Yankees broke and fled. A Rebel exclaimed with exaggeration, "our whole force went tearing after them like so many blood-hounds after fear stricken deer." Stuart slowed the pursuit at the bridge over Totopotomoy Creek, expecting the enemy to defend the crossing. When dismounted skirmishers seized the structure, the Confederates proceeded east, following a narrow tree-lined road. Royall, meanwhile, had sent forward reinforcements for Leib.[44]

Twice, between the creek and Old Church, Royall's troopers made stands. In the final clash, Captain William Latane, charging ahead of his squadron from the 9th Virginia, was killed, struck by three bullets. Latane was the same age as Stuart and had been a physician before the war. The death of "the lamented Captain Latane," in Stuart's words, was soon immortalized for Southerners in an elegy, "The Burial of Latane," by John Reuben Thompson, in the July–August 1862 issue of the *Southern Literary Messenger*.[45]

A hand-to-hand struggle ensued, with sabers and pistols. Confederate numbers prevailed, and a wounded Royall and his Regulars fled. Stuart's horsemen entered Old Church, where the Southerners "reveled in the captured supplies." Stuart was seventeen miles from Hanover Court House and had accomplished the expedition's primary purpose—the Federals had not fortified the Chickahominy-Pamunkey watershed. He either could retrace his march or ride south, through Tunstall's Station on the York River Railroad, McClellan's supply line, to the Chickahominy, encircling the Union army. "Here was the turning point of the expedition," as he stated in his report.[46]

When Stuart and Robert E. Lee met on June 10, the cavalry officer had broached the idea of a ride around the enemy; Lee thought otherwise. Now, however, the opportunity glistened before him. In his report, Stuart listed the difficulties of a return march, but whether he considered them seriously at the time cannot be ascertained. As he said, "my favorite scheme" was to march to the Chickahominy. He discussed the idea with Fitz and Rooney Lee. Fitz Lee opposed it; Rooney Lee favored

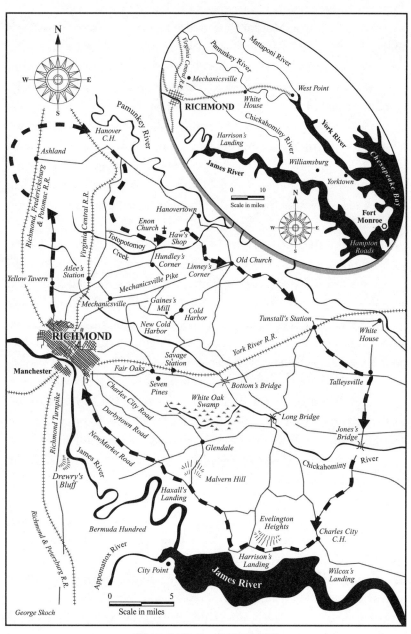

Stuart's Ride, June 1862

it. They would go forward. The decision, stated John Mosby, was not only "the turning point in the expedition, but in Stuart's life."[47]

Colonel Thomas Munford asserted after the conflict, "Stuart was ambitious as Caesar," adding that he "was as full of dash as he was ambition. He always took special care of himself." Ambition was not an uncommon commodity of the era, but Stuart's flamed more intensely. Almost certainly it mattered in his decision at Old Church. The undertaking was not, however, a rash venture. The distance to the Chickahominy was less than to Hanover Court House, and scouts had informed him that few enemy troops barred the route. The Federals, most likely, would not expect him to move in that direction, and the wooded, swampy region, with narrow roads, favored concealment as the column marched.[48]

Late in the afternoon of June 13, the Rebels rode out of Old Church, with "the hope of striking a serious blow at a boastful and insolent foe," in Stuart's words. Mosby, Farley, Burke, and Private Richard E. Frayser, a local man in the 3rd Virginia, scouted ahead, while Will Martin and the Jeff Davis Legion covered the rear. After a few miles, Stuart ordered a squadron from each of the 1st and 9th Virginia to Garlick's Landing on the Pamunkey River. At the small Union supply depot, the Virginians burned two transports and some wagons, seized prisoners, horses, and mules, and then started back toward the main force. Stuart, meanwhile, had sent Mosby and the others ahead to report on the situation at Tunstall's Station. When the scouts captured a sutler's wagon en route to the railroad stop, Mosby scribbled a message to Stuart to quicken the march as "the woods were full of game."[49]

The vanguard of the Confederate force swept into Tunstall's Station, bagging a handful of infantry guards and a park of sutler's wagons. Men piled logs across the rails, but before they had finished, a train approached from the west. Stuart arrived and watched as the locomotive plowed through the obstruction under gunfire from the Rebels. The marksmen wounded a number of crew members and passengers. The train escaped, clanging toward White House, the main Union supply base on the Pamunkey. A Northern newspaper termed the Southerners' action as "their infernal work."[50]

Details cut down telegraph poles and tore up the tracks while the majority of men ransacked the sutlers' wagons. Private John H. Timberlake of the 4th Virginia bragged: "We broke up the sutlers and got all their good eating. . . . We had a gay time." They carried away clothing, shoes, whiskey, pistols, and cigars before torching the wagons and the remaining supplies. A member of the Jeff Davis Legion argued later, "it would of been a loss of everything if we had of attempted to bring off wagons it was all that we could do to get through with the prisoners, horses & mules." With the work finished, Stuart headed them south to Talleysville, where they halted at 8:30 P.M. for a few hours of rest and for the rear of the column to close up. They had covered forty miles since daylight.[51]

The march resumed in the early minutes of June 14, for the Chickahominy. A moonlit night brightened the road, but men "went to sleep in the saddle" from exhaustion. An aide held Stuart on his horse as he slept. Lieutenant Jones Christian guided the column toward his family's home, Sycamore Springs, where a private ford lay. When the Confederates arrived, they encountered a swollen Chickahominy from the recent rains. Although a contingent of men managed to swim across to the southern bank, the main body, cannon, and the prisoners mounted on the mules could not risk a passage. "Anxiety at this time was reflected on the face of every one of these dusty and begrimed rebels," recalled a trooper.[52]

Stuart arrived and learned the news. In the judgment of a staff officer, "Stuart was, by nature, intended to lead and command men." He was "rarely excited by anything" and was able "to *think* with entire calmness." He sent a courier with a message to Robert E. Lee, requesting a diversion against the Union lines along Charles City Road. Scouts informed him of the destroyed Jones or Forge Bridge, a mile downstream where a road from Providence Forge, a local plantation, to Charles City Court House crossed the river. Stuart led the column to the site.[53]

Using a small skiff as a pontoon, the men stripped boards from a nearby warehouse and built a rickety bridge. Stuart watched from the bank "in the gayest humor I have ever seen him," noted Mosby. The Confederates walked over in a single file, carrying their saddles and holding the reins of their mounts, which swam the stream. Once across, they learned that they were on an island. A search located a swampy crossing site at the island's western end. After about half the column had managed to reach the southern bank, it was determined that the artillery pieces could not make their way through the shallows. The men erected a second makeshift bridge with the timbers, needing three hours. By 1:00 P.M., everyone had crossed, burning the structure behind them. A cavalryman admitted in a letter that the general "ran great risks but achieved much."[54]

Less than two hours later, Colonel Richard Rush and the 6th Pennsylvania clattered up to Sycamore Springs, where the Union horsemen soon learned that their quarry had eluded them. It was the closest the Federal pursuers came to overtaking the Confederates. Stuart's father-in-law, Philip St. George Cooke, commanded the Federal force. Conflicting orders slowed the pursuit, but Cooke acted neither with decisiveness nor celerity. His lackluster performance characterized the Union effort. McClellan's policy of parceling out mounted commands to infantry corps left them with no concentrated force to interdict the 1,200 Rebels. "The pursuit was not managed well," a general stated.[55]

The Confederate cavalrymen halted on the outskirts of Charles City Court House—Stuart and staff at the home of Judge Isaac Christian; the main body at Buckland, the residence of J. M. Wilcox. At 6:00 P.M., Stuart, Private Richard Frayser, and a courier started for Richmond, leaving orders for Fitz Lee to follow with the men five hours later. Refreshed with a few hours' sleep and a brief stop for coffee, Stuart and his companions rode through the night, avoiding enemy picket posts during the roughly thirty-mile ride. They reached the city about sunrise on June 15. Stuart sent Frayser to inform Virginia governor John Letcher of their return while he reported to army headquarters.[56]

Stuart rode out and met his exhausted officers and men as they came in later that morning. It had been a difficult ride, moving between enemy infantry works and gunboats on the James River. "Once more within our lines," recounted a trooper, "all went merry as a marriage bell." They rested for a few hours before passing through the city to their camps. Throngs of residents lined the streets, with girls laying flowers before Stuart's horse. One young woman placed a garland around the mount's neck. Another woman recorded in her diary that the procession produced "quite a sensation," noting that many of the riders were eating a loaf of bread as they passed.[57]

A Texan saw Stuart and recounted years later: "He looked like a prince as he rode by our camp, mounted on a splendid bay, wearing a hat with a black plume pinned back with a gold star." He wore a splendid uniform, but the infantryman thought, "he appeared to take but little care of fine clothes." "Somebody once said of Stuart," added the Texan, "'He is a dandy on dress parade, a belle at a ball, a boy in a possum hunt, and a hero in a fight.'"[58]

John Mosby in a letter written the next day exclaimed to his wife, "Our exploit is all the talk here & has produced more sensation than anything you ever saw." The Richmond *Examiner* called the enterprise "one of the most brilliant affairs of the war, bold in its inception and most brilliant in its execution." The Richmond *Dispatch* stated, "Stuart and his troopers are now forever in history." Even the caustic Major General D. H. Hill declared, "no more dashing thing done in the war," while a Georgia soldier asserted, "The whole seems fabulous."[59]

Robert E. Lee wrote that the expedition "was executed with great address and daring by that accomplished officer." Governor Letcher wrote to Jefferson Davis, requesting Stuart's promotion to major general. Gustavus Smith, James Longstreet, and Joseph E. Johnston endorsed Letcher's recommendation. "In my opinion," Johnston stated, "Brig. Genl. Stuart has fully earned promotion. No officer of his grade has performed more or better service than he."[60]

Several months later, Stuart confided to a staff member that the exploit "was the most perilous and most successful of all" of his operations until then. His command had captured 165 Federals, 260 horses and mules, and quartermaster and ordnance supplies. Union engineers, however, readily repaired the damage to the railroad, and the ride alerted McClellan to the vulnerability of his supply line. On June 18, he began transferring supplies to City Point on the James River. But the expedition's primary goal had been achieved—the confirmation that, as Stuart reported, "the enemy had no defensive works with reference to attack from the direction" that Jackson's force would approach from the Valley.[61]

The reaction to the expedition revealed a deeply felt need of the Southern people. Since First Manassas in July 1861, they had witnessed the loss of cities, battlefield victories by their opponents, and the possible capture of their national capital. The daring, if not brash, ride around the Army of the Potomac, with the loss of only one man killed, electrified them in these dark days. Stuart attained what he so coveted—he had become a Confederate hero. The flowers strewn before his horse and the official and newspaper praise were not lost upon Stuart. A deed such as this could enhance or restore a soldier's reputation. "Stuart wanted to be admired," John Thomason, a biographer, has written, "and himself saw to it that he was always admirable."[62]

He did not forget the officers and men who had been with him on the enterprise. On June 17, he issued a congratulatory order, stating in part: "History will record in imperishable characters and a grateful country will remember with gratitude that portion of the First, Fourth, and Ninth Virginia Cavalry, the Jeff. Davis Legion, and the section of the Stuart Horse Artillery engaged in the expedition. What was accomplished is known to you, to the public, and to the enemy." He closed with, "Proud of his command, the general trusts that it will never lose sight of what is at stake in this struggle—the reputation now its province to maintain."[63]

In his report on the operation, Stuart commended the regimental commanders and his staff officers. Among the aides cited were two new members to the staff—Lieutenant John Esten Cooke and Captain Heros von Borcke. Cooke was Flora Stuart's cousin and had been serving with the Richmond Howitzers. He had frequented Stuart's headquarters during the previous months, moving the general to tell Flora: "Jno. Esten is a case & I am afraid I cant like him. He is like your Pa in some peculiarities." Later, perhaps after Flora wrote to him about her cousin, Stuart assured her, "you need not fear any difference" between him and Cooke, and "by no possible chance with me." In May, despite his misgivings, Stuart assigned Cooke to the staff as an ordnance officer.[64]

Johann August Heinrick Heros von Borcke had passed recently through the Union naval blockade from his native Prussia. A former lieutenant in the Prussian cavalry, the twenty-six-year-old von Borcke had been promised a commission in the Confederate army by a Southern representative in Europe. When he arrived in Richmond, Secretary of War George Randolph assigned him as a volunteer aide-de-camp to Stuart. "It was no easy matter to find General Stuart," von Borcke wrote in his memoirs.[65]

"Von Borcke was a powerful creature," testified an officer, "a tall, blonde, active giant." He stood six feet, two inches tall, and his weight was described as between 250 and 280 pounds. Moxley Sorrel, Longstreet's chief of staff, called him "an ambulating arsenal," with a double-barreled shotgun, a carbine, and three revolvers. He also possessed a "ponderous saber . . . long and straight, and of a size no ordinary man could handle." When he joined Stuart, he knew not "a word of English," but in time he learned to speak it well. He had the curious habit of filing his fingernails to points. Stuart liked him at once, and von Borcke became devoted to the general.[66]

After the ride around the Union army, Captain William Blackford rejoined the staff as an engineer officer. Another Virginian, Norman R. FitzHugh, replaced Luke Brien as assistant adjutant general or chief of staff. Brien had assumed his duties as lieutenant colonel of the 1st Virginia. The thirty-year-old FitzHugh was a "tall, red-bearded" man, who had served as a corporal in the 9th Virginia. FitzHugh proved to be a capable, hardworking, and popular staff member.[67]

With the return of cavalry from the expedition, the officers and men enjoyed a period of relative quiet. They complained about the flies that encircled the camps and about mosquitoes, which they called "*gallon-sippers*." Stuart continued to impose strict limits on the troopers' off-duty times. "We cant go to town," grumbled a private to his mother, "and only two miles from it. I despise to be under Genl Steward he has no feeling Cares nothing for the Comfort of his men he is much disliked by his men." Another cavalryman noted that "the fool pickets" raised alarms nearly every night, "scared to death afraid the Yankees will try the same trick" of riding around the Confederates. Some regiments received new flags, and Stuart held reviews of units.[68]

Robert E. Lee, meanwhile, met with four of the army's senior generals at the Dabbs house on June 23. Present were Longstreet, D. H. Hill, A. P. Hill, and Stonewall Jackson, who arrived about midday after a sixty-mile horseback ride. An eyewitness who had seen Jackson just days before thought that the hero of the Shenandoah Valley Campaign looked like "an awkward, tired, humpshouldered, careworn looking man, dressed in the very plainest garb." A week earlier, a day after Stuart had completed his mission, Lee ordered Jackson to bring his command east "to unite with this army," advising the subordinate, "the movement must be secret." While his troops marched toward Richmond, Jackson had ridden ahead to be at the conference.[69]

Lee outlined to the generals his plans for an offensive strike against George McClellan's right flank in the vicinity of Mechanicsville. With the confirmation of the enemy's vulnerability brought by Stuart, he believed that Jackson could roll up the Federal flank north of the Chickahominy. When Lee finished, he left the room to allow the generals to discuss freely the proposal. Longstreet asked Jackson when he thought that he could be ready to attack. Daylight of June 25, replied Jackson. Longstreet countered that he might require more time for his troops to be in position. Jackson concurred, and they settled on daybreak, June 26. Lee returned, and more discussion ensued before Lee issued verbal orders with the promise of written orders to follow.[70]

The audacity that had concerned Porter Alexander was at hand. In the orders, dated June 24, Lee assigned the infantry divisions of major generals Benjamin Huger and John Magruder the duty of demonstrating against the Union works south of the river. If the Federals advanced on them, Huger's and Magruder's troops comprised the Confederates' main line of defense for the capital. While A. P. "Powell" Hill's division moved directly on the enemy's position behind Beaver Dam Creek at Mechanicsville, Jackson's command would turn McClellan's flank, moving toward Cold Harbor. D. H. Hill and Longstreet were directed to support Powell Hill's and Jackson's movements. The orders specified that the infantrymen should have three days' cooked rations.[71]

Lee divided Stuart's brigade. The 3rd and 5th Virginia, 1st North Carolina, and a squadron of the Hampton Legion were ordered to cover the roads on the south side of the Chickahominy. The 10th Virginia was to act as a reserve on Nine Mile Road. Lee instructed Stuart, with the 1st, 4th, and 9th Virginia, Cobb's Legion, Jeff Davis Legion, and the Stuart Horse Artillery, to march on June 25, to "take position to the left of Genl Jackson's line of march," and to cooperate with his force. Scouts should roam well beyond the infantry column in the front and on the left flank.[72]

Stuart rode forth with his command on June 25, following, in part, the route they had taken thirteen days earlier. By evening, they had reached Jackson's command at Ashland. It had been a long, exhausting day for Jackson's so-called foot cavalry. The infantrymen had marched twenty miles in stifling heat. The troops' physical condition forced Jackson to halt at Ashland, six miles short of the planned destination. He sent a note to Lee, informing the commander that he would resume the march at 2:30 A.M. on June 26, or as he said, "early dawn."[73]

Stuart met briefly with Jackson. When the cavalryman arrived at the headquarters, nearby infantrymen cheered. The friends were undoubtedly pleased to be reunited. They had not seen each other since the previous autumn. Now, both of them were Confederate heroes—Jackson for his victories in the Valley, Stuart for his ride around the Union army. Leaving Jackson, Stuart rejoined his command for the night.[74]

Much has been written about Jackson's lackluster performance during the forthcoming Seven Days' Campaign. The primary interpretation has argued that physical exhaustion smothered the usual fire within him. Whatever the reason or reasons, Jackson's difficulties began from the outset on this critical day of June 26. It was as though the devout soldier and his "army of the living God" were cursed: the march started at 8:30 A.M., six hours behind schedule; aware of his approach, the Federals skirmished with the van, felled trees across the roads, and lobbed artillery shells toward the ranks; and the swelling heat drained further the stamina from bone-weary men. At sundown, after covering sixteen miles, Jackson halted the column at Hundley's Corner, a mile past Pole Green Church.[75]

In defense of Jackson, Lee had never specified a destination for him. Using a faulty map, Lee concluded that if Jackson reached Pole Green Church he would be beyond Beaver Dam Creek and on the Union flank. Instead, the church lay three miles from the stream and farther from the enemy's position. In his orders, Lee expected Jackson to turn the Federal flank, but Jackson seemed to believe that his goal for the day was Cold Harbor. Although Jackson sent two messages to Brigadier General Lawrence Branch of Powell Hill's division with whom he was to link up, neither he nor Lee communicated with each other during the day. The misunderstanding and miscommunication boded ill for Lee's army.[76]

Hundreds of Confederate troops paid dearly for the failings on this

day. Impatient at Jackson's nonappearance, Powell Hill sent his brigades across the Chickahominy, through Mechanicsville, and toward
the Union line behind Beaver Dam Creek. Porter Alexander declared
that the enemy position was "absolutely impregnable to a frontal
attack." In all, five Confederate brigades charged into a furnace of
musketry and artillery fire. The Yankees, troops of Major General Fitz
John Porter's Fifth Corps, erased the oncoming ranks. A Union officer
remarked that on the lower plain the Southern dead appeared "like
flies in a bowl of sugar." Their casualties amounted to 1,400; Porter's to
fewer than 400.[77]

Stuart, meanwhile, performed his duty routinely on June 26. His
cavalrymen protected Jackson's left flank, roaming far to the north.
They had brushes with Union troopers and rebuilt a bridge over Totopotomoy Creek. But there seemed to be no urgency or aggressiveness
to Stuart's actions. He met Jackson at Hickory Well, the home of Dr.
Edwin T. Shelton, before the infantry reached Hundley's Corner. Jackson's uniform, said William Blackford, "looked as if they formed no part
of his thoughts." Stuart ringed Jackson's troops with pickets during the
night.[78]

Lee had gambled when he assumed the offensive that George
McClellan would not assail the undermanned Confederate works south
of the Chickahominy. Stuart and others in Lee's army believed that
McClellan should have advanced on the capital. Instead, when the
Union commander learned of the attack on Porter and Jackson's presence in the area, he ordered Porter to retreat to a stronger defensive position at Gaines's Mill, on a wooded plateau above Boatswain's Swamp,
four miles to the southeast. Porter's thirty thousand troops abandoned
their position east of Mechanicsville at daylight on June 27.[79]

Lee's 55,000 officers and men closed on Porter's position throughout
the morning. Confusion plagued the Confederates once again as Boatswain's Swamp was not on their maps. Jackson's column encountered
delays, not arriving on the field until after A. P. Hill opened the battle.
A Pennsylvanian exclaimed that the fighting was "as terrible as human
beings can make it." Rebel units breached the enemy line only to be
blasted back. Veterans in both armies had never experienced such a
fearful and bloody struggle.[80]

Stuart brought his cavalry onto the field behind Jackson's deploying units. The cavalry had circled to the left of Jackson's line of march, sparring with Federal horsemen. Stuart found Jackson sitting on a log near an "old tumble down log house." Stuart itched to get into the fight, but Jackson ordered him to place the cavalry in reserve on the left flank. Union artillery fire began striking close by. William Blackford maintained that Jackson and Stuart "were the only two men I ever knew whom I thought unconscious of the feeling of fear. There were many as brave, but these two never seemed to feel that danger existed." Nevertheless, both men moved from the shellfire.[81]

Stuart rode away, searching for a place to use cannon from the horse artillery. John Esten Cooke wrote in his diary that the staff "followed Stuart here, there, everywhere." Finally, he brought John Pelham forward with two guns, and the crews soon opened fire on Union batteries. Federal cannon responded, disabling one of Pelham's pieces within minutes. With only a 12-pound Napoleon, Pelham kept firing. Stuart described the artillerists' efforts as "one of the most gallant and heroic feats of the war." He asked Jackson to send additional guns. A trooper posted in support of Pelham's Napoleon swore, "I never did hear balls burst and whistle so in all my life before." When a shell howled close to Stuart and the staff, Cooke fell off his horse. Stuart asked if the aide had been hit. "Oh, no General, I only dodged a little too far." His comrades laughed aloud, and for months afterward, Stuart greeted Cooke in the morning with his words.[82]

Stuart rejoined Jackson as his infantrymen advanced. "With cheers our lines moved forward," recalled one of Jackson's aides. "Stuart clapped his hands with delight." On the right front of the Confederate line two of Longstreet's brigades broke through Porter's line. The Union ranks splintered, but the fighting was hand-to-hand at places. More Confederates surged onto the plateau, sweeping the Yankees south toward the Chickahominy. Blue-coated reserves fashioned a rear guard, allowing Porter's troops to cross the stream throughout the night. Stuart's cavalrymen pursued for about three miles to the east, found no enemy troops, and halted in the darkness. He returned to Jackson, and the pair of generals slept on the ground with Esten Cooke between them.[83]

The Battle of Gaines's Mill cost Porter's Fifth Corps twenty-two cannon and 6,837 casualties. Confederate losses amounted to 8,700. The defeat left McClellan with two choices—he could attack the enemy works held by Huger's and Magruder's divisions or he could abandon his campaign by retreating. He chose the latter course, and by it, this cautious officer defined his generalship. He ordered an abandonment of the army's supply base at White House and a withdrawal to the James River. He seemed incapable of doing what Lee had done—undertake a risky operation that might salvage his campaign. In a meeting with his ranking generals, he said, "If we were defeated, the Army and the country would be lost."[84]

Lee spent June 28, trying to get confirmation about McClellan's movements. He was reluctant to believe that his opponent would abandon the supply base and retreat either down the Peninsula or to the James. Stuart reported to army headquarters in the morning and received orders to march to the York River Railroad and to sever the enemy's supply line. Lee also sent Richard Ewell's infantry division in that direction. Perhaps one or both of them could uncover vital intelligence.[85]

The cavalry angled southeast, passing through the region used during the final ride to the Chickahominy a fortnight earlier. Stuart sent a dispatch to Lee that the enemy had destroyed the railroad bridge over the river, providing more evidence of a Union retreat. Stuart pushed on to Tunstall's Station, while Ewell halted at Dispatch Station. Ewell forwarded a report from a subordinate that indicated an enemy withdrawal. At Cold Harbor, Lee still hesitated to commit his army to a pursuit, uncertain of the direction of McClellan's movement. Dust clouds from the south, made by men and wagons on the march, offered further proof. Lee decided, however, to wait until the next morning to issue orders.[86]

At Tunstall's Station, Stuart's men tore up the railroad tracks and bivouacked for the night. To the northeast, a red glow in the night sky could be seen as fires consumed the vast stockpile of supplies at White House. Stuart moved toward the site on the morning of June 29. The Rebels advanced cautiously to within a quarter mile of the supply base, where a Union gunboat was moored in the Pamunkey River. Stuart had a howitzer fire artillery rounds at the vessel, which soon steamed downriver. Despite the Federals' efforts, "provisions and delicacies of every description lay in heaps," reported Stuart. White House was the home of Rooney Lee, and the Yankees torched it before departing. Stuart bristled at the sight, calling the residence's destruction "the deceitfulness of the enemy's pretended reverence for everything associated with the name of Washington." Lee's mother was a Custis, the daughter of Martha Washington's grandson and the first president's adopted son.[87]

Large amounts of rations and forage had not been destroyed, all of which were needed badly by the men and their mounts. Sometime during the morning, Stuart received a dispatch from Colonel R. H. Chilton, the army's chief of staff. "The Gen'l. Comd'g," wrote Chilton, "requests that you will watch the Chicahominy as far as Forge Bridge, ascertain if any attempt will be made in that direction by the enemy, advising Gen'l Jackson, who will resist their passage until reinforced. If you find that they have passed down below where they cannot cross, leave a force to watch movements which may be made & recross yourself to this side for further operations."[88]

Stuart complied with the orders by sending Fitz Lee and the 1st Virginia to picket the river from Bottom's Bridge to Forge Bridge. In his report, Stuart wrote, "There was no evidence of a retreat" by the Federals toward Yorktown, and "that I had no doubt the enemy since his defeat was endeavoring to reach the James as a new base." He claimed that he sent this information to army headquarters, but when or whether Lee received the message is uncertain as no copy of it appears to exist. Stuart remained at White House, overseeing the destruction of the supplies not commandeered by his men. He forwarded a copy of Chilton's dispatch to Jackson.[89]

The note to Stuart attested to an uncertainty in Lee's mind to McClellan's destination. He had acted, however, on the belief that the Federals were marching toward the James River. Longstreet's and Powell Hill's divisions moved in a "forced march" to be in position south of the river to interdict the Union retreat on June 30. The commands of Magruder, Huger, and Theophilus H. Holmes advanced east to slow the enemy columns. Magruder encountered the Federal rear guard at Savage Station, bringing on a "severe action" in the late afternoon.[90]

Jackson's assignment was to repair Grapevine Bridge, crossing the river when completed, and "to push the pursuit vigorously." Magruder expected assistance from Jackson. When Magruder asked for support, Jackson replied that he had "other important duty to perform." Jackson had received a copy of Chilton's dispatch from Stuart and interpreted it as requiring him to remain on the north bank and to resist any Federal crossing attempt. Jackson misread, however, the intent of Lee's instructions to Stuart. Left alone, Magruder's men suffered a repulse. It was not until hours later that Jackson's divisions filed over the bridge.[91]

Porter Alexander, the preeminent historian of the army who served in its ranks, wrote of June 30, 1862, "But never, before or after, did fates put such a prize within our reach." Despite the command problems that had hampered, if not crippled, operations, Lee stood poised to inflict a decisive defeat on McClellan's army. Union infantry and artillery held the vital crossroads of Glendale, where three roads, coming in from the west, intersected the route of the Federals to the James River. If the Rebels seized the crossroads, McClellan's army could be divided and vulnerable to piecemeal destruction.[92]

The fates, however, ignored Lee's legions. Longstreet's and Powell Hill's veterans charged the Union defenses with a valor and ferocity similar to that at Gaines's Mill. Hand-to-hand combat characterized some of the fury. Once more, Jackson remained out of the fighting, thwarted by a Union force across White Oak Swamp from him. After failed attempts to locate other crossing sites and against enemy resistance, Jackson sat against a tree and slept. At Glendale, nearly 7,500 men, Northern and Southern, had been killed, wounded, or captured. The Yankees held the crossroads at dark, and during the night marched south—a soldier compared it to "a funeral procession"—to a strong defensive position on Malvern Hill.[93]

With the infantry divisions and artillery batteries united at last, Lee's army trailed the Federals to Malvern Hill. It took the Southerners most of July 1 to deploy into battle ranks below the massed Union cannon and rows of infantry on the plateau. Lee hesitated to attack, but two erroneous reports that the enemy was retreating opened the doors to a slaughterhouse. Fifteen Confederate brigades—at times alone, at other times in pairs—ascended the slope into a furnace of canister and musketry. The words of the attackers convey, as well as words can, how terrible Malvern Hill was—a Georgian: "a tempest of iron and lead was sweeping over it cutting down every living thing. . . . Nothing but a kind Providence saved any of us"; a Virginian: "At no other time did I so realize the horrors of a battlefield"; division commander D. H. Hill: "It was not war—it was murder."[94]

Lee attributed the battle's outcome to the "want of concert among the attacking columns." In fact, despite a magnificent display of valor by Confederate officers and men, a gale of iron and lead had engulfed them, seizing them in its grip and leaving behind "rivers of good blood." A gunner in Lee's army offered a fair assessment of Malvern Hill: "The battle ought never to have been fought where it was."[95]

Stuart and the cavalry arrived at Malvern Hill late in the day of July 1. While the Battle of Glendale had raged, the horsemen watched the crossings of the lower Chickahominy. Stuart had addressed a message to Fitz Lee with "Hd Qrs Army of Observation," indicating the duty his men were performing. During the night of June 30–July 1, he received orders to cross the river and to join the army. In the dispatch, chief of staff Chilton instructed him: "move up and cooperate on our left. By threatening this the defeat will be more complete and you can follow after them." After a march of forty-two miles, the cavalry came up on the army's left flank. With the Federals victorious and still on the plateau, the horsemen encamped. A drenching rain fell overnight.[96]

Jackson and Stuart rode together to army headquarters on the morning of July 2. The two generals, Lee, Longstreet, and President Jefferson Davis, who had joined Lee on June 30, were discussing the army's condition when they learned that the Federals had resumed their withdrawal to the James River. Stuart hurried back to his command and went in pursuit. His troopers captured many enemy stragglers along the route. At nightfall, Stuart sent John Pelham with a cannon and squadron of the 1st Virginia farther down the road. At 10:00 P.M., Stuart informed Lee by courier that he would continue the pursuit at daylight, noting, "McClellan is doubtless awaiting for his transports."[97]

Early on the morning of July 3, Stuart received a message from Pelham. A civilian had told the artillerist that the Union army had ended its retreat on "a beautiful plain" at Harrison's Landing on the James River. According to the citizen, the broad lowland lay beneath Evelington Heights, which extended for a mile. "He says," wrote Pelham, "that guns placed on the hill commands every thing as far as the river." Stuart forwarded Pelham's note to Lee, who replied that the cavalry should "retard" the enemy until the infantry, who were on the march, joined them. Lee was "much pleased at the vigorous pursuit."[98]

Stuart and Pelham rode on to Evelington Heights at mid-morning. Beneath them sprawled the Army of the Potomac with its vast train of wagons and artillery. Stuart could not resist the temptation. "Stuart's fondness for the use of artillery was almost excessive," asserted a staff officer. A crew rolled forward a howitzer and began shelling the campsite. Union gunboats in the river answered with a "few shells as big as flour barrels," in the description of a trooper. Stuart's hasty action alerted the Federals to the tactical importance of the heights, and they advanced infantry to retake the ground. "We skedaddled," declared one of Stuart's men.[99]

"I had the infinite gratification of skipping around the enemys rear and shelling his camp at Westover," Stuart boasted to Flora. "If the army had been up with me we would have finished his business." But the infantry, slowed by the muddy roads, was not up when the howitzer opened fire. Stuart's impatience, if not rashness, squandered perhaps an excellent opportunity for the Confederates. Although McClellan and his generals might have realized their army's vulnerability without Stuart alerting them to it, Major Charles Venable of Lee's staff called Stuart's action "a grave error." His fellow aide, Major Walter Taylor, concluded, "Those heights in our possession, the enemy's position was altogether untenable, and he was at our mercy; unless they could be recaptured his capitulation was inevitable."[100]

Lee, Longstreet, and Jackson surveyed the Union position on Evelington Heights the next day, deciding that McClellan's army was secure from attack. Leaving some mounted units behind to observe the enemy, Lee withdrew the army to reserve positions during the next week, ending the Seven Days' Campaign. Lee stated in his report, "the Federal army should have been destroyed." According to Porter Alexander, the commanding general was "deeply, bitterly disappointed." Perhaps Lee expected too much from an army not yet forged into the weapon it would become. But Richmond had been saved, although at a cost of more than twenty thousand casualties.[101]

As the campaign progressed, the region's terrain limited the role of Stuart and the cavalry. In the operation's origin, they had rendered valuable intelligence service with the expedition around the enemy. The Southern populace acclaimed Stuart a hero. At campaign's end, he committed a serious misjudgment. Another Union army was forming, however, on ground favorable for mounted warriors.

Chapter Seven

"Great Spirits of the Land"

A CANVAS FLY TENT marked the headquarters of Jeb Stuart on a farm of a Mr. Timberlake near Atlee's Station on the Virginia Central Railroad north of Richmond. Beneath the canvas a chair and a desk served as furnishings, while outside a flag hung in the July heat. Nearby sprawled the camps of the cavalry regiments. Except for picket duty, drills, and the hordes of flies, the officers and men enjoyed the respite from active campaigning. But in the words of a captain, "a rigid discipline" prevailed.[1]

Flora Stuart and the children came from the city for a visit. Four-year-old Flora and two-year-old Jimmie stayed with their mother, whom they called "Ma Ma," at an adjacent house. Heros von Borcke noted that the youngsters "were the pets of the whole camp." The Stuart family welcomed a stream of visitors from the capital for the drills, reviews, and social affairs. Stuart was the Confederacy's newest hero, and he relished the attention and renown.[2]

It seemed that wherever Stuart went during these days he garnered attention. A diarist recorded that he saw the general in the city. When duty permitted, Stuart attended Sunday services at St. Paul's Episcopal Church. An eyewitness wrote that he "would stalk down the aisle to a seat near the front, with his spurs jingling and swinging his cavalier's hat with an enormous plume, so that it was impossible to take him all in." When he and Stonewall Jackson stopped at the War Department together, they "attracted much attention," remarked a clerk. "Everybody wished to see them." Stuart took time to visit former army friends who were prisoners in Libby Prison.[3]

Confederate authorities rewarded Stuart officially for his performance during the recent operations with a promotion to major general, dated July 25. General Robert E. Lee congratulated Stuart, remarking, "It is deserved though it has been somewhat tardy." Similarly, Jackson wrote to his friend, "Permit me to congratulate you upon your well earned promotion." "I am desirous of seeing you along the front of my lines," added Jackson. "Nothing has yet given a fair opportunity for our cooperation, should any exist, you may expect to hear from me."[4]

In his letter, which he marked "Private," Lee informed Stuart, "I am endeavoring to put the Cavl on a good footing." Jackson had suggested to Lee that Stuart should be assigned "to the command of all the cavalry" in the army. On July 28, Lee approved the formation of Stuart's regiments into two brigades. Lee also ordered that the new major general "will take General direction of all the Cavalry of this army."[5]

The brigades were commanded by brigadier generals Wade Hampton and Fitz Lee. Stuart proposed that Lee should lead the First Brigade and Hampton the Second. Robert E. Lee, however, reversed this as Hampton was senior in rank to Fitz Lee. Hampton's brigade consisted of the 1st North Carolina, 2nd South Carolina, 10th Virginia, Cobb's Georgia Legion, and Jeff Davis Legion. Lee's command contained five Virginia regiments—1st, 3rd, 4th, 5th, and 9th. A third brigade, originally under Turner Ashby in the Shenandoah Valley, was now led by Brigadier General Beverly Robertson. Ashby had been killed in an action at Harrisonburg on June 6. Five Virginia units comprised Robertson's brigade—2nd, 6th, 7th, 12th, and 17th battalions—and were serving with Jackson. Two batteries of the Stuart Horse Artillery completed Stuart's command.[6]

The appointment of Wade Hampton brought to the cavalry one of the South's wealthiest slaveowners. A member of one of South Carolina's most distinguished families, Hampton owned more than 12,000 acres and hundreds of slaves in several plantations. When the war began, he organized and mainly funded the Hampton Legion of infantry, artillery, and cavalry companies. He had suffered a slight wound at First Manassas and had been hit in the foot at Seven Pines. While on leave, he accepted promotion to brigadier general, to date from May 23, after previously declining the appointment. He held temporary command of an infantry brigade during the Seven Days' Campaign. When the campaign concluded, Lee proposed his transfer to the cavalry, and with apparent reluctance, Hampton agreed.[7]

Hampton was a man who appeared comfortable with the responsibilities of leadership. He was forty-four years old, slightly under six feet tall, physically strong, and athletic. A superb horseman, he was equally skillful with a sword, rifle, or pistol. A reserve and dignity encased Hampton, and he was unfailingly courteous and gentlemanly with strangers. Among friends, he could be frank and congenial. Staff officers and ranking subordinates were devoted to him.[8]

James Longstreet's chief of staff, Moxley Sorrel, claimed that on a battlefield Hampton was "of the most undaunted courage." Unlike Stuart, however, war never held for him a grandeur or chivalric illusions. He saw the conflict darkly as a grim and deadly business. He served, thought John Esten Cooke, "from a sense of duty, and not from passion, or to win renown." To him, the struggle "was hard work—not sought, but accepted." Military service was an obligation to be fulfilled, perhaps even a debt to be paid for what he had been given.[9]

Hampton and Stuart forged a professional relationship but not a personal friendship. They shared an adherence to duty and to the cause. But the contrasts between them in style and in personality were undeniable. Stuart wore a resplendent uniform; Hampton preferred a "dingy" gray coat. Stuart relished the pageantry of a review; Hampton viewed it as another onerous task for himself and his men. Hampton possessed a quiet self-assurance, rooted in wealth, stature, and achievement; Stuart had a clanging self-confidence, stoked by ambition and wrapped in flamboyance. In the end, however, each respected the other man's personal bravery and talent as a cavalry leader.[10]

Fitz Lee's ascension to brigade command carried with it promotion to brigadier general. Although no record of his view seems to exist, Grumble Jones must have been galled by the news. But Lee had been one of Stuart's favorites for nearly a year, and Stuart and Lee's uncle, the army commander, recommended him for the rank. Stuart's proposal to designate Lee's regiments as the First Brigade indicated his preference for him. In a private postwar letter, Longstreet argued that Lee "was anything but an efficient cavalryman." Over time, other officers came to share Longstreet's estimation of him. Not long after Hampton's and Lee's appointments, Stuart endeavored to have a fourth brigade organized, with Rooney Lee as commander, but his recommendation was not acted upon.[11]

Stuart's efforts on behalf of another officer ignited a furor within a regiment that led to a court-martial. Since the minor affair at Lewinsville in September 1861, Stuart had been impressed with Thomas Rosser, who commanded artillery on that day. When the War Department organized the 5th Virginia in June 1862, Stuart lobbied for and secured Rosser's promotion to colonel and command of the regiment. "I pushed through your Colonelcy of the 5th Virginia Cavalry," he declared in a June 23 letter to Rosser. "Today the commission is ordered by the Secretary. Come to me at daylight in the morning and I will give you the particulars. You are in my brigade and must play an important part in the next battle. 'Come a-runnin.'"[12]

The 5th Virginia had been formed around a five-company battalion under Lieutenant Colonel Henry Clay Pate. When Pate learned of Rosser's appointment, he was furious, believing that he deserved the post. "Colonel Pate contended," recalled an officer in the regiment, "that a great injustice was done him." An enlisted man, while describing Pate as "a brave man," argued that he "was of a domineering disposition with a faculty for getting into trouble." It was one thing, however, to find trouble, it was another matter to seek it.[13]

Pate alleged that Rosser was "prejudiced against me" when he joined the regiment and abetted "a conspiracy to rob me of my command." In fact, it was Stuart who most likely "prejudiced" Rosser against Pate. Stuart and Pate had a history stretching back to Kansas, where the army, with Stuart present, secured the release of Pate and his men from John Brown. As the controversy brewed, Stuart remarked that "Pate could not be a Corporal in the Missouri Army," and "we know Pate about here." Stuart had tried to have him removed when the regiment was organized, but Secretary of War George Randolph overruled Stuart.[14]

On July 10, Pate charged Rosser with intemperance while on duty, claiming that several officers in the 5th Virginia asked him to do so. When Stuart received Pate's report and letters from the officers, he rejected the charge for not being filed through Rosser. In an effort to avoid a formal hearing, Stuart asked Rosser to sign "a written obligation to abstain from intoxicating drink whilst in the army of the Confederacy." Rosser refused to sign a formal pledge but wrote a letter to that effect. Stuart dismissed Pate's charge.[15]

Weeks later, Rosser arrested Pate, citing him with five violations that included "disrespectful conduct and disobedience of orders." Rosser declared to an officer at the time that if Pate "knew what was best for him, he would resign, that these were charges enough against him to sink him to hell." Instead, Pate demanded a court-martial to refute the charges. The court convened, listened to testimony for four days, and was disbanded when the cavalry received orders to march. Pate was sent home to await further orders. Not until the spring of 1863 would a court-martial clear him, at which time he returned to duty.[16]

Pate had committed a grave mistake—he had opposed one of Stuart's favored officers and, by implication, Stuart himself. As Esten Cooke had stated, Stuart was "a thoroughly good hater" who brooked little, if any, resistance to his will. His prejudices ran deep and remained with him for a long time. In his estimation, Pate's surrender to abolitionists in Kansas had been shameful, and he regarded Pate with contempt. Pate's charges against Rosser might have had some basis in fact as the latter indulged in alcoholic drink. But it was Stuart's handling of the dispute that revealed his dark motives.[17]

At the time, Major William G. Deloney of Cobb's Legion addressed a problem that would simmer within the ranks of the cavalry far into the future. Writing to his wife, he grumbled, "It is a great misfortune not to be a Virginian." He asserted that the Virginia regiments "had a good time on easy duty," while the mounted units from the lower South spent two weeks on picket duty. "The truth," he contended, was "that in this war the post of honor is to be a Virginian & the post of labor & danger is to be a Georgian." A Virginia regiment had replaced Cobb's Legion on picket duty because, Deloney claimed, it "is in disgrace with Stuart" as "every officer in it has applied to be transferred to Genl. Robertson's brigade." Whether Deloney's complaint was just or not, the perception festered that Stuart assigned the onerous duties to non-Virginians.[18]

When Deloney wrote his letter on July 21, the relative quiet after the Seven Days' Campaign was ending for the cavalry. A second Union army was advancing south into central Virginia, and General Robert E. Lee wanted Stuart to march north toward the North Anna River, where he could observe the enemy and protect the Virginia Central Railroad. Earlier, Lee had dispatched Jackson with two infantry divisions and an artillery battery to Gordonsville to confront this Federal command. With Major General George B. McClellan's Army of the Potomac still encamped at Harrison's Landing, Lee concluded that the pressing threat lay in the region along the Rapidan and Rappahannock rivers.[19]

The Union force before Jackson was the newly organized Army of Virginia. At the end of June, the administration in Washington merged three departments together to form the new command and appointed Major General John Pope to lead it. A West Point roommate of Longstreet, Pope had achieved modest success along the Mississippi River and seemed to possess an aggressiveness sorely lacking in McClellan. Brash and egotistic, Pope announced to the army upon assuming command that he had come from the West "where we have always seen the backs of our enemies." "Let us look before and not behind," he declared. "Success and glory are in the advance."[20]

By mid-July the vanguard of Pope's fifty-thousand-man army had crossed the Rappahannock and Rapidan, arriving at Culpeper Court House, thirty miles north of Gordonsville. The Virginia Central Railroad and the Orange & Alexandria Railroad intersected at Gordonsville, making the town vital to the Confederacy. Lee sent a third infantry division to Jackson, telling the general, "I want Pope to be suppressed." An 11,000-man Union division occupied Fredericksburg, which had moved Lee to order Stuart north.[21]

Leaving Hampton's brigade on picket duty east of Richmond, Stuart led Fitz Lee's regiments to Hanover Court House, where he established his headquarters on the courthouse lawn. Lee instructed Stuart to resist any enemy movement from Fredericksburg and to stop Yankee cavalry raids against the railroad. In one raid, the blue-jacketed horsemen captured John Mosby while he waited for a train at Beaver Dam Station. Mosby had with him a letter from Stuart to Jackson, whom he was en route to join as a scout. "He is bold, daring, intelligent and discreet," Stuart wrote of Mosby. "The information he may obtain and transmit to you may be relied upon, and I have no doubt that he will soon give additional proofs of his value." Although his captors secured the letter, they exchanged Mosby for an infantry lieutenant within ten days. They would come to regret their decision.[22]

Heros von Borcke remembered the weeks at Hanover Court House as a time of "great comfort and enjoyment." While in the town, Stuart acted as godfather at the baptism of Captain Norman FitzHugh's son. Operations against the Federals, however, kept Stuart and his troopers busy. Twice he conducted expeditions toward Fredericksburg, clashing with enemy infantry and cavalry units and capturing prisoners and wagons. "The greatest benefit you can do," Lee wrote to him on August 7, "is what you are now doing, cutting up their communications, trains, &c. Keep me informed of events." Two days later, Stuart boarded a train for Gordonsville, with orders from Lee to inspect Jackson's cavalry.[23]

Jackson had requested Stuart's services. "Old Jack," as his men called him, had become displeased with Beverly Robertson as his cavalry commander. Jackson was, according to an officer, "mad about" Robertson's assignment to his command. During the first week of August, he had asked Robertson, "Where is the enemy?" When the cavalry officer replied, "I really do not know," Jackson wired Lee for Stuart. Jackson wrote to Stuart directly after Lee agreed, stating, "I desire you to make it [an inspection] during active operations, as I may thereby secure your services for the time being."[24]

Stuart joined Jackson on the morning of August 10 near Cedar Mountain, south of Culpeper Court House. The day before, Jackson had attacked Pope's advanced units, under Major General Nathaniel P. Banks, at Cedar Mountain. The fighting began in the afternoon and continued into darkness. Despite confusion and tactical errors, the Confederates prevailed, driving the Yankees north toward Culpeper Court House. Jackson's casualties amounted to more than 1,400, including the death of the able Brigadier General Charles S. Winder, commander of the Stonewall Brigade. Union losses reached 2,400.[25]

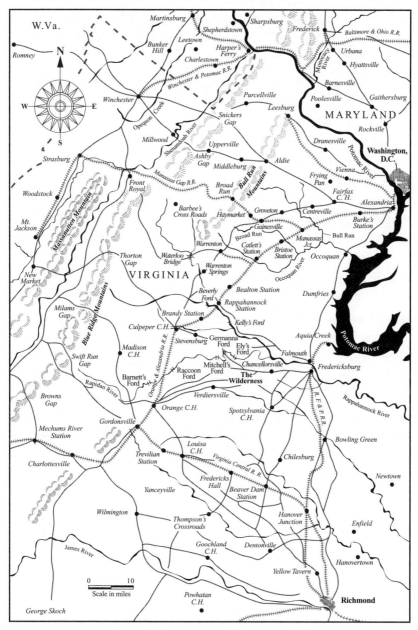

Area of Operations, Summer 1862

When Stuart arrived, Jackson gave him command of the cavalry and ordered him to conduct a reconnaissance on the Union left flank. Jackson was contemplating a renewal of attacks until Stuart confirmed reports that Banks's corps had been reinforced. Rebel skirmishers sparred with enemy soldiers as Jackson withdrew his command to the Cedar Mountain battlefield, where details began burying the dead. Stuart spent the rest of the day and part of the next inspecting Robertson's cavalry brigade.[26]

On the morning of August 11, the Federals requested a truce to inter their fallen. Jackson agreed and directed Stuart and Brigadier General Jubal A. Early to supervise the truce. A Confederate trooper recounted that the Northerners placed their slain comrades in mass graves, kicking some of the corpses into the pits. "The live Yankees seemed to be in good spirits," he stated, "and did not evince the least sympathy for their friends who lay disfigured on the field." Stuart lunched with friends from West Point and the antebellum army. According to an eyewitness, he "had a long chat" with his former comrades, wagering that Northern newspapers would describe Cedar Mountain as a Union victory. He allegedly bragged about his ride around McClellan's army, asserting, "That performance gave me a Major-Generalcy."[27]

Stuart returned to Hanover Court House on August 13, and prepared his inspection report for Lee on Robertson's brigade. "I observed closely their conduct on reconnaissance, the march and in evolution." He noted that the 7th Virginia "had entirely reconciled" to their new commander, Grumble Jones. As for Robertson, he "deserves much credit for the discipline and instruction in his command. Awarding him full credit for these I regard his transfer to another command as an important measure for the public good. Frankly and fairly he does not possess some of the indispensable requisites of a Cavalry commander, particularly, on outpost duty." He "did not for some reason inspire his command with confidence in him but rather the contrary."[28]

Robertson had served as a colonel under Stuart, the report noted, and "I was convinced of his deficiency in the qualities essential to a bold, vigorous, and successful cavy commander in the ever-changing and complicated and extended operations of campaign." The "want of confidence" in him by his officers and men was "very perceptible." "It is still more important therefore that he should be replaced," concluded Stuart, by an officer who possesses the requisite attributes "in an eminent degree." Stuart's letter was a severe indictment of Robertson, who seemed to be better suited as an instructor than as a commander leading men along the edge of an army.[29]

While Stuart was inspecting Robertson's brigade, Lee began shifting Longstreet's divisions to Gordonsville. The army had received intelligence reports that Major General Ambrose E. Burnside's Union command, coming from North Carolina, had reached Fredericksburg, and was marching toward Pope's Army of Virginia. On the Peninsula, information indicated that McClellan's host had begun a withdrawal down the region toward Fort Monroe with the intent of also joining Pope. "It therefore seemed that active operations on the James were no longer contemplated," wrote Lee, "and that the most effectual way to relieve Richmond from any danger of attack from that quarter would be to reenforce General Jackson and advance upon General Pope."[30]

Most of Longstreet's troops reached Gordonsville by railroad on August 13. "Old Pete," as his men called him, conferred with Jackson. To the north, Pope's Army of Virginia rested in a large V laid on its side, formed by the Rapidan and Rappahannock rivers. Both generals saw an opportunity to inflict a grievous blow upon the enemy in that position between the two rivers. Longstreet wrote to Lee, proposing a strike against Pope's right or western flank. Lee, meanwhile, boarded a train, arriving in the town on August 15.[31]

Lee, Longstreet, and Jackson met and finalized an offensive operation against Pope. Instead of adopting Longstreet's plan, Lee decided to assail the Federals' eastern flank or closed end of the V, isolating the enemy from reinforcements from Fredericksburg. Longstreet's divisions would cross the Rapidan at Raccoon Ford, Jackson's upriver at Somerville Ford. Stuart and the cavalry would use Morton's Ford, east of Longstreet, march north through Stevensburg, and seize the railroad bridge at Rappahannock Station in the enemy's rear. If the movement went as planned, Pope's army could be trapped and destroyed between the rivers. They agreed on August 18 for the bold strike.[32]

Lee issued the necessary orders, directing Stuart to march Fitz Lee's brigade to the vicinity of Raccoon Ford. Before boarding a train for

Gordonsville with his staff, Stuart rode to Dundee, the home of his aunt and uncle, Dr. and Mrs. Lucien B. Price. Flora Stuart and the children had come from Richmond, wanting to be near him, and were staying with the Price family. The Prices' nineteen-year-old son, R. Channing Price, had joined his cousin's staff as an aide-de-camp just days earlier. Young Price soon proved to be gifted at transferring Stuart's oral orders into a written form with remarkable accuracy. A daughter, Ann Overton "Nannie" Price, described Stuart's visits as "the bright sunshine he always carried with him."[33]

Stuart remembered the parting from Flora and the children as difficult. Little Flora climbed onto his horse, flung her arms around her father's neck, and gave him "tearful kisses till forced-away." Stuart said later that the thought "flashed" through his mind that "we may not meet again." Leaving his family at Dundee, he rode to Beaver Dam Station and entrained for Gordonsville. He and his staff found room in the tender car as more of Longstreet's troops filled the other cars. The train steamed into Gordonsville at daybreak on August 17.[34]

Stuart reported before noon to army headquarters located at Meadow Farm, the home of Erasmus Taylor, outside Orange Court House. From there, he accompanied Jackson's topographical engineer, Jedediah Hotchkiss, to Clark's Mountain, the highest peak in the area south of the Rapidan. To the north, they viewed the campsites of Pope's army, to the south, Jackson's and Longstreet's troops closing on their crossing points on the river. Finally, during the evening, Stuart rode with Heros von Borcke, John Mosby, and Lieutenant St. Pierre Gibson of the 4th Virginia to Verdiersville, where Stuart expected to meet Fitz Lee and his brigade.[35]

The party of horsemen arrived at the crossroads village after nightfall. Verdiersville, dubbed "My Dearsville" by soldiers, consisted of "an old-looking hotel and a dwelling house," in the words of an artillerist. Norman FitzHugh and Chiswell Dabney of the staff joined Stuart and reported that Lee's regiments were nowhere to be found. Stuart decided to send FitzHugh in search of the missing command. With the other men, he stopped at the brick two-story farmhouse of Catlett Rhodes several hundred yards outside the crossroads. The group bedded down on the house's front porch.[36]

The Confederate officers awoke before daylight on August 18, greeted by a heavy fog. The sound of approaching horses and wagons had aroused them. Thinking it was Lee's missing brigade, Mosby and Gibson rode to meet their comrades. Within minutes, pistol shots were heard, with Mosby and Gibson soon appearing through the mists, shouting that Yankee cavalry were behind them. Stuart, von Borcke, and Dabney ran to their horses. "I just had time to mount my horse and clear the back-fence," Stuart told Flora. He and Dabney raced across a field into woods, while von Borcke fled on Orange Plank Road under gunfire from the Northerners. Stuart described their escapes as "miraculous." On the porch, the enemy troopers found Stuart's hat, cloak, and haversack.[37]

The Federals, members of the 1st Michigan and 5th New York, had crossed the Rapidan at unguarded Raccoon Ford. Longstreet had sent an order to Brigadier General Robert A. Toombs's headquarters assigning two Georgia regiments from the brigade to picket the road from the shallows. Toombs was visiting a local friend when the dispatch arrived. Upon his return to his headquarters, the brigadier recalled the regiments to camp. Toombs, a former United States senator, allegedly complained that the road could be guarded "with an old woman and broomstick." When Longstreet learned the details, he arrested the Georgian. The Yankees had nearly bagged one of the Confederacy's most valuable generals.[38]

En route to Verdiersville, however, the Union cavalrymen nabbed Norman FitzHugh, who was returning to Stuart. FitzHugh had with him Robert E. Lee's orders to Stuart about the movement against the Federal army. Pope received the document shortly after noon. Realizing the danger that he faced, Pope ordered a withdrawal. Shielded by darkness, the Army of Virginia filed across the Rappahannock.[39]

"It can hardly be denied however," concluded Major Charles Venable of Robert E. Lee's staff, "that if the cavalry had been sooner up . . . there would have been a good opportunity for striking Pope a heavy blow in Culpeper." Fitz Lee's tardy arrival forced his uncle to delay, and then to postpone, the offensive. When the cavalry brigade appeared on the night of August 18, its commander reported that the horses were exhausted and needed a day's rest. By the time the Confederates marched in pursuit, Pope's army had burned the bridges over the Rappahannock and rimmed the stream's northern bank at the fords with artillery batteries. Robert E. Lee confided to Longstreet when the two men saw the abandoned enemy lines along the Rapidan, "General, we little thought that the enemy would turn his back upon us this early in the campaign."[40]

In his report, Stuart criticized Fitz Lee: "Not appreciating the necessity of punctuality in this instance," wrote Stuart, Lee had detoured through Louisa Court House to collect provisions, adding twenty miles to his march. "By this failure to comply with instructions," Stuart declared, "not only the movement of the Cavalry across the Rapidan was postponed . . . but a fine opportunity lost to overhaul a body of the enemy's cavalry on a predatory excursion far beyond their lines." Stuart's orders to his subordinate, however, had apparently been less than explicit as to the urgency of Lee being up on August 17. For this, Stuart deserved a share of the blame.[41]

With Fitz Lee's brigade present and rested, the Army of Northern Virginia waded through the Rapidan's fords on the morning of August 20—Jackson on the left, Longstreet in the center, and Stuart on the right. "An army fording a river is a sight worth seeing," a Georgia infantryman noted two days later. "Some of the men just walked in with shoes & all on, but most of them were guiltless of any clothing below the waist." Stuart accompanied Beverly Robertson's brigade, which encountered Union cavalry near Brandy Station, north of Culpeper Court House. Grumble Jones's 7th Virginia spearheaded the mounted charges, twice driving the Federals rearward. Stuart's friend from the academy and frontier army Brigadier General George Bayard led the Yankees.[42]

Clashes occurred along the Rappahannock during the next day as Jackson's and Longstreet's troops moved into position along the southern bank of the river. Pope's line, braced by cannon, precluded a frontal assault, so throughout August 22, Lee shifted Jackson's and Longstreet's divisions upstream. By day's end, Jackson had reached Warrenton Sulphur Springs Ford beyond the Union right flank and pushed eight regiments and two batteries across the river. Longstreet halted opposite Freeman's and Beverly's fords, repulsing an afternoon crossing by the

Federals. Stuart, meanwhile, had proposed a raid behind the enemy's line to cut the Orange & Alexandria Railroad, Pope's supply line. Lee approved.[43]

Stuart took with him 1,500 officers and men of Fitz Lee's and Robertson's brigades and a pair of artillery pieces, riding forth at ten o'clock on the morning of August 22. Striking west, the cavalrymen passed through Jeffersonton, cleared the Rappahannock at Waterloo Bridge and Hart's Mill, and entered Warrenton. In the town, according to Chiswell Dabney, the women were "nearly going into hysterics with joy and telling us never to take a prisoner." They distributed apple pies and smoked fish to the troopers. The Rebels rode out of Warrenton about 5:00 P.M., proceeding toward Auburn. They had not gone far when a violent thunderstorm, with lightning and heavy downpours, rumbled in, lashing the column. Once through Auburn, they approached Catlett's Station and halted. It was nearly 7:30 P.M.[44]

"It was so dark that I could not see a man by my side," swore a Virginian. Men from the 5th Virginia stalked ahead and scooped up enemy pickets. The rain still poured down. Unwilling to charge without knowing the situation at the station, Stuart sent William Blackford forward to reconnoiter. Returning soon, Blackford had discovered, in his words, "a vast assemblage of wagons and a city of tents, laid out in regular order and occupied by the luxuriously equipped quartermasters and commissaries . . . but no appearance of any large organized body of troops." One of Stuart's men also captured the black servant of a Union officer. The fellow said that Pope's headquarters wagons were at the station and offered to guide the Southerners to them. Stuart assigned two guards to him.[45]

The thunder and rain muffled sounds, allowing the Confederates to deploy for the attack one hundred yards from the station. Stuart assigned Colonel Rooney Lee's 9th Virginia to lead the charge, while the 1st and 5th Virginia hit a second camp south of the depot. Riding along the ranks, Stuart encouraged the men to yell when the bugles sounded. He turned to his chief bugler and said, "Sound the charge, Freed."[46]

Blackford compared the men's yells to "a roar like Niagara." It must have seemed like an instant to the stunned Federals before the Confederates were among them, firing pistols and wielding sabers. "Never had I seen anything like it," exclaimed Chiswell Dabney. "The Yankees were perfectly frantic with fear." The horsemen laughed at their foes. A small group of infantry guards, members of the 13th Pennsylvania Reserves, rallied at the depot, triggered a volley, and then scattered. To the south, Northerners in the second camp extinguished their lights at the first sounds of yells and gunfire, blanketing their campsite in darkness and foiling an attack by the 1st and 5th Virginia. Colonel Thomas Rosser, leading the two regiments, abandoned the attempt over the difficult ground.[47]

The raiders cut telegraph wires, rifled through the laden wagons, located Pope's headquarters wagons with the assistance of the black servant, and found his uniform coat, hat, and dispatches. But, as Stuart reported, "The great object of the expedition—the destruction of the Cedar Run railroad bridge"—defied the strenuous labor of ax-wielding members of the 4th Virginia. The rain had soaked the timbers and trestles, preventing the burning of it. "The commanding general will, I am sure," wrote Stuart, "appreciate how hard it was to desist from the undertaking, but to any one on the spot there could be but one opinion—its impossibility. I gave it up."[48]

If the Confederates could have destroyed the bridge, Pope's supplies would have been curtailed and might have forced him to abandon his Rappahannock lines. Instead, with more than three hundred prisoners, the raiders rode away from Catlett's Station about three o'clock on the morning of August 23. Stuart halted the return march at Warrenton Sulphur Springs, where Jackson's men were building a bridge over the rain-swollen Rappahannock to extricate the units that had crossed over the previous day. The mud-splattered, weary troopers bivouacked north of the stream, crossing over the next day. "Raiding with General Stuart is poor fun and a hard business," confessed one of them. "Thunder, lightning, rain, storm nor darkness can stop him when he is on a warm fresh trail of Yankee game."[49]

Stuart had vowed to Flora after his near capture and loss of his hat at Verdiersville, "I intend to make the Yankees pay for that hat." For days prior to the raid, he had been greeted with "Where's your hat?" Now, upon his return, he bragged to his wife, "I have had my revenge out of Pope." Moxley Sorrel remembered that Stuart "was highly tickled at the capture of Pope's wagons and personal effects." Stuart sent the Union general's uniform coat and hat on to Governor John Letcher, who hung them in the library of the state capitol. He also wrote a note to Pope and had it passed through the lines: "General: Your cavalry have my hat and plume; I have your best coat. I have the honor to propose a cartel for the exchange of these prisoners." He signed it, "Very respectfully, J. E. B. Stuart, Major General, Confederate States Army." The message even amused Jackson, who read it before Stuart forwarded it.[50]

Stuart probably saw the comment of a New York *Herald* correspondent on the raid, "The Rebel cavalry are smart fellows—great on the dash—here to-day and there tomorrow." More pertinent, however, Robert E. Lee told President Jefferson Davis that the expedition to Catlett's Station "accomplished some minor advantages." The captured dispatches confirmed for Lee what he had calculated—the enemy planned a juncture of McClellan's army, coming from the Peninsula, with Pope's command. Lee either had to strike Pope or alter the strategic or operational situation in the region before the Union forces combined.[51]

Lee explained his strategic goals to Davis in an August 23 letter: "If we are able to change the theater of the war from James River to the north of the Rappahannock we shall be able to consume provisions and forage now used in supporting the enemy. This will be some advantage and prevent so great a draft upon other parts of the country." Lee preferred to avoid a battle by using maneuver to draw Pope farther away from Fredericksburg and reinforcements.[52]

Lee met with Jackson the next afternoon in an open field outside Jeffersonton. In front of them stood a table with a map on it; in the distance, opposing artillery crews dueled. At some point, Longstreet and Stuart joined them. An enlisted man described them as the "great spirits of the land." Lee proposed another bold movement—Jackson would take his three infantry divisions and artillery, roughly 24,000 men, march up the Rappahannock beyond the enemy's flank, and descend upon the Orange & Alexandria Railroad. Lee left the details to his subordinates as to where the Rebels would sever Pope's supply and communications link. Longstreet's units would follow, while Stuart's cavalry screened Jackson's march.[53]

Once again, as he had done against McClellan, Lee fashioned an audacious maneuver. He understood that the division of the army, with one wing executing a broad flanking movement, was a hazardous undertaking. Lee reasoned, however, that he had few choices. After the war he justified his decision, stating that "the disparity . . . between the contending forces rendered the risks unavoidable."[54]

The primary execution of the plan rested with Jackson. According to Stuart, after the Seven Days' Campaign Lee had "rather a low estimate of Jackson's ability." Since then, however, Lee's judgment changed as Jackson appeared to be reinvigorated in his confrontation with Pope at Cedar Mountain. He had acted aggressively as he had done in the Shenandoah Valley. A civilian visitor with the army at this time informed newspaper readers at home that Jackson was "the idol of the army. . . . He is the great dread of the Yankees. . . . When the old hero passes along the lines there is always a long, continuous shout of joy."[55]

A member of Jackson's staff recorded in his journal that Stuart told him that Jackson had persuaded a reluctant Lee to attempt the daring operation. In turn, Jackson had remarked to Stuart just days earlier "that he would be willing to follow him [Lee] blindfolded." So it seemed with the rank and file. "Great confidence in the abilities of our Generals pervades the whole army," wrote an officer. "It is the general impression, too, that the mass of the Yankee Army is much demoralized and will not fight too well."[56]

Jackson's command started forth before dawn on August 25. Colonel Thomas Munford's 2nd Virginia rode ahead of the miles-long column, picketing the roads until the infantry, artillery, and wagons passed. From Jeffersonton to Amissville, across the Rappahannock at Hinson's Mill, through Orleans toward Salem (present-day Marshall), the Confederates marched. The men could only speculate about the destination. "None of Jackson's old officers even try to divine his movements," grumbled a subordinate. All day long, officers pressed men to "Close up." "Close up." When the van of the column approached Salem, Jackson stood on a large rock beside the road, watching them pass. Turning to his aides, he said, "Who could not conquer with such troops as these?" By nightfall, the column stretched from Salem to Orleans.[57]

The march resumed at daylight on August 26, through the Bull Run Mountains at Thoroughfare Gap and down its eastern slope. Late in the afternoon the Confederates arrived at Gainesville, where clattering on another road came Stuart with the brigades of Fitz Lee and Beverly Robertson. The cavalry had ridden out at two o'clock that morning, following Jackson's route. When they reached Salem, they overtook the wagon train, which clogged the road to Thoroughfare Gap. Using a guide, the horsemen proceeded on back roads, passing through the mountains, most likely at Glascock's Gap, a mile and a half south of Thoroughfare Gap.[58]

Although the story is probably apocryphal, an infantryman with the column's van recounted that when Stuart rode up, he called out: "Hello, Jackson! I've got Pope's coat; if you don't believe it, there's his name." Stuart held up the uniform coat for Jackson's inspection. "General Stuart," replied Jackson, "I would much rather you brought General Pope instead of his coat."[59]

Stuart's cavalrymen flanked the column from Gainesville as the infantry tramped south toward Bristoe Station on the Orange & Alexandria Railroad. Jackson surmised that the depot would be defended with few Union troops. A former VMI student of Jackson, Munford led the advance with the 2nd Virginia. Munford was thirty-one years old, a lean man with a distinguished bearing, drooping mustache, and prematurely graying hair. He had served directly under Jackson during the Shenandoah Valley and Seven Days' campaigns. He was a highly capable cavalry officer, earning Jackson's respect and trust.[60]

Munford's Virginians swept into the station. Federal cavalrymen fled while their infantry comrades, sheltering themselves behind buildings, fired on the Rebels. Coming in behind Munford's men was a brigade from Major General Richard Ewell's division, which ended the action. Within minutes, the Rebels heard the approach of a train and scrambled to pile wood on the tracks. The engineer, seeing the danger, steamed through the barrier under a fusillade of gunfire. The soldiers then lifted rails along a section of track and waited. A second train approached, encountered gunfire, and sped past the station, careening into a bank when it struck the gap in the rails. Finally, a third train slammed into the rear of the wrecked one. The Rebels swarmed over the broken cars.[61]

Old Jack's "foot cavalry" had accomplished a remarkable feat.

Marching fifty-four miles in thirty-six hours, they had seized the main supply line of Pope's army. Moxley Sorrel declared that their grueling pace and toil "in swiftness, daring, and originality of execution, were almost extraordinary." Five miles down the railroad to the north lay Pope's supply base at Manassas Junction, with its warehouses and railroad cars bulging with quartermaster and commissary stores. With its capture, Pope would have no choice but to abandon the Rappahannock position.[62]

"I deemed it important that no time should be lost in securing Manassas Junction," Jackson reported. Sixty-year-old Brigadier General Isaac Ridgeway Trimble volunteered to take the 21st North Carolina Infantry and 21st Georgia Infantry from his brigade and seize the supply base. When Jackson questioned that he might need more than two regiments, Trimble answered, "I beg your pardon, General, but give me my two Twenty-ones and I'll charge and capture hell itself." Jackson assigned Stuart to overall command of the movement. Stuart ordered Colonel Williams Wickham and the 4th Virginia to circle behind Manassas Junction, while he led detachments from Robertson's brigade in front of Trimble's two infantry regiments.[63]

The Southerners captured Manassas Junction at about two o'clock on the morning of August 27. Stuart said that they accomplished it "with so little difficulty." The North Carolinians and Georgians overwhelmed the 115 Union infantrymen and artillery crews and chased away a new regiment of Pennsylvania cavalrymen. In all, the Rebels bagged more than three hundred prisoners, eight cannon, nearly two hundred horses, and the vast stockpiles of supplies.[64]

Trimble's subsequent report on the affair ignited a feud between him and Stuart. Trimble charged: "I had no assistance from artillery or from any part of General Stuart's cavalry. . . . General Stuart himself did not arrive until 7 or 8 o'clock in the morning." He accused the cavalrymen of "an indiscriminate plunder of horses." Trimble was twice Stuart's age and might have resented the younger man's authority over him.[65]

When he read Trimble's report, Stuart rebutted the claims, "I was in plain view all the time, and rode through, around, and all about the place soon after its capture." Unquestionably, Stuart's horsemen had made initial contact with enemy pickets, withdrew, and then Trimble's two regiments, advancing on both sides of the railroad tracks, captured the supply base. Stuart was right when he argued, "I commanded in the capture of Manassas quite as much as either General Jackson or General Lee would have done had either been present."[66]

Leaving Ewell's division and some cavalry at Bristoe Station to protect the rear, Jackson marched his other two infantry divisions and artillery to Manassas Junction on the morning of August 27. At the junction, the Confederates discovered a cornucopia of foodstuffs and equipment. "What a time that was . . . ," exclaimed a Virginian, "half-starved and worn out, we suddenly found ourselves turned loose among car loads of everything good to eat and drink and smoke." They feasted on mounds of food, grabbed shoes, clothing, and candles. Some of them uncovered barrels of whiskey, filled their canteens with it, and "were as happy as a lamb with two mammies."[67]

While the Southerners scavenged among the stores, Brigadier General George Taylor's New Jersey Brigade marched toward the junction from Centreville. Earlier, Jackson had brought forward artillery and infantry when a Union regiment crossed Bull Run. The Rebels sent the Federals scurrying rearward before Taylor approached. Believing only enemy cavalry roamed in his front, Taylor led his troops into a cauldron of hellfire. Jackson's artillery crews unleashed canister into the Federals' flanks, and infantrymen lashed them with musketry. The New Jerseymen staggered, retreated, and then fled. "The enemy seemed to run, every man for himself," boasted a Confederate, "and we ran right after them, shooting as we ran." Taylor's casualties exceeded four hundred, more than one-third of his command.[68]

Stuart wrote that detachments from Lee's and Robertson's regiments spent the day in "great sport chasing fugitive parties of the enemy's cavalry." He remained at the junction most of the time. It was there that Stuart's childhood friend David French Boyd, now a Confederate officer, saw him. "I recognized Stuart on the platform," remembered Boyd, "fighting jacket on, black plume in his hat, and literally dancing—as on the old chicken coop years before." Nearby, leaning on a barrel was Jackson, with his "old hat pulled down over his eyes, arms folded, and evidently in deep meditation." If Boyd and Stuart took time for reminiscences, Boyd did not relate it.[69]

In the early minutes of August 28, Jackson's troops marched away from Manassas Junction. Behind them, fires lit the night sky as the remaining stores burned. Through the darkness the Southerners plodded. Units became scattered across the countryside, but by mid-morning Jackson had gathered them on a wooded ridge north of Warrenton Turnpike near Groveton. Stuart's cavalrymen patrolled south and east of the position, forming a broad arc from beyond Bull Run to Haymarket. The troopers skirmished with enemy detachments. Late in the day, Jackson attacked a Federal division near Groveton at Brawner's Farm, provoking a fierce two-hour engagement.[70]

Jackson's seizure of the railroad and destruction of the supply base rendered Pope's position along the Rappahannock untenable. He could either move downriver to Fredericksburg or retire northward, concentrating his units against Jackson. Lee had obviously divided his army, and Pope saw an opportunity, as he stated, to "crush any force of the enemy that had passed through Thoroughfare Gap." The retrograde movement began on August 27, and by nightfall of August 28, Pope's corps were closing on the old killing ground of Manassas. To the west, meanwhile, Lee and Longstreet's wing of the army bivouacked in or near Thoroughfare Gap after taking the defile from an outmanned Union force.[71]

The reckoning came on August 29, as the armies converged on Jackson's lines. His troops manned a fine defensive position behind an unfinished railroad embankment. Despite reports of the approach of Longstreet's divisions, Pope focused on Jackson. The Federals moved to the attack about mid-morning, with the combat lasting until sundown. Jackson's veterans clung to the embankment, repulsing a series of assaults. At one point in the fury, a Rebel volley, in the words of a Yankee, "seemed to create a breeze that made the leaves upon the trees rustle, and a shower of small boughs and twigs fall upon the ground."[72]

Stuart met with Jackson at eight o'clock in the morning. The friends had shared a house at Sudley Mills during the previous night. With the mounted regiments covering Jackson's flanks, Jackson directed Stuart to "establish communication with Longstreet." Riding south with Robertson's troopers, Stuart met Lee and Longstreet and the van of Longstreet's column between Haymarket and Gainesville about nine o'clock in the morning. Lee inquired of Jackson, and Stuart described his position. They examined a map, with Stuart suggesting that Longstreet's men use Warrenton Turnpike to come in on Jackson's right flank. Lee ordered Stuart to reconnoiter south and east toward Manassas Junction, protecting Longstreet's flank from that direction.[73]

By noon, Longstreet's units had filed into position on a ridge south of Jackson. Woods screened his ranks from Union view. "*We all were particularly anxious to bring on a battle after 12m.,*" Longstreet wrote after the war. "General Lee more so than the rest." While Lee and Longstreet surveyed the enemy lines, a bullet grazed the cheek of the commanding general. Lee "expressed his wish" that Longstreet attack as soon as possible, but Longstreet cautioned against it. Stuart had already forwarded a report of an unknown Federal force on Gainesville–Manassas Road, beyond the Confederates' flank. Lee reluctantly agreed, with both generals conducting further reconnaissances.[74]

The Yankees belonged to Major General Fitz John Porter's Fifth Corps of the Army of the Potomac. When Stuart detected Porter's troops, he had his cavalrymen drag brush along roads to create the deception of marching infantrymen. He notified Lee "that Longstreet's flank and rear were seriously threatened." Longstreet sent three brigades and several cannon to a ridge, blocking Porter's advance. Confederate gunners lobbed shells toward the Federal columns. Porter halted. In time, Pope blamed Porter for failing to attack the enemy flank, preferred charges against him, and a court-martial cashiered him from the army. It took the disgraced soldier fifteen years before he received exoneration from all charges and restoration of his name to the army register.[75]

Longstreet conducted a reconnaissance-in-force along Warrenton Turnpike near Groveton at sunset. The Confederates shoved back the surprised Union defenders, with darkness snuffing out the action. At Union army headquarters, Pope clung to the myopic belief that Longstreet's divisions lay behind Jackson's lines, not extending them southward. His senior generals tried to convince him otherwise, but he remained unmoved. In the Confederate lines, Stuart and his staff bedded down on the army's right near the turnpike. Fitz Lee's brigade was posted on Jackson's left, while Robertson's troopers covered Longstreet's right flank. Silence had come to the familiar landscape as if it were a hushed warning before the storm.[76]

A Virginian remembered August 30 as "a lovely day." "The morning was so still and quiet," he wrote, "that everybody seemed to be on his good behavior." The hours passed with a calmness as Pope wrestled with conflicting reports of a Confederate retreat. It was not until three o'clock in the afternoon when the Federals, Porter's veterans from the Peninsula, advanced. Jackson's ranks exploded in sheets of musketry and artillery fire. "The first line of the attacking column," stated a defender, "looked as if it had been stuck by a blast from a tempest and had been blown away." At points along the embankment, however, the Northerners penetrated Jackson's ranks. Jackson requested help from Longstreet.[77]

At four o'clock, "my whole line," wrote Longstreet, "was rushed forward at a charge. The troops sprang to their work, and moved forward with all the steadiness and firmness that characterizes war-worn veterans." For the next four hours, in one of the conflict's most fearful counterattacks, successive waves of Longstreet's units hammered back the Union left flank. Federal officers shifted troops from the other flank to oppose the onslaught. The Confederates rolled forward to a climax on Henry House Hill, where the Yankees held, securing the army's retreat route to Centreville.[78]

Stuart trailed Longstreet's advance, bringing forward artillery batteries to cover the flank. When the gun crews opened fire, Stuart ordered Robertson's brigade toward Bull Run to intercept the enemy's retreat. Thomas Munford's 2nd Virginia led the brigade and came upon Brigadier General John Buford's four regiments of Union cavalry. Robertson sent in Munford's men, who were overwhelmed in a fierce struggle with the 1st Michigan and 4th New York. While Munford's horsemen fled rearward, "old Stuart," according to a trooper, ordered the 7th and 12th Virginia forward from a reserve position. The Yankees' uncharacteristic aggressiveness might have surprised Robertson.[79]

The pair of Virginia regiments charged the enemy's ranks. Buford's men, most of whom had not been in combat, broke and plunged down a ridge, splashing across the run at Lewis's Ford. The Southerners pursued through the stream, overtaking and capturing three hundred Federals, their horses, and accoutrements. Darkness ended the pursuit.[80]

Rain fell overnight as if it were cleansing man's bloody work. The carnage was, however, too massive for one rainfall. Union casualties exceeded 13,800; Confederate, more than 8,300. By the next day's light, details of Southerners buried the dead, gathered up the wounded, and harvested weapons and equipment discarded by their foes. During a reconnaissance, Fitz Lee injured both his hands in a fall. He sprained his left hand and fractured a small bone in his right. A surgeon applied splints, and Lee would have to travel in an ambulance.[81]

Stuart, meanwhile, with the brigades of Fitz Lee and Robertson, started in pursuit of Pope's army before daylight on August 31. Riding north and then east, the cavalrymen rounded up blue-coated stragglers, captured wagons and ambulances, and scouted. For the next two days, Stuart's men roamed along the edges of the enemy columns in the Ox Hill–Fairfax Court House area. Stuart managed a visit to "my Fairfax sweethearts," Laura Ratcliffe and Antonia Ford.[82]

Ordered by Lee to try to intercept the Federal retreat toward Washington, Jackson's troops followed the cavalrymen. Late on the afternoon of September 1, at Chantilly, Jackson's veterans fought Pope's rear guard in a nasty engagement during a thunderstorm. By nightfall of September 2, the Yankees were safely within the defenses of the capital, and the Second Manassas Campaign had ended.[83]

Brigadier General William Dorsey Pender, Stuart's academy classmate and friend, professed to his wife in a letter: "Gen. Lee has shown great Generalship and the greatest boldness. There never was such a campaign, not even by Napoleon." Longstreet came to regard the operations as Lee's masterpiece. In two months, Lee and the army had shifted the conflict from the outskirts of Richmond to the doorstep of Washington. Porter Alexander wrote afterward that the campaign had been conceived by Lee and "was executed with a dash & brilliancy equaled by few campaigns in the world, & with as much success as could possibly have been hoped for, considering the odds & all the circumstances."[84]

In their reports, Lee and Jackson praised Stuart and his troopers. The cavalry "rendered most important and valuable service," stated Lee. "It guarded the flanks of the army, protected its trains, and gave information of the enemy's movements." Jackson wrote of Stuart, "I shall more than once have to acknowledge my obligations for the valuable and efficient aid which he rendered." To D. H. Hill, Jackson remarked, "'Jeb' Stuart is my ideal of a cavalry leader, prompt, vigilant, and fearless."[85]

Except for the raid on Catlett's Station, Stuart found few, if any, opportunities for further glory. But he and his officers and men had performed the invaluable services of reconnaissance and screening the army's movements. On September 2, Wade Hampton's brigade arrived from its picket duty outside Richmond. Stuart now had with him his entire command. The next day, Lee wrote to Jefferson Davis, "The present seems to be the most propitious time since the commencement of the war for the Confederate Army to enter Maryland."[86]

Chapter Eight

"We Cannot Afford to Be Idle"

THE RUBICON HAS been crossed," exclaimed Lieutenant Channing Price of Jeb Stuart's staff to his mother on September 10, 1862. It had been five days since the Army of Northern Virginia had entered Maryland by fording the Potomac River. The recent victory at Second Manassas or Bull Run had instilled further confidence in the rank and file, who cheered when they waded into the river. Bands struck up "Maryland, My Maryland." "Our army is in fine trim and spirits," attested Major Walter Taylor. Another staff officer believed, "I was beholding what must be the turning point of the war," as he viewed the passage onto Northern soil.[1]

Once more, General Robert E. Lee had chosen boldness. Believing that the enemy was "much weakened and demoralized" by the defeat at Manassas, Lee saw an opportunity beyond the Potomac. Although he had concerns about subsistence for his troops in Maryland and the reduced stores of ammunition, he explained to President Davis that the time for such an offensive was at hand. "We cannot afford to be idle," Lee contended, "and though weaker than our opponents in men and military equipments, must endeavor to harass, if we cannot destroy them. I am aware that the movement is attended with much risk, yet I do not consider success impossible, and shall endeavor to guard it from loss."[2]

The previous campaign against Major General John Pope's Union Army of Virginia had forged the Confederate legions into a formidable weapon. The confusion, misunderstandings, and poor staff work of the Seven Days had been corrected for the most part. Under Stonewall Jackson and James Longstreet, the army's two wings had performed with mounting skill. Now, with perhaps seventy thousand officers and men in the ranks, Lee intended to retain the strategic or operational initiative that his army had wrested from the Federals.[3]

Before the army marched into Maryland, Jeb Stuart met twice with Lee on September 5 at army headquarters in the residence of Henry T. Harrison in Leesburg. Lee assigned to Stuart the crucial role of screening the army's movement in the state by placing the cavalry between it and Washington. At the meeting, Stuart might have voiced a desire to remove Beverly Robertson from command of his brigade. Stuart's inspection report on Robertson in August had been highly critical, and Jackson probably had expressed his concerns about the brigadier to Lee. Regardless, later in the day, Lee removed Robertson from command, assigning him to the Department of North Carolina.[4]

Colonel Thomas Munford of the 2nd Virginia assumed temporary command of the brigade. Munford claimed after the war that Jackson believed that the cavalry regiments remained under his authority as they had been during the Shenandoah Valley and Cedar Mountain campaigns. "He was jealous of his command," Munford wrote of Jackson. "Wanted it all, at all times and under all circumstances, and got very mad at *me* because I failed to report to *him*." When Lee came to Gordonsville in mid-August, however, he appointed Stuart to command of all the cavalry units with the army. Whether Munford's recollection was accurate about Jackson's view, his mounted regiments served under Stuart during the campaign.[5]

Lee's army began its passage of the Potomac that same day, Thursday, September 5. Jackson's infantry and artillery units and Stuart's horsemen used White's Ford northeast of Leesburg. Major William G. Deloney of Cobb's Legion described the crossing: "As soon as we came in sight of the Potomac the boys gave one of the loudest most long protracted & glorious shouts you ever heard. We crossed by moonlight and the whole scene was one of the most inspiring I have ever witnessed."

The Rebels camped at Poolesville, where the men purchased boots, hats, and gloves with Confederate money "at very low prices."[6]

While Jackson's and Longstreet's troops marched to Frederick and halted, the cavalry veered north and east. Stuart's three brigades and three batteries of horse artillery numbered about 4,500 officers and men. Fitz Lee's regiments guarded the left flank toward Baltimore at New Market on the Baltimore & Ohio Railroad; Hampton's, the center at Hyattstown; and Munford's, the right flank in the Urbana-Barnesville area. After visiting with Lee in Frederick and receiving orders to confuse the Federals by threatening Baltimore and Washington, Stuart established his headquarters in Urbana, "a pretty village of neat white houses," according to Heros von Borcke.[7]

The cavalry remained posted along this broad arc for the next five days. "It would have amazed you to see how astonished the people were at our appearance," a man in the 9th Virginia informed his wife. "It was entirely unexpected." A trooper in the 12th Virginia thought "more than two thirds of the people are Union. . . . I don't want to stop in Maryland five minutes longer than I can help." With their supply wagons far to the rear, the cavalrymen and their mounts lived off of green corn and what the Rebels managed to get from local folks.[8]

Except for the need to forage and the demands of picket duty, the men spent the first couple of days in the border state in relative quiet. Morale was high with the belief that the campaign's outcome could be decisive in ending the conflict. "Our officers & men are all in fine spirits," commented Major Deloney, "and all are determined to do all that men can do to end the war with a clap of thunder."[9]

At Urbana, Stuart savored the renown of a Confederate hero. "Ladies of Maryland make a great fuss over your husband," he wrote to his wife, "loading me with bouquets, begging for autographs, buttons, etc. What shall I do?" He purchased clothing items and cloth for Flora and the children. He wondered how little Flora and Jimmie were "getting along." He also noted in the letter that Robertson had been transferred to North Carolina, adding: "'Joy's mine.' My command is now okay."[10]

He and his staff decided to enjoy the respite by holding a "Sabers and Roses Ball" at the deserted Shirley Female Academy in Urbana. Stuart could hardly resist such a festivity even in the midst of active operations. "He was a *light-hearted dashing rollicking* young fellow," asserted Thomas Munford in a postwar letter, "devoted to admiration, fond of *dancing* and pretty young girls—fond of music & full of fun." He sent out invitations to residents of the town and surrounding countryside on the morning of September 8.[11]

The guests arrived at seven o'clock that night. The cavalrymen had decorated the large eastern room of the two-story academy with regimental flags, sabers, and roses. Candles lit the room in an amber glow. Stuart hauled in the band of the 18th Mississippi Infantry to provide the music. The officers and female attendees danced until nearly midnight when a courier interrupted the gala with news that the Yankees had attacked Hampton's pickets. Stuart and his staff hurried to the site only to learn that the 1st North Carolina had repulsed the enemy. Returning to the academy, they joined the guests, and the ball resumed until daylight.[12]

Earlier on September 8, Union cavalrymen had entered Poolesville. Munford and the 7th and 12th Virginia attacked the Federals but failed to drive them out of the town. The presence of enemy horse soldiers in Poolesville and against Hampton near Hyattstown indicated that the Yankees were reacting at last to the Rebel incursion into Maryland. In fact, the Union army's infantry and artillery units were advancing in three columns along a broad front, protecting the capital and Baltimore. The Federal response had been delayed by controversy within the administration.[13]

President Lincoln and several cabinet members believed that during the days preceding the Battle of Second Manassas, Major General George B. McClellan deliberately withheld reinforcements from the Army of the Potomac to John Pope's army. Four of Lincoln's department heads wanted McClellan charged with incompetence and disobedience of orders. But with the Confederates poised apparently to enter Maryland, Lincoln reluctantly restored McClellan to command on September 2. As the president confided to a secretary: "I must have McClellan to reorganize the army and bring it out of chaos. McClellan has the army with him."[14]

With his talent for organization, McClellan integrated Pope's three corps of the Army of Virginia and dozens of new regiments into the Army of the Potomac. He revamped and increased the artillery batteries and formed the twelve cavalry regiments into a division of five brigades, commanded by Brigadier General Alfred Pleasonton. Leaving two corps in the capital's defenses, McClellan marched forth with 95,000 officers and men on September 6 and 7. By the third day, Pleasonton's troopers had skirmished with Munford's and Hampton's men, and the Union infantry corps were within a two days' march from Frederick.[15]

While the Federals lumbered toward Frederick, Lee recast the campaign. Meeting with Longstreet and Jackson at his headquarters south of the town, the Confederate commander finalized plans for another daring movement. To secure his line of communications and rear for a possible march into Pennsylvania, Lee wanted to capture the Union garrisons at Martinsburg and Harper's Ferry, Virginia. He proposed dividing his army into five segments, with the bulk of forces committed to the seizure of the two garrisons. Although sources conflict, Longstreet and Jackson voiced opposition to the plan—Longstreet arguing against a dangerous division of the army and Jackson advocating an offensive strike into Pennsylvania with the entire army.[16]

Lee issued Special Orders No. 191 to the army on September 9. In them, he committed six infantry divisions, moving in three separate columns, to the capture of Martinsburg and Harper's Ferry. Longstreet and two divisions, with the army's wagon trains, would cross South Mountain and halt at its western base in Boonsborough. D. H. "Harvey" Hill's division, following Longstreet's column, would act as rear guard. After detaching units to operate with the infantry commands, Stuart, "with the main body of the cavalry, will cover the route of the army, bringing up all stragglers that may have been left behind." The orders specified that the movement would begin early on September 10.[17]

Historian Joseph Harsh has concluded in his study of the campaign that by dividing his army Lee "put at risk his campaign in Maryland and possibly even the safety of his army." Lee had predicated the enterprise on two assumptions. He explained his thinking in his subsequent report: "The advance of the Federal Army was so slow at the time we left Fredericktown as to justify the belief that the reduction of Harper's Ferry would be accomplished and our troops concentrated before they would be called upon to meet it."[18]

Lee's understanding of the progress of McClellan's army resulted from an apparent lack of vigilance on the part of Stuart. While at Urbana, Stuart enjoyed five leisurely days, highlighted by the Sabers and Roses Ball. He must have sent dispatches to Lee during this time, and twice visited Frederick, where he probably spoke with the commanding general. It seems clear, however, that Stuart failed to detect the advance of McClellan's infantry corps along the three routes of march. Writing to his family on September 10, staff officer Price noted, "The main body of the enemy is about 10 miles from Washington at a place called Rockville, which they are fortifying rapidly." But on that day, the "main body" of Federals was approaching Stuart's lines from New Market, through Hyattstown, to Buckeystown.[19]

While Stuart effectively screened Lee's army from the enemy, the assessment of historian Harsh seems fair: "there is no indication that Stuart undertook any special measures to gain information or to increase security" as the Confederate infantry and artillery marched from Frederick. A feeling of nonchalance apparently pervaded Stuart's headquarters at Urbana. He made no mention in his campaign report of scouts or patrols sent out to gather intelligence. Lee's venture in Maryland relied upon timely and accurate information, and during its earliest stages, Stuart was remiss in providing it. The reasons for Stuart's performance remain elusive.[20]

The final contingent of Confederate infantry marched out of Frederick on September 11. To the east, McClellan's infantry corps appeared, forcing Stuart to contract his lines. Fitz Lee's brigade retired from New Market, crossing the Monocacy River at Liberty, while Hampton's troopers withdrew to Frederick, and Munford, left with only two regiments, rode west toward Frederick. That night, at 8:40, Stuart wrote a note to Robert E. Lee. Although the message has not been found, Stuart indicated, by Lee's subsequent response, that the cavalry would hold Frederick for a few more days. Why Stuart thought that possible with the enemy nearby and "in force" is difficult to understand. Later that night, according to Heros von Borcke, the general and staff members danced with "spirited Irish girls" at a farmhouse.[21]

Lee replied to Stuart the next day, "I do not wish you to retire too fast before the enemy, or to distribute your cavalry wide apart." By the time Stuart received the dispatch, however, the Federals had entered

Frederick, shoving Hampton's rear guard out of the town. Hampton's veterans engaged Union cavalrymen before retreating to Middletown and encamping. Stuart, meanwhile, instructed Fitz Lee to move beyond the enemy's right flank and to operate in its rear. Recrossing the Monocacy, the brigadier marched twenty-five miles to Westminster, removing his regiments from the campaign for the next two days. By nightfall of September 12, Stuart had been forced out of Frederick and scattered his mounted units.[22]

In his message, Lee informed his cavalry commander that Harper's Ferry had not fallen to the Confederates as Lee had expected by September 12. The army's infantry divisions and artillery batteries remained widely separated with six divisions near Harper's Ferry, Longstreet's two divisions at Hagerstown, and D. H. Hill's at Boonsborough. If the enemy advanced more rapidly than anticipated, Lee's army either had to abandon the campaign in Maryland or face piecemeal destruction before the divisions could be reunited. Lee needed Stuart to slow the Federal march and not "to retire too fast."[23]

In Stuart's defense, he had operated on the assumption that the Harper's Ferry garrison had surrendered, or as he stated, "I supposed the object already accomplished." "I, nevertheless, felt it important to check the enemy as much as possible in order to develop his force," he contended in his report. With Fitz Lee on a fruitless mission and with Munford posted miles away to the south, however, Hampton's men simply could not contend with the sheer numbers of the Federals in their front. Stuart maintained in his report that he notified army headquarters of the enemy occupation of Frederick and that he planned to contest an advance where the National Road passed through a gap in the Catoctin Mountains west of Frederick.[24]

At daylight on September 13, Union cavalrymen appeared before Hagan's Gap in the Catoctins. Lieutenant Colonel Will Martin's Jeff Davis Legion and a section of horse artillery held the defile. Throughout the morning, the Rebels defended their position. About 2:00 p.m., a pair of Federal infantry brigades entered the action and wrested the gap from Martin's men. Stuart, who had remained nearby at Middletown, made another stand with Hampton's brigade at the village. When the blue-coated infantrymen attacked, breaking the ranks of the 1st North

Carolina, Stuart withdrew to near the eastern base of Turner's Gap in South Mountain. Roughly six miles to the south, Munford and the 2nd and 12th Virginia occupied Crampton's Gap after being pushed back by enemy horsemen.[25]

While Stuart's cavalry opposed the Federal thrusts, the main contingent of McClellan's army converged on Frederick. During the morning, a soldier in the 27th Indiana Infantry found, wrapped around three cigars, a lost copy of Lee's Special Orders No. 191. McClellan received it as he spoke to a group of local citizens. After reading it, he exclaimed to them, "Now I know what to do!" The fortuitous discovery, one of the most significant intelligence finds in American military history, confirmed that Lee had divided his army. The Union general telegraphed Lincoln: "I think Lee has made a gross mistake and that he will be severely punished for it. . . . I have all the plans of the Rebels and will catch them in their own trap if my men are equal to the emergency."[26]

Seeking further corroboration of the lost order's details, McClellan pressed Hampton's and Munford's lines during the afternoon. He ordered his cavalry commander, Alfred Pleasonton, a woeful intelligence officer, "to ascertain whether this order of march has thus far been followed by the enemy." When Pleasonton reported late in the day that the Confederates had evidently followed the routes, McClellan decided to advance on Turner's and Crampton's gaps the next day. If successful, his army could relieve the Harper's Ferry garrison through Crampton's Gap, and assail Lee's rear guard at Boonsborough through Turner's Gap. It might have been better for McClellan, however, if he had acted more aggressively throughout the afternoon of September 13.[27]

When Stuart halted east of Turner's Gap about five o'clock in the afternoon of September 13, a Marylander rode up. The civilian had been standing outside McClellan's tent when the Union general read the lost order and made his exclamation about knowing what to do. If Stuart surmised at this time that the document was a copy of Special Orders No. 191 remains uncertain, but he concluded that McClellan had to be aware of at least some of the Confederate dispositions. He sent a courier with a note to army headquarters at Hagerstown. Lee admitted later, based on Stuart's message and a similar one from Hill, that McClellan's change in tactics surprised him.[28]

Stuart, then, made a serious miscalculation. During the day's action he had seen only Union cavalry and the two infantry brigades, "which was the only force we were yet able to discover," as he put it. Based on this, he decided that the main Federal movement would be against Crampton's Gap, "the weakest point in the line." If the Federals broke through the mountain pass, they could march down Pleasant Valley and assail the rear of the Confederate forces on Maryland Heights, which towered above Harper's Ferry on the north side of the Potomac. Consequently, Stuart ordered Hampton's brigade, except for the Jeff Davis Legion and a battery, to reinforce Munford's two regiments at Crampton's Gap. Even as Hampton's men started south, the valley below Turner's Gap was filling with an entire Union corps and a pair of cavalry brigades.[29]

Accompanied by his staff, the Jeff Davis Legion, and the artillery crews, Stuart ascended Turner's Gap. On the crest, he met Colonel Alfred Colquitt and his brigade of Georgia infantrymen and a battery. Colquitt had been ordered by his division commander, Harvey Hill, to the mountaintop as support for Stuart's cavalry. Stuart and Colquitt conferred briefly. In a postwar account, Colquitt stated that Stuart "informed me that he could not remain—that he should move his cavalry towards Harper's Ferry—that I would have no difficulty in holding my position—that the enemy's forces he thought consisted of cavalry and one or two brigades of infantry." The colonel asked for two companies of cavalry to guard the flanks, but Stuart refused.[30]

After meeting with Colquitt, Stuart rode down the western slope to Boonsborough. In the village he found Colonel Thomas Rosser and the 5th Virginia, which had been detached from Fitz Lee's brigade. Stuart ordered Rosser's men and a battery of horse artillery up South Mountain to Fox's or Braddock's Gap, located a mile south of Turner's Gap. In a postwar letter, Rosser asserted, "Stuart did not expect the enemy would advance on Boonsboro, and was careless in guarding the roads leading that way."[31]

Heros von Borcke recalled that when they reached Boonsborough, "we were glad enough to rest our weary limbs and exhausted horses." Fatigue might explain why Stuart did not seek out Harvey Hill, whose headquarters were close to the village. Instead, before he slept, Stuart sent a message to Hill in which he probably reiterated that one of Hill's brigades "would be sufficient to hold the pass." Stuart adhered to the belief that the main Federal effort would be the relief of Harper's Ferry.[32]

On the crest of South Mountain, however, Colquitt looked down in the valley upon countless enemy campfires, indicating the presence of many more Yankees than Stuart had reported to him. Colquitt forwarded the information to Hill, who ordered a brigade and a battery to Colquitt's support. Hill also sent a dispatch to Hagerstown, relaying the intelligence. Lee decided to make a stand at Turner's and Crampton's gaps, delaying McClellan's army until the Confederates forced the surrender of Harper's Ferry. He directed Longstreet, who argued for a concentration at Sharpsburg, to march with two divisions toward Boonsborough at daylight. To Hill, Lee replied that he "was not satisfied with the conditions of things" at Turner's Gap, and "suggested" that Hill should proceed personally to the crest and "assist Stuart in its defense."[33]

When Hill received Lee's message, he shifted Brigadier General Roswell S. Ripley's four regiments closer to the western base of Turner's Gap and instructed Ripley "to get information about roads and gaps" on the mountain from Stuart. Ripley arrived at Stuart's headquarters about midnight, had him awakened, and spoke with him. Before lying down again, Stuart prepared a dispatch to Lee. He repeated what the Southern sympathizer had told him and either implied or stated positively—the dispatch is missing—that McClellan had been given a copy of Special Orders No. 191. This second communication from Stuart confirmed for Lee that McClellan was acting with unaccustomed aggressiveness.[34]

If Stuart had deduced that the document described by the civilian was a copy of the orders, why he waited more than seven hours to inform Lee remains within history's shadows. Lee replied soon after receiving the letter. "The gap must be held at all hazards," the army commander declared, "until the operations at Harper's Ferry are finished." Although unspecified, Lee meant Turner's Gap. "You must keep me informed," added Lee, "of the strength of the enemy's forces moving up by either route." In this response and in the one to Hill, Lee expected Stuart to direct, at least with Hill, the defense of Turner's Gap. Stuart, however, thought differently.[35]

Soon after dawn on September 14, Stuart, his staff, and the Jeff Davis Legion headed south toward Crampton's Gap. Stuart departed from Boonsborough evidently without notifying Hill. En route, he received a note from Rosser that the enemy was advancing on his position at Fox's Gap. But Stuart rode on, unwilling, it would seem, to be swayed in his conviction that the Federals intended their major offensive thrust toward Harper's Ferry. His misjudgment of the situation had not ended.[36]

Behind him, at Turner's and Fox's gaps, a billowing storm was forming. By nine o'clock in the morning, the Federals were advancing, first at Fox's Gap and then at Turner's Gap. Two Union corps led the offensive, climbing the rugged, heavily forested mountainside. Hill, whom a soldier described as "a born fighter—as aggressive, pugnacious and tenacious as a bull-dog," and Alabamians, Georgians, and North Carolinians fought valiantly, clinging to the gaps and crest until darkness. The arrival of Longstreet's troops stabilized the lines before the Confederates retreated down the western slope after nightfall. Longstreet's chief of staff, Moxley Sorrel, wrote later that Hill's men "made a magnificent defense, but [were] terribly mauled and broken up."[37]

While the fighting ignited and raged at the mountain passes above Boonsborough, Stuart arrived at Crampton's Gap, where he met Hampton and Munford. As he reported, he learned "that the enemy had made no demonstration toward Crampton's Gap up to that time." Once again, Stuart made a critical misjudgment. The lack of enemy activity persuaded him that the Federals intended to march directly along the Potomac River, bypassing South Mountain, to Harper's Ferry. He ordered Hampton's 1,200 men south to cover the roads along the river, leaving Munford with four hundred troopers, three hundred infantrymen, and six cannon to defend the defile. He told Munford to "hold it against the enemy at all hazards," and then rode away to determine the progress of Major General Lafayette McLaws's command on Maryland Heights.[38]

Stuart left Munford after midday, and before long the valley in front of Crampton's Gap darkened with Union troops. An onlooking Rebel said that the Yankees "were so numerous that it looked as if they were creeping up out of the ground." Munford wrote later that Stuart's order was "easier said than done with such odds." The colonel grumbled, "there never was any excuse for Genl. Stuart being off at Maryland Heights with McLaws."[39]

When Stuart joined McLaws on the heights, the two generals could see smoke in the sky above Crampton's Gap. Stuart claimed that earlier he had requested reinforcements for Munford from McLaws, who sent Brigadier General Howell Cobb's infantry brigade to the gap. The amount of smoke indicated to McLaws heavy cannon fire and a serious attack by the Federals. If the enemy seized the pass, the Yankees could assail McLaws's rear as his troops battled for control of Maryland Heights. According to McLaws in a postwar letter, Stuart assured him that it was only a single Union brigade. McLaws decided to see for himself. Stuart, wrote McLaws, "tried to persuade me not to go."[40]

Accompanied by staff officers, McLaws and Stuart descended the heights, mounted their horses, and rode toward Crampton's Gap. As they neared the pass, they met a stream of fleeing troops. Howell Cobb was, stated Channing Price, "so violently excited as to add to the confusion prevailing." McLaws and Stuart tried to rally the Southerners. They had been overwhelmed by Union numbers—troops of the Sixth Corps—after two hours of courageous resistance. Munford described the combat as "the heaviest I ever engaged in, and the cavalry fought here with pistols and rifles." Darkness prevented a Federal pursuit. "Well General," McLaws said to Stuart, "we are in a pen, how am I to get out of it?"[41]

McLaws patched together a defensive line across Pleasant Valley, using brigades from his division and Major General Richard H. Anderson's. Stuart remained at this position until 10:00 P.M. and then rode to McLaws's headquarters. He sent couriers to Lee, informing the army commander of the enemy capture of Crampton's Gap. When he rejoined McLaws, the latter said that he planned to offer battle to the Federals in the morning. Stuart, wrote McLaws later, "appeared to be completely dazed" when he heard this. In reality, McLaws could only bluff the Yankees while operations continued on Maryland Heights.[42]

Beneath Maryland Heights, meanwhile, Stonewall Jackson had rolled cannon onto Bolivar Heights, west of Harper's Ferry. When the fog lifted on the morning of September 15, dozens of Confederate guns opened fire on the Union garrison. In Pleasant Valley, recalled Heros von Borcke, the sound of the artillery "reverberated like rolling thunder through the surrounding mountains." Before nine o'clock the Federal commander surrendered the post, with its 11,500 troops, seventy-three cannon, thousands of weapons, and hundreds of wagons and their teams. During the night, Colonel Benjamin F. "Grimes" Davis, a native Mississippian who had remained loyal to the Union, had led the garrison's 1,300-man cavalry contingent out of the town, using an unguarded road below Maryland Heights. Munford blamed Stuart for the escape of the Northern horsemen, arguing that by scattering his cavalry units he could not seal off the roads from Harper's Ferry.[43]

Stuart entered Harper's Ferry later that morning. Federal prisoners lined the streets, and, wrote William Blackford, "their appearance was 'dapper' in the extreme." Stuart met Jackson, who asked his friend to ride to Sharpsburg and report the capture of the town to Lee. Leaving behind his staff to assist with surrender details, Stuart, with his escort and probably the Jeff Davis Legion, headed for Sharpsburg, seventeen miles away. Arriving early in the afternoon, Stuart found Lee as the army commander was supervising the deployment of Longstreet's and Harvey Hill's troops on the hills above Antietam Creek.[44]

Lee had withdrawn Longstreet's and Hill's veterans from the western base of South Mountain during the morning. Fitz Lee and three regiments had reached Boonsborough on the previous evening after their fruitless effort to harass McClellan's columns. Posted as a rear guard, the Virginia cavalrymen were surprised by Union troopers about noon, and "a general stampede" ensued through Boonsborough. Fitz Lee rallied his men, counterattacking with the 4th and 9th Virginia. In the swirling action, Colonel Rooney Lee had his horse killed under him and had to flee on foot to escape capture. A Virginian declared, "This was an awful day for our Brigade as the loss was heavy & injury inflicted on the enemy must have been slight."[45]

When Robert E. Lee crossed Antietam Creek that morning, he remarked to a group of soldiers, "We will make our stand on those hills." He had passed two difficult days on September 13 and 14, his plans hampered by inadequate intelligence from Stuart and concern for the slowness of operations at Harper's Ferry. The valiant defense of South

Mountain by Hill's division gave him precious time until Jackson forced the surrender of Harper's Ferry. Despite McClellan's good fortune of being given the lost copy of Special Orders No. 191, Lee's army could have abandoned the Maryland campaign before being overtaken by the Federals. Instead, Lee chose to offer battle, explaining, "it was better to have fought the battle in Maryland than to have left it without a struggle."[46]

From the outset, Lee's entry into Maryland, with the division of his army, had been attended with risks. Now Lee took the most dangerous gamble of the campaign. Sharpsburg and the surrounding farmers' fields and woodlots lay in a bend of the Potomac River. The knolls and ravines could conceal bodies of troops, but the terrain possessed no dominant natural eminence. With the river to his rear, Lee risked the destruction of his army. Porter Alexander thought that Lee's decision to stand and fight along Antietam Creek "the greatest military blunder that Gen. Lee ever made." At best, argued Alexander, Lee could achieve a drawn battle for a "*possible* outcome."[47]

The danger to the army was compounded by its reduced numbers. Thousands of men had straggled while in Maryland, with many of them returning to Virginia. A woman who lived across the Potomac and watched troops pass her home for four years commented afterward on Lee's veterans at this time, "never were want and exhaustion more visibly put before my eyes, and that they could march or fight at all seemed incredible." When all the commands at Harper's Ferry reached Sharpsburg—the final one did not arrive until late in the afternoon of September 17—Lee counted barely forty thousand officers and men in the ranks.[48]

Throughout September 16, most of the units in the opposing armies gathered along Antietam Creek—the Federals to the east of the stream, the Confederates to the west. McClellan spent hours examining the Rebel position before deciding on an attack against Lee's left flank for the next day. Lee, meanwhile, deployed his infantry divisions and batteries in a rough, inverted L. Longstreet's troops manned the army's right on the bluffs along the creek, while Jackson's troops formed the base of the L in the fields and woods beside Hagerstown Turnpike, which followed a ridge from north to south. Where the line bent westward, Harvey Hill's division manned a sunken road. The nature of Lee's position allowed for the shifting of units along interior lines.[49]

Stuart spent most of September 16 on horseback. He posted Fitz Lee's regiments on the army's left flank in the vicinity of West Woods and Munford's regiments on the opposite end of the Confederate line at the lower fords of Antietam Creek. On instructions from Robert E. Lee, he conducted a reconnaissance on the roads to the north and northwest of Sharpsburg. At some point during the day, Jackson evidently assigned Stuart to command of the ground beyond the infantry's left flank. Stuart placed artillery batteries and brought up more than a dozen cannon from the horse artillery, parking them on the reverse or western base of Nicodemus Heights. An artillery officer noted, "Genl Stuart is galloping around."[50]

About mid-afternoon, pickets of the 9th Virginia reported to Stuart the movement of Union troops across the creek beyond the Confederate center. The Federals belonged to the three divisions of Major General Joseph Hooker's First Corps. Rebel infantry and cavalry skirmishers and artillery crews fired on the enemy column, which eventually halted on the Joseph Poffenberger farm, a mile north of Jackson's lines. After nightfall, Major General Joseph Mansfield's two divisions of the Twelfth Corps crossed the stream, moving up in support for Hooker's planned attack.[51]

When Stuart received the intelligence of the enemy movement, he rode into town to the brick home of Dr. Jacob Grove, where Lee, Longstreet, and Jackson were conferring. The news ended the meeting, with the generals returning to their commands. Stuart remained along Jackson's lines until after dark when he came back to the Grove residence to talk with Lee and Jackson. He might have informed Lee at this time that he had sent a courier to Wade Hampton to hurry his brigade's march to Sharpsburg. While Jackson slept on a sofa in the house, Stuart rejoined his men, bedding down probably near West Woods or Nicodemus Heights.[52]

A fog settled in overnight, filling the hollows and woodlots, as if the forthcoming tragedy needed a natural curtain. With the morning's light the mist began to dissipate across the benign landscape. Skirmishers triggered shots at dimly seen figures, and gun crews rammed in charges. Men stepped out, coming from the north, and soon this good Maryland ground was transformed into haunting names—Miller's Cornfield, East Woods, West Woods, Dunker Church, "Bloody Lane," and Burnside's Bridge.

Stuart was up well before dawn and awakened Major John Pelham. The Alabamian was, wrote Henry Kyd Douglas of Jackson's staff, Stuart's "artillery pet." Pelham had earned Stuart's "unlimited confidence," and according to Blackford the general "loved him dearly." Pelham's courage was unquestioned, and his skill in managing artillery in combat "amounted to genius" in the judgment of the chronicler of the army's artillery. It was to be a day for gun crews, and Pelham was at his finest.[53]

Under Stuart's direction, Pelham's gunners shouldered fifteen cannon, mostly from Jackson's batteries, onto Nicodemus Heights before dawn. The ridge ran from north to south, west of Hagerstown Turnpike and directly opposite farmer David R. Miller's twenty-acre cornfield— the Cornfield. The artillerists opened fire as Hooker's Union infantrymen prepared to advance, drawing counterbattery fire from enemy cannon. When Hooker's nine thousand officers and men moved to the attack, Pelham's crews directed their shells and solid shot on the blue-coated ranks. For the next three hours, 27,000 Northerners and Southerners ravaged each other in an area of less than two square miles.[54]

The fury was nearly all-consuming, as if an enraged giant reached out, gathered clumps of men in his hand, and flung them to the ground. The musketry and cannon fire was deafening, ripping apart lines of soldiers. A Virginian described the Cornfield as "those corn acres of hell." A Yankee confided to his family, "I thought I had seen men piled up and cut up in all kindes of shape, but never anything in comparison to that field." The carnage flowed through the Cornfield, engulfed East Woods, covered a wedge-shaped pasture between the turnpike and Smoketown Road, and surrounded the whitewashed brick Dunker Church, where German Baptist Brethren worshipped a pacifist Lord. When Brigadier General John B. Hood's Confederates retired after a counterattack, Hood was asked where his division was. "Dead on the field," replied the intrepid fighter.[55]

As Hood's veterans dragged themselves back to Dunker Church, Stuart was pulling Pelham's guns off Nicodemus Heights due to the Union counterbattery fire. For ninety minutes, Pelham's crews had laced

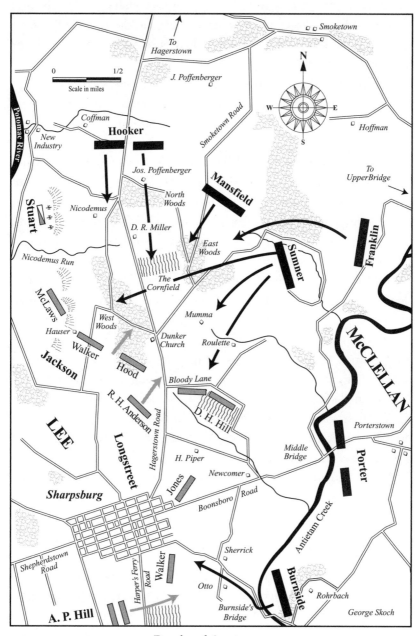

Battle of Antietam

Union infantry commands and withstood the concentrated fire of Federal cannon. Stuart now shifted them south to Hauser's Ridge behind West Woods and brought forward more guns. He also ordered Brigadier General Jubal Early's brigade, which had been sent to him earlier by Jackson, into West Woods.[56]

Stuart's new line of artillery fired on Mansfield's Twelfth Corps troops as the Federals advanced through East Woods into the pasture. After Mansfield's attack stalled, a brief lull ensued until Major General John Sedgwick's 5,200-man Second Corps division, stacked in three lines, marched directly toward West Woods. Stuart probably did not know that the oncoming Yankees were commanded by his former senior officer and close friend in Kansas. From the south and west, meanwhile, Confederate infantry reinforcements were striding toward West Woods. When Sedgwick's veterans neared the turnpike, the Southerners ringed the woods, waiting for them.[57]

Within minutes, the Confederates turned West Woods into a slaughterhouse. The cannon on Hauser's Ridge, numbering at least twenty-four, unleashed "a seamless wall of canister" into the Union ranks. Rebel musketry, seemingly from the depths of hell, scourged the Yankee lines. "For a time the loss of life was fearful," stated a Massachusetts soldier. "We had never before seen anything like it." When Sedgwick's left flank regiments disintegrated under the merciless gunfire, the Federals streamed from the woods. In twenty minutes, Sedgwick's division suffered 2,200 casualties. No command in the army incurred greater losses on this day.[58]

With the repulse of Sedgwick's division, the combat shifted to the Confederate center, where Harvey Hill's brigades manned a sunken roadbed. The fighting abated around Dunker Church and East and West woods, but was not stilled. Jackson and Stuart examined together Jackson's battered ranks. Later Stuart and Lafayette McLaws, whose troops had arrived on the field to join the action in West Woods, conducted a reconnaissance along Jackson's left flank. When enemy gunners spotted the generals and staff officers, they targeted the group, forcing the Confederates to withdraw. It was the second time Stuart escaped harm. He had had a horse shot under him and a courier killed by his side while near Dunker Church.[59]

By mid-afternoon Lee's Army of Northern Virginia teetered on the edge of defeat. Union assaults on the sunken road or Bloody Lane had wrenched it from Hill's troops. Only a patchwork of Confederate infantrymen and a few cannon limited the breakthrough. Along Jackson's lines additional Federal units had arrived, but McClellan decided against a renewal of attacks. But on Lee's right flank, officers and men of the Union Ninth Corps had seized the Lower or Burnside's Bridge and were advancing northwest toward Sharpsburg. To relieve pressure on his right, if not in desperation, Lee directed Jackson to strike the enemy right flank and rear with cavalry and artillery. If successful, Jackson was to charge, using the depleted ranks in West Woods.[60]

Jackson assigned Stuart to command of the turning movement and alerted his infantry commanders to be prepared to advance. Stuart gathered three regiments from Fitz Lee's brigade, Hampton's brigade—which had arrived during the morning—three infantry regiments, and twenty-one cannon under Pelham's direction. The force numbered more than four thousand officers and men and assembled west of Nicodemus Heights on a farm along River Road. Before the force started out, Stuart sent two batteries onto Nicodemus Heights and placed the infantry regiments behind the ridge in support of the gun crews.[61]

Fitz Lee's Virginians led the march, following River Road for about a mile to a cluster of houses known as New Industry. Here, the Potomac River bowed eastward—"a remarkable bend" in Jackson's words—narrowing the gap between its banks and Hagerstown Turnpike to within seven hundred yards. Evidently both Jackson and Stuart were unaware of the confining nature of the terrain. Stuart could have, however, proceeded north to Bakersville, then east, bringing him beyond the Union right flank as Lee had directed. A ridge to his right would have concealed the movement from the enemy. Instead, as he was seemingly disposed to do, Stuart ordered Pelham forward with nine cannon to develop the Federal position. "No explanation has ever been offered why Stuart did not continue northward to Bakersville," historian Joseph Harsh has written.[62]

Pelham rolled the artillery pieces on to a wooded rise. To the east, roughly nine hundred yards away and in view, were thirty Union cannon at the Poffenberger farm. Artillery officers protested to Pelham against opening fire on this array of guns. Laughing, Pelham replied, "Oh, we must stir them up a little and then slip away." The initial salvo by the Confederates achieved what Pelham and Stuart intended. The enemy batteries responded with a "murderous fire," which drove Pelham's artillerists off the hill in less than fifteen minutes. The Federals then directed their fire on the pair of batteries on Nicodemus Heights, clearing the ridge of the cannon.[63]

Captain William T. Poague of the Rockbridge Artillery commanded one gun under Pelham. At the time, he and other officers blamed Pelham for "a most indiscreet proceeding." But in his memoirs, written years later, Poague assigned the responsibility to Stuart, who "took this method of determining whether McClellan's flank could be turned." "I suppose Pelham knew what he was sent there for," concluded the artillery captain. Poague was undoubtedly correct. By directing Pelham to "stir them up"—the words seem fitting for Stuart—Stuart failed in his primary mission. About 4:00 P.M., Stuart led his command back toward Jackson's lines.[64]

As the cavalry and batteries withdrew, the battle neared a climax on the Confederate right flank. Major General A. P. Hill's division, marching from Harper's Ferry, smashed into the Union Ninth Corps, unraveling the Federal ranks. Hill's attack salvaged a tactical victory for Lee's army. Sporadic rifle and artillery fire ended the bloodiest day in American history. Combined casualties exceeded 23,000 in killed, wounded, and missing. The carnage enveloped the ground. Lieutenant Richard H. Watkins of the 3rd Virginia offered an explanation for the staggering bloodshed, writing five days after the battle, "The feeling of hatred on both sides is becoming intensified and the battles more fierce and desperate."[65]

During the night, according to Henry Kyd Douglas of Jackson's staff, "Half of Lee's army were hunting [for] the other half." But the rank and file, with courage and skill, and at a fearful cost, had given Lee and the cause their finest hour. "The fight of the 17th," declared Major Walter Taylor in a letter, "has taught us the value of men—who can even when weary with constant marching & fighting & when on short rations, contend with and resist three times our number." Although the disparity in numerical strength was not as great as Taylor believed, the Rebels had exploited interior lines, plugged gaps in thinning ranks, and advanced into the fury with élan. "The result," stated Robert E. Lee, "reflects the highest credit on the officers and men engaged."[66]

After nightfall Lee met with his senior officers. While most of them anticipated a retreat across the Potomac during the night, Lee announced that the army would hold its position for another day. He issued orders for rations to be cooked, units redeployed, and stragglers herded back to their regiments. Lee's decision surprised his generals, including Stuart. He made it, however, "without apprehension," calculating that McClellan would not renew the struggle until reinforcements joined the Union army.[67]

A truce on September 18 allowed burial details and ambulance crews to collect the human wreckage. Lee discussed with Jackson an offensive strike against the Union right, but a reconnaissance precluded the idea. Throughout the day wagons and ambulances creaked south, crossing the Potomac at Boteler's Ford. Early on September 19, Confederate infantry and artillery units marched to the ford and into Virginia. Longstreet admitted privately, "All that we can claim is that we got across the Potomac with an organized army." Porter Alexander maintained after the war that Lee "fought where he could have avoided it & where he had nothing to make & everything to lose—which a general should not do."[68]

During the afternoon, before the retreat began, Lee summoned Stuart to army headquarters. The commanding general instructed Stuart, with a combined force of cavalry, infantry, and artillery, to march up the Potomac and to occupy Williamsport, Maryland. Despite the depletion of the army's ranks from straggling and Sharpsburg's grievous casualties, Lee intended to reenter Maryland and to threaten McClellan's supply and communications lines. Lee's aide Walter Taylor admitted in a letter that such an undertaking, given the army's condition, "would have indeed been hazardous."[69]

With the main army using Boteler's Ford, the cavalry needed another crossing site. Stuart chose his aide Captain William Blackford to locate a shallow passage. Accompanied by twenty men, Blackford followed the river's bank, testing the stream's depth at various locations. Finally, he came upon "a fish trap," a dam of loosely piled stones, which created

shallows below it. The staff officer led his horse into the current, crossing and recrossing the river several times. "The place was very rough
and the water swift," wrote Blackford, "but it was the best that could be
had." Posting men along the route, he reported to Stuart.[70]

While Fitz Lee's brigade covered the main army's retreat as a rear
guard, Blackford guided Wade Hampton's regiments to the site. A heavy
night fog set in. As the lengthy column entered the river, the current
began to push the riders farther away from the dam into deeper water.
Several men drowned and their horses were lost. "The right thing would
have been to post men all along the ford on the lower side," admitted
Blackford in his memoirs, "but this no one thought of until too late."[71]

Stuart, with his staff, the 12th Virginia, and Pelham's gun crews
started for Boteler's Ford about ten o'clock. "I can safely say," remembered Heros von Borcke, "that the ride to the Potomac was one of the
most disagreeable of my life." The fog and a misty rain churned the road
into mud. The group threaded their way among wagons, artillery trains,
and infantry columns. The Prussian aide and his mount floundered and
fell at least five times. Before they reached the ford, Stuart met Jackson's topographical engineer, Jedediah Hotchkiss, who was returning to
the Maryland side after a reconnaissance. Stuart asked him to guide his
party across the river.[72]

"The General was in great haste," wrote von Borcke, "and was calling out continually to those in front of him in somewhat angry tones."
Teamsters and soldiers, not recognizing Stuart, answered him in a
"rough manner" to the amusement of his staff. Either in the river or
before it, Stuart's horse stumbled and fell, throwing its rider beneath a
wagon's wheels. Von Borcke stopped the vehicle before its wheels seriously injured Stuart. After an hour's halt in Shepherdstown, Stuart led
his column toward Williamsport. The 12th Virginia crossed the Potomac at Light's Ford and scattered a squadron of Union cavalry out of
the town. Hampton's brigade, following an all-night ride, arrived, along
with infantry troops and cannon from Martinsburg.[73]

The next day, September 20, Stuart moved on Hagerstown. Late in
the afternoon, he readied Hampton's men for an attack, but by then,
two Federal cavalry brigades and a pair of infantry brigades had arrived.
Skirmish and artillery exchanges marked the encounter before Stuart

withdrew. The Confederates returned to Virginia after nightfall. At Shepherdstown, meanwhile, Jackson's troops fought a brief, fierce rear-guard engagement with troops from the Union Fifth Corps. With the repulse of the Yankees at Shepherdstown and Stuart's recrossing, the Maryland Campaign ended.[74]

The Confederate army concentrated at Martinsburg in the lower Shenandoah Valley and encamped. "The condition of our troops now demanded repose," Lee stated. From his headquarters, Stuart wrote to Flora on September 22 that they "were in Va again but only for a short time, we hope to be in Penna. Very soon." He had heard that the "Yankees claim a glorious victory," but he assured her that Lee's army had retreated from Maryland not because it had been defeated. He could not have known, however, when he wrote to her that in Washington, Abraham Lincoln, using the Rebel withdrawal into Virginia as a strategic victory, issued the preliminary Emancipation Proclamation. Lincoln's act coupled human freedom with the restoration of the union as the administration's war aims.[75]

In their reports on the Battle of Antietam or Sharpsburg, Lee and Jackson praised Stuart's conduct during the engagement. "General Stuart, with the cavalry and horse artillery," wrote Lee, "performed the duty intrusted to him of guarding our left wing with great energy and courage, and rendered valuable assistance in defeating the attack on that part of our line." Jackson put it tersely of Stuart, "This officer rendered valuable service throughout the day." Stuart's handling of the artillery on Nicodemus Heights and Hauser's Ridge had been excellent. He ably assisted Jackson by shifting infantry units, conducting reconnaissances, and inspiring the troops. Amid the shifting currents on a battlefield, he demonstrated an ability to adapt, to exploit tactical advantages, and to utilize terrain features.[76]

It was in the days preceding the battle, however, when Stuart's efforts were wanting. To be sure, misfortune—the lost copy of Lee's orders—redirected the course of the campaign, which had been a risky endeavor from the outset. Although Stuart surmised correctly the contents of the document handed to George McClellan in Frederick, he supplied army headquarters with faulty intelligence, sent Fitz Lee's command on an ill-conceived mission, misjudged enemy intentions, and rode away from Turner's and Crampton's gaps as struggles for them loomed. Finally, on the afternoon of September 17, as Lee sought a possible movement around the Federal right flank, Stuart mishandled the operation by sending forward Pelham's gun crews to engage numerically superior Union artillery batteries. The blizzard of enemy fire silenced Pelham's cannon and ended Stuart's attempt.

Months later, Stuart remarked to John Esten Cooke, "If Harper's Ferry had not surrendered, we would have been in a bad way." It might have been as he thought. If so, part of the responsibility would have rested with him. Instead, the Union garrison surrendered, and Lee attempted to salvage the campaign with his bold stand at Sharpsburg. On that bloodiest of days, Stuart's "valuable service" overshadowed other aspects of his performance during the entire campaign in Maryland. But as he had mentioned to Flora, he hoped to be in Pennsylvania "very soon."[77]

Chapter Nine

To Pennsylvania and Back

Wの HEN JEB STUART rode across a countryside, noise seemingly encircled him. He was "never quiet, never depressed," always whistling, singing, or laughing, wrote Henry Kyd Douglas of Stonewall Jackson's staff. When the cavalryman came to their camp, he "was generally heard afar off." In the weeks after the campaign in Maryland, Jackson and his aides probably could distinguish his approach as Stuart visited often with his friend at the latter's headquarters near Bunker Hill, Virginia.[1]

The recent campaigns of Second Manassas and Sharpsburg in which Stuart served closely with Jackson surely deepened the bond between them. "The intimacy between these two officers, so dissimilar in every respect," asserted Douglas, "was the cause of much comment—they seemed to have so little in common. . . . But Jackson was more free and familiar with Stuart than with any other officer in the army, and Stuart loved Jackson more than he did any living man." D. H. Hill, Jackson's brother-in-law, noted that Jackson's "fondness for Stuart was very great, and it was cordially reciprocated. Their meeting after a temporary absence was affectionate and brotherly in the extreme."[2]

Like a brother, Stuart eased the reticent and reserved Jackson and took liberties with him that no one else dared. One night Stuart arrived at headquarters when Jackson and his aides were asleep. He entered Jackson's tent, unbuckled his saber belt, and crawled into bed beside his friend. The next morning when Jackson appeared at the campfire, Stuart greeted him, "Good morning, General Jackson, how are you?"

Looking at his friend, Jackson replied: "General Stuart, I'm always glad to see you here. You might select better hours sometimes, but I am always glad to have you." Pausing, rubbing his legs, and managing to elicit the humor so well hidden inside, Jackson added, "But, General, you must not get into my bed with your boots and spurs on and ride me around like a cavalry horse all night!"[3]

While at Bunker Hill, Stuart presented Jackson with a new general's uniform coat. Unlike Stuart, Jackson wore an "old weather-stained coat," whose buttons had been long removed by women admirers of the Confederate hero. Stuart commissioned a Richmond tailor to make one of fine wool, with gilt buttons and lace. He sent Heros von Borcke with it and messages to his friend's headquarters. Von Borcke handed the package to Jackson without revealing its contents. When Jackson opened it, recalled von Borcke, "I was heartily amused at the modest confusion with which the hero of many battles regarded the fine uniform from many points of view, scarcely daring to touch it." After a while, he carefully folded it and laid it in his portmanteau.

"Give General Stuart my best thanks, Major," Jackson said to the aide. "The coat is much too handsome for me, but I shall take the best care of it, and shall prize it highly as a souvenir. And now let us have dinner." Von Borcke insisted, however, that he try it on so he could tell Stuart if it fit. Jackson assented, and wearing the "handsome suit," walked outside his tent to the dinner table. His appearance stunned his staff. When Jackson's servant came with a roast turkey, he nearly dropped the dish when he saw the general. The news raced through the camps. Flocks of soldiers "came running to the spot desirous of seeing their beloved Stonewall in his new attire."[4]

Jackson stored it away and did not wear the coat again for more than two months. The gift undoubtedly pleased him, and he wrote to Stuart: "I am much obliged to you for the beautiful coat you have presented to me. Your injunction will be heeded. My lost buttons have been replaced. We learn by experience. When you come near don't forget to call & see me."[5]

Stuart's frequent visits to Jackson's headquarters occurred during an interlude in active operations, a time of rest and healing for both armies after the carnage along Antietam Creek. Within days of the Confederates return to Virginia, thousands of stragglers who had abandoned the army in Maryland rejoined the ranks. "Our Army has been increased by the poor barefooted fellows," testified an officer. Porter Alexander recalled that after a few weeks, "It was really wonderful how our numbers increased during this month. . . . We began to feel that again we had an army." By early October, the army counted 65,000 officers and men in the ranks.[6]

The cavalry had left Maryland, in the words of a Virginian, "terribly taxed and exhausted." The bounty of harvested corn and hay in the lower Shenandoah Valley, however, restored their horses' health within days. Recruits, riding fresh mounts, arrived. Stuart reported nearly six thousand officers and men present for duty within a few weeks. His troopers manned picket posts along the Potomac River from opposite Williamsport, Maryland, to outside Harper's Ferry, Virginia. The Federals had reoccupied the latter town, and Stuart proposed to Robert E. Lee an attack on the garrison. Lee suggested that Stuart confer with Jackson about the idea, but nothing came of it.[7]

A clash occurred on October 1, when Union cavalry crossed the Potomac at Shepherdstown, and proceeded into Martinsburg. When Stuart learned of their presence south of the river, he gathered Fitz Lee's and Wade Hampton's brigades, leading them north. A week earlier, Lee had been kicked by a mule and "badly hurt." His cousin, Colonel Rooney Lee, commanded the brigade in his absence. The Confederates encountered the Yankees, backed by artillery, south of Martinsburg.[8]

Determined to attack, Stuart deployed Lee's regiments to strike the enemy center and left, while Hampton's men swung out to hit the Union right. But confusion among Lee's regiments stalled the attack along Valley Pike. Only a squadron of the 1st Virginia had formed when Stuart rode up and shouted to the Virginians, "Charge them men, charge them, take that battery." When none of the troopers moved, Stuart said, "What is the matter with the First, I never saw her refuse to obey my orders before." He sent for the 5th Virginia, but it could not be found.[9]

Eventually, Stuart and officers rectified the confusion, and the pair of brigades advanced. Confronted by the Confederate cavalry, the Federals withdrew through Martinsburg and recrossed the river at Shepherdstown. The Rebels pursued to the Potomac. While in Shepherdstown, Stuart visited Mrs. Lily Parran Lee, the widow of William F. Lee, Stuart's West Point classmate, who had been killed at Manassas. When the word spread through the town, a cluster of girls and young women came to Mrs. Lee's home, with each one giving the general a kiss. It was late at night before Stuart reached his headquarters at The Bower.[10]

Stuart had selected The Bower as his headquarters site on September 28. Located about ten miles west of Charlestown in Jefferson County, the stately, fourteen-room brick home stood on a hill above Opequon Creek. Adam Stephen Dandridge II and his wife, Serena, owned the beautiful house. A carriage house, brick smokehouse, and woodshed comprised the outbuildings, with a formal flower garden lying to the rear of the house and a stand of towering oak trees gracing the front. Five daughters and two young boys lived with their parents, while three older sons served in the Confederate army.[11]

Stuart pitched his tent at the southern end of the grove beneath a majestic tree that became known as "Stuart's Oak." His staff members erected their tents farther away from the house. The Bower served as headquarters for a month, and in their contemporary letters and postwar writings, the aides recalled fondly their stay with the Dandridges. When duty permitted, they enjoyed afternoon teas and evening music, dances, and skits with the family. "We spend a very gay time dancing with the ladies every night," Chiswell Dabney told his mother. In one skit, the huge Prussian von Borcke dressed and played the role of a woman.[12]

Stuart described The Bower to Nannie Price as "a charming place, full of pretty girls, all dear friends of mine." To Flora, he wrote, "It is very much such a place as Dundee." In the letter to his wife, he added, "The good people of Berkeley & Jefferson [counties] treat me with far more consideration than anywhere else in the state." But despite all the attention given to him, "my heart ever turns to my Darling & loved ones pratting at her knee." He ended it, undoubtedly to her disappointment, "The idea of my paying you a visit is you know as well as I do out of the question."[13]

While at The Bower, Stuart purchased a small five- or six-year-old sorrel mare from Dandridge and gave her as a gift to Robert E. Lee. Named Lucy Long, the horse had a blaze forehead and white hindlegs. Traveller remained Lee's favorite mount, but he came to like Lucy Long's "fast walk, easy pace, and short canter." Like Jackson with the coat, Lee appreciated Stuart's generosity and thoughtfulness.[14]

During the first week of October, Stuart met with Lee and Jackson for discussions about a mounted raid into Pennsylvania. Stuart had, according to Channing Price, "long expressed [a] desire to pay a visit" to the Keystone State, particularly the south-central town of Chambersburg. He received a stream of daily reports from his picket posts and sent out scouts, who probably roamed beyond the Potomac River. Major General George McClellan's Army of the Potomac remained in the Sharpsburg area, and as James Longstreet noted at the time, McClellan "has shown no particular desire to cross" the river. After lengthy talks, Lee approved the operation.[15]

Terming it "an expedition into Maryland with a detachment of cavalry," Lee directed Stuart on October 8, to take with him "1,200 to 1,500 well-mounted men," gather information on enemy positions and movements, seize horses, and destroy a railroad bridge near Chambersburg. If the cavalry encountered state or federal government officials, they should be taken as hostages to be used in an exchange for Southern citizens arrested by Union troops. "Having accomplished your errand," cautioned Lee, "you will rejoin this army as soon as practicable. . . . It is not intended or desired that you should jeopardize the safety of your command, or go farther than your good judgment and prudence may dictate."[16]

When Stuart received Lee's orders, he made the preparations. He instructed Wade Hampton, Rooney Lee, and Grumble Jones to select the officers and men from their brigades and have them cook five days' rations. When the assignments were completed, the force consisted of 1,800 cavalrymen drawn from eight Virginia regiments, 1st and 2nd South Carolina, 1st North Carolina, and Phillips Legion, accompanied by four cannon under John Pelham. Stuart ordered the three columns to rendezvous south of the Potomac at Hedgesville by nightfall on October 9. He also chose four guides, a native of western Maryland and three former residents of Pennsylvania. Stonewall Jackson evidently supplied him with a map of the region, adding in a note that he hoped "the 'war path' will lead to a good terminus."[17]

Stuart and his staff enjoyed a night of dancing and music on October 8 at The Bower, ending the festivities by serenading the Dandridge family. They waited until nightfall the next day to ride to Hedgesville to join the command. There had been much speculation among the men as to their destination. "Some said one thing," wrote a Virginian, "and some said another until in the confusion of opinions, and ideas the mystery was made deeper, and deeper and the excitement grew higher."[18]

At some time during October 9, Stuart issued a proclamation to the officers and men, which read in part: "You are about to engage in an enterprise which, to insure success, imperatively demands at your hands coolness, decision, and bravery; implicit obedience to orders without question or cavil, and the strictest order and sobriety on the march and in bivouac. The destination and extent of this expedition had better be kept to myself than known to you."[19]

About midnight Stuart and Hampton rode to the river to examine McCoy's Ford as the crossing site. Returning, Stuart slept briefly in a strawrick. At three o'clock on the morning of October 10, with fog hanging over the river, a detail of about thirty men, led by Lieutenant Hopstill R. Phillips of the 10th Virginia, crossed the Potomac two hundred yards upstream from the ford, moved down the north bank, and scattered a Federal picket post. The Union officer at the site escaped and sent the initial warning of the Rebels' movement.[20]

At daylight, Hampton's command, leading the lengthy column, splashed through the shallows, entering Maryland. Guided by Captain Benjamin S. White, a Marylander, the Confederates marched almost directly north and crossed National Road west of North Mountain. A detail captured an enemy signal station on Fairview Heights, and local residents reported that a Union infantry force had passed recently on the turnpike en route toward Hancock. Using narrow country roads, the raiders reached Blair's Valley, following it into the Keystone State, where they halted at ten o'clock.[21]

Maryland Campaign and Stuart's Ride, October 1862

While the column halted, officers read Stuart's orders to the troopers. The instructions assigned one-third or two hundred of the six hundred men in each brigade to the duty of seizing horses. Stuart admonished them to treat any hostages with respect and to give a receipt for all captured property. "Individual plunder for private use is positively forbidden," he stated, "and every instance must be punished in the severest manner, for an army of plunder consummates its own destruction." If they encountered Union forces, "The attack, when made, must be vigorous and overwhelming, giving the enemy no time to collect, reconnoiter, or consider anything except his best means of flight." He enjoined them to maintain an "unceasing vigilance."[22]

A light rain began falling as they proceeded north toward Mercersburg, Pennsylvania. Native Pennsylvanians, brothers Hugh and Alexander Logan, succeeded White as guides. The horse details separated from the main column, roaming across the countryside as if on a Virginia fox hunt. "Over every field and in every direction," wrote Lieutenant Richard Watkins of the 3rd Virginia, "men could be seen chasing horses, each one trying to catch the most. They would meet wagons in the road, take the horses and leave the poor wagoner either swearing with rage or mute with astonishment. Citizens on horses or in buggies were dismounted and turned loose afoot. Any threat or exhibition of rage was only laughed at. Every trooper seemed to be in the best humor imaginable and it was really the greatest frolic I ever witnessed."[23]

Some of the citizens mistook the Confederates initially for Federals. One woman, with a baby in her arms, ran through the rain to greet the horsemen. "You can imagine," recounted Watkins, "what a change came over the spirit of her dream when our boys laughed at her and told her we were live rebels." When the reality of the situation became clear, "we met with no smile of welcome," according to Private Julian Edwards, "but were greeted every where with sour looks and dark frowns." Many of the folks were, wrote another raider, "frightened almost to deth they thought we were going to kill all of them."[24]

The farms, particularly the barns, impressed the Rebels, but the inhabitants, in the words of Private William Corson, "are principally Dutch. The men are as ugly as sin and the gals fat and greasy. Lagerbeer and Sourcrout are the staple commodities." Private Edwards was more charitable than Corson, thinking that the women were "sadly wanting in those qualities peculiar only to the southern girl, and which are so attractive to the southern youth."[25]

The Confederates entered Mercersburg about noon to the astonishment of its residents. Stuart used the stone home of George and Katherine Steiger as headquarters. The Steigers' sons had measles, so Stuart and his staff remained outside, eating a lunch on the porch. Despite orders, the men cleaned store shelves of goods, removing four hundred to six hundred pairs of shoes and boots from one establishment. A Mercersburg physician noted that the Confederates "behaved very decently. They were gentlemen's robbers." Stuart obviously ignored the disobedience as the men tied the stolen property to their saddles. Pelham's artillerists found straw hats, put them on, which led Stuart to joke with Pelham about where he had located so many farmers. Stuart, however, directed officers to examine the men's canteens for whiskey and to pour out any that they discovered.[26]

With male hostages along, the Southerners rode out of Mercersburg in mid-afternoon, angling northeast toward Chambersburg. The rain had increased, falling heavily, and the details continued to collect horses. Stuart accelerated the march's pace on the muddy roads. At the small village of St. Thomas, a handful of local Home Guards fired on the column and then fled. Late in the afternoon, a solitary horseman, wearing a blue overcoat, rode into Chambersburg. Stopping at the store of Jacob Hoke, the man asked for a pair of socks. When Hoke inquired if he belonged to the Union army, he answered, "No, sir, I'm from Virginia." Remounting, the scout spurred away to report on what he had seen in the town. Before long, the van of the Confederate column approached from the west, confirming an earlier report of their presence in Mercersburg.[27]

In Chambersburg, the Franklin County courthouse bell tolled, and seventy-five members of the Home Guard assembled to the beating of a drum. A delegation of town officials and leading citizens, "looking as amiable and noncombative as a parcel of sheep," according to an eyewitness, gathered. Escorted by the Home Guard, two members of the delegation, Colonel Alexander K. McClure and Thomas B. Kennedy, proceeded out of town and met an approaching group of Confederate cavalrymen. Led by Wade Hampton, whom Stuart had appointed military governor of the town, McClure negotiated Chambersburg's unconditional surrender. Hampton assured him that private property would be unmolested. About 8:00 P.M., the 2nd South Carolina led the raiders into the town. Rain poured down as more Rebels rode in, filing "off into the different streets like a star," in the description of a resident.[28]

Lieutenant Watkins thought that Chambersburg was "one of the most beautiful places that I ever saw." Stuart and his staff followed the vanguard into the town, halted at the Franklin Hotel, where they signed the register, and then rode to Chambersburg's eastern edge, stopping at a toll house. A Virginian described the night as "miserable" with the rain, but the Southerners collected an array of goods, from more shoes and boots to Union overcoats to calico, silk, coffee, sugar, molasses, hats, drawers, and undershirts. They found five hundred revolvers and a number of sabers, which they loaded into wagons. The horse details scoured stables and the surrounding countryside. They opened a bank vault, but the specie had been sent on to Philadelphia. "The men got every thing they wanted & a great many things they did not want," wrote Chiswell Dabney.[29]

A primary goal of the expedition was the destruction of the Cumberland Valley Railroad bridge over Conococheague Creek, located about five miles outside Chambersburg. Grumble Jones assigned Captain Thomas Whitehead and a detachment from the 2nd Virginia to carry out the duty. En route to the site, the Virginians inquired about the bridge from citizens, who told them that the structure was built of iron. With the rain pouring down, the Confederates abandoned the effort without riding to the stream and verifying the civilians' description. In fact, the bridge was wooden, and the locals had duped the Rebels. Another body of Southern cavalry destroyed it during the Gettysburg Campaign in June 1863.[30]

Before daylight, Stuart's troopers formed ranks to leave Chambersburg. While the main body, with captured horses and items, rode out, troopers from the 2nd South Carolina and 1st North Carolina tore up tracks and burned the Cumberland Valley Railroad depot, machine shops, nearby barns, and a warehouse full of ordnance ammunition that had been captured from the Confederates by Union cavalry during the

Antietam Campaign. When the flames reached the ammunition, explosions shook adjacent buildings. "We had a good view of the conflagration," stated a civilian, "and truly it was awful." Before they departed, the Confederates paroled more than 250 sick and wounded Union soldiers who were in the town.[31]

In his report, Stuart wrote "after mature consideration," he decided to return to Virginia by crossing the Potomac near Leesburg, instead of retracing the march back to McCoy's Ford. According to Colonel Williams Wickham, Stuart told him later that he had selected the eastward movement from "gut intuition," believing that he could deceive Federal pursuers. But in his orders to Stuart, Lee had suggested the possibility of return by way of Leesburg. For whatever reason or reasons, Stuart started his five-mile-long column east, with Jones's men in the lead, followed by Rooney Lee's command, the horse herd and seized goods, and Hampton's troopers as a rear guard.[32]

Union commanders and authorities had known of the Confederates' initial crossing at McCoy's Ford within hours, and subsequent reports accurately placed them at Mercersburg and Chambersburg. From Washington, Major General Henry W. Halleck, the government's general-in-chief, wired George McClellan: "Not a man should be permitted to return to Virginia. Use any troops in Maryland or Pennsylvania against them." McClellan ordered Potomac fords guarded and mounted units from the Army of the Potomac and from Pennsylvania to various towns in Maryland. McClellan claimed, however, that he had fewer than one thousand cavalrymen with him for the operation as regiments had been sent toward Cumberland, Maryland, to oppose the Rebel force that had been sent by Lee to draw Federals away from Stuart.[33]

Companies of Yankee cavalrymen fanned out across Maryland from Hagerstown to Frederick. Reports kept coming in of the Rebels' location, with one accurately stating that they were moving toward Frederick and Leesburg. Scouts roamed ahead of the main bodies, covering a wider arc of territory. McClellan wrote afterward, "After the orders were given for covering all the fords upon the river, I did not think it possible for Stuart to recross, and I believed that the capture or destruction of his entire force was perfectly certain."[34]

It was not to be, however. Williams Wickham described the march from Chambersburg to the Potomac as "dull hard marching." The Confederates stopped briefly in Cashtown, Pennsylvania, across South Mountain from Chambersburg. While the men fed their mounts, numbers of troopers depleted the Cashtown Inn of its liquor supply. Turning south, the raiders rode through Fairfield before crossing the Mason-Dixon Line and entering Emmitsburg, Maryland, where the townsfolk welcomed them with cheers and food. An hour or so earlier, four companies of the 6th Pennsylvania had passed through the town, riding north toward Gettysburg. It was after sundown when the Rebels continued south.[35]

When they entered Maryland, Benjamin White resumed the duty as guide. Stuart rode with the van, while his aides passed along the column, urging the men to close up ranks. Blackford called it a "terrible night march." Mounts broke down and had to be abandoned, with the riders taking another horse. South of Emmitsburg, they captured a Federal courier with a dispatch. Its contents, wrote Stuart, "satisfied me that our whereabouts was still a problem to the enemy." Through Mechanicstown (present-day Thurmont), Woodsboro, Liberty, and New Market they rode. At the last town, they wrecked a section of Baltimore & Ohio Railroad track. Here, Stuart, with Blackford and an escort, detoured to Urbana to visit with a family he had met a month ago. Somewhere along the march route, Stuart's servant Bob, leading a pair of the general's horses, strayed from the column, allegedly drunk at the time. He would not rejoin Stuart until late November.[36]

Stuart overtook his men at Hyattstown about dawn on October 12. A staff member wrote of him: "His physical constitution was superb, and his powers of endurance defied fatigue. Simple existence was to him a pleasure." From Hyattstown, White led the column down back roads and a "cart track" through woods toward White's Ford on the Potomac. Before they reached the crossing, Rooney Lee's troopers clashed with Union cavalry, driving the Yankees rearward. When they reached the ford, they saw a contingent of fewer than two hundred untested infantrymen of the 99th Pennsylvania Infantry on the Virginia side of the river.[37]

"The moment seemed to be a critical one indeed," asserted Richard Watkins, "but General Stuart remained perfectly composed." Stuart ordered Wickham to engage the enemy with skirmishers while Pelham hurried forward cannon. When Pelham's guns opened fire, the Pennsylvanians fled. With Hampton's regiments protecting the rear, the Confederates began crossing the river. On the Virginia side, Pelham redeployed his cannon and covered Hampton's passage through the stream. Federal cavalry soon appeared and were met by artillery fire from Pelham. "But all were over and safe," declared Watkins.[38]

The Confederate cavalrymen rode triumphantly into Leesburg and were met by jubilant townsfolk. Women and girls surrounded Stuart, hugging and kissing him until he "looked really mean," in the words of a private. In less than sixty hours, they had ridden 120 miles, seized about 1,200 horses, inflicted property damage estimated at a quarter of a million dollars, secured caches of revolvers, sabers, and uniform coats, and returned with thirty to forty civilian hostages, without the loss of a man killed or seriously wounded. One of the raiders exclaimed to his father, "it was one of the greatest scouts Gen Stuart ever took."[39]

The expedition received almost universal praise from within the army and the Confederacy. Like the June 1862 ride around the Union army on the Peninsula, the boldness of the operation, the destruction of property, the minor casualties, and the embarrassment to the Union army and administration boosted Southern morale, enforcing a favorable view of the campaign into Maryland. In forwarding Stuart's report to Richmond, Robert E. Lee wrote, "I take occasion to express to the Department, my sense of the boldness, judgment and prowess he [Stuart] displayed in its execution, and cordially join with him, in his commendation of the conduct and endurance of the brave men he commanded." Lee termed the enterprise "eminently successful."[40]

Other voices echoed Lee's assessment. Lee's adjutant, Walter Taylor, declared, "It was an entirely successful expedition and executed in Jeb's usual & unequalled style." A War Department clerk called it "a most brilliant affair," while Major William Deloney of Cobb's Legion described it as "another of Stewart's brilliant reconnaissances." Wade Hampton admitted that it was a "well-managed affair," but complained: "Stuart will as usual give all the credit to his Virginia Brigades. He praises them on all occasions, but does not give us any credit." In his report, however, Stuart commended all of the units with him, stating that they "are entitled to my lasting gratitude for their coolness in danger and cheerful obedience to orders."[41]

There were others who questioned the raid's material benefits. Cantankerous Jubal Early dubbed it "the greatest horse stealing expedition" that only "annoyed" the enemy. Hundreds of the men's horses had broken down and were left behind, while the majority of the captured Pennsylvania farmers' animals were more fit for artillery batteries than cavalry mounts. The officers and men returned to Virginia physically exhausted. When they reached Leesburg, according to an artillerist with Pelham, the troopers "actually fell off their horses, not having enough strength to unsaddle them, and slept until next morning." As for intelligence garnered, Stuart informed Lee "no material portion" of McClellan's army had left the Sharpsburg area since the battle on September 17.[42]

Stuart rode out of Leesburg on the morning of October 13, and while passing by his men, received three cheers. He crossed the Blue Ridge and reported to Lee's headquarters in the Shenandoah Valley, giving the army commander a personal account of the excursion. Most likely the next morning he went to Stonewall Jackson's camp. As he approached his friend's tent, Jackson shouted to him, "How do you do, Pennsylvania." Dismounting, Stuart handed Jackson a picture that he had found on the raid. The caption read, "Where is Stonewall Jackson?" Even Jackson enjoyed a hearty laugh over it. Before Stuart left, Jackson joked whether he had found the hat lost at Verdiersville. "No, not yet," replied Stuart. By midday, he had reunited with his staff at The Bower.[43]

That night at The Bower, Stuart and his staff had a "gay time." On the following night, they held a "grand ball" to celebrate the expedition. At it, Stuart received a pair of golden spurs, sent to him as a gift from some women in Baltimore. Heros von Borcke probably presented the spurs to Stuart. The Prussian had not accompanied the cavalry on the raid as he had no mount in good condition. "Von B. sat a horse well," recalled Blackford, "but had not the slightest idea of caring for one." His weight, reckless riding, and "utter neglect" ruined horses.[44]

The next day, October 16, Stuart wrote a letter to Flora. He had assured her earlier by telegram, "I am safe & well." In the letter, he described the raid as "the second 'grand rounds' of McClellan's Army." "It did me good," he added, "to run the squirt Pleasonton (who commands a Brigade of Cavalry) across the Potomac some time ago with his Brigade and since foiled him in recrossing the Potomac. I know my last Cavalry expedition is without parallel in history. Whether it will be appreciated as highly as Chickahominy and Catlett by our people I can't tell of course. But if my wifey is proud of me I am satisfied." He had asked an aide while in Pennsylvania to secure a silk dress for her, but he failed. He ended it with, "God bless you—Your loving husband."[45]

After their return from Pennsylvania, Stuart's cavalrymen resumed their picket duty along the Potomac. On October 16, a Union force of cavalry, infantry, and artillery, upward of ten thousand officers and men, advanced in a reconnaissance-in-force into the lower Shenandoah Valley. The Federals marched south in two wings—one from Harper's Ferry to Charlestown, the second from Shepherdstown to Kearneysville. Stuart, with the brigades of Fitz Lee and Grumble Jones, opposed the column from Shepherdstown. For two days, Stuart's horsemen skirmished with Yankees, slowing their advance. Casualties were minor, and the Northerners withdrew on the night of October 17.[46]

A week later, on October 24, Stuart filed a return of his command to the War Department, accompanied with letters requesting the promotion of several officers. For his "conspicuous gallantry, ability and efficiency" during the Battle of Sharpsburg or Antietam, Stuart wrote, John Pelham deserved promotion to lieutenant colonel and appointment as chief of the horse artillery. Few, if any, subordinate officers had secured Stuart's respect and affection more than Pelham. The young Alabamian was a gifted artillerist, unquestionably fearless in combat, and worthy of promotion.[47]

For command of the brigade temporarily under Grumble Jones, Stuart recommended Colonel Thomas Munford. In his endorsement of Munford, Stuart stated, "He is a gallant soldier, a daring and skillful officer, and is thoroughly identified with the brigade as its leader. . . . With Munford in command of that brigade I shall expect hearty cooperation, zealous devotion, and indefatigable attention to his duty."[48]

Although Munford deserved a brigadiership, Stuart's motives in recommending the capable colonel possessed a dark cast. He wanted to prevent Jones's permanent assignment to the brigade, or as he told Flora, "I don't want him in the Cavalry." The relationship between the two men remained marked by mutual dislike. In his letter to Lee on Munford, Stuart declared: "I do not regard Brigadier General Jones as deserving this command or as a fit person to command a Brigade of Cavalry. . . . With Brigadier General Jones I feel sure of opposition, insubordination, and inefficiency to an extent that would in a short time ruin discipline and subvert authority in that brigade." Finally, "I must beg the Commanding General to avert such a calamity from my division and if there are any who entertain different views in regard to General Jones, let such have the benefit of his services and his talents."[49]

Unfortunately for Stuart, his friend Jackson and Lee held "different views" about Jones's abilities. Jackson wrote of Jones: "I have found him prompt and efficient. . . . I am not acquainted with any other field officer of cavalry whom I regard as so well qualified for commanding a Brigade." Sharing Jackson's estimation of Jones, Lee had him assigned to the brigade. Lee transferred Munford and the 2nd Virginia to Fitz Lee's command.[50]

Stuart also urged the formation of a fourth brigade. Expecting that Rooney Lee was to be assigned to command of cavalry units in eastern Virginia, Stuart recommended the promotion of Thomas Rosser to brigadier general and as commander of the new brigade. Instead, Rooney Lee received the brigade, and regiments were reassigned within the division. Georgian Major William Deloney of Cobb's Legion wrote afterward: "Stuart is an ambitious man—he wants those about him who are his friends. This is the first consideration—talent is the next. . . . A little flattery & a daring spirit will bring promotion."[51]

Unquestionably, Stuart had favorites, whose advancement he sought. They might have curried his favor, but the ability to lead men and courage in combat mattered foremost to him. As Deloney and Hampton complained, more times than not Virginians received Stuart's recommendations for promotion over non-Virginians. The highly capable Grumble Jones, a fellow West Pointer and Virginian, was a decided exception.

The changes in the cavalry division coincided with the official organization of the army's infantry units into corps. James Longstreet and

Stonewall Jackson were promoted to lieutenant generals and assigned command of the First Corps and Second Corps, respectively. Longstreet's rank predated Jackson's by a day, making Old Pete the senior subordinate officer in the army. With the influx of stragglers in the weeks after the army's return to Virginia, the number of officers and men in the ranks surpassed eighty thousand by October's end. A staff officer noted that brigades appeared once more like brigades.[52]

The reorganization of the infantry and cavalry commands had not been completed when the Union Army of the Potomac began crossing the Potomac at Berlin, Maryland, on October 26. Lincoln had been urging such a movement for weeks after the Battle of Antietam. Lincoln had visited the army in early October, meeting with George McClellan and prodding the army commander to act during the autumn's fair weather. Once started, however, the passage into Virginia took six days.[53]

When Robert E. Lee learned of the Union advance, he waited until additional reports confirmed that it was a major movement, not a diversion. On October 28, he started Longstreet's First Corps toward Front Royal and passage through the Blue Ridge. Lee held Jackson's Second Corps in the Shenandoah Valley for the present and instructed Stuart to cross the mountains with Fitz Lee's and Wade Hampton's brigades. Grumble Jones's regiments remained with Jackson.[54]

Ordering Hampton to follow, Stuart rode forth with Fitz Lee's five regiments, numbering about one thousand, and six guns under John Pelham on October 30, crossing the Blue Ridge at Snicker's Gap. They bivouacked at Bloomfield in the Virginia Piedmont. During the night, scouts informed Stuart of a Union detachment at Mountville. Early on the morning of October 31, Colonel Williams Wickham—Fitz Lee remained disabled by the mule kick—led the brigade toward the hamlet. The Rebels surprised the Federals, about one hundred members of the 1st Rhode Island, capturing most of them and chasing the others toward Aldie. A second encounter with more Union cavalry occurred at Aldie, until Stuart withdrew after scouts reported—erroneously— that the enemy had reoccupied Mountville in his rear. The Southerners retired west of Middleburg for the night.[55]

For the next three days, in a rough triangle with the village of Philo-

mont at the point and the base between the towns of Aldie and Upperville, Wickham's horsemen and Pelham's artillerists fought against
numerically superior Union cavalry and infantry units. The Confederate cavalrymen engaged the Yankees mounted and dismounted, often
manning the numerous stone walls in the fertile farming region. Stuart
was constantly along the front lines, directing the action and inspiring
the men. Their duty was to screen the movement of Longstreet's corps
farther to the south and the possible march of Jackson's troops from the
Valley, and to impede the enemy advance.[56]

By nightfall of November 3, Stuart had divided his force, with two
regiments guarding his flank between Piedmont and Markham, and
three regiments at the eastern base of Ashby's Gap at Paris. During the
day's fighting, Wickham suffered a neck wound from a piece of artillery
shell, and Stuart assigned Rosser to temporary command of the brigade.
While at Paris, Stuart learned that Jackson had his headquarters at
Millwood, several miles west of Ashby's Gap. Thinking that his friend's
orders had been changed, Stuart decided to cross the Blue Ridge and
to confer personally with Jackson. Accompanied by staff members and
couriers, Stuart rode west about midnight. Heros von Borcke remembered that the waters of the Shenandoah River were frigid when they
forded it.[57]

Arriving while Jackson and his staff members were asleep, Stuart and
his party rested until daylight. The generals and aides shared breakfast,
and Stuart learned that Jackson's corps was to remain in the Valley for
the present, which relieved the cavalry of holding Ashby's Gap. Wade
Hampton and his brigade had reached Millwood, so Stuart ordered it to
join Rosser at Markham. While Hampton passed through the mountains
at Manassas Gap, Stuart used a trail to cross the Blue Ridge. Approaching Markham, he discovered that the Federals had pushed Rosser south
and occupied the town. Riding on, he met Hampton at Linden Station on the Manassas Gap Railroad and directed the brigade to Barbee's
Crossroads, where Rosser had retreated.[58]

Determined "to give battle" to the Federal cavalry on the morning
of November 5, Stuart deployed Pelham's guns and dismounted sharpshooters on a hill north of Barbee's Crossroads. Rosser's and Hampton's
brigades formed in support on both sides of the road that led from the

hamlet south to Orleans. About mid-morning the Yankees appeared. In Stuart's words, "a fierce engagement" ensued between artillery crews and skirmishers that lasted into the afternoon. When Stuart received a report—again inaccurate—that the enemy had occupied Warrenton beyond his right flank and rear, he concluded that the hours-long action was only a demonstration by the Federals. He ordered a withdrawal to Orleans, where the Southerners camped for the night.[59]

For the next five days, with Robert E. Lee urging Stuart to "get exact information of the strength & movements of the enemy," the Confederate horsemen skirmished with their opponents. Stuart kept Lee informed, despite the deteriorating health of his men's horses. But as the Union infantry corps penetrated deeper into central Virginia toward the Rappahannock River, they pushed the Southern horsemen across the stream toward Longstreet's corps at Culpeper Court House. By November 10, Rosser's and Hampton's brigades lay south of the Hazel River.[60]

It was during these autumn days, in the opinion of a 3rd Virginia private, "that Genl. Stuart acquitted himself with real credit." He and his cavalrymen parried Union advances and gathered valuable intelligence on enemy movements. At one point, Lee wrote to Stuart, "I am glad that you have operated to check the advance of the enemy with your usual skill." In his report, Stuart praised the conduct of his officers and men, stating accurately, "In all these operations I deem it my duty to bear testimony to the gallantry and patient endurance of the cavalry, fighting every day most unequal conflicts, and successfully opposing for an extraordinary period the onward march of McClellan."[61]

On November 3, in the midst of the actions, Stuart sent a telegram to Flora, who was in Lynchburg, Virginia: "I have come through four days hard fighting unscathed. How is my little Flora." His query about his daughter resulted from two dispatches he had received from Dr. Charles Brewer, husband of Flora's sister Maria. Brewer was attending to the sick child, told Stuart that her "case was doubtful," and urged him, in Flora's name, to come to Lynchburg. When he received the second dispatch on November 2, Stuart wrote to his wife from "the field of battle": "I was at no loss to decide that it was my duty to you and to Flora to remain. I am entrusted with the conduct of affairs the issue of which *will* affect you, her and the mothers and children of our country much more seriously than we can believe. I wonder if Dr. Brewer really thinks with you that I ought to leave my post under existing circumstances."[62]

He went on, perhaps trying to convince himself and to persuade Flora of the rightness of the trying decision. "If my Darling daughter's case is hopeless," he wrote, "there are ten chances to one that I would get to Lynchburg too late—If she be convalescent why should my presence be necessary. She was sick nine days before I knew it." Then, in an effort to console her if the worst occurred, he wrote: "My darling let us trust in the Good God who has blessed us so much, to spare our child to us—but if it should please him to take her from us let us bear it with Christian fortitude and resignation. It is said that woman is better at bearing misfortune than man—I hope you will exemply it. At all events remember that Flora was not of this world, she belonged to another and will be better off by far in her heavenly habitation."[63]

On the morning of November 6, a telegram reached Stuart with the terrible news—his "La Pet" Flora had died on November 3. His staff was with him, and turning to them, straining for words with tears on his face, he said, "I will never get over it—never!" Von Borcke remembered: "My dear general never recovered from this cruel blow. Many a time afterwards, during our rides together, he would speak to me of his lost child. Light-blue flowers recalled her eyes to him; in the glancing sunbeams he caught the golden tinge of her hair; and whenever he saw a child with such eyes and hair, he could not help tendering embracing it." Months later, he remarked to Esten Cooke: "I shall never get over it. It is irreparable."[64]

Little Flora Stuart died of typhoid fever at the age of four years, eleven months, and twenty days. When her father learned of it, he wrote a letter to her heartstricken mother: "I was sometime expecting it and yet it grieves me more the more I think of it. When I remember her sweet voice, her gentle ways and strong affection for her Pa, and then think she is *gone* my heart is ready to burst. I want to see you so much to know what her last words were. She is better off I know but it is a hard blow to us. She is up in heaven where she will still pray for her Pa, and look down upon him in the day of Battle. Oh, if I could see her again! no child could ever have such a hold on my affections as she had. She was not of earth, however."[65]

Ten days later, Stuart informed his friend Mrs. Lily Parran Lee of Shepherdstown, Virginia, of his child's death. "Since we parted," he confided, "the hand of affliction has laid heavily on me, in the loss of my darling little daughter whom I loved too well." He thought of "her sweet little face, sweet temper and nature and extraordinary susceptibilities and weep like a child to think that their embodiment who loved her Pa like idolatry is now lifeless clay. May you never feel such a blow."[66]

Seven members of the general's staff extended their "deepest sympathy" to Flora in a letter. It read in part: "We feel that the right to call ourselves *friends* has been given us by both yourself and the General: Your kindness has proven it and we cannot but feel individually bound to him who daily manifests his friendship to one and all of us. As friends we desire to express to you our sincere condolence with you and to assure you that our prayers shall ascend to a kind Providence that he will give both of you and our General strength to bear this heavy blow."[67]

Stuart wired Flora on November 8, asking her to join him at Culpeper Court House. "I can see you there for a short time," he wrote. Within days, she and Jimmie arrived. Stuart assigned a trooper to be his son's personal escort and tried to console Flora. He admitted to Lily Lee, "Mrs. Stuart is near me but is not herself since the loss of her little companion." Less than three weeks later, Stuart learned that his brother William's son, Sandy, had died of whooping cough on December 2. "He was my favorite," confessed William, who had lost his wife, Mary, to illness in July.[68]

While Flora and Jimmie visited with Stuart, the Union movement toward the Rappahannock stalled temporarily in the Warrenton area because of a change in army commanders. Lincoln's patience with George McClellan's intransigence to act had been drained away at last. During his visit to the army, Lincoln had warned McClellan that he would be "a ruined man if he did not move forward, move rapidly and effectively." The pace of the army's advance into Virginia at the end of October had not satisfied the president. On November 5, a day after gubernatorial and congressional elections in the North, Lincoln relieved McClellan of command and appointed Major General Ambrose Burnside as his successor. Two days later, in an autumn snowstorm, a War Department officer delivered the order to McClellan.[69]

A close friend of McClellan, Burnside accepted the command reluctantly. He confessed to a fellow officer, "I don't feel equal to it." Within the army's ranks, the removal of McClellan lit a firestorm of protest. Some officers growled that the army should march on Washington and demand his restoration to command. The anger subsided, but in a sense the army would always belong to Little Mac. His greatest failing as a general was that after he had forged them into a formidable weapon he refused to unsheathe it. He boarded a train for the capital on November 11, leaving behind a career encased in controversy.[70]

Burnside understood that the administration expected an advance against Lee's army before winter weather limited movement. He reorganized the infantry units into grand divisions, assigning two corps to each one. With the approval of Lincoln, Burnside started the army east toward Fredericksburg on November 15. Within two days, the army's vanguard reached Falmouth, across the river from Fredericksburg. Burnside had ordered a pontoon train to meet the army at Falmouth. The Federals had stolen a march on the Rebels, but General-in-Chief Henry Halleck failed to ensure the prompt execution of the orders. Instead, Burnside's army stopped on the eastern bank of the Rappahannock. By the time the pontoon train arrived on November 25, Confederate infantry and artillery manned the hills west of Fredericksburg. To the watching Yankees, it should have been an omen.[71]

When Lee learned of McClellan's removal, he wrote to Stuart: "I am in doubt, whether the change from him to Burnside, is a matter of congratulation or not. I have some acquaintance with McClellan and knew where to place him. Burnside has to be studied." Consequently, Lee instructed his cavalry commander to "ascertain the position of the enemy." In turn, Stuart conducted reconnaissances and raids across the Rappahannock, with scouts roaming far in the rear of the enemy army.[72]

For a week, while the Federals marched downriver to Falmouth, Stuart's men gathered up stragglers and engaged their mounted opponents. The duty was onerous, dangerous, and exhausting to men and horses. The blue-jacketed horsemen fought with a new tenacity that had been evident earlier in the clashes in the Piedmont. In one fight, a bullet clipped off part of Stuart's mustache. Wade Hampton remarked, "This sort of work is very hard." A private in the 10th Virginia declared to his wife, "our camps of nights after fighting in the day would be more like Church than camp every body praising god for his kind protection men praised god that never thought of him before."[73]

The strain on Stuart's men and mounts was evident. Major Deloney of Cobb's Legion groused to his wife, "in a little while longer if we have not rest, there will be none left." He counted only 150 of 700 officers and men in the command fit for duty. Hampton exclaimed to his sister: "The country is exhausted and I do not see how we are to live. But Gen. Stuart never thinks of that; at least as far as my Brigade is concerned."[74]

Although Stuart reported an increase of more than 1,800 officers and men present for duty in a ten-day span in mid-November, thousands more remained dismounted. Sore tongues and scratches or "mountain itch" disabled their horses. Stuart established a recruitment and remount camp in Albemarle County, but after three weeks it was disbanded as impracticable. The condition of the cavalry's horses moved Lee to warn the War Department, "Unless some means can be devised of recruiting the cavalry, I fear that by spring it will be inadequate for the service of the army."[75]

Despite the difficulties and enemy opposition, Stuart confirmed to Lee on November 18 that Burnside's entire army was in motion eastward. Earlier, Lee had started two of Longstreet's divisions in that direction. Now, he ordered his subordinate's entire corps to Fredericksburg. By November 22, Longstreet's troops had filed into position west of the historic town. The next day, Lee directed Jackson, "I wish you to move east of the Blue Ridge, and take such a position as you may find best." According to Lieutenant Chiswell Dabney of Stuart's staff, "The men say they are going to walk right through Burnside and *gobble him up*."[76]

Chapter Ten

Winter War

F IVE CONFEDERATE HORSEMEN reined up in front of Gay Mont
on the afternoon of November 30, 1862. Dismounting, Jeb Stuart, Major John Pelham, and three staff officers entered the house. Gay
Mont was the home of the Bernard family and was located outside the
village of Port Royal, Virginia, roughly twenty miles down the Rappahannock from Fredericksburg. The Bernards prepared tea and beds for
their guests. But as a family member recalled, "Like a comet Gen. Stuart
was gone, nor would he allow any of his train to remain saying that it
was unsoldierly to sleep in a house."[1]

Days earlier, Stuart had stopped at Gay Mont and chatted with the
family. Now, he had come to establish temporary headquarters and to
erect a signal station on a nearby hill. He was to remain in the Port
Royal area for the better part of two weeks, along with Pelham's artillery crews and Rooney Lee's cavalry regiments. Stuart visited frequently
with the Bernards, preferring to sneak into the house and to announce
his presence by "playing the music-box in the library."[2]

On December 2, the Bernards hosted a dinner for Stuart, Rooney
Lee, Pelham, and aides. Afterward, Helen Bernard, writing with a
tinge of snobbishness, described the three renowned guests. Lee was,
she noted, "Tall, robust, athletic, yet polished, courteous & with a

gentleness of manner almost like a woman's." Stuart, however, "does not impress me so favorably, a bold dashing soldier, he doubtless is, but without the striking marks of high breeding which distinguished Gen. Lee." As for the handsome Pelham, he "pleased us extremely, a mere youth apparently, beardless & slender almost to a fault, but quick & energetic in his movements & with an eagle eye that shows his spirit."[3]

While they dined, Stonewall Jackson arrived at the nearby signal station, where he was mistakenly told that Stuart was elsewhere. The vanguard of Jackson's Second Corps had reached Fredericksburg the day before, with the remaining units coming on, completing a 175-mile march from the Shenandoah Valley. When Jackson rode in ahead of his troops, Robert E. Lee directed him to extend the army's position at Fredericksburg, south to Port Royal. Although Jackson did not confer with Stuart, he examined the miles of ground to be held by his units. He assigned D. H. Hill's infantry division to the Port Royal area with Rooney Lee's cavalrymen and Pelham's gunners.[4]

With the arrival of Jackson's veterans, the Confederate front sprawled for thirty miles west of the Rappahannock. Fitz Lee's and Wade Hampton's mounted brigades protected the army's left flank near the confluence of the Rapidan and Rappahannock rivers. Since their arrival at Fredericksburg, James Longstreet's First Corps troops held three hills outside the city, crowning the heights with batteries. Longstreet's position was a formidable one, which Union commander Ambrose Burnside had planned to occupy until the pontoon train failed to arrive in time. Beyond Longstreet's right, Jackson's infantrymen and artillerists covered the river's course to Port Royal, where Rooney Lee's troopers guarded the flank.[5]

At Port Royal, during the first week of December, Stuart oversaw the placement of batteries and conducted scouting missions along the river. On December 4, four Union gunboats steamed upriver past Port Royal and were met with solid shot from Pelham's and Hill's batteries. The naval vessels withdrew, steaming back downriver beyond Port Royal. The gunboats' appearance, however, alerted Jackson to a gap in his lines at Skinker's Neck, where Burnside had planned a crossing of the river. When Union infantry approached the site the next day, the opposite bank bristled with Rebel infantrymen. Burnside abandoned the effort, remarching his troops to Falmouth.[6]

At the opposite end of the Confederate line, Wade Hampton led his troopers on reconnaissances and raids across the Rappahannock behind the Union army. The Rebels captured enemy supply wagons and prisoners and relayed intelligence reports on Federal movements. The duty brought a recurring complaint from William Deloney of Cobb's Legion: "Hampton keeps the enemy worried and is constantly on the move. The Virginia Brigades are having a fine time behind the Infantry lines. . . . We are doing the work and they are reaping the rewards."[7]

The efforts of Hampton's brigade and the Virginia regiments did not pass unnoticed by the army commander during the latter days of November and the initial fortnight of December. In general orders and in his report, Lee praised the mounted units, twice citing specifically the raids conducted by Hampton's officers and men. As for the cavalry division, Lee wrote: "To the vigilance, boldness, and energy of General Stuart and his cavalry is chiefly due the early and valuable information of the movements of the enemy. His reconnaissances frequently extended within the Federal lines, resulting in skirmishes and engagements, in which the cavalry was greatly distinguished."[8]

Stuart left Port Royal for Fredericksburg on either December 9 or 10. Before he departed, he received the news of Captain Redmond Burke's death. The Irish immigrant had been one of Stuart's finest and most trusted scouts. While serving on detached duty in the Shenandoah Valley, Burke and five comrades were surprised at a house in Shepherdstown by a party of Federals on the night of November 24. The other five men were captured, but Burke ran from the house. A pistol shot struck him in the back, passing through the right side of his chest and killing him.[9]

Stuart called Burke's death "a severe blow to us and to our cause." He issued a general order to his division, announcing the scout's fall. To Flora, he said: "He died as he lived, true as steel. . . . His childlike devotion to me is one of those curious romances of this war which I will cherish next to my heart while I live."[10]

By the time Stuart arrived at Fredericksburg, a foreboding hung over the historic river city, located midway between Washington and Richmond. Across the Rappahannock, Burnside had sought a crossing site for weeks. But time and again, as they had at Skinker's Neck, Confederate troops barred the way. On December 9, Burnside held a council of war with his senior generals. He informed them that the army would cross at Fredericksburg, arguing that the enemy "did not expect us to cross here." If the Federals acted swiftly, they could attack the Rebels before Lee consolidated his lengthy front. When Burnside was told of opposition to his plan, he held a second meeting with some generals the next day, but was not dissuaded by their objections.[11]

With a heavy, cold fog enveloping the river, Union engineers began constructing pontoon bridges at three sites—two opposite the city and one downriver—in the predawn darkness of December 11. Before long, gunfire blazed from buildings, behind street barricades, and along the rifle pits in Fredericksburg. Fifteen hundred Mississippians from Brigadier General William Barksdale's brigade occupied the city and scattered the Federal bridge builders. Repeated attempts by the engineers failed. A frustrated Burnside ordered his artillery commander to bombard Fredericksburg. For an hour, the gunners hurled solid shot and shells into the buildings and streets, gouging holes in structures, toppling chimneys, collapsing walls, and igniting fires, which consumed squares of homes and businesses.[12]

In the wake of the fury, blue-coated infantrymen piled into pontoon boats to be ferried across the river. Under a fusillade of rifle fire, the Yankees secured a lodgment on the bank, fanned out, and engaged the defenders in a vicious street-to-street, house-to-house fight that lasted until darkness. Behind the Federal troops, the engineers completed the pontoon bridges. But the Mississippians' stalwart defense wrecked Burnside's plan, delaying the army's crossing until the next day.[13]

On December 12, appearing like ribbons of dark blue, seventy thousand Northerners filed across the spans. A Confederate prisoner watching them pass shouted, "Never mind, Yanks, you chaps will ketch hell over there." Once in Fredericksburg, inexplicably, the Federals engaged in a frenzy of pillaging and destruction. They hauled possessions into the streets, smashing them into pieces. They looted residences of valuables, and after some soldiers discovered caches of whiskey and ale, hundreds of drunken men staggered through the streets. Streams of civilians fled the city. Stuart told Flora afterward: "Fredericksburg is in ruins. It is the saddest sight I ever saw."[14]

Stuart spent the two days frequently in the company of Lee and Jackson, riding along the army's lines and watching the Union crossings. He wore a cape made for him by Flora over his uniform. Lee complimented him on it, which moved Stuart to suggest to her, "I think one like it would be very acceptable to him, you are at liberty to use the cloth for it if you choose." At one point, he and Jackson dismounted, walked to an old fence row, and viewed the enemy ranks four hundred yards away.[15]

Through December 11 and 12, the Confederates strengthened their position and realigned units. Jackson brought forward A. P. Hill's division to Prospect Hill at the southern end of the line and ordered his other three divisions, posted downriver, to march to Fredericksburg. The mounted brigades of Fitz Lee and Rooney Lee covered Jackson's flank beyond Hamilton's Crossing. On Marye's Heights, the center of Longstreet's position, the corps commander suggested to Porter Alexander, his artillery commander, that more cannon might be needed on the hill. Alexander answered: "General, we cover that ground now so well that we will comb it as with a fine-tooth comb. A chicken could not live on that field when we open on it."[16]

A morning's fog lifted slowly on December 13, as if it were unwilling to usher in the tragedy that awaited. When the mists dissipated, the sun warmed the air and muddied the ground. Vague orders and miscommunication delayed the Union attacks. Skirmishers plied their work as Federal units aligned ranks in front of Jackson's position on Prospect Hill. On the Confederate right, John Pelham, watching the enemy formation, saw an opportunity to harass the Yankees with artillery fire. With Stuart's permission, he rolled forward a 12-pounder Napoleon, concealing it in a swale behind a cedar hedgerow. The flank of Major General George G. Meade's Union division lay four hundred yards away.[17]

Stuart was nearby at the junction of Bowling Green and Hamilton's Crossing roads when Pelham's gun crew opened fire about ten o'clock. The initial shot stunned the Federals. Pelham's gunners unleashed two more rounds before enemy artillerists could reply. Batteries with Meade and from across the river on Stafford Heights hurled heated iron toward the Confederates. The low ground and hedge shielded Pelham's crew, with most of the enemy fire passing overhead. Robert E. Lee witnessed the action from Prospect Hill and remarked, "It is glorious to see such courage in one so young." After thirty minutes of firing, Pelham ordered Captain Mathis W. Henry and his gunners to lie down.[18]

Rooney Lee advanced dismounted skirmishers in support of Pelham. Union infantry skirmishers countered, pushing Lee's men rearward into a wooded ravine. Additional Federals entered the action and cleared the woods of the Confederates. Now, more Union gun crews joined in the pounding of Pelham's solitary cannon. The concentrated fire forced Pelham to relocate, moving the Napoleon from one position to another as his gunners kept fighting. When Stuart sent a courier to ask "how he was getting on," Pelham answered, "I am doing first rate."[19]

Stuart ordered Captain John Esten Cooke forward with a Blakely rifle. Unlimbering the cannon at an exposed spot, Cooke's gunners fired one shot before Union artillery disabled the piece. Despite running low on ammunition and suffering a half-dozen casualties, Pelham maintained his defiant stand, even helping to serve the Napoleon. It took three orders from Stuart before he withdrew. He and Captain Henry's crew had been in action for an hour. Their valiant effort had disrupted enemy preparations for an assault and had unmasked their numbers. In his report, the army commander referred to the major as "the gallant Pelham." Channing Price, however, overheard Lee remark "that the young major general (alluding to Gen. Stuart) had opened on them too soon."[20]

Two hours later, at 1:00 P.M., Meade's division of Pennsylvania Reserve troops crossed the plain toward Jackson's ranks on Prospect Hill. Earlier in the morning, Jackson, supported by Stuart, proposed that the Confederates strike first, but the army commander rejected the idea. When Jackson came to Lee's headquarters, he had on the uniform coat given to him by Stuart. The officers present had never seen him in it and congratulated him on his appearance. He replied, "it was some of his friend Stuart's doings." With his proposal for an offensive dismissed, Jackson returned to Prospect Hill, readying his veterans for an enemy advance.[21]

Meade's 4,500 Pennsylvanians stepped out into a storm of cannon fire and musketry. A lieutenant in the ranks stated, "The undertaking seemed like madness." On their left flank, Stuart pushed forward at least a dozen cannon, which enfiladed the Federal ranks. But the Pennsylvanians kept coming, across the tracks of the Richmond, Fredericksburg & Potomac Railroad and into the wooded slope of Prospect Hill. "The work of death began," exclaimed a gray-coated defender."[22]

Meade's veterans surged into a six-hundred-yard gap in the enemy's line. They raked the exposed flanks of Confederate regiments, with the combat mounting into a ferocity. Jackson ordered in reserves, and Brigadier General John Gibbon's Union division advanced in support of Meade's beleaguered ranks. The Rebel counterassault was, however, powerful and relentless, driving the Yankees out of the woods and beyond the tracks. Union artillery and infantry stopped the Confederate pursuers, and the fighting subsided into the familiar duel between skirmishers.[23]

But it was to the north, on the open ground in front of Marye's Heights, where the name Fredericksburg became seared into a nation's memory. Minutes before noon, columns of Federal infantrymen marched forth on a pair of city's streets, striding toward hell. The hill brimmed with cannon, and along its base, a stone wall edged a sunken road, with its top blending into the landscape. Behind it, Longstreet's seasoned fighters jammed the roadbed. The doors of a slaughterhouse were opening.[24]

At midday, through the afternoon and on into the darkening of day, six Union divisions and units from another one, between 35,000 and 40,000 officers and men, advanced up the long slope into the withering Confederate fire. A survivor of a charge warned those coming on: "It's no use, boys; we've tried that. Nothing living can stand there; it's only for the dead." Hundreds of Yankees were pinned to the ground beneath a curtain of gunfire, unable to move forward or to retire safely. "It was not a battle," insisted a Federal soldier, "it was a wholesale slaughter of human beings."[25]

Burnside contemplated with stubborn delusion a renewal of the attacks on the morning of December 14, until a council of his generals convinced him to abandon the idea. The opponents negotiated an informal truce, allowing the Federals to gather up their wounded comrades. The defeated army refiled across the Rappahannock during the night of December 15–16. The Battle of Fredericksburg had cost more than 12,500 casualties against Confederate losses of barely 5,300.[26]

During the fighting, Lee commented to a group of officers, "It is well that war is so terrible—we should grow too fond of it." Afterward, he commended his redoubtable veterans in a congratulatory order for "the fortitude, valor, and devotion displayed by them." He reminded them, however: "The war is not yet ended. The enemy is still numerous and strong, and the country demands of the army a renewal of its heroic efforts in her behalf."[27]

As for the conduct of Stuart's command, Lee stated: "In the battle of Fredericksburg, the cavalry effectually guarded our right, annoying the enemy and embarrassing his movements by hanging on his flank, and attacking when the opportunity occurred. The nature of the ground and the relative positions of the armies prevented them from doing more." If Stuart prepared a report on the engagement, it has not been found. He wired Flora the next day, telling her of the victory and noting, "I got shot through my fur collar but am unhurt."[28]

The destruction of the homes and businesses in Fredericksburg appalled Stuart. He issued a circular to the division, requesting that a subscription be taken up for the townsfolk. In the 2nd Virginia, for instance, the men raised $2,037 within an hour. Similar monetary drives were conducted among the infantry and artillery units.[29]

After the battle, Stuart established his headquarters about five miles from the city along Telegraph Road in a stand of pine trees. In time, men erected a chimney to his tent, and he dubbed the site "Camp No Camp." Flora and Jimmie arrived on December 23 and boarded initially nearby at the residence of a Mrs. French. On Christmas Eve, Stuart hosted a dinner at his tent for cavalry officers. They dined on turkey, ham, chicken, sweet potatoes, eggs, and apple brandy. They might have feasted more sumptuously had not thieves—allegedly from the Texas Brigade—pilfered some of the turkeys. Guards then watched the fowl until the dinner.[30]

On Christmas Day, Stuart joined Lee, William N. Pendleton, the army's artillery chief, and staff officers for dinner at Stonewall Jackson's headquarters at Moss Neck Manor, the plantation of Richard and Roberta Corbin. The Corbins' home was an imposing brick house, measuring 250 feet from wing to wing. Jackson used the family's three-room wooden office as his headquarters. Corbin served as a private in the 9th Virginia in Rooney Lee's brigade. He had rejoined the regiment three months earlier after being exchanged from a Union prison.[31]

Lee and Stuart seemed to take particular delight in the occasion. When Lee saw the well-furnished office, he teased Jackson that he should come to army headquarters and "see how a soldier ought to live." Stuart noticed paintings of thoroughbred horses and prize bulls on the walls and feigned shock at Jackson's taste in art. A member of the host's staff recalled, "Stuart was in great glee, ridiculing the white apron [worn by a servant] and playfully chiding Jackson for his bottle of wine." The butter was stamped with the print of a rooster, and Stuart "pronounced it to be Jackson's coat of arms."[32]

The Christmas festivities offered a brief respite for both generals and their troops. Since the battle, Stuart's horsemen had resumed picket duty along stretches of the river. In some areas, the opposing pickets agreed to "no firing" arrangements. The 2nd Virginia's Colonel Thomas Munford complained that the men lacked adequate rations and the horses suffered from a scarcity of forage. Wade Hampton conducted a raid behind Union lines, bagging supply wagons and prisoners.[33]

Within a week of the battle, Lee offered Hampton command of an infantry brigade. "When I proposed your transfer to the cavalry," wrote the army commander, "I understood you, in giving your assent, to say that you did not desire it to be permanent." With the mortal wounding of Brigadier General Maxcy Gregg at Fredericksburg, the infantry brigade of Hampton's fellow South Carolinians needed a commander. "If it is agreeable to your wishes," continued Lee, "and will not do violence to the feelings of others, I will propose to the Department your permanent transfer to the brigade."[34]

Since his assignment to the cavalry in July, Hampton had emerged as Stuart's most capable and reliable brigade commander. Although the two men had not enjoyed a warm personal friendship, they worked well together professionally. Hampton disliked, as he saw it, Stuart's favoritism toward Virginians for promotion and official praise. His belief had some merit, but on his return from this recent raid, Stuart endorsed his report, "General Hampton has again made a brilliant dash into the enemy's communications . . . and I cordially commend his conduct and that of his command to the favorable notice of the commanding general." Hampton declined Lee's offer of a transfer to the infantry.[35]

In his excursion behind Union lines, Hampton had approached the town of Dumfries on Telegraph Road, north of Fredericksburg. Telegraph Road ran from Alexandria to the outskirts of Richmond, and was used as a supply route for Burnside's army. On December 23, three days after Hampton's return, Lee ordered Stuart to "penetrate the enemy's rear, ascertain if possible his position & movements, & inflict upon him such damage as circumstances will permit." Most likely, Lee directed the raid after discussions with Stuart. Hampton's men believed that Stuart originated the plan, because "he was jealous," in Hampton's words, of their recent exploit.[36]

Stuart assigned 1,800 officers and men from his three brigades and a battery of horse artillery to the operation. The contingents from Fitz Lee's and Rooney Lee's commands and the battery marched upriver on Christmas Eve to near Brandy Station, where Stuart and his staff joined them after his Christmas dinner at Moss Neck Manor. Hampton's troopers arrived on the morning of December 26, after which the Confederates crossed the Rappahannock and rode on to near Morrisville and encamped for the night.[37]

The march resumed before daybreak on December 27, with the Rebels moving in three parallel columns toward Dumfries, twenty miles away. Stuart accompanied Rooney Lee's men in the center. Lee arrived first at Dumfries, which was defended by Union infantry and artillery. A brief skirmish ensued before the Federals withdrew to a ridge that overlooked the town. Stuart engaged the enemy with cannon, and when Fitz Lee's command came up, considered an attack. But he dismissed the idea, writing, "the capture of the place would not have compensated for the loss of life which must have attended the movement." With the day's seizures of twenty wagons, one hundred prisoners, and 150 horses and mules, the Rebels rode away, halting at Cole's Store, roughly eight miles northwest of Dumfries.[38]

Hampton's force, meanwhile, moving to the left of the Lees, scattered Union cavalry and entered the town of Occoquan, north of Dumfries on Telegraph Road. When Stuart and the other two commands did not appear as Hampton expected, he retreated from the town, reuniting with Stuart at Cole's Store. During the night, Stuart sent two gun crews whose ammunition had been nearly expended, the wagons, and prisoners back with an escort to the army. It was not much of a haul for a force of 1,800 raiders.[39]

The next morning, Stuart considered abandoning the raid until a civilian and scouts reported the approach of Union cavalry. Heading north, with Fitz Lee's brigade in advance, the Confederates rode to Greenwood Church, where Stuart detached Colonel Matthew Calbraith Butler and the 2nd South Carolina to cut off the enemy retreat from the northwest. Slightly beyond Greenwood Church, Lee encountered the Yankee horsemen, members of the 2nd and 17th Pennsylvania, numbering between five hundred and six hundred officers and men. The Pennsylvanians were in line of battle in a woods.[40]

The 1st Virginia spearheaded Lee's charge, followed by the 2nd, 3rd, and 5th Virginia. The Pennsylvanians triggered a volley with their pistols, then broke and fled. Lee described the attack as "one of the most admirable performances of cavalry I ever witnessed." The Virginians raced in pursuit, overtaking about one hundred Federals. Splashing across the Occoquan River at shallow, rocky Selectman's Ford, the Rebels reached the enemy's abandoned camp. In their flight, the Northerners left behind "a great many spoils of every description." Hampton's and Rooney Lee's men followed across the river. Butler's South Carolinians rejoined the column after a narrow escape from another body of Union cavalry.[41]

Burning what they could not take with them, the Confederates marched north to Burke's Station on the Orange & Alexandria Railroad, fewer than a dozen miles west of Alexandria and four miles south of Fairfax Court House. A detail seized the telegraph office before the operators could warn authorities in Washington. With his own telegrapher with him, Stuart intercepted messages between Union commanders. Before he departed, Stuart sent a telegram to Union quartermaster General Montgomery C. Meigs, "Gen. Meigs will in the future please furnish better mules; those you have furnished recently are very inferior." Stuart signed his name to the message.[42]

Details tore up the tracks at Burke's Station, and a small party, led by

Fitz Lee, damaged the railroad bridge over Accotink Creek. It was well after nightfall when Stuart resumed the march, moving toward Fairfax Court House. Striking Little River Turnpike three miles west of the town, Stuart halted. He led Fitz Lee's Virginians down the road "with the view, if practicable," as he reported, "of surprising and capturing the place." The town was held by Brigadier General Edwin H. Stoughton's brigade of Vermont regiments. A volley from the Vermonters in the darkness ended Stuart's attempt.[43]

The cavalry commander decided upon a return to Confederate lines. Little more, if anything, could be accomplished without jeopardizing the command's safety. The men and horses needed rest. Acting as a rear guard, Hampton's troopers built large campfires as a deception. The Southerners rode through the night as the men slept in the saddles, finally halting at dawn on December 29, at Frying Pan, near Chantilly. While the men rested and fed their mounts, Stuart visited with Laura Ratcliffe.[44]

At 11:00 A.M., the column re-formed, continuing west on Little River Turnpike. The Confederates arrived at Middleburg at sunset and bivouacked for the night. Stuart and his staff found lodging at Oakham, the home of the Hamilton Rogers family. The next morning, John Mosby came to Stuart's room. The scout, in whom Stuart had "unlimited confidence," asked for a detail of men from the 1st Virginia to operate as partisans or guerrillas in Fauquier and Loudoun counties during the winter. "I did not want to rust away my life in camp," Mosby explained later. Stuart consented to the temporary service. It proved to be one of his wisest decisions.[45]

From Middleburg, the riders marched south through White Plains (today, The Plains) and on to Warrenton. As they passed his home outside of White Plains, Edward Carter Turner noted, "The soldiers so far as I have seen are well clothed and well shod." By New Year's Eve, they had crossed the Rappahannock and halted at Culpeper Court House. The men were able to enjoy coffee, cakes, cheeses, nuts, oranges, and lemons from the captured sutler wagons. Some of the "well shod" troopers, whom Turner noticed, were probably wearing boots taken from their Yankee prisoners.[46]

The raid had cost Stuart a captain killed and about a dozen men wounded. According to Channing Price, the Confederates seized 250 men and their mounts, more than one hundred arms, and twenty wagons. In his report, Stuart listed the incursion's results as the destruction of the telegraph line, the captures, the dispersal of enemy, and the "impression" of a movement into Maryland. In fact, the raid accomplished minimal benefits, except to embarrass further the Union administration and to delight Southerners when they read of Stuart's telegram. It had, however, expended valuable horseflesh, an increasingly precious commodity for Stuart and for the cause.[47]

Stuart returned to his headquarters outside Fredericksburg on New Year's Day, likely receiving a welcome from Flora and Jimmie. His wife and son would remain near him, boarding with a Mrs. Alsop, until mid-February. Flora's grief over the death of their daughter could hardly have eased. It must have stalked her mind like a dark, recurring dream. Apparently she had expressed often to her husband her fears about Jimmie's health and his safety. Weeks earlier in a reply to her dire concerns, he wrote that she should "not allow imaginary cares to annoy you. That is my greatest apprehension."[48]

When duty did not pull Stuart away from Camp No Camp, during these winter months, he enjoyed not only Flora's and Jimmie's company but the camaraderie of army life. With Jackson's headquarters an easy ride away, Stuart visited frequently with his friend. "No more welcome guest ever came than General J. E. B. Stuart," asserted James Power Smith of Jackson's staff. "With clanking saber and spurs and waving black plume he came," added Smith, "and was warmly greeted at the door. Papers and work were all hastily laid aside."[49]

Stuart's aide and kinsman John Esten Cooke thought their affection for each other striking because of their contrasts in "character and temperament." "Stuart was the most impulsive and Jackson the most reserved and reticent of men," Cooke remembered. Cooke noted, however, the two men "seemed to have a sincere friendship for each other, which always impressed me as a very singular circumstance indeed; but so it was." The staff officer believed that "a strong bond of mutual admiration and confidence united them." Stuart regarded his friend as a *"military genius."*[50]

Jackson's medical director, Dr. Hunter McGuire, recalled that during the stay at Moss Neck "there was a great increase in his [Jackson's] sociability: and he unbent much more, as at table, & in enjoying an innocent jest." McGuire continued, "Maj. Gen. Stuart especially used to break the ice & make him laugh, sometimes uproariously, at his grotesque raillery." Jedediah Hotchkiss, Jackson's topographer, described Stuart as "the genuine soul, always full of life & humor." Stuart kept an autograph book, gathering signatures of his fellow generals and aides. In one of the few written sentiments, Jackson wrote "Your much attached friend."[51]

During these weeks, Stuart also enjoyed relaxed moments with the army commander. On one occasion he and Lee, with their aides, visited the home of a Mr. and Mrs. William P. Taylor. Staying with the Taylors were their nieces, thirteen-year-old Fannie and fourteen-year-old Bessie Gwathmey. When Lee was introduced to the teenagers, he said he had brought kisses for them from another aunt and asked their permission to give them. "He gave us two for our aunt and two for himself," wrote Fannie later. Standing nearby, Stuart said to Lee: "General, I don't think it fair for you to get all the kisses. I would like to kiss these little girls too."

"General Stuart," rebutted Fannie, "I would love dearly to kiss you but I just can't let any one take General Lee's kisses off my lips." Her words brought loud laughter from Stuart's staff officers.[52]

Stuart's admiration of Lee's character and confidence in his generalship had deepened. Writing of Lee, he stated, "to his wisdom, patriotism, and self-abnegation we owe much and will owe more before this war was over." Stuart was not alone in the army in his view. Major Deloney of Cobb's Legion, after meeting Lee for the first time, declared to his wife, "Gen. Lee is one of the most courteous, pleasant & simple in his manner of any of the Old Army officers I have met." The common soldiers now called him "Marse Robert."[53]

A South Carolina captain left a vivid description of the men's reaction to Jackson, Stuart, and Lee. Writing to a fellow officer during the previous fall, the South Carolinian contended: "Whenever Jackson is seen every soldier's mouth flies wide open—you can always tell whenever Jackson is coming. General Stuart also creates a considerable enthusiasm." When Lee passed by, however, "the soldiers gaze at him in silent admiration. . . . Of all the generals I think General Lee by far the most superior. He has not equal in this continent in my estimation."[54]

It was at Camp No Camp where Stuart's zest for life and boyish nature were most evident. "He is charming when he throws off business," Esten Cooke said of his commander. "The days and night," recounted Cooke, "were full of song and laughter." One night Stuart returned to his headquarters at midnight, and according to a staff member, "had a great romp with his two aides, and roused up the whole camp by his singing and shouting."[55]

Stuart relished playing practical jokes on and teasing his staff officers. Heros von Borcke and Channing Price appeared to receive the brunt of Stuart's mischief. The Prussian blushed readily, which made him a frequent mark for Stuart. He needled Price by calling the young lieutenant "Major Price." Price's remarkable ability to remember Stuart's oral orders and to put them accurately on paper moved Stuart to describe him as "invaluable to me." Ironically, the one staff officer he could barely abide was Flora's cousin Esten Cooke. "I wish I could get rid of John Esten," he complained to his wife, "he is the greatest bore I ever met, and is disagreeable to everybody, but we must all suffer some."[56]

During the previous weeks and months, the composition of the staff had changed. Major Norman FitzHugh, captured at Verdiersville in August 1862, had been exchanged and rejoined Stuart as adjutant general or chief of staff. When Major Samuel Hairston left in March 1863, Stuart appointed FitzHugh as his commissary chief and named Price as his new adjutant. Heros von Borcke, Esten Cooke, William Blackford, Chiswell Dabney, and William Farley continued serving in various capacities.[57]

New members included captains Andrew Reid Venable, Jr., James M. Hanger, and Richard Frayser; lieutenants Frank Robertson, Walter Q. Hullihen, whom Stuart nicknamed "Honey-bun," and Thomas R. Price, Jr., Channing's brother; and, Dr. John B. Fontaine. All of the men were Virginians, and Venable, Robertson, and Hanger served with Stuart until May 1864. Thomas Price remained until June 1863, when the publication of his captured diary by the New York *Times*, with its critical comments on Stuart, caused his resignation. Fontaine acted as the cavalry division's medical director and Stuart's personal surgeon.

During the winter, Stuart attended the wedding of Fontaine and Elizabeth Price, Channing and Thomas's sister, at Dundee.[58]

While at Camp No Camp, Stuart resumed his efforts to promote John Pelham and Thomas Rosser. "I have already made several urgent recommendations for the promotion of Pelham," he wrote to Adjutant General Samuel Cooper. "The battle of Fredericksburg, form[ed] a fresh chapter in his career of exploits without a parallel," Stuart affirmed. "It has been alleged that he was too young. Though remarkably youthful in appearance *there are Generals as young* with less claim to that distinction, *and no veteran in age has ever shown more coolness and better judgment in the sphere of his duty.*" But despite this and earlier letters from Stuart to the War Department, Pelham remained a major.[59]

The six-foot, two-inch, broad-shouldered Rosser had acted, from time to time, as temporary commander of Fitz Lee's brigade in that officer's absence. In a letter to Flora, Stuart called Rosser "my right hand man." It seemed to be well known in the division that the Virginian, as an officer stated it, "has always been a very great favorite of Stuart's." The cavalry commander now proposed the organization of a new brigade, formed around Rosser's 5th Virginia and drawing units from the other brigades. In his endorsement of Rosser's promotion to brigadier, Stuart wrote that he had "vindicated his claims" with his conduct on outpost duty, in combat, and as "a rigid disciplinarian." The War Department ignored Stuart's recommendations.[60]

Stuart then proposed to Robert E. Lee that Rosser, who was "most suitable for such a command," replace Grumble Jones as brigade commander. When Jackson's Second Corps left the Shenandoah Valley in November 1862, Jones's brigade stayed in the region. Jackson and Lee thought highly of Jones's abilities as a cavalry officer. Once again, Stuart allowed his personal dislike of Jones to cloud his judgment of him.[61]

On February 11, Flora and Jimmie traveled to Richmond, accompanied by Stuart. He remained in the capital only a day or two. While there, he was presented to the Virginia Senate and House of Delegates and was offered a seat in the lower body. He thanked the members. As he was leaving, Peter Dabney, brother of Chiswell Dabney, introduced himself, remarking that he should know the general. "I suppose I should," replied Stuart, "as you married my old *sweet-heart.*"[62]

When Stuart left Richmond, he traveled to Culpeper Court House, with orders from Lee to determine if they could strike "a damaging blow" against the Federals, either along the Potomac River or in the Shenandoah Valley. Lee's instructions marked a departure from the relative quiet during the preceding seven or eight weeks. Through much of that time, the cavalry performed picket or vidette duty on a line, which stretched from Culpeper County to below Fredericksburg. Stuart held only a pair of reviews and spent his days away from headquarters checking on the picket posts. An infantryman saw him for the first time in January and was surprised at his youthful appearance, writing, "I have always heard him spoken of as 'Old Stuart.'"[63]

Activity had quickened temporarily on January 20, when Union Major General Ambrose Burnside undertook an offensive movement, marching his army up the Rappahannock to outflank the Confederate defenses. Unfortunately for the luckless Burnside, a winter storm brought a deluge of rain, miring the Federals in their tracks. Dubbed the "Mud March," the failed movement finished Burnside. When he demanded the removal of several generals, Lincoln refused. Burnside tendered his resignation from the service, but the president declined it, granting him a thirty-day leave of absence. Lincoln appointed Major General Joseph Hooker as commander of the Army of the Potomac.[64]

It was three weeks after the doomed Mud March when Lee instructed Stuart to ascertain the possibilities of an operation against the enemy. Wade Hampton's brigade had been posted in Culpeper County. Hampton and Stuart had had their differences during the winter weeks. "All my time & correspondence of late," the South Carolinian wrote on January 27, "have been taken up in quarreling with Stuart, who keeps me here doing all the hard work while his Virginia Brigades are quietly doing nothing." A lack of forage for the horses particularly galled Hampton, who appealed directly to Lee about the conditions. Stuart's perceived partiality toward his Virginians Hampton described as "disgusting," and "it constantly makes me indignant." He even sarcastically suggested to a Confederate senator that Stuart should have a command composed of only Virginians as it "would be a great matter of him, *if he ever runs for Gov. of Va.*"[65]

Hampton's criticisms of Stuart were too harsh. Not only his men's mounts, but Fitz Lee's and Rooney Lee's lacked adequate forage. Stuart had spread out the units to alleviate the shortages, while fulfilling the demands of picket duty. Robert E. Lee alerted President Jefferson Davis to the worsening problem: "There has been great scarcity of forage in the whole army, & requires the greatest care of officers & men to keep the horses in condition."[66]

The Confederate cavalrymen's letters home were replete with the words "starve" and "starving" to describe their horse's conditions. "The men look very well but the horses sorry," claimed a Georgian. "I did not know mine at first sight." When forage details went into the country-side to find hay and corn, their mounts usually consumed it before they returned to camp. Thomas Rosser reported the 5th Virginia "unfit for duty" because of the weakness of the horses. A member of Cobb's Legion grumbled to his father, "This way of belonging to cavalry or artillery and having sorry horses I don't like, and I can't stand the infantry." Across the Rappahannock, Federal mounts appeared to be equally thin, moving an observer to write, "The cavalry horses look as if they came from Egypt during the seven years' famine."[67]

Official returns from the cavalry division indicated the extent of the problem during these months. Stuart reported nearly 9,500 officers and men present for duty on December 31, 1862. By the end of February, that number had been reduced to barely 6,300, with one regiment on detached duty and not included. For each of those months, roughly 2,000 men were present, but unable to perform duty. Disabled mounts accounted for some of the depletion of troopers present for duty, but the horse policy of the Confederate government added to the rolls of those men not on duty.[68]

When the conflict began, the eleven states that comprised the Confederacy were home to 2.5 million horses and mules. Of that number, about 1.1 million animals were in Texas, Tennessee, and Virginia. Confederate officials decided to purchase horses and mules for artillery batteries and for supply wagons, but required cavalry officers and men to provide their own mounts. The government was responsible for horseshoes and feed, while paying each cavalryman 40 cents a day for "the use and risk of their horses." If a horse were killed in action, the trooper received a payment based upon "a fair valuation" of the animal at the time of the man's muster into the service. If the horse were captured, disabled, or worn out, the loss fell to its owner.[69]

Consequently, when Southern men and boys joined cavalry units, they generally rode their family's finest horse. But the war's rigors, compounded by disease and malnourishment, made many animals unserviceable, which left their riders either seeking another mount or transferring to the artillery or infantry. Horses were to be fed fourteen pounds of hay and twelve pounds of oats, barley, or corn each day. As commissary officers were unable to fill the amount of forage, as happened during this winter, the number of horses unfit for service rose. For instance, approximately one-fourth of the mounts in the 3rd Virginia were classified as unserviceable.[70]

Henry B. McClellan, who joined Stuart's staff in April 1863, stated in his memoirs, "That the government should have adopted such a policy at the beginning of the war was a misfortune; that it should have adhered to it to the very end was a calamity against which no amount of zeal or patriotism could successfully contend." The theory had been if a man owned the horse he would take special care of it. In fact, many men did, but the physical demands upon their horses, inadequate forage, disease, and combat left many men riderless.[71]

When men needed to replace their mounts, they secured furloughs— the troopers called them "horse details"—to go home. They were away from the army generally from thirty to sixty days before returning with another horse. For Hampton's men, who came from the lower South, the furloughs usually were longer. A lieutenant with Stuart declared after the war: "This method of keeping up cavalry was subject to *very great* abuse. Men would purposely neglect their horses to break them down and get these details." The number of absentee troopers on furloughs increased progressively, while the quality of Southern horseflesh decreased.[72]

And with the winter, a foretelling came to the cavalry. By mid-February, conditions in Hampton's brigade forced Robert E. Lee to relieve the command of duty. At least one-half of the members were dismounted, with hundreds having been sent home on horse details. An officer in the Jeff Davis Legion believed, "Clearly the Legion was in no condition to cope with any attack the Federals might make." The situation with Hampton's command and Lee's suggestion about a possible raid thus brought Stuart to Culpeper County.[73]

Stuart replaced Hampton's depleted ranks with Fitz Lee's five Virginia regiments. Stuart withdrew Hampton's command to recuperate, with some units sent to the Shenandoah Valley and others to beyond the James River in southeastern Virginia. The army commander's proposal of a cavalry foray either into the Valley or toward the Potomac was abandoned. On February 23, however, Robert E. Lee ordered a reconnaissance across the Rappahannock with men from his nephew's brigade. In his endorsement to the instructions, Stuart wrote to Fitz Lee, "The commanding general is aware of the extraordinary obstacles and difficulties in the way of success—a swollen river, snow, mud, rain, and impracticable roads, together with distance."[74]

Fitz Lee selected four hundred officers and men from the 1st, 2nd, and 3rd Virginia, starting across the river at Kelly's Ford on the morning of February 24. More than a foot of snow lay on the ground. The troopers thought Lee was, wrote a captain, either "drunk" or "a fool" to undertake such a mission at this time. Despite the grumbling, the brigadier was well liked and respected by his men. His genial disposition, concern for their welfare, and personal bravery endeared him to them. "If he ever punished a man, during the entire war," noted a member of the 1st Virginia, "I have not heard of it."[75]

The next morning the Rebel column rode downriver until it met a force of Union cavalry at Hartwood Church. The brick Presbyterian church marked the end of the Federal army's right flank, about eight miles in the rear of Falmouth. Troopers from the 1st and 2nd Virginia charged the Yankees, members of the 3rd and 16th Pennsylvania. Shouting, "Surrender you dog," the Southerners routed the enemy, but blue-jacketed reserves counterattacked. A charge by the 3rd Virginia ended the action and covered the withdrawal of the Confederates. Lee's men rode away with nearly 150 prisoners, horses, and gear.[76]

Before he departed, Lee learned from the captives that they belonged to the command of his West Point classmate and friend Brigadier General William W. Averell. Lee left behind a note for his academy friend: "I wish you would put up your sword, leave my state, and go home. You ride a good horse, I ride a better. Yours can beat mine running. If you won't go home, return my visit, and bring me a sack of coffee."[77]

Lee's cavalrymen returned to Culpeper County in a rainstorm on February 26. That same day, Stuart arrived back at Camp No Camp, "wet as a *submerged* rat," as he told Flora. The inclement weather stalled active operations for more than a fortnight. With Flora and Jimmie away from him, Stuart wrote to her, "I want to see you dear one to talk over matters—hold a council of war." She sent him a wreath, and in reply, he stated, "If you dote on me too much I will be taken from you— think of me as the *hard case* you know I am and then you wont miss me so much."[78]

On March 11 or 12, Stuart, John Pelham, and Heros von Borcke traveled to Culpeper Court House on court-martial duty. When they arrived at the railroad station, Mosby met them. Stuart had not seen Mosby since he had granted the lieutenant permission to conduct guerrilla operations in northern Virginia. For the past two months, Mosby and, in Stuart's phrase, "his band of a dozen chosen spirits" had attacked Union picket posts and wagon trains. Mosby had come to Culpeper to deliver his latest haul of Union captives and horses.[79]

On the night of March 8–9, Mosby and twenty-nine men penetrated Union lines around Fairfax Court House, entered the village, and captured fifty-eight horses and thirty-three prisoners, including Union general Edwin Stoughton. Mosby personally awakened Stoughton in his bed and led away the commander of the Vermont Brigade. Without firing a gun or suffering a casualty, the raiders disappeared into the morning darkness. Reaching Culpeper, Mosby handed over Stoughton and the others to Fitz Lee. From their time together in the 1st Virginia, Mosby and Lee had developed a mutual dislike for each other. When Mosby presented the captured general to Lee, the Confederate brigadier "could not have treated me with more indifference," wrote Mosby later. In fact, Lee asked that Mosby return to him the men from the 1st Virginia. Stuart rejected the request.[80]

Stuart was "overjoyed" with the audacious feat. He called it "unparalleled in the war," while Robert E. Lee stated, "Mosby had covered himself with glory." Commissioned a captain within days, Mosby gave Stoughton's saddle to Stuart. Afterward, Stuart directed Mosby to organize a "band of permanent followers for the war," but added a caution, "Be vigilant about your own safety, and do not have any established headquarters anywhere but 'in the saddle.'" Years later, Mosby wrote of Stuart, "He was the best friend I ever had and made me all that I was in the War."[81]

While in Culpeper, Stuart boarded at the residence of a Confederate officer. Local citizens entertained him and his companions at parties. When the general attended Sunday services at St. Stephen's Episcopal Church, the pews filled. On the night of March 16, Stuart, Pelham, and von Borcke visited the home of Judge Henry Shackleford. Pelham was dating the jurist's daughter, Bessie, and the group enjoyed music, coffee, and crackers. That night, Pelham shared a couch in another house with his West Point classmate, now Colonel Pierce M. B. Young of Cobb's Legion.[82]

North of the Rappahannock meanwhile, a Union force of 2,100 cavalrymen and six artillery crews had gathered throughout the day. After Joseph Hooker assumed command of the Army of the Potomac, he organized its mounted units into a separate corps. Hooker appointed Major General George Stoneman as its commander. Hooker talked aggressively and expected the army, particularly the cavalry, to act aggressively. Fitz Lee's attack at Hartwood Church angered the Union commander, who berated Stoneman: "We ought to be invincible, and by God, sir, we shall be! You have got to stop these disgraceful cavalry 'surprises.' I'll have no more of them."[83]

When information placed Fitz Lee's troopers still in Culpeper County, Hooker ordered Lee's opponent at Hartwood Church, William Averell, to attack the Rebels. Drawing officers and men from five regiments, Averell led them across the river at Kelly's Ford on the morning of March 17, 1863. The Yankees scattered an enemy picket post, passed through the tiny village of Kellysville, and deployed in line beyond it. The gunfire from the river had alerted Lee, who gathered about eight hundred men from his five regiments and rode to meet the Federals. A battery of horse artillery joined the Confederate horsemen.[84]

Duels between dismounted skirmishers, artillery exchanges, and mounted charges and countercharges marked the engagement at Kelly's Ford. Stone walls and ditches across farmers' fields disrupted the attacks on horseback. The clang of sabers and the blasts of pistols at close range echoed across the fields. A Yankee called it "a square, stand-up, cavalry fight."[85]

Stuart, Pelham, and von Borcke followed the Confederate cavalrymen to the battlefield. Lee offered to relinquish command to Stuart, who declined, saying afterward, "I determined not to interfere with his command of the brigade as long as it was commanded so entirely to my satisfaction." Pelham decided, however, to join in the fight and rode with the 3rd Virginia in its initial attack. Pelham trailed the Virginians as they filed through a gate in a stone wall on the G. W. Wheatley farm. Suddenly, an enemy artillery shell burst above the Alabamian, with a piece striking him in the head. Some troopers held the wounded major on his horse and led him to the rear. They lay Pelham in an ambulance, which carried him to the Shackleford home in town.[86]

Stuart was informed of Pelham's fall but remained on the battlefield. Averell's numbers prevailed, breaking Lee's lines in a final assault. Confederate horse artillery crews stopped the Union pursuit. Averell still held the advantage, but instead of renewing the attacks on Lee's broken ranks, he was unwilling "to make a direct and desperate attack," as he put it. He ordered a withdrawal across the river.[87]

Although Stuart claimed a victory by holding the field against superior numbers, a more aggressive Averell might have routed Lee's command. Hooker rebuked the brigadier for his caution. Total casualties in the action amounted to slightly more than two hundred. Before he rode away, Averell left behind a sack and a note, which read: "Dear Fitz, Here's your coffee. Here's your visit. How did you like it? How's that horse? Averell."[88]

Stuart arrived at the Shackleford home at two o'clock on the morning of March 18. Expecting to find Pelham alive, he "was dreadfully shocked to see his dead body," in the words of Channing Price. The piece of artillery shell had crushed part of his skull. He did not regain consciousness and died an hour before Stuart reached the house. When he saw his body, Stuart, with "his eyes full of tears," kissed Pelham's forehead, cut a lock of hair from his head, and whispered, "Farewell."[89]

Pelham's death stunned the army and the Southern people, casting, as Stuart wrote, "a shadow of gloom over us not soon to pass away." His friend Pierce Young said of him: "He was brave as Caesar and gentle as a

girl. . . . I never knew a better friend, a braver soldier." Henry Kyd Douglas called him "the pet of Jeb Stuart & of all who knew him." Channing
Price told his mother that Pelham was "one of the noblest specimens
I ever had the pleasure of meeting with." "Nothing," Price wrote in
another letter, "has happened in the progress of the war which I have
felt more keenly than his death." Robert E. Lee confided to his wife: "I
grieve over the loss of Major Pelham. He had been stricken down in the
midst of his career of usefulness and honour."[90]

Jennings Cropper Wise, historian of the artillery of the Army of
Northern Virginia, contended that the horse artillery under Pelham's
leadership achieved "an independence of action and celerity of movement." "Pelham's skill in its management amounted to genius," concluded Wise. Colonel Thomas Munford believed that Stuart could not
have accomplished what he did without Pelham. As Stuart said, "His
loss to the country is irreparable."[91]

Stuart and the ladies of Culpeper placed his body in a coffin and
covered it with a wreath of evergreens. A train carried it to Richmond
and then on to Alabama. Stuart sent a telegram on March 18 to Confederate Congressman J. L. M. Curry: "The noble, the chivalric, the gallant Pelham is no more. He was killed in action yesterday. His remains
will be sent to you today. How much he was beloved, appreciated and
admired, let the tears of agony we have shed, and the gloom of mourning throughout my command bear witness."[92]

Officially, Stuart issued a general order to his division, announcing
Pelham's death. In it, he called him "the gallant Pelham," and asked of
his men, "In mourning his departure from his accustomed post of honor
on the field, let us strive to imitate his virtues." He directed his staff
members to wear mourning badges for thirty days in Pelham's memory.
He and John Esten Cooke wrote a eulogy, which was published anony-
mously in newspapers.[93]

Privately, Stuart's grief was profound. A day after Pelham's death, he
told Flora, "You must know how his death distressed me." In another letter, written weeks later, he asserted, "I want Jimmie to be just like him."
Flora was pregnant, and if she had a boy, he wanted him to be named
John Pelham Stuart. "I have thought of it much—it is *my* choice," he
declared. "His record is *complete*, and it is spotless, it is *noble*. His family

was the very best. His character pure his disposition as sweet & innocent as our own Little Flora's. You have no idea how I will feel to know
that if a boy, I will have an heir named John Pelham." If the child were
a girl, Maria Pelham Stuart.[94]

Stuart also wrote to Pelham's parents, enclosing a ring taken from
his finger for his mother. "I know that man's sympathy is emptiness, to
one, who has lost as you have the promise and hope of a noble son," he
professed in part, "but when I tell you, I *loved him as a brother*, you will
permit me to share with you a grief so sacred, so consoling." Later, the
Pelhams sent Stuart sleeve buttons and studs for a uniform that they
had had made for their son. He had been slain before they were finished, and they wanted Stuart to have them.[95]

Frequently, amid the fury of combat, Stuart and Pelham were by
each other's side. "General Stuart loved him like a younger brother,"
attested William Blackford, "and could not bear for him to be away
from him." This time, the separation would be permanent.[96]

Daguerreotype of George Washington Custis Lee, James E. B. Stuart, and Stephen D. Lee after their graduation from West Point in June 1854. (VIRGINIA HISTORICAL SOCIETY [VHS])

Daguerreotype of Flora Cooke Stuart, who married J. E. B. Stuart after a whirlwind romance on November 14, 1855. After the war, she dedicated her life to his memory, education, and her family. (VHS)

Stuart Leading a Cavalry Charge, the *Autumn Mural* from Charles Hoffbauer's *Four Seasons of the Confederacy*. (VHS)

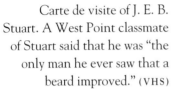

Carte de visite of J. E. B. Stuart. A West Point classmate of Stuart said that he was "the only man he ever saw that a beard improved." (VHS)

General Robert E. Lee, commander of the Army of Northern Virginia. Upon learning of Stuart's death, Lee said of his cavalry commander, "He never brought me a piece of false information." (UNITED STATES ARMY MILITARY HISTORY INSTITUTE [USAMHI])

Lieutenant General Thomas J. "Stonewall" Jackson, commander of the Second Corps, Army of Northern Virginia. Jackson and Stuart's friendship was unique among senior officers in the army. Stuart called his best friend's death a "national calamity." (USAMHI)

Lieutenant General James Longstreet, commander of the First Corps, Army of Northern Virginia. Stuart served under Longstreet during the late summer and early fall of 1861, and the two developed a close friendship. (USAMHI)

A photograph of Stuart probably taken later in the war. The burdens of command and the weariness of war are evident in his face. (USAMHI)

Brigadier General Wade Hampton, a wealthy South Carolina planter who emerged as Stuart's finest subordinate commander. His and Stuart's relationship was more professional than personal. (USAMHI)

Brigadier General Fitzhugh Lee, nephew of Robert E. Lee and one of Stuart's closest subordinates. Fitz Lee shared with Stuart a zest for life and good times on the march and around a campfire. (USAMHI)

Brigadier General William E. "Grumble" Jones, a talented horse soldier, respected by Robert E. Lee and Stonewall Jackson. Jones and Stuart had an abiding hatred for each other, which resulted in a court-martial of Jones. (USAMHI)

Brigadier General Thomas L. Rosser, one of Stuart's favorite officers. An inordinately ambitious man, Rosser blamed Stuart for not securing sooner Rosser's promotion to brigadier. (USAMHI)

Colonel Thomas T. Munford in the uniform of a brigadier general. Stuart repeatedly recommended the highly capable Munford for promotion to brigadier. The paperwork was submitted but the rank was never officially awarded. (USAMHI)

Brigadier General Lunsford L. Lomax, a friend of Stuart from the antebellum army. Lomax commanded a brigade under Stuart and was with him at Yellow Tavern. (USAMHI)

Brigadier General William Henry Fitzhugh "Rooney" Lee in the uniform coat of a colonel. The second son of Robert E. Lee, Rooney Lee proved to be one of Stuart's best cavalry officers. (USAMHI)

Colonel John Singelton Mosby, commander of the 43rd Battalion of Virginia Cavalry, or Mosby's Rangers. An invaluable scout for Stuart, Mosby rendered greater service as a partisan officer. He called Stuart "his best friend" in the army. (USAMHI)

Union Brigadier General George Armstrong Custer in his conspicuous uniform of black velvet. Custer's Michigan Brigade opposed Stuart's horsemen on several fields of battle. One of Custer's men fatally shot Stuart at Yellow Tavern. (USAMHI)

A charge of Union cavalry up Fleetwood Hill at the Battle of Brandy Station, June 9, 1863. Southern newspapers criticized Stuart for being "surprised" in the largest cavalry engagement of the Civil War. (USAMHI)

A postwar statue of Stuart, showing his familiar uniform, with high-topped boots, sword, revolver, and plumed hat. (USAMHI)

Uniform jacket and yellow sash of Major General J. E. B. Stuart. This fine uniform enhanced his carefully crafted image as a bold and dashing cavalryman. (VHS)

Chapter Eleven

"Right Noble Did Stuart Do"

C APTAIN JUSTUS SCHEIBERT, an engineer officer in the Prussian army, arrived at the headquarters of the Cavalry Division, Army of Northern Virginia in April 1863. Sent by his government as an observer of the conflict in America, Scheibert came to Virginia, where he sought out the Confederate army. When Scheibert appeared at the cavalry camps, his fellow Prussian, Major Heros von Borcke, welcomed him and offered to share his quarters, which Scheibert described as "a round tent with holes in it like a sieve—it was the only one of its type in the army."[1]

Von Borcke introduced Scheibert to Jeb Stuart. In his memoir of his travels through the Confederacy, Scheibert recounted his meeting with the renowned cavalryman: "In a simple tent, which also seemed to be his office, I found a young man in his thirties, with bold, flashing eyes and full beard, who looked very well in his gray jacket with the insignia of a general, in gray trousers tucked in his high boots. He greeted me with frank and noble propriety." During their conversation, Stuart, pointing at von Borcke, remarked to Scheibert, "If you have any more like him over there, send them all over here!"[2]

The jacket noted by Scheibert had been sent to the general recently by Flora Stuart. He told her, "it was *beautiful*." His boots, size nine, were made of Russian leather, and the gloves he wore had been given to him by a woman in Madison County. He carried with him a brass compass and French-made binoculars in a red velvet-lined case from Chevalier Opticien of Paris. Stuart used a gold, intricately engraved mechanical pencil for correspondence.[3]

For arms, Stuart had chosen a LeMat revolver. Invented by Dr. Jean Alexandre François LeMat, a New Orleans physician, the revolver held ten shots—nine .42-caliber ball cartridges and one revolving cylinder on a center barrel for .66-caliber grapeshot. A French firm had contracted with the Confederate government for five thousand revolvers, using Dr. LeMat's 1856 patent. Like most officers of Stuart's rank, he rarely used the weapon.[4]

Scheibert arrived at Stuart's headquarters about a month after the engagement at Kelly's Ford. Since that action and the death of John Pelham, Stuart had reconstituted the horse artillery batteries into a separate command, no longer assigned to a particular brigade as in the past. When a battery served with a cavalry brigade in a fight or operation, however, its officers remained subject to the orders of the brigade commander.[5]

As a successor to the fallen Pelham, Stuart recommended Major Robert F. Beckham. The twenty-five-year-old Beckham, an 1859 West Point graduate, had commanded a pair of cannon at First Manassas and had served as an ordnance officer for an infantry division. In his request for Beckham's appointment, Stuart wrote, "I have known Major Beckham from the beginning of the war—he fought at my side at the first Manassas—and I am satisfied of his fitness for the place." Beckham joined his new command during the early days of April.[6]

By mid-month, the brigades of Fitz Lee and Rooney Lee were in Culpeper County, with Stuart's headquarters located one-half mile south of Culpeper Court House. Wade Hampton's command remained off active duty, as its men returned from horse details at home and officers recruited volunteers. In letters and in personal interviews, Robert E. Lee expressed to President Davis the critical need for more cavalry units as the spring campaign season approached. He requested that a brigade in North Carolina and one in western Virginia be assigned to Stuart. Lee stated his concern to Stuart, "I do not see how you are to keep the cavalry together before the grazing season opens."[7]

The army commander informed Davis that cavalry pickets extended from the Blue Ridge Mountains east to the Chesapeake Bay. The majority of the duty fell to the troopers with the two Lees and primarily along the Rappahannock. The work was dangerous for men on both banks of the river. Colonel Thomas Munford of the 2nd Virginia noted that when his pickets manned the posts they excelled in the deadly game. "I had a great many Mountaineers that could kill a running deer with their rifles or cut off a wild turkey's head," Munford declared in a postwar letter, "and if well posted, it was not safe for any man, especially an officer, to come within range of their rifles. It was a *cruel kind of fun*, but it was war, and they would *enjoy* the *practice*."[8]

Beyond the Rappahannock, Federal horsemen continued the aggressiveness they had shown at Kelly's Ford. Clashes flared at the fords as the Yankees attempted crossings. In two days, Rooney Lee's troopers repulsed three forays by the enemy. Stuart joined Lee's men at one of the actions, and in Lee's words, "his presence gave confidence and stability to the command." At Kelly's Ford, Stuart led a charge against the Union cavalrymen.[9]

The increased activity along the river foretold a resumption of operations. Robert E. Lee directed Stuart to watch for enemy movements, and if possible, to inflict "a damaging blow" upon the Federals. Lee cautioned, however, "that you will not necessarily expose yourself or men." Stuart forwarded to army headquarters a copy of the New York *Herald* in which the newspaper urged Union army commander Joseph Hooker to advance upon the Confederates. "He is not a man," Lee wrote of Hooker in reply, "I think to resist popular clamor."[10]

Stuart's efforts to gather information about enemy plans and movements extended into the rear of Hooker's army. His intelligence operations relied heavily upon the work of scouts, who maintained a constant presence behind enemy lines. "General Stuart was particularly happy in the selection of scouts," contended a staff officer. He sought men who possessed equanimity, discretion, and discernment. He studied or learned of a man's character before assigning him to scout duty. Stuart directed them to roam as far as necessary, even to the outskirts of Washington, to gather information, to observe Federal camps, and to follow the enemy on the march, reporting numbers and the direction of the movement.[11]

The scouts worked singly, in pairs, or in groups of various sizes. An officer boasted that one fifteen-man detail had captured "a great many prisoners" and "are a terror to the Yankees." They wore their Confederate uniforms, but at times, circumstances required them to conceal their identities. They depended on their own skills and information gleaned from civilians. A lieutenant in the 3rd Pennsylvania, writing about the residents of central Virginia, grumbled: "Every inhabitant in this country was in full sympathy with the enemy, and no matter how frequently the posts of our videttes were changed and the reserves moved, it was but a short time until the precise location was known at the headquarters on the other side of the river. Women and children as well as men took a patriotic pride in giving information to our movements."[12]

With the increasing likelihood of a Union movement, the demands on the scouts rose. A scout recalled of such times, "When Stuart gave orders for certain information wanted, it was a fair certainty that the scouts so detailed found but little sleep until he was satisfied as to the intent of the Federal general commanding." For instance, on April 26, Stuart wrote to John Mosby, whose partisan rangers were watching enemy activity along the Orange & Alexandria Railroad: "Information of the movements of large bodies is of the greatest importance to us just now. The marching or transportation of a Division will often indicate the plan of a campaign. Be sure to give dates & numbers & names as far as possible."[13]

Two days after Stuart sent the dispatch to Mosby, a stream of reports from scouts and pickets flowed into cavalry headquarters. Justus Scheibert was present and recalled: "I noticed that there was a mysterious restlessness in the air on April 28. General Stuart received a number of messages, dispatched couriers, and had a pensive look." Staff members were occupied with work. During the evening and night, reports came in stating that Federal infantry units were marching up the Rappahannock River and engineers were laying a pontoon bridge at Kelly's Ford.[14]

Stuart had expected an enemy offensive for some time. He had issued general orders to his command, addressing the need for inspections of horses and arms. Earlier, when John Esten Cooke asked about the probability of a spring campaign, Stuart responded, "If there is a spring campaign it will last through the year, and if so, it will go on to the end of Lincoln's time." More recently, he asked his brother William to pray for him, saying, "With me, no moment of the battle has ever been too momentous for prayer."[15]

Similarly, he wrote to Flora: "I go forth into the uncertain future. My saber will not leave my hand for months. I am sustained in the hour of peril by the consciousness of right, and upheld by the same Almighty hand, which has thus far covered my head in the day of battle, and in whom I put my trust." In another letter, Stuart asked of her, "When I am gone train up my boy in the footsteps of his father and tell him never to falter in implicit faith in Divine Providence." Having lost her beloved daughter and pregnant with another child, Flora could not have been reassured by the fearful possibility implied by her husband's words.[16]

But the reports hurried to Stuart's headquarters on April 28 indicated that the time had come again to unsheathe the sword. Three Union infantry corps, about 43,000 officers and men, were on the march, striding toward crossings of the Rappahannock and Rapidan rivers beyond the Confederate army's left flank. Hooker had wanted to undertake an offensive at the beginning of April, but inclement weather canceled the movement. At mid-month a rainstorm halted a planned cavalry raid behind enemy lines. More bad weather delayed Hooker's advance until the final days of April.[17]

Hooker fashioned a plan that required coordinated movements across a broad swath of the countryside. While the Fifth, Eleventh, and Twelfth corps turned the Rebel left flank, the First and Sixth corps would cross the Rappahannock below Fredericksburg and threaten the opposite flank. Hooker held the Second and Third corps in reserve and dispatched George Stoneman and six cavalry brigades on a raid against the enemy railroad connections to Richmond. Hooker calculated that Robert E. Lee would either have to abandon his lines and retreat or offer to give battle against a force of 135,000 Federals. Before the movement began, "Fighting Joe" Hooker, as he had been nicknamed, bragged to a colonel: "that he was just as sure that he was going to whip the rebels as he was a living man. He said all he was afraid of was that they would run before he got a chance to fight."[18]

The three corps of the main turning column had started forth from their winter camps, which were distant from Rebel picket posts, on

April 27. The march proceeded well the next day, and by nightfall, the Yankees had bivouacked at Kelly's Ford while engineers spanned the crossing with a pontoon bridge. It was the movement of these Northerners that Stuart's scouts and videttes had detected and relayed the information to headquarters.[19]

At daybreak on April 29, according to Scheibert, Stuart opened the tent of his staff members and announced, "Gentlemen, everyone will be in the saddle in a quarter of an hour." By mid-morning, Stuart had gathered the brigades of Fitz and Rooney Lee in the Brandy Station area. He received dispatches from the army commander, instructing him, "if you are forced back try to guard our left, & detain them all you can." As reports filtered back to Stuart and as details brought in Federal prisoners for interrogation, Stuart ordered Rooney Lee, with the 9th and 13th Virginia and six cannon, to march toward Gordonsville and to interdict and harass Stoneman's mounted raiders. With Fitz Lee's four regiments and the 5th Virginia, roughly 1,600 officers and men, Stuart rode for Raccoon Ford on the Rapidan River.[20]

During the day, the three Union infantry corps filed over the pontoon bridge across the Rappahannock and marched toward Germanna and Ely's fords on the Rapidan. The recent rains had swelled the river, but into the night, with bonfires lighting the darkness, the Federals waded through the current. At Fredericksburg, the Yankees, laying down pontoons, secured a lodgment on the west bank of the Rappahannock. Robert E. Lee, meanwhile, had wired Richmond, informing Davis that the enemy's "intention, I presume, is to turn our left, and probably get into our rear. . . . Our scattered condition favors their operations."[21]

Ahead of the blue-coated flanking column loomed the Wilderness of Spotsylvania, a seventy-square-mile swath of stunted trees, snarled undergrowth, ravines, and bogs fed by small streams, with only a scattering of open fields and a handful of dwellings. Narrow roads and old lumbering paths crisscrossed the tangled landscape. Two main roads, Orange Turnpike and Orange Plank Road, passed through the Wilderness, linking Fredericksburg to the Virginia Piedmont. The two roads merged for a distance of two miles before parting again at Chancellorsville, an imposing name for only a large brick house sitting in a seventy-acre clearing. An army caught within the confines of the Wilderness

would have its advantages in numbers and artillery negated by the fore-
bidding terrain.[22]

Toward the Wilderness, then, came the three Union corps, reaching Chancellorsville at mid-afternoon on April 30. Fifth Corps commander Major General George Meade argued for a continuation of the
march eastward to "get out of this Wilderness." Hooker's orders, however, had been to halt at Chancellorsville until the Second and Third
corps joined the column. The army commander and his staff arrived at
Chancellorsville that evening. He was exultant over the initial execution of his offensive. He had planned boldly, and the army had executed
it. After the war, Confederate artillerist Porter Alexander asserted, "On
the whole I think this plan was decidedly the best strategy conceived in
any of the campaigns ever set on foot against us."[23]

An aide with Stuart remembered April 30: "Things were lively in
the cavalry division that day. Staff and couriers were kept busy." With
orders from army headquarters "to ascertain the route of the enemy,"
Stuart had Fitz Lee's horsemen gnawing at the edges of the Union infantry ranks. The Rebels delayed part of the Federal column for two hours
in a minor clash at Wilderness Tavern. When Stuart learned that the
Yankees had reached Chancellorsville, he led Lee's troopers to Todd's
Tavern, located several miles southwest of Chancellorsville. Here, Lee's
men halted, encamping for the night.[24]

"Anxious to know what the commanding general desired me to do
further," as he stated in his report, Stuart decided to ride through the
night to army headquarters. With staff members, he started on Brock
Road toward Spotsylvania Court House. After proceeding a short distance, Stuart halted. "Things are not quite right up front," he remarked.
He sent majors Heros von Borcke and Lewis Terrell ahead as scouts.
The pair of Confederates soon encountered pickets of the 6th New
York. Firing a few pistol shots at the Yankees, von Borcke and Terrell
raced away, pursued by the Union cavalrymen. When the aides and the
oncoming New Yorkers appeared out of the moonlit night, Stuart and
his other officers bolted toward the rear, barely escaping capture.[25]

Stuart ordered forward Fitz Lee's weary troopers. The Confederates
advanced down the road, bagging the enemy pickets, and found the 6th
New York, under Lieutenant Colonel Duncan McVicar, in a field at the

house and shop of Hugh Alsop. The outnumbered New Yorkers repulsed
attacks of the 5th Virginia and then 3rd Virginia. McVicar ordered a
counterattack against the two Rebel regiments. In the swirling action
in the field and along the road, McVicar was killed, but his men pushed
the Rebels farther to the rear.[26]

By now, Thomas Munford's 2nd Virginia had arrived behind the
battered ranks of the other two regiments. The able Munford ordered
a charge, and his veterans shattered the New Yorkers' final line. The
Southerners chased the Federals toward Chancellorsville until members of the 1st Virginia mistakenly fired into Munford's column. While
Fitz Lee's Virginians bivouacked for the night near Spotsylvania Court
House, Stuart and a few staff officers continued on, arriving at army
headquarters at sunrise on May 1.[27]

By the time Stuart met with Robert E. Lee, the Confederate commander had readied the army to move against the Federals at Chancellorsville. The fifty-six-year-old general still suffered from the effects
of a serious illness that had afflicted him since March. Believed to be
either angina pectoris or possibly pericarditis, an inflammation of the
membrane encasing the heart, the disease had confined him to a room
for two weeks. On April 19, he had written to his wife, "I am feeble &
worthless & can do but little." Now, with his army between two wings
of Hooker's army, the physically weakened Lee chose boldness once
again.[28]

Lee explained his decision later: "The enemy in our front near
Fredericksburg continued inactive, and it was now apparent that the
main attack would be made upon our flank and rear. It was, therefore,
determined to leave sufficient troops to hold our lines, and with the
main body of the army to give battle to the approaching column." Lee
counted barely 56,000 officers and men in the ranks—James Longstreet
and two divisions remained in southeastern Virginia, collecting vital
supplies. Leaving Major General Jubal Early and 12,400 troops to hold
Marye's Heights behind Fredericksburg, Lee ordered his other divisions,
fewer than 44,000 men, toward Chancellorsville.[29]

Stonewall Jackson and the Second Corps marched west at dawn on
May 1. Riding ahead of his column, Jackson met with Major Generals
Richard Anderson and Lafayette McLaws, whose divisions, sent forward

earlier by Lee, manned a ridge roughly three miles east of Chancellorsville. Porter Alexander recounted that when he saw the van of Jackson's veterans appear, he knew, "We were not going to wait for the enemy to come & attack us in those lines, we were going out on the warpath after them."[30]

The Confederate infantry, supported by artillery, advanced along Orange Turnpike and Orange Plank Road against troops of the Union Fifth Corps, which had cleared the Wilderness. A fierce struggle ensued, but Jackson and the others pressed the assault. When Hooker learned of the situation, he ordered a withdrawal into the Wilderness. The Rebels pursued, gaining possession of a ridge located slightly more than a mile east of the Chancellorsville clearing. Hooker had reacted with caution, which belied his previous boastfulness. More critically, he had ceded the tactical initiative to an audacious opponent.[31]

Jeb Stuart spent the day at the front, often with Jackson. Munford's 2nd Virginia and six guns of the horse artillery were at hand. Fitz Lee's other regiments covered the infantry flanks, reconnoitering and sending back reports. Hooker's decision to send Stoneman and six brigades of cavalry on the raid allowed Stuart's horsemen to dominate the edges of the battlefield, probing Union lines and sealing off the roads. An early distinguished historian of this campaign, John Bigelow, concluded, "It was a capital mistake of Hooker's to detach the cavalry corps."[32]

Late in the afternoon, Brigadier General Ambrose R. Wright's Georgia brigade of Anderson's division joined Stuart at Catharine Furnace at a road intersection about one and a half miles southwest of the Chancellor house. Stuart informed Wright that the enemy were in force in the woods north of the furnace. While the Georgians moved to the attack, Stuart ordered Robert Beckham and four cannon forward in support of the infantrymen. The woods resounded with musketry and the discharges of artillery. The density of the trees restricted Beckham to firing one cannon at a time, but his shots brought a furious response from ten Union gun crews. "I do not think that men have been often under a hotter fire than that to which we were here exposed," stated Beckham.[33]

During the fighting, Jackson and a staff officer reined up. He, Stuart, and their aides walked to the crest of a knoll to view the Federal lines. When Union artillery shells began exploding close to the group, Stuart shouted to his friend, "General Jackson, we must move from here!" As they descended from the knoll, another artillery round burst above them, with a piece of it striking one of Stuart's adjutant general Channing Price's legs. At first, Price dismissed the wound as slight and mounted his horse. He rode only a few paces before falling from the saddle. Fellow staff officers took him south to the brick home of Charles and Evelina Wellford.[34]

The iron shard had struck Price behind the knee, severing an artery. Remarkably, if not inexplicably, no one on the staff had a tourniquet that could have stanched the flow of blood. As the twenty-year-old's condition worsened, he talked incoherently. Stuart came to the house and learned that the wound was mortal. He stood beside Price, held the aide's head tenderly in his hands, and cried. Duty called him away before the end. Dr. Beverley Tucker Lacy, Jackson's chaplain, performed last rites. The cavalry's chief of staff died minutes before midnight. Fellow staff officer William Blackford called him "the best Adjutant General I ever saw."[35]

Ten days later, Stuart wrote to Price's mother. "Let me share with you the deep grief for the fate of your dear boy, whose loss to me is scarcely less than to you," he began the letter. He assured her, "As an Adjutant General he had no superior, and his reputation as an able and efficient staff officer had already spread through the army." "I have no hesitancy in saying," Stuart continued, "no one about me could have been less spared, and I miss him hourly." He had ordered his staff to wear mourning badges for thirty days. "Channing's place," he ended it, "can never be filled."[36]

The duty that had pulled Stuart away from the Wellford house was evidently a dispatch from Fitz Lee. He rode to the intersection of Furnace Road and Orange Plank Road, where the commanding general and Jackson were meeting. The two generals had been discussing plans for the next day. Jackson believed that Hooker would retreat across the river during the night; Lee doubted it. Lee had conducted a personal reconnaissance, concluding that assaults on the Union center and left flank would be costly and uncertain of success.[37]

Stuart, however, brought promising information. Fitz Lee's cavalrymen had discovered that Hooker's right flank, extending along Orange Turnpike, was unsecured by any terrain feature and vulnerable to an attack. The army commander asked Stuart if he knew whether a road network existed that would allow for a broad turning movement beyond the enemy's flank. He did not know, Stuart answered, but he would find out. Remounting, Stuart rode back up Furnace Road.[38]

Details had to be finalized, but Lee had decided upon perhaps the boldest of his gambles. He had divided his army once, now he would divide it again in front of a numerically superior foe. He told Jackson, "We must attack on our left as soon as practicable." With only a few hours left before down, Lee and Jackson lay dawn to sleep amid a grove of pine trees.[39]

Stuart returned to the Wellford house, where his staff had encamped. Undoubtedly, he sent out riders to examine the roads that cut through the Wilderness. Evelina Wellford stated in a letter that the general and his aides "slept under the trees in the yard and seemed to have a good time." If her observation were accurate, the mood at headquarters was surprising considering the death of Channing Price.[40]

At some point during the night or the next morning, Stuart named Major Henry McClellan to succeed Price as adjutant general. A native of Philadelphia, Pennsylvania, and a cousin of Union general George McClellan, the twenty-two-year-old McClellan had been a private tutor in Virginia when the war began. Enlisting as a private in the 3rd Virginia, he was appointed regimental adjutant in May 1862. Fitz Lee recommended him to Stuart, writing that he "will make an excellent aide." McClellan joined the staff on April 20. When Stuart asked for his appointment, he cited as reasons, "the signal gallantry displayed by him in the field and his efficiency and zealous devotion to duty as a Staff Officer."[41]

Before sunrise on May 2, Jedediah Hotchkiss, Jackson's topographical engineer, came to the Wellford house. He spoke with Stuart and Charles Wellford and learned from them that a route led to the Union right flank and rear. Returning to army headquarters, Hotchkiss traced the roads on a map to Lee and Jackson, who were seated on discarded "Yankee Cracker boxes."[42]

In the discussion, Lee inquired, "General Jackson, what do you propose to do?" Pointing to the route marked by Hotchkiss, Jackson answered, "Go around here."

"What do you propose to make this movement with?" asked Lee.

"With my whole corps," came the response—three divisions and artillery, 28,000 officers and men.

The audacious Lee was taken aback. "What will you leave me?"

"The divisions of Anderson and McLaws," replied Jackson.

The commanding general hesitated, knowing that he would have fewer than 16,000 troops to demonstrate against the Union center. "Well, go on," Lee said, adding that Stuart's cavalry would lead the march and cover the column's flank. If the Yankees detected and understood the import of Jackson's movement, the Confederate army faced destruction.[43]

The Second Corps stepped off about 7:30 A.M. on May 2. The 2nd Virginia led the column, while the other mounted regiments screened the route. Within an hour, the Federals sighted the marchers. When the information reached army headquarters, Hooker alerted commanders to push forward skirmishers and to take protective measures. As additional reports filtered to the Chancellor house, Hooker and others thought that Lee was retreating. An advance by some Union troops resulted in a clash at Catharine Furnace, but it did not halt the movement.[44]

The march became an ordeal for the men. "It was through brushes swamps and hills we marched in the heat of the day," complained a veteran in a subsequent letter, "I thought that he [Jackson] would kill all of us before we would get to the enemy. Men laid by the bushey rode side." Late in the afternoon, Munford's cavalrymen turned the column onto Orange Turnpike, moving east. Stuart rode most of the miles with Jackson and a coterie of officers near the head of the column before joining Munford at the front. He sent a message back to Jackson, writing, "there seem to be few of the enemy about." Stuart and his aides watched as the infantrymen entered the turnpike, continued on about a mile, and filed into battle ranks on a low, wooded ridge. When completed, the line stretched for a mile on both sides of the roadbed, with additional ranks aligned to the rear.[45]

It was about 5:30 P.M. when Jackson turned to Brigadier General Robert E. Rodes, commander of the leading division, and said, "You can go forward then." A pair of Robert Beckham's horse artillery guns, under Stuart's orders, rolled forward on the turnpike with the infantry. Through the forest the Rebels strode in one of the conflict's greatest assaults. They cleared the woodline, "yelling like devils let loose." Like a terrible wind, volleys swept over the surprised troops, members of the Union Eleventh Corps. Despite warnings from Hooker's headquarters, the corps commander, Major General Oliver Otis Howard, Stuart's old academy friend, had done virtually nothing to prepare his defenses.[46]

Although many men in the Eleventh Corps—known in the army as the "damned Dutch" because of its German members—fled in a panic, some regiments and gun crews fought valiantly against Jackson's veterans until outflanked. Additional Union batteries and troops from the Third and Twelfth corps blunted the Rebel tide, but it had been a stunning Confederate success. Disorganization in the Southern ranks and nightfall halted further advances. Jackson's attack inflicted more than 2,400 casualties, captured nine cannon, and seized a mile and a half of enemy fieldworks along the Turnpike and Plank roads. Hooker's right flank had collapsed under an avalanche of gray-coated soldiers.[47]

Stuart and his staff had followed the attackers on the turnpike. The 2nd Virginia moved forward through the difficult terrain on the infantry's left flank. It was after dark when Stuart requested permission from Jackson to take the cavalry and an infantry regiment to secure Ely's Ford Road, a possible retreat route for the Federals. Jackson approved, and Stuart rode away from his friend. Sporadic gunfire flashed and resounded between the opposing lines. Night in the Wilderness could be a haunting time.[48]

Stuart took with him the 1st Virginia and 16th North Carolina Infantry. When the road had been secured, Stuart and his staff officers rested in a nearby ravine. Sometime before midnight, Captain Richard H. T. Adams, Major General A. P. Hill's signal officer, located the group. Adams handed Stuart a message, which he read with aid of a candle. Both Jackson and Hill had been wounded, the note stated, and Stuart was ordered to assume command of the Second Corps. After telling von Borcke to remain behind and to act in his stead, Stuart mounted and rode away at "topmost speed." Whether during the ride he learned the details of what had befallen his friend and Powell Hill is unknown.[49]

After the fighting had subsided, Jackson decided to conduct a personal reconnaissance of the Union line. With an escort of eight officers and men, Jackson followed Orange Plank Road toward the front; Hill and another group trailed well behind. Earlier in the afternoon, Stuart had sent Private David Kyle, a prewar resident of the region, to Jackson as a guide. Now, in the darkness, Kyle led the general and his party onto Mountain Road, a narrow trace through the woods and parallel to the Plank Road. The mounted party passed beyond the Confederate infantry line. After listening a few minutes to voices from the Union works, two hundred to three hundred yards away, the mounted Southerners turned back.[50]

For the soldiers in the opposing lines, it was a difficult night. Times of stillness occurred only to be shattered by outbursts of gunfire. As Jackson proceeded rearward, a single rifle shot ignited a swelling round of volleys. When the musketry reached the 18th North Carolina Infantry, lying directly in front of Jackson, its members triggered a blast into the woods. Three smoothbore balls struck Jackson—one in the right hand and two in the left arm. In Hill's group on Orange Plank Road farther to the rear, the gunfire mortally wounded one of Hill's aides and killed Captain James Keith Boswell of Jackson's staff.[51]

Hill was untouched by the musketry and rode to Jackson's assistance. He and Jackson had had a difficult relationship, but had seemed to have resolved their differences during the preceding weeks. Hill and a few officers collected a litter party, which carried Jackson to the rear. The musketry exchanges, however, drew artillery fire from Union batteries. A piece of a shell struck Hill in the leg, disabling him. Hill then summoned Stuart to take command of the corps.[52]

"I did not like Genl Stuart & did not want to see him command that corps," wrote Major William H. Palmer, Hill's chief of staff, after the war. But Palmer admitted, "I think it was wise in that emergency after Hill to select Stuart for the command. . . . Stuart was well known in our corps." In his report, Robert Rodes, Hill's senior division commander and successor by rank in the corps, stated that he yielded command to Stuart, "not because I thought him entitled to it," but because he believed it had been the desire of Jackson and Hill. A Second Corps staff officer, who knew Rodes well, argued, "Rodes distrusted his ability to take command," attributing this to the general's "modesty."[53]

When Stuart reached Orange Plank Road in the early minutes of May 3, he found Jackson's chief of staff, Major Alexander "Sandie" Pendleton. Palmer alleged that Pendleton shared his personal dislike of the cavalry commander. Captain Henry Kyd Douglas, writing years later, stated, "Personally I never liked or admired Stuart & still believe he was vain & pretentious & greatly overrated as a soldier." But, added Douglas, "Genl Stuarts reputation in the corps then was, in some respects only second to Jacksons. Jackson had great admiration for him as a soldier . . . [and] knew the men of his corps would have more confidence in him than any man who would take his place." Stuart was "the best man" at the time.[54]

Stuart sent Pendleton to his wounded friend to learn if Jackson had any instructions for him. He also met with Porter Alexander and learned that the corps's chief of artillery, Colonel Stapleton Crutchfield, had been wounded. Stuart assigned Alexander to command of the artillery and ordered him to conduct a reconnaissance. Knowing nothing himself of the deployment of the Confederate units, Stuart rode to the front through the woods. Under daunting circumstances, he managed to restore some order in the ranks and to shift units.[55]

Pendleton rejoined Stuart, who had set up temporary headquarters along Orange Plank Road. Pendleton had located his commander at the corps hospital near Wilderness Tavern. Jackson was sleeping after the amputation of his left arm by Dr. Hunter McGuire. The staff officer implored McGuire to allow him to speak to the general. The surgeon refused until Jackson awoke while being examined. Describing the situation at the front, Pendleton asked if Jackson had any orders for Stuart. "I don't know, I can't tell; say to General Stuart he must do what he thinks best," the wounded general replied weakly.[56]

Alexander came back before dawn from his reconnaissance and described for Stuart the tactical importance of Hazel Grove. An elevated, open plateau, extending for five hundred yards, Hazel Grove anchored the southern end of the Union line astride Orange Plank Road and dominated the surrounding terrain. Alexander wrote later

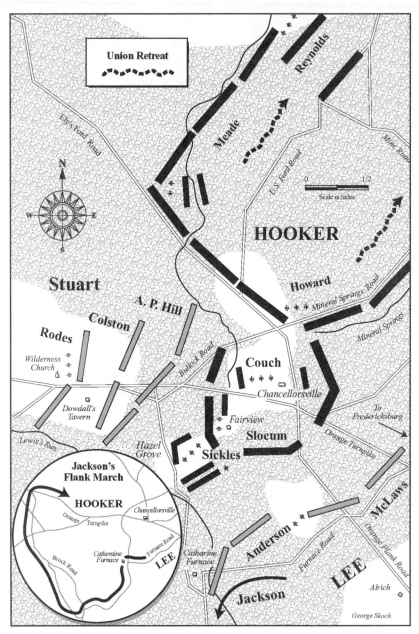

Battle of Chancellorsville

that he "convinced" Stuart that Hazel Grove was the key to this section of the battlefield.[57]

Sometime about four o'clock in the morning, Stuart received the first of two messages from Robert E. Lee. A staff officer had informed Lee of Jackson's and Hill's wounding and of Stuart's temporary assignment to corps command. When Lee heard the sobering news, he "was very much distressed and said he would rather a thousand times it had been himself" than Jackson. Hotchkiss arrived later at army headquarters and reported on Jackson's condition. Lee, said the engineer, "did not wish to converse about it."[58]

In the first dispatch, dated 3:00 A.M., Lee wrote: "It is necessary that the glorious victory thus far achieved be prosecuted with the utmost vigor, and the enemy given no time to rally. As soon, therefore, as it is possible, they must be pressed, so that we can unite the two wings of the army." "Let nothing," continued the message, "delay the completion of the plan of driving the enemy from his rear and from his positions." Lee's concern for the gap between the Second Corps and Anderson's and McLaws's divisions was manifest as he prepared a second dispatch a half-hour later. In it, he repeated the need to "unite both wings of the army," urging Stuart to "proceed vigorously."[59]

Stuart and members of the corps awaited daylight. He had stacked the divisions in three lines—from front to rear, Brigadier General Henry Heth's, replacing Hill in command of the Light Division; Brigadier General Raleigh E. Colston's Stonewall Division; and Robert Rodes's Georgians, North Carolinians, and Alabamians. Heth's ranks lay about five hundred to seven hundred yards from the Federal works. The Yankees, officers and men of the Third and Twelfth corps, had spent the night felling trees, digging a trench, and piling logs and dirt to the height of three feet. They cleared the ground in front of the works, lacing it with abatis. The Union position extended from Hazel Grove north to beyond Orange Plank Road. Additional entrenchments scarred the ground farther to the rear.[60]

The Confederates' task was starkly simple—step forward in headlong attacks through dense woods and across gnarled ground against veteran foes behind earthworks. The nature of the terrain precluded complicated tactics and strained the efforts of commanders to maintain coordination between the attacking units. It was to be a bloody, grim slugging match. "Whichever side displayed more tenacity," historian Earl Hess has written, "would win a contest like this." But, as a North Carolina lieutenant affirmed, "The assault had to be made."[61]

Before daybreak, opposing skirmishers, exchanging gunfire, presaged the coming onslaught. The sun brought with it "a beautiful morning," a Sabbath. "It was as calm as could be and it did look like a pity to disturb its hallowed name," remembered a Southerner, "but such is war. It was so still; not a bit of wind, but soft and warm." A South Carolinian described it "as beautiful and bright a day as one could desire." Only the stench from yesterday's fallen fouled the air. It would become worse.[62]

Stuart ordered forward Heth's troops. The watchword was, Stuart told them, "Charge, and remember Jackson." Then it began. "The scene was terrific," exclaimed a North Carolinian, "it seemed as if heaven and earth were coming together." When the Union batteries opened fire, "it was absolutely deafening," recounted an Alabama major, "& the limbs from the trees fell as fast as if axemen were at work." For two hours the fighting raged as each of the three Confederate divisions entered the struggle. It was the worst Chancellorsville had to offer with the opposing ranks separated at times by only the log breastworks.[63]

Stuart had a horse killed from under him during the combat's initial thirty minutes. He borrowed a bay named Josh from a courier and rode him. But he was in his element. "In a charge," asserted John Esten Cooke, "Stuart seemed on fire." Lieutenant Frank Robertson of his staff declared: "He rode the lines with flashing eyes and heroic courage, exhorting, commanding, inspiring. He seemed tireless, he seemed everywhere. . . . He noticed the passage of shot and shell with absolute indifference."[64]

Wearing a new blue uniform coat, with a red artillery sash around his waist, Stuart indeed "seemed everywhere." The woods limited his range of vision, so he roamed along the fringes of the firing lines. His aides and couriers were constantly on the move, delivering orders. He upbraided division commander Colston for some mistake, changed the attack path of a brigade, and rallied the Stonewall Brigade after a repulse, leading the Virginians with a shout "for the Old Stonewall to follow." Twice he directed the charge of the 28th North Carolina Infantry. When a young artillery officer had found the range of the enemy, Stuart yelled above the din: "You've got it, kid! Give it to them!"[65]

Accounts testify to Stuart's inspirational leadership during the fighting. He rode along the ranks singing "Old Joe Hooker, won't you come out' the Wilderness—Come out' the Wilderness." Men joined him in the verses as they loaded and fired. "The personal bearing of Stuart," attested Henry McClellan, "created great enthusiasm among the troops." Porter Alexander proclaimed, "There can be no doubt that his personal conduct had great influence in sustaining the courage of the men."[66]

A cavalry officer claimed that Stuart possessed a "self-contained and buoyant manner in the presence of the greatest danger," which endeared him to the men. On this morning, when men stepped into hell's grasp, his bearing amid the fury helped to steel them. Those who saw him during the fighting afterward used descriptions of him such as "his usual happy manner," and "with reckless valor." His academy classmate and friend William Dorsey Pender, now a brigade commander with Heth, averred to his wife, "right noble did Stuart do."[67]

After two hours of grievous combat the fortunes on the battlefield shifted dramatically in favor of the Confederates. Union commander Joseph Hooker committed a critical error by ordering his blue-coated defenders to abandon Hazel Grove in a consolidation of their lines. When Stuart learned of the withdrawal, he sent Alexander and thirty cannon onto the plateau. Within minutes of unlimbering on the high ground, Alexander's gun crews began, as he said, "to shake the Federals' lines." The artillery fire blasted enemy batteries on Fairview to the northeast and rained down upon the Chancellorsville clearing. One round struck a porch pillar on the Chancellor house, splitting it and knocking Hooker unconscious for at least thirty minutes.[68]

Stuart ordered the battered ranks of the Second Corps and Richard Anderson's division on the right forward. The Confederates surged over the final line of Union works, swept across the crest of Fairview, and rushed forward toward Chancellorsville. Stuart rode close behind the ranks shouting: "Go forward boys! We have them running, and we'll keep them at it!" The Rebel momentum stalled finally against Union reserves, but the Southerners stood amid the wreckage around the Chancellor house.[69]

Before long Lee and Stuart approached the clearing, riding together on Orange Plank Road. Officers and men removed the dead and wounded from the road ahead of the generals. Soldiers, including wounded, removed their hats as they passed. Lee and Stuart returned the salutes. When they reached the Chancellor house, the troops cheered, their voices rising above the ongoing clamor of gunfire. "I thought that it must have been such a scene that men in ancient days rose to the dignity of gods," wrote Major Charles Marshall of Lee's staff. Against formidable odds, Lee and his army had achieved perhaps his greatest tactical victory.[70]

A Confederate staff officer wrote several days later: "How our men ever drove them out of such fortifications as they had is a mystery to me. The Yankee army ought to be ashamed of itself." The Union resistance had been fierce, however, until the withdrawal from Hazel Grove. The day's casualties attested to the intensity of the struggle—more than 17,000, shared almost equally by both armies. The percentage of losses among several Southern units exceeded one-fourth their numbers. "The Rebels fought desperately," a Yankee professed. "They evidently made up their minds to conquer or die and die they did."[71]

The leadership of Stuart and his subordinate commanders and the valor and spirit of the men in the ranks had prevailed, uniting the wings of the army and staving off a possible disaster. In a postwar letter Porter Alexander assessed Stuart's generalship: "Altogether, I do not think there was a more brilliant thing done in the war than Stuart's extricating that command from the extremely critical position in which he found it as promptly and as boldly as he did. . . . But Stuart never seemed to hesitate or to doubt for one moment that he could just crash his way wherever he chose to strike." Indeed, May 3, 1863, had been Stuart's finest day as a Confederate officer.[72]

While the Confederate forces achieved a victory at Chancellorsville, Major General John Sedgwick's Union Sixth Corps wrenched Marye's Heights at Fredericksburg from its defenders. From there, Sedgwick's troops moved west and engaged Rebel units at Salem Church, three miles east of Chancellorsville. On May 4, Lee shifted more troops against Sedgwick and assumed personal direction of the operations. Stuart was left in command of half of the army at Chancellorsville. The

Rebels constructed fieldworks and blocked the roads. After dark, Stuart wrote to Lee that the enemy was "still fortifying and chopping."[73]

Early on May 5, Stuart sent a dispatch to Lee, proposing an assault on the Union lines. Lee replied at 8:15 A.M.: "I do not know the circumstances which induce your wish to attack the enemy. With your present strength as reported in field returns, it might be beyond us. If the Enemy is recrossing the Rappk or attempting to do so, or if other circumstances warrant the attack, you can withdraw Heth. If you have to storm entrenchments, unless the Enemy can be driven from them by cannon, I cannot recommend an attack except under very favorable circumstances."[74]

Lee sent another message during the morning, instructing Stuart to have his batteries fire on the enemy for "several hours." "If you can attack to advantage," added Lee, "you can do so." By then, he had been informed that Sedgwick's command had withdrawn across the Rappahannock at Banks's Ford during the night. Anderson's and McLaws's divisions began their return march to Chancellorsville, and Early's troops to Marye's Heights. A heavy rain began falling during the afternoon, and shielded by it and darkness, the Union forces in front of Stuart recrossed the river at U.S. Ford during the night of May 5–6. Nearly 31,000 Northern and Southern men had been killed, wounded, or captured during the campaign.[75]

On the morning of May 6, Lee met with Stuart and Hill, the latter now fit to resume command. The troops were ordered back to their old camps, and Lee issued a special order, appointing Hill to temporary command of the Second Corps and Stuart back to the cavalry. There is no evidence that Lee contemplated keeping Stuart with Jackson's corps. It must be surmised that Lee was unwilling to lose Stuart's unmatched talents as a cavalry commander. Furthermore, at the time Lee had been told that Jackson's condition was improving. He probably expected him to return to duty when he had recovered.[76]

"I always thought it an injustice to Stuart," Porter Alexander contended in a postwar letter, "and a loss to the army he was not from the moment *continued in command of Jackson's corps.* He had won the right to it. I believe he had all of Jackson's genius and dash and originality, without that eccentricity of character which sometimes led to disappointment. . . . That Sunday morning's action [on May 3] ought to rank with whatever else of special brilliancy can be found in the annals of the Army of Northern Virginia."[77]

Lee was generous in his praise of Stuart in his report, which was prepared months later. The cavalry commander, stated Lee, "ably discharged the difficult and responsible duties which he was thus unexpectedly called to perform. . . . General Stuart exhibited great energy, promptness, and intelligence." In turn, Hill commended Stuart's performance, writing, "with indomitable energy he surmounted all difficulties and achieved a glorious result."[78]

Late in the day on May 7, Stuart joined Rooney Lee's regiments west of Chancellorsville. For more than a week, Lee's horsemen had harassed George Stoneman's column of 7,400 Union troopers. Joseph Hooker expected much from this raid, but Stoneman's force inflicted only slight damage to railroads, burned some supply wagons, and had little effect on Lee's operations at Chancellorsville. The Yankees crossed the Rappahannock during the night of May 7–8. Stuart abandoned the pursuit and led Rooney Lee's command to Orange Court House.[79]

While at Orange Court House on May 8, Stuart prepared a preliminary report on cavalry operations in the Chancellorsville Campaign. In it, he expressed the belief that the cavalry could have prevented Stoneman's raid, except for the "entire inadequacy in numbers" in his division. "With Cmdg. Genl, who is aware of all the facts, we are content to rest our vindication—if the pursuit of the plain path of duty needs vindication."[80]

Stuart wrote a brief letter to Lee the next day. The letter has not been found, but from Lee's reply to it, Stuart apparently thought that his performance at Chancellorsville merited more public commendation. "As regards the closing remarks of your note," Lee answered, "I am at a loss to understand their reference or to know what has given rise to them. In the management of the difficult operations at Chancellorsville, which you so promptly undertook and creditably performed, I saw no errors to correct, nor has there been a fitting opportunity to commend your conduct. I prefer your acts to speak for themselves, nor does your character or reputation require bolstering by out-of-place expression of my opinions." Lee's words were a rebuke to Stuart's ambition and need for acclaim.[81]

At the end of the letter, Lee wrote: "I regret to inform you that the great and good Jackson is no more. He died yesterday at 3:15 P.M., of pneumonia, calm, serene, and happy. May his spirit pervade our whole army; our country will then be secure." The Confederate hero's condition had worsened during the previous days, the pneumonia draining away his strength. With his wife, Mary Anna, by his side, he succumbed, as he had wished, on a Sabbath, saying before the passage, "Let us cross over the river, and rest under the shade of the trees."[82]

First John Pelham, then Channing Price, now Stuart had lost "the dearest friend I had." Theirs had been a singular, if not unique, friendship among the senior officers of the army. Despite their quite different personalities, the bond between them had been affectionate and deep. They had shared a devotion to the cause and a profound religious faith. "His example, his Christian and soldiery virtue," Stuart said of his friend, "are a precious legacy to his countrymen and to the world."[83]

Stuart told his staff that Jackson's death "is a national calamity." Lee confided to his son, "I do not know how to replace him." Jackson's remains were laid in state in the Virginia capitol and then carried to Lexington, where he was buried on May 15. Five days later, Jedediah Hotchkiss admitted to his wife, "everything wears an altered and lonely look" without Jackson at the head of the Second Corps. His memory, it seemed, never left the infantry.[84]

In time, Stuart wrote a sympathy note to Mary Anna Jackson. She replied on August 1: "Your kind words of sympathy for me, & your tribute of admiration to my noble Husband were warmly appreciated. I need not assure you of which you already know, that your friendship & admiration were cordially reciprocated by him. I have frequently heard him speak of Gen'l Stuart as one of his warm personal friends, & also express admiration for your Soldierly qualities."[85]

Chapter Twelve

"The Hardest Cavalry Fight"

R OBERT E. LEE, thought a clerk at the War Department in
Richmond, "looked thinner, and a little pale" when the general
visited on May 15, 1863. The army commander had arrived in the capital the day before and would stay until May 18, sequestered much of the
time in meetings with President Jefferson Davis and cabinet members.
Although Chancellorsville had been a tactically brilliant victory, it had
not resulted in the decisive defeat of the Union army that Lee sought.
He knew that with time the Yankees would advance once more against
his army.[1]

Lee had come to the city with a bold proposal. The recent victory
had given him the strategic initiative in the region, and he wanted to
exploit it by carrying the war beyond the Potomac into Pennsylvania.
In the meetings with Davis and the department heads, Lee argued that
such an offensive would garner vital supplies, spare Virginia for a time
from the conflict's ravages, and disrupt enemy campaign plans for the
summer. After much discussion, the president and cabinet approved the
operation. Secretary of War James A. Seddon confided later that Lee's
opinion "naturally had great effect in the decisions of the Executive."[2]

Upon his return to the army, Lee began preparations for the movement. He wrote to Davis on May 20: "I have for the past year felt that

the corps of the army were too large for one commander. Nothing prevented my proposing to you to reduce their size and increase their number but my inability to recommend commanders." With the death of Stonewall Jackson, Lee suggested that the infantry be reorganized into three corps instead of the present two. The plan necessitated a reshuffling of divisions and brigades, with each corps consisting of three divisions.[3]

A rumor or "a great deal of talk" persisted that Jeb Stuart would replace Jackson. Stuart believed otherwise, telling Flora that such speculation was "I think without any foundation in fact." At cavalry headquarters, a story circulated that on his deathbed Jackson expressed a desire that his friend should succeed him in command of the Second Corps. When told of this, Stuart allegedly remarked, "I would rather know that Jackson said that, than have the appointment."[4]

As Stuart surmised, it was not to be. Instead, Lee recommended Richard S. Ewell, who had had a leg amputated from a wound at Second Manassas, as Jackson's successor, and A. P. "Powell" Hill as commander of the newly created Third Corps. Each man was promoted to lieutenant general. Both Ewell and Hill were Virginians, which rekindled "no little discontent," in the words of First Corps commander James Longstreet, a non-Virginian. Although a majority of the regiments hailed from outside the Old Dominion, Virginians dominated the army's senior leadership at corps and division levels. It was a resentment similar to that expressed by Wade Hampton against Stuart and his preference for fellow Virginians.[5]

If Lee were to undertake an offensive strike into Pennsylvania, he had to increase the size of Stuart's command. The problems that had plagued the cavalry during the winter had persisted to some extent into the spring. Hundreds of men remained at home on horse details, their efforts to secure another mount hampered by the steeply rising price of horseflesh. Regimental officers were absent on recruiting duty. While horses fed on spring grasses, shortages of forage continued. Lieutenant Robert Hubard, Jr., of the 3rd Virginia blamed government quartermaster and commissary officers for the lack of grain, calling them "the white livered sons of bitches."[6]

Lee and Stuart tried to address the issues. Lee asked the administration to consider the formation of a second cavalry division and sent Stuart to Richmond to plead the case. When this effort brought no results, Lee refused to add new brigades to the cavalry division before increasing the strengths of the current ones. Interestingly, officers of the 1st, 4th, and 5th Texas Infantry, the heart of the Texas Brigade, petitioned the War Department to be converted into mounted regiments. Their request went unheeded.[7]

In the end, Lee drew upon what he could to augment Stuart's force. From North Carolina, he secured the transfer of two of Beverly Robertson's five regiments, the 4th and 5th North Carolina. Robertson came to Virginia with the pair of regiments although Lee and Stuart wished otherwise. The army commander ordered Brigadier Albert G. Jenkins and his small brigade, operating in western Virginia, to relieve Grumble Jones's troopers in the Shenandoah Valley. Lee then directed Jones to cross the Blue Ridge "by easy marches" and to join Stuart.[8]

The possibility of Jones serving with Stuart again moved the latter to suggest that the brigadier be assigned to the Stonewall Brigade, whose commander had been so recently killed at Chancellorsville. Lee answered, "I am perfectly willing to transfer him [Jones] . . . if he desires it; but if he does not I know of no act of his to justify my doing so." Well aware of the personal animosity between the two men, Lee advised Stuart, "Do not let your judgment be warped."[9]

Lee's orders to leave the Valley were as unwelcome to Jones as they were to Stuart. Historian Edwin Coddington has contended that Jones "had a hatred for Stuart which bordered on the pathological." A day after he received Lee's dispatch, Jones wrote to Secretary of War Seddon: "I most especially tender my resignation as Brigadier General in the P.A.C.S. [Provisional Army of the Confederate States]. My reason for so doing is my conviction that where I am now ordered my services cannot be serviceable to my country. Other reasons not necessary to mention exist. Being of conscript age I will not escape service." Seddon apparently filed the letter away.[10]

Stuart, meanwhile, readied the cavalry for the forthcoming campaign. Hampton's brigade joined Fitz Lee's and Rooney Lee's in Culpeper County. Stuart increased drills and inspections and had the men refurbish their arms and equipment. "A vast amount of 'spit and polish,'" complained a Georgian. He also admonished officers to use the "utmost diligence . . . to preserve the Horses of this Command, as the success of the summer campaign depends much upon their good condition and efficiency."[11]

The three brigades staged reviews on May 20 and 22. At both affairs, generals and officers joined civilians in watching the horsemen conduct drills and participate in a sham battle. An officer in the 3rd Virginia called the second review "the most magnificent sight I ever witnessed." An infantryman watching the cavalry speculated, "it may prove that there is going to be a wild promiscuous ride by 'our Jeb,' in retaliation for what Stoneman has done." A Virginian repeated the rumor of "a ride round in Pennsylvania."[12]

Flora Stuart and Jimmie visited briefly in Culpeper County, probably leaving after the reviews. When they had gone, Stuart wrote to her. A newspaperman had come to headquarters, he informed her, and sought permission to accompany the cavalry during its operations. "I *politely* declined," Stuart recounted, "he returns tomorrow with a *flea in his ear*. Look to see me *abused* for it." "You know," he went on, "I make *duty* paramount to everything."[13]

By early June, Stuart counted more than ten thousand officers and men in five brigades and five batteries of horse artillery in Culpeper County. On June 3, elements of Lee's army marched away from their lines at Fredericksburg, moving up the Rappahannock River. Two weeks before, Lee declared in a letter to one of his generals: "I agree with you in believing that our army would be invincible if it could be properly organized and officered. There never were such men in an army before. They will go anywhere and do anything if properly led."[14]

As the van of the infantry column reached Culpeper Court House on June 4, special trains of the Orange & Alexandria Railroad, brimming with passengers, rolled into the town. Stuart planned to hold a cavalry review the next day and had spread the news as far south as Charlottesville. He invited former Secretary of War George Randolph as his special guest. That night, with many women in attendance for the review, Stuart and the officers held a ball in the courthouse. It was, reported a newspaper correspondent, a "gay and dazzling scene, illuminated by floods of light from numerous chandeliers."[15]

The crowd gathered throughout the next morning on a plain north of the town and about a mile southwest of Brandy Station. Stuart reveled in such events. The pageantry of war stirred his soul and affirmed his status as a Confederate hero. Being surrounded, as he was on this day, by an "immense concourse of ladies" fueled his vanity. He wore, said an eyewitness, a "short grey jacket, wide-brimmed whitish hat with long black plume." An artilleryman thought, "He is the prettiest and most graceful rider I ever saw."[16]

Mounted on "his big bay," Stuart rode past the massed regiments, inspecting the serried ranks. His staff officers or "bodyguard," according to a gunner, accompanied him. Returning to a knoll, the general and aides joined the spectators. Three bands played music as Major Robert Beckham's batteries led the martial procession. Behind them came the cavalry in columns of squadrons, first at a walk, then a trot, and finally at a gallop. Dust billowed and rolled across the plain. The review ended with cannon booming and the horsemen charging.[17]

Writing in his diary, a Virginia artilleryman enthused about the review, "It is one of the most sublime scenes I ever witnessed." A newspaperman described the parade of batteries and mounted regiments as "a beautiful sight," while stating, "I have no patience with such tomfooleries." He called Stuart "the Prince of showy men" and his aides, "a collection of pretty men, dressed in their best." He reported that Stuart held another ball that night for the "young and thoughtless beauties," who had attended the review.[18]

Stuart had invited the commanding general to the review, but Lee begged off, explaining, "there is so much work to be done here." When Lee arrived at Culpeper Court House, he agreed to review the cavalry, wanting to observe for himself the condition of the men and horses. Stuart's men grumbled, however, at the order to clean and to polish their equipment for a second display. Stuart held it on the same site of the previous review, at Auburn, the farm of John Minor Botts, an avowed Unionist. Lee, Longstreet, Ewell, other generals, and a cloud of staff officers joined another crowd of civilians on June 8.[19]

Fitz Lee had invited Major General John B. Hood and "any of his people" to the event. Hood arrived with ten thousand hardened veterans in his infantry division. Infantrymen scoffed at the idea that their comrades on horseback performed difficult and dangerous service. They dubbed the cavalrymen "Grub scout," "Kitchen ranger," "Bomb Proof," "Buttermilk spies," and "Loonies." Often when horsemen passed a column of foot soldiers, a shout went up, "Where's your mule?" On this day, as Stuart's troopers rode by the infantry, one of them said, "Wouldn't we clean them out, if old Hood would only let us loose on 'em." A Georgia cavalryman complained later that Hood's men were "hardly the most appreciative audience."[20]

Lee and his staff, accompanied by Stuart, rode rapidly past the lines of horsemen, as the officers and men saluted with their sabers. Lee and the assemblage of officers watched from the knoll while the ranks of troopers wheeled into a column of squadrons. When the van of the cavalry approached the knoll, Stuart rode in front. According to one of his men, he "came out with his bridle reins and everything about him wreathed with flowers." At one point, Grumble Jones's brigade failed to advance. Stuart sent an aide to the brigadier, who was lying on the ground and "apparently oblivious of everything that was going on." The staff officer delivered Stuart's message, and Jones, remembered the aide, "blazed all sorts of language at me."[21]

Unlike the previous review, the cavalry did not stage a mounted charge nor did the artillerists fire their cannon. Stuart's engineer, Captain William Blackford, remembered it as "the most magnificent sight I ever witnessed." Writing the day of the review, Lee told his wife: "It was a splendid sight. The men and horses looked well. They have recuperated since last fall. Stuart was in all his glory."[22]

At the time of the June 8 review, Lee had concentrated Ewell's three divisions of the Second Corps and two of Longstreet's First Corps divisions in Culpeper County. Powell Hill's Third Corps troops still manned fieldworks at Fredericksburg. The halt in Culpeper was only a pause in the initial leg of the march northward. When the advance resumed, Ewell's corps was to lead the movement, with Stuart's cavalry preceding and screening the infantry columns. Stuart had orders to start on June 9.[23]

After the review, the five cavalry brigades returned to their widely dispersed campsites. Stuart scattered them for grazing the horses and in preparation for the movement. Robertson's pair of North Carolina regiments remained on the Botts farm. To the southeast, Hampton's brigade lay encamped between Brandy Station and Stevensburg. Jones's brigade covered Beverly Ford on the Rappahannock, resting near St. James church, two miles from the river. Two miles north and west of the church, at Welford's Ford on the Hazel River, Rooney Lee had his five regiments. Across the Hazel River and eight miles from Brandy Station were Fitz Lee's Virginians. Lee was confined to a bed with "inflammatory rheumatism," and Thomas Munford of the 2nd Virginia commanded the brigade in his absence. Beckham's horse artillery crews were bivouacked between St. James church and Beverly Ford. At the time, a gunner with Beckham contended that the artillery "has been permitted to roost a little too near the lion's den."[24]

Stuart had his headquarters in the yard of Henry Miller's home, Fleetwood. The Miller house stood on Fleetwood Hill, a ridge that lay a half-mile north of Brandy Station. Rising 150 feet above the surrounding countryside, Fleetwood Hill possessed a commanding view of the farmers' fields and woodlots. Stuart had used the Miller place for several days, but on this night, only a pair of fly tents marked the site. His headquarters and camp equipage had been packed in wagons for the anticipated march.[25]

Across the Rappahannock, the Federals had known of the presence of Stuart's cavalry in Culpeper County for some time. Recent reports indicated that the Confederate horsemen were preparing for a raid into Maryland, or as an intelligence officer told Union commander Joseph Hooker, "the most important expedition ever attempted in this country." Estimates placed Stuart's command at between 12,000 and 15,000 officers and men. On June 7, Hooker ordered Brigadier General Alfred Pleasonton "to disperse and destroy the rebel force assembled in the vicinity of Culpeper." Hooker assigned the entire Cavalry Corps—three divisions of eight thousand troopers—three thousand infantrymen in two brigades and four artillery batteries, to the offensive movement.[26]

Pleasonton had held temporary command of the army's cavalry for fewer than three weeks. After his raid during the Chancellorsville Campaign, George Stoneman was granted a medical leave of absence. Hooker had been critical of the general's performance, and Stoneman had suffered excruciating pain from hemorrhoids during the raid. Hooker preferred Brigadier General John Buford for Stoneman's position, but Pleasonton's commission predated Buford's. A laconic, no-nonsense man, Buford was the finest horse soldier in the army. Instead, Pleasonton, a bantam-sized man with burning ambition whose embellished reports mixed fact with fiction, received the appointment.[27]

A Union cavalry officer professed later, "From the day of its reorganization under Hooker, the cavalry of the Army of the Potomac commenced a new life." Another one likened its formation into a corps to "an emancipation" from the restricted roles under George McClellan and Ambrose Burnside. The Yankee troopers had shown signs of their increasing prowess at Kelly's Ford in March. Now, for the first time in the cavalry's history, it was to go "into action as a body."[28]

Throughout June 8, the Union cavalry closed on the Rappahannock crossings. Buford's First Cavalry Division, an infantry brigade, and artillery batteries halted opposite Beverly Ford. Eight miles downstream, the Second and Third Cavalry divisions, under the overall command of Brigadier General David McM. Gregg, arrived at Kelly's Ford. Like Buford, Gregg was a capable and reliable officer; unlike Pleasonton, he disliked newspapermen. An infantry brigade and a battery of horse artillery joined Gregg.[29]

At 4:30 A.M., June 9, the 8th New York, leading Colonel Benjamin F. "Grimes" Davis's brigade of Buford's division, plunged down the steep banks of Beverly Ford, splashed through the shallows, and was met with scattered fire from Rebel pickets. Company A of the 6th Virginia manned the crossing and retired fighting. The gunfire must have sounded like a thunderclap in a clear sky to the sleeping cavalrymen and artillerists in camp between the ford and St. James Church. The Yankees "surprised us in bed," recorded a Southern gunner in his diary afterward. Officers rallied their men, and Beckham's artillery crews scrambled to limber up the cannon.[30]

Two companies or a squadron of the 6th Virginia surged down the road initially to stall the oncoming New Yorkers. Behind the squadron came troopers of the 7th Virginia. Many of the Confederates were half-dressed and rode bareback, as they had left their horses unsaddled to graze. On the road from the ford, two guns of Captain James F. Hart's

Washington Battery deployed. Hart's South Carolinians fired on the Federals as their comrades in the horse artillery lashed the other teams rearward.[31]

Like the men, Stuart and his staff were awakened by the gunfire. As a precaution, Stuart sent the headquarters baggage wagons to the rear. A courier soon arrived, reporting that enemy cavalry "in heavy force" had crossed the river and were advancing. Stuart directed Lieutenant Chiswell Dabney to ride to the front and to ascertain the situation. According to Lieutenant Frank Robertson, Stuart remained on Fleetwood Hill for "some time." Wade Hampton joined him and received orders to move his brigade to the support of Jones's regiments and Beckham's guns at St. James Church.[32]

Dabney found, in his words, "an enormous column of the Yankees" engaged with Jones's troopers and Beckham's gun crews. The staff officer sent a courier to headquarters with the information. Most likely, by then Stuart had issued a flurry of orders, directing Rooney Lee and Thomas Munford to the church and shifting Beverly Robertson's two North Carolina regiments toward Kelly's Ford, thinking that the enemy might be coming also from that direction. He instructed Hampton to detach the 2nd South Carolina and to post it at Stevensburg, south of Brandy Station. Leaving Major Henry McClellan and a string of couriers behind on Fleetwood Hill, Stuart rode to the front at the church.[33]

Stuart came upon a burgeoning engagement being waged by Jones's troopers and Beckham's gunners. The counterattack by companies of the 6th and 7th Virginia and the stand of Hart's two guns secured the escape of the batteries. In the swirling melee between the Virginians and the New Yorkers, Grimes Davis and Lieutenant Robert Owen Allen of Company D of the 6th Virginia had fought head-to-head. Allen eluded a saber blow by Davis and fired his pistol, killing the Union colonel.[34]

The brick St. James Church marked the center of the Confederate line. Hampton's troopers came up on the batteries' right flank, filing into the line with dismounted skirmishers edging the front. Farther to the north and west, beyond Jones's left flank, Rooney Lee's command arrived on Yew Ridge. Lee strung out a line of sharpshooters behind a stone wall along the ridge's eastern base. A section or two of guns from Captain James Breathed's 1st Stuart Horse Artillery battery supported

Lee's men. Toward the river, meanwhile, Buford's other two mounted brigades, infantry regiments, and an artillery battery were deploying.[35]

Stuart's ordnance officer, Captain John Esten Cooke, maintained that the general "preferred pure cavalry fighting" rather than sharpshooting between opposing lines. "Stuart was born to fight cavalry," believed Cooke, with an instinct during combat that "was unfailing." He possessed an "unshrinking nerve" and "equanimity" during the worst of times on a battlefield. Cooke's fellow staff officer William Blackford wrote: "It was in action Stuart showed to the greatest advantage. I have never seen his superior on a battlefield." Now, in his first major cavalry engagement, those qualities attributed to him by Cooke and Blackford were to be tested.[36]

On came the Yankees, directing their mounted attacks against Beckham's row of cannon. The Confederates responded, and the combat intensified into a series of mounted charges and countercharges. Private William H. Ware of the 3rd Virginia left a graphic description of such mounted warfare: "A cavalry charge is a terrible thing. Almost before you can think, the shock of horse against horse, the clash of steel against steel, crack of pistols, yells of some poor lost one, as he lost his seat and down under those iron shod hoofs that knew no mercy, or the shriek of some horse overturned and cut to pieces by his own kind. It is Hell while it lasts."[37]

Into this maelstrom and blasts from Beckham's guns rode the 8th Illinois, 17th Pennsylvania, 6th Pennsylvania, and 6th United States in a wave of successive charges. Grumble Jones's Virginians—members of the 11th, 12th, and 35th battalions—met them in swirling clashes. A trooper in the 12th Virginia attested to the fierceness, "It was then warm work, hand to hand, shooting and cutting each other in desperate fury, all mixed through one another, killing, wounding, and taking prisoners promiscuously." On the Confederate flanks, Hampton's and Lee's sharpshooters repulsed attacks of Union dismounted cavalrymen and infantrymen.[38]

A Virginia sergeant recalled, "I saw General Stuart that day riding out on the field where shot and shell were raining around, and he didn't seem to bat an eye." While the fighting raged, Stuart seemed to be, as he had been at Chancellorsville on May 3, everywhere along his line. He

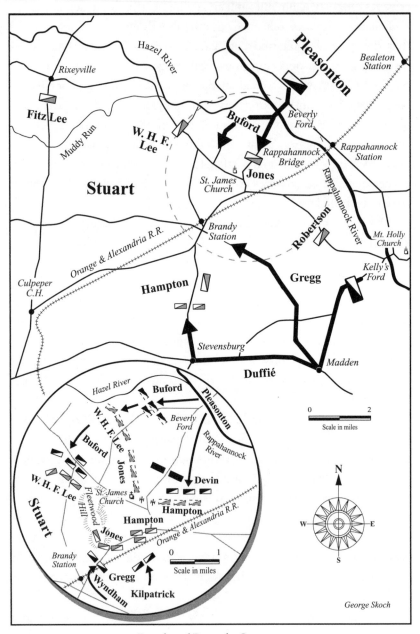

Battle of Brandy Station

issued a series of orders to his commanders, shifting units and artillery crews. At such time, wrote Cooke, Stuart's "voice was curt, harsh, imperious, admitting no reply." He looked "dangerous," thought Cooke.[39]

The action subsided about eleven o'clock, extending into an hour-long lull. During this respite, a courier from Jones reported to Stuart that additional Federal units were approaching Brandy Station. According to Captain Hart, who was with Stuart, the cavalry commander "angrily dismissed the informant." "Tell General Jones," Stuart was to have said, "to attend to the Yankees in his front, and I'll watch the flanks." When Jones heard Stuart's reply, he barked: "So he thinks they ain't coming, does he? Well, let him alone; he'll damn soon see for himself."[40]

Before long, a courier reined up with a similar message from Henry McClellan on Fleetwood Hill. Stuart turned to Hart, "Ride back there and see what all that foolishness is about." Minutes later, a third courier arrived, confirming the presence of enemy cavalry at Brandy Station behind Stuart's line at St. James Church. McClellan learned later that Stuart appeared "incredulous" at the news. Frank Robertson was with him and stated afterward, "For the first time the Gen. looked excited." He rushed orders to Jones and Hampton to withdraw and to "move like lightning on those people in our rear."[41]

In fact, two columns of Union cavalry were approaching Brandy Station—one by a more direct road to the railroad station, the other by a circuitous road toward Stevensburg. The Yankees belonged to the Second and Third Cavalry divisions, under David Gregg. Their crossing of Kelly's Ford had been delayed because of the tardy movement of Colonel Alfred N. Duffié's Second Division. Once across, Gregg sent Duffié toward Stevensburg, while his Third Division moved on another road east of Duffié's column. The infantry regiments, led by Brigadier General David A. Russell, marched on Kelly's Mill Road, the shortest route from the ford to Brandy Station, covering Gregg's right flank.[42]

When the fighting erupted at Beverly Ford, Stuart dispatched Beverly Robertson and his inexperienced 4th and 5th North Carolina to cover the right flank on Kelly's Mill Road, and the 2nd South Carolina, followed by the 4th Virginia, to Stevensburg. Stuart expected the regiments to oppose an enemy advance from that direction and to inform him of the situation. Although Robertson reported the enemy's advance, he did virtually nothing to impede Gregg's march.[43]

Robertson, whom an infantryman called "a bon vivant and ornament of the boudoir . . . but not a success as a cavalry officer," had his skirmishers engage Russell's infantrymen. "Had I pursued the flanking party [Gregg's column]," Robertson contended in his report, "the road I was ordered to defend would have been left utterly exposed. I acted according to orders and the dictates of judgment." In his report, Stuart stated that Robertson "did not conform to the movement of the enemy to the right, of which he was cognizant, so as to hold him check or thwart him by a corresponding move of a portion of his command in the same direction." It was much to ask of the North Carolinians to oppose Gregg's superior numbers, but the result was that Robertson suffered a handful of casualties and Stuart's rear lay open to the Federals.[44]

At Stevensburg, against Duffié's Second Division, Colonel Calbraith Butler and 220 officers and men of the 2nd South Carolina made a valiant, but hopeless, stand. The Union attacks were spirited, with overwhelming numbers. When the 4th Virginia joined the South Carolinians, the Yankees routed the regiment in what its commander, Colonel Williams Wickham, termed "so disgraceful" a rout. A Northerner called the pursuit of the Virginians "a regular steeple chase," and according to a Confederate, "the Yankees *cut them in the back* as they ran." The enemy charges also broke Butler's ranks, scattering the Rebels, except for a small contingent that rallied and defiantly stood as a rear guard.[45]

The South Carolinians' defense came with a high price. Lieutenant Colonel Frank Hampton, Wade Hampton's brother, fell mortally wounded, and Butler had his right leg above the ankle struck by an artillery round. Captain Will Farley, one of Stuart's finest scouts, was mounted beside Butler when the colonel was wounded. The shell cut off one of the captain's legs at the knee before plowing through his horse and hitting Butler. When the men picked up Farley to carry him away, he reportedly joked: "Bring along my leg too. I wish to have that along any how." Farley died soon afterward. Stuart wrote to his mother: "He had served without emolument, long, faithfully and always with distinction. No nobler champion has fallen."[46]

To the north, on Fleetwood Hill, the Battle of Brandy Station was swirling to a resolution. When Henry McClellan notified Stuart of the Union movement, the chief of staff had with him only a few couriers and a cannon from Captain R. Preston Chew's battery, under Lieutenant John W. Carter. The artillery crew had expended its ammunition, except for defective ones, in opposing Buford and had withdrawn. It was, declared McClellan, "a circumstance which proved to be our salvation." As the van of Gregg's force reached Brandy Station, Carter's men fired deliberately their few faulty rounds on the Yankees, delaying their advance for vital minutes.[47]

A solitary artillery piece, however, could not stall for long the Union horsemen. The 1st New Jersey led the attack, ascending the hill's southern slope. But then, like a drama staged in an American theater, clearing Fleetwood's crest, charged the 12th Virginia. The foes met in a crash of horses, sabers, and pistols. Frank Robertson witnessed it from a distance and exclaimed in a letter to his sister, "From where I was I could see the most exciting scene I ever witnessed."[48]

Behind the Confederates came their fellow Virginians in Lieutenant Colonel Elijah V. "Lige" White's 35th Battalion. In time, White's men were to earn the nickname "Comanches." It might have had its beginnings here. They plowed into the New Jerseymen in another whirlwind of close-in fighting. The Federals shoved the Rebels down the eastern slope, where they rallied. The 1st Pennsylvania joined the New Jerseymen, only to be met with a counterattack by the 6th Virginia and the pair of re-formed units. A Virginian described the struggle: "On each side, in front, behind, everywhere on top of the hill the Yankees closed in upon us. [W]e fought them single-handed, by twos, fours and by squads, just as the circumstances permitted."[49]

Stuart arrived on Fleetwood Hill as the Virginians counterattacked. One of his men averred, "Genl Stuart always fought the hardest when things looked the worst." He rode back and forth, giving orders and looking for reinforcements. A cavalryman stated that he was "coldly furious" and was "here, there and everywhere . . . his black plume floating . . . where the battle was fiercest." He shouted to his men, "give them the saber boys."[50]

As the Federals were prevailing against Jones's Virginians, the leading units of Hampton's brigade—Cobb's Legion and 1st South Carolina—stormed up the hill's eastern slope and into the enemy's ranks. Led by Colonel Pierce M. B. Young, John Pelham's friend, the Georgians in the Legion "went in with a rousing cheer." "It was the first time we have ever met the enemy in an open field in a charge," Lieutenant Colonel William Deloney told his wife. The Georgians and the South Carolinians swept the Yankees off the hill. Stuart brought forward sections of artillery to open on the enemy. Young asserted in his report, "I do claim that this was the turning point of the day."[51]

The Confederates secured Fleetwood Hill when the 1st North Carolina and the Jeff Davis Legion arrived. Hampton led the North Carolinians in their charge, moving a cavalryman to proclaim, "Never did an officer exhibit more cool, daring gallantry, on any occasion, than was shown by Gen. Wade Hampton." In a final attack, the 11th Virginia, led by Stuart's friend Colonel Lunsford Lomax, captured three cannon of the 6th New York Independent Battery. Earlier, White's Virginians had overrun the gun crews in a spirited assault, shooting and slashing the Union artillerists, but were repulsed by a counterattack of the 1st Maine.[52]

The fighting at Brandy Station ended on Yew Ridge in a desperate struggle by Rooney Lee's men to protect the Confederate left flank and rear. When Union infantrymen enfiladed Lee's flank, Buford ordered a cavalry charge. Once again, the combat was marked by mounted thrusts and counterthrusts. At one point, a trooper in the 10th Virginia shouted to his comrades as they met the Yankees, "Hurrah for Hell, Wade in." The 2nd North Carolina's Colonel Soloman Williams was killed as he re-formed his ranks. Williams had been married for only two weeks.[53]

A lieutenant in the 9th Virginia wrote of his brigade commander, "General Lee's coolness and courage were of a high order, and his presence in battle was an inspiration to the bravery and constancy of his men." But late in the action, Rooney Lee suffered a serious leg wound from a pistol ball. Afterward, he was taken to Hickory Hill, his wife, Charlotte Wickham's, family home, north of Richmond, to recover. When the Federals learned from Richmond newspapers of his location, they came to Hickory Hill and captured him on June 26. Lee would not be exchanged until February 25, 1864. While he was imprisoned, his wife died on Christmas Day 1863.[54]

While the contest raged for possession of Fleetwood Hill and Yew Ridge, Gregg directed Duffié to march to Brandy Station from Stevensburg. Instead of taking the direct road, Duffié took a roundabout route, coming up on Gregg's rear too late to join in the fighting. Had Duffié brought the Second Division onto the field expeditiously, the Federals might have prevailed and uncovered the presence of Confederate infantry in Culpeper County. Instead, with Stuart's veterans holding the high ground, Pleasonton ordered a withdrawal across the Rappahannock.[55]

The Battle of Brandy Station was the largest cavalry engagement of the war. Union casualties exceeded 850 killed, wounded, and missing, while Confederate losses amounted to more than 425. A trooper in the 10th New York entered into his diary, "i think it was the hardest Cav fite we hav had." Southerners shared the New Yorker's view, with one of Grumble Jones's Virginians nothing in his diary, "We were on the field all the day it was the hardest cavalry fight that Steward [Stuart] ever witnessed." A Rebel artillerist confided to his journal, "As we move back to camp the boys are too tired to joke and were very quiet."[56]

As was his habit, Alfred Pleasonton exaggerated Stuart's numerical strength by threefold and his command's disruption of enemy plans. He had failed, however, in wrecking Stuart's force, his primary mission. An officer contended, "I am sure a good cavalry officer would have whipped Stuart out of his boots; but Pleasonton is not and never will be that." The day's accomplishments belonged not to Pleasonton, but to the officers and men in the corps.[57]

The blue-jacketed horse soldiers had fought with skill, valor, and tenacity. A member of the 1st Maine wrote afterward: "All mouths are full of praise for our gallant actions. . . . The Cavalry is getting to be as much a valued branch of the service as heretofore it has been a ridicule." Stuart's adjutant, Henry McClellan, probably overstated the result when he argued in his memoirs that Brandy Station "made the Federal cavalry." McClellan's fellow staff officer William Blackford was closer to the truth, "The cavalry of the enemy were steadily improving and it was all we could do sometimes to manage them."[58]

From the surprise at Beverly Ford, to the bloody work around St. James Church, and to the fierce defense of Fleetwood Hill and Yew Ridge, Stuart owed the outcome to his subordinate commanders and the veterans in the ranks. In a larger sense, his command's performance could be attributed to him. From the spring of 1861, when he assumed command of volunteer companies at Harper's Ferry, he had instituted drills and training, demanded discipline, and instilled a spirit for combat that proved vital at Brandy Station. When the fighting concluded, he and Hampton rode by Cobb's Legion. "As they passed," stated a Georgian, "three cheers were given to each of them. Such cheering I never heard before."[59]

Robert E. Lee had watched the battle from a distance. He was concerned that the Federals might discover Confederate infantry in the area and expressed this in a message to Stuart during the fighting. Lee brought forward an infantry division if needed to support the cavalry, but it remained concealed from the enemy. A week later on June 16, after Lee read Stuart's report, the army commander wrote: "The dispositions made by you to meet the strong attack of the enemy appear to have been judicious and well planned. The troops were well and skillfully managed, and, with few exceptions, conducted themselves with marked gallantry."[60]

Within the army, however, criticism of Stuart arose, centered on the cavalry being surprised by the enemy. "Genl Stewart [Stuart] it is said," one Rebel informed his father, "has been paying more attention to the Ladies at Culpepper than to his business as a soldier." Another army member stated that officers and men "are hard on Stuart." A Georgia infantryman wrote, "I am sorry to state that from all I can learn they [the enemy] caught our dragoons napping." Another foot soldier maintained: "Genl Stuart was beautifully surprised & whipped the other day. . . . It is amusing to hear the cavalry fellows trying to bluff out of it."[61]

Some of the army's generals expressed similar observations. "Think Stuart had best stop his reviews and look to his laurels," jotted George T. Anderson in his diary. Lafayette McLaws, who had called Stuart "a buffoon to attract attention" in an earlier letter, complained to his wife, "Our cavalry were surprised yesterday by the enemy and had to do some desperate fighting to retrieve the day." James Longstreet stated that it was "well known as a surprise" in the army.[62]

How "well known" it was to Stuart is uncertain. He unquestionably knew, however, of the judgment of the Southern press. In editorials across the Confederacy, newspapers condemned Stuart for an obvious lack of vigilance. The Charleston *Mercury* used the words "ugly surprise." The Savannah *Republican* opined: "There is little doubt, from all accounts, that our cavalry, resting secure in believing there was no danger with so much infantry surrounding them, allowed the enemy to surprise them everywhere. . . . The whole affair was, to say the least, very discreditable to somebody."[63]

The Richmond newspapers were particularly acerbic in their comments. The *Examiner* attributed the surprise to "negligence and bad management" by "a few vain and weak-headed officers," who had conducted cavalry operations as if it were "a tournament." The *Sentinel* argued: "Vigilance, vigilance, more vigilance, is the lesson taught us by the Brandy surprise, and which must not be forgotten by the victory which was wrested from defeat. Let all learn it, from the Major General down to the picket." The *Dispatch* reported erroneously that Stuart's headquarters had been shelled by artillery before the Rebels knew of the Yankees' crossing of the river. The paper then repeated a rumor that Stuart and his staff had been "rollicking, frolicking and running after girls."[64]

The Richmond *Enquirer* was caustic in its comments: "If Gen. Stuart is to be the eyes and ears of the army we advise him to see more, and be seen less." The newspaper asserted, "Gen. Stuart has suffered no little in public estimation by the late enterprises of the enemy." Reflecting current opinion in the capital, a War Department clerk, J. B. Jones, wrote in his diary, "The surprise of Stuart, on the Rappahannock, has chilled every heart." A week after the engagement, however, the *Whig* speculated, "We shall be surprised, if the gallant Stuart does not, before many days, make the enemy repent solely the temerity that led them to undertake as bold and insulting a feat."[65]

Stuart learned of the newspapers' articles and editorials within days of the battle. Writing on June 12 to Flora, he averred: "The papers are in great error as usual about the whole transaction. It was no surprise the enemy's movement was known, and he was defeated." The "great error" referred to a report in the Richmond *Examiner* that the Federals had captured official papers at his headquarters. "I will of course take no notice of such base falsehoods," he swore.[66]

In fact, Stuart took considerable notice of the press's censure of him. Flora Stuart forwarded copies of the newspapers to her husband. He denied again to Flora that he had been surprised. "The newspapers are false *in every statement* except as to the victory. . . . The papers ought to apologize." He sent a copy of Lee's June 16 note—"a very handsome letter," in his words—to Dr. Charles Brewer, his brother-in-law. Brewer was to distribute copies to the newspapers. The letter was, he assured Flora, "the only one I ever allowed to be published." He regarded the battle at Brandy Station as "the greatest triumph I ever had."[67]

The Richmond *Sentinel* published a copy of Lee's letter in its June 22 edition. In his letter to Flora, Stuart declared, "I *pleasure myself on my vigilance.*" When the press accused him, with sound reason, for being caught unprepared, Stuart was incensed. According to Longstreet, Stuart tried "to stave it off on others," but the effort failed, at least within the army. In Longstreet's estimation the facts could not be denied.[68]

The newspapers' reaction to Brandy Station entailed more than the question of whether the cavalry had been surprised. It threatened to damage what Stuart coveted—public acclaim. "He ardently desired the applause of his superiors and his country," admitted Henry McClellan, "and was keenly alive to adverse criticism. . . . He could never see or acknowledge that he was worsted in an engagement." A Confederate cavalryman writing of Brandy Station argued, "I can't imagine anyone more likely to suffer in his own feelings than Gen Jeb from the withdrawal of that popular applause which he is so fond of sunning himself in."[69]

Historian Douglas Southall Freeman believed that Stuart "was humiliated more deeply than ever he had been in his campaigning" by the battle's contentious aftermath. The tone of his letters to Flora indicated anger and resentment of the press's treatment of him. Even the Federals, who had read the Southern newspapers, expected Stuart "to do something to retrieve his reputation."[70]

Chapter Thirteen

To Gettysburg

J EB STUART GAZED northward. Writing to his brother William about a week after Brandy Station, he proclaimed: "I am standing on the Rappahannock, looking beyond . . . and feel not unlike a tiger pausing before its spring . . . that spring will not be delayed much longer. . . . I ask now, my dear brother, and best friend, that you will pray for me in the coming struggle."[1]

When Stuart wrote to his brother, the Confederate movement toward Pennsylvania had resumed. With Richard Ewell's Second Corps leading the march, the army's vanguard had entered the Shenandoah Valley. On June 13 and 14, Ewell's veterans routed a Union force at Winchester, capturing wagons, guns, supplies, and nearly four thousand prisoners. Within days, James Longstreet's First Corps crossed the Blue Ridge; Ewell pushed a division across the Potomac into Maryland, and A. P. Hill's Third Corps was en route to the Valley. From central Virginia to beyond the Potomac, the Rebel column stretched for more than one hundred miles.[2]

While the infantry units filled the roads, appearing like ribbons of dirty gray amid the summer's foliage, Stuart led three brigades of cavalry across the Rappahannock. Ordered by Robert E. Lee to secure the gaps of the Blue Ridge to screen Longstreet's troops from the Federals,

Stuart moved into the Virginia Piedmont. Wade Hampton's and Grumble Jones's regiments remained south of the Rappahannock until Hill's corps passed into the Valley. It was a welcome movement, according to one of Stuart's aides, as "we breathed the fresh air of the Blue Ridge."[3]

Stuart's horsemen covered Ashby's and Snicker's gaps in the Blue Ridge. On June 17, he ordered Fitz Lee's brigade, under Colonel Thomas Munford, and Rooney Lee's brigade, led by Colonel John R. Chambliss, Jr., east toward the gaps of the Bull Run Mountains. Stuart held Beverly Robertson's North Carolina regiments in reserve as support. With his staff, Stuart rode to Middleburg, where, in his words, "I remained to close up the command, and keep in more ready communication with the rear."[4]

Meanwhile, Joseph Hooker, commander of the Army of the Potomac, had been slow in reacting to the signs of the Confederate movement. It was not until June 13 that intelligence reports convinced him that Lee's legions were in the Shenandoah Valley. The Union army started northward the next day in grueling marches amid stifling heat. The advance halted on June 16 as Hooker wrestled with conflicting information about the Rebels' whereabouts. Seeking reliable intelligence, Hooker directed Alfred Pleasonton's cavalry units, supported by infantry, toward the Blue Ridge gaps.[5]

Brigadier General Judson Kilpatrick's four regiments led the Federal march toward the mountain passages. About mid-afternoon on June 17, the Yankee cavalrymen reached Aldie, where Munford's Virginians had been sent by Stuart. The surprise encounter sparked a bloody action. Dismounted skirmishers manned stone walls, and mounted horsemen met in a series of attacks and counterattacks. An officer in the 2nd Virginia, whose sharpshooters held a stone wall, believed that the Federals "charged up to as I suppose a dozen times. I don't remember the exact number, and each time we piled yankees and horses in the road until it was blockaded." Another Confederate asserted, "I had never known the enemy's cavalry to fight so stubbornly or act so recklessly."[6]

Stuart remained in Middleburg, five miles west of Aldie, during the fighting. Major John Mosby joined him in the town. A week earlier, at nearby Rector's Cross Roads (present-day Atoka), Mosby had organized officially his partisans into Company A, 43rd Battalion of Virginia Cavalry, which was assigned to Stuart's command. When Mosby entered Middleburg, he found Stuart in the main street, surrounded by a group of ladies. The scene reminded Mosby of "a dance around a Maypole." Mosby and his Rangers had been scouting, and he brought with him information about the enemy for Stuart.[7]

In the evening after Mosby had reported, a courier galloped into Middleburg, exclaiming, "A regiment of Yankees are coming into town at a trot." Stuart and his staff officers ran for their mounts and raced away to the west, meeting the van of Robertson's pair of North Carolina regiments. In Middleburg, the Federals, Colonel Alfred Duffié's 1st Rhode Island, were barricading the streets. It was nearly nightfall when Robertson's North Carolinians attacked.[8]

The Rebels came from the north, east, and west, jumping their horses over the barricades and scattering the Federal skirmishers. A confused struggle in the darkness ensued before the Union colonel tried to lead his beleaguered command away. The Confederates bagged dozens of prisoners, and scores of Yankees spent the night in the woods, surrounded by the enemy. Discovered the next morning as they rode out, the Northerners were nearly all captured by men of Chambliss's brigade, which had arrived during the night and camped outside town. The 1st Rhode Island lost a few men killed or wounded, but more than two hundred were listed as captured or missing.[9]

June 18 was oppressively hot, with the temperature approaching one hundred degrees. Stuart avoided an engagement with the enemy, waiting until Hampton's and Jones's men, en route from the south, joined him. Munford's Virginians, having withdrawn after the fight at Aldie, covered the left flank toward the town of Union, while Robertson's and Chambliss's troopers abandoned Middleburg to the Federals. About dawn, Stuart received dispatches from one of Mosby's men that had been taken from a captured officer on Hooker's staff. Stuart hurried the documents on to Lee. A heavy rain fell late in the day and continued intermittently for two more days.[10]

The Federals advanced toward the Blue Ridge gaps on June 19. David Gregg's cavalrymen came from Middleburg and were met by Robertson's and Chambliss's dismounted men and two batteries west of town on a ridge. Stuart remained close to the action. When the Yankees pressed the attack, Stuart withdrew his line to a second ridge. His purpose was to delay the enemy, and he succeeded. Before the Southerners retired, a bullet struck Heros von Borcke in the neck, ripped his windpipe, and lodged in his right lung.[11]

When the bullet hit the Prussian, recalled Lieutenant Frank Robertson, "The impact was so loud that I thought a fragment of shell had struck a fence near us." Robertson and William Blackford helped von Borcke off his horse, and he was carried into Upperville to the home of Dr. Talcott Ellison, a cavalry surgeon. Blackford admitted that they "had little hope for him." Ellison thought the wound to be mortal. But the powerfully strong man survived and was eventually taken to Dundee, where the Price family cared for him.[12]

Von Borcke never returned to duty with the Confederacy. He had served with Stuart for a year as an amiable companion around a campfire and as a fearless staff officer in battle. Stuart was very fond of the Prussian despite the aide's healthy ego and strutting manner. In time, he returned to Prussia, married, and wrote his memoirs, which were lavish in praise of Stuart and of himself.[13]

By the morning of June 20, Wade Hampton's and Grumble Jones's brigades had arrived. Desultory skirmishing between the foes characterized the action on this day. Rain hampered operations, but as Stuart reported, "I was extremely anxious now to attack the enemy as early as possible." He added, however, that since June 21 was a Sabbath, "I recognized my obligation to do no duty other than what was absolutely necessary." His opponents had no such intentions of rest on a Sunday.[14]

Union batteries opened fire at eight o'clock in the morning of June 21. Behind them, David Gregg's brigades advanced west from Middleburg, while from the northwest John Buford's division moved forward. Using the terrain and stone walls, dismounted Confederate sharpshooters and horse artillery crews slowed the Yankees. The Federals shoved the Rebels back to the fields and woodlots north and east of Upperville. Jones's and Chambliss's troopers opposed Buford's cavalrymen north of the village as Hampton's and Robertson's regiments engaged Gregg's command at Upperville's eastern edge. Munford's Virginians guarded the approaches to Snicker's Gap and were not involved in the action.[15]

As they had at Brandy Station twelve days earlier, the foes bloodied each other in mounted charges and countercharges while dismounted skirmishers raked their enemy. Against Buford's men, a Confederate artillerist declared, "We are firing faster than I ever saw artillery fire." For Jones's and Chambliss's veterans, it was a fighting withdrawal against the Yankees. East of town, the combat was fierce at points. Shouting, "Charge them, my brave boys, charge them!," Hampton led the 1st North Carolina in a counterattack. Stuart personally ordered in the 5th North Carolina and Jeff Davis Legion, riding forward with the Legion. "The 1st Dragoons tried very hard to kill me the other day," he informed Flora later. "Four officers fired deliberately at me with their pistols several times, while I was putting a regiment at them which routed them."[16]

At the end, Stuart ordered a withdrawal to the foot of the Blue Ridge at Ashby's Gap. The Yankees occupied Upperville and the bloody fields around it. The next morning Pleasonton countermarched to the east, passing through Middleburg and Aldie. Although the Confederate cavalry had prevented the Federals from reaching the mountain defiles, Pleasonton reported, based on information gleaned from prisoners and local citizens, "The main body of the rebel infantry is in the Shenandoah Valley." He conjectured that Lee's army would cross the Potomac and march toward Pittsburgh, Pennsylvania.[17]

Pleasonton's troopers could claim tactical victories in these engagements, but Stuart's horsemen fulfilled their mission of screening the army's infantry and artillery units from the enemy. Stuart incurred slightly more than five hundred casualties from June 17 to June 21. Criticism of Stuart's conduct of the operations arose among some in the army. It was, however, unwarranted. Two years of Southern dominance by its mounted units had ceased, giving the appearance of poor leadership. Stuart could no longer dictate, with little concern about the outcome, the shape and terms of an engagement. His cavalry remained a vaunted force, but no longer an unchallenged one.[18]

Stuart spent the night of June 21–22 in Paris. In a postwar letter, Henry McClellan claimed that Stuart rode the next morning to army headquarters, located a mile north of Berryville in the Shenandoah Valley. McClellan, however, made no mention of such a meeting in his memoirs. In fact, Stuart had met with Lee and Longstreet in Paris on

June 18, while the two generals were passing through to the Valley. The discussion must have centered upon the cavalry's role in the unfolding campaign. It also must have been at this time when Stuart proposed, in Lee's words, "that he could damage the enemy and delay his passage of the river [Potomac] by getting in his rear."[19]

Lee waited to act on Stuart's suggestion until the cavalry clashes east of the mountains ended. Stuart wrote a note to Longstreet, dated 7:45 A.M., June 22 that is missing. In it, Stuart likely reported the withdrawal of the Union cavalry from his front and might have restated his proposal for the movement by the Federal army's rear. Longstreet forwarded the note to Lee, who had his military secretary, Major Charles Marshall, prepare a reply. Written in the afternoon, the message's key portion read, "If you find that he [the enemy] is moving northward, and that two brigades can guard the Blue Ridge and take care of your rear, you can move with the other three into Maryland, and take position on General Ewell's right, place yourself in communication with him, guard his flanks, keep him informed to the enemy's movements, and collect all the supplies you can for the use of the army." Lee also sent a dispatch to Ewell in which he repeated the instructions given to Stuart.[20]

A courier delivered two letters to Longstreet's headquarters at Millwood—one for the First Corps commander and one to be forwarded to Stuart across the mountains. Longstreet wrote his own letter to Stuart:

> General Lee has inclosed to me this letter to you, to be forwarded to you, provided you can be spared from my front, and provided I think that you can move across the Potomac without disclosing our plans. He speaks of you leaving, via Hopewell Gap [in the Bull Run Mountains], and passing by the rear of the enemy. If you can get through by that route, I think that you will be less likely to indicate what our plans are than if you should cross by passing to our rear. I forward the letter of instructions with these suggestions.
>
> Please advise me of the condition of affairs before you leave, and order General Hampton—whom I suppose you will leave here in command to report to me at Millwood, either by letter or in person, as may be most agreeable to him.

Longstreet then added a postscript:

I think that your passage of the Potomac by our rear at the present moment will, in a measure, disclose our plans. You had better not leave us, therefore, unless you can take the proposed route in rear of the enemy.[21]

In turn, Longstreet notified Lee that his letter had been sent on to Stuart, "with the suggestion that he pass by the enemy's rear if he thinks that he may get through." The next day, Lee ordered Marshall to compose a second letter to Stuart. Dated 5:00 P.M., June 23, this letter has formed the basis of the controversy over Stuart's actions in the Gettysburg Campaign. Marshall wrote, in part:

If General Hooker's army remains inactive, you can leave two brigades to watch him, and withdraw with the three others, but should he not appear to be moving northward, I think you had better withdraw this side of the mountain to-morrow night, cross at Shepherdstown the next day, and move over to Fredericktown [Frederick, Maryland].

You will, however, be able to judge whether you can pass around their army without hindrance, doing them all the damage you can, and cross the river east of the mountains. In either case, after crossing the river, you must move on and feel the right of Ewell's troops, collecting information, provisions, &c.

Give instructions to the commander of the brigades left behind, to watch the flank and rear of the army, and (in the event of the enemy leaving their front) retire from the mountains west of the Shenandoah, leaving sufficient pickets to guard the passes, and bringing everything clear along the Valley, closing upon the rear of the army.

In a final admonition, Marshall stated for Lee, "I think the sooner you cross into Maryland, after to-morrow, the better."[22]

If Lee wanted clarity on the cavalry's mission, the June 23 letter provided confusion, if not contradiction. The phrase "should he not appear" contravened the previous wording, "If General Hooker's army remains inactive." Marshall either might have made an unintended mistake or possibly meant the word "now" instead of "not." A clerk at army headquarters recorded the letter in Lee's letterbook faithfully, with the word "not." Furthermore, the orders specified multiple duties for the cavalry during the movement, was vague about where east of the mountains Stuart should cross, and designated no time for the cavalry to be in Maryland if it passed around the Federal forces.[23]

Despite the order's "ambiguous and uncertain" nature, in the words of historian Alan Nolan, Lee intended for Stuart to cross the Potomac as soon as possible and join Ewell's corps, which was spearheading the Confederate offensive into Pennsylvania. In their postwar writings, Marshall and fellow staff officer Armistead L. Long argued that had been their commander's plan. To be sure, Lee granted Stuart the authority to march east of the mountains and around the Union army but only if he could do so "without hindrance." The statement, "I think the sooner you cross into Maryland, after to-morrow, the better," was forthright.[24]

In his report on the campaign, Lee was clear in his understanding of the orders, "it was left to his [Stuart's] discretion whether to enter Maryland east or west of the Blue Ridge; but he was instructed to lose no time in placing his command on the right of our column as soon as he should perceive the enemy moving northward." When asked in a postwar interview the reasons for the Confederate defeat at Gettysburg, Lee attributed one of them to, in the interviewer's phrase, "Stuart's failure to carry out his instructions."[25]

Why Lee considered and then approved, with restrictions, such an enterprise is difficult to understand. When he had the June 23 orders prepared, he knew that the Federals were laying a pontoon bridge at Edwards Ferry on the Potomac, indicative of a crossing into Maryland. Although Hooker's corps were scattered across north-central Virginia, they were closing on the Potomac. Despite Lee's subsequent averral that he wanted to avoid a battle in Pennsylvania, he sought such an engagement, hoping to strike Hooker's units in detail as they marched north. Intelligence on Union movements overrode any gains derived from an operation in their rear. Cavalry was vital in gathering information along his army's edges.[26]

Lee's regard for and confidence in Stuart's judgment and skill almost assuredly factored into Lee's granting such latitude. Thomas Munford wrote, "R. E. Lee was *intensely fond*" of the cavalry commander. Moxley Sorrel, Longstreet's chief of staff, believed that Stuart was the "true body and soul to Lee." In a postwar letter, writing of Stuart, Longstreet contended: "I often spoke of him to General Lee, as of the best material for cavalry service, but needing an older head to instruct and regulate him. The General was fond of him, and gave way to him to the disadvantage of both."[27]

Another factor might have been Longstreet's argument that with the cavalry passing around the Union army's rear they could deceive the enemy. It was, at best, a weak proposition. Ewell's leading elements had entered Pennsylvania, a fact reported to Hooker. When Longstreet's and Hill's corps crossed the Potomac, Union signalmen at Harper's Ferry detected the movement. By the time Stuart was ready to march, the Federals possessed reliable information on the direction of march of Lee's army. On the day Stuart departed, June 25, three Union corps filed across the pontoons at Edwards Ferry and entered Maryland. Lee's "plan was working," Nolan has written, "the enemy was following him across the Potomac and out of Virginia."[28]

Armistead Long of Lee's staff maintained later that had the Confederate commander known of the Federals' passage of the Potomac, "he would hardly have given his approval to the course Stuart pursued" as it "was too hazardous to be undertaken at the most critical period of the campaign." But Lee informed Jefferson Davis on June 23 that he believed the enemy was preparing to cross the river. Porter Alexander's assessment seems fair, "When one compares the small beneficial results of raids, even when successful, with the risks here involved, it is hard to understand how Lee could have given his consent."[29]

As noted, Lee's consent and orders imposed conditions if Stuart were to pass around the Union army. In the end, however, the decision rested with Stuart. It would appear that before he received Lee's June 23 letter that night, he had concluded to march east around the Federals. Earlier in the day, John Mosby arrived at cavalry headquarters at Rector's Cross Roads and met with Stuart. Mosby and/or his scouts had discovered a corridor between the Union corps through which the

Confederates could pass. Mosby suggested that Stuart use unguarded Hopewell Gap in the Bull Run Mountains, proceed north, passing west of Centreville, and cross the Potomac at Seneca Ford, twenty miles upriver from Washington.[30]

"I was present in the room when the plan was adopted to go to Ewell by Hooker's rear," Mosby wrote in a postwar letter. In another account, he claimed that Hampton and Fitz Lee, who had returned to duty, joined him and Stuart. Evidently, Stuart discussed his plans with his two sub-ordinates and sent a courier with a dispatch to the army commander. Stuart sent a pair of notes to army headquarters on this day, dated 9:00 A.M. and 10:30 A.M., but neither has been found. From Lee's response, one dealt with the purchase of tobacco for the cavalrymen, the other might have asked for further clarity on Stuart's proposal and Lee's June 22 letter. One of the notes could have been the message Mosby recalled. If it were, Stuart had settled upon the attempt to ride around Hooker's army hours before he received Lee's second letter.[31]

"A pitiless rain," in Henry McClellan's description, fell on the night of June 23–24. He urged Stuart to sleep on the porch of the Clinton Caleb Rector home in the village. "No!" answered Stuart, "my men are exposed to this rain, and I will not fair any better than they." He retired to a tree behind the house, while ordering his adjutant general to bed down on the porch, where if a courier arrived with a message he could find McClellan. Later that night, according to McClellan in his memoirs, he received a dispatch, marked "confidential," from Robert E. Lee.[32]

McClellan opened the dispatch, and taking it with him, woke Stuart and read the contents. Stuart mildly rebuked the aide for opening a confidential message and then resumed his sleep. According to McClellan, the letter stated that Jubal Early's division of Ewell's corps was to march to York, Pennsylvania, and Stuart should join him as soon as possible. "The whole tenor of the letter gave evidence that the commanding general approved the proposed movement, and thought it might be productive of the best results, while the responsibility of the decision was placed upon General Stuart himself."[33]

McClellan claimed that this important dispatch was subsequently lost. McClellan's postwar account seems questionable as to the existence of this letter. There is no copy of it in Lee's headquarters letter-book as there is with the June 22 and 23 orders. McClellan is the only source for its existence. In his report, Stuart used language similar to that cited by McClellan when he stated, "after crossing, to proceed with all dispatch to join the right (Early) of the army in Pennsylvania." He also used language similar to that of Lee in the 5:00 P.M., June 23, letter. No other member of the staff mentioned the reception of a second June 23 letter in his postwar writings.[34]

The timing and the contents of the dispatch also raise questions as to its existence. Charles Marshall dated the June 23 orders at 5:00 P.M. It probably took a courier a few hours to cover the thirty or so miles from beyond Berryville to Rector's Cross Roads in "a pitiless rain." Is it creditable then to believe that Lee decided to have a second letter composed within a few hours of the first one and sent on to Stuart later that night?[35]

McClellan's contention that Stuart should join Early at York is dubious. At the time, neither Lee nor Ewell had mentioned York in their correspondence or that Early's division had been assigned to that destination. In fact, it was not until June 25 that Ewell ordered Early to march to the south-central Pennsylvania city. Although the wording cited by McClellan varies considerably, he might have been referring to the documented June 23 orders. If not, the loyal chief of staff invented a second letter, which presented a reasonable defense for the course Stuart chose. The latter appears more likely to be the case.[36]

Stuart spent June 24 readying his command for the march. "He needed not only veteran troops," recalled McClellan, "but officers upon whose hearty cooperation he could confidently rely." He chose the brigades of Hampton, Fitz Lee, and Rooney Lee, still led by John Chambliss, to accompany him. He ignored Longstreet's recommendation to leave Hampton behind in command to guard the gaps and to observe the Federals. Instead, Stuart assigned the duty to Beverly Robertson and Grumble Jones. As senior officer, Robertson had overall command of both brigades.[37]

Undoubtedly, the personal animosity between Jones and Stuart governed the latter's decision not to take Jones with him. Jones's regiments were the equal of any in the cavalry on a battlefield. But the abiding dislike between the two men remained a festering sore. In Stuart's mind, he could not expect "hearty cooperation" from the brigadier. Stuart, however, had called Jones *"the best outpost officer"* in the cavalry division, and the assignment would utilize Jones's skills. Unfortunately for Stuart, Jones was to serve under Robertson's authority.[38]

Robertson's limitations as a commander of cavalry in the field had been reexposed at Brandy Station. He lacked aggressiveness and vigilance, attributes vital to the duty Stuart expected him to perform. "Your object will be to watch the enemy," Stuart instructed him in orders on June 24, "deceive him as to our designs, and harass his rear if you find he is retiring. Be always on the alert; let nothing escape your observation, and miss no opportunity which offers to damage the enemy." Robertson should maintain a picket line from Ashby's and Snicker's gaps through the Valley to the Potomac, and "report anything of importance" to Longstreet.[39]

When the enemy had withdrawn from his front, continued the orders, Robertson and Jones should enter the Valley, march north across the river, and "follow the army, keeping on its right and rear." While moving down the Shenandoah, the two brigades should "sweep the Valley clear of what pertains to the army."[40]

Throughout June 24 then, the officers and men of Hampton's, Fitz Lee's, and Chambliss's command descended upon the rendezvous site at Salem (present-day Marshall), Virginia. Some of the cavalrymen had been told that they were only relocating their camps. "We began to imagine that a little rest was in store for us," remarked an officer. Instead, Stuart issued orders for the men to cook three days' rations as no supply wagons were to accompany the column. He assigned six cannon from the horse artillery to the force of approximately 5,500 officers and men. A Virginian admitted, however, "our men and horses were already worn and jaded."[41]

Stuart and his staff clattered away from Rector's Cross Roads at one o'clock on the morning of June 25. Mounted on his bay horse, Virginia, Stuart allegedly shouted as he departed: "Ho! for the Valley!" The party rode west initially, as if heading across the Blue Ridge, before turning south toward Salem. When Stuart joined the three brigades, the officers and men filed into a column of fours. Lieutenant George Beale of the 9th Virginia noted that the men had been astonished as they rode south to Salem during the previous day. With the main army en route north, it was a "mystery of which none of us could understand." Now, wrote Beale, "the fact that General Stuart headed the expedition led many of us to understand that our journey southward would not continue long."[42]

The route was, as Beale and his comrades soon saw, toward the east and the morning's sun. The Confederates passed through White Plains (present-day, The Plains) and entered Glascock's Gap in the Bull Run Mountains. Stuart had probably used this route when he had joined Stonewall Jackson's command in the Second Manassas Campaign. It was after sunrise when the van of the column, descending the mountains' eastern face, approached Haymarket. The Southerners halted. Before them stretched Union infantrymen, wagons, and artillery pieces, filling the road and plodding northeast. The Yankees belonged to the Second Corps and were marching from their campsites at Thoroughfare Gap, a mile and a half north of Glascock's Gap, to Gum Springs.[43]

Stuart brought forward cannon, and the guns fired on the enemy column. "We could see the dust of the shells fall among them & the scattering of the blue jackets," stated a Confederate surgeon. Union gun crews responded, and they continued until, as the doctor remembered, "We soon found we were wasting ammunition & let things done." Stuart sent Fitz Lee's troopers on a reconnaissance toward Gainesville, and withdrew the main body several miles rearward to Buckland, where the men rested and grazed their horses.[44]

"It was now clearly impossible for Stuart to follow the route originally intended," professed Henry McClellan in his memoir. He either had to retrace his route and cross the Blue Ridge into the Shenandoah Valley or make "a wider *detour*," in McClellan's words. From Buckland, by whatever route he chose, the distance to the Potomac fords, either in the Valley or northwest of Washington, were roughly equal, nearly sixty miles. John Mosby, who would become Stuart's staunchest postwar defender, admitted, "It was all important for the success of Stuart's plan that the status quo should be preserved until at least he could get partly through Hooker's army." But the status quo had changed. The Union army was on the march; Stuart had encountered hindrance.[45]

The cavalry commander consulted with no ranking subordinate or staff member. When he had his troopers unsaddle their mounts to graze, he had decided to wait until the enemy passed before he resumed the movement around the Federal army. As his friend Fitz Lee noted later, Stuart was "free to act" on the discretion given to him by Robert E. Lee. While the evidence is not conclusive—it may never be—it can be argued that Stuart had determined before he left his headquarters at Rector's Cross Roads to conduct another ride around an opponent he seemed to regard with scant respect, perhaps even contempt. In his report, he gave no indication that he considered turning around and moving west.[46]

Was Stuart "free to act" as Fitz Lee stated? Charles Marshall fervently thought otherwise. When the cavalry encountered the Union troops, Marshall averred "the discretion so given him by General Longstreet was at an end, and there was yet time for General Stuart to retrace his steps and obey the order he had received from General Lee in the letter of June 23rd to cross the Potomac west of the Blue Ridge and move until he felt the right of Ewell's column." After the campaign had ended and during the postwar years, Marshall was a harsh critic of Stuart's conduct, but his argument was valid. Stuart could pass around Hooker's army but only "without hindrance." With the Federals on the march and with his intended route blocked, the restrictions in the June 23 orders applied. This might have been the reasoning behind Robert E. Lee's postwar statement that Stuart failed to obey his instructions.[47]

If Stuart had begun a retrograde march on June 25 when stopped at Haymarket, he could have probably reached Robert E. Lee at Chambersburg, Pennsylvania, no later than June 28. In a reminiscence, Private John Z. H. Scott of the 10th Virginia claimed that he was a member of a detail sent to picket Thoroughfare Gap after Stuart withdrew to Buckland. The Virginians remained in the gap during the night of June 25–26, and then rode to Buckland. When they arrived, the three brigades were gone. They decided to head west, pass through Ashby's Gap, and follow the army into Pennsylvania. Scott wrote that the detail reached Chambersburg when Lee, Longstreet, and A. P. Hill were there, which indicated June 28. A detail was not a 5,500-man force, but Stuart would have three full days and part of another one to complete the march.[48]

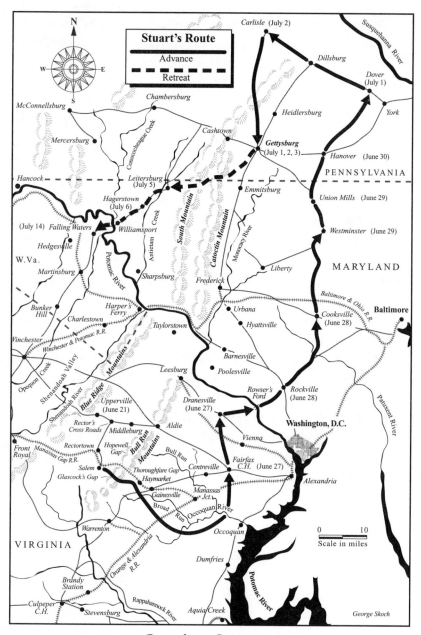

Gettysburg Campaign

Fitz Lee wrote subsequently, "I think the move selected was not the best under the circumstances." In his report, however, Stuart justified his decision as "practicable to move entirely in the enemy's rear," and "the results abundantly confirms my judgment as to the practicability as well as utility of the move." He buttressed his argument by claiming he "was directed to communicate" with Jubal Early at York, Pennsylvania. As noted previously, except for McClellan's alleged receipt of a second June 23 letter, no written evidence exists ordering Stuart to unite with Early other than Stuart's report. Early made no mention of a juncture with the cavalry in his report. When questioned later why he had not sent out scouts to establish contact with Stuart, Early denied that he received such instructions. By his own admission, Stuart learned of Early's arrival in York from captured Northern newspapers.[49]

History has been burdened ever since with the controversy that has encased Stuart's decision. It was the most fateful, and arguably most consequential, act of his cavalry career. Douglas Southall Freeman, the renowned historian of Lee and his army, termed the enterprise "a reckless adventure," and concluded, "Stuart almost certainly was prompted to undertake a long ride in order to restore the reputation he felt had been impaired in the Battle of Brandy Station." Freeman believed that Stuart had been humiliated by the criticism of him in the Southern press.[50]

Lieutenant Theodore S. Garnett, Jr., a clerk at cavalry headquarters, offered an explanation of Stuart's motives in a postwar newspaper article. "Raiding was Stuart's hobby," wrote Garnett, "and one which he *rode* with never failing persistence." Garnett stated that Stuart knew that he could ride through or around the Union army. "What a glorious opportunity was now offered for the indulgence of his love!" proclaimed the aide. "What a tempting prize lay within his reach. . . . Here was an undertaking which . . . would eclipse in brilliance and real importance any exploit of the war."[51]

He determined then, most likely before he left Rector's Cross Roads, to execute another ride around the Yankees. Another successful expedition, like those of the previous year, could restore his reputation and might further enhance his fame, precious commodities that he coveted. After Brandy Station, the prospects must have glimmered to him. His devotion to the Confederate cause was undeniable. Now, however, devotion to his reputation and stature as a Confederate hero overrode his better judgment. It was as though he could not turn back, for the road ahead offered more than the one behind. Consequently, Stuart disobeyed the spirit, if not the letter, of Lee's orders. In his mind, he might have had but one choice—he went on.

John Mosby and a small band of Rangers, meanwhile, had tried to unite with Stuart's brigades throughout June 25. Stuart had ordered Mosby to gather fresh intelligence on the location of Federal units and to rendezvous with him at Gum Springs. After escaping from an enemy ambush, the Rangers heard the artillery fire from Haymarket and rode toward the sounds. But Union troops clogged the roads, forcing Mosby to seek concealment. They stayed the night, before returning to Fauquier County and then to Snicker's Gap. Grumble Jones's troopers picketed the mountain pass. Whether Mosby informed his former commander that Hooker's army was on the march north is uncertain.[52]

A heavy rain fell during the night of June 25–26. Like the men, Stuart and his staff slept on the sodden ground. The march resumed early the next morning. Angling southeast and then north in a wide arc, the column moved slowly, mainly at a walk. When the riders reached the southern bank of the Occoquan Creek at Wolf Run Shoals, Stuart halted to allow the horses to graze. "The country that we passed through was desolate in the extreme," wrote an artilleryman, "having been the camping ground for both Confederates and Federals for nearly three years."[53]

The Southerners remounted at four o'clock on the morning of June 27, splashed across the creek, and rode north toward Fairfax Court House. As they neared the village, the advance guard was attacked by a squadron of the 11th New York on a reconnaissance mission. The 1st North Carolina rushed forward and engaged the New Yorkers. The mounted clash was fierce for a brief time until the North Carolinians overwhelmed the Yankees, killing, wounding, or capturing nearly the entire two Union companies. Farther east at Annandale, troopers from Fitz Lee's brigade seized a train of sutlers' wagons.[54]

In Fairfax Court House, the Confederates ransacked a pair of warehouses and cleaned out the sutlers' wagon. An officer noted in a letter that they "obtained a large supply of valuable edible stores which were most opportune, we being very hungry." While Stuart watched the activities, he prepared a dispatch for Robert E. Lee: "General: —I took possession of Fairfax C.H. this morning at nine o'clock, together with large quantity of stores. The main body of Hooker's army has gone toward Leesburg, except for the garrison of Alexandria and Washington, which has retreated within the fortifications."[55]

A courier rode away with the letter. By now, nearly all the units of the Army of the Potomac had entered Maryland, located between Stuart's command and Lee's headquarters at Chambersburg, Pennsylvania. The courier never delivered Stuart's message to Lee. A clerk in the War Department at Richmond, however, recorded it in his diary under the July 1 entry. The department employee did not note how the original dispatch or a copy of it reached the Confederate capital. Consequently, Lee learned nothing of Stuart's whereabouts for another four days.[56]

From Fairfax Court House, the horsemen rode toward the Potomac, passing through Dranesville and arriving at Rowser's Ford on the river at sundown. A Virginia sergeant described the site as "an old deer crossing." The Potomac was a half-mile wide at the ford, with the river's waters two feet higher than normal. Stuart had an aide cross, testing the depth, which rose nearly to his saddle. With the 1st North Carolina leading, Hampton's brigade entered the river, crossing in a single file.[57]

The Chesapeake and Ohio Canal edged the north bank of the river. Once across, Hampton's men seized canal boats, placed them against each other, and laid planks crosswise on them for the use of the men. Hampton notified Stuart that it was impossible for the artillery to ford the river. After a fruitless search for another site, Stuart ordered the artillery ammunition distributed among the riders. The current submerged the cannon and caissons, but the six guns made it across. "No more difficult achievement was accomplished by the cavalry during the war," boasted Henry McClellan.[58]

Stuart rested his weary men and horses for a few hours. Details of troopers captured more canal boats and their passengers and wrecked the locks and boats. He learned that the Union army was marching toward Frederick. "I realized the importance of joining our army in Pennsylvania," he wrote later, "and resumed the march northward." Dividing the command into two columns, Stuart led them toward Rockville. The 9th

Virginia, leading Chambliss's brigade, encountered and scattered the 2nd New York in "a running fight," as Stuart put it. When the Southerners rode into the town, they were greeted with "the wildest demonstration of welcome," according to Northern newspapers. The residents offered food to the famished Rebels.[59]

It was past noon when Stuart entered the town. His men cut the telegraph line that linked Frederick to the Federal capital. As he relaxed in a house, a scout arrived and reported the approach of a large train of supply wagons on the pike from Washington. Stuart mounted and raced toward the prize. He and his staff followed closely as horsemen descended on the train. "A circus was on that I have never seen paralleled," exclaimed Frank Robertson.[60]

The Confederates swarmed among the eight-mile-long train of 140 wagons. Panic-stricken teamsters careened the wagons off the road, wrecking them, while others set them on fire to prevent their capture. According to Stuart, "Not one escaped. . . . More than one hundred and twenty-five best United States model wagons and splendid teams with gay caparisons were secured and driven off. The mules and harness of the broken wagons were also secured." The wagons were hauling foodstuffs, oats, hay, and other items to Hooker's army. The Rebels grabbed bacon, ham, crackers, and bread and fed their mounts the oats and hay. "Here was a godsend for our poor horses," declared William Blackford. "It did one's heart good to see the way the poor brutes got on the outside of those oats."[61]

Stuart contemplated and then dismissed a daring attack on the defenses of Washington, realizing that it could not be undertaken before nightfall. He was determined, however, not to relinquish the wagons and teams. His men worked for hours regrouping the train, hitching a pair of mules to each wagon, and herding together more than two hundred additional mules. Writing about the captured vehicles, a captain asserted, "at first they were regarded as a prize, they soon became a great burden." In his memoir, Henry McClellan admitted, "it must be acknowledged that the capture of this train of wagons was a mistake."[62]

The ponderous column lumbered out of Rockville that evening. When the Southerners reached Brookeville at ten o'clock, Stuart rested the command for three hours. Since Fairfax Court House, the Rebels had amassed about four hundred prisoners, including a number of black contrabands. During the halt, Stuart used the porch of Reverend W. Kent Boyle's home to parole most of the Union captives, completing the task the next day in Cooksville. As the people in Rockville had done, the residents of Brookeville welcomed the Confederates and shared food with them.[63]

The march northward resumed at one o'clock on the morning of June 29. Through the night the cavalrymen rode, moving at "a slow gait," in the words of one of them, because of the captured wagons. The strain on the riders and their mounts was becoming evident. They had covered more than one hundred miles since leaving Salem. Horses broke down and were abandoned, with their riders scouring the countryside for replacements. With each successive mile, the problem worsened.[64]

A dozen or so miles north of Brookeville, the Confederates struck the tracks of the Baltimore & Ohio Railroad at daylight. Details of troopers cut down telegraph lines, wrecked tracks at Hood's Mill, and burned a wooden bridge at Sykesville. The damage inflicted and service disrupted was minimal. The next day, after the Rebels had moved on, repair crews restrung the wire and rebuilt the bridge in twenty minutes at a cost of $44.50. Stuart stayed in the area until 10:30 A.M., hoping to intercept a passing train. When none appeared, he left a detachment behind to watch for later ones and led the main body toward Westminster.[65]

"The enemy was ascertained to be moving through Frederick City northward," Stuart explained in his report, "and it was important for me to reach our column with as little delay as possible, to acquaint the commanding general with the nature of the enemy's movements, as well as to place with his column my cavalry force." Stuart's actions belied his concern for a swift juncture with Lee's army. From the capture and retention of the wagon train to the hours spent tearing up railroad tracks, the march possessed the characteristics not of a rapid movement into Pennsylvania, but of a raid. Stuart and his later defenders could justify the damage inflicted upon the Union army's rear by Lee's June 23 orders. But events in Pennsylvania and to the west of Stuart's command in Maryland were transforming the unfolding campaign.[66]

At Confederate army headquarters in Chambersburg, Pennsylvania, meanwhile, Lee expressed to various officers his disquietude over Stuart's whereabouts. He inquired of others: "Can you tell me where General Stuart is?" "Have you any news of the enemy's movements?" Staff member Walter Taylor noted, "The absence of that indispensable arm of the service was most seriously felt by General Lee." Charles Marshall described it as Lee's "apprehension," adding that it "was due entirely to his hearing nothing from General Stuart." On June 27, Lee ordered scouts from the 1st South Carolina to try to establish communication with Stuart's brigades.[67]

About ten o'clock on the night of June 28, Henry Harrison, a Confederate spy hired by Longstreet, arrived at Chambersburg. The Yankees were in Maryland, reported Harrison to Longstreet, and were moving toward Pennsylvania. When Lee interrogated the spy, he was reluctant to accept the news until one of Longstreet's staff officers vouched for Harrison. Lee's initial wariness or disbelief about the vital intelligence is difficult to understand. For nearly a week, he had known of the construction of Union pontoons at Edwards Ferry indicative of a crossing of the Potomac by Hooker. In the intervening days, he must have surmised, regardless of a lack of information from Stuart, that the Federals had entered Maryland. He had predicated his campaign, in part, on the enemy following him into the Keystone State, where he hoped to achieve a decisive victory. Perhaps it was the nearness of the blue-clad units to Pennsylvania that surprised Lee.[68]

With the leading elements of Ewell's Second Corps near the Susquehanna River, Lee ordered a concentration of his scattered divisions east of South Mountain at either Cashtown or Gettysburg. Lee's instructions to Ewell were sent on the morning of June 29. The movement required time to be accomplished. If Lee needed to expedite the concentration, seven of his nine infantry divisions and most of the army's artillery batteries and wagons would have to march on Chambersburg Pike across South Mountain to either of the towns.[69]

While Confederate infantrymen filed onto the roads of south-central Pennsylvania, their opponents edged closer to the state's border. The Union army, however, had undergone a change in commanders. Joseph Hooker and General-in-Chief Henry Halleck had been entwined in a dispute over the garrison at Harper's Ferry. Hooker wanted the ten thousand troops attached to the army and the place abandoned. Halleck opposed the idea. Hooker pressed the issue by submitting his resignation. Halleck forwarded the telegram to Lincoln, who accepted Hooker's resignation.[70]

In Hooker's place, the president appointed Major General George Meade, commander of the Fifth Corps. Lincoln had never met the forty-seven-year-old Pennsylvanian, but he had learned that most of the army's senior officers favored Meade as a successor to Hooker. Meade received the order early on the morning of June 28, outside Frederick, Maryland. No army commander in the country's history faced a more critical and untimely burden than Meade. One of his division commanders, Brigadier General Alpheus S. Williams, writing on June 29, stated: "we run a fearful risk, because upon this small army everything depends. If we are badly defeated the Capital is gone and all our principal cities and our national honor."[71]

Halleck instructed Meade that the army must cover Washington and Baltimore and engage the Rebels. "My endeavor will be in my movements," replied Meade, "to hold my force well together, with the hope of falling upon some portion of Lee's army in detail." Along a broad front, with the cavalry roaming ahead, the army resumed its march north on June 29. When Lee learned of the change in commanders, he supposedly remarked, "General Meade will commit no blunder in my front, and if I make one, he will make haste to take advantage of it."[72]

As a collision between the two armies beckoned with a seeming inevitability, Stuart's horsemen plodded toward Westminster. Leading the mounted column, Fitz Lee's Virginians entered the town from the east late on the afternoon of June 29. On the previous day, Major Napoleon Bonaparte Knight and companies C and D of the 1st Delaware had arrived in Westminster. Knight strung out pickets on the roads into the town, but the oncoming Southerners captured the videttes on their route. Fortunately for the Federals, a local resident alerted them to the Rebels' approach. Knight, who reportedly was drunk in a tavern, ordered Captain Charles Corbit to charge the enemy cavalrymen.[73]

Corbit led his men down East Main Street in a valiant but hopeless attack. The Delaware volunteers fought obstinately in the mounted fight but were overpowered when the Confederates struck in a counterattack. The Union companies, numbering nearly one hundred, lost sixty-seven members killed, wounded, or captured. Two lieutenants of the 4th Virginia, St. Pierre Gibson and John W. Murray, were killed in the fray. The Southerners also captured a detachment of the 150th New York Infantry, which had been posted in the town for a few weeks.[74]

Stuart followed his men and "was greeted with hearty cheers whenever he was recognized." One woman, holding stones in an apron, threw them at the Confederates while shouting, "go back, go back, you nasty rebels." Stuart's men found forage for their horses at the Western Maryland Railroad depot and seized a United States flag, sewn by local women, from the vault in the courthouse. Stuart conferred with Fitz Lee, Hampton, and Chambliss before starting their officers and men toward Union Mills, a few miles south of the Pennsylvania border.[75]

The cavalry commander remained in Westminster for several hours as the miles-long string of horsemen, captured wagons, and herd of mules passed through the town. A Confederate sympathizer invited Stuart to his home for tea. A fellow guest thought that the general "seemed to have a heavy load of care on his mind, and whilst at tea it was noticed that, though at times full of spirits, he occasionally grew abstracted and thoughtful." Like his men, Stuart suffered from exhaustion. His renowned stamina was being drained away, causing him to fall asleep in the saddle at times. When this occurred, staff members held him on his horse by each coat sleeve.[76]

A group of ladies came to Stuart and inquired if they could bury the bodies of Gibson and Murray in the cemetery of the Ascension Episcopal Church. Stuart consented. Four years later, the family of Gibson had his remains disinterred and returned to Virginia. Murray's grave still lies beneath a tree close to the sanctuary.[77]

During the tea, the host asked Stuart if he had concerns about the outcome of an impending battle. "None at all," he responded. "I have the utmost confidence in our men, and I know that if they are given a ghost of a chance they are sure to win." Sometime after midnight he mounted his horse, and with members of his staff, followed his troopers.[78]

Through the early morning darkness of June 30, Stuart's party rode, weaving its way through the strung-out column bivouacked along the road from Westminster to Union Mills. Arriving at daybreak, Stuart and aides joined Fitz Lee for a breakfast of biscuits and shortcakes at the home of William Shriver in the village. When Lee's troopers reached Union Mills before midnight, the Shrivers, who were pro-Confederate, distributed slices of bread to between two hundred and three hundred hungry men. Across the road from William's house was the home of his brother, Andrew, who supported the Union cause. The Shrivers owned and operated the mill at the village.[79]

"Genls. Lee and Stuart were both in the kitchen and everywhere; up stairs, and all around," wrote Miss S. C. Shriver. A Mrs. Heard came to the home, and she and Henry McClellan played a piano while the others sang. "I wish you had heard Genl. Stuart sing, accompanied by all the rest,—'If you want to be a bully boy join the cavalry' to the tune of 'Great Big House and Nobody Living,'" added Miss Shriver. "If you had seen him, he put as much enthusiasm in that song as I know he does into matters of a much more serious nature, his eyes sparkled; and he kept time with his foot, he was the very personification of fun and spirit."[80]

While at Union Mills, scouts reported the presence of Union cavalry at Littlestown, Pennsylvania, several miles to the north on the road to Gettysburg. Stuart asked William Shriver if his sixteen-year-old son, T. Herbert Shriver, could act as guide as the Confederates entered Pennsylvania. In return, Stuart promised to secure admission for the teenager into the Virginia Military Institute. The father consented, and Stuart fulfilled his pledge. Herbert Shriver would enter the school and be in the cadet ranks at the Battle of New Market on May 15, 1864.[81]

Henry McClellan argued subsequently that when they stopped at Union Mills "it would have been better had Stuart here destroyed the captured wagons." "But it was not in Stuart's nature to abandon an attempt until it have been proven to be beyond his powers," explained the chief of staff, "and he determined to hold on to his prize until the last moment. This was unfortunate."[82]

When the Confederates left Union Mills, Stuart detached Lee's brigade to cover their left flank toward Littlestown, while the main body proceeded on the road toward Hanover, Pennsylvania. Chambliss's regiments led the column toward Hanover, followed by the wagons, and then Hampton's brigade. An officer described the advance as a "hurried march" up and over steep hills that "prostrated men & horses." Stuart took three local men from their homes to act as additional guides. The van of Chambliss's brigade approached Hanover, a town of about 1,600 residents, about ten o'clock in the morning of June 30. Before them, the Rebels saw Federal cavalrymen in the streets.[83]

The Yankees belonged to Brigadier General Elon J. Farnsworth's brigade of Judson Kilpatrick's Third Cavalry Division. They were the enemy that Stuart's scouts had detected at Littlestown. Kilpatrick's 3,500-man division had been ordered toward York, to locate units of Richard Ewell's Confederate Second Corps. With two regiments of Brigadier General George A. Custer's Michigan Brigade leading the march from Littlestown, most of Kilpatrick's regiments had already passed through Hanover when a detachment from the 13th Virginia struck part of the 18th Pennsylvania southwest of the town. Neither side expected such an encounter.[84]

The Virginians routed the Pennsylvanians, sending them, in Stuart's words, "pell-mell through the town." Chambliss unlimbered a battery, and the gunners began shelling the place. When Stuart heard the gunfire, he hurried forward John Esten Cooke to ascertain the situation. When Cooke returned with the news that Chambliss was driving the enemy, Stuart said: "Good! Tell him to push on and occupy the town, but not to pursue them too far." By then, however, the Virginians had come upon the 5th New York, whose members were mounted and dismounted in the town square. In Cooke's retelling, "We had supposed their force to be small, but it was now seen to be heavy."[85]

The New Yorkers blasted the Virginians with a volley and counterattacked. Perhaps one hundred men of the 2nd North Carolina had joined the Virginians and were also hit by the gunfire and enemy attack. Troopers from the 18th Pennsylvania rallied and charged along with the 1st West Virginia and 1st Vermont. The Rebels broke under the onslaught. But the 9th Virginia, numbering nearly five hundred officers and men, had been sent forward, and a volley from its members stalled briefly the Federal assault.[86]

Stuart, staff members, and couriers spurred forward to rally the shattered ranks. The Rebels were in "confusion," recounted William Blackford. The 9th Virginia was fleeing, and it became a race to escape capture. After his horse stumbled, Lieutenant Colonel William H. F. Payne, temporarily commanding the North Carolinians, fell into a vat of brown dye at a tannery and was taken prisoner. Stuart, Blackford, and others rode into a field, where "before we were aware of it," wrote Blackford, "we found ourselves at the head of the enemy's charging column."[87]

The Confederates bolted for the rear amid a string of pistol bullets. Stuart, Blackford, and several riders eluded the Yankees by jumping their mounts over a fifteen-foot-wide gully. Others in the party plunged their horses into the ditch but escaped. The pursuers reined up. It had been the narrowest of escapes for the renowned cavalryman. Minutes before, Chambliss had been told by one of his Virginians that Stuart had been surrounded and probably taken prisoner. With the flight of the Southerners, the fighting subsided.[88]

"If my command had been well closed now," argued Stuart in his report, "this [Union] cavalry column, which we had struck near its rear, would have been at our mercy." Instead, he found his command entangled in an untimely engagement, with Hampton's brigade miles away behind the wagon train and Fitz Lee's regiments also en route. Uncertain of the enemy force in his front, Stuart had urged Chambliss to seize the town. But the Union counterattacks scattered Chambliss's ranks, secured Hanover, and blocked a direct route northward for the Confederates.[89]

When Hampton's and Lee's troopers arrived, they formed a line on Chambliss's flanks. Throughout the afternoon the Rebels engaged Kilpatrick's entire division in skirmishes and artillery exchanges. During the action, Stuart was given a newspaper, which reported that Jubal Early's division had been in York but had marched away. The article did not specify in which direction the infantrymen went. After nightfall, Stuart's command pulled away, marching east and then north in an arc around Hanover. Casualties in the fight had amounted to fewer than three hundred combined.[90]

In his report, Stuart confessed, "Our wagon train was now a subject of serious embarrassment, but I thought, by making a *détour* to the right by Jefferson, I could save it." Unwilling then to abandon the captured vehicles and teams, Stuart had no other choice but to make a wide swing away from Kilpartrick's command. At Jefferson, he planned to turn north, stating, "every accessible source of information" placed the Confederate army near the Susquehanna River. His men were also burdened with nearly four hundred prisoners, who had been taken since he paroled the other captives in Maryland. Stuart had asked much of his veterans in the past; now he demanded even more.[91]

Away from Hanover and into the night, the Confederates marched. Fitz Lee led, followed by the wagons, mule herd, and prisoners, then Chambliss, and finally Hampton. To Jefferson and a bend north, past the western edges of York, and on to Dover, they crawled. At points, the column stretched for ten miles. Horses broke down, their backs raw with saddle sores. Their riders used the wagons, mounted mules, or secured one of the confiscated animals. Starved for water and forage, the mules became unmanageable. Overcome by exhaustion, the men fell asleep in their saddles.[92]

In their letters and reminiscences, the officers and men recounted the ordeal of this march. A North Carolinian echoed the words of many in a letter to home, "I thought I knew some thing of the hardships of a soldier's life before but must confess that I did not." They spoke of "perishing" and "starving." Stuart had forbidden pillaging, but many men ignored the order, breaking into stores in the towns and carrying away items. Some of them begged for food and noted the generosity of Pennsylvanians. A member of Hampton's brigade asserted: "We fared first rate in Pennsylvania. The Citizens gave us plenty of Bread and milk." He seemed, however, to be an exception. More typically was the experience of a Virginian, "Some of us nearly starved."[93]

Stuart wrote afterward, "The night's march over a very dark road was one of peculiar hardship." He accompanied Fitz Lee's brigade at the head of the lengthy column. When the Virginians entered the village of Dover on the morning of July 1, he ordered a halt. Stuart paroled the Union prisoners. While in the town, he learned—probably from citizens—that Early's division had marched toward Shippensburg on the previous day. With Early's troops or other units in Ewell's corps perhaps only miles away, he sent out Major Andrew Venable, Jr., of his staff and a party of couriers in search of the infantry commands.[94]

Believing that elements of Ewell's corps might be in Carlisle, Stuart resumed the march, angling northwest, passing through Dillsburg. Once more, the Confederates rode as if in a stupor. "The men were overcome and so tired and stupid," averred a lieutenant, "as almost to be ignorant of what was taking place around them." Nevertheless, the seizure of civilian horses continued, called "a very disagreeable necessity" by a Virginian. Late in the afternoon, Fitz Lee's vanguard reached the outskirts of Carlisle. Instead of finding their comrades in Ewell's Second Corps in the town, the horsemen encountered a force of 2,400 New York militiamen and Pennsylvania emergency troops.[95]

Stuart came forward. Rations had been exhausted, and his men and mounts needed food and forage. "I disliked to subject the town to the consequences of attack," he declared, "at the same time it was essential to us to procure rations." Under a flag of truce, he demanded an unconditional surrender. If refused, he would order his artillery to fire upon the town. The Union commander was Major General William F. "Baldy" Smith, a West Point graduate and career soldier, who had commanded the Sixth Corps at Fredericksburg. Ordered to pursue Ewell's troops when they withdrew from the Susquehanna River opposite Harrisburg, Smith and his command had arrived in Carlisle a short time before Stuart's cavalrymen appeared from the southeast.[96]

When Smith heard Stuart's demand and threat, he replied, "Shell away and be damned!" Stuart ordered the cannon deployed and sent in a second surrender demand. Once more, Smith refused. "I thought some time," conjectured Major Norman FitzHugh of Stuart's staff in a letter, "that the General meant to pay them back for . . . Fredericksburg." When Stuart received the final refusal, in FitzHugh's words, "he ordered everything let loose upon the town."[97]

The Confederate gun crews unleashed their rounds. The shells screeched into homes and businesses, battering down walls. Despite the cannon's roar, the Southerners heard the screams of women and children. The bombardment was intermittent. A cavalryman commented that he and his comrades were so exhausted that they fell asleep during the shelling while lying near the guns. He also related that one man dozed off as he climbed over a fence. "It is impossible for me," swore an officer in a letter, "to give you a correct idea of the fatigue and exhaustion of the men and beasts at this time."[98]

About ten o'clock Lieutenant Frank Robertson carried an order from Stuart to Colonel Williams Wickham of the 4th Virginia. Stuart directed Wickham to burn Carlisle Barracks, the Regular Army's cavalry school. Wickham's Virginians torched seven of the post's eleven buildings, destroying officers' quarters, barracks, and stables. The loss was later estimated at $47,600. A detail from another of Fitz Lee's regiments burned the town's gas works and outbuildings. Stuart justified the destruction by arguing, "the place resisted my advance instead of peaceable surrender."[99]

As flames from the fires glowed in the night, Major Venable returned from his search for Ewell's troops. The staff officer had ridden to Gettysburg, where he found the Confederates engaged with two corps of the Army of the Potomac in a fierce battle north and west of the town. With the infantry divisions still not concentrated, Robert E. Lee had wanted to avoid a general engagement. A collision had occurred, and subordinate generals had entangled the army in the unexpected, but burgeoning, struggle.[100]

During the morning, Lee had inquired of Major Campbell Brown, Ewell's assistant adjutant general and stepson, if the Second Corps commander "had heard anything" from Stuart. Brown, who was delivering a message to Lee, related afterward that Lee's question was asked "with a peculiar searching, almost querulous impatience." When Brown responded that they knew nothing of Stuart's whereabouts, Lee stated, "that Gen'l Stuart had not complied with his instructions." Instead of remaining in constant communication with the army, Stuart had marched around the rear of the Union army. Lee knew this only through Northern newspapers. The army commander was, thought Brown, "really uneasy & irritated by Stuart's conduct & had no objection to his [Brown's] hearing of it."[101]

Lee's demeanor and tone surprised Brown. Other officers likewise noted the commanding general's anxiety about the cavalry's absence on this morning. Similarly, he inquired: "Have you heard anything about my cavalry? Any news to give me about General Stuart?" Before Brown rode away, he directed the aide to have Ewell send out a mounted patrol in search of the missing three brigades. Ewell complied, dispatching a nine-man detail.[102]

When Venable arrived at Second Corps headquarters and reported that Stuart was at Carlisle, Ewell directed him to Lee. The Confederate commander gave Venable orders for Stuart to march to Gettysburg. Carlisle was roughly thirty miles north of Gettysburg, and Venable rejoined Stuart about midnight. Stuart acted at once—Fitz Lee, Chambliss, and the horse artillery would follow the road from Carlisle; Hampton and the wagon train, to the rear at Dillsburg, would move from that village and proceed ten miles during the night. In the early minutes of July 2, Stuart and a coterie of staff officers started ahead of the cavalry for Gettysburg.[103]

Esten Cooke believed, "This night march was the most severe I ever experienced." At dawn, Stuart halted and announced that he was going to sleep for two hours. "Everybody imitated him," recalled Cooke. After two hours, Stuart awoke, mounted his horse, and continued alone to Gettysburg. He reached the battlefield probably between noon and 1:00 P.M. When he reported personally to Lee, the army commander purportedly remarked, "Well, General Stuart, you are here at last." Although no record exists of their conversation, the meeting was, according to Henry McClellan, "painful beyond description."[104]

Afterward, at Lee's direction, Stuart rode to the army's left flank along York Road. Throughout the afternoon, Fitz Lee's and Chambliss's troopers and horse artillerymen reached Confederate lines. When they passed the infantry, "such joyful shouts as rent the air I never heard," proclaimed Major Norman FitzHugh, "the cavalry for once was well received." A private in the 2nd Virginia, describing their exhaustion, wrote, "The men would reel in their saddles like drunken men." Late in the afternoon, Hampton's veterans fought a rearguard action with Judson Kilpatrick's Union horsemen at Hunterstown, a few miles northeast of Gettysburg. The Georgians of Cobb's Legion repulsed the enemy attack, and the fighting frittered away.[105]

Sleep came easily that night to the Confederate cavalrymen. They had been on the march for eight days, suffering from hunger and numbing fatigue, contending with fractious mules, and clashing several times with their foes. By one estimate, they had covered 250 miles. The journey had been long. For their commander, Jeb Stuart, the journey would be beyond measurement in miles.[106]

Chapter Fourteen

"I Have Been Blessed with Great Success on This Campaign"

T HE STENCH OF death hung over the battlefield of Gettysburg, Pennsylvania, on the night of July 2–3, 1863. Amid the foul odor, "a low, steady, indescribable moan," in the words of a Union lieutenant, rolled across the fields and woodlots. The sound came from the pleading voices of dying and wounded men. Their curses, prayers, and groans were, said the officer, "literally heart rending." The red lights of ambulance lanterns dotted the moonlit darkness, marking each stop in a plentiful harvest of human wreckage. Two days of fighting had exacted a staggering toll of nearly 34,000 killed, wounded, and missing, but the battle's outcome remained unresolved.[1]

On July 1, Robert E. Lee's Army of Northern Virginia, as it had so often in the past year, achieved a signal victory. The Confederates battered the Union First and Eleventh corps, swept them through the town, killed Major General John F. Reynolds, and corralled four thousand prisoners. Through the ensuing night and next day, the armies gathered. As Lee wrote, "A battle thus became, in a measure, unavoidable."[2]

Major General George Meade, commander of the Army of the Potomac, rode onto the battlefield in the early hours of July 2. Subordinate officers informed him that the army's position was good ground upon which to wage a defensive struggle. As Meade's five remaining infantry corps arrived, the Union line extended from Culp's Hill on the right flank, west to Cemetery Hill, and then south along Cemetery Ridge to the base of Little Round Top. Described eventually as a fishhook, it possessed natural strengths and a convex character that could expedite the shifting of units from one threatened section to another.[3]

Against the objections of First Corps commander James Longstreet, Lee decided to assail the Union ranks on July 2. Late in the afternoon, the Confederates advanced against the Federal left flank. The divisions of major generals John Hood and Lafayette McLaws of Longstreet's corps carried out the assault. Through the Peach Orchard, across Stony Hill, into the Wheatfield, beyond Devil's Den, up the slopes of Little Round Top, and onto the crest of Cemetery Ridge, the Rebels charged. The combat was savage and bloody, with Union reserves sealing breaches in the line and clinging to the high ground. A pair of evening and night-time attacks by the Southerners against East Cemetery Hill and Culp's Hill resulted in more casualties and few gains. "The fighting was most desperate," admitted a Rebel in a letter, "the enemy fighting much harder on their own soil & having the best position."[4]

Lee's vaunted infantry had come remarkably close to achieving a tactical victory. Longstreet praised his veteran soldiers, calling their efforts "the best three hours' fighting ever done by any troops on any battle-field." Lee believed, as he put it, "with proper concert of attack," his army could break the enemy lines. Before midnight, he issued orders for a renewal of the offensive against both Union flanks. "The general plan was unchanged," wrote Lee. Longstreet's third division, under Major General George E. Pickett, had reached the battlefield late in the afternoon of July 2, and was to be added to the attack force.[5]

Jeb Stuart's role in the July 3 operations remains ill-defined. Evidently, Lee gave him verbal orders, as no written ones or dispatches seem to exist. In his report, Stuart wrote only, "pursuant to instructions from the commanding general." Unquestionably, the cavalry was to protect the army's left flank, while moving on the Union right flank. He must have been informed of Lee's offensive plans for the day, but whether the cavalry was to have any active part in the operations appears doubtful.

Most likely, based upon the day's events, Stuart was directed to seek an opportunity for a strike against the enemy or possibly to seize Baltimore Pike, the main Union supply line.[6]

A cavalry sergeant contended that dawn of July 3 "found our command in a poor condition to undergo the hardship of a battle with credit either to themselves or their country." Hundreds, if not thousands, of Stuart's men had abandoned ranks during the ride, had their mounts break down, or were physically unable to perform their duties. Robert E. Lee stated that the cavalry ranks were "much reduced." Although a modern study has calculated Stuart's "engaged strength" in the three brigades on July 3 at 4,836 officers and men, accounts by members of the command offer a much lower figure. A reasonable estimate would be fewer than three thousand in the saddle on this morning.[7]

Stuart's numerical strength was augmented by Brigadier General Albert Jenkins's brigade of Virginia regiments and battalions. Officially assigned to the cavalry division, Jenkins's troopers had accompanied Ewell's corps into Pennsylvania. On July 2, Jenkins had been knocked unconscious by a shell fragment, and Colonel Milton J. Ferguson assumed command. On this day, however, various companies from the brigade guarded Union prisoners, and Ferguson stayed in the rear with them. Lieutenant Colonel Vincent A. Witcher of the 34th Virginia Battalion commanded the remaining companies. Witcher wrote later that he had barely 350 officers and men with him when he joined Stuart.[8]

The cavalry marched early on July 3. Hampton's brigade backtracked through Hunterstown before turning south toward York Road. Witcher's, Chambliss's, and Fitz Lee's commands rode across the fields north of York Road, crossed it, and then followed narrow country roads south toward Hanover Road. Witcher's Virginians led the column, trailed by Chambliss's troopers. When the two brigades reached the western base of wooded Cress Ridge, they halted and dismounted. It would be an hour or more until Hampton's and Fitz Lee's regiments came up, stopping on the farms of a Miller and a Stallworth, north of the ridge.[9]

Stuart and his staff accompanied the leading units. While the troopers rested, he rode onto the crest of the ridge. Before him, stretching southward, lay the farms of John Rummel and Jacob Lott. John and

Sarah Rummel owned Cress Ridge, and the stand of trees on it was known locally as Rummel's Woods. In the distance, at the intersection of Low Dutch Road and Hanover Road, Stuart saw Union cavalry and a battery.[10]

The Federals belonged to the Michigan Brigade of Brigadier General George Custer. Promoted from brevet captain to brigadier on June 29, Custer was at twenty-three the youngest general in the Union army. He wore a uniform of black velvet trimmed with gold lace, a wide-collared blue navy shirt with silver stars sewn at the points of the collar, a red necktie, and a wide-brimmed felt hat. Like Stuart, he was ambitious, fearless, and seemed to be a knight-errant born in the wrong century. At Hunterstown, he had had a horse shot from under him while leading a charge. With his long blond hair, his Michiganders called him "the boy General of the Golden Lock."[11]

Ordered to hold the crossroads, Custer arrived about an hour before the Confederates. Low Dutch Road continued past the intersection for a few miles to Two Taverns on Baltimore Pike. If Stuart intended as one of his objectives the seizure of Baltimore Pike in the Union rear, the Low Dutch Road–Hanover Road intersection was vital to the Northerners. The march of the Confederate cavalry had been detected by Federals on Culp's Hill, and an advance guard from Custer had also reported the Rebels' approach. Custer deployed the 5th Michigan, armed with Spencer rifles, a .56-caliber weapon with a seven-shot magazine, as skirmishers and unlimbered the six rifled cannon of Lieutenant Alexander C. M. Pennington's Battery M, 2nd United States Artillery.[12]

Before noon, Stuart advanced five companies of the 34th Virginia Battalion to the Rummel farm buildings, where these dismounted troops occupied the barn and manned a stone wall. On the crest of the ridge, a pair of ten-pound Parrott cannon of the Louisiana Guard Artillery, a Second Corps battery temporarily attached to the cavalry, unlimbered. Stuart ordered the gun crews to open on the enemy. Henry McClellan claimed in his memoir that after their arrival on Cress Ridge, Stuart had a cannon fire "a number of random shots in different directions." Neither Stuart nor other participants substantiate McClellan's account.[13]

Pennington's artillerists soon forced the Louisiana gun crews off the crest. Before long, Brigadier General David Gregg, commander of the Second Cavalry Division, the mounted brigade of Colonel John B. McIntosh, and Captain Alanson M. Randol's Batteries E and G, 1st United States Artillery, joined Custer. Gregg assumed command on the field and ordered Custer, whose brigade served in Judson Kilpatrick's Third Cavalry Division, to remain on the field. Gregg had about 3,000 cavalrymen and artillerists to oppose Stuart's approximately 3,200 to 3,500 Confederates.[14]

For the next three hours—as the foes heard distinctly the cannonade before Pickett's Charge, the sound of which a Pennsylvania trooper described "as tho there were thousands of acres of timber on fire"—the Yankees and Rebels conducted a deadly prelude of skirmishing and artillery duels. Gregg funneled units—the 1st New Jersey and four companies of the 6th Michigan—onto the skirmish line with the 5th Michigan. More of Witcher's Virginians clustered around the Rummel buildings and along the stone wall. Nine Confederate artillery pieces rolled onto Cress Ridge and three more cannon unlimbered behind the rise to oppose Pennington's and Randol's crews. The superior Union ordnance prevailed, disabling cannon and killing and wounding gunners and horses.[15]

Stuart watched the action with increasing frustration. He had planned to hold the enemy skirmishers in place, and moving south behind Cress Ridge, strike Gregg's left flank. But when a portion of Witcher's Virginians withdrew after expending their ammunition and the New Jerseymen and Michiganders pressed forward, he decided to sweep them from the field with a mounted charge. "I would have preferred a different method of attack," explained Stuart, but the enemy's aggressiveness changed his plans and he was "determined to make the best fight possible."[16]

The 9th and 13th Virginia of Chambliss's brigade cleared Rummel's Woods and descended the sloping ground past the Rummel house and outbuildings. The dismounted Union skirmishers fled before the Confederates on horseback. When Gregg saw the Virginians, he ordered forward the 7th Michigan in a counterattack. The Michiganders formed ranks into a close column of squadrons and advanced. Suddenly, Custer rode up to the head of the regiment. He had much to prove to his new command. As the pace of the regiment quickened, he turned in his saddle and shouted, "Come on, you Wolverines!"[17]

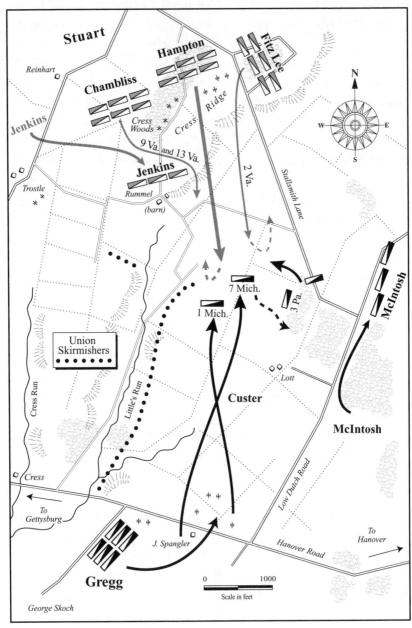

Cavalry Fight, July 3, 1863

"We stopped to see that charge," exclaimed a skirmisher of his fellow Michiganders. The charging horsemen collided at a post-and-rail fence in a wild melee of sabers, pistols, and carbines at close range. A Federal lieutenant averred, "It was kill all you can do your best each for himself." The Yankees broke through the jumbled mass of Virginians, driving toward Rummel's Woods. On came the 1st North Carolina and the Jeff Davis Legion, blunting the enemy's pursuit and tumbling them rearward.[18]

Hampton, meanwhile, rode forward to recall the 1st North Carolina and Jeff Davis Legion. He had been searching unsuccessfully on Cress Ridge for Stuart, who by one account was near the Rummel barn. As Hampton was returning with his units, the other regiments in his command—the 1st and 2nd South Carolina and the Phillips Legion—and the 1st Virginia of Fitz Lee's brigade advanced in a second attack. Their drawn sabers, "glistening like silver in the bright sunlight," gave them a formidable appearance. Hampton joined his men in the charge.[19]

The Confederates started at a walk, increased to a trot, and then "yelling like demons," charged at a gallop. A Michigander, watching them, admitted, "It was an inspiriting and imposing spectacle." The Rebels surged toward the Union cannon, whose crews switched the ammunition to canister. From the south, once again, came a Union regiment—the 1st Michigan—to meet them. And for a second time, Custer rode in the front and shouted, "Come on, you Wolverines!"[20]

The foes crashed together in a tangle of somersaulted horses and unsaddled riders. An onlooker likened the noise of the collision to "the falling of timber." The opposing cavalrymen slashed with swords and fired revolvers at point-blank range. On the edges of the mass, dismounted Union troopers laced the Confederates with rifle fire. A squadron of the 3rd Pennsylvania knifed into the Rebel left flank, forging a lane through the jumbled ranks. Hampton reeled in the saddle from two saber cuts to the head and a bullet wound. His men extricated him from the fighting, taking him to the rear and placing him in an ambulance. Hampton thought initially that he was dying.[21]

The Confederate attack broke, with the Rebels "sweeping back to the rear." The Federals pursued to the Rummel farm and then retired. Both sides had had enough. Gregg reported casualties of 254; Stuart,

182. Although the combined losses amounted to less than 10 percent of those engaged, a Virginian claimed, "Mounted fights never lasted long, but there were more men killed and wounded in this fight than I ever saw on any field where the fighting was done mounted." A Michigander bragged afterward, "Cavalry never did such fighting before in America."[22]

Stuart waited until nightfall before withdrawing to York Road. Whatever designs he had, Custer's and McIntosh's horse soldiers thwarted them. Stuart maintained in his report that he had secured the army's left flank and "commanded a view of the routes leading to the enemy's rear." "Had the enemy's main body been dislodged, as was confidently hoped and expected," he continued, "I was in precisely the right position to discover it and improve the opportunity." He attributed the change in his plans to his cavalry "being exposed to view" of the Federal horsemen, who stayed and contested the ground.[23]

The cavalry engagement was, however, eclipsed by the drama that unfolded in the fields between Seminary Ridge and Cemetery Ridge south of Gettysburg. Minutes after two o'clock in the afternoon, nine Confederate infantry brigades, upward of 13,000 officers and men, stepped forth in one of the war's most renowned attacks, Pickett's Charge. The assault had not been Robert E. Lee's original plan for the day. But when James Longstreet failed, either through misunderstanding or miscommunication, to order George Pickett's division to be on the field at daybreak, Lee was forced to refashion his offensive on this section of the battlefield. Longstreet objected fervently to a frontal attack, but Lee was unswayed in his determination to strike the Union center.[24]

Prior to the infantry advance, Lee's artillerists, manning more than 160 guns, pounded the enemy line in a cannonade unparalleled in the annals of the Confederate army. Then came the infantry—Pickett's division of Virginians; Brigadier General J. Johnston Pettigrew's division of North Carolinians, Virginians, Mississippians, Alabamians, and Tennesseeans; and two brigades of North Carolinians under Major General Isaac Trimble. Valor meant much on this afternoon, but it was not enough as Union guns crews and veteran infantrymen ripped apart the oncoming ranks with shellfire, canister, and musketry. A few hundred of the Southerners breached the Union line only to be overwhelmed and forced back. Lee rode out to his retreating men, saying to them, "It was not your fault this time."[25]

Lee consolidated his lines during the night of July 3–4, preparatory to a return march to Virginia. If Meade did not attack on July 4, Lee planned to begin the withdrawal during the day. A retreat meant an admission of defeat and an abandonment of thousands of wounded men, but the Confederate commander had no other choice. The army's ammunition stores had been seriously reduced, its supplies nearly consumed, and its casualties staggering. Confederate killed, wounded, and missing exceeded 28,000, while Union losses amounted to slightly more than 23,000. The carnage surpassed in total casualties any engagement in the war.[26]

The cavalry would have to protect the army's miles-long trains of wagons and ambulances and screen its rear. Lee now had seven mounted brigades to perform the duty. The commands of brigadier generals John Imboden, Beverly Robertson, and Grumble Jones had joined the army during July 3. Imboden's brigade, an independent unit not under Stuart's authority, had trailed the army into Pennsylvania, protecting its rear, gathering supplies, and guarding the wagon train. Robertson and Jones had marched from the Blue Ridge gaps and arrived at Cashtown. During the day, Jones's Virginians routed the 6th United States in a clash at Fairfield, several miles southwest of Gettysburg.[27]

It is unlikely that at this time Stuart learned how Robertson had failed so miserably in his assigned mission along the Blue Ridge. His primary duty, as designated in orders from Stuart, had been to hold Ashby's and Snicker's gaps, to watch closely for enemy movements, and to keep Lee and Longstreet informed of a Federal march northward. Robertson claimed that he sent a number of dispatches by couriers to army headquarters. No such messages have been found either from him or Jones. It would have been uncharacteristic of Jones not to comply with orders, but he might have passed on intelligence to Robertson, his superior officer, assuming it would be relayed into Pennsylvania.[28]

In a postwar interview, when asked if he had obeyed Stuart's instructions, Robertson answered, "I did, literally and promptly." The facts and evidence, however, belie his assertion. Neither he nor Jones appear to have detected the movement of the Union army toward the Potomac River and into Maryland—a critical task. Then when Lee summoned them to Pennsylvania on June 29, after the spy Harrison reported his information, their brigades took four days to reach Cashtown, evidently marching, as Longstreet put it, in "a slow ride." Robertson had ill-served Lee, Stuart, and the cause.[29]

But Stuart's responsibility in this matter cannot be dismissed. He knew well Robertson's weaknesses as a cavalry officer and ignored Longstreet's suggestion of assigning Hampton to the mission. In Stuart's defense, he expected rightfully that Robertson would be active and obey his explicit orders. Conversely, his decision to leave Robertson and Jones behind suggests further Stuart's determination, made at Rector's Cross Roads, to conduct another ride around the Union army, accompanied by officers he trusted. John Mosby, who defended Stuart's performance in the Gettysburg Campaign after the war, told Henry McClellan, "The only thing I blame Stuart for, was not having him [Robertson] shot."[30]

A judgment on Robertson's conduct awaited a later time. For the present, Lee needed the services of all of his mounted units during the retreat. The growing prowess of Union cavalry was evident. The return march to Virginia, with a passage across the Potomac, was a difficult and dangerous undertaking. Miles of supply and ordnance wagons and ambulances required protection during the lengthy journey, in addition to the army itself. The duty was to be demanding for Stuart's command.[31]

Lee issued the retreat instructions on July 4. The army's three infantry corps, artillery battalions, Second Corps wagons and reserve train, and 5,500 Federal prisoners were to march through Fairfield, Pennsylvania, on the direct road to Hagerstown, Maryland. The wagon trains and ambulances of the other two infantry corps and cavalry division were to move on Chambersburg Pike across South Mountain, escorted by Imboden's independent brigade. Finally, Lee designated the duties for the cavalry, while allowing Stuart to make the assignments.[32]

Two mounted squadrons accompanied the main body of the army, covering the front and rear. Stuart ordered the brigades of Fitz Lee and Hampton, the latter now under the command of Colonel Laurence Baker of the 1st North Carolina, to follow Imboden's trains and guard the right flank and rear during the retreat. Robertson's and Jones's commands were directed to proceed to the gaps of Jack's Mountain, part of the South Mountain chain, above Fairfield, and to hold them. With Chambliss's and Ferguson's troopers, Stuart and his staff were to screen the retreating columns' left flank and rear, moving south toward Emmitsburg, Maryland.[33]

A drenching rain began falling on the afternoon of July 4, churning roads into sloughs of mud and adding to the misery of the wounded men still lying on the battlefield. The Southern army's wagon trains rolled forth during the day, followed after dark by the infantry and cavalry. Stuart and the two brigades had a difficult ride, slowed by the rain, darkness, and unfamiliarity with the country roads. He halted for several hours of rest and employed a guide before proceeding on. They reached Emmitsburg at dawn, on July 5, where they secured rations and learned that a Union cavalry division had passed through the previous afternoon.[34]

The Yankees were Judson Kilpatrick's horse soldiers, moving in pursuit of the Confederate wagon trains. From Emmitsburg, the Yankees rode toward Waynesboro, Pennsylvania. Before midnight on July 4, they overtook a train at Monterey Pass west of Jack's Mountain. George Custer's Michiganders led the attack "into a boiling pot of hell," according to one of them. A battalion of Southern cavalrymen resisted stubbornly in the night's blackness and pouring rain until overwhelmed and routed. The Federals swept into the train of wagons and ambulances. In all, Kilpatrick's men either wrecked or seized about 250 vehicles and bagged nearly 1,300 prisoners. Grumble Jones barely escaped capture in the wild melee on the mountain.[35]

From Monterey Pass, Kilpatrick's cavalrymen and the captured wagons, ambulances, and prisoners descended the western face of the mountain, moving southwest. During the march Kilpatrick ordered many of the Confederate wagons burned. The column arrived about nine o'clock on the morning of July 5, at Smithsburg, Maryland. Kilpatrick halted, resting the men and animals. Isolated from other units of the Union army, Kilpatrick encircled the town with scouts and pickets.[36]

Across the mountains to the east, meanwhile, Stuart and the two brigades left Emmitsburg. The Rebels plodded south to Mechanicstown

(present-day Thurmont), and turned west into a gap in the Catoctin
Mountains, another section of the South Mountain range. Late in the
afternoon, they debouched from the mountains and encountered Kilpatrick's videttes, which fled to Smithsburg to alert their comrades. The
road forked as it neared the mountain's base, and Stuart sent Chambliss's veterans to the right and Ferguson's Virginians to the left toward
the Yankees. He also brought forward a battery of horse artillery.[37]

Across the rolling fields the Federals stood on hills, their lines
braced with cannon and dismounted skirmishers to the front. Ferguson's men advanced on foot, engaging the Yankees. Gun crews worked
their pieces. Stuart, who accompanied Chambliss's Virginians, sent
them in dismounted against Kilpatrick's left flank. The aggressive move
collapsed the Union flank, with the blue-jacketed troopers streaming
rearward. Kilpatrick ordered a hurried withdrawal, and his brigades rode
south toward Boonsborough. Behind them, the Rebels occupied the
town.[38]

While the Confederates rested in Smithsburg, Captain George M.
Emack rode in. Emack had commanded the companies of Marylanders
at Monterey Pass and brought word to Stuart of the Federals' capture.
"It was nearly night," related Stuart, "and I felt it of the first importance
to open communication with the main army." He chose Private Robert
Goode of the 1st Virginia, "a trusty and intelligent soldier," to deliver
the information to Robert E. Lee. Stuart remounted the brigades, and
they rode north through the night to Leitersburg.[39]

By daybreak on July 6, the gray ribbon of retreating Confederate
infantrymen and artillerists still extended for about twenty miles, from
Waynesboro to outside Fairfield, Pennsylvania. Ahead of them, the
main caravan of wagons rolled on, nearing Hagerstown, and moving
toward Williamsport, the planned crossing site on the Potomac. At Williamsport, a huge park of wagons and ambulances, including the train
escorted by Imboden's brigade, awaited passage across the rising waters
of the river. The cavalrymen of Fitz Lee and Laurence Baker guarded
the northern approaches to the town.[40]

A key juncture on the retreat route was Hagerstown, toward which
Stuart marched on the morning of July 6. Robertson's and Jones's brigades joined him at Leitersburg. Stuart ordered Chambliss's command,

trailed by Robertson's two regiments, on the direct road to Hagerstown, while sending Jones by Cavetown to Funkstown, south of Hagerstown on the road to Boonsborough. Stuart, with Ferguson's Virginians, followed Jones to Cavetown, and then headed west toward Hagerstown. The three routes of advance gave Stuart flexibility in the event of an enemy movement on Hagerstown.[41]

When Chambliss's horsemen entered Hagerstown, they dismounted and barricaded the streets. About midday, Chambliss learned of the approach of Judson Kilpatrick's mounted division on the road from Boonsborough, where the Federals had withdrawn after the encounter with Stuart at Smithsburg. The Virginia colonel hastened a courier to Stuart, with a plea for reinforcements. While Robertson's North Carolinians came up behind Chambliss, Stuart led Ferguson's troopers toward the town. Jones's brigade, meanwhile, spurred ahead to Funkstown, in the rear of Kilpatrick's force.[42]

The initial Union assault by the 18th Pennsylvania broke through the barricades and routed the 9th and 10th Virginia. The Southerners rallied, however, fighting from street to street, house to house. Stuart rode ahead of Ferguson's men, who deployed on the town's eastern edge and began pressing forward against the enemy's right flank. In the town, Stuart rode up to the 5th North Carolina as it prepared to counterattack and shouted to its members, "We've got 'em now, boys."[43]

The North Carolinians met the Yankees in a mounted brawl of sabers and pistols. The charge stalled the Federal drive, with the fighting spiraling into an action between dismounted cavalrymen behind buildings and walls. When Brigadier General Alfred Iverson, Jr.'s Confederate infantry brigade appeared and triggered volleys at the Northerners, Kilpatrick retreated, moving south on the road to Sharpsburg. Stuart's veterans pressed the rear of Kilpatrick's command[44]

Six miles to the southwest at Williamsport, meanwhile, Imboden's and Fitz Lee's cavalrymen, some infantry commands, artillery crews, and a ragtag collection of convalescent wounded soldiers, clerks, and teamsters had been making a valiant stand against John Buford's Union cavalry division. George Custer's Michigan Brigade joined Buford's troopers after Kilpatrick withdrew from Hagerstown, but the patchwork Confederate line held. At nightfall, Buford and Custer abandoned the effort. Farther east, Stuart's veterans lashed the rear guard of Kilpatrick's column, pushing the Yankees through the night to Jones's Crossroads, where Buford's and Kilpatrick's worn-out horse soldiers bivouacked for the night. In Hagerstown, the vanguard of Robert E. Lee's infantry was marching into the town.[45]

The Confederate army's vast array of wheeled vehicles and the route of the retreat march had been secured. Stuart and his horsemen, aided by some infantry and a motley gang of defenders, had parried the Union thrusts. Stuart's deft handling of his command showed once more his skill at screening the army and protecting critical places. Historian Ted Alexander has contended that Stuart was "the key commander during the retreat."[46]

Stuart's mission, however, had not been completed with the contests at Hagerstown and Williamsport. The recent heavy rains had swollen the Potomac's waters, preventing a crossing of the Southerners into Virginia. As the army's foot soldiers and artillerists constructed an extensive and formidable line of earthworks from around Williamsport downriver to Falling Waters, Stuart's cavalry covered the front, engaging the enemy in a series of fights. At times, gray-coated infantrymen supported the mounted units in the clashes.[47]

From July 8 through July 12, as a Virginia horseman grumbled in a letter, "We have a cavalry fight nearly every day." The engagements occurred primarily in the countryside between Hagerstown, through Funkstown, to Boonsborough. The fighting consisted mainly of dismounted skirmishing and artillery exchanges with Buford's and Kilpatrick's troopers. One day's action was characterized in the diary of a horse artillerist, "Battle opened ugly and early." At other times, the participants used words such as "very sharp" and "galling" in describing the gunfire between the opposing ranks. The Confederate cavalrymen fulfilled Robert E. Lee's instructions to their commander, "Keep your eye over the field, use your good judgment, and give assistance where necessary."[48]

Stuart remained constantly at the front. He was obviously exhausted, said Henry McClellan, and the staff had to rouse him from a deep sleep at night and make him eat some of their "scanty rations." The general had a horse killed from under him on July 10. "These days," claimed

McClellan, "will be remembered by the members of General Stuart's staff as days of peculiar hardship."[49]

On the day Stuart had his mount slain at Funkstown, he came upon one of his batteries of horse artillery. The gunners had expended their ammunition and were lying on the ground until the ordnance chests were refilled. When a lieutenant explained the situation to him, Stuart replied, "Then let them stand up for moral effect." "The boys stood up all right," recounted the officer, "but always referred to the general as 'Moral Effect' after that, but never without respect and admiration, because he never failed to go where the battle was raging hottest."[50]

During these days, a British observer with the army, Lieutenant Colonel Arthur James Lyon Fremantle of Her Majesty's Coldstream Guards, was introduced to the renowned cavalryman. "He is a good-looking, jovial character, exactly like his photographs," Fremantle wrote of Stuart. "He has certainly accomplished wonders, and done excellent service in his peculiar style of warfare. He is a good and gallant soldier, though he sometimes incurs ridicule by his harmless affectation and peculiarities. . . . No one can deny that he is the right man in the right place."[51]

On July 10, descending South Mountain, at last came the infantry of George Meade's Army of the Potomac. The Federals approached the nine miles of Confederate works and halted. Meade conferred with his corps commanders on the night of July 12, proposing a reconnaissance-in-force or an attack the next day. A majority of his senior generals however, voted against the plan. Meade agreed to postpone it until he could conduct a personal examination of the Rebels' lines. Meade did so the next day and then issued orders for an advance on July 14. By then, it was too late.[52]

The Potomac River had subsided enough for the Confederates to ford its waters at Williamsport, and engineers had completed a pontoon bridge at Falling Waters. After dark on July 13, in a heavy rainstorm, the Rebels began wading through and filing across the river. Stuart's cavalry covered the passage. In his instruction to Stuart, Robert E. Lee wrote, "Direct your men to be very vigilant and bold, and not let the enemy discover that our lines have been vacated." Lee added, "I know it to be a difficult, as well as delicate, operation to cover this army and then withdraw your command with safety, but I rely upon your good judgment, energy, and boldness to accomplish it, and trust you may be successful as you have been on former occasions."[53]

The rain muffled the sounds of an army on the march. As a ruse, Stuart, his staff, and couriers rode along a section of the works and sang loudly. By daylight on July 14, nearly every unit in the army had returned to Virginia. The Rebels escaped nearly unscathed, except for a clash between Southern infantrymen and Custer's cavalrymen at Falling Waters. In the brief, bloody encounter, Confederate brigadier Johnston Pettigrew suffered a fatal wound. When the Yankees discovered the empty trenches, a sergeant groused, "I do not think Lee will ever be catched up in as tight a place again."[54]

Upon his return to Virginia, Stuart rode through Martinsburg with "a large cavalcade of staff and couriers and two bugles blowing most furiously." They rode to The Bower, where Stuart reestablished his headquarters at the Dandridge family home. His cavalrymen patrolled the Potomac crossings as the main army settled into camps in the lower Shenandoah Valley. For the next ten days or so, occasional clashes flared between Stuart's men and their mounted foes as the Yankees probed south of the Potomac. In one action, an enemy bullet cut through Stuart's oilcloth. That night after a staff officer recounted the incident for fellow aides, Stuart remarked, "Well, I expect to be killed ere this war ends."[55]

The picket duty and the brushes with the Yankees denied the cavalrymen and their mounts an extended period of rest and recuperation after the rigors of the campaign in Maryland and Pennsylvania. "Last years campaign was child's play to this, so far as cavalry is concerned," asserted a Virginian after the return to his native state. "We have lost more men and suffered more hardships than in the past two years put together," claimed another horse soldier. A Georgian described the campaign as "a terrible one," while a member of the 2nd Virginia reported, "I never had my saddle of[f] ove my horse one hour at a time for three weeks and the most sleep that I got was on my horses back."[56]

A month after the crossing of the Potomac, Colonel John Logan Black of the 1st South Carolina wrote of his fellow officers and men in Wade Hampton's command: "The Brigade was rough in appearance, dirty, ragged and worn from the effects of the long Pennsylvania Campaign. They had been back so short a time that the men and horses were not rested & washed up." Thomas Munford attributed the loss of so many broken-down mounts to Stuart, who *did not foster* his *horses; worked* them *for glory* & newspaper notoriety."[57]

Lieutenant Colonel J. Fred Waring of the Jeff Davis Legion described the cavalry operations during the Gettysburg Campaign as "our disgusting raid." Waring believed that Stuart "seemed positively to enjoy the dirty business." Upon the army's return to Virginia, recalled Waring, "Stuart certainly did not carry himself as if he felt ashamed or defeated." The general still retained his "immense cheerfulness."[58]

If Waring had asked Stuart, the Georgian would have learned that the cavalry commander regarded the campaign as a "great success." During the retreat, he wrote to Flora twice, on July 10 and 13. In the first, brief letter, he boasted, "My Cavalry has nobly sustained its reputation and done better and harder fighting than it ever has since the war." In the lengthier second one, after listing the items he had purchased for Flora and Jimmie, he proclaimed, "I had a grand time in Penna. and we return without *defeat*." He noted that his men had captured nine hundred prisoners and two hundred wagons. "I have been blessed with great success on this campaign," he assured her, "and the accidents and losses in the way of captives are no way chargeable to my command." "We must invade again—it is the only path of peace," Stuart affirmed.[59]

Within the army, however, a different judgment on Stuart's operations emerged soon after the campaign's conclusion. Writing four days after the Potomac crossings, a staff officer with Longstreet noted, "General Stuart is much criticized for his part in our late campaign, whether rightfully I cannot say." Summarizing what he heard, the aide stated that the cavalry had "played a small part in the great drama either as the 'eyes of the army' or any other capacity. In his anxiety to 'do some great thing' General Stuart carried his men beyond the range of usefulness and Lee was not thereafter kept fully informed as to the enemy's movements as he should have been, or as he would have been had Stuart been nearer at hand."[60]

The censure of Stuart must have been prevalent and voiced aloud. Mosby acknowledged that Stuart heard the criticisms and that they "almost broke his heart." Henry Heth, whose division initiated the

Confederate action on July 1, contended in a postwar account, "The failure to crush the Federal army in Pennsylvania in 1863, in the opinion of almost all of the officers of the Army of Northern Virginia, can be expressed in five words—*the absence of the cavalry*." Moxley Sorrel, Longstreet's chief of staff, "never doubted" that the cause of the army's difficulties was Stuart's enterprise, which Sorrel called "a useless, showy parade." Even Stuart's valued subordinate Thomas Rosser declared in a later speech that his commander did "on this campaign, *undoubtedly*, make the fatal blunder which lost us the battle of Gettysburg."[61]

The sentiment among Stuart's critics in the army managed to reach the War Department in Richmond. An official in the Bureau of War recorded in his diary on July 26: "The battle was fought *when*, and it was, *in* consequence of Stuart's disobedience of orders. Instead of finding the enemy and keeping Lee advised, he went off on a raid towards Washington, and the armies blundered on one another."[62]

Robert E. Lee filed a preliminary report on the campaign on July 30. In addressing Stuart's movements prior to the battle, Lee commented, "the absence of the cavalry rendered it impossible to obtain accurate information." He then explained: "By the route he [Stuart] pursued, the Federal Army was interposed between his command and our main body, preventing any communication with him until his arrival at Carlisle. The march toward Gettysburg was conducted more slowly than it would have been had the movements of the Federal Army been known."[63]

The commanding general submitted his final report six months later in January 1864. His military secretary, Charles Marshall, gathered the reports of subordinates and prepared the document. Lee, said Marshall, "weighed every sentence I wrote." Characteristically, according to Marshall, Lee "struck from the original draft many statements which he thought might affect others injuriously, his sense of justice frequently leading him to what many considered too great a degree of lenience." Marshall admitted, however, "The official report of General Lee is I believe substantially true, as far as it goes."[64]

After the war, Marshall claimed that in the original draft he charged Stuart with "explicit disobedience of orders, and laid the full responsibility at his door." But Lee "was unwilling . . . to adopt my draft." Marshall purportedly told Lee that Stuart should be court-martialed and shot. If true, Lee discounted such an idea. In Marshall's judgment, the commanding general's personal fondness for Stuart, whom Marshall thought "a most noble, loveable man," mattered for much.[65]

In the final and official version, Lee stated that the cavalry commander, "in the discretion given him," decided "to pass around the rear of the Federal army." Consequently, since Lee had not heard from Stuart in days, "it was inferred that the enemy had not yet left Virginia." Then in words that constituted a rebuke of Stuart's conduct, the commanding general wrote, "The movements of the army preceding the battle of Gettysburg had been much embarrassed [affected adversely] by the absence of the cavalry."[66]

Although dated August 20, Stuart's report was not delivered to army headquarters until months later. Covering cavalry operations from June 16 to July 24, the document was the lengthiest—twenty-four printed pages in the *Official Records* published after the war by the U.S. War Department—filed by him in Confederate service. The narrative consisted of descriptions of engagements, embellishments of achievements, praises of subordinates, assignments of failures to others, and justifications of his actions. "It was a strange document," historian Edwin Coddington has written in his masterful study of the campaign, "more of an apology than a report, in which he tried to prove the virtues of his venture."[67]

Stuart presented a forthright defense of his conduct of operations from the time the cavalry left Salem on June 25 until its arrival at Gettysburg on July 2. Refusing to accept the responsibility for the eight days when the three brigades were out of contact with the army, he pointed the blame elsewhere: it was not his fault that the army was not where he thought it should be; Jubal Early made no effort to locate the cavalry; and the army did not suffer from "want of cavalry" with Jenkins's brigade with the main body. Furthermore, by moving in the rear of the Union army, he had "spread terror and consternation" into Washington and Baltimore, and had an impact on the operations of the Federal army before Gettysburg. The statements were not only a denial of his accountability, but of reality.[68]

Stuart had convinced himself—and seemed unwavering in that conviction—that he had been unjustly criticized "by those who knew nothing about it." He was steadfast in his report, "The result abundantly confirms my judgment as to the practicability as well as utility of the move." He justified his actions by arguing that he had exercised "the discretion vested in me by the commanding general." The discretionary orders were the crux of his defense and the source of the controversy ever since.[69]

Ultimately, what matters in history's long reach seems undeniable—Stuart failed Lee and the army in the reckoning at Gettysburg. Lee was, however, not blameless. He approved a plan that entailed much risk with few benefits. Porter Alexander had it right: "it was bad play to let our cavalry get out of touch & reach of our infantry. . . . Such a raid could cut no real figure on the grand result, & was taking chances for no good." Lee couched his approval by preparing discretionary instructions with limits. Stuart could pass behind the Union army only if the movement encountered no hindrance. When the cavalry did, Lee expected Stuart to abandon the endeavor and to follow the army down the Shenandoah Valley.[70]

During the retreat, however, Stuart rendered invaluable service in screening the army. Historian Ted Alexander has stated that Stuart "deserves much of the credit for the successful withdrawal." But it was earlier, on the morning of June 25 at Haymarket, where history glares the hardest at him. The evidence indicates that he was determined to conduct a raid, and he went forth. It was a misjudgment with consequences. A veteran cavalryman with him understood the choice before Stuart, "His hard horse sense ought to have told him to stick to Lee."[71]

Events consist of threads, intricately woven. The Confederate defeat and Union victory at Gettysburg possess their own patchwork of reasons. To charge Stuart with primary responsibility for the battle's outcome ignores the failings of fellow officers, including Lee, and the stalwart fight given by the Army of the Potomac. History offers only what was, not what might have been. Why Stuart chose his course eludes certainty. Lee trusted him and gave him discretion, but Stuart acted injudiciously. As Coddington has concluded, "Therein lies the tragedy of 'Jeb' Stuart in the Gettysburg Campaign."[72]

Chapter Fifteen

Corps Command

D UTY BROUGHT CONFEDERATE signal corpsman Charles E. Taylor frequently to headquarters of the Cavalry Division, Army of Northern Virginia during July and August 1863. "I like being at HdQrs," Taylor professed to his family. "Here we get all the news, and every hour or two prisoners are brought in and pumped by Gen. S. or some of his staff. Every night we have fine music. You know how fond Gen. S. is of music. Every night he gets his aides & escort in front of his tent, and has them at it till 10 o'ck."[1]

The headquarters visited by Taylor was located in Culpeper County, Virginia. Unlike George McClellan after the Battle of Antietam in September 1862, Union army commander George Meade trailed Robert E. Lee's veterans into Virginia, crossing the Potomac River east of the Blue Ridge and marching south. By the end of July the two armies had returned to the familiar ground of central Virginia drained by the Rappahannock and Rapidan rivers and their tributaries. "There is a time for all things," mused a Yankee, and after Gettysburg's carnage, the time came for a relative quiescence.[2]

Despite the nighttime camaraderie and lively atmosphere witnessed by Taylor at Jeb Stuart's headquarters, questions about and criticism of the general's performance during the campaign hung over the campsite.

Rumors filtered out from the army that Stuart was to be replaced by John Hood as cavalry commander. The Richmond *Dispatch* pronounced the speculation as "sensation news." The *Dispatch* and the Richmond *Whig* printed letters from army members who supported Stuart. One writer proclaimed that "Gen. Stuart . . . is a commander of incomparable excellence in his arm of the service, and his services have been so great, that to put this slight upon him would be regarded as unpardonable, not only by his comrades of the army, but by the whole country."[3]

Lee's preliminary Gettysburg report fueled the talk. At the War Department in the capital, the rumor circulated of Hood succeeding Stuart. A diarist in the department ascribed the cause to "absence of cavalry before and at battle of Gettysburg against orders, to which absence General Lee in his report of that battle is said . . . to attribute the loss of the battle or rather the campaign."[4]

Stuart heard the gossip but assured Flora, "It is *all bosh*." He called it "the Hood imbroglio," blaming the matter on "the busy cravings of some of his eager friends. I do not believe *he* [Hood] ever gave the matter countenance. I am begged to give myself no uneasiness on the subject for a private note by Gen. Lee." He warned his wife: "As for the growlers, who come back, pay no attention to them, they had hard long & harassing marches but they *were necessary* indeed *indispensable* as my report will show, and rest assured, the Cavalry has no record brighter than that of June & July's Campaign. I will gladly rest my name & reputation on the achievements of those two months."[5]

As Stuart predicted, the rumor dribbled away and died. In the campaign's aftermath, however, changes occurred within the cavalry division. On July 15, a day after the army's return to Virginia, Beverly Robertson wrote to Lee's chief of staff: "I consider it an injustice to myself and the service to remain longer in my present position. . . . I think my services would be of more avail elsewhere." When Robertson delivered the letter to Stuart, the cavalry commander endorsed it, "Respectfully forwarded, and recommended that he be relieved from duty with this command accordingly." Lee approved, and Robertson was gone. William Blackford assessed the brigadier well, "General Robertson was an excellent man in camp to train troops, but in the field, in the presence of the enemy, he lost all self-possession, and was perfectly unreliable."[6]

At the same time, Stuart moved against his old nemesis Grumble
Jones. Stuart relieved the brigadier of command for the loss of the wagons at Monterey Pass. When Jones responded with "a very disrespectful
letter," Stuart placed him under arrest. Stuart then submitted a list of
three charges against Jones and requested a court-martial, which Lee
acceded to and appointed officers to a court.[7]

There was, it seemed, an inevitability to this legal resolution between
these personal enemies. Their hatred for each other had simmered for
more than two years, awaiting a time when it would boil openly to the
surface. Henry McClellan recalled that since his appointment as Stuart's adjutant general in May 1863, he had received almost daily "official papers containing proof of Jones' idiosyncrasies." A staff officer who
knew Jones well noted, "never was a needle truer to the pole, than he,
to what he conceived to be his duty." Jones had, said the aide, "contempt for all kinds of display."[8]

The court convened, with six generals and a colonel on the board,
at Orange Court House, during the final week of August. The officers
absolved Jones of disobedience of orders and conduct prejudicial to
military order and discipline. The court found him guilty of the third
charge—"Behavior with disrespect to his commanding officer"—
and ruled that he be "privately reprimanded by the Commanding
General."[9]

When Lee received the court's verdict, he confided to President Jefferson Davis: "I consider General Jones a brave and intelligent officer,
but his feelings have become so opposed to General Stuart that I have
lost all hope of his being useful in the cavalry here. . . . I understand he
will no longer serve under Stuart, and I do not think it would be advan-
tageous for him to do so, but I wish to make him useful." On October 9,
the War Department assigned Jones to command of the cavalry in the
Department of Western Virginia and East Tennessee. For vastly different reasons, Robertson and Jones were gone from Stuart's division.[10]

While newspapers published rumors and the cavalry leadership
roiled with controversy, Stuart's horse soldiers recovered slowly from
the rigors of the Gettysburg Campaign and protected the army's front
along the Rappahannock River. The combat and the marches over
the span of more than two months had reduced the cavalry's ranks by

roughly 1,500 to nearly 8,600 officers and men. Despite the hardships and casualties, morale in the ranks remained good. "As for the demoralization of our army," declared William Deloney of Cobb's Legion in a typical letter, "it is nonsense to talk about it. It is confined to a few croakers. I have never seen the slightest symptom of it nor have I seen any one who has."[11]

A common complaint among the rank and file was a lack of food for themselves and forage for their horses in the previously occupied region. A sergeant in the 1st North Carolina grumbled about the constant duty, "with out one bite to eat." A Virginia trooper swore, "I got so weak I could hardly get on my horse." A private in the 3rd Virginia growled: "our rations is just three crackers and a greasy spot [of meat] a day. Our horses look like graven images and are living on their constitutions and the hope of a better day coming."[12]

Stuart reinstituted daily drills and addressed discipline concerns with the division. When not on picket duty—"We never fire at each other on picket line, unless the Yanks advance," wrote a trooper—the officers and men drilled twice each day for about six hours. Horses were grazed in the morning and at night. While in camp, men were restricted to an area within five miles from brigade headquarters. Stuart also created provost guard details, ordering that malingerers, stragglers, and deserters be arrested and returned to their units.[13]

Two days after Stuart issued the orders about the provost guards, on August 1, John Buford's Union cavalry division crossed the Rappahannock on a reconnaissance-in-force. Hampton's brigade, led by Colonel Pierce M. B. Young, fought a delaying action against the Federals until Stuart arrived with Grumble Jones's brigade, under Colonel Laurence Baker. Again the opponents engaged in mounted charges and countercharges. When infantry regiments from the Confederate Third Corps appeared, Buford withdrew and recrossed the river. Colonels Young, Baker, and John L. Black of the 1st South Carolina suffered wounds in the engagement. After it, Stuart wrote Flora: "My own escape untouched is most extraordinary. I was as much exposed as any, and we have reason to be thankful to God for his deliverance."[14]

On the same day of the clash with Buford, Robert E. Lee wrote a letter to Jefferson Davis proposing a reorganization of Stuart's command into a corps of two divisions. "I think the brigades, as now composed, even with the reduced numbers in the regiments, are too large for one commander," explained Lee. He recommended the assignment of four regiments to each brigade, noting, "I think by reducing the number of regiments in a brigade we shall get more men into the field." Some units would have to be transferred or consolidated into a new command.[15]

Lee suggested the appointment of Wade Hampton, who was still recovering from his Gettysburg wounds, and his nephew Fitz Lee as commanders of the two new divisions, with promotions to major general. He also recommended the promotion of four colonels—Matthew Calbraith Butler, Williams Wickham, Laurence Baker, and Lunsford Lomax—to brigadier generals and their assignment to command of a brigade. "I believe these four officers are the best qualified and most deserve promotion," wrote Lee.[16]

It took several weeks before the reorganization of the cavalry had been completed, with army headquarters announcing it officially on September 9. As Lee recommended, the newly created Cavalry Corps had two divisions, each comprised of three brigades. Hampton's First Division consisted of the brigades of Grumble Jones, Laurence Baker, and Matthew Butler. It would be more than a month before a permanent successor to Jones was appointed. Butler was in South Carolina, recovering from the amputation of a leg after Brandy Station, and Pierce Young assumed temporary command of his units. Like Butler, Baker was unfit for duty from his wound on August 1, and Colonel James B. Gordon of the 1st North Carolina replaced Baker at the head of four regiments.[17]

Young and Gordon had rendered distinguished service and merited the assignments. The twenty-six-year-old Young had attended West Point, where he roomed with George Custer and forged a lasting friendship. He had battled his friend at Hunterstown and led Hampton's brigade in the action on August 1, until slightly wounded. Unlike Young, the tall, raw-boned thirty-year-old Gordon had no military education but had proved to be a natural leader of men. Stuart praised his service. Before long, both received promotion to brigadier general.[18]

Ten Virginia regiments, 1st South Carolina, and 1st Maryland Battalion formed Fitz Lee's Second Division. With the army commander's

endorsement, Lunsford Lomax and Williams Wickham secured briga-
dierships and brigade command. Both appointments pleased Stuart,
particularly that of his good friend Lomax. As for Wickham, the only
objection to his assignment seemed to be, at least from one trooper, "his
profanity." The third brigade officially remained with the commanding
general's son, Rooney Lee. The younger Lee still languished in a Union
prison, and Colonel John Chambliss continued to lead the unit.[19]

The promotions and appointments elicited some complaints about
favoritism to West Pointers and Virginians. No two men felt more
aggrieved about being passed over than Thomas Munford and Thomas
Rosser. Although Stuart regarded Lomax as "Munford's superior as a
colonel," he had recommended Munford twice in the past for command
of Jones's brigade. "No man," wrote Stuart of Munford, "has such claims
to command *that* Brigade as himself." Stuart's ardent desire to rid his
command of Jones factored clearly in his effort on Munford's behalf.[20]

The ambitious Rosser, one of Stuart's favorites, reacted with anger to
not receiving a promotion. In letters to his wife—he had been married
in the previous spring—he accused Stuart of deceiving him. Rosser had
"a long conversation" with Stuart on the matter, telling his wife afterward, "His arguments I thought quite silly, he seems to hate the way that
he has treated me but that is too late you now know." Stuart assured him
in a letter that when Jones's transfer was official, "You are my choice
for the post." Finally, with Lee's and Stuart's recommendations, Rosser
would receive a brigadiership and command of Jones's brigade in mid-
October. His private correspondence revealed his ungratefulness for all
that Stuart had done for him in the past.[21]

For Stuart, the formation of a corps brought with it the prospect of
a lieutenant generalcy for himself. Since October 1862, infantry corps
commanders had been appointed to the rank. "Rumor is quite rife that
I have been actually appointed Lieutenant General," he informed Flora
on September 4. "I think it must be so. I wish you were here to receive
and hand me the commission as you have twice done heretofore." A
week later after the reorganization had been announced, he wrote to
her: "I am not promoted. Whether I am or not remains to be seen. Gen
Lee said nothing to me about it nor I to him, of course. Every one seems
to think it will come. I am not sanguine."[22]

Stuart's instincts in the matter were correct. Whether Lee considered a promotion for his cavalry commander is unknown. No correspondence or official documents have been found that indicate Lee either broached or proposed the idea. No evidence supports the speculation that Lee withheld promotion because of Stuart's performance during the Gettysburg Campaign. It is more likely that Lee thought the responsibilities in command of a cavalry corps did not equal those of an infantry corps.[23]

Before the reorganization of the cavalry units had been completed, the weeks of unusual quiet ended. Ironically, some of Stuart's veterans had been complaining of "monotonous camp life" and strict orders that confined them to camp. A captain in the 4th Virginia stated in a letter in early September, "While the Yanks are in sight of us on the other side of the river they give us no trouble, they keeping on their side and we on ours." Trouble was, however, at hand.[24]

The Federals had learned of the detachment of two infantry divisions and an artillery battalion from Lee's army. In Tennessee, a Union force had captured Knoxville, and another was threatening Chattanooga. The administration in Richmond regarded the crisis in Tennessee of paramount importance. With Lee's reluctant acquiescence, Confederate authorities decided to send James Longstreet and his veteran troops as reinforcements to General Braxton Bragg's beleaguered Army of Tennessee. Longstreet's movement began on September 9, the initial leg in a trip of roughly 775 miles. "We all disliked very much to see this splendid section of our army leave us," wrote Walter Taylor of Lee's staff.[25]

The Yankees came on September 13, three divisions of cavalry splashing through the Rappahannock fords at daylight. A civilian who resided north of the river had passed through the Union lines and alerted Stuart of the enemy advance minutes after midnight. Stuart relayed the information to Lunsford Lomax, who was acting as temporary commander of Grumble Jones's brigade as the reorganization of the cavalry had not been fully completed. Lomax's veteran horsemen were in the saddle by dawn. With the Confederate infantry south of the Rapidan, where they had been posted since the army's return to the region, Lomax could not expect support from those commands. At best, he could fight a delaying action against the numerically superior enemy force.[26]

Lomax made an initial stand at Brandy Station, but the enemy shoved his troopers south to a ridge outside Culpeper Court House. Three cannon of horse artillery supported the Rebels and engaged the Union guns. The Federals possessed a confidence, if not arrogance. "We can lick any division of rebels that ever straddled a horse," one of them boasted. A charge by the 2nd New York unhinged Lomax's line and resulted in the capture of the three artillery pieces.[27]

Judson Kilpatrick's Federals, leading the pursuit, passed through Culpeper Court House. Lomax rallied his regiments on a hill south of town, where Stuart joined him with another battery of horse artillery. The Rebels clung to the hill for a while before being forced back to Pony Mountain, a four-hundred-foot height. Rooney Lee's brigade, under Colonel Richard L. T. Beale, arrived, forming on Lomax's line. But this day belonged to the Yankees, who drove the Southerners off the mountain. Darkness halted the fighting.[28]

The valiant defense by the outnumbered Confederates saved Stuart's wagon trains from capture. The next morning brought another advance by the Union horsemen, and Stuart withdrew across the Rapidan. Skirmishing flared along the river, moving a New Yorker to jot in his diary, "The rebels were good shots." Behind the blue-jacketed cavalrymen, George Meade's infantry corps marched into the region between the Rappahannock and Rapidan on the ground where John Pope's army was nearly trapped in August 1862.[29]

Once across the Rapidan, Stuart ringed the army's front along the river, with Hampton's division covering the left flank and Fitz Lee's the right. Cavalry scouts and patrols crossed the stream, gathering intelligence on the Federals. On the night of September 21, Stuart received a report of Union cavalry movement from Madison Court House against the army's left flank. He issued orders for Hampton's three brigades to move at daybreak. His plan was, as he told Flora, to "put after him [the enemy] to attack and frustrate his purpose."[30]

Stuart assumed personal command of Hampton's division in that officer's absence and led the two thousand officers and men northward on the morning of September 22. The Confederates encountered John

Buford's Union horsemen at Jack's Shop, a tiny cluster of two or three houses located five miles south of Madison Court House on the road to Gordonsville. Dismounted skirmishers on both sides opened the fighting. At such times, according to a Virginian, the foes typically lie down upon the ground and fire "at the puffs of smoke." "It doesn't rise to the dignity of a battle," he noted, "but is called skirmishing." Union and Confederate artillery crews backed the skirmishers.[31]

Early in the afternoon, Buford pressed an attack against Stuart's right flank. About the same time, Brigadier General Henry E. Davies, Jr.'s, brigade of Judson Kilpatrick's division advanced on the Confederate left flank and rear, having approached Stuart's ranks undetected. The Rebels were, in the words of a captain, "almost encompassed." A counterattack by the 1st and 5th North Carolina against Davies's men ended in a repulse. "When we saw how many men and guns were there," recounted a North Carolinian, "it looked so awful that we fell back slowly to our main line."[32]

Stuart hurried a staff officer with orders for another charge to the regrouped 5th North Carolina and 9th Virginia. The aide rode along the ranks, telling them that they were nearly surrounded, and then exclaimed, "Boys, it is a fight to captivity, death or victory." The men cheered and spurred ahead only to be stopped again. Now, recalled a North Carolinian, "We were pressed back by sheer brute force and deadly fire." Stuart retired to a hill, where the artillery crews fired their cannon in three directions. "General Stuart always fought the hardest when things looked the worst," declared one of his veterans. "The man in the ranks knew that they were surrounded."[33]

An officer believed "the coolness and gallant bearing of Stuart" steadied the men. The cavalry commander and staff officers fashioned an attack force of the 7th, 11th, and 12th Virginia and led them in another charge on Davies's horse soldiers. The assault buckled back the Federal line, opening an escape route. Stuart had a horse shot beneath him. With Cobb's Legion and the 2nd South Carolina acting as rear guards, the Southerners recrossed the Rapidan at Liberty Mills. "A few more such fights," complained a Georgian in Cobb's Legion, "& we placed next to the enemy & there will be nothing left for us." A North Carolinian called it "a shameful affair on our side."[34]

The Confederate troopers credited their escape to the fact that the Northerners "cant stand the saber, & I've heard that they curse us bitterly for yelling so much when we charge." Stuart recrossed the river the next day and pursued the retreating Yankees until they forded Robertson's or Robinson River beyond Madison Court House. Stuart told Flora, contrary to the facts, that he "did not 'fall back' as the papers have it." He called it "a grand success."[35]

Robert E. Lee sent a message to Stuart, praising him: "I congratulate you on defeating his [the enemy's] and arresting his advance. The energy and promptness of yourself and command elicits my high admiration." To Jefferson Davis, Lee wrote on September 23, "General Stuart showed his usual energy, promptness, and boldness in his operations yesterday; keeping with the front line of his troops."[36]

Another interlude followed the engagement at Jack's Shop, lasting for a fortnight or so. Stuart established his headquarters at Brampton, the home of Dr. Andrew Grinnan, outside Orange Court House not far from his outposts. With the respite, Stuart worried increasingly about Flora, who was in her final days of pregnancy and staying in Lynchburg. Earlier, he had asked her: "How are you this bright morning? Well, I hope and pray. Do let me hear from you. Maria [Flora's sister] will doubtless be with you at the proper time." In another letter, he reaffirmed his love for her: "Your picture is a great comfort to me as *lip salve*. I carry it next to my heart, but do not need it my love, to keep *you* ever vividly before me."[37]

Stuart reported to Flora that he had found "a nice quiet little house and farm for sale, such as you and I have often pictured in our imaginations." He wrote to his brother William, asking if he would purchase the property for them. William Stuart served as administrator of the Confederate salt works in Saltville, Virginia, and as Stuart explained to his wife, "he invests wherever he can." Jeb Stuart wanted to acquire the house because "I would like to have you located here."[38]

As the time neared for him to be a father again, he thought of the daughter he had lost ten months ago. He remembered the parting at Dundee before the campaign against John Pope when "Little Flora" clung to him. "Ah! little did I think *I* was to be *spared* and *she* taken," he wrote to Nannie Price. "I dare not write to Flora as I have written to you," he confessed to his cousin. "I have to restrain my grief, my feelings, my language on that subject (little Flora) and she little dreams what agony in lone bivouac and even on the march those choking memories have caused me."[39]

Military matters consumed his days, however. He prodded the War Department for more cavalry regiments, "My cavalry force has been always inadequate in number to the work to be performed." He had been unable to complete his reports on the previous campaign and requested that John Esten Cooke, his ordnance officer, be promoted to major and assigned as assistant adjutant general to prepare the documents. Henry McClellan said in a letter, "We are all well, we laugh & grow fat."[40]

By the first week of October, the inactivity along the Rappahannock and Rapidan rivers was nearing an end. Except for the cavalry clashes, the two armies had passed the two months and more since Gettysburg in a stalemate. In particular, shortages of arms, ammunition, and supplies had hampered operations by the Confederates. Robert E. Lee had suffered from a recurrence of his springtime heart ailments and had offered to relinquish command of the army, telling President Davis "that a younger & abler man than myself can readily be attained." When Davis read the letter, he responded by calling Lee "my dear friend" and asserting, "To ask me to substitute you by some one in my judgment more fit to command, or who would possess more of the confidence of the army, or of the reflecting men in the country is to demand an impossibility."[41]

Events in Tennessee, however, gave Lee a strategic opening in Virginia. On September 19–20, Bragg's army and Longstreet's divisions achieved a signal victory at Chickamauga in northern Georgia, driving William S. Rosecrans's Union forces into Chattanooga. The Southerners followed, filed onto the heights south and east of the city, and began siege operations. In reaction, the administration in Washington ordered George Meade to send the Eleventh and Twelfth corps to the capital for transfer to the West. The veteran troops marched away from their camps during the final week of September. Their detachment left Meade with 80,000 officers and men present for duty, opposed to Lee's 48,000 troops.[42]

"With the design of bringing on an engagement with the Federal army," as he stated it, Lee undertook a broad turning movement beyond

Meade's right flank during the second week of October, similar to the campaign against John Pope's army in August 1862. Stuart, leading Hampton's division, was directed to lead the march and to screen the flank of the trailing Confederate infantry. Lee assigned the cavalry division of his nephew Fitz Lee and a pair of infantry brigades the duty of holding the ground south of the Rapidan while Stuart and the army swung northwest through Madison Court House and James City to the Rappahannock fords. If successful, Lee intended to strike Meade's retreating columns on the march.[43]

Stuart rendezvoused the brigades of James Gordon, Pierce Young, and Oliver R. Funsten on the evening of October 9, near Madison Court House. Colonels Young and Funsten were serving as temporary commanders. At daylight the next day, Stuart, with Gordon's and Young's horsemen, rode toward James City. Funsten's troopers accompanied the infantry columns in the flanking movement. Crossing Robertson's River at Russell's Ford, Stuart and the two brigades routed an advance guard of Union cavalrymen, chasing them to James City. Beyond the town, the Southerners came upon Judson Kilpatrick's Union horse soldiers, an infantry division, and a battery of six cannon. "I did not attempt what would have been impossible—with my force to dislodge the enemy," reported Stuart, who settled for skirmishing with the Yankees until darkness.[44]

During October 10, Meade received confirmation of the Confederate flank movement and, early on the next morning, ordered a withdrawal of his army across the Rappahannock. When Stuart arose on October 11, he discovered that the enemy force in his front had retreated during the night. Leaving Young's command at James City, he and Gordon's North Carolinians headed toward Culpeper Court House. At Griffinsburg, Stuart met Funsten and the 7th and 12th Virginia, which joined the column. By the time the Confederates reached Culpeper Court House, Kilpatrick's Yankees were retiring north toward Brandy Station. Stuart pressed against Kilpatrick's rear guard, but Union cannon dissuaded him from undertaking a frontal attack. Stuart swung west in an attempt to pass around the enemy flank and to cut him off from the river.[45]

To the north and east, meanwhile, Fitz Lee's cavalrymen were pushing John Buford's mounted Union division toward Brandy Station. On the previous day, Buford had forded the Rapidan on a reconnaissance and engaged Lee's troopers and Confederate infantry. Ordered to withdraw, Buford pulled back on this morning, trailed closely by Lee. From two directions then, the opponents converged on the old killing ground around Brandy Station. When they met, remarked a Virginian, a "very severe fight" erupted.[46]

The combat possessed that deadly familiarity of such an encounter—gun crews working their cannon, dismounted skirmishers stalking each other, and charges and countercharges thundering across the ground. For Kilpatrick's Yankees, it became a bloody passage between the closing wings of enemy horsemen. The 2nd New York and 18th Pennsylvania, buying time, routed the 4th and 5th North Carolina. On came the 7th Virginia, shattering the ranks of the New Yorkers and Pennsylvanians and driving them back. While a band played "Yankee Doodle," George Custer's Michiganders rolled up Lee's left flank, cutting an opening for the rest of Kilpatrick's command to unite with Buford's division on Fleetwood Hill. A Southern officer, writing after the war, asserted that Custer "was by far the best cavalry officer in the Federal Army."[47]

"An engagement ensued of the most obstinate and determined character," wrote Stuart. Confederate sharpshooters occupied woods near the railroad station, and the fighting swirled around them. The Rebels met enemy attacks with counterattacks. Stuart reported "five distinct charges" were made by Chambliss's and Lomax's men. When Fitz Lee threatened the Federal left flank on the hill, the Northerners abandoned the elevation and retreated across the Rappahannock. A Virginian summarized the action well, recording in his diary that the Yankees "made a stand and fought stubbornly for awhile we finally driving them across the river."[48]

"And now commenced the rase for Bull Run and Manasses," in the description of a Pennsylvania cavalryman. On October 12, Confederate infantry forded the Rappahannock, their passage cleared by Stuart's troopers and artillery. Throughout the day, the horsemen preceded the long strings of foot soldiers and rimmed their flanks. By nightfall, the bulk of the Rebel units were concentrated near Warrenton. A handful of miles to the south and east, Meade's Union army lay encamped, its bivouac sites along either the tracks of the Orange & Alexandria Railroad or nearby roads.[49]

Uncertain about the locations of Meade's units, Robert E. Lee sent Stuart on a reconnaissance toward Catlett's Station on the morning of October 13. Lomax's regiments went ahead, trailed by Stuart and the brigades of Gordon and Funsten. At Auburn, Stuart halted Lomax to secure his rear as the other units proceeded toward the railroad. When Stuart approached Catlett's Station, he saw a vast park of Union wagons that extended south to Warrenton Junction, and signs of a Federal retrograde movement. He dispatched Major Andrew Venable with the information to army headquarters.[50]

The prize tempted Stuart but, as he explained, "a more decided result could be obtained by a movement of our whole army." Concealing his force, he waited for darkness. A courier from Venable arrived, reporting that enemy troops occupied Auburn. Earlier Captain William Blackford and a detail had ridden away on a reconnaissance and, upon their return, confirmed Venable's news. Stuart led his column back toward Auburn.[51]

In the darkness, Stuart's outriders stumbled upon enemy pickets, which sparked a brief exchange of gunfire. One of Gordon's men recounted in a letter that Stuart came forward and "soon found out what a trap we had thrown ourselves into, and put his *Mentals* to work, to continue a way to get out." Stuart had with him about three thousand officers and men, seven cannon, and a mule-drawn wagon train. Ahead, the distinct sound of men on the march could be heard. A gunner stated, "This was the only occasion in which I have ever seen Stuart give outward manifestations of deep concern."[52]

Scouts located a small valley, with woods covering its entrance. Stuart turned the string of horsemen, cannon, and wagons off the road and into it. When they had halted, he told officers to apprise the men of the situation. "Not a word was allowed except in whispers," wrote a trooper, "not a spark of fire could be struck." Stuart held them in line, either standing or kneeling throughout the night. "You were hungry, and so was the mule," recalled an enlisted man, "and there were more Yankees around you than you believed were left in the world after Get-

tysburg." If a mule brayed, the men had orders to knock down the animal with a club.[53]

Stuart purportedly remarked, "If the Yankees will let us alone, I shall
certainly not disturb them to-night." He picked six "bold men" and had
them ride out with messages on "the state of affairs." A heavy fog developed toward dawn, but the Confederates could hear distinctly the voices
of enemy troops as they boiled coffee and ate breakfast on a nearby hill.
Stuart instructed Major Robert Beckham and the seven artillery crews
to load their cannon. Funsten's men deployed into a dismounted battle
line while Gordon's North Carolinians mounted.[54]

After dawn, gunfire erupted in the distance, indicating the presence of other Confederate troops. One of Stuart's couriers had delivered his dispatch to Richard Ewell, commander of the Second Corps.
Ewell started his infantry forward at once. With Ewell's veterans came
Fitz Lee's cavalrymen. Lee had received an earlier message from Stuart
and marched. The Southerners closed on Auburn from the north and
west.[55]

When Stuart heard the artillery booms and musketry, he directed
Beckham to open fire with shells on the unsuspecting Yankees on the
hill. The Federals scrambled for cover under the sudden explosion of
shells. The Union force at Auburn consisted of three divisions of the
Second Corps, David Gregg's cavalrymen, and batteries. On the rise, a
dozen enemy gun crews targeted Beckham's pieces. Stuart ordered them
to withdraw and to limber up. Funsten's men, fighting on foot, engaged
oncoming blue-coated infantrymen. "The fields were darkened with
them," averred a Rebel horseman of the Yankees, "and they were fast
gaining the rear of our artillery and our only route of retreat."[56]

With sabers drawn and mounted, the 1st North Carolina charged
the enemy infantry, plowing into the ranks. A North Carolinian
described the fighting as "wild disorder and turmoil." The regiment's
commander, Colonel Thomas Ruffin, fell mortally wounded, and his
men retired. Gordon rallied the horsemen and led them forward a second time. Behind "this Spartan band," in Stuart's phrase, the cannon,
wagons, and Funsten's troopers passed through the gap. As the North
Carolinians fell back, Funsten's Virginians covered the rear of the column. Stuart led them south on the road a short distance before veering

off into the fields. They circled around the Federals and linked up with Lee's and Ewell's men.[57]

It had been the narrowest of escapes while saving all of the cannon and vehicles. When the campaign concluded, a member of the 11th Virginia wrote an account of the episode for readers of the Richmond *Sentinel*. "Let me add, in closing," the soldier correspondent wrote, "in view of aspersions lately made, that Gen. Stuart has, throughout these late dangerous scenes, conducted himself so nobly as to put down all slanders, and endear himself more than ever to his command. His coolness in difficulty, his perfect fearlessness, his boldness in the face of dangers, and his kind and gentle manner to his troops, and his inspiring confidence in himself, have won the highest praise even from those who spoke ill of him before."[58]

The "rase" noted by the Pennsylvanian quickened later on October 14. Meade's army followed the Orange & Alexandria Railroad northward. The two Confederate infantry corps, with Stuart's cavalry roaming along each flank, marched toward the tracks from the west. A Union officer compared movements to "the old game of 'hide-and-go-seek.'" Late in the afternoon at Bristoe Station, A. P. Hill's Third Corps overtook units of the Federal Second Corps, the troops who had been at Auburn in the morning. Hill rushed forward a pair of brigades, and Yankee rifles and cannon shredded the ranks. When Robert E. Lee came upon the bloody debacle, he censured Hill in "the most bitter terms."[59]

The engagement at Bristoe Station was the only serious encounter during Meade's retrograde movement. When the Federals crossed Bull Run and reached Centreville, they won the race. The Confederates followed, but Lee was unwilling to assail the enemy behind fieldworks. Stuart's cavalry probed the flanks of Meade's lines for two days. Rain, falling heavy at times, hampered operations. Finally, Lee started his army south. The Southerners tore up the tracks of the railroad during the march. By nightfall of October 18, Lee's infantry had forded the Rappahannock, leaving Stuart's horsemen north of the stream. Stuart and the three brigades of Hampton's division encamped at Haymarket; Fitz Lee's command, at Bristoe Station.[60]

During the night, scouts informed Stuart of a planned advance by Judson Kilpatrick's cavalry and an infantry force the next morning.

Early the next morning, October 19, the Northerners—George Custer's Michigan Brigade—appeared. Stuart withdrew south to behind Broad Run at Buckland, where the Rebels thwarted Custer's efforts throughout the morning. Stuart alerted Fitz Lee of the enemy presence. In reply, Lee reported that he was moving forward to Auburn and suggested that Stuart draw the Yankees farther west where Lee would strike their flank. Stuart agreed to the plan and, about midday, began slowly receding before the Federals, halting finally at Chestnut Hill, a few miles from Warrenton.[61]

At Buckland, meanwhile, Kilpatrick, a sprig of a man known as "Kil-Cavalry" for his aggressive tactics, joined Custer. Kilpatrick directed Custer to follow Henry Davies's brigade in pursuit of Stuart. Custer refused until his men and horses had been fed. He cautioned Kilpatrick that his scouts had sighted a Confederate force—mistakenly identified as infantry—on their flank. The division commander rejected the information and sent Davies's men ahead. Kilpatrick should have heeded the warning.[62]

Stuart's slow withdrawal pulled Davies into the trap. When the Confederate commander heard Lee's guns fire on Custer, he wheeled around his three brigades on Chestnut Hill and charged. Davies's ranks broke under the attack and fled precipitately toward Buckland. "It was very exciting," exclaimed a pursuing Rebel, "and afforded us as much amusement as *fox chase*." Custer's hardened troopers were holding back Lee's advance until Davies's routed horsemen crossed Broad Run. Custer's men "were obliged to fall back pretty lively," admitted one of them. They managed to retreat in fairly good order. In the confusion, however, an isolated battalion of the 5th Michigan was captured.[63]

The pursuit continued for several miles until the Confederates came upon Union infantry near Gainesville. The Rebels seized scores of prisoners and a few wagons, including Custer's headquarters wagon. A sergeant in the 5th North Carolina called the fight "a real good thrashing." Lieutenant Colonel William R. Carter of the 3rd Virginia stated later, "This was quite a successful affair & particularly gratifying, as the braggart Kilpatrick was completely outgeneraled and badly defeated." In his report, Stuart could not restrain himself, "I am justified in declaring the rout of the enemy at Buckland the most signal and complete that any

cavalry has suffered during the war." Robert E. Lee congratulated Stuart
and his men, noting, "The plan was well conceived and skillfully executed." Among the victors, the affair became the "Buckland Races."[64]

Stuart led his command across the swollen Rappahannock on October 20, marking the end of the Bristoe Campaign. Within days, Meade's
army returned to the river's north bank, and the stalemate resumed.
Lee's offensive had garnered scant results, except for the capture of
2,400 prisoners, the majority of which had been taken by the cavalry. "I
know of no advantages gained by the late move of Lee's army," opined
a member of the 3rd Virginia. "I do not even know the object of the
advance."[65]

The campaign had been hard on the cavalry. Although the casualties amounted to fewer than four hundred, the strain on the men and
mounts had been onerous. "I don't think I ever had such a time as this
before—cold, rain and fatigue," Private James A. Tompkins of the
5th Virginia complained to his mother. The 3rd Virginia's Lieutenant
Colonel Carter argued, "I consider this the hardest campaign we have
ever been engaged in; consequently men & horses were both very much
exhausted." Carter added, however, "It has been a very brilliant campaign for the cavalry."[66]

Indeed it had been. Jedediah Hotchkiss, formerly Stonewall Jackson's topographer, now serving with Richard Ewell, rendered a fair
assessment of Stuart's horsemen: "In fact all the glory of this movement,
if there is any, belongs to the cavalry. They fought elegantly, charging
the enemy on all occasions and carrying everything before them, capturing hundreds of Yankees." The mounted units did all that was expected
of them and more. They screened the army, gathered intelligence, and
defeated the numerically superior Union cavalry. Even the escape from
the near trap at Auburn showed their mettle. Stuart praised his officers
and men for their "patient endurance as well as heroic daring."[67]

The cavalry commander's performance had been masterful, leading
personally three brigades and guiding the movements of Fitz Lee's division. In his report, Colonel Oliver Funsten attributed the cavalry's success "to the generalship, boldness, and untiring energy of Major-General
Stuart, for it was he who directed every movement of importance, and
his generalship, boldness, and energy won the unbounded confidence of

officers and men, and gave the prestige of success." "The whole tone" of Richmond newspapers, according to a former aide, seemed to change toward Stuart after the campaign ended. The criticism leveled at him for months had been stilled for the present.[68]

Upon the cavalry's return, Stuart received a gratifying letter from James Longstreet in Tennessee. Writing of the mounted command in Braxton Bragg's army, Longstreet informed his friend: "It seems to be about equal to what yours was when we first served together at Falls Church [in the summer and fall of 1861]. I have seen enough of your cavalry to know that you have improved vastly since that time. As I have to *deal a little with* the Cavalry here I think that you had better send me a few suggestions occasionally instead of hoping to get any from this Service."[69]

The most joyous news came from Flora. She had given birth to a daughter on October 9, 1863, in Lynchburg. The parents named her Virginia Pelham Stuart, "after my mother state and one of her bravest defenders," in the words of her father. Flora sent him a lock of the baby's hair and promised to bring the children to him when she was able to travel. He learned from her, as he stated in a letter to a cousin: "Jeb Jr. is so demonstrative towards his sister, that one of his squeezes very nearly finishes her. . . . She is said to be like Little Flora. I hope she is."[70]

While Stuart awaited a visit from the family, he held another review of the cavalry and horse artillery near Brandy Station on November 5. Robert E. Lee, "all the big generals," Virginia governor John Letcher, and a host of ladies attended it. William Carter of the 3rd Virginia wrote of it: "Grand affair! Stuart appeared in all his glory!" The horsemen executed a mock charge, which an onlooker called "quite amusing and animating." To Stuart, "Gen. Lee was the grand central figure."[71]

Two days after the review, the situation along the Rappahannock changed. Union infantry overran Confederate defenses at Rappahannock Station in a surprise assault. Swarming over rifle pits and a redoubt, the Federals captured 1,600 Southerners, two thousand stands of arms, four cannon, and eight battle flags. "It was *fun* for *us* to see the stew they were in," boasted a Yankee of his foes. The affair compelled Lee to withdraw behind the Rapidan into works that had been manned before the Bristoe Campaign.[72]

Once across the Rapidan, Stuart chose a small valley, edged by a stand of cedar, oak, and pine trees and located about a mile or so north-east of Orange Court House, as a headquarters site. He and his staff would stay here for nearly six months. A large hospital tent marked Stuart's office and living quarters. Rows of smaller tents held aides and couriers. The cavalry general designated the site Camp Wigwam for his years on the frontier. Army headquarters lay about two miles away.[73]

Wade Hampton returned to active duty during the early days of November. The South Carolinian's Gettysburg wounds had mended, and with the rank of major general, he assumed command of his division. Among the veterans from the lower South states, whom he had led directly, Hampton's respect of and popularity with exceeded Stuart's. Unlike Stuart, Hampton eschewed pomp and pageantry and newspaper acclaim if he believed others more deserving. A fellow South Carolinian portrayed him well: "Gen Hampton is a most excilent general . . . he is a brave man himself, but prudent and careful of his men. he is polite and affable in his desporson [sic] and a perfect gentleman in manners."[74]

On November 26, a few weeks after Hampton's return, the Army of the Potomac filed across the Rapidan's fords east of the Confederate main lines. Prodded by the Lincoln administration to assume the offensive before the advent of inclement weather, George Meade decided to turn Lee's right flank and attack the enemy or force Lee to assail Meade's superior numbers. When reports of the Union movement reached Lee, he reacted swiftly, marching his infantry and artillery east to Mine Run, about seven or eight miles southwest of the old Chancellorsville battle-field. The gray-coated veterans dug an extensive line of entrenchments behind the stream. Rain fell on November 28, as the Yankees aligned themselves opposite the Rebel works in the heavily wooded terrain.[75]

Meade ordered an assault for the morning of November 30, assigning 28,000 troops to the effort under Major General Gouverneur K. Warren, Second Corps commander. During the previous night, however, the Confederates strengthened and extended their fieldworks. When a Union sergeant saw them in the morning's light, he thought the position was "worse than Fredericksburg, I felt death in my very bones." Warren agreed with the sergeant after he and a staff officer had crawled forward on their hands and knees for a better view. The general canceled the attack and informed army headquarters. Meade, who had an explosive temper, rode to Warren.[76]

Meade conducted his own examination of the enemy works and reluctantly concurred with Warren. An assault would incur only heavy casualties, and the army commander was unwilling to sacrifice the lives of his men. Meade thought that the decision might cost him command of the army. The men in the ranks, however, praised Meade for the moral courage it took in avoiding the needless bloodletting. There was nothing else left but to recross the river.[77]

The cavalry's role in the week-long Mine Run Campaign was limited. Stuart, with Hampton's division, operated on the army's right flank and toward the enemy's rear. Thomas Rosser's brigade had minor affairs with Union horsemen, but that was the extent of the actions. The Federals withdrew on December 2 in bitterly frigid weather. For men in both armies the plummeting temperatures portended a cessation of active operations and winter quarters. For Jeb Stuart, they held the promise of a family reunion.[78]

Chapter Sixteen

"Grand Jeb Stuart"

I N THE PRIVATE correspondence of Jeb Stuart there exists no known letter in which he recounted the first time that he held his baby daughter in his arms. Like much of history, the scene is presumably lost, hidden behind time's impenetrable curtain. But it must have been a precious moment for him, with the memory of Little Flora ever present. The child could not replace the one death had taken, but she could assuage some of the pain.

Flora, Jimmie, and baby Virginia Pelham arrived at Orange Court House sometime after the end of the Mine Run Campaign. He had "engaged" for them "a large spacious house, with two old people and no children. the room for you is remarkably snug, has a stairway leading to it by a separate door from the rest of the house." The house was "quiet and convenient" to his headquarters, and it had taken "a great deal of diplomacy" on his part before the owners, a Mr. and Mrs. Scott, "surrendered" to his requests. In the "snug little room," he told Flora, he could "clasp my darling to these arms and consign to oblivion the cares & anxieties of separation."[1]

Their presence so close at hand undoubtedly brought Stuart joy. He must have visited the Scott residence frequently, if not nightly. The settlement of both armies into winter encampments reduced the demands on his time. Duty eased, and the work at headquarters slowed. The family's arrival coincided, however, with a crisis in the cavalry corps.[2]

On December 9, a week after Mine Run, Robert E. Lee wrote to Stuart, "Please look out for positions for the cavalry, where they can be foraged, and be not too far away from the field of operations." The shortage of grain for the horses that had stalked the camps during the previous winter foretold this day. The region occupied by Lee's army south of the Rappahannock and Rapidan rivers could not sustain Stuart's entire command through the cold weather months. Units would have to be dispersed farther south if the animals were to survive.[3]

Fitz Lee and the brigades of Williams Wickham and John Chambliss, with batteries of horse artillery, left during the second week of December. Lunsford Lomax's regiments remained with the main army, picketing the Rapidan fords. At first, Wickham's and Chambliss's men marched south toward Albermarle County but were rerouted to the Shenandoah Valley to interdict a Union force on a raid through western Virginia. When that operation ended, Fitz Lee scattered the regiments on both sides of the Blue Ridge. In time, however, he disbanded them, allowing the officers and men to go home until recalled. The horse artillerymen, meanwhile, had constructed winter quarters at Charlottesville. Their horses were, professed one of them, "weak, worn out, worthless and false."[4]

Stuart sent Thomas Rosser's brigade, Grumble Jones's former command, to Augusta County in the Shenandoah Valley. The majority of the officers and men hailed from the region and had served there throughout most of 1861 and 1862. Rosser had been in command of the brigade less than a month, but one of his troopers noted already, "We like our present commander (Gen Rossear) very well only he puts on more extras than *Old pap Jones* did." Stuart wrote to his cousin Alexander H. H. Stuart before the brigade arrived: "General Rosser is a cavalier of the right stamp—very different from Jones. I promise you people of Augusta no stampedes or false alarms from him."[5]

Rosser's move to the Valley left Wade Hampton with the brigades of James Gordon and Pierce Young. Both commands stayed with the army, performing picket duty along the rivers. Many of the officers and men, however, were or would be going home on horse details, an "absolutely necessary process," stated an aide of Stuart. If they were unable to secure new mounts, Hampton wrote, "I greatly fear many of my best men will be forced to go into the infantry." He recommended to army headquarters that entire regiments or battalions be sent south, where the forage was abundant.[6]

By Christmas, then, Stuart had fewer than half of the officers and men in the Cavalry Corps under his immediate supervision. Flora and the children resided still with the Scotts, remaining with him through the holidays. On Christmas Eve, Stuart hosted a party at headquarters for FitzGerald Ross, an Englishman who had served in the Austrian Huzzars; Francis Lawley, correspondent for the London *Times*; and Frank Vizetelly, another Englishman who was a sketch artist for the *Illustrated London News*. Sam Sweeney played for the guests, who joined Stuart in songs.[7]

The three Englishmen returned for a Christmas dinner. "Stuart's camp is always one of the jolliest," Ross thought, "as the General is very fond of music and singing, and is always gay and in good spirits himself, and when he laughs heartily, as frequently happens, he winds up with a shout very cheering to hear." At night, Stuart and staff members ended the day's celebration with music by Sam Sweeney and his cousin Bob Sweeney. One of the songs they might have sung was "Cavalier's Glee," composed by William Blackford and quite popular within the cavalry.[8]

The Stuart family boarded a train on New Year's Eve, traveling east— the general to Richmond, Flora and the children to Dundee, the Price family home. For the next month Stuart shuttled back and forth between Fredericksburg and Charlottesville, where he inspected his units, and the Confederate capital. While he was away from his headquarters, Sam Sweeney contracted smallpox and died. "His loss is deeply felt," Stuart said of the accomplished musician when he heard the news.[9]

During the stopovers in Richmond, Stuart indulged in the capital's social life. "Stewart [Stuart] is fond of society," Confederate Chief of Ordnance Josiah Gorgas jotted in his diary, "but entirely abstemious as to drinks." A woman who saw him at a party described him as "gilt-edged with stars." He sang, danced, and flirted with young women. Mary Chesnut, the wife of an advisor to Jefferson Davis, recounted in her diary that at one party Stuart "was devoted to Hetty Cary," the beautiful reigning belle of Richmond society.[10]

Charades had become the rage of the city's elite, and its members prepared elaborate settings for the game. At one party, with the audience sitting in front of a curtained stage, an orchestra played "Hail, The Conquering Hero Comes!" The curtain parted and, in the words of an attendee: "Forth strode grand Jeb Stuart in full uniform, his stainless sword unsheathed, his noble face luminous with inward fire. Ignoring the audience and its welcome, he advanced, his eyes fixed upon the shrine [a cross and altar] until he laid the blade, so famous, upon it. Then he moved to a group, and never raised his eyes from the floor as he stood with folded arms."[11]

Flora, Jimmie, and Virginia Pelham traveled to Richmond, where they stayed with her sister and brother-in-law, Dr. Charles and Maria Brewer. By then, however, Stuart had gone on to Charlottesville to send companies from Fitz Lee's divisions home on recruiting duty. While in the college town, he and John Esten Cooke attended a ball. At the dance, Stuart told Cooke that he had heard that "an old lady" had warned her daughters before the affair "not to dance round dances or let General Stuart kiss them." In a letter to Flora, he thought that Charlottesville would make a fine permanent home for the family. By the beginning of February, he was back with the army at Orange Court House.[12]

Soon after his return to Camp Wigwam, Stuart received a letter from his wife. Flora had heard gossip about her husband at the parties and believed that she was the subject of cruel jest because of it. He replied: "As to being laughed at about your husband's fondness for society and ladies, all I can say is that you are better off in that than you would be if I were fonder of some other things that excite no remark in others. *The society of ladies will never injure your husband*, and ought to receive your encouragement." His correspondence with various ladies was due "to the position I hold." Then, he reassured her, "I am thankful to say I have—and I hoped that my wife could not for one moment be made a prey to any twinge or unpleasant feeling at anything of the kind."[13]

Flora's reaction to the chatter of Richmond's fashionable set was understandable. Apparently, within a week or so after he had written to her, Stuart decided to allay further her concerns. He took a three-day leave of absence and traveled to the capital. A staff member believed that it was the only time during the war that the general went on leave. Whether Flora and the children returned with him to Orange Court House at the time is unclear. They were there, presumably staying at the Scotts' again, by early March.[14]

Once back at Camp Wigwam, Stuart attended to the duties of a corps commander. He conferred with Robert E. Lee, whose headquarters lay not too distant on the farm of a Rogers family. Stuart's primary responsibility, in Lee's instructions to him, was to "endeavor to find out enemy's intention & direction." Stuart maintained his network of scouts and spies, with some of them ranging as far north as the lower Shenandoah Valley and to the outskirts of Washington. He rode frequently to the signal station on Clark's Mountain, a 1,100-foot-high elevation behind Confederate lines, and interrogated the signal corpsmen on Federal movements.[15]

"I am getting my staff straightened gradually," Stuart boasted to Flora, "and soon will have the best in the Army." New members joined, and old members departed. Captain William Blackford secured an appointment to the 1st Regiment of Engineers as a major and left for Richmond. Blackford had been with Stuart since the Seven Days' Campaign. Private Theodore Garnett, who had been serving as a courier, was promoted to first lieutenant and appointed aide-de-camp. In his letter recommending Garnett's assignment, Stuart wrote that the Virginia private deserved it based upon "gallantry in action,—irreproachable character, and qualifications." Other additions, made during the previous months, included Dr. John Fontaine as medical director of the corps and Major Charles Grattan as ordnance officer.[16]

As a reward for the services of his very able chief of staff, Henry McClellan, Stuart requested that McClellan be appointed to a vacancy in the Adjutant General's Department of the Confederate Regular Army. The appointment would secure for McClellan a permanent rank in the army if the Confederacy achieved its independence. "With the exception of Major W. H. Taylor on General Lee's staff," stated Stuart of his aide in the letter to the War Department, "I know no one equal to him as an Assistant Adjutant General in the field." Evidently, another officer secured the vacancy.[17]

Confederate Congressman Alexander R. Boteler had joined Stuart's staff during the previous summer as a volunteer aide-de-camp. A former Whig politician and member of the United States House of Representatives, Boteler had served in the same capacity with Stonewall Jackson. He regarded Stuart as "a good friend" and presented to the cavalryman a gold-mounted "Washington Cane" as a gift. The cane had been crafted from a cedar tree at Mount Vernon, and had been given to Boteler by the stepgrandson of the Revolutionary War hero and first president.[18]

With Boteler still holding his seat in the Congress in Richmond during the winter, Stuart approached his influential friend about a concern that had gnawed at the general for months. When Stuart read that John Hood, his junior in rank, had been promoted to lieutenant general, he declared in a letter to Boteler: "For my part, I *yield to no man in the Confederacy in quantity and quality* of service. I know that General Lee would not have another in my place." He commanded two divisions, and "Withholding the rank of Lieutenant General seems to me a mere quibble, for a corps is two or more divisions by accepted military definition."

He went on, "while rank should be *no* patriot's *motive*, it is nevertheless the acknowledged evidence of appreciation, and when withheld from one occupying a position corresponding to higher rank the influence is against the officer and prejudiced to him." Stuart thought it "curious" that Congress had not extended to him and his command its formal "thanks."[19]

Four days later in a second letter, Stuart renewed his argument to Boteler: "A military man without aspirations is like a vessel without sail—a compass without the needle. It is farcical to say it is impracticable to make me Lieut. Genl. . . . If it is decided never to give a Lt. General to the cavalry, it is perhaps better that I should know it at once. My age is urged by the interested, as a reason for my not being promoted, but let it not be forgotten that I am with one exception the oldest (in rank) Major Gen'l on duty in either army." He joked, "When I lose my *head* however I hope to be *promoted*." He noted at the end, "Of course what I write on such subjects is *private*."[20]

His admonition about confidentiality notwithstanding, Stuart almost assuredly wanted Boteler to use the arguments in the letters for his pro-

motion. He had prized a lieutenant generalcy since the organization of
cavalry corps. But it was not to be. Instead, the legislature voted him
"the thanks of Congress" for the June and October 1862 raids, Catlett's
Station, Brandy Station, Chancellorsville, "and other places." Gettysburg was not cited.[21]

At this time, Colonel William H. Stiles, Jr., of the 60th Georgia
Infantry visited Camp Wigwam. "I went over to see Gen Stuart short
time ago," Stiles related to his father, "& he is fixed up more comfortably than any General in the field unless it is Gen. Lee." Two African-
Americans, Jake and Bob, acted as his servants. Music at night had not
ceased with the death of Sam Sweeney. Stuart enjoyed particularly sitting around "our merry camp-fire," as he called it, drinking coffee from a
silver cup. He was, said an aide, "an ardent lover of coffee."[22]

It might have been during one night's festivities at Camp Wigwam—
the date is uncertain—that the headquarters flag toppled into the fire
and a corner of it was burned. The banner was thirty-four inches square,
with a "red bunting field," edged in white, and a blue St. Andrew's
Cross. Flora had sewn it for Stuart. After the accident, he returned it to
her, writing, "It has proudly waved over many battlefields and if ever I
needed a motive for braving danger and trails I found it by looking upon
that symbol placed in my hands by my cherished wife."[23]

At the end of February, Union Brigadier General George Custer
undertook a mounted raid on Charlottesville. Custer's movement was
intended as a diversion for a four-thousand-man raid, led by Judson
Kilpatrick, on Richmond, where the Yankees planned to free Federal
prisoners held in Libby Prison and on Belle Isle. When Stuart learned
of Custer's movement, he gathered up companies of the 1st and 2nd
Virginia and rode south from Orange Court House. The Virginians met
Custer's four regiments on their return march near Standardsville. A
minor clash ensued, but the Northerners eluded the Rebels after repulsing a charge. Earlier, at Charlottesville, the gunners of Stuart's horse
artillery batteries had blunted the enemy advance north of the town.
Meanwhile, Kilpatrick's raid ended in failure, with the Confederates
seizing papers that allegedly outlined a plot to burn Richmond and
assassinate Confederate officials.[24]

The routine of winter quarters resumed after the Federal Charlottesville raid. In mid-March, Stuart welcomed back Rooney Lee, who had been exchanged as a prisoner of war. "Words cannot express the joy your safe return to us caused me," Stuart professed to the son of the army commander, "and I assure you I have never failed to improve everything tending to effect your rescue from a position most galling a soldier is ever called to endure." Lee had spent eight months in captivity at Fort Lafayette in New York.[25]

Stuart took the opportunity of Rooney Lee's return to duty by rec-ommending the brigadier's promotion to major general and by propos-ing the organization of a third cavalry division. Lee merited the higher rank, argued Stuart, for his "heroic" conduct at Brandy Station on June 9, 1863. The formation of a third division would require a reshuffling of brigades in the corps, and Stuart suggested dividing Calbraith Butler's command into two brigades. Under the plan, Fitz Lee and Rooney Lee would command two brigades, and Wade Hampton, three.[26]

When Hampton learned of Stuart's proposal for Butler's brigade, the South Carolinian objected. The relationship between Stuart and Hampton seemed to have soured during the winter. At the end of Feb-ruary, Stuart had written to Custis Lee, his friend and military advi-sor to Jefferson Davis, about a transfer of Hampton to the West. Two weeks later, Hampton fumed over the assignment of Butler's troopers to picket duty along the lower Rappahannock River. He voiced his disap-proval directly to Robert E. Lee, which elicited a response from Stuart: "I cannot conceive what object General Hampton has in submitting my telegram and his answer to the Commanding General. I certainly have no objection to the Commanding General's strictest scrutiny into every official act of mine."[27]

Hampton spoke personally to Robert E. Lee, expressing his opposi-tion to the reorganization. In a rare blunt reaction to a subordinate, Lee told Hampton, "I would not care if you went back to the South with your whole division." Afterward, Hampton confessed that Lee's "man-ner made this speech immensely mortifying." Mary Chesnut, to whom Hampton related the incident, noted in her diary: "It seems General Lee has no patience with any personal complaints or grievances. He is all for the cause, and cannot bear officers to come to him with any such matters as Wade Hampton had come about."[28]

The War Department approved the expansion of the cavalry corps into three divisions before the opening of the spring campaign. Rooney Lee's new division consisted of the brigades of John Chambliss, now a brigadier, and James Gordon, while Fitz Lee retained the commands of Lunsford Lomax and Williams Wickham. As Stuart proposed, the brigade of Calbraith Butler was broken up and reorganized into two units, one under Butler, and the other under Pierce Young. The 1st and 2nd South Carolina were ordered to their home state and were replaced by the 4th, 5th, and 6th South Carolina, which formed Butler's command. Thomas Rosser's three regiments and a battalion of Virginians completed Hampton's division.[29]

Like the mounted units, the horse artillery underwent command changes. In February, Robert Beckham was promoted to colonel and assigned to the Army of Tennessee. Stuart recommended Lieutenant Colonel James Dearing, who had commanded a First Corps artillery battalion, for the post. When Dearing expressed no desire for the command, Stuart endorsed Major R. Preston Chew, arguing that the twenty-one-year-old Virginian would make "an excellent commander." Chew had commanded a battery of horse artillery since November 1861, and was highly regarded within the cavalry corps. Colonel Thomas Munford thought his battery "was good, better, best." An artillery lieutenant said of Chew, "A more gallant or braver officer never wore sword." Chew received the appointment.[30]

At this time, Stuart sent an intriguing letter to Custis Lee, marking it "*Confidential.*" An opening in command of the Trans-Mississippi Department had arisen. If President Davis believed, wrote Stuart, "that my promotion with the view to assignment . . . would be productive of more good to the interests of the Confederacy at large, than my continuance in this Army, I shall cheerfully accept it." "I shall bring to the *faithful* discharge of its difficult duties whatever of energy and ability I possess," affirmed Stuart.[31]

Stuart then added a lengthy postscript to the letter. It revealed him at his scheming best. If his appointment raised objections in the Confederate Senate and among the public, President Davis might consider James Longstreet, Richard Ewell, or A. P. Hill, infantry corps commanders in the Army of Northern Virginia. "As Gen'l Lee has done me the honor to mention my name favorably in connection with the command of an Infy Corps," explained Stuart, "is it not probably that he has reference to one of the Corps in this Army, where I am no doubt more favorably known than anywhere else. In this connection might not the transfer of one of these Lt. Generals to the command of so important a Dept, better accommodate discontent and rivalries out there than the appt of myself."[32]

"Now a few words as regards my own command—the Cavalry," continued Stuart. He stated unequivocally whom he did not want as his possible successor. "Hampton is not the man for such a command," he declared, "and I know he will not suit Gen'l Lee, nor the peculiar requisites of such a station. Hampton is a gallant officer, a nice Gentleman, and has done meritorious service, but there you *must stop*." The South Carolinian "has frequently expressed to me the desire to serve in the west, and if there is the remotest intention to promote me, it would be a measure highly conducive to the public interest to assign him to the command of the District of the Mississippi."[33]

What should be made of this letter? Unquestionably, it reaffirmed the depth and intensity of Stuart's ambition and craving for promotion to lieutenant general. By writing to Custis Lee, his close friend from their academy days, Stuart hoped to exploit Lee's influence with Davis. He gave the departmental vacancy a good deal of thought and posited different scenarios that might result in his promotion. By raising objections to Hampton as his successor, Stuart opened the possibility of Fitz Lee, Custis Lee's cousin, as commander of the cavalry corps. Whether his friend discussed the matter with the Confederate president is unknown.

In the letter to Custis Lee, Stuart prophesized, "I think there is very little room for doubt that old Virginia will again be bathed in blood this spring & summer." It was this belief in the approaching fury that kept Stuart attentive to preparations throughout the weeks of command reorganization, difficulties with subordinates, and his quest for promotion. Daily drills and dress parades were reinstituted. Officers inspected arms and equipment and read the Articles of War each Monday to the men. Stuart issued orders to subordinate commanders, stressing the importance of maintaining active picket outposts and obtaining accurate information on enemy movements.[34]

The activity of scouts and spies increased. Stuart doled out money for civilian informers "in ragged bank notes in $1 & $2 denominations." His scouts ranged as far north as along the Potomac River. Private Channing Smith led the scouts, who operated in the rear of the Army of the Potomac. The twenty-one-year-old Smith had been serving as a scout and was, in Stuart's words, "cool, courageous and self-possessed—a perfect nonchalance under circumstances of great personal danger calculated to shake the stoutest hearts." Smith sent Stuart detailed reports on the Federals across the Rapidan and Rappahannock rivers.[35]

Beyond the streams, the Yankees had been amassing a formidable force. George Meade's five infantry corps had been consolidated into three, and the administration had ordered Major General Ambrose Burnside's Ninth Corps from Tennessee to operate with Meade's Army of the Potomac. By the time the spring warmth hardened the roads, the Federals numbered 119,000 "present for duty equipped."[36]

More important, the operations of the Union force were under the direction of Ulysses S. Grant. The victor at forts Henry and Donelson, Shiloh, Vicksburg, and Chattanooga, Grant had been appointed general-in-chief with the newly authorized rank of lieutenant general. He possessed an aptitude, if not genius, for warfare. As he had demonstrated in the West, Grant was a relentless enemy, undeterred by setbacks or defeats. "The art of war is simple enough," he explained later. "Find out where your enemy is. Get at him as soon as you can. Strike at him as hard as you can and often as you can, and keep on moving." With him, there would be no turning back regardless of the reversals or costs in casualties.[37]

Grant retained Meade in command of the army but removed Alfred Pleasonton as commander of the Cavalry Corps. The general-in-chief named Major General Philip H. Sheridan as Pleasonton's successor. Like Grant, Sheridan had served in the West, leading an infantry division at Chattanooga. His energy and fiery temperament impressed Grant. Physically short, looking like a tree stump attached to sawed-off legs, the thirty-three-year-old Sheridan was a man of action. Grant hoped that the subordinate would instill an aggressiveness into the cavalry's nearly 12,500 officers and men.[38]

Robert E. Lee watched closely the billowing storm across the rivers and understood well the stakes involved in the conflict's fourth spring. It would take time before he had the measure of Grant, but his redoubtable army of approximately 75,000 officers and men exuded confidence in him and the cause. He had no illusions about the task before them. To Jedediah Hotchkiss, Lee asserted that he "wanted every man to his post, that we had hard work to do this year." To his adjutant, Walter Taylor, he declared, "we have got to whip them, we must whip them."[39]

During the winter, Lee attended Sunday services at St. Thomas Episcopal church in Orange Court House. As the prospect of a spring campaign neared, "a solemn communion" was held on a Sabbath in the crowded sanctuary. "After the services had begun," recounted a surgeon in attendance, "all eyes were turned to a person who came clattering up the aisle with his jingling spurs, to be Genl. Jeb Stuart the Cavalry Commander. He was handsomely dressed for a Confederate, with buff coat facings and collar and embroidered wreath around the three stars on his collar, full gold braid on his sleeves, and a bouquet in his button hole. His felt hat adorned with a plume he carried on his arm in a conspicuous way, and was altogether 'loud.' I had never seen Jeb Stuart before and was not surprised from what I had heard of him."[40]

Although the doctor who recorded Stuart's noisy entrance did not specify the exact Sabbath day, the solemn worship was held probably on May 1. From the minister's sermon, through the fervency of the prayers, to the quiet taking of the sacrament, a foreboding must have hung over the congregation. In the eternal cycle of seasons, spring held a renewal of life, a promise of future bounty. But with an enemy movement expected soon, this spring portended another grim harvest of death.[41]

On Monday, May 2, Lee rode to the summit of Clark's Mountain, where his corps commanders and eight infantry division commanders joined him. Beneath them, to the north, against the background of greening fields, the army's senior generals surveyed the tented camps of the Union army. Lee told the assembled officers that preparations for a swift movement should be completed. The Federals, he said, will likely march beyond the Confederate right flank, crossing the Rapidan at Germanna and/or Ely's fords. If they came that way, Lee intended to strike them before they cleared the Wilderness, the vast tract of stunted trees and gnarled undergrowth where the Rebels had achieved a stunning victory the year before at Chancellorsville.[42]

The next night, Channing Smith, Private Benjamin Franklin Stringfellow, and other scouts rode into Camp Wigwam. They reported that the enemy planned to march the next morning, May 4, and numbered roughly 120,000 officers and men. Stuart relayed the information to army headquarters and alerted his division commanders. The cavalry lay scattered from along the Rapidan to below Fredericksburg on the Rappahannock.[43]

Confirmation of the scouts' intelligence came on the morning of May 4, when cavalry pickets at Germanna and Ely's fords fired on the advancing Yankees and then retreated. At Camp Wigwam, Stuart shouted to his staff and couriers "Pack up." "Our tents were struck," recorded Alexander Boteler, who had joined Stuart on May 2, in his diary, "wagons loaded and long before noon everything was in its proper place and everybody about the camp ready for active operations. Our mid-day meal was a merry one for all seemed glad to be relieved from the monotony of camp life in Winter Quarters."[44]

Stuart and his staff headed for army headquarters, riding across the countryside and testing their horses by jumping them over fences. Lee and his aides greeted the cavalrymen. "Everything betokened an immediate movement at Headquarters," noted Boteler. Lee's well-known mount, Traveller, had been saddled and awaited the general. Lee was, thought Boteler, "looking remarkably well and as calm, as courteous and considerate today as on the most ordinary occasions. No one would suppose from his demeanor that great events are in the gale or vast responsibilities weighing on his mind."[45]

After conferring with Lee, Stuart spurred east on Orange Plank Road. Behind him, Richard Ewell's Second Corps and A. P. Hill's Third Corps were on the march, following Orange Turnpike and Plank Road, respectively. Cavalry screened the infantry advance, and farther east, cavalry scouts from Fitz Lee's division hung on the edges of the enemy columns, sending back reports. Throughout the afternoon and evening, as the messages reached Stuart, he forwarded them to army headquarters. The news was good—the enemy had halted for the day in the Wilderness.[46]

Ewell's and Hill's infantrymen stopped for the night behind Mine Run. Stuart and his staff passed through the infantry ranks after dark, stopping on Orange Plank Road. Campfires brightened the darkness. Coming toward him were Hampton's veterans. When they recognized Stuart, the horse soldiers "greeted him with enthusiastic shouts as regiment after regiment, following each other, filed off before him along the rear of the infantry. It was an impromptu ovation to the Chief of the Cavalry Corps."[47]

Holding his plumed hat in his hand, Stuart looked, in Boteler's description, "like an equestrian Statue, —both man and horse being as motionless as marble." The scene moved Boteler, "it was really a grand spectacle to see these gallant horsemen coming toward us out of the gloom of night into the glare of the fire, making their welkin ring with their mild war cries and the earth to tremble beneath their horses hoofs."[48]

Stuart and his aides bivouacked for the night at Verdiersville. Another morning's sun would bring certainly a renewal of fighting, perhaps even slaughter. Whether Stuart thought of the dangers that might await cannot be known. Weeks earlier, Flora had repeated her fears for his safety that so haunted her thoughts. He tried to assuage them, writing: "I conjure you, if *you love me*, to 'cast the shadow from the brow.' 'Be gay & happy.' Tomorrow will bring its own cares without torturing the imagination to day to divine what *may* happen. By all means avoid *'pet miseries'* and cultivate a little merry heart, with cheerful resignation to the decree of Providence."[49]

He had looked to the future in his letter as he thought of his daughter, Virginia Pelham. "I am delighted to hear my pet is such a belle," Stuart enthused, "she will be a greater one if she lives to reach sweet sixteen, at which time we can *establish our Rules & Regulations* for the government of young ladies in search of husbands."[50]

He had tried comforting her in the past without success as the dark dreams kept recurring. Missing from this letter, and in all that he had written to her, were the words he had spoken to Esten Cooke, "I never expect to come out of this war alive."[51]

Chapter Seventeen

"I Had Rather Die, Than Be Whipped"

FOLKLORE HELD THAT the Rapidan River owed its name to "a fast young lady of the primitive time." A captivating beauty named Ann, she drew many suitors. She rejected each beau, however, with rapidity. When one of the forlorn swains nearly drowned crossing the stream, he thought of her and dubbed the river Rapid Ann.[1]

The Rapidan had served as a divide between fellow Americans during the months of winter encampments. Across its waters, they conversed, traded coffee for tobacco, and warned their foes if they were to fire. So much bound them together, and so much had brought them to opposite banks along a Virginia river. They spoke to each other of home, of an end to this terrible war. Each side knew that there must be a settlement before they could return to families and homes. When the Federals crossed the Rapidan on May 4, 1864, the beginning of the end had come.

The long road ahead passed first through the hellish confines of the Wilderness. Opposing skirmish lines sounded the warnings at mid-morning on May 5. The presence of Confederates surprised the Federals, whose planned march through the Wilderness halted. Union army commander George Meade ordered assaults, and throughout the afternoon, the fighting raged on both sides of the Orange Turnpike and Orange Plank Road. The combat was, exclaimed a Yankee, "a blind and bloody hunt to the death, in bewildering thickets, rather than a battle."[2]

From their bivouac at Verdiersville, Jeb Stuart and his staff rode toward the action on Orange Turnpike, passing through the columns of Richard Ewell's Second Corps. At Locust Grove or Robertson's Tavern, the party of cavalrymen veered southeast to Orange Plank Road, where A. P. Hill's Third Corps veterans filled the roadway. About noon, Stuart joined Robert E. Lee and a cluster of generals and officers at the Widow Tapp farm, one of the clearings in the miles of unbroken forest in the Wilderness. Within minutes, a line of Union skirmishers appeared across a field along the treeline. The group of Confederates scattered immediately, fleeing into the nearby woods. Had the Yankees fired their rifles, thought Alexander Boteler, the result "might have been of most disastrous consequences to the Confederate cause."[3]

Stuart remained behind Hill's battle ranks throughout the afternoon and evening. To the south, Thomas Rosser's brigade sparred with the van of Brigadier General James H. Wilson's Union cavalry division on Catharpin Road. When Wilson retreated after repulsing a Rebel charge, Rosser followed toward Todd's Tavern. Fitz Lee's division, meanwhile, passed through Spotsylvania Court House, moving toward Todd's Tavern from the south. Skirmishes flashed between the mounted foes.[4]

Stuart camped with his staff for the night at Parker's Store on the Plank Road. He rose before daylight on May 6, and according to his quartermaster officer, rode "off in fine spirits to lead his cavalry." Joining Rosser's brigade, he ordered the brigade mounted. Stuart "appeared to be in a great hurry," wrote Rosser later. Rosser was one of Stuart's favorites, but during the winter while in the Shenandoah Valley, the brigadier had received a reprimand from Stuart for disobedience of orders. In one letter to Rosser, Stuart rebuked him sharply, "if subordinates undertake to hold all orders in abeyance which affect them unpleasantly or do not meet their approval, then good bye to discipline and an effective army."[5]

The censure from Stuart must have fueled even more of Rosser's resentment toward his superior officer. Rosser believed, unfairly, that Stuart had deceived him over a promotion during the previous fall. As

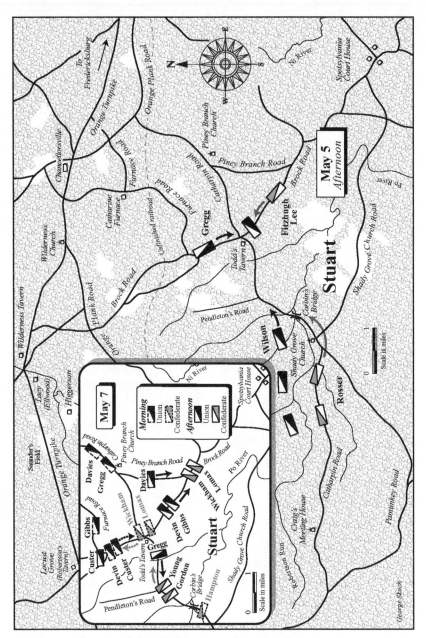

Battle of the Wilderness, Cavalry Operations

noted, Rosser was ungrateful for Stuart's efforts on his part. The brigadier had been given one of the corps's finest combat units, Grumble
Jones's former brigade. In fact, before his Virginians left the Valley,
Rosser christened them the "Laurel Brigade," in recognition of their
fighting prowess. He instructed each member of the brigade to wear two
or three laurel leaves on his hat or coat.[6]

From the Laurel Brigade's campsite on Catharpin Road southwest
of Todd's Tavern, Stuart directed the command north on country roads
toward the Union infantry's left flank. As the Confederates neared
Brock Road, they encountered George Custer's Michigan Brigade,
which held the Brock Road–Catherine Furnace Road intersection. An
extensive field sprawled along the Michiganders' line. Rosser had been
Custer's closest friend at West Point.[7]

The 35th Virginia Battalion, nicknamed the "Comanches" by Rosser
for their martial spirit, opened the fighting with a charge. The Federals,
armed with Spencer carbines, blasted back the Virginians. Rosser sent
in the 7th, 11th, and 12th Virginia in a succession of piecemeal attacks
only to suffer repulses. Colonel Thomas C. Devin's Union brigade came
up in support of Custer. When Rosser tried a flank attack, his academy
friend counterattacked, driving the Confederates from the field. Fortunately for the Virginians, two batteries of Preston Chew's horse artillery
arrived and held the Federals in check. Stuart stood among the cannon,
exhorting the gunners to stand fast. But more Union pieces opened on
Chew's gun crews and forced them rearward.[8]

The Laurel Brigade was, declared a sergeant in the 11th Virginia,
"badly cut to pieces." Although outnumbered, the Virginians blamed
Rosser for the defeat. "My bright dream that Rosser was one of the first
calvery Generals in our service is gone," proclaimed an officer in a letter. "He is no general at all. As brave a man as ever drew breath, but
knows no more about putting a command into a fight than a school boy.
We have lost confidence in him so fast that he can't get a good fight out
of us any more unless we know positively what we are fighting."[9]

Late in the day, Stuart pushed Rosser's brigade forward again toward
Brock Road. Stuart admitted in a message to army headquarters that
the command was "very much reduced." At Todd's Tavern, Fitz Lee's
horse soldiers, manning fieldworks they had built overnight, dueled

with David Gregg's troopers. Neither side gained an advantage. About mid-afternoon, Gregg retired, having been ordered back. A short time later, Stuart received a dispatch from the commanding general: "It is very important to save your Cavalry & not wear it out. . . . You must use your good judgment to make any attack which may offer advantages."[10]

When Robert E. Lee sent the note to Stuart, the second day of fury in the Wilderness spiraled to a climax. The day had begun with a massive Union assault along Orange Plank Road, which routed two of Hill's divisions and threatened Lee's entire line. The dramatic arrival on the battlefield of James Longstreet's First Corps divisions blunted the Union attack and then rolled it up, sending the Yankees rearward. The carnage was staggering. As Longstreet oversaw another advance, he was severely wounded, his party mistakenly fired into by his own men. A series of Confederate assaults against Federal works along Brock Road and on Meade's right flank ended the fighting. The Rebels achieved a tactical victory, but the bloodletting on both sides exceeded 28,000. "This war is horrid," a surgeon recorded in his diary that night.[11]

The gunfire and artillery charges had ignited the underbrush. When the evening breezes increased, the woods burned, smothering the wounded and charring the remains of the dead. Stuart was well removed from the fiendish work, encamped at Parker's Store. He sent a telegram to Flora, "I am safe and well." When he had ridden out in the morning, Major Philip Powers, his quartermaster, beseeched, "May God protect him this day is my earnest prayer."[12]

For the main armies locked together in the Wilderness, May 7 passed with a series of skirmishes, with each side probing the other's lines for indications of a possible movement. Concluding that his adversary would retreat south, Ulysses Grant issued orders for a night march to Spotsylvania Court House, intending, if possible, to place the Union army between the Confederates and Richmond. Later in the day, Robert E. Lee surmised that the enemy was heading toward the crossroads village. After nightfall, the First Corps, now under Major General Richard Anderson in place of the wounded James Longstreet, stepped off.[13]

The direct route for the Federals to Spotsylvania Court House was Brock Road. For much of May 7, Fitz Lee's Confederate cavalrymen fought against Philip Sheridan's Union horsemen. "Off and on we drove them and they drove us," stated a Virginian. The Rebels fought tenaciously from behind their fieldworks. At one point in the action, the log works caught on fire, forcing Lee's men to abandon them and retire. When the combat subsided at sundown, Sheridan made an unwise decision by withdrawing to Todd's Tavern. Lee's men still blocked Brock Road between Spotsylvania Court House and the tavern.[14]

As he had done on the previous day, Stuart was present during the engagement but left Fitz Lee in command. Rebel scouts worked on the fringes of the Union lines and examined the road network for the march of Confederate infantry. All of Wade Hampton's division joined Stuart at last and was posted at Shady Grove Church on Catharpin Road, approximately two miles southwest of Todd's Tavern. That night, Stuart sent a second telegram to Flora: "I am safe and well—Saturday. We have beaten the enemy badly but he is not yet in full retreat."[15]

Stuart rose before daylight on May 8, and then headed for Spotsylvania Court House with his staff and couriers. Along the way, the coterie of horsemen passed the veteran troops of the First Corps. The infantrymen had been marching through the night. With fires smoldering in the woods beside the road, Anderson kept them moving instead of halting for a few hours' rest as he had been instructed by the army commander. His decision proved to be a fateful one for the army.[16]

Riding to the front of Anderson's column, Stuart led the infantrymen, the division of Brigadier General Joseph B. Kershaw. While the Confederate foot soldiers plodded down the road, gunfire rolled back from Brock Road, where Fitz Lee's brigades were delaying the Union Fifth Corps. The Rebel horsemen felled trees across the road and undertook counterattacks. A battery of horse artillery supported the troopers. A member of the 5th Virginia thought that their two-day stand on Brock Road was "some of the hardest fighting . . . that they have ever done since the war commenced." At last, they fell back to a low ridge known as Laurel Hill. Their valiant defense, however, had delayed the Yankees for nearly five precious hours.[17]

Coming up the reverse slope of Laurel Hill were South Carolinians and Mississippians from two of Kershaw's brigades. Stuart directed them there, riding in front of them and singing to them: "The sun's low down the sky, Lorena/The frost is on the grass again." Now, he pointed them to the crest. "He was a fine looking officer and rode a fine dark dapple-gray horse," remembered a South Carolinian of the famous cavalryman. "He, the general, wore a black plume in his hat."[18]

As Kershaw's crack foot soldiers hurried past, Stuart said to them: "Hush, hush, boys. Be quiet. Don't say a word." On the crest was a makeshift barricade of fence rails. Pointing to them, Stuart said: "Run for the rail piles. The Federal infantry will reach them first if you don't run." A Rebel infantryman thought that Stuart was as "cool as a piece of ice, though all the time laughing."[19]

The Confederates won the race for the rail works. To their front, a division of the Union Fifth Corps, veterans like Kershaw's men, were crossing Spindle Field and beginning their ascent of the hillside. Stuart seemed to be all along the growing Southern line, deploying the regiments and placing two batteries into position. "Hold your fire until the Federals are well within range," he admonished the waiting riflemen, "and then give it to them and hold this position to the last man. Plenty of help is near at hand."[20]

Smoke and flames from the muzzles of rifles and cannon suddenly creased the hilltop. The initial volley blew over the heads of the Yankees, but not the second or third or more. The blue-coated ranks staggered, with men going down in clumps. More Federal units stepped forth into the withering musketry and artillery fire. "We continued our rain of lead into their ranks," a Rebel averred. "The field in our front was blue with dead and wounded Federals."[21]

Kershaw's South Carolinians and Mississippians were as fine a body of troops as the army possessed. They had fought on some of the bloodiest battlefields and knew bravery and leadership. Stuart's conduct impressed them, and they remembered it. He rode behind their ranks, waving his hat and inspiring them. An infantryman recounted seeing the general "sitting on his horse amidst a storm of bullets, laughing and joking with the men and commending them highly for their courage and for the rapidity and accuracy of their fire." He rode to a battery crew, and gesturing toward enemy artillery pieces, said: "Boys, I want you to knock them all to pieces. So go to work."[22]

The Confederates held Laurel Hill against the initial Union attacks, but additional Yankees were coming down Brock Road. At Spotsylvania Court House, meanwhile, Kershaw's remaining two brigades chased James Wilson's Union cavalry division out of the town. Wilson had swung around, entering the crossroads from the north and threatening the enemy's rear on Laurel Hill. When the Southern infantry appeared, Wilson extricated his command from the closing vise. Spotsylvania, Grant's objective for the day, belonged to his foe.[23]

Throughout the rest of the day, the area around the village filled with troops from both armies. Men dug trenches and piled logs on the dirt, reshaping the face of the killing and maiming. The Confederates had beaten their enemy to the battleground by the narrowest of margins. Anderson's decision to continue the march during the night had been critical, and the delaying tactics and obstinate defense by Fitz Lee's cavalrymen had been, in the judgment of historian Gordon Rhea, "magnificent."[24]

Stuart's conduct of the fight for Laurel Hill harked back to his performance at Chancellorsville on May 3, 1863. He had handled the deployment of the units skillfully, using the ground's contours to advantage. His fearlessness, buoyant manner, and reassuring words inspired Kershaw's veterans and earned their admiration. War suited him. With Stonewall Jackson dead and James Longstreet badly wounded, Stuart now stood unmatched among Robert E. Lee's lieutenants.

That night, Stuart and his aides camped at the "Old *Block House*" outside the village. The army commander and other senior officers bivouacked nearby. For whatever reason, Stuart did not send another telegram to his wife with comforting words about his safety. In his reminiscences, Theodore Garnett noted that this was the last night that all of the staff members and their leader were together.[25]

Once again, as he had done for several days, Stuart was mounted and on his way soon after daybreak. He passed through Spotsylvania Court House, riding out Fredericksburg Road, where he joined Fitz Lee. Lee's troopers were fighting dismounted, harassing the van of the Union Ninth Corps with the same grit that they had shown on Brock Road. Stuart stayed awhile and then rode back into the village.[26]

Robert E. Lee had entered the town and set up headquarters beside a church near the courthouse. Stuart clattered up to the location and dismounted. He and Lee spent the next hour or so together. The army's operations undoubtedly dominated their conversation. But the personal warmth and mutual respect between them would have been evident to an observer. Since Stuart's cadet days at West Point, Lee had taken a liking to the vibrant young man. Stuart owed Lee much; Lee owed Stuart much. While they were together, cavalry scouts arrived, reporting that a large column of Union horsemen was marching south away from their army.[27]

On the previous morning, the commander of the Army of the Potomac, George Meade, rode to Todd's Tavern, where he expected to find the route to Spotsylvania open. Instead, he discovered two of Philip Sheridan's cavalry divisions without orders and the passage down Brock Road barred by Fitz Lee's troopers. Meade had an ill temper on good days, and this was not one of them. By the time Sheridan appeared, Meade "had worked himself into a towering passion," in the words of a staff officer.[28]

A mutual antipathy had developed between Meade and Sheridan by this time. Meade tore into the diminutive cavalry commander with "hammer and tongs." But the fuse on Sheridan's temper was clipped as short as Meade's. The Irishman shot back with curses, accusing Meade "of mixing up infantry with cavalry." "If he could have matters his own way," snarled Sheridan, "he would concentrate all the cavalry, move out in force against Stuart's command, and whip it."[29]

Later that day, Meade related the encounter with Sheridan to Grant. He repeated the subordinate's vow about whipping the Confederate cavalry. "Did Sheridan say that?" asked Grant. "Well, he generally knows what he is talking about. Let him start right out and do it." That night Meade issued an order for Sheridan's horsemen to "proceed against the enemy's cavalry." In Sheridan's reasoning, a raid against Confederate supply and railroad lines would almost certainly draw a response from Stuart. Then, he would "whip" the vaunted Southern mounted units.[30]

Before daylight on May 9, the Yankee troopers marched. Sheridan kept one mounted regiment with the army and led three divisions, more than ten thousand officers and men, and six batteries of horse artillery south on Telegraph Road. By nightfall, the Federals had crossed the North Anna River and descended upon Beaver Dam Station on the Virginia Central Railroad. At the station, they seized a train carrying three thousand Union prisoners, destroyed more than one million rations and a load of medical supplies for Lee's army, and burned the depot. These raiders, in the estimation of historian Robert E. L. Krick, "tried the Confederate cavalry as never before."[31]

It was one o'clock in the afternoon of May 9 before Fitz Lee's brigades of Williams Wickham and Lunsford Lomax started after Sheridan's command. Lee's men had remained at the front, skirmishing with the enemy, until relieved by Confederate infantrymen at noon. Stuart also assigned James Gordon's brigade from Rooney Lee's division to the chase. In all, ten cavalry regiments, about three thousand officers and men, were sent to intercept a force more than three times their numbers. Robert E. Lee decided to retain part of Stuart's corps with the army for reconnaissance and flank protection.[32]

"We in the ranks did not know what for," wrote a corporal in the 1st Virginia, "but as we became extended on the way south word came along the line that the Yankee cavalry had been despatched on a raid to Richmond, that city being, as it was supposed, but weakly defended. We were to follow up the Yankees and put them out of business before they got to Richmond." Late in the afternoon Fitz Lee's column overtook Sheridan's rear guard at Mitchell's Store, north of Chilesburg, and a clash ensued. The Federals held, and Lee halted for the night.[33]

Stuart remained at Spotsylvania Court House until 3:00 P.M. The artillerist Porter Alexander visited with him before he left, and recalled that Stuart "was in his usual high spirits & cheerful mood." Stuart instructed some aides to stay behind with the army, telling Major Norman FitzHugh that he wanted the staff officer to tend "to the wants of our people." As Stuart and a few staff members rode away, an onlooker heard the general sing, "Take your time Miss Lucy and pour your coffee out."[34]

Descriptions of Stuart's mood conflict. During the sixteen-mile ride to Mitchell's Store, the general was, contended his aide-de-camp, Lieutenant Theodore Garnett, "exceedingly depressed, anxious, troubled, even feverish." When he arrived at Fitz Lee's camp after dark, the division commander thought that Stuart seemed in "good spirits, always incident to a prospect for a fight." He laughed, joked, and sang, recalled Lee. Earlier, he had exchanged friendly words with Lee's pickets after one of them, recognizing the general, shouted: "Hurrah boys! Here's old Jeb!"[35]

At Mitchell's Store, Lee, Wickham, and Lomax talked with Stuart. During the meeting, someone suggested that their outnumbered men could not stop Sheridan. According to Lomax, Stuart "exclaimed abruptly and almost in anger, 'No sir, I'd rather die than let him go on!'" When they had finished, Stuart remounted Lee's weary troopers and led them south on an all-night march.[36]

The column of gray-jacketed horsemen passed through Chilesburg, forded the North Anna River, and proceeded to the ruins of Beaver Dam Station. If Stuart had had any uncertainty about Sheridan's objective, reports indicated that the Union cavalry had continued on toward the capital's defenses. Although Stuart could not have known it, Sheridan's goal was not Richmond, but the pursuing Confederates. As he had declared to Meade, he wanted to "whip" Stuart. The Federals' march on this day was described as "leisurely," a slow pace that would give the Southerners time to close the gap between the two forces.[37]

Given the information, Stuart decided that he must harass Sheridan's force and intercept the enemy's route of march before the Yankees approached the capital. While Gordon's North Carolinians, who were coming on through Chilesburg, pressed the Federal rear, Lee was ordered to move east to Telegraph Road at Hanover Junction, and then to turn south. Before he left the railroad station, Stuart alerted General Braxton Bragg, now military advisor to Jefferson Davis, about the impending threat, stating in the dispatch, "I am pursuing closely." He sent a second message to Colonel Bradley T. Johnson, commander of the Maryland Line at Hanover Junction, requesting that Johnson loan the Baltimore Light Artillery battery to Lee's division.[38]

When Fitz Lee resumed the march, Stuart and Major Andrew Venable rode a mile from the station to the home of Colonel Edmund Fontaine, president of the Virginia Central Railroad. Flora Stuart and the children had been staying with the Fontaines for several weeks. Fontaine and his wife, the former Maria Louisa Shackleford, were both second cousins of Stuart. Fontaine had named his fine home Beaver Dam.[39]

Stuart halted in front of the house but did not dismount. Flora, probably holding Virginia Pelham, and Jimmie came out to see him.

Someone handed him "a little poodle dog," which he held in his lap for a while. Mollie Fontaine, a daughter, brought a kettle of stewed asparagus to him. As he ate them, gravy dripped on the dog's head. Stuart must have cradled his daughter, who he had bragged was "now a great beauty," in his arms and lifted up Jimmie into the saddle. He and Flora had "a few words of private conversation" and then he rode away. "After riding some distance in silence," Venable wrote of the general, "he told me he never expected to live through the war, and that if we were conquered, that he did not want to live."[40]

Stuart and Venable overtook Fitz Lee's cavalrymen between Hanover Junction and Taylorsville late in the afternoon. A member of the 5th Virginia, watching Stuart pass, wrote later that his commander "looked worn out from fatigue." It was not until 9:00 P.M. before Lee's exhausted men and mounts halted for the night, after more than thirty hours on the march. Stuart notified Bragg that a citizen had informed them that Sheridan's force was several miles to the southwest of Lee's position at Ground Squirrel Bridge over the South Anna River. "There is none of our cavalry from this direction," Stuart stated, "between the enemy and Richmond." "I am very anxious to give my command a night's rest, if compatible with duty," he concluded.[41]

Bradley Johnson and the Baltimore Light Artillery came from Hanover Junction to Taylorsville during the night. Johnson was led to where Stuart and his staff had bedded down. The cavalry commander was, remembered Johnson, "asleep with his head on his saddle. We could not wake him." The colonel left a note behind, telling Stuart, "he must take care of" the battery.[42]

The showdown sought by both Sheridan and Stuart began in the predawn darkness of May 11. The Yankees were on the move by 2:00 a.m., riding east. Brigadier General Henry Davies's brigade rode toward Ashland and the Richmond, Fredericksburg & Potomac Railroad. Another detachment filed southeast to Hungary Station on the railroad. Finally, after sunrise, the main body of Union horsemen, led by Sheridan, followed Mountain Road toward its intersection with Telegraph Road at Yellow Tavern. "All the information that could be obtained led me to believe that the Rebel General was concentrating his cavalry at Yellow Tavern," reported Sheridan.[43]

The Confederates were, in fact, on the march south on Telegraph Road, having remounted at three o'clock. When they reached Ashland, they found Davies's Yankees tearing up the rails and torching a few buildings. The 2nd Virginia of Wickham's brigade attacked dismounted, engaging the 1st Massachusetts in the streets and from houses and yards. Women residents cheered the Virginians, who captured some prisoners before Davies withdrew. Stuart sent a dispatch to Bragg, briefly summarizing the fighting in the town before stating: "I intersect the road of the enemy is marching at Yellow Tavern (Head of Turnpike 6 miles of Richmond). My men & horses though tired hungry & jaded are *all right*."[44]

Lomax's Virginians had ridden at a trot, even at a gallop at times, directly from Taylorsville to Yellow Tavern, arriving at eight o'clock. After the fight at Ashland, Wickham hurried to reunite with Lomax. Stuart's chief of staff, Henry McClellan, rode beside the general. "We conversed on many matters of personal interest," testified the aide in his memoirs. "He was more quiet than usual, softer, and more communicative. It seems now that the shadow of the near future was already upon him."[45]

Theodore Garnett claimed many years after the war that as Stuart and his aides neared Yellow Tavern, his longtime bugler, Private George Freed, remarked, "General, I believe you love bullets." Stuart turned his head sharply, and looking at Freed, shot back, "No, Freed, I do not love bullets any better than you do; I go where they are because it is my duty, and I do not expect to survive this war."[46]

Stuart arrived at Yellow Tavern between nine and ten o'clock. The building for which the area had been named was now a dilapidated shell of a structure. Originally built in the 1830s as a stagecoach stop, the three-story tavern, measuring fifty feet by thirty feet, had been abandoned for years. During the war, soldiers had stripped boards from its sides, doors, and windows, using them for firewood. Its yellow color had faded along with the clamor of former guests.[47]

Yellow Tavern sat on the east side of Brook Turnpike, several hundred yards south of the juncture of Telegraph Road and Mountain Road. Brook Turnpike ran from the intersection of the two roads into Richmond. Coming from the northwest, Mountain Road joined Telegraph Road at a sharp angle. Lomax's three regiments had halted along Telegraph Road a half-mile or more north of the tavern. When Stuart came up, he decided to deploy the two brigades north of the juncture on the flank of the Federals as they marched on Mountain Road. As a precaution, he sent McClellan into the capital to learn from Bragg if the city's defenses were adequately manned.[48]

The Confederate line formed in the shape of an inverted and upside-down L. Lomax's 6th, 5th, and 15th Virginia dismounted and manned the bed of Telegraph Road, facing west. When Wickham's troopers arrived, Stuart placed them on a wooded rise in a line perpendicular to Lomax's ranks, with Wickham's left flank connecting with Lomax's right or northern flank. Wickham dismounted his four regiments and deployed them from left to right: 1st, 3rd, 4th, and 2nd Virginia. These veteran horse soldiers were concealed among the trees and faced south.[49]

With Bradley Johnson's loan of Captain William H. Griffin's Baltimore Light Artillery, Stuart had ten cannon. It would seem that Captain Philip P. Johnston's 1st Stuart Horse Artillery of four guns unlimbered initially on Wickham's right flank on the wooded ridge. A two-gun section of Captain James Hart's South Carolina Horse Artillery covered the left end of Lomax's line along Telegraph Road. Griffin's four cannon were placed in reserve to the rear. The very capable Major James Breathed, whom Stuart called "Old Jim Breathed," commanded the artillery. A member of the 5th Virginia wrote later: "We thought we had Sheridan safe and sound. Our position was a good one."[50]

Before the Confederate deployment had been completed, the van of Sheridan's command, Brigadier General Wesley Merritt's First Division, came into view on Mountain Road. Merritt shook out a dismounted skirmish line, using the troopers from the brigades of colonels Alfred Gibbs and Thomas Devin. Lomax countered by advancing companies from his ranks into woods several hundred yards west of Telegraph Road. For the next few hours, the Yankees and Virginians fought for possession of the woods. Finally, about noon, the Federals cleared the Rebels from among the trees, pushing them through a five-hundred-yard field to Telegraph Road.[51]

The fighting subsided temporarily with the retreat of Lomax's men. Stuart had been, recalled Garnett, "on the spot, and as usual, among

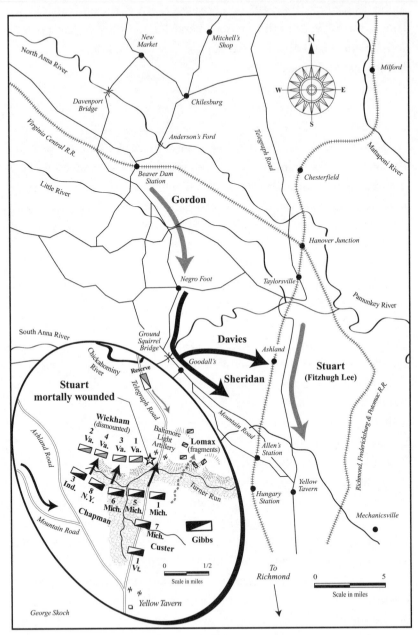

Battle of Yellow Tavern

the skirmishers, directing their fire." He left them finally and superin-
tended the final disposition of the regiments. He rode then to a rise east
of Telegraph Road from which he could view most of the battlefield.
Before long, Gibbs's and Devin's Union troopers advanced on Lomax's
line from the west and south. A section of a Federal battery unlimbered
just north of the tavern and began shelling Lomax's left flank.[52]

When Stuart saw the oncoming dismounted Yankees, he turned to
Garnett and said, "Go and tell Colonel Pate to hold that position *at
all hazards*." For some unexplained reason, Lomax had assigned Colonel
Henry Clay Pate of the 5th Virginia to command of the brigade and
went to the rear, where he could observe the combat. Pate was Stuart's
old nemesis who had applied for a court of inquiry in the summer of
1862 when Stuart secured the appointment of Thomas Rosser to command of the regiment. The story is most likely apocryphal that Stuart
rode to Pate, and the two of them mended their differences and shook
hands before the Federals struck.[53]

Garnett found Pate in the roadbed, the colonel standing among his
men and holding his unsheathed sword. "I delivered the order in the
very words I had received it," recounted the aide in his memoir, "and I
can see Col. Pate as he now stood, looking me square in the eye, with his
cold grey eyes and pallid face, (not from fear for his was habitually pale)
but uttering no response." Garnett repeated the order, but still Pate said
nothing. "But I saw he had heard and understood my orders in their
full significance, as a veritable 'death-sentence.'" In an unpublished
account, Garnett attributed Pate's reaction to being "quite deaf."[54]

Garnett scurried away moments before Merritt's Northerners—New
Yorkers and Pennsylvanians—closed on Pate's ranks. The pair of Union
cannon near the tavern raked the left flank of the Confederate line in
the road, punishing the 6th Virginia. The Virginians held on until the
dismounted attackers charged up the road. The 6th Virginia broke and
fled rearward. The 5th and 15th Virginia still clung to the roadbed, but
the Yankees were coming on, lashing the Rebels' front and flank. "Our
fire, protected as we were, did not seem to check their advance in the
least," wrote a 5th Virginia man of the enemy.[55]

Amid the collapsing ranks stood Pate. Waving his hat, the colonel
encouraged the men, "One more round boys, and then we'll get to the

hill." He had barely shouted the words when a bullet struck him in the forehead, killing him. His Virginians scrambled for the hill, but dozens were trapped in a cut in the road and were captured. A Pennsylvanian grabbed Pate's "silver-mounted" Colt revolver and had it in his possession years later. Wickham's troopers counterattacked from the hill, driving the Yankees back across the field and down Telegraph Road.[56]

Lomax, Stuart, and fellow officers rallied the fleeing Virginians on the rise east of Telegraph Road. When told of Pate's fall, Stuart said with emotion that he "died the death of a gallant soldier." Stuart ordered forward Griffin's Baltimore Light Artillery, placing the four guns astride the road between Wickham's and Lomax's lines. It was about two o'clock in the afternoon, and a calm settled in for a second time.[57]

Stuart established his command post near Griffin's battery. He had been concerned for several hours about James Gordon's brigade, which had been trailing Sheridan's column. During the morning, the Confederates at Yellow Tavern had heard gunfire from the distant west. Shortly after the shattering of Lomax's line in the road, a courier delivered a message from Gordon. Stuart read it, and according to Theodore Garnett, "It seemed to put him in a very good humor." The general said to Garnett, "I wish Gordon was here."[58]

Gordon's North Carolinians had been dogging the Federals' rear for two days. Early this morning, Gordon bypassed enemy pickets along the South Anna River and led his men across the stream at an unguarded location. Once on the southern bank, the Confederates attacked the rear guard of David Gregg's Second Division. The surprised Yankees rallied, and the combat escalated around Ground Squirrel Church and Goodall's Tavern. "We had the most desperate hand-to-hand conflict I ever witnessed," proclaimed the colonel of the 1st North Carolina. Gordon's aggressive tactics prevented Gregg's brigades from joining Sheridan at Yellow Tavern.[59]

Although Gordon's dispatch eased one concern for Stuart, officers reported that their men had spent nearly all of their carbine ammunition. He then sent Garnett to a nearby house to inquire if there were any byroads or "bridle paths" that a detail of horsemen could use to reach the capital and to return with boxes of ammunition. For most of the time during the lull, however, Stuart relaxed. A courier brought him a piece of bacon, hoe cake, and rye coffee, which the trooper had acquired at a log farmhouse. Chief of staff Henry McClellan came back from Richmond, and he and Stuart "sat quietly near one of the batteries for more than an hour."[60]

At 3:00 P.M., Stuart wrote a message to Braxton Bragg. "The enemy now has the Yellow Tavern and hold on to Old Mountain road for some distance above," he began. He noted the location of Gordon's brigade and suggested that Bragg advance Brigadier General Eppa Hunton's infantry brigade out Brook Turnpike into the rear of the Federals. "I cannot see how they can escape," if Hunton joined him. "I have attacked once and feel confident of success," he professed. "They drove our extreme left back little, but we have been driving their rear and left. As soon as Gordon joins my right I will try them again, and expect to get so as to command the intersection. . . . The enemy fights entirely as infantry today."[61]

The Confederates at Yellow Tavern needed time before Gordon's North Carolinians reached them. It was not to be, however. Sheridan had hesitated in making a mounted and dismounted assault on Stuart's line until Brigadier General James Wilson's Third Division appeared on the field. When Wilson's horsemen rode in during the break in the fighting, Sheridan prepared for an attack. George Custer's four Michigan regiments and the 1st Vermont would lead the charge, supported on both flanks by some of Wilson's regiments and Gibb's and Devin's troopers in Merritt's division.[62]

Custer, whom his men now called "Old Curly," readied his command. The 5th and 6th Michigan were dismounted west of Telegraph Road and were to advance against Wickham's troopers. In the roadbed, Custer stacked in column of squadrons the 1st and 7th Michigan and the 1st Vermont. They were to charge mounted up the road toward the Baltimore Light Artillery. "The situation at 3:30 P.M. was one of anxiety to all," remembered Merritt's chief of staff, Theodore W. Bean, "and all believed that the crisis was near at hand."[63]

Thirty minutes later, Custer rode to the front of the 1st Michigan. Bugles sounded, and the mounted Yankees moved at a walk and then at a trot, like a blue lance toward Griffin's guns. From the ridge, a courier with Stuart thought the Federals "resembled a great gang of black birds at a distance." In the fields beside the road, more Northerners advanced on foot. Confederate gunners fired their cannon, and the cavalrymen blazed away with their carbines. A member of the 2nd Virginia asserted, "Our recruits fought like old men."[64]

A narrow bridge over Turner's Run at the base of the ridge momentarily slowed the 1st Michigan. On the crest, Griffin's artillerists switched from shells to canister. But the Michiganders surged up the hillside, "yelling like demons," according to one of the Confederate gunners. Within minutes, the saber-wielding attackers were among the cannon, slashing Griffin's Marylanders. "We emptied more than one Yankee saddle while they were charging us, but there were too many for us," wrote a battery member. East and west of the road, dismounted Northerners pressed forward against Wickham's and Lomax's troopers.[65]

Stuart had held companies of the 1st, 2nd, and 6th Virginia in a mounted reserve. When the Michiganders overran Griffin's battery, he ordered them forward in a counterattack. Lomax led Company D of the 6th Virginia into the jumbled ranks of the 1st Michigan. Behind the men of the 6th Virginia came companies B and G of the 1st Virginia. The roadbed was jammed with foes locked in a frenzied melee. "The dull sound of sabers descending upon hapless heads could be heard amid the rattle of carbines and the cracking of pistols," attested a combatant.[66]

It was toward this confusing, roiling combat that Stuart spurred his large gray horse. "As he always did," Henry McClellan explained in a letter to Flora Stuart, "the General hastened to the point where the greatest danger threatened." He came alone—his staff members were scattered, giving orders or rallying men, and McClellan's mount was too exhausted after the round-trip ride to Richmond for his chief of staff to accompany him.[67]

Stuart reined up along the edge of pine woods near Company K of the 1st Virginia, whose seventy or so members were firing from behind a fence along Telegraph Road. One of the Confederates believed that above the din he heard Stuart whistling as he arrived. Stuart shouted to them: "Steady, men, steady. Give it to them." He carried a .36-caliber Whitney revolver on this day, drew it from the holster, and emptied its six shots at the Michiganders in the road.[68]

The Yankees were retreating on horseback and on foot, some of them turning about and firing at the Rebels. Drawing his sword, Stuart exclaimed: "Bully for old K. Give it to them, boys!" A Virginian swore later that he told Stuart "to go away several times that was no place for [him]." Then, as McClellan related the event afterward to Flora, "one man who had been dismounted in the charge & was running out on foot, turned as he passed the General and discharging his pistol inflicted the fatal wound."[69]

In his report, Colonel Russell A. Alger of the 5th Michigan claimed that one of his men, Private John A. Huff of Company E, shot Stuart. Alger stated that the Confederate officer whom Huff fired at was carrying a flag and had with him "a large staff and escort." This could not have been Stuart. Furthermore, the 5th Michigan attacked on foot against the front of Wickham's line, not toward Griffin's battery. Confederate accounts agree that the Yankee had been dismounted and was fleeing on foot, as McClellan described. The evidence points to a trooper in either the 1st or 7th Michigan.[70]

Whoever fired the shot, his .44-caliber pistol ball struck Stuart in the left side, at "the top of his breaches pocket," sliced through his stomach, and passed out his back, one inch to the right of his spine. He reeled in the saddle when hit, with his plumed hat falling to the ground. Captain Gustavus W. Dorsey, commander of Company K, rushed to his aid. Dorsey seized the reins of the wounded general's mount, trying to lead the animal to the rear. But the horse became "so restive and unmanageable" that Stuart "insisted upon being taken down."[71]

Dorsey helped Stuart from the horse and placed him against a tree. Stuart told the captain to leave him alone, rejoin his men, and repulse the Yankees. He feared that the wound was mortal, said Stuart, and Dorsey could be of no further assistance. Dorsey replied that he could not obey the order until he had the general taken to safety. By now, a few of Dorsey's men—members of Company K were Marylanders— had gathered around Stuart. "I saw that his whole side was soaked with blood," recounted Private Frederick Pitts.[72]

Dorsey asked for another horse upon which to put Stuart. Pitts volunteered his mount, and several men lifted their commander into the saddle. Pitts and privates Charles Wheatley and Robert Bruce held Stuart on the horse and led him to the rear. The three enlisted men found a mule-drawn ambulance and lay the general in it. The fighting still raged along the ridge and in the road.[73]

Fitz Lee and members of Stuart's staff hurried to the fallen general after receiving the news from a messenger sent by Dorsey. Lee spoke briefly to his friend, who relinquished command to the subordinate. Stuart said: "Go ahead, Fitz, old fellow. I know you will do what is right!" Lee wrote later, "My own time was so much occupied, I could not give more of it to his comfort . . . and did not well know the extent of his wound."[74]

Henry McClellan, Andrew Venable, Theodore Garnett, and Dr. John Fontaine reached the ambulance. Stuart was, said Garnett, "lying on his back and very pale." A cavalryman in the 6th Virginia recalled that he and comrades saw "one of our head surgeons riding rapidly down the road with his sleeves rolled up and his arms all bloody from his attendance on our wounded. A soldier standing by me said that some big man had been wounded, to see one of the head surgeons coming like that." The rider almost certainly was Dr. Fontaine.[75]

It was decided that Venable, Garnett, and Captain Walter Hullihen, a former aide of Stuart now serving on Lomax's staff, would accompany the ambulance. McClellan would stay behind and assist Fitz Lee. Repeatedly in the past, Stuart had told his chief of staff that if he were wounded, McClellan should report for duty to the senior commander on the field. McClellan complied—undoubtedly with reluctance—to his beloved general's wishes. Fontaine, Venable, and Hullihen rode in the ambulance with Stuart, while Garnett and three couriers acted as mounted escorts.[76]

Before the ambulance rolled away, a party of Union horsemen charged up the road, threatening to overrun the vehicle. Major James Breathed, the artillery commander, rallied some mounted Confederates and repulsed the enemy. Fleeing troopers passed around the ambulance. Seeing some of them, Stuart raised himself up, and with a weakened voice, urged them: "Go back! go back! and do your duty as I have done mine, and our country will be safe, Go Back! go back! I had rather die, than be whipped."[77]

The escort and the ambulance headed northeast to a crossing on the Chickahominy River. With Sheridan's horsemen in control of Brook

Turnpike, the direct road to Richmond was closed. Stuart asked if he could be taken to Flora and the children at Edmund Fontaine's home, but the distance was too far, the journey too dangerous. A thunderstorm broke over the region. At Yellow Tavern the Confederates ripped apart a final Union attack and then filed across the Chickahominy for the night. By now, many of them had heard about Stuart. A veteran cavalryman professed, "I never saw such a distressed looking body of men in my life . . . many of them shedding tears."[78]

Before the ambulance departed the battlefield, Stuart asked Venable, "Old fellow, I know you will tell me the truth, tell me, is the death pallor on my face?" Venable hoped not, he answered, that "there was some flush on his forehead." But now with seemingly each rotation of the ambulance's wheels on the muddy rutted road, Stuart's pain intensified. Dr. Fontaine offered him a drink of whiskey, but he refused at first. He had kept his childhood vow to his mother not to use alcohol. Stuart relented at last, took a sip, and the agony worsened. He turned to Hullihen, whom he called "Honey-bun," and spoke, "Well, I don't know how this will turn out; but if it is God's will that I shall die I am ready." Hullihen spared him the truth in reply.[79]

Fontaine halted the ambulance two or three times because of Stuart's distress. Once across the river, they struck a good road, and the mules moved at a "brisk trot." At Atlee's Station, one of the escorts secured some ice, and Stuart sucked on it. A civilian volunteered, at the Confederates' request, to ride ahead to Mechanicsville, and to have a resident make coffee for the general. When the party reached the town, Stuart drank half a cup. At Mechanicsville, on Stuart's instructions, Garnett proceeded alone to the capital to inform Braxton Bragg of the general's wound and to alert Dr. Charles Brewer that Stuart would be brought to his house.[80]

The ambulance stopped before 11:00 P.M. at 206 West Grace Street, the Brewer residence in Richmond. The detail of men carried the wounded general to an upstairs room that had been prepared for him. Dr. Brewer served in the Confederate Surgeon General's office in the capital. His wife, Maria Cooke, was Flora's devoted sister and best friend. Her grief at the sight of her brother-in-law must have been heartrending.[81]

Fontaine and Brewer tended to Stuart's wound. How the patient spent the night went unrecorded. Thursday, May 12, dawned cloudy, with rain and thunder resuming during the morning. "The streets have a quiet deserted sort of look," noted a neighbor lady of the Brewers. Later, an ambulance passed along Grace Street, carrying James Gordon, the fine commander of the North Carolina cavalrymen. Gordon had been wounded in another action with Sheridan's Federals on this day, and would succumb to his wounds on May 18.[82]

During the morning, a distraught Heros von Borcke came to the Brewer house. When he arrived, Stuart seemed to rally, and the physicians expressed some hope that the wound might not be fatal. Garnett remained behind, and he and von Borcke took turns sitting beside the general's bed. Von Borcke related that he gave ice to Stuart frequently and applied some of it to the wound. Stuart asked him and the others about Flora and the children.[83]

Henry McClellan arrived sometime after von Borcke. Fitz Lee, with obvious regard for McClellan's concerns, sent the staff officer with a dispatch for Braxton Bragg in Richmond. When McClellan entered the bedroom, he found Stuart "calm and composed, in full possession of his mind." They talked for an hour, interrupted at times as "paroxysms of suffering" seized Stuart.[84]

Stuart delegated his trusted chief of staff to attend to his possessions. He wanted Andrew Venable to have his gray horse since he was a larger man, McClellan his bay. A woman in Columbia, South Carolina, had made for him a small Confederate flag, which he carried in his hat, and he wanted it returned to her. Mrs. Lilly Lee, widow of his old friend on the frontier William Fitzhugh Lee, should have his spurs. His son, Jimmie, should be given his sword. His personal effects belonged to Flora—oval gold cuff links, a key-wind gold pocket watch with his initials, "JEBS," inscribed within a shield, his gauntlets, LeMat revolver, and, the famous plumed hat.[85]

McClellan's parting with Stuart could only have been emotional for the young staff officer. "More than any brother did I love him," he confessed to Flora later. He left before noon, when Jefferson Davis stopped by for a brief visit. The tall, gaunt president sat beside the bed, and holding Stuart's hand in his, inquired "How do you feel?" "Easy," replied

Stuart, "but willing to die, if God and my country think I have fulfilled my destiny and my duty."[86]

At the same time, more than thirty miles northwest of Richmond, a telegram was delivered to the home of Edmund Fontaine. Sheridan's cavalry had cut the direct telegraph line to the city, and the message had been sent on a circuitous route through Lynchburg and Charlottesville to Beaver Dam Station. One account states that Flora Stuart was upstairs at the Fontaine house, bathing a child, when she received the news of her husband's wounding. Immediately, Fontaine arranged a special train and brought Flora and the children to the station in his carriage. His daughters, Mollie and Lucie, and Dr. George Woodbridge, rector of the Monumental Church in Richmond and a guest of the Fontaines, boarded the train with the Stuart family.[87]

The train carried them as far as Ashland. The tracks wrecked by the Union horsemen had not been repaired. Borrowing an ambulance offered by wounded officers, they set out for the capital. The morning's rain intensified, with thunderstorms rumbling across the countryside. It was, or it must have seemed to be, the slowest and longest journey of Flora Stuart's life. Her nights, even days, had been haunted with her worst fear. This time his reassuring words could not allay the reality.[88]

Back at the Brewer residence, Stuart's condition began deteriorating through the afternoon. He passed in and out of consciousness, was delirious at times, asked for his family, spoke of Little Flora, gave orders to couriers, and in "broken sentences," talked of battles and campaigns. He writhed in agony at times. In the evening, he asked his brother-in-law if he would live through the night. No, replied Brewer, death was "rapidly approaching." "I am resigned, if it be God's will," Stuart said, "but I should like to see my wife. But God's will be done."[89]

About seven o'clock, Brewer, Fontaine, Garnett, Reverend Joshua Peterkin of St. James's Episcopal Church, a Reverend Keppler, and "a circle of sorrow-stricken comrades and friends," in the words of a newspaper, crowded into the bedroom. Peterkin prayed with Stuart, and at the general's request led the group in singing "Rock of Ages." The dying Confederate hero turned to Brewer and said: "I am going fast now. I am resigned; God's will be done." Then, he was gone at 7:38 P.M., Thursday,

May 12, 1864. James Ewell Brown Stuart was thirty-one years, three months, and six days old.[90]

Dr. Brewer gave an interview afterward to a city newspaper correspondent. "The immediate cause of death," the physician stated, "was mortification of the stomach, induced by the flow of blood from the kidneys and intestines into the cavity of the stomach."[91]

About ten o'clock, an ambulance pulled up in front of 206 West Grace Street. Flora Stuart stepped out and entered the house of her sister and brother-in-law. She was too late. The dreams that had so haunted her nights now had become real. Flora Cooke Stuart "plunged into the greatest grief."[92]

Chapter Eighteen

"The Greatest Cavalry Officer Ever Foaled in America"

R AIN FELL FROM darkened skies on the capital of the Confederacy on Friday, May 13, 1864. On West Grace Street, at the home of Dr. Charles and Maria Brewer, a queue of visitors offered condolences and passed by the body of Major General James Ewell Brown Stuart. His mortal remains lay on a billiards table, amid arrangements of yellow roses. The legs had been covered with a white sheet, and the bare torso was, noted an onlooker, "as smooth as marble & contrasted vividly with his wiry red beard." Later in the day, the body was prepared for burial and placed in a metallic coffin.[1]

The publicly announced funeral service was held at 5:00 P.M. in St. James's Episcopal church at the corner of Marshall and Fifth streets. A crowd of mourners joined Flora Stuart, their children, Jimmie and Virginia Pelham, and the Brewers. President Jefferson Davis, General Braxton Bragg, Major General Robert Ransom, Jr., Stuart's friend and former subordinate Heros von Borcke, and members of Congress were in attendance. At the appointed hour, as an organist played a dirge, the pallbearers—among whom were former Secretary of War George Randolph and generals Joseph R. Anderson, John H. Winder, and Alexander R. Lawton—carried the coffin up the center aisle and placed it before the altar. Wreaths and a cross of evergreens, "interwoven with delicate lilies of the valley, laurel and other flowers of purest white" lay upon the casket.[2]

Reverend Joshua Peterkin, who had been with Stuart at the end, conducted the Episcopal services. When Peterkin finished, a choir sang an anthem. The pallbearers lifted the coffin, proceeded slowly down the aisle, and walked outside into the rainy evening. A hearse draped with black plumes and drawn by white horses led a long procession of carriages to Hollywood Cemetery. Reverend Charles F. E. Minnegerode of St. Paul's Episcopal church read passages at the gravesite. Then, with artillery booming in the distance against the Federals, the body of Jeb Stuart was lowered into the soil of Virginia.[3]

Stuart's death elicited immediate and sorrowful reactions from within the Confederacy and the army. On the day after his funeral, the Richmond *Whig* editorialized: "Never, before, nor certainly since the death of Stonewall Jackson, has the demise of any Southern leader produced so profound a sensation among all classes of our community. They seem reluctant to realize the painful truth that the gallant and dashing cavalier . . . had at last fallen." A North Carolina newspaper stated: "The death of such a man as General Stuart would be a great loss to any country at any time. What a great calamity then, it might be to our young Confederacy, in the midst of its desperate struggle for freedom, to have this 'Giant in arms' forever lost to his comrades."[4]

Poetic tributes to his memory appeared in newspapers within weeks of his burial. Former Virginia governor John Letcher, writing to Stuart's brother William, declared, "The people of the whole Confederacy and especially of Virginia, feel and deplore his loss as a great calamity which has fallen upon us at a moment, when it was least expected, and when we could illy afford to spare his invaluable services." In Patrick County, Virginia, his birthplace and childhood home, a five-member committee drafted resolutions at a public gathering, extending the "sincere condolence of the good people of this county" to Stuart's mother, Elizabeth Pannill Stuart, and to Flora Stuart.[5]

At a May 14 meeting, the Richmond City Council adopted resolutions "in behalf of the Citizens thereof." The council offered "their deepest and most heartfelt condolence" to Stuart's family and "earnestly request that the remains of their great benefactor may be permitted to remain under the eye and guardianship of the people of Richmond and that they may be allowed to commemorate by a suitable Monument this gratitude."[6]

When Flora Stuart received a copy of the document, she replied to the council president: "I beg you to communicate to the council of the City of Richmond the earnest assurance that I most gratefully appreciate the kindness and sympathy expressed in their resolutions adopted on the 14th inst. To my children and myself the knowledge that such sentiments are entertained by the people of Richmond, constitute a precious inheritance! I acknowledge the claim of the Capital of Va to retain the remains of one who freely gave his life as an offering of affection and devotion to his native state."[7]

The editorials and resolutions conveyed a nation's grief and gratitude, but it was among Stuart's comrades in the army that the magnitude of his death was most keenly understood and felt, personally and professionally. According to Major Charles Marshall, Robert E. Lee "was affected at hearing of Stuart's death, leaning forward and putting both hands over his face for some time to conceal his emotion." Lee purportedly remarked of his cavalry commander to another officer, "*He never brought me a piece of false information.*"[8]

Privately, Lee confided to his wife, "A more zealous, ardent, brave & devoted soldier, than Stuart, the Confederacy cannot have." Officially, the commanding general issued General Orders No. 44 to the army on May 20, announcing Stuart's death. "Among the gallant soldiers who have fallen in this war," the proclamation read, "General Stuart was second to none in valor, zeal, and unfaltering devotion to his country. His achievements form a conspicuous part of the history of this army, with which his name and services will be forever associated. . . . To his comrades in arms he has left the proud recollection of his deeds, and the inspiring influence of his example."[9]

Members of the army's rank and file expressed similar sentiments. Henry Kyd Douglas, formerly of Jackson's staff and who cared little for Stuart personally, called the general's loss "simply irreparable." Jackson's topographer, Jedediah Hotchkiss, writing of "my friend," asserted:

"A great loss, surely, to the Confederacy. He was a noble man, a true soldier." James Longstreet's chief of staff, Moxley Sorrel, stated that Stuart's mortal wounding "caused an indescribable feeling in the army." "Deep was our grief," professed Sorrel. An artillery sergeant, reflecting shared views, averred, "A braver and nobler cavalier never drew a sword or wielded a saber."[10]

Grumble Jones, Stuart's bitter antagonist, said to his adjutant when he heard the news, "You know I had little love for Stuart, and he had just as little for me; but that is the greatest loss that army has ever sustained except the death of Jackson." Conversely, Thomas Rosser, who owed much of his advancement to brigadier general to Stuart, mentioned not a word of his death in letters to his wife in the weeks after the event.[11]

In the Cavalry Corps, Fitz Lee paid tribute to his fallen commander in a general order. "Great, glorious and good—his loss to his country— to our army—Especially to his troopers, is inconsolable," wrote Lee. "Whilst his bright, glancing Eye can no longer see—his clear, ringing voice no longer be heard by his mourning followers—may the principles he has taught us—the Example he has shown us not be lost. Stuart had no superior as a soldier." In his campaign report, Lee characterized Stuart's death as an "irreparable loss."[12]

Except for Flora Stuart, no one more personally lamented the general's passing than members of his staff. His couriers wept when they learned of it. His quartermaster, Philip Powers, exclaimed to his wife: "I have lost my best friend in the army. I cannot realize he is *gone*, that I am to see his gallant figure, nor hear his cheering voice no more." Norman FitzHugh wrote to Flora Stuart of her husband, "I loved him as tho' he were my own Mothers son."[13]

Like FitzHugh, Henry McClellan wrote to his commander's widow. In a September 1864 letter, the former chief of staff mentioned that he and her husband's aides were now serving with Wade Hampton, who had succeeded Stuart in command of the Cavalry Corps. McClellan confessed: "But every day we miss our chief—our friend—our brother. Every day the contrast between the present and the past returns to us, and time does not seem to soften that contrast. Oh! Mrs. Stuart, we did love him, how much, I knew not until he was taken away from us—to me he was the kindest friend I have ever known."[14]

For Flora Stuart, time might soften the deep pain, but it could not heal what was irretrievable. She had the comfort of the children and of her sister Maria. Shortly after the funeral she received a letter passed through the lines from her father, Philip St. George Cooke. So far as is known, they had not been in contact for three years. Her father implored her: "Come to us, with your two orphans. Your Mother knows not yet of this, but you know her heart." She and the children could be escorted, under a flag of truce, into Union lines outside of Richmond. Whether Flora replied in writing is uncertain.[15]

Instead, at some later time, Flora, Jimmie, and Virginia Pelham traveled to Saltville, Virginia, to the home of William Stuart. Jeb had always turned to "Alick" for business advice and loans. In early 1862, Jeb had bought a $10,000 life insurance policy, explaining in a letter to his brother, "For I may be killed or captured tomorrow or any day, and they [his family] must look to you for support." Unfortunately, settlement of the policy would have been in Confederate currency, whose value decreased with each successive month until it became worthless with the war's end.[16]

William Stuart, who had been widowed and remarried, informed his brother in 1863, "You may rest perfectly assured that as long as I have anything it shall be shared with you and yours." In his will, dated November 16, 1861, Jeb named Flora and William as executors. The will, which bequeathed Jeb's entire estate to his wife, was not probated until September 18, 1865. More important for Flora and the children after the war, William secured the $5,000 that Jeb had received for his patent and had deposited in a St. Louis bank prior to the conflict. Flora gave William some of the money as a repayment for all of his financial assistance.[17]

Virginia was to be Flora's home for the rest of her life, fulfilling the request of her husband. In the spring of 1863, she had written to him about the upbringing of Jimmie and the child she was bearing in the event of her death. "I shall religiously observe your wishes respecting ours in case I should survive you, which is so extremely improbable," Stuart replied, "but I wish an assurance on your part in the other event your surviving me, that *you will make the land for which I have given my life your home, and keep my offspring on southern soil.*" Although he did not limit her to his native state, she must have known that Virginia would have been his preference.[18]

For most of the fifteen years immediately after the war, the Stuart family resided in Saltville. William Stuart assisted Flora in opening a school in a log cabin. Education became her livelihood and career for the next four decades. While Flora and the children lived in Saltville, her mother-in-law, Elizabeth Stuart, moved in with William's family. Interestingly, Jeb rarely corresponded with his mother or mentioned her in his wartime letters. Elizabeth Stuart died at William's home on August 20, 1884, and was buried in Saltville. In her will, she gave a gold watch to her grandson, James E. B. Stuart, Jr.[19]

At the time of Elizabeth Stuart's death, Flora lived in Staunton. In 1880, she accepted the principalship of the Virginia Female Institute, founded in 1844 and the oldest school for girls in the state. More than a decade before, Robert E. Lee, a member of the school's board of visitors, had recommended her for the post. The Lee family's affection for her husband had been manifest. Mary Custis Lee, the general's wife, had written to Flora after Stuart's death, "For myself, I could scarcely grieve more deeply if one of my own sons had fallen."[20]

Under Flora's leadership, the institute revised its curriculum, created a music department, and constructed four new buildings. From requiring uniforms to prescribing rules for behavior, Flora was involved closely in the students' education and training as young ladies. She established an aid program for girls from poor families. The students called her "Mrs. General Stuart," and she signed papers formally as "Mrs. J. E. B. Stuart," the name she preferred to be addressed.[21]

It tooks several years, but Flora reconciled eventually with her parents. She and the children visited the Cooke home and vacationed with her parents. Her pride was, however, her son and daughter. Responding to an inquiry about the family in April 1887, Flora wrote: "It is not indelicate of me to say, that I have great satisfaction in seeing my children—well educated, and established in life—and much of it owing, or due to my own efforts. They are 'poor' as the world knows them—but with a *noble* inheritance."[22]

At the time Flora wrote the letter, her son and daughter were married. James E. B. Stuart, Jr., forged a career mainly in banking and served as a captain in the army during the Spanish-American War. He wed Josephine Phillips in July 1886. The couple had five children, four daughters and a son, who was named James Ewell Brown Stuart III. James Stuart, Jr., died on November 26, 1930.[23]

Virginia Pelham Stuart married Robert Page Waller in Staunton, in January 1887. The union resulted in three children, two daughters and a son. Virginia Waller died from complications in childbirth on January 9, 1898. When her daughter passed away, Flora resigned the principalship at the institute and moved to Norfolk, Virginia, where she assisted her son-in-law in the upbringing of her grandchildren. In honor of her service to the Virginia Female Institute, the school's board renamed it Stuart Hall, which it remains to this day.[24]

Flora Stuart spent the final two decades and more of her life in Norfolk. She died on May 10, 1923, after striking her head in a fall on a city sidewalk. She was buried beside her husband and "Little Flora" or "La Pet" in Hollywood Cemetery in Richmond. His grave had been moved to a more prominent location in the grounds. Her estate was valued at $6,794.19, and was divided equally among her eight grandchildren.[25]

Flora Stuart outlived her husband by almost exactly fifty-nine years, wearing mourning clothes for all that time. While she lived, she guarded his reputation with fervency. She never wrote a memoir or a book about Stuart's career, leaving that task to those who had served with him. She supported efforts by his former officers and men to honor his memory in stone. A new headstone replaced a plain wooden one over his grave. On June 18, 1888, Flora attended the unveiling of a monument at Yellow Tavern that marked the site of his mortal wound.[26]

The major project to enshrine Stuart belonged to the Veteran Cavalry Association of the Army of Northern Virginia. The leadership of the association included Fitz Lee, Wade Hampton, Lunsford Lomax, M. Calbraith Butler, Thomas Munford, and Henry McClellan. Poverty in the postwar South and a national depression in the 1890s hampered fund-raising for a monument to be erected on Monument Avenue in Richmond. Eventually, with money from the state legislature and private contributions, the association hired Frederick Moynihan as the sculptor.[27]

The dedication of the Stuart monument took place on May 30,

1907. Seventeen years earlier, a monument of Robert E. Lee was dedicated on the same avenue. Flora Stuart and her granddaughter Virginia Stuart Waller attended. Reverend Walter Hullihen, who had ridden in the ambulance with the wounded general from Yellow Tavern to Richmond, offered the dedicatory prayer. A host of former veterans of the army and a huge crowd looked on as Jeb and Flora Stuart's granddaughter unveiled the mounted statue of the Confederate cavalryman. The monument is, perhaps, where it should be—on the flank of Robert E. Lee.[28]

Writing nearly thirty years before the statue towered above passersby, John Esten Cooke said of his former commander: "Everything about Stuart was broadly and vividly defined. There were no half tints or negative colors either in his personal appearance or his character, and he stood out from the great war canvas like a prominent figure in some painting, brilliant and imposing, catching and holding the eye."[29]

On that canvas, Stuart had been the Confederacy's knight-errant, the bold and dashing cavalier, attired in a resplendent uniform, plumed hat, and cape. Amid a slaughterhouse, he had embodied chivalry, clinging to the pageantry of a long-gone warrior. He crafted the image carefully, and the image befitted him. He saw himself as the Southern people envisaged him. They needed a knight; he needed to be that knight.[30]

Since his youth, Stuart had seized life, draining it of sustenance, craved attention and approval, and fueled an intense flame of ambition. He chose the soldier's trade because it fulfilled all of those desires. When war came, it brought with it the possibilities of greater fame and reputation. He embraced the cause of Southern independence as zealously as anyone who wore a Confederate uniform. Before him lay a quest, a knight's mission that offered personal glory.[31]

For Stuart, however, the quest was inextricably linked to the cause. "His faith in the justice of the struggle was absolute," declared Esten Cooke, "and he never, to my knowledge, had one moment's doubt as to the result of the war." His abiding religious faith and devotion to duty defined him far more than the vanity and the pleasure from the fawning presence of young women. Blessed with a remarkable physical stamina, he worked tirelessly in the defense of the Confederacy.[32]

Beneath the veneer of a cavalier was a student of warfare, a firm disciplinarian, a realist who schooled his officers and men in drills and tactics. It has been argued that Stuart failed to adapt to the evolving nature of Civil War combat and the role of cavalry operations in it. On the contrary, Stuart organized his regiments into brigades months before his opponent, issued detailed instructions on dismounted and mounted tactics, and trained the rank and file in them. No cavalry commander in the East matched the mobility and audacity of Stuart while he lived. The dominance that his horsemen achieved and held for two years gave way not to his failings, but to superior Union numbers, weaponry, and horseflesh. The Federals emulated Stuart.[33]

Cavalry doctorine of the era and the reluctance of army commanders on both sides restricted the role of the mounted arm in major battles. Stuart's raids, which brought him fame, were of limited strategic value. Nevertheless, they were valuable for they inspired the Southern populace and enhanced Confederate nationalism. He was, however, unequaled in cavalry's traditional role—reconnaissance and screening an army. "Our sense of security against surprise [was] so confident with him in the saddle," attested Moxley Sorrel. His network of scouts and spies was invaluable to Robert E. Lee. In turn, Stuart possessed a keen aptitude for deciphering conflicting intelligence reports. A former lieutenant in the 3rd Virginia believed that Stuart "made his cavalry more completely and thoroughly [to] be the 'eyes and ears' of the army than any other officer I ever knew."[34]

Ironically, it was Stuart's skill in reconnaissance and timely intelligence that lay at the crux of the controversy over his conduct during the Gettysburg Campaign. His eight-day absence from the army shaped, in part, the course of events. When he decided, either at Rector's Cross Roads or at Haymarket, to undertake another circuit of the Union army, he committed a critical misjudgment for which he was condemned at the time and since. Fairly or unfairly, in the long shadow of history, Stuart and Gettysburg will be inexorably linked.

Nevertheless, a singular fact remains—Jeb Stuart was one of the finest light cavalrymen in American history. Fitz Lee presented an appraisal of his friend and commander that is honest and astute. Writing in an official report after Stuart's death, Lee stated: "his rare genius, hightoned spirit, indifference to danger, indefatigable energy, wonderful endurance in the saddle, supreme coolness in action, and enthusiastic devotion to the cause in which he offered up his life are too well known, and form too large a part of 'the history of the times' for me to dwell upon them here."[35]

Porter Alexander fought with Stuart on the battlefield of Chancellorsville on May 3, 1863, when the cavalryman led Stonewall Jackson's Second Corps in the assaults. It was one of Stuart's most remarkable accomplishments, and it convinced Alexander that Stuart could have led an infantry corps and could have excelled in independent command. Similarly, Joseph E. Johnston, who served in the two main theaters during the war and commanded Western cavalry leaders such as Nathan Bedford Forrest and Joseph Wheeler, said in a conversation, "he had never seen any one he considered his [Stuart's] equal in our Cavalry service."[36]

A Federal cavalry officer, writing after the war, argued that Stuart "made" the Confederate cavalry, noting: "He died at a good time for his own fame, for not even he could have changed the inevitable result that followed. It is no discredit that it was so." Perhaps the most fitting epitaph for James Ewell Brown Stuart came from his dear friend from their days together in Kansas. Union general John Sedgwick said that his old comrade was "the greatest cavalry officer ever foaled in America."[37]

Notes

Abbreviations

Works cited will be found in full in the Bibliography. The following abbreviations are used in the Notes:

ACHS	Augusta County Historical Society
ACW	*America's Civil War*
ADAH	Alabama Department of Archives and History
AHS	Atlanta Historical Society
AIGO	Adjutant and Inspector General's Office
ANB	Antietam National Battlefield
B&G	*Blue & Gray Magazine*
B&L	*Battles and Leaders of the Civil War*
BU	Boston University
CMU	Central Michigan University
CR	Compiled Records
CSA	Confederate States of America
CSR	Compiled Service Records
CV	*Confederate Veteran*
CW	*Civil War: The Magazine of the Civil War Society*
CWTI	*Civil War Times Illustrated*
DU	Duke University
ECU	East Carolina University
EU	Emory University
FM	Franklin and Marshall College

FSNM	Fort Sumter National Monument
FSNMP	Fredericksburg-Spotsylvania National Military Park
GHS	Georgia Historical Society
GM	*Gettysburg Magazine*
GNMP	Gettysburg National Military Park
HL	Huntington Library
HU	Harvard University
JEBS	James Ewell Brown Stuart
JML	Jones Memorial Library
JSH	*Journal of Southern History*
KHQ	*Kansas Historical Quarterly*
KHS	Kittochtinny Historical Society
LC	Library of Congress
LSU	Louisiana State University
LVA	Library of Virginia
MC	Museum of the Confederacy
MDHS	Maryland Historical Society
MJCHS	*Magazine of the Jefferson County Historical Society*
MNBP	Manassas National Battlefield Park
MOLLUS	*Military Order of the Loyal Legion of the United States*
NA	National Archive
N&S	*North & South*
NC	Navarro College
NCHR	*North Carolina Historical Review*
NYHS	New-York Historical Society
NYPL	New York Public Library
OR	*The War of the Rebellion: A Compilation of the Official Records of the Union and Confederate Armies*
RML	Rosenbach Museum and Library
RNBP	Richmond National Battlefield Park
SHSP	*Southern Historical Society Papers*
SOR	*Supplement to the Official Records of the Union and Confederate Armies*
UCB	University of California, Berkeley
UGA	University of Georgia
UM	University of Michigan
UNC	University of North Carolina

UND   University of Notre Dame
USAMHI United States Army Military History Institute
USC   University of South Carolina
USM   University of Southern Mississippi
USMAA United States Military Academy Archives
USMAL United States Military Academy Library
UVA   University of Virginia
VATU   Virginia Tech University
VHS   Virginia Historical Society
VMHB   *Virginia Magazine of History and Biography*
VMI   Virginia Military Institute
VSL   Virginia State Library
WFU   Wake Forest University
WLU   Washington and Lee University
WMU   Western Michigan University
YU   Yale University

Chapter 1: Son of Virginia

1. Richard H. Watkins–[Wife] July 18, 1863, Watkins Papers, VHS; A. H. Byars–Ma & Sisters, June 24, 1863, Byars Letter, USAMHI.
2. Busey and Martin, *Regimental Strengths and Losses*, pp. 246–49.
3. OR, v. 27, pt. 3, pp. 315, 323.
4. Extract, Stuart Family Bible, Stuart Papers, VHS; Perry, *Ascent*, pp. 3, 9, 10; Catherine N. Trevillian–Author, January 23, 2006, letter in possession of author; Thomas, *Bold Dragoon*, p. 7.
5. Perry, *Ascent*, p. 20; Thomason, *Jeb Stuart*, p. 16; Pedigo and Pedigo, *History*, pp. 263, 264; Robertson, *Alexander Hugh Holmes Stuart*, p. 1.
6. Thomason, *Jeb Stuart*, pp. 16, 17; Pedigo and Pedigo, *History*, p. 264; Bobrick, *Angel in the Whirlwind*, pp. 431–32; Robertson, *Alexander Hugh Holmes Stuart*, pp. 4, 7.
7. Thomason, *Jeb Stuart*, p. 17; Perry, *Ascent*, p. 20; Robertson, *Alexander Hugh Holmes Stuart*, pp. 4, 10; Undated fragment of a letter by Flora Cooke Stuart, Stuart Papers, VHS.
8. Thomason, *Jeb Stuart*, p. 17; McClellan, *I Rode*, p. 2; Perry, *Stuart's Birthplace*, pp. 17–20.
9. Perry, *Stuart's Birthplace*, p. 38; Mitchell, ed., *Letters . . . Stuart*, p. 13; SHSP, v. 8, p. 435.
10. Perry, *Ascent*, pp. 9, 27; Thomason, *Jeb Stuart*, p. 18; Perry, *Stuart's Birthplace*, pp. 27–28.

11. Perry, *Stuart's Birthplace*, pp. 30–32.

12. Ibid., pp. 32–34.

13. Ibid., p. 43; *SHSP*, v. 8, p. 435; Thomason, *Jeb Stuart*, p. 18.

14. *SHSP*, v. 8, p. 435; Thomason, *Jeb Stuart*, p. 17; Perry, *Stuart's Birthplace*, pp. 41, 42, 43, 46, 53, 55.

15. Perry, *Stuart's Birthplace*, pp. 39, 40, 44, 47, 48; Shepard, "Breaking into the Profession," *JSH*, v. 48, no. 3, p. 393.

16. Perry, *Stuart's Birthplace*, pp. 39, 40.

17. Ibid., pp. 44, 51, 52; Pedigo and Pedigo, *History*, pp. 1, 3, 11; Thomas, *Bold Dragoon*, pp. 7, 8.

18. McClellan, *I Rode*, p. 5; Davis, *Jeb Stuart*, p. 18; JEBS–My beloved Sister, October 24, 1856, *Catalog No. 157*, No. 276; Perry, *Stuart's Birthplace*, pp. 51, 52.

19. JEBS–My beloved Sister, October 24, 1856, *Catalog No. 157*, No. 276.

20. Perry, *Ascent*, pp. 9, 10.

21. Ibid., p. 10; Hairston, ed., "J. E. B. Stuart's Letters," *NCHR*, v. 51, no. 3, pp. 270n, 306; JEBS–My Darling One, March 4, 1863; JEBS–My Dear *Dear* Wife, August 26, 1863, Stuart Papers, VHS.

22. Boyd, "Boyhood," pp. 17, 18, Boyd Papers, LSU.

23. Mitchell, ed., *Letters . . . Stuart*, p. 228; Duncan, ed., *Letters*, p. 21; Perry, *Stuart's Birthplace*, p. 95; Thomas, *Bold Dragoon*, p. 10.

24. Boyd, "Boyhood," pp. 19, 20, 21, 29, 30, Boyd Papers, LSU.

25. Ibid., pp. 17, 27.

26. Carter, "Works Progress Administration: Shepard Farm," p. 2, copy in possession of Krick; Catherine N. Trevillian–Author, January 23, 2006, in possession of author; Perry, *Ascent*, p. 9; Boyd, "Boyhood," p. 1, Boyd Papers, LSU.

27. JEBS–[Mother], Wednesday night [n.d.], Stuart Papers, VHS; Reed, *David French Boyd*, p. 3; Mitchell, ed., *Letters . . . Stuart*, p. 12.

28. Catherine N. Trevillian–Author, January 23, 2006, in possession of author; Boyd, "Boyhood," pp. 30, 31, Boyd Papers, LSU; Mitchell, ed., *Letters . . . Stuart*, pp. 5, 8, 10, 398n; Carter, "Works Progress Administration: Shepherd Farm," pp. 1, 2, copy in possession of Krick.

29. Boyd, "Boyhood," pp. 18, 19, 22, Boyd Papers, LSU; Thomas, *Bold Dragoon*, p. 10; Mitchell, ed., *Letters . . . Stuart*, pp. 3, 9.

30. Thomas, *Bold Dragoon*, pp. 12, 13; Reed, *David French Boyd*, p. 281; Boyd, "Boyhood," pp. 19, 20, 23, Boyd Papers, LSU.

31. Mitchell, ed., *Letters . . . Stuart*, p. 4.

32. Ibid., p. 6; Thomas, *Bold Dragoon*, pp. 11, 12; Hairston, ed., "J. E. B. Stuart's Letters," *NCHR*, v. 51, no. 3, pp. 288, 288n; Cashin, "Structure," *JSH*, v. 56, 1, pp. 59, 63, 64, 67, 69.

33. Perry, *Stuart's Birthplace*, p. 49; Mitchell, ed., *Letters . . . Stuart*, pp. 9, 10.

34. Thomason, *Jeb Stuart*, p. 19; Thomas, *Bold Dragoon*, p. 13; Stevenson, *Increase in Excellence*, p. 206.

35. Stevenson, *Increase in Excellence*, pp. 5, 6, 34, 49, 50, 59, 73.

36. Ibid., pp. 50–56, 58.

37. Ibid., pp. 206, 207; Mitchell, ed., *Letters . . . Stuart*, p. 11.

38. McClellan, *I Rode*, p. 6; JEBS–Milt, January 25, 1851, Stuart Papers, VHS.

39. JEBS–Milt, January 25, 1851, Stuart Papers, VHS; Stevenson, *Increase in Excellence*, p. 207.

40. JEBS–Captain, December 30, 1859, Stuart Papers, USMAL; Hairston, ed., "J. E. B. Stuart's Letters," *NCHR*, v. 51, no. 3, pp. 270n, 271, 271n.

41. Mitchell, ed., *Letters . . . Stuart*, pp. 12, 13; Appointment of the President of the United States, June 30, 1850, Stuart Papers, VHS.

42. Tucker, *Lee and Longstreet*, p. 202; Hairston, ed., "J. E. B. Stuart's Letters," *NCHR*, v. 51, no. 3, p. 293; McClellan, *I Rode*, p. 6; Boyd, "Boyhood," p. 19, Boyd Papers, LSU.

Chapter 2: West Point and Texas

1. Davis, *Jeb Stuart*, p. 19; Mitchell, ed., *Letters . . . Stuart*, pp. 15, 16.

2. Mitchell, ed., *Letters . . . Stuart*, pp. 13, 14, 15, 20, 21.

3. Ibid., p. 21; Wert, *General James Longstreet*, p. 26.

4. Wert, *General James Longstreet*, pp. 26–28.

5. Ibid., p. 27; "Sherman on West Point," *CWTI*, v. 10, no. 9, p. 22.

6. Waugh, "Life at the Point," *CWTI*, v. 41, no. 2, p. 36.

7. Wert, *General James Longstreet*, p. 27; Freeman, *R. E. Lee*, v. 1, pp. 319, 321; Hairston, ed., "J. E. B. Stuart's Letters," *NCHR*, v. 51, no. 3, pp. 284, 286, 287.

8. Mitchell, ed., *Letters . . . Stuart*, p. 21; Howard, *Autobiography*, v. 1, p. 48.

9. Mitchell, ed., *Letters . . . Stuart*, p. 20; Hairston, ed., "J. E. B. Stuart's Letters," *NCHR*, v. 51, no. 3, p. 265.

10. Freeman, *R. E. Lee*, v. 1, p. 319; Howard, *Autobiography*, v. 1, p. 49; Mitchell, ed., *Letters . . . Stuart*, p. 27.

11. Freeman, *Lee's Lieutenants*, v. 3, p. 419; Thomas, *Bold Dragoon*, pp. 18, 19.

12. McClellan, *I Rode*, pp. 7, 8; Ferguson, Memoir, p. 8, FSNM.

13. Mitchell, ed., *Letters . . . Stuart*, p. 236; Hairston, ed., "J. E. B. Stuart's Letters," *NCHR*, v. 51, no. 3, p. 300; Cullum, *Biographical Register*, v. 1, pp. 515, 524, 548, 550, 567, 572–603, 613, 615, 630.

14. Hairston, ed., "J. E. B. Stuart's Letters," *NCHR*, v. 51, no. 3, pp. 300, 314; Mitchell, ed., *Letters . . . Stuart*, p. 236; Styple, ed., *Generals in Bronze*, p. 176; Howard, *Autobiography*, v. 1, p. 53.

15. Carpenter, *Sword and Olive Branch*, pp. 8, 9; Styple, ed., *Generals in Bronze*, p. 179; McClellan, *I Rode*, p. 7; Howard, *Autobiography*, v. 1, pp. 51, 52, 380.

16. JEBS–Milt, January 25, 1851, Stuart Papers, VHS; Hairston, ed., "J. E. B. Stuart's Letters," *NCHR*, v. 51, no. 3, pp. 268, 274.

17. JEBS–Milt, January 25, 1851, Stuart Papers, VHS.

18. Freeman, *R. E. Lee*, v. 1, p. 326; Register of Merit, No. 2, USMAA; Hairston, ed., "J. E. B. Stuart's Letters," *NCHR*, v. 51, no. 3, pp. 290, 290n.

19. Register of Delinquencies, p. 137, USMAA.

20. Mitchell, ed., *Letters . . . Stuart*, pp. 36–37, 50; "Private accounts" book, *passim*, Stuart Papers, VHS.

21. Freeman, *R. E. Lee*, v. 1, p. 319; Warner, *Generals in Gray*, pp. 180–81.

22. Freeman, *R. E. Lee*, v. 1, pp. 319, 320; Waugh, "Life at the Point," *CWTI*, v. 41, no. 2, pp. 37, 62; Mitchell, ed., *Letters . . . Stuart*, p. 91.

23. Freeman, *R. E. Lee*, v. 1, pp. 319, 325; Lee, *Recollections*, p. 18; Thomas, *Robert E. Lee*, p. 156.

24. Freeman, *R. E. Lee*, v. 1, p. 323; Hairston, ed., "J. E. B. Stuart's Letters," *NCHR*, v. 51, no. 3, p. 297; Mary Custis Lee–[Flora Stuart], [1864], Lee Family Papers, VHS; JEBS–My Darling Wife, August 11, 1863, Stuart Papers, VHS.

25. Mitchell, ed., *Letters . . . Stuart*, p. 91; Register of Merit, Nos. 2 and 3; Register of Delinquencies, p. 137, USMAA.

26. Mitchell, ed., *Letters . . . Stuart*, p. 93.

27. Hairston, ed., "J. E. B. Stuart's Letters," *NCHR*, v. 51, no. 3, pp. 296–300.

28. Ibid., p. 305; Register of Merit, No. 3, USMAA; J. E. B. Stuart III, "A Profile," p. 2, USMAL.

29. Mitchell, ed., *Letters . . . Stuart*, pp. 102, 104.

30. Ibid., pp. 103, 104.

31. Ibid.

32. JEBS–Sir, February 20, 1854, typed copy in possession of Krick; Thomas, *Robert E. Lee*, p. 164.

33. Register of Merit, No. 3, USMAA; *Heritage Auction Galleries*, p. 54.

34. Hairston, ed., "J. E. B. Stuart's Letters," *NCHR*, v. 51, no. 3, p. 285.

35. JEBS–Friend, June 19, 1854, Stuart Collection, MC; JEBS–My Dear Cousin, December 18, 1863, Alexander H. H. Stuart Papers, UVA; Duke Records, v. 1, pp. 195, 196, 201, UVA; Mitchell, ed., *Letters . . . Stuart*, p. 81; Commission, Brevet Second Lieutenant, Regiment of Mounted Riflemen, August 14, 1854, Stuart Papers, VHS; Hairston, ed., "J. E. B. Stuart's Letters," *NCHR*, v. 51, no. 3, pp. 316–17, 317n.

36. Hairston, ed., "J. E. B. Stuart's Letters," *NCHR*, v. 51, no. 3, pp. 316–18.

37. Mitchell, ed., *Letters . . . Stuart*, p. ix.

38. Ibid., pp. 123, 124; Hairston, ed., "J. E. B. Stuart's Letters," *NCHR*, v. 51, no. 3, p. 319.

39. Mitchell, ed., *Letters . . . Stuart*, pp. 125–36; JEBS–Captain, December 30, 1859, Stuart Papers, USMAL; Billings, *Report*, pp. 215, 217; Hairston, ed., "J. E. B. Stuart's Letters," *NCHR*, v. 51, no. 3, pp. 319–25.

40. Utley, *Frontiersmen*, pp. 18, 19, 22, 24, 29, 74; Billings, *Report*, pp. 215, 217; Chappell, "United States Dragoons," *Denver Westerners Roundup*, v. 30, no. 2, pp. 18, 41.

41. Mitchell, ed., *Letters . . . Stuart*, pp. 136, 137; JEBS–Captain, December 30, 1859, Stuart Papers, USMAL; Commission, Second Lieutenant, January 10, 1855, Stuart Papers, VHS.

42. Mitchell, ed., *Letters . . . Stuart*, pp. 136–47, 229; Hairston, ed., "J. E. B. Stuart's Letters," *NCHR*, v. 51, no. 3, pp. 328–29.

43. Hairston, ed., "J. E. B. Stuart's Letters," *NCHR*, v. 51, no. 3, p. 328; Mitchell, ed., *Letters . . . Stuart*, p. 143.

44. Hairston, ed., "J. E. B. Stuart's Letters," *NCHR*, v. 51, no. 3, pp. 328–29; Mitchell, ed., *Letters . . . Stuart*, pp. 138, 139, 149.

45. Utley, *Frontiersmen*, p. 20; Mitchell, ed., *Letters . . . Stuart*, p. 154; JEBS–Sir, April 26, 1855, Letters Received Adjutant General, 1822–1860, NA.

46. John S. Simonson–JEBS, May 8, 1855, Stuart Papers, HL.

Chapter 3: "I Go with Virginia"

1. Billings, *Report*, pp. 284, 286, 287; *Outline Descriptions*, pp. 102, 103, 141; Chalfant, *Cheyennes*, pp. 12, 18, 24.

2. Chalfant, *Cheyennes*, p. 319; McKale and Young, *Fort Riley*, p. 6; Utley, *Frontiersmen*, p. 64.

3. Chalfant, *Cheyennes*, pp. 14, 27–44; Utley, *Frontiersmen*, pp. 7, 8.

4. Annual Return of the First Regiment of Cavalry, 1855, Returns . . . Fourth Cavalry, NA; Utley, *Frontiersmen*, p. 54; Chalfant, *Cheyennes*, pp. 319, 320; McKale and Young, *Fort Riley*, p. 6.

5. Annual Return of the First Regiment of Cavalry, 1855, Returns . . . Fourth Cavalry, NA; Warner, *Generals in Blue*, p. 490; Chalfant, *Cheyennes*, p. 321; Wert, *Sword of Lincoln*, p. 86.

6. Returns of the First Regiment of Cavalry, April–July, 1855, Returns . . . Fourth Cavalry, NA; Mitchell, ed., *Letters . . . Stuart*, p. 157.

7. J. E. B. Stuart III, "A Profile," p. 1, Stuart Papers, USMAL; Boyd, "Boyhood," p. 2; Flora Cooke Stuart–My dear Col., April 28, 1896, Boyd Papers, LSU.

8. Thomas, *Bold Dragoon*, pp. 41, 307n; Davis, *Jeb Stuart*, p. 36; McClellan, *I Rode*, p. 424n; Mitchell, ed., *Letters . . . Stuart*, p. 159.

9. Extract, Stuart Family Bible, Stuart Papers, VHS; Perry, *Ascent*, p. 4; Cooke Family Tree, Stuart Collection, MC.

10. Davis, *Jeb Stuart*, pp. 36, 37; Thomas, *Bold Dragoon*, p. 41.

11. Boyd, "Boyhood," p. 23, Boyd Papers, LSU; Hairston, ed., J. E. B. Stuart's Letters," *NCHR*, v. 51, n. 3, pp. 272, 275, 283, 294, 300; Mitchell, ed., *Letters . . . Stuart*, p. 113.

12. Mitchell, ed., *Letters . . . Stuart*, pp. 159, 160, 163; Davis, *Jeb Stuart*, p. 38; Flora Stuart–My Dear Sir, n.d., Stuart Papers, VHS.

13. Returns of the First Regiment of Cavalry, August–December, 1855, Returns . . . Fourth Cavalry, NA; Chalfant, *Cheyennes*, pp. 29–31.

14. Returns of the First Regiment of Cavalry, August–December, 1855, Returns . . . Fourth Cavalry, NA; Mitchell, ed., *Letters . . . Stuart*, p. 161.

15. Extract, Stuart Family Bible, Stuart Papers, VHS; Mitchell, ed., *Letters . . . Stuart*, pp. 159, 160, 161, 162; Returns of the First Regiment of Cavalry, January–September, 1856, Returns . . . Fourth Cavalry, NA.

16. Extract, Stuart Family Bible, Stuart Papers, VHS; Thomason, *Jeb Stuart*, p. 10; Davis, *Jeb Stuart*, p. 37; Returns of the First Regiment of Cavalry, January–September, 1856, Returns . . . Fourth Cavalry, NA.

17. Commission, First Lieutenant, April 30, 1856, Stuart Papers, VHS; Annual Return of the First Regiment of Cavalry, 1856, Returns . . . Fourth Cavalry; JEBS–Sir, June 13, 1855, Letters Received Adjutant General, 1822–1860, NA.

18. Returns of the First Regiment of Cavalry, January–September, 1856, Returns . . . Fourth Cavalry; L. Thomas–Sir, December 21, 1855, JEBS–Col., December 31, 1855, Letters Received Adjutant General, 1822–1860, NA; Mitchell, ed., *Letters . . . Stuart*, pp. 164, 165.

19. Reynolds, *John Brown*, pp. 112, 140, 141.

20. Ibid., pp. 139–43, 145, 157, 171, 176, 184, 185.

21. Ibid., pp. 187, 188.

22. Ibid., p. 187; *Proceedings*, pp. 67, 73, 85.

23. Thomason, *Jeb Stuart*, p. 29; *Catalog No. 157*, No. 276, letter dated October 24, 1856; *CV*, v. 32, p. 10; Goodwin, *Team of Rivals*, p. 228.

24. *Catalog No. 157*, No. 276.

25. Ibid.

26. Chalfant, *Cheyennes*, p. 50; Returns of the First Regiment of Cavalry, October 1856–May 1857, Returns . . . Fourth Cavalry, NA; Utley, *Frontiersmen*, pp. 45, 46; Ross, *Cities and Camps*, p. 171.

27. Returns of the First Regiment of Cavalry, October 1856–May 1857, Returns . . . Fourth Cavalry, NA; Chalfant, *Cheyennes*, pp. 64–65, 67, 68; Schaefer, "Tactical and Strategic Evolution," Ph.D. diss., p. 24.

28. Chalfant, *Cheyennes*, pp. 5, 7, 39, 53, 300, 303, 305, 315; Utley, *Frontiersmen*, p. 62.

29. Chalfant, *Cheyennes*, p. 68; JEBS–Sir, June 1, 1857, Letters Received Adjutant General, 1822–1860, NA.

30. JEBS–Sir, June 1, 1857, Letters Received Adjutant General, 1822–1860, NA.

31. Ibid.

32. Returns of the First Regiment of Cavalry, June–December 1857, January–December 1858, NA; JEBS–My Dear Custis, February 11, 1860, copy in possession of Krick; Chalfant, *Cheyennes*, p. 105; Diary, p. 61, Long Papers, USAMHI.

33. Notes from Diary, Stuart Papers, VHS; Chalfant, *Cheyennes*, pp. 132–60, 176–86; Diary, pp. 61, 62, Long Papers, USAMHI.

34. JEBS–[Flora], July 30, 1857, Stuart Papers, VHS; Chalfant, *Cheyennes*, pp. 195, 197, 199; *National Tribune*, May 23, 1901; Diary, pp. 63, 64, Long Papers, USAMHI.

35. JEBS–[Flora], July 30, 1857; Notes from Diary, Stuart Papers, VHS; Chalfant, *Cheyennes*, pp. 204, 271, 274.

36. Notes from Diary, Stuart Papers, VHS.

37. Ibid.; Utley, *Frontiersmen*, p. 30.

38. Notes from Diary, Stuart Papers, VHS.

39. Eckert and Amato, eds., *Ten Years*, pp. 89–90; Chalfant, *Cheyennes*, p. 268; Returns of the First Regiment of Cavalry, June–December, 1857, Returns . . . Fourth Cavalry, NA; Extract, Stuart Family Bible, Stuart Papers, VHS.

40. Returns of the First Regiment of Cavalry, January 1858–December 1860, Returns . . . Fourth Cavalry, NA; JEBS–Capt., December 30, 1859, Stuart Papers, USMAL; *Outline Descriptions*, p. 142; Utley, *Frontiersmen*, p. 67; Chalfant, *Cheyennes*, p. 21; Billings, *Report*, p. 287; McKale and Young, *Fort Riley*, pp. 11, 15, 16, 18, 20; Morrison, ed., *Memoirs*, p. 119.

41. Returns of the First Regiment of Cavalry, January–December, 1858, Returns . . . Fourth Cavalry, NA; Drake, "Old Army," *MOLLUS*, Massachusetts, v. 1, p. 149.

42. JEBS–My Dear Cousin, January 28, 1857, Alexander H. H. Stuart Papers, UVA; "Private accounts book," Stuart Papers, VHS; JEBS–Lowe, March 14, April 2, May 10, 1858, Perry Collection, VATU; Russell, "Jeb Stuart on the Frontier," *CWTI*, v. 13, no. 1, pp. 15, 16.

43. Returns of the First Regiment of Cavalry, January–December 1858, Returns . . . Fourth Cavalry, NA; Boyd, "Boyhood," p. 59, notation by Flora Stuart, Boyd Papers, LSU; JEBS–Capt., December 30, 1859, Stuart Papers, USMAL.

44. W. H. Emory–Hardee, September 14, 1858, Stuart Papers, VHS.

45. *Auction Catalog No. 41—Part I*, p. 67; Returns of the First Regiment of Cavalry, January–December 1859, Returns . . . Fourth Cavalry, NA; JEBS–My Dear Sister, November 10, 1859, Stuart Papers, VHS.

46. Lomax, *Leaves*, p. 104; Thomas, *Bold Dragoon*, pp. 53, 54; Speech to Hermesian Society, [1859], Stuart Papers, VHS.

47. Mitchell, ed., *Letters . . . Stuart*, p. 176; J. E. B. Stuart, Belt. No. 25,684, Stuart Papers, VHS; Patent, October 22, 1859, Stuart Papers, HL.

48. Mitchell, ed., *Letters . . . Stuart*, pp. 177, 183, 184; Patent, October 22, 1859, with contract, November 2, 1859, Stuart Papers, HL; JEBS–My Dear Sister, November 10, 1859, Stuart Papers, VHS; Thomas, *Bold Dragoon*, p. 59.

49. JEBS–General, October 3, 1859, *Autograph Catalog*, Alexander Autographs; Thomas, "'Greatest Service,'" *VMHB*, v. 94, no. 3, p. 352.

50. Goodwin, *Team of Rivals*, p. 2; Thomas, "'Greatest Service,'" *VMHB*, v. 94, no. 3, p. 352; Freeman, *R. E. Lee*, v. 1, p. 394.

51. Freeman, *R. E. Lee*, v. 1, p. 395; Thomas, "'Greatest Service,'" *VMHB*, v. 94, no. 3, p. 352.

52. Freeman, *R. E. Lee*, v. 1, p. 395; Thomas, "'Greatest Service,'" *VMHB*, v. 94, no. 3, p. 352.

53. Reynolds, *John Brown*, pp. 310–15.

54. Ibid., pp. 316–21.

55. Freeman, *R. E. Lee*, v. 1, pp. 396, 397; Thomas, "'Greatest Service,'" *VMHB*, p. 94, no. 3, pp. 352, 356.

56. Freeman, *R. E. Lee*, v. 1, pp. 398, 399; Reynolds, *John Brown*, p. 397; Thomas, "'Greatest Service,'" *VMHB*, v. 94, no. 3, p. 355.

57. Freeman, *R. E. Lee*, v. 1, pp. 399–400; Reynolds, *John Brown*, pp. 327–28, 337, 371, 373.

58. Thomas, "'Greatest Service,'" *VMHB*, v. 94, no. 3, p. 355; *National Tribune*, May 16, 1901; White, Memoir, copy in possession of Krick.

59. Reynolds, *John Brown*, pp. 387, 388, 391, 394–97.

60. Ibid., Chapter 16; Davis, *Jeb Stuart*, p. 43.

61. Returns of the First Regiment of Cavalry, January–December 1859, January–December, 1860, Returns . . . Fourth Cavalry, NA; JEBS–My Dear Sister, November 10, 1859, Stuart Papers, VHS; Goodwin, *Team of Rivals*, p. 228; Davis, *Jeb Stuart*, p. 43; JEBS–My Dear Custis, February 11, 1860, typescript copy in possession of Krick.

62. JEBS–My Dear Custis, February 11, 1860, typescript copy in possession of Krick; Thomas, "'Greatest Service,'" *VMHB*, v. 94, no. 3, p. 351.

63. Returns of the First Regiment of Cavalry, January–December, 1860, Returns . . . Fourth Cavalry, NA; JEBS–My Dear Custis, February 11, 1860, typescript copy in possession of Krick.

64. Root, ed., "Extracts," *KHQ*, v. 1, no. 3, p. 206; Stuart, "Journal," YU; Extract, Stuart Family Bible, Stuart Papers, VHS.

65. Stuart, "Journal," YU; Root, ed., "Extracts," *KHQ*, v. 1, no. 3, pp. 206–10;

Russell, "Jeb Stuart's Other Indian Fight," *CWTI*, v. 12, no. 9, pp. 11, 12; JEBS–My Dear Sir, October 8, 1860, Stuart Collection, MC.

66. Stuart, "Journal," YU; Diary, 1860, Stuart Papers, UVA.

67. Extract, Stuart Family Bible, Stuart Papers, VHS; Perry, *Ascent*, p. 4; JEBS–My Dear Sir, October 8, 1860, Stuart Collection, MC.

68. JEBS–My Dear Sir, October 8, 1860, Stuart Collection, MC; Diary, June 14, 1857, Long Papers, USAMHI; Root, ed., "Extracts," *KHQ*, v. 1, no. 3, p. 207n.

69. JEBS–My Dear Sir, October 8, 1860, Stuart Collection, MC; JEBS–My Dear Sir, December 20, 1860, Perry Collection, VATU.

70. JEBS–Major, January 11, 1861, Stuart, Letter . . . Hill, UVA; JEBS–My Dear Brother, January 18, 1861, Stuart Papers, VHS; Duncan, ed., *Letters*, p. 9.

71. General Orders, No. 12, February 2, 1861, endorsement, March 4, 1861, Stuart Papers, HL; Thomason, *Jeb Stuart*, p. 59; JEBS–My Dear Brother, March 14, 1861, Stuart Papers, VHS.

72. JEBS–My Dear Brother, March 14, 1861, Stuart Papers, VHS; Boyd, "Boyhood," p. 38, notation by Flora Stuart, Boyd Papers, LSU.

73. JEBS–My Dear Friend, March 23, 1861, Stuart Papers, VHS.

74. Reynolds, *John Brown*, p. 395.

75. McClellan, *I Rode*, p. 31; Styple, ed., *Generals in Bronze*, p. 74; Diary, Boteler Papers, LC.

76. Lunsford L. Lomax–Bayard, April 21, 1861, Lomax Family Papers; Cooke family tree, VHS; Duncan, ed., *Letters*, p. 9; Diary, Cooke Papers, DU.

77. McClellan, *I Rode*, p. 31; Mitchell, ed., *Letters . . . Stuart*, p. 194; JEBS–Samuel Cooper, May 3, 1861, Stuart Collection, MC.

78. Carmichael, *Last Generation*, pp. 7, 9, 10–14, 18, 112.

Chapter 4: "A Rare Man"

1. JEBS–My Darling Wife, May 13, [1861], Stuart Papers, DU; Driver, *1st Virginia Cavalry*, p. 1; Wert, *Brotherhood*, p. 13.

2. McClellan, *I Rode*, p. 32; JEBS–My Darling Flora, March 30, 1863, Stuart Papers, VHS.

3. Richmond *Dispatch*, May 10, 1861; Commission, Lieutenant Colonel, May 10, 1861; Special Orders, No. 34, May 9, 1861; JEBS–My Dear Flora, May 9, 1861, Stuart Papers, VHS.

4. JEBS–My Dear Flora, May 9, 1861, Stuart Papers, VHS; Thomas, *Bold Dragoon*, p. 67; Krick, *Staff Officers*, p. 145; Trout, *They Followed the Plume*, p. 171; Peter W. Hairston–My Dear Fanny, May 9, 1861, Hairston Papers, DU.

5. Driver, *1st Virginia Cavalry*, p. 1; OR, v. 2, p. 868; Johnston, *Narrative*, p. 16; Wayland, *Virginia Valley Records*, p. 242; Wert, *Brotherhood*, p. 30.

6. Wert, *Brotherhood*, pp. 26, 27.

7. Freeman, *Lee's Lieutenants*, v. 1, p. xlii; Greene, *Whatever You Resolve to Be*, p. 170; Randolph Barton–A. C. Hamlin, August 31, 1892, Hamlin Papers, HU; Colt, ed., *Defend the Valley*, p. 70; Duke, Recollections, v. 1, p. 84, UVA; Sutherland, "Stars in Their Courses," *ACW*, v. 4, no. 4, p. 45.

8. *Annals*, p. 647; Robertson, *Stonewall Jackson*, pp. 226, 237, 238; Howard, *Recollections*, p. 80; Smith, *With Stonewall Jackson*, p. 2; Blackford, *War Years*, p. 81; Randolph Barton–A. C. Hamlin, August 31, 1892, Hamlin Papers, HU.

9. Greene, *Whatever You Resolve to Be*, pp. 15–17; Wert, *Brotherhood*, p. 97; Taliaferro, "Personal Reminiscences," *CWTI*, v. 34, no. 2, p. 18.

10. Boyd, "Boyhood," pp. 46, 47, Boyd Papers, LSU; Robertson, *Stonewall Jackson*, p. 235; CV, v. 5, p. 551.

11. Boyd, "Boyhood," p. 47, Boyd Papers, LSU; Smith, *With Stonewall Jackson*, p. 73; Robertson, *Stonewall Jackson*, p. 235.

12. Wert, *Brotherhood*, p. 30; Eggleston, *Rebel's Recollections*, p. 64; JEBS–My Darling Wife, May 13, [1861], Stuart Papers, DU.

13. Driver, *1st Virginia Cavalry*, pp. 1–3; JEBS–My Darling Wife, May 16, 1861, Stuart Papers, DU; Brennan, "Best Cavalry," *N&S*, v. 2, no. 2, p. 12; *Annals*, p. 666; Thomason, *Jeb Stuart*, p. 83.

14. Driver, *1st Virginia Cavalry*, p. 3; Mitchell, ed., *Letters . . . Stuart*, p. 200.

15. Johnston, *Narrative*, p. 14; Warner, *Generals in Gray*, p. 161; Gallagher, ed., *Fighting For*, pp. 48, 49.

16. Johnston, *Narrative*, p. 16; OR, v. 2, pp. 470, 471, 867, 868, 869.

17. Blackford, *War Years*, pp. 15, 16; Von Borcke, *Memoirs*, v. 1, pp. 21, 22; Thomason, *Jeb Stuart*, p. 1; Freeman, *Lee's Lieutenants*, v. 1, p. xlix; Sorrel, *Recollections*, p. 19.

18. Blackford, *War Years*, p. 89; Cooke, *Wearing*, p. 205; Thomason, *Jeb Stuart*, p. 3; Hopkins, *From Bull Run to Appomattox*, p. 268; Mitchell, ed., *Letters . . . Stuart*, p. 205; Benjamin Franklin Cochran–Mother, June 12, 1861, Cochran Family Papers, VATU; Robert Hooke–Father, June 6, 11, 1861, Hooke Papers; JEBS–Col. Allen, June 10, 1861, Stuart Papers, DU.

19. JEBS–My Darling Pet, June 11, 1861, Stuart Papers, DU; Davis, *Jeb Stuart*, p. 52.

20. JEBS–My Darling Wife, May 13, 16, 23, 26, 30, 31, June 1, 5, 7, 11, 1861, Stuart Papers, DU; Mitchell, ed., *Letters . . . Stuart*, p. 207.

21. JEBS–My Darling Flora, May 26, 30, 1861, Stuart Papers, DU; Adjutant General's Office–JEBS, May 14, 1861, Stuart Papers, VHS; Mitchell, ed., *Letters . . . Stuart*, pp. 201, 203.

22. JEBS–My Darling One, May 31, 1861; JEBS–My Dearest One, June 13, 1861, Stuart Papers, DU.

23. Symonds, *Joseph E. Johnston*, pp. 104, 106, 108.

24. Robertson, *Stonewall Jackson*, p. 236; Longacre, *Lee's Cavalrymen*, pp. 6, 7.

25. *SOR*, v. 1, p. 182; *OR*, v. 2, p. 934; Peter W. Hairston–My Darling Pet, June 18, 1861, Hairston Papers, UNC; Mitchell, ed., *Letters . . . Stuart*, pp. 207, 209.

26. *SOR*, v. 1, p. 182; Thomason, *Jeb Stuart*, p. 9.

27. Brennan, "Best Cavalry," *N&S*, v. 2, no. 2, pp. 12, 13; Hudgins and Kleese, eds., *Recollections*, p. 51; Opie, *Rebel Cavalryman*, p. 91; Eggleston, *Rebel's Recollections*, pp. 111, 112, 113, 115, 116, 118, 124.

28. Eggleston, *Rebel's Recollections*, p. 119; Robert Hooke–Father, June 7, 23, 1861, Hooke Papers, DU; *OR*, v. 2, pp. 471, 472; Johnston, *Narrative*, p. 34; Peter W. Hairston–My Darling One, June 5, 18, 1861, Hairston Papers, UNC.

29. Joseph E. Johnston–JEBS, June 22, 1861, Stuart Papers, HL.

30. Wert, *Brotherhood*, p. 33; *SOR*, v. 1, p. 198; Gimbel, "End of Innocence," *B&G*, v. 22, no. 4, p. 16.

31. Wert, *Brotherhood*, pp. 33, 34; *OR*, v. 2, pp. 185, 186; Gimbel, "End of Innocence," *B&G*, v. 22, no. 4, p. 16; *CV*, v. 11, p. 351; Philip H. Powers–My Dear Wife, July 4, 1861, Powers Letters, USAMHI.

32. *OR*, v. 2, p. 186; Philip H. Powers–My Dear Wife, July 4, 1861, Powers Letters, USAMHI; Gimbel, "End of Innocence," *B&G*, v. 22, no. 4, p. 16.

33. Gimbel, "End of Innocence," *B&G*, v. 22, no. 4, pp. 16, 17; Duncan, ed., *Letters*, p. 13; Philip H. Powers–My Dear Wife, July 4, 1861, Powers Letters, USAMHI; *OR*, v. 2, p. 186.

34. *SOR*, v. 1, pp. 184, 198, 199; JEBS–My Darling Wife, July 4, 1861, Stuart Papers, VHS; Driver, *1st Virginia Cavalry*, pp. 7, 8, 9; *OR*, v. 2, pp. 962–63.

35. Robert Hooke–Father, July 12, 1861, Hooke Papers, DU; Turner, ed., *Ted Barclay*, p. 17; Peter W. Hairston–My Dear Fanny, July 12, 1861, Hairston Papers, UNC.

36. General Orders, No. 1, July 7, 1861, Stuart Papers, HL.

37. *SOR*, v. 1, p. 199; Wert, *Sword of Lincoln*, pp. 12–13, 16.

38. Wert, *Sword of Lincoln*, pp. 12, 13.

39. *OR*, v. 2, p. 473; Johnston, *Narrative*, pp. 32–35; JEBS–[Flora], July 19, 1861, Stuart Papers, DU; John O. Collins–Wife, July 19, 1861, Collins Papers, VHS; William W. Blackford–Uncle John, August 6, 1861, Blackford Letter, USAMHI; *SOR*, v. 1, p. 199.

40. William W. Blackford–Uncle John, August 6, 1861, Blackford Letter, USAMHI; Wert, *Brotherhood*, pp. 36, 46.

41. William W. Blackford–Uncle John, August 6, 1861, Blackford Letter, USAMHI; Driver, *1st Virginia Cavalry*, p. 12; Blackford, *War Years*, p. 17; Trout, *They Followed the Plume*, p. 288; Commission, Colonel, July 16, 1861, Stuart Papers, VHS.

42. Wert, *Sword of Lincoln*, pp. 18, 19.

43. Ibid., pp. 20–25, quotes on pp. 22, 24.

44. Blackford, *War Years*, p. 26; OR, v. 2, pp. 481, 482, 483, 488, 497; Lee, Reminiscences, p. 10, WLU; Martinsburg (West Virginia) *Statesman*, June 8, 1906; SOR, v. 81, p. 664.

45. OR, v. 2, pp. 408, 483; William W. Blackford–Uncle John, August 6, 1861, Blackford Letter, USAMHI; Mitchell, ed., *Letters . . . Mosby*, p. 114; Wert, *Sword of Lincoln*, p. 23; Scott, ed., *Forgotten Valor*, pp. 290, 291.

46. OR, v. 2, p. 483; SOR, v. 81, pp. 657, 664; Compiled Records: Virginia Cavalry, NA; *Southern Bivouac*, v. 2, p. 530; William W. Blackford–Uncle John, July 27, 1861, Blackford Papers, UNC.

47. OR, v. 2, pp. 408, 483; SOR, v. 81, p. 664; Martinsburg (West Virginia) *Statesman*, June 8, 1906; CV, v. 4, p. 155; William W. Blackford–Uncle John, July 27, 1861, Blackford Papers, UNC; Driver, *1st Virginia Cavalry*, p. 14; William W. Blackford–Uncle John, August 6, 1861, Blackford Letter, USAMHI.

48. Wert, *Sword of Lincoln*, pp. 25–26; OR, v. 2, pp. 476, 483, 484, 534, 557; Lee, Reminiscences, p. 11, WLU; Philip H. Powers–My Dearest Wife, July 23, 1861, Powers Letters, USAMHI; Helm, *Black Horse Cavalry*, pp. 36, 38; Driver, *First and Second Maryland Cavalry*, pp. 8–9.

49. Wert, *Sword of Lincoln*, pp. 27, 28.

50. OR, v. 2, pp. 477, 500; JEBS–My Darling Wife, July 27, 1861, Stuart Papers, DU.

51. OR, v. 2, p. 995; Wert, *Sword of Lincoln*, p. 28.

52. Wert, *General James Longstreet*, p. 81.

53. OR, v. 51, pt. 1, p. 38; SHSP, v. 9, p. 132; Blackford, ed., *Letters*, p. 42; Daniel G. Cushwa–My Dear Father, August 29, 1861, Cushwa Papers, VHS; Cooke, *Wearing*, p. 204; Philadelphia *Weekly Times*, October 5, 1878; Mitchell, ed., *Letters . . . Mosby*, p. 16; Colt, ed., *Defend the Valley*, p. 99.

54. Lee, Reminiscences, pp. 17, 31, 32, WLU; Driver, *First and Second Maryland Cavalry*, p. 11.

55. Thomas G. Rhett–JEBS, August 15, 1861, Stuart Papers, HL; Brennan, "Best Cavalry," *N&S*, v. 2, no. 2, p. 13; SHSP, v. 9, p. 132.

56. Robert Hooke–Father, August 8, 1861, Hooke Papers, DU; Driver, *1st Virginia Cavalry*, p. 20; Younger, ed., *Inside*, pp. 3, 4, 5.

57. Driver and Howard, *2nd Virginia Cavalry*, p. 26; Compiled Records: Virginia Cavalry, NA; Robert Hooke–Father, August 13, 1861, Hooke Papers, DU; Thomason, *Jeb Stuart*, p. 11.

58. Turner, ed., *Ted Barclay*, p. 26; Turner, ed., *Old Zeus*, p. 80; Roper, ed., *Repairing*, p. 136; Hassler, ed., *General to His Lady*, pp. 50–51.

59. Johnston, *Narrative*, p. 16; OR, v. 5, p. 777.

60. Wert, *General James Longstreet*, Chapters 1–3, pp. 80–81, 252.

61. Ibid., pp. 82, 84; Lord, ed., *Fremantle Diary*, p. 196; Blackford, *War Years*, p. 47.

62. Wert, *General James Longstreet*, p. 85; Blackford, *War Years*, p. 47; OR, v. 5, p. 182.

63. OR, v. 5, pp. 175–78, 182, 183; Mitchell, ed., *Letters . . . Stuart*, pp. 214–15; Johnston, *Narrative*, p. 73; General Orders, No. 19, September 12, 1861; General Orders, No. 2, September 13, 1861, Stuart Papers, HL.

64. Orlando M. Poe–My Dear Beauty, September 11, 1861, Stuart Papers, VHS.

65. James Longstreet–JEBS, September 14, 1861, two letters, Stuart Papers, HL; P. G. T. Beauregard–James Longstreet, September 15, 1861, Stuart Papers, HL.

66. OR, v. 5, p. 181.

67. Wert, *Sword of Lincoln*, pp. 41, 95; Griffith, *Battle Tactics*, p. 182.

68. Commission, Brigadier General, September 24, 1861, Stuart Papers, VHS; J. E. Johnston–JEBS, [September 24, 1861], Stuart Papers, VHS; Stuart file, CSR, NA; JEBS–My Darling Wife, July 31, 1861, Stuart Papers, DU; Hassler, ed., *General to His Lady*, p. 80.

Chapter 5: "I Will Not Leave the Van of Our Army"

1. Hartley, *Stuart's Tarheels*, p. 72.

2. Wert, *General James Longstreet*, p. 91.

3. OR, v. 5, pp. 913–14, 922, 930, 935, 938; P. R. Reamy–My Dear Sallie, July 25, 1861, Reamy Papers, NC.

4. Mitchell, ed., *Letters . . . Stuart*, p. 219; SOR, v. 1, p. 407; Thomason, *Jeb Stuart*, p. 131; Johnson, *In the Footsteps*, p. 11.

5. Davis, *Jeb Stuart*, pp. 74–75; Duncan, ed., *Letters*, p. 16; OR, v. 5, pp. 932, 1015.

6. OR, v. 5, p. 181.

7. Warner, *Generals in Gray*, pp. 166–67; Lambert, *Grumble*, pp. 2, 3; Driver, *1st Virginia Cavalry*, p. 192.

8. Mosgrove, *Kentucky Cavaliers*, p. 85; Haden, *Reminiscences*, p. 27; Joseph H. Trundle–My Darling Mother, November 24, 1863, Trundle Letters, USAMHI; Opie, *Rebel Cavalryman*, p. 54.

9. McClellan, *I Rode*, p. 320; Blackford, *War Years*, p. 16.

10. Richmond *Dispatch*, November 7, 1861; Duncan, ed., *Letters*, p. 16.

11. OR, v. 5, p. 181; v. 51, pt. 2, p. 316; Longacre, *Fitz Lee*, pp. 14, 28, 30, 32.

12. Lee, Reminiscences, p. 32, WLU; Andrews, ed., *Scraps of Paper*, p. 149; Freeman, *Lee's Lieutenants*, v. 1, p. liv; Styple, ed., *Generals in Bronze*, p. 217.

13. *SHSP*, v. 35, p. 143; Longacre, *Fitz Lee*, pp. 5, 10; Blackford, *War Years*, p. 50.

14. Driver and Howard, *2nd Virginia Cavalry*, pp. 29, 252, 263; Thomas T. Munford–My dear General, September 4, 1912, Lomax Family Papers, VHS; Duncan, ed., *Letters*, p. 16.

15. Stiles, *4th Virginia Cavalry*, pp. 6, 7; Hartley, *Stuart's Tarheels*, p. 66; Warner, *Generals in Gray*, p. 259; JEBS–My Dear Robertson, November 13, 1858, *Auction Catalog No. 41—Part I*, p. 67.

16. Duncan, ed., *Letters*, p. 16; Stiles, *4th Virginia Cavalry*, pp. 2, 3, 7, 10; Helm, *Black Horse Cavalry*, p. 48.

17. Warner, *Generals in Gray*, p. 253; Mosgrove, *Kentucky Cavaliers*, p. 85; Hartley, *Stuart's Tarheels*, pp. 13, 14, 19, 36, 54, 55, 66.

18. SOR, v. 44, pp. 469–84; Musick, *6th Virginia Cavalry*, p. 7; Warner, *Generals in Gray*, p. 214.

19. Wise, *Long Arm*, pp. 302, 349; Bridges, *Fighting with JEB Stuart*, pp. 27–28, 34; Duncan, ed., *Letters*, p. 26.

20. Krick, *Staff Officers*, p. 145; Blackford, *War Years*, p. 50; Thomason, *Jeb Stuart*, pp. 120, 121; Trout, *They Followed the Plume*, p. 28; Cooke, *Wearing*, pp. 23, 24.

21. *Annals*, p. 672; Richmond *Dispatch*, October 31, 1861; Blackford, *War Years*, pp. 90, 93.

22. Richmond *Dispatch*, October 31, November 27, 1861.

23. General Orders, No. 1, October 2, 1861, Stuart file, CSR, NA; Krick, *Staff Officers*, pp. 66, 83, 87, 108, 144, 275, 288; CV, v. 21, p. 176; Mitchell, ed., *Letters . . . Stuart*, pp. 228, 235, 237.

24. Longacre, *Lee's Cavalrymen*, p. 31; Trout, ed., *With Pen and Saber*, p. 49; Knapp, *Confederate Saddles*, p. 20.

25. Knapp, *Confederate Saddles*, p. 20; Longacre, *Lee's Cavalrymen*, p. 38.

26. OR, v. 51, pt. 2, p. 349; newspaper clipping, Hotchkiss Papers, LC; CV, v. 22, p. 320.

27. L. Tiernan Brien–Colonel, December 3, 1861, Stuart Papers, DU; JEBS–General, October 10, 1861, Early Family Papers, VHS; Ross, *Cities and Camps*, p. 173; JEBS–Sir, December 21, 1863, Samuel H. Hairston file, CSR, CSA Generals, NA.

28. Colt, ed., *Defend the Valley*, p. 104; Blackford, ed., *Letters*, pp. 52, 53; Richmond *Disptach*, November 7, 1861; Daniel G. Cushwa–Father, November 1, 1861, Cushwa Papers; JEBS–My Dear Darling, December 23, 1861, Stuart Papers, VHS; Duncan, ed., *Letters*, p. 27.

29. SOR, v. 1, pp. 407–9; Duncan, ed., *Letters*, p. 17; JEBS–Miss Mary, December 17, 1861, Lee Family Papers, VHS; OR, v. 5, pp. 439–42, 446–47; v. 51, pt. 1, p. 50.

30. OR, v. 5, p. 490; Philadelphia *Weekly Times*, October 31, 1885, January 9,

1886; JEBS–My Dear Darling, December 23, 1861, Stuart Papers, VHS; Hartley, *Stuart's Tarheels*, pp. 75, 77.

31. OR, v. 5, pp. 490–92; Philadelphia *Weekly Times*, October 31, 1885; JEBS– My Dear Darling, December 23, 1861, Stuart Papers, VHS; Styple, ed., *Writing and Fighting*, p. 78.

32. Styple, ed., *Writing and Fighting*, pp. 78, 79; OR, v. 5, pp. 492, 494; Phila- delphia *Weekly Times*, October 31, 1885; Hartley, *Stuart's Tarheels*, p. 77; Younger, ed., *Inside*, p. 20; JEBS–My Dear Darling, December 23, 1861, Stuart Papers; Chiswell Dabney–Mother, December 24, 1861, Saunders Family Papers, VHS.

33. JEBS–My Dear Darling, December 23, 1861, Stuart Papers, VHS.

34. Younger, ed., *Inside*, p. 20.

35. Duncan, ed., *Letters*, p. 30; Paxton, ed., *Civil War Letters*, p. 20; Peter W. Hairston–My Dear Fanny, September 24, 1861, Hairston Papers, UNC; Mitchell, ed., *Letters . . . Stuart*, p. 237.

36. Duncan, ed., *Letters*, pp. 21, 27; Mitchell, ed., *Letters . . . Stuart*, pp. 227–28, 236.

37. Davis, *Jeb Stuart*, p. 87; Duncan, ed., *Letters*, p. 23; Will, November 16, 1861, Stuart Papers, VHS.

38. Blackford, ed., *Letters*, pp. 57, 58; Duncan, ed., *Letters*, pp. 17, 19.

39. Duncan, ed., *Letters*, pp. 21, 22n, 26; Thomason, *Jeb Stuart*, p. 206; Will, November 16, 1861, Stuart Papers, VHS; Mitchell, ed., *Letters . . . Stuart*, pp. 228, 229, 234.

40. Duncan, ed., *Letters*, p. 24.

41. Davis, *Jeb Stuart*, p. 87; Thomason, *Jeb Stuart*, p. 128; Withers, Diary, UNC; JEBS–My Darling One, January 16, 1862, Stuart Papers, VHS.

42. Blackford, *War Years*, pp. 50, 51; Driver and Howard, *2nd Virginia Cavalry*, p. 273; Thompson, *Horses*, p. 8; Garnett, *Riding with Stuart*, p. 30; CV, v. 30, p. 344.

43. JEBS–My Darling One, January 16, 1862, Stuart Papers; Daniel G. Cushwa– Father, January 21, 1862, Cushwa Papers, VHS; Haskell, *Haskell Memoirs*, pp. 19–20.

44. JEBS–My Darling Wife, February 17, 1862, Stuart Papers, VHS.

45. JEBS–My Darling Wife, January 16, 24, February 1, 14, 17, 26, 1862, Stuart Papers, VHS; Wert, *General James Longstreet*, pp. 96–97.

46. Rust, "Portrait of Laura," *Virginia Cavalcade*, v. 12, no. 3, pp. 34, 35; Wash- ington *Times*, December 12, 2001; Low, "Letters to Laura," *CWTI*, v. 32, no. 3, p. 58.

47. Peter W. Hairston–My Dear Fanny, September 4, 1861, Hairston Papers, UNC; Thomason, *Jeb Stuart*, p. 124; Low, "Letters to Laura," *CWTI*, v. 32, no. 3, p. 58.

48. JEBS–My Darling One, February 14, 1862, Stuart Papers, VHS; *SHSP*, v. 8, p. 453.

49. Blackford, *War Years*, pp. 89, 90; Smith, ed., "Watching Lee's Lieutenants," *CW*, v. 10, no. 4, p. 55.

50. Wert, *General James Longstreet*, pp. 97, 98.

51. Ibid., pp. 98, 99.

52. Ibid., p. 99; Younger, ed., *Inside*, pp. xi, xxv, 46, 50.

53. "Appeal," March 5, 1862, Stuart Papers, HL; Johnston, *Narrative*, p. 103; Blackford, *War Years*, pp. 59, 60; Robert Randolph–Bro Alfred, March 7, 1862, Minor Family Papers; JEBS–My Darling Wife, March 16, 1862, Stuart Papers, VHS; *OR*, v. 12, pt. 1, p. 333.

54. Nisbet, *4 Years*, pp. 26, 27; J. E. Johnston–JEBS, March 17, 1862, Stuart Papers, HL; O'Neill, "Cavalry on the Peninsula," *B&G*, v. 19, no. 5, p. 15.

55. Wert, *Sword of Lincoln*, pp. 65–68.

56. Wert, *General James Longstreet*, pp. 101–2; Joseph E. Johnston–General, March 29, 1862, Johnston Letter, NYHS; Bridges, *Fighting with JEB Stuart*, p. 35; Blackford, *War Years*, p. 61; Bill, *Beleaguered City*, p. 118.

57. Wert, *General James Longstreet*, pp. 102–3.

58. JEBS–My Darling One, April 18, 1862; JEBS–My Darling Wife, April 21, 1862, Stuart Papers, VHS; Lasswell, ed., *Rags and Hope*, p. 78; Miller, ed., *Peninsula Campaign*, v. 3, p. 140; Driver and Howard, *2nd Virginia Cavalry*, pp. 40, 41; Hartley, *Stuart's Tarheels*, p. 83.

59. Krick, *Staff Officers*, pp. 83, 145, 246.

60. Wert, *Brotherhood of Valor*, p. 94.

61. JEBS–My Darling Wife, April 29, 1862, Stuart Papers, VHS; W. E. Jones–Hon. J. P. Benjamin, February 26, 1862; W. E. Jones–Hon. G. W. Randolph, April 28, 1862, copies in possession of Krick; McClellan, *I Rode*, p. 320; Blackford, *War Years*, p. 51.

62. W. E. Jones–Hon. G. W. Randolph, April 28, 1862, copy in possession of Krick.

63. Driver, *1st Virginia Cavalry*, p. 193; Cooke, *Wearing*, p. 17.

Chapter 6: "Our Exploit Is All the Talk Here"

1. Dubbs, *Defend This Old Town*, pp. 1–5.

2. Ibid., p. 94; Wert, *General James Longstreet*, pp. 104–5.

3. Wert, *General James Longstreet*, pp. 103–4; *OR*, 11, pt. 3, pp. 469, 485.

4. Wert, *General James Longstreet*, p. 104; Gallagher, ed., *Fighting For*, pp. 77, 78, 79; Dubbs, *Defend This Old Town*, p. 77.

5. *OR*, v. 11, pt. 1, p. 444; JEBS–Thomas G. Rhett, May 8, 1862, Stuart Papers, HL; Hubard, "Civil War Reminiscences," p. 12, UVA; Nanzig, *3rd*

Virginia Cavalry, pp. 4, 12–14; Musick, *6th Virginia Cavalry*, p. 1; Hudgins and Kleese, eds., *Recollections*, p. 51.

6. OR, v. 11, pt. 1, pp. 444–45; JEBS–Thomas G. Rhett, May 8, 1862, Stuart Papers, HL.

7. Wert, *Sword of Lincoln*, pp. 76, 77; OR, v. 11, pt. 1, p. 564.

8. OR, v. 11, pt. 1, pp. 570, 571, 574, 585, 606; Wert, *General James Longstreet*, p. 106; Coski, "Forgotten Warrior," *N&S*, v. 2, no. 7, p. 78; JEBS–My Darling Wife, May 9, 1862, Stuart Papers, VHS; William H. F. Payne–Father, June 19, 1862; Mary Payne, "Search for My Wounded Husband," Hunton Family Papers, VHS.

9. OR, v. 11, pt. 1, pp. 565, 570–72; JEBS–My Darling Wife, May 9, 1862, Stuart Papers; Scott, Memoir of Service, p. 5; J. O. Collins–Wife, May 5, 1862, Collins Papers, VHS; Cadmus M. Wilcox–My Dear Sir, February 6, 1869, Alexander Papers, UNC; Wert, *Sword of Lincoln*, p. 78.

10. OR, v. 11, pt. 1, pp. 568, 585, 606.

11. Trout, *They Followed the Plume*, pp. 106, 108; Krick, *Staff Officers*, p. 125; OR, v. 11, pt. 1, p. 573; JEBS–Thomas G. Rhett, May 8, 1862, Stuart Papers, HL.

12. Vogtsberger, ed., *Dulanys*, pp. 50–51; Von Borcke, *Memoirs*, v. 2, p. 10n; Philadelphia *Weekly Times*, April 26, 1879.

13. Corson, *My Dear Jennie*, p. 77; Driver, *1st Virginia Cavalry*, p. 34; Chiswell Dabney–Mother, May 18, 1862, Saunders Family Papers, VHS; Richard H. Watkins, May 20, 1862, Watkins Papers, VHS; John Price Kepner–[Parents], May 12, 1862, Kepner Letters and Diary, VHS.

14. Philip H. Powers–My Dear Wife, May 15, 1862, Powers Letters, USAMHI.

15. G. W. Smith–JEBS, May 16, 17, 19, 1862, Stuart Papers, HL; OR, v. 11, pt. 1, p. 628; Wert, *Sword of Lincoln*, pp. 81–83.

16. Gilbert J. Wright–Dorothy, May 16, 1862, Wright Papers, VHS; Wert, *General James Longstreet*, pp. 107, 108.

17. Wert, *Sword of Lincoln*, pp. 82–83.

18. Wert, *General James Longstreet*, pp. 111–14, Gallagher, ed., *Fighting For*, p. 85.

19. Wert, *General James Longstreet*, pp. 114–21.

20. Ibid., pp. 120–22.

21. JEBS–My Dearest Wife, May 28, June 4, 1862, Stuart Papers, VHS; OR, v. 11, pt. 1, pp. 941, 994.

22. Wert, *General James Longstreet*, pp. 122–23; JEBS–My Darling Wife, June 4, 1862, Stuart Papers, VHS.

23. Wert, *General James Longstreet*, pp. 126, 127.

24. Warner, *Generals in Gray*, pp. 180–82; Thomas, *Robert E. Lee*, pp. 187, 188.

25. Gallagher, ed., *Richmond Campaign*, p. 11.

26. Roland, *Reflections*, p. 90; Maurice, ed., *Aide-de-Camp of Lee*, p. 74; Gallagher, ed., *Fighting For*, pp. 89, 91.

27. Freeman, *R. E. Lee*, v. 4, p. 174; Gallagher and Glatthaar, eds., *Leaders*, pp. 11, 35; Maurice, ed., *Aide-de-Camp of Lee*, p. 74; Roland, *Reflections*, p. 99.

28. Freeman, *R. E. Lee*, v. 4, pp. 170, 181, 183, 184; Roland, *Reflections*, pp. 96, 99, 100, 101; Taylor, *Four Years*, p. 77; John S. Mosby–James Keith, January 27, 1906, Mosby Papers, NC.

29. Freeman, *R. E. Lee*, v. 4, pp. 171, 172.

30. Dowdey and Manarin, eds., *Wartime Papers*, pp. 182, 187; OR, v. 12, pt. 3, p. 910; Wert, *General James Longstreet*, pp. 129–32.

31. JEBS–R. E. Lee, June 4, 1862, Stuart Papers, HL.

32. John S. Mosby–My dearest Pauline, June 16, 1862, Mosby Papers, VHS; CV, v. 6, p. 421; Wert, *Mosby's Rangers*, pp. 28–29.

33. John S. Mosby–James Keith, January 27, 1900, Mosby Papers, NC; Wert, *Mosby's Rangers*, pp. 27–33.

34. John S. Mosby–My dearest Pauline, June 16, 1862, Mosby Papers, VHS; Diary, Cooke Papers, DU; Von Borcke, *Memoirs*, v. 1, p. 34.

35. John S. Mosby–My dearest Pauline, June 16, 1862, Mosby Papers, VHS; OR, v. 11, pt. 2, p. 514; Mewborn, "A Wonderful Exploit," *B&G*, v. 15, no. 6, p. 9.

36. OR, v. 11, pt. 2, p. 514; R. E. Lee–JEBS, June 11, 1862, Stuart Papers, HL; Dowdey and Manarin, eds., *Wartime Papers*, p. 188.

37. Rawleigh Dunaway–My Dear Sister, June 8, 1862, Forrester, Excerpts, RNBP; Murray, *My Mother*, p. 130; John C. Edrington–My Dear Girls, June 4, 1862, Edrington Papers, VHS.

38. OR, v. 11, pt. 1, pp. 1036, 1042, 1044; Freeman, *Lee's Lieutenants*, v. 1, p. 280; Scott, ed., "Two Confederate Items," *Bulletin of the Virginia State Library*, v. 16, nos. 2 and 3, p. 67.

39. Von Borcke, *Memoirs*, v. 1, p. 37; Thomason, *Jeb Stuart*, p. 2; Freeman, *Lee's Lieutenants*, v. 1, p. 283; JEBS–My Darling One, May 22, 1862, Stuart Papers, VHS; Cooke, *Wearing*, pp. 7, 8, 9.

40. Miller, ed., *Peninsula Campaign*, v. 3, pp. 79, 186; OR, v. 11, pt. 1, p. 1036; Chewning, Journal, p. 4, Handley Library; Scott, ed., "Two Confederate Items," *Bulletin of the Virginia State Library*, v. 16, nos. 2 and 3, pp. 67, 68; Shepherdstown *Register*, April 1, 1882; Natchez *Courier*, July 3, 1862; Cozzens and Girardi, eds., *New Annals*, pp. 101, 102.

41. Cooke, *Wearing*, p. 167; Brooksher and Snider, "Stuart's Ride," *CWTI*, v. 12, no. 1, p. 6.

42. OR, v. 11, pt. 1, p. 1037; Miller, ed., *Peninsula Campaign*, v. 1, pp. 82, 88; Mewborn, "A Wonderful Exploit," *B&G*, v. 15, no. 6, p. 16.

43. *OR*, v. 11, pt. 1, pp. 1020, 1037; Miller, ed., *Peninsula Campaign*, v. 1, pp. 84, 84n, 86.

44. *OR*, v. 11, pt. 1, pp. 1020, 1037, 1043; Cozzens and Girardi, eds., *New Annals*, p. 102; Natchez *Courier*, July 3, 1862.

45. *OR*, v. 11, pt. 1, pp. 1021, 1037, 1042, 1043; *CV*, v. 5, p. 53; R. P. Baylor–My Dear Father, June 15, 1862, Baylor Letter; Chiswell Dabney–Mother, June 18, 1862, Saunders Family Papers, VHS; Miller, ed., *Peninsula Campaign*, v. 1, p. 93.

46. *OR*, v. 11, pt. 1, pp. 1021, 1037; Pitts, "Stuart's Raid," USM; Cozzens and Girardi, eds., *New Annals*, pp. 102, 103; Miller, ed., *Peninsula Campaign*, v. 1, p. 93.

47. *OR*, v. 11, pt. 1, p. 1038; Freeman, *Lee's Lieutenants*, v. 1, p. 289; Pitts, "Stuart's Raid," USM; Mitchell, ed., *Letters . . . Mosby*, pp. 221–22; *SHSP*, v. 26, p. 250.

48. Thomas Munford–Jedediah Hotchkiss, August 19, 23, 1896, Hotchkiss Papers, LC; *OR*, v. 11, pt. 1, p. 1038; Freeman, *Lee's Lieutenants*, v. 1, p. 289; Thomason, *Jeb Stuart*, p. 153.

49. *OR*, v. 11, pt. 1, p. 1038; McClellan, *I Rode*, p. 62; *SHSP*, v. 11, p. 507; *SHSP*, v. 26, p. 250; Mewborn, "*From Mosby's Command*," p. 114.

50. *OR*, v. 11, pt. 1, pp. 1038, 1039; Richmond *Dispatch*, June 17, 1862; Franklin and Pruett, eds., *Civil War Letters*, p. 7; New York *Daily Tribune*, June 17, 1862; New York *Tribune*, June 18, 1862.

51. *OR*, v. 11, pt. 1, p. 1039; John H. Timberlake–Gertie, June 16, 1862, Timberlake Letters, RNBP; Robert S. Young–Brother, June 18, 1862, Timberlake Letters, RNBP; Richmond *Dispatch*, June 16, 1862; *SHSP*, v. 11, pp. 508–9.

52. *OR*, v. 11, pt. 1, p. 1039; McClellan, *I Rode*, pp. 62, 63; *SHSP*, v. 11, p. 510; Cozzens and Girardi, eds., *New Annals*, pp. 105, 106; Mewborn, "A Wonderful Exploit," *B&G*, v. 15, no. 6, pp. 46, 47; Cooke, *Wearing*, p. 177.

53. *Annals*, pp. 669, 670; Shepherdstown *Register*, April 1, 1882; *OR*, v. 11, pt. 1, p. 1039.

54. *OR*, v. 11, pt. 1, p. 1039; Natchez *Courier*, July 3, 1862; Philadelphia *Weekly Times*, July 19, 1879; Newborn, "A Wonderful Exploit," *B&G*, v. 15, no. 6, pp. 47, 48.

55. *OR*, v. 11, pt. 1, pp. 1005–8, 1011–14, 1017, 1018; Miller, ed., *Peninsula Campaign*, v. 3, p. 120; Mewborn, "A Wonderful Exploit," *B&G*, v. 15, no. 6, pp. 50, 51; *SOR*, v. 2, p. 76.

56. *OR*, v. 11, pt. 1, p. 1039; *SHSP*, v. 11, p. 512; Cozzens and Girardi, eds., *New Annals*, pp. 107, 108; Copland, ed., *Confederate History*, p. 9; Richmond *Dispatch*, June 17, 1862; Mewborn, "A Wonderful Exploit," *B&G*, v. 15, no. 6, p. 49.

57. OR, v. 11, pt. 1, p. 1039; McCabe, *Grayjackets*, p. 365; Bill, *Beleaguered City*, p. 132; Fletcher, Diary, DU.

58. Lasswell, ed., *Rags and Hope*, p. 79.

59. John S. Mosby–My dearest Pauline, June 16, 1862, Mosby Papers, VHS; Longacre, *Lee's Cavalrymen*, p. 93; Bridges, *Lee's Maverick General*, p. 61; Styple, ed., *Writing and Fighting*, p. 110; Wiggins, ed., *Journals*, p. 45.

60. OR, v. 11, pt. 2, p. 490; John Letcher–Mr. President, June 15, 1862, Stuart file, CSR, NA.

61. Trout, *They Followed the Plume*, p. 227; J. O. Collins–Wife, June 18, 1862, Collins Papers, VHS; Freeman, *Lee's Lieutenants*, v. 1, p. 301; Mewborn, "A Wonderful Exploit," *B&G*, v. 15, no. 6, pp. 53, 54; OR, v. 11, pt. 2, p. 514.

62. Thomason, *Jeb Stuart*, p. 137.

63. OR, v. 11, pt. 1, pp. 1041–42.

64. Ibid., p. 1040; Trout, *They Followed the Plume*, pp. 89, 91; Duncan, ed., *Letters*, pp. 25–26; JEBS–My Darling One, January 16, March 20, 1862, Stuart Papers, VHS.

65. Krick, *Staff Officers*, p. 78; Slivka, "Heros Von Borcke's Home," *B&G*, v. 22, no. 4, p. 29; OR, v. 11, pt. 1, p. 1040; Von Borcke, *Memoirs*, v. 1, p. 19.

66. Sorrel, *Recollections*, p. 66; Blackford, *War Years*, p. 69; SOR, v. 2, p. 783; Cleneay, "A Child's Recollection;" Blackford, Annotations, UVA.

67. Blackford, *War Years*, p. 85; Krick, *Staff Officers*, pp. 75, 129; JEBS–General, June 21, 1862, FitzHugh file, CSR, CSA Generals, NA; Eby, ed., *Virginia Yankee*, p. 85; Trout, *They Followed the Plume*, p. 116.

68. Charles E. Bates–Parents, June 19, 1862, Bates Letters, VHS; John O. Collins–Wife, June 18, 21, 1862, Collins Papers, VHS; Driver, *10th Virginia Cavalry*, p. 21; William G. Deloney–My Dear Rosa, June 23, 1862, Deloney Family Papers, UGA; Beale, *Lieutenant of Cavalry*, p. 33.

69. Wert, *General James Longstreet*, pp. 133–34; OR, v. 12, pt. 2, p. 913.

70. Wert, *General James Longstreet*, p. 134; D. H. Hill–My Dear Genl, May 5, 1876, Hill Papers, NC.

71. Dowdey and Manarin, eds., *Wartime Papers*, pp. 198–200.

72. Ibid., p. 199; OR, v. 11, pt. 2, pp. 513, 521, 523; Hartley, *Stuart's Tarheels*, p. 100.

73. Robertson, *Stonewall Jackson*, pp. 468–69; OR, v. 11, pt. 2, pp. 513, 514.

74. Robertson, *Stonewall Jackson*, pp. 429, 469; Freeman, *Lee's Lieutenants*, v. 1, p. 505; OR, v. 11, pt. 2, p. 514; Joseph Jones–Father, July 25, 1862, Jones Papers, NC.

75. Freeman, *Lee's Lieutenants*, v. 1, p. 659; Gallagher, ed., *Richmond Campaign*, pp. 79, 82, 83; Robertson, *Stonewall Jackson*, pp. 470–72.

76. OR, v. 11, pt. 2, pp. 489, 552; Dowdey and Manarin, eds., *Wartime Papers*,

p. 199; analysis of Jackson's performance in Robertson, *Stonewall Jackson*, pp. 471–73.

77. Gallagher, ed., *Fighting For*, pp. 95, 100; Wert, *General James Longstreet*, p. 136.

78. *OR*, v. 11, pt. 2, p. 514; Freeman, *Lee's Lieutenants*, v. 1, p. 633; *Old Homes*, pp. 25, 36; Blackford, *War Years*, p. 71.

79. Wert, *Sword of Lincoln*, pp. 102–3; Diary, Cooke Papers, DU.

80. Wert, *Sword of Lincoln*, pp. 103–5.

81. *OR*, v. 11, pt. 2, pp. 514, 515; Diary, Cooke Papers, DU; Blackford, *War Years*, p. 79.

82. *OR*, v. 11, pt. 2, p. 515; Diary, Cooke Papers, DU; Murray, *My Mother*, p. 131; Blackford, *War Years*, pp. 73–74.

83. R. L. Dabney–My Dear Sir, March 3, 1896, Hotchkiss Papers, LC; Memoir, Allan Papers, UNC; *OR*, v. 11, pt. 2, p. 515; Diary, Cooke Papers, DU; Gallagher, ed., *Richmond Campaign*, p. 77.

84. Wert, *Sword of Lincoln*, pp. 106–7.

85. Wert, *General James Longstreet*, pp. 139–40; *OR*, v. 11, pt. 2, p. 515.

86. *OR*, v. 11, pt. 2, pp. 493, 515; Maurice, ed., *Aide-de-Camp of Lee*, pp. 104, 105; Freeman, *R. E. Lee*, v. 2, pp. 159–65; Murray, *My Mother*, p. 131.

87. *OR*, v. 11, pt. 2, pp. 516, 517; William G. Deloney–My Dear Rosa, June 29, 1862, Deloney Family Papers, UGA; Beale, *Lieutenant of Cavalry*, p. 36.

88. *OR*, v. 11, pt. 2, p. 517; Blackford, Annotations, UVA; R. W. Chilton–JEBS, June 29, 1862, Stuart Papers, HL.

89. *OR*, v. 11, pt. 2, p. 517; Robertson, *Stonewall Jackson*, p. 488.

90. Wert, *General James Longstreet*, pp. 140–41; Greene, *Whatever You Resolve to Be*, p. 60; *OR*, v. 11, pt. 2, pp. 494, 556.

91. *OR*, v. 11, pt. 2, pp. 494, 680, 687; a defense of Jackson's actions is presented in Robertson, *Stonewall Jackson*, pp. 488–90.

92. Gallagher, ed., *Fighting For*, p. 109; Wert, *Sword of Lincoln*, pp. 113–14.

93. Wert, *Sword of Lincoln*, pp. 113–17, quote on p. 117; Freeman, *Lee's Lieutenants*, v. 1, pp. 575, 576; Robertson, *Stonewall Jackson*, pp. 493–96.

94. Wert, *General James Longstreet*, pp. 146–47, 148, 149.

95. Ibid., pp. 148, 149; *OR*, v. 11, pt. 2, p. 496.

96. *OR*, v. 11, pt. 2, pp. 517, 518; JEBS–Col. Lee, July 1, 1862, Stuart Letter . . . Fitz Lee, NYHS; R. H. Chilton–JEBS, July 1, 1862, Stuart Papers, HL; Von Borcke, *Memoirs*, v. 1, p. 73.

97. *OR*, v. 11, pt. 2, p. 519; Memo, July 1, 1862, Stuart Papers, HL; JEBS–General, July 2, 1862, Stuart Letter . . . R. E. Lee, NYHS.

98. John Pelham–JEBS, July 3, 1862, Stuart Papers, DU; *OR*, v. 11, pt. 2, p. 519; Special Orders, July 2, 1862; R. E. Lee–JEBS, July 3, 1862, Stuart Papers, HL.

99. OR, v. 11, pt. 2, p. 520; McClellan, I Rode, p. 173; SOR, v. 2, p. 89; Murray, My Mother, p. 133.

100. JEBS–My Darling Wife, July 5, 1862, Stuart Papers, VHS; Wise, Long Arm, p. 233; Venable, "Personal Reminiscences," p. 51, UVA; Taylor, Four Years, p. 41.

101. Wert, General James Longstreet, pp. 150, 151; OR, v. 11, pt. 2, pp. 497, 521; Gallagher, ed., Fighting For, p. 96; Gallagher, ed., Richmond Campaign, pp. 13, 17, 79, 82, 83; Freeman, Lee's Lieutenants, v. 1, pp. 633, 659.

Chapter 7: "Great Spirits of the Land"

1. Von Borcke, Memoirs, v. 1, p. 82; Annals, p. 672; Blackford, War Years, p. 87; William G. Deloney–My Dear Rosa, July 15, 1862, Deloney Family Papers, UGA; John O. Collins–Wife, July 21, 1862, Collins Papers, VHS; Leonard Williams–My Dear Anna, July 19, 1862, "Civil War Letters," USAMHI.

2. Blackford, War Years, p. 87; Von Borcke, Memoirs, v. 1, p. 82; JEBS–My Darling One, February 14, 1862, Stuart Papers, VHS; Bill, Beleaguered City, p. 141.

3. Pearce, ed., Diary, p. 51; Haskell, Haskell Memoirs, p. 20; Jones, Rebel War Clerk's Diary, v. 1, p. 147; Priest, ed., One Surgeon's Private War, p. 39.

4. Stuart file, CSR, NA; Commission, Major General, July 25, 1862; R. E. Lee–JEBS, July 27, 1862; T. J. Jackson–JEBS, July 31, 1862, Stuart Papers, VHS.

5. R. E. Lee–JEBS, July 27, 1862; T. J. Jackson–JEBS, July 31, 1862; A. L. Long–JEBS, July 27, 1862, Stuart Papers, VHS; OR, v. 12, pt. 3, p. 920.

6. OR, v. 12, pt. 2, p. 550; pt. 3, p. 920; Krick, Stonewall Jackson, pp. 8, 9.

7. Cisco, Wade Hampton, pp. 17, 31, 83, 85, 86, 91; Longacre, Gentleman, pp. 81, 83, 123; James Griffin–My Darling Wife, July 27, 1861, Griffin Letters, USAMHI.

8. Freeman, Lee's Lieutenants, v. 1, pp. 93, 94; Sorrel, Recollections, p. 249; Cooke, Wearing, p. 54; William G. Deloney–My Dear Rosa, August 29, 1862, Deloney Family Papers, UGA.

9. Sorrel, Recollections, p. 249; Cooke, Wearing, pp. 48, 49, 52; Freeman, Lee's Lieutenants, v. 1, p. 94.

10. Cooke, Wearing, pp. 49, 51, 52; Longacre, Lee's Cavalrymen, p. 105.

11. R. E. Lee–JEBS, July 27, 1862, Stuart Papers, VHS; JEBS–My Dear General, July 24, 1862, Heritage Auction Galleries, p. 61; James Longstreet–My Dear General Munford, September 9, 1894, Munford–Ellis Family Papers, DU; Burton H. Harrison–JEBS, August 12, 1862, Stuart Papers, HL.

12. Driver, 5th Virginia Cavalry, pp. 1, 2; Proceedings, pp. 48, 70, 71; Mitchell, ed., Letters . . . Stuart, p. 257.

13. *Proceedings*, p. 7; Fitzhugh, Memoirs, p. 18, MC; Anderson, War Record, p. 3, VHS.

14. *Proceedings*, pp. 7, 56, 67, 73; JEBS–George W. Randolph, June 26, 1862, Letters Received . . . Confederate AIGO, NA.

15. *Proceedings*, pp. 5, 11, 14, 52, 53.

16. Ibid., pp. 3, 4, 6–9, 24, 68, 69.

17. Cooke, *Wearing*, p. 17; Thomas L. Rosser–My Dearest Wife, November 18, 1863, Gordon and Rosser Family Papers, UVA.

18. William G. Deloney–My Dear Rosa, July 21, 1862, Deloney Family Papers, UGA.

19. Trout, ed., *With Pen and Saber*, p. 84; OR, v. 12, pt. 3, p. 916; Wert, *General James Longstreet*, p. 157.

20. Wert, *General James Longstreet*, pp. 156–57.

21. Ibid., pp. 156, 157; Dowdey and Manarin, eds., *Wartime Papers*, p. 239.

22. Blackford, *War Years*, p. 88; R. E. Lee–JEBS, July 22, 23, 1862, Stuart Papers, HL; OR, v. 12, pt. 2, pp. 119, 725; v. 51, pt. 2, p. 594; Wert, *Mosby's Rangers*, p. 30.

23. Von Borcke, *Memoirs*, v. 1, p. 86; Trout, ed., *With Pen and Saber*, pp. 84, 90; OR, v. 12, pt. 2, pp. 119–21, 177; pt. 3, p. 925; R. E. Lee–JEBS, July 30, 1862, Stuart Papers, HL; Carter, *Sabres*, pp. 7, 8.

24. Thomas Munford–Jedediah Hotchkiss, August 23, 1896, Hotchkiss Papers, LC; Krick, *Stonewall Jackson*, p. 9; T. J. Jackson–JEBS, August 7, 1862, Stuart Papers, HL.

25. SOR, v. 2, p. 592; the finest account of Cedar Mountain is Krick, *Stonewall Jackson*, Chapters 7–14, casualty figures on pp. 372, 376.

26. OR, v. 12, pt. 2, p. 184; Pfanz, *Richard S. Ewell*, p. 243; McDonald, ed., *Make Me a Map*, p. 67; JEBS–General, August 13, 1862, Stuart Papers, VHS.

27. OR, v. 12, pt. 2, p. 143; SOR, v. 2, p. 592; Blackford, *War Years*, p. 111; Eby, ed., *Virginia Yankee*, p. 80; Chiswell Dabney–Mother, August 13, 1862, Saunders Family Papers, VHS; Turnwold, *Countryman*, August 23, 1862; Sutherland, *Seasons*, p. 162.

28. Trout, ed., *With Pen and Saber*, p. 90; JEBS–General, August 13, 1862, Stuart Papers, VHS.

29. JEBS–General, August 13, 1862, Stuart Papers, VHS.

30. OR, v. 12, pt. 2, pp. 551–52.

31. Wert, *General James Longstreet*, pp. 157–58.

32. Ibid., p. 158.

33. Mitchell, ed., *Letters . . . Stuart*, pp. 259, 419n; Krick, *Staff Officers*, p. 247; Freeman, *Lee's Lieutenants*, v. 2, pp. 442, 443; Nannie O. Price–Mrs. Stuart, May 15, [1864], Stuart Papers, VHS.

34. Mitchell, ed., *Letters . . . Stuart*, p. 343; Blackford, *War Years*, p. 97; Hennessy, *Return to Bull Run*, p. 43; Von Borcke, *Memoirs*, v. 1, pp. 102–3.

35. Von Borcke, *Memoirs*, v. 1, pp. 103, 104; Wert, *General James Longstreet*, p. 158; OR, v. 12, pt. 2, p. 726; Mewborn, ed., "*From Mosby's Command*," pp. 118, 119.

36. OR, v. 12, pt. 2, p. 726; Scott, *History of Orange County*, p. 179; Neese, *Three Years*, p. 213; Mitchell, ed., *Letters . . . Stuart*, p. 247.

37. OR, v. 12, pt. 2, p. 726; Mewborn, ed., "*From Mosby's Command*," p. 119; JEBS–My Dear Wife, August 19, 1862, Stuart Papers, VHS.

38. Mewborn, ed., "*From Mosby's Command*," p. 141; Hennessy, *Return to Bull Run*, pp. 42, 46, 47, 48; Wert, *General James Longstreet*, pp. 158, 159.

39. OR, v. 12, pt. 2, p. 726; Hennessy, *Return to Bull Run*, pp. 48, 49; Wert, *General James Longstreet*, p. 160.

40. Venable, "Personal Reminiscences," p. 53, UVA; OR, v. 12, pt. 2, pp. 552, 726; pt. 3, p. 934; Maurice, ed., *Aide-de-Camp of Lee*, p. 125; Wert, *General James Longstreet*, p. 160.

41. OR, v. 12, pt. 2, p. 726; Alexander, *Military Memoirs*, p. 187; Freeman, *Lee's Lieutenants*, v. 2, p. 60.

42. OR, v. 12, pt. 2, pp. 726, 728, 745, 746; SOR, v. 2, pp. 594, 783, 784; Neese, *Three Years*, pp. 96, 97; Wert, *General James Longstreet*, p. 160; Freeman, *Lee's Lieutenants*, v. 2, pp. 68, 69.

43. OR, v. 12, pt. 2, pp. 553, 730; Wert, *General James Longstreet*, pp. 160–61.

44. OR, v. 12, pt. 2, p. 731; Sutherland, *Seasons*, p. 185; Trout, ed., *They Followed the Plume*, p. 254; Hennessy, *Return to Bull Run*, pp. 74, 76; Stiles, *4th Virginia Cavalry*, p. 17.

45. OR, v. 12, pt. 2, p. 731; Franklin and Pruett, eds., *Civil War Letters*, p. 18; Blackford, *War Years*, p. 101; Hennessy, *Return to Bull Run*, pp. 76, 77; Scheel, *Civil War in Fauquier County*, p. 33.

46. OR, v. 12, pt. 2, p. 731; Newspaper clipping, Hotchkiss Papers, LC; Driver, *1st Virginia Cavalry*, p. 44; CV, v. 36, p. 303; Blackford, *War Years*, p. 102.

47. OR, v. 12, pt. 2, p. 731; Chiswell Dabney–Father, September 10, 1862, Saunders Family Papers, VHS; Blackford, *War Years*, pp. 102–3.

48. OR, v. 12, pt. 2, p. 731; Blackford, *War Years*, pp. 105–7; Dowdey and Manarin, ed., *Wartime Papers*, p. 262.

49. OR, v. 12, pt. 2, pp. 731–32; Neese, *Three Years*, p. 102.

50. JEBS–My Dear Wife, August 19, 25, 1862, Stuart Papers, VHS; Sorrel, *Recollections*, p. 92; Douglas, *I Rode*, p. 133; Blackford, *War Years*, p. 107; Freeman, *Lee's Lieutenants*, v. 2, p. 72; Cozzens and Girardi, eds., *New Annals*, p. 115.

51. Scheel, *Civil War in Fauquier County*, p. 34; Dowdey and Manarin, eds., *Wartime Papers*, p. 262; Wert, *General James Longstreet*, pp. 161–62.

52. *OR*, v. 12, pt. 3, p. 941; Freeman, *R. E. Lee*, v. 2, pp. 298, 299.

53. *OR*, v. 12, pt. 2, pp. 553, 554; Cozzens and Girardi, eds., *New Annals*, p. 113; Driver and Howard, *2nd Virginia Cavalry*, p. 55; Wert, *General James Longstreet*, p. 162.

54. McDonald, ed., *Make Me a Map*, p. 118; Wert, *General James Longstreet*, p. 162.

55. McDonald, ed., *Make Me a Map*, p. 118; Columbus *Daily Sun*, August 28, 1862.

56. *SOR*, v. 4, p. 499; John S. Mosby–General Fitzhugh Lee, December 28, 1895, Coleman Papers, VHS; James Power Smith–My dearest Sister, August 19, 1862, Smith Correspondence, MC.

57. *OR*, v. 12, pt. 2, pp. 643, 747; Hassler, ed., *General to His Lady*, p. 164; Wert, *General James Longstreet*, pp. 162–63.

58. *OR*, v. 12, pt. 2, pp. 643, 733, 734; *SOR*, v. 2, p. 597.

59. *CV*, v. 34, p. 221; Robertson, *Stonewall Jackson*, p. 551.

60. *OR*, v. 12, pt. 2, pp. 633, 734; Wert, "His Unhonored Service," *CWTI*, v. 24, no. 4, pp. 29, 30, 33.

61. *OR*, v. 12, pt. 2, p. 643; Hennessy, *Return to Bull Run*, pp. 111–12.

62. Wert, *General James Longstreet*, p. 163; Sorrel, *Recollections*, p. 90.

63. *OR*, v. 12, pt. 2, pp. 643, 734; Warner, *Generals in Gray*, p. 310; Hennessy, *Return to Bull Run*, p. 113.

64. *OR*, v. 12, pt. 2, pp. 643, 720, 721, 734, 741.

65. *OR*, v. 12, pt. 2, pp. 721, 741–42; Hennessy, *Return to Bull Run*, pp. 113–15.

66. *OR*, v. 12, pt. 2, pp. 721, 742.

67. Wert, *Brotherhood*, pp. 141, 142; Robertson, *Stonewall Jackson*, p. 557.

68. Wert, *Brotherhood*, p. 141; Hennessy, *Return to Bull Run*, pp. 125–27.

69. *OR*, v. 12, pt. 2, p. 734; Boyd, "Boyhood," p. 44, Boyd Papers, LSU.

70. Wert, *Brotherhood*, p. 142; *OR*, v. 12, pt. 2, pp. 644, 645, 734; Taliaferro, "Personal Reminiscences," *CWTI*, v. 34, no. 2, p. 64.

71. Hennessy, *Return to Bull Run*, pp. 116–17; Wert, *General James Longstreet*, pp. 163–66.

72. Hennessy, *Return to Bull Run*, Chapters 11–16, quote on p. 248. Hennessy's book is the finest work on the campaign.

73. Ibid., p. 225; *OR*, v. 12, pt. 2, p. 736; McDonald, ed., *Make Me a Map*, p. 73; C. L. Gatewood–My Dear Sister, September 3, 1862, Gatewood Papers, VMI; Gallagher, ed., *Lee the Soldier*, pp. 16–17.

74. Wert, *General James Longstreet*, pp. 167–69; James Longstreet–Fitz John Porter, September 23, 1866, Daniel Papers; Venable, "Personal Reminiscences," pp. 55, 56, UVA.

75. *OR*, v. 12, pt. 2, pp. 565, 736; Wert, *General James Longstreet*, pp. 169–72; Blackford, *War Years*, pp. 126–27.

76. Wert, *General James Longstreet*, pp. 170–71; Blackford, *War Years*, pp. 128, 130; OR, v. 12, pt. 2, p. 736.

77. Wert, *General James Longstreet*, pp. 175, 176.

78. Ibid., pp. 177, 178; OR, v. 12, pt. 2, p. 565.

79. OR, v. 12, pt. 2, pp. 737, 746; Hennessy, *Return to Bull Run*, pp. 430–32; Thomas Garber–Father, September 25, 1862, Garber Family Papers, ACHS.

80. OR, v. 12, pt. 2, pp. 737, 746, 747, 748; Thomas Garber–Father, September 25, 1862, Garber Family Papers, ACHS; Hennessy, *Return to Bull Run*, pp. 433–35.

81. Wert, *General James Longstreet*, p. 178.

82. OR, v. 12, no. 2, pp. 737, 743–45; JEBS–My Darling One, September 4, 1862, Stuart Papers, VHS.

83. Harsh, *Taken at the Flood*, pp. 11–12, 16–19; SOR, v. 2, p. 601.

84. Hassler, ed., *General to His Lady*, p. 173; Wert, *General James Longstreet*, p. 179; Gallagher, ed., *Fighting For*, p. 128.

85. OR, v. 12, pt. 2, pp. 558, 641; Cozzens, ed., *B&L*, v. 5, p. 135.

86. OR, v. 12, pt. 2, p. 744; v. 19, pt. 2, p. 590.

Chapter 8: "We Cannot Afford to Be Idle"

1. R. Channing Price–Mother, September 10, 1862, Price Papers, UNC; Carter, *Sabres*, p. 12; Tower, ed., *Lee's Adjutant*, p. 43; Wert, *Brotherhood*, p. 163.

2. Dowdey and Manarin, eds., *Wartime Papers*, pp. 292, 293, 294.

3. Harsh, *Taken at the Flood*, pp. 150–51, 162.

4. Ibid., pp. 71, 86, 89, 93; Gallagher, ed., *Lee the Soldier*, p. 8; OR, v. 19, pt. 2, p. 595.

5. Thomas T. Munford–E. A. Carman, April 7, 1896; Thomas T. Munford–George B. Davis, December 16, 1894, Carman Papers, NYPL; OR, v. 12, pt. 3, p. 934; v. 19, pt. 1, p. 810.

6. Von Borcke, *Memoirs*, v. 1, pp. 182–87; William G. Deloney–My Dear Rosa, September 10, 1862, Deloney Family Papers, UGA; Richard H. Watkins–Darling, September 7, 1862, Watkins Papers, VHS; Carter, *Sabres*, p. 12.

7. OR, v. 19, pt. 1, pp. 810, 815, 825; SOR, v. 3, p. 498; Map, Fitz Lee's Cav & Rosser, LC; Harsh, *Taken at the Flood*, pp. 104, 107, 108, 162; Von Borcke, *Memoirs*, v. 1, pp. 187, 188.

8. Richard H. Watkins–Darling, September 7, 1862, Watkins Papers, VHS; OR, v. 19, pt. 1, pp. 815–16, 828; Thomas Garber–Sister, September 17, 1862, Garber Family Papers, ACHS; Harrison A. Shuler–Father, September 9, 1862, Shuler Letters, EU; Klein, ed., *Just South*, pp. 25, 38; Richmond *Dispatch*, July 16, 1897.

9. OR, v. 19, pt. 1, p. 815; Harsh, *Taken at the Flood*, p. 115; William G. Delo-ney–My Dear Rosa, September 10, 1862, Deloney Family Papers, UGA.

10. JEBS–My Darling One, September 12, 1862, Stuart Papers, VHS.

11. Johnson, *In the Footsteps*, p. 116; Thomas T. Munford–My dear Sir, January 21, 1898, Ropes Papers, BU; Von Borcke, *Memoirs*, v. 1, pp. 192, 193.

12. Stanicoff House description, copy in possession of Krick; Von Borcke, *Memoirs*, v. 1, pp. 194–97.

13. OR, v. 19, pt. 1, pp. 815, 825; Harsh, *Taken at the Flood*, pp. 121, 122; Wert, *Sword of Lincoln*, pp. 137–38, 147.

14. Wert, *Sword of Lincoln*, pp. 138, 139.

15. Ibid., pp. 144–47; Schildt, *Roads to Antietam*, pp. 43–44.

16. Wert, *General James Longstreet*, pp. 182–83.

17. OR, v. 19, p. 2, pp. 603–4.

18. An analysis of Lee's plans for Special Orders No. 191 is in Harsh, *Taken at the Flood*, Chapter 3, quote on p. 167; OR, v. 19, pt. 1, p. 145.

19. OR, v. 19, pt. 1, p. 815; Harsh, *Taken at the Flood*, pp. 68, 121, 122, 130, 148; R. Channing Price–Mother, September 10, 1862, Price Papers, UNC; Schildt, *Roads to Antietam*, pp. 57, 60.

20. Gallagher, ed., *Lee the Soldier*, pp. 25–26; Harsh, *Taken at the Flood*, pp. 180, 181; Von Borcke, *Memoirs*, v. 1, p. 198; OR, v. 19, pt. 1, pp. 815, 821.

21. OR, v. 19, pt. 1, pp. 815–16, 822; R. E. Lee–JEBS, September 12, 1862, Stu-art Papers, HL; Augusta *Daily Constitutionist*, October 2, 1862; Bryce, "Battle of South Mountain," p. 11, ANB; Von Borcke, *Memoirs*, v. 1, pp. 201–2.

22. R. E. Lee–JEBS, September 12, 1862, Stuart Papers, HL; OR, v. 19, pt. 1, p. 816; Harsh, *Taken at the Flood*, pp. 205–6; G. F. Beale–E. A. Carman, June 30, 1897, Carman Collection, NA.

23. R. E. Lee–JEBS, September 12, 1862, Stuart Papers, HL; OR, v. 19, pt. 2, p. 603; Harsh, *Taken at the Flood*, pp. 196–97.

24. OR, v. 10, pt. 1, p. 816.

25. OR, v. 19, pt. 1, pp. 816, 817, 824, 825; Bryce, "Battle of South Mountain," p. 13, ANB; Harsh, *Taken at the Flood*, pp. 231, 232; Von Borcke, *Memoirs*, v. 1, pp. 209–12.

26. Wert, *Sword of Lincoln*, pp. 148, 149; OR, v. 19, pt. 2, p. 281.

27. Wert, *Sword of Lincoln*, pp. 49–51.

28. Harsh, *Taken at the Flood*, pp. 232–33; R. E. Lee–JEBS, September 14, 1862, Stuart Papers, HL; Gallagher, ed., *Lee the Soldier*, p. 26.

29. OR, v. 19, pt. 1, pp. 417, 817, 823; Harsh, *Taken at the Flood*, p. 236.

30. OR, v. 19, pt. 1, pp. 817, 1052; Harsh, *Taken at the Flood*, p. 234; Bryce, "Battle of South Mountain," p. 13, ANB.

31. OR, v. 19, pt. 1, p. 817; Von Borcke, *Memoirs*, v. 1, p. 212; Harsh, *Taken at the Flood*, p. 244.

32. Von Borcke, *Memoirs*, v. 1, p. 213; R. Channing Price–Mother, September 18, 1862, Price Papers, UNC; *OR*, v. 19, pt. 1, p. 1019.

33. *OR*, v. 19, pt. 1, p. 1019; Wert, *General James Longstreet*, pp. 187–88; D. H. Hill–James Longstreet, February 11, 1885, Longstreet Papers, DU.

34. *OR*, v. 19, pt. 1, p. 817; Gallagher, ed., *Lee the Soldier*, p. 26.

35. R. E. Lee–JEBS, September 14, 1862, Stuart Papers, HL; R. Channing Price–Mother, September 18, 1862, Price Papers, UNC.

36. R. Channing Price–Mother, September 18, 1862, Price Papers, UNC; Von Borcke, *Memoirs*, v. 1, p. 213; *OR*, v. 19, pt. 1, p. 817; Bridges, *Lee's Maverick General*, p. 103; Harsh, *Taken at the Flood*, p. 275.

37. Wert, *General James Longstreet*, pp. 189–90; Stiles, *Four Years*, p. 65; Sorrel, *Recollections*, p. 101.

38. *OR*, v. 19, pt. 1, pp. 818, 824, 826; Harsh, *Taken at the Flood*, p. 275; R. Channing Price–Mother, September 18, 1862, Price Papers, UNC; Thomas T. Munford–E. A. Carman, December 10, 1894, Carman Papers, NYPL.

39. Von Borcke, *Memoirs*, v. 1, p. 215; Wert, *Sword of Lincoln*, p. 154; Thomas T. Munford–E. A. Carman, December 10, 1894, Carman Papers, NYPL.

40. Von Borcke, *Memoirs*, v. 1, p. 216; R. Channing Price–Mother, September 18, 1862, Price Papers, UNC; *OR*, v. 19, pt. 1, pp. 818, 854; Lafayette McLaws–My Dear McBride, July 3, 1895, McBride Papers, AHS.

41. R. Channing Price–Mother, September 18, 1862, Price Papers, UNC; *OR*, v. 19, pt. 1, pp. 819, 827, 854; Lafayette McLaws–My Dear McBride, July 3, 1895, McBride Papers, AHS.

42. *OR*, v. 19, pt. 1, pp. 819, 855; R. Channing Price–Mother, September 18, 1862, Price Papers, UNC; Von Borcke, *Memoirs*, v. 1, pp. 218–19; Lafayette McLaws–My Dear McBride, July 3, 1895, McBride Papers, AHS.

43. Wert, *Brotherhood*, p. 173; Robertson, *Stonewall Jackson*, pp. 602–5; Von Borcke, *Memoirs*, v. 1, p. 219; Thomas T. Munford–My dear Sir, January 21, 1898, Ropes Papers, BU.

44. *OR*, v. 19, pt. 1, p. 819; Blackford, Annotations, UVA; R. Channing Price–Mother, September 18, 1862, Price Papers, UNC; *National Tribune*, October 5, 1893; Harsh, *Taken at the Flood*, p. 323; Anderson, War Record, p. 6, VHS.

45. *OR*, v. 19, pt. 1, p. 819; Carter, *Sabres*, p. 15; Richmond *Dispatch*, July 16, 1897; R. B. Lewis–E. A. Carman, May 8, 1897; G. F. Beale–E. A. Carman, June 6, 30, 1897; Account of James W. Moore, n.d., Carman Collection, NA; Richard H. Watkins–Darling, September 18, 1862, Watkins Papers, VHS; Nanzig, *3rd Virginia Cavalry*, p. 21.

46. Wert, *Sword of Lincoln*, pp. 150, 155; R. E. Lee–My dear Mrs. Jackson, January 25, 1866, Lee Letter, WLU.

47. Wert, *Sword of Lincoln*, p. 155; Gallagher, ed., *Fighting For*, pp. 145–47.

48. Wert, *Sword of Lincoln*, p. 155; Wert, *Brotherhood*, p. 174.

49. Wert, *Sword of Lincoln*, pp. 155–57.

50. *OR*, v. 19, pt. 1, p. 819; Harsh, *Taken at the Flood*, pp. 333, 337; Gallagher, ed., *Antietam Campaign*, p. 198; R. Channing Price–Mother, September 18, 1862, Price Papers, UNC; Krick, *Parker's Virginia Battery*, p. 49.

51. Harsh, *Taken at the Flood*, pp. 344, 354; Wert, *Sword of Lincoln*, p. 157.

52. Harsh, *Taken at the Flood*, p. 355; Von Borcke, *Memoirs*, v. 1, p. 229; Wade Hampton–JEBS, September 16, 1862, Stuart Papers, HL; R. Channing Price–Mother, September 18, 1862, Price Papers, UNC.

53. Douglas, *I Rode*, p. 196; Cooke, *Wearing*, p. 120; Blackford, *War Years*, p. 90; Wise, *Long Arm*, p. 349.

54. *OR*, v. 19, pt. 1, pp. 819–20; Gallagher, ed., *Antietam Campaign*, pp. 196, 201, 202; Wert, *Sword of Lincoln*, pp. 159, 160.

55. Wert, *Sword of Lincoln*, p. 159; Wert, *Brotherhood*, p. 185.

56. *OR*, v. 19, pt. 1, pp. 820, 956, 968, 969; Gallagher, ed., *Antietam Campaign*, pp. 204, 205.

57. *OR*, v. 19, pt. 1, pp. 820, 969; Gallagher, ed., *Antietam Campaign*, pp. 206, 207.

58. Gallagher, ed., *Antietam Campaign*, pp. 208, 210; Wert, *Sword of Lincoln*, pp. 162–63.

59. *OR*, v. 19, pt. 1, pp. 820, 956; Gallagher, ed., *Antietam Campaign*, p. 211; Carman, "Maryland Campaign," Chapter 18, Carman Papers, LC; Lafayette McLaws–General Heth, December 13, 1894, Carman Papers, NYPL; R. Channing Price–Mother, September 18, 1862, Price Papers, UNC.

60. Wert, *Sword of Lincoln*, pp. 163–67, 168–69; *OR*, v. 19, pt. 1, p. 956; Harsh, *Taken at the Flood*, pp. 407–9.

61. In his report Stuart erroneously placed this movement on September 18, *OR*, v. 19, pt. 1, p. 820; Harsh, *Taken at the Flood*, pp. 410–11; Gallagher, ed., *Antietam Campaign*, p. 211.

62. Carman, "Maryland Campaign," Chapter 18, Carman Papers, LC; *OR*, v. 19, pt. 1, pp. 956–57; Harsh, *Taken at the Flood*, p. 411; Poague, *Gunner with Stonewall*, p. 47.

63. Poague, *Gunner with Stonewall*, p. 47; *OR*, v. 19, pt. 1, p. 1010; Carman, "Maryland Campaign," Chapter 18, Carman Papers, LC; Lafayette McLaws–General Heth, December 13, 1894, Carman Papers, NYPL.

64. Poague, *Gunner with Stonewall*, pp. 47, 48; Carman, "Maryland Campaign," Chapter 18, Carman Papers, LC; Harsh, *Taken at the Flood*, p. 413.

65. Wert, *Sword of Lincoln*, p. 169; Richard H. Watkins–[Wife], September 22, 1862, Watkins Papers, VHS.

66. Douglas, *I Rode*, p. 174; Tower, ed., *Lee's Adjutant*, p. 44; *OR*, v. 19, pt. 1, p. 151.

67. OR, v. 19, pt. 1, p. 151; Wert, *General James Longstreet*, pp. 200–201; Harsh, *Taken at the Flood*, p. 429.

68. Harsh, *Taken at the Flood*, pp. 441–43; Wert, *General James Longstreet*, p. 201; Gallagher, ed., *Fighting For*, p. 92.

69. OR, v. 19, pt. 1, pp. 142, 151, 820; Blackford, *War Years*, p. 152; R. E. Lee–My dear Mrs. Jackson, January 25, 1866, Lee Letter, WLU; Tower, ed., *Lee's Adjutant*, p. 46.

70. Blackford, *War Years*, p. 152.

71. Ibid., pp. 152–53; OR, v. 19, pt. 1, pp. 820, 824.

72. Von Borcke, *Memoirs*, v. 1, pp. 240, 241; McDonald, ed., *Make Me a Map*, p. 83.

73. Von Borcke, *Memoirs*, v. 1, pp. 241–43; McDonald, ed., *Make Me a Map*, p. 83; OR, v. 19, pt. 1, pp. 820, 824; Blackford, *War Years*, p. 153; Harsh, *Taken at the Flood*, pp. 450, 451; Pierce, "Autobiography," pp. 21, 22, Handley Library.

74. R. H. Chilton–JEBS, September 20, 1862, Stuart Papers, HL; OR, v. 19, pt. 1, pp. 152, 820, 821, 824; v. 51, pt. 1, p. 851; Von Borcke, *Memoirs*, v. 1, pp. 252–53, 255, 256; William G. Deloney–My Dear Rosa, September 23, 1862, Deloney Family Papers, UGA; Harsh, *Taken at the Flood*, p. 466.

75. OR, v. 19, pt. 1, p. 152; R. Channing Price–Sister, September 25, 1862, Price Papers, UNC; JEBS–My Darling Wife, September 22, 1862, Stuart Papers, VHS.

76. OR, v. 19, pt. 1, pp. 151, 957.

77. Diary, Cooke Papers, DU.

Chapter 9: To Pennsylvania and Back

1. Douglas, *I Rode*, p. 193.

2. Ibid., p. 193; Cozzens, ed., *B&L*, v. 5, p. 135.

3. Douglas, *I Rode*, p. 196; Greene, *Whatever You Resolve to Be*, p. 172.

4. Von Borcke, *Memoirs*, v. 1, pp. 295–96; Smith, *With Stonewall Jackson*, p. 22.

5. T. J. Jackson–JEBS, September 30, 1862, Stuart Papers, HL.

6. William G. Deloney–My Dear Rosa, October 6, 1862, Deloney Family Papers, UGA; Gallagher, ed., *Fighting For*, p. 155; OR, v. 19, pt. 2, p. 660.

7. John Bolling–Sir, September 24, 1862, Armistead and Blanton Family Papers, VHS; Harrison A. Shuler–Father, September 25, 1862, Shuler Letters, EU; Blackford, *War Years*, p. 154; OR, v. 19, pt. 2, p. 660; R. E. Lee–JEBS, September 23, 1862, Stuart Papers, HL.

8. Von Borcke, *Memoirs*, v. 1, p. 273; John Bolling–Sir, September 24, 1862, Armistead and Blanton Family Papers, VHS; Driver, *1st Virginia Cavalry*, p. 47.

9. Von Borcke, *Memoirs*, v. 1, pp. 273, 274; Driver, *1st Virginia Cavalry*, pp. 47, 48.

10. Driver, *1st Virginia Cavalry*, p. 48; CV, v. 37, p. 198; Von Borcke, *Memoirs*, v. 1, pp. 275, 276.

11. Blackford, *War Years*, p. 154; Chiswell Dabney–Mother, October 21, 1862, Saunders Family Papers, VHS; Thompson, *Horses*, p. 2; "Album," *MJCHS*, v. 24, pp. 9, 11.

12. "Album," *MJCHS*, v. 24, p. 10; Blackford, *War Years*, pp. 154–58; Von Borcke, *Memoirs*, v. 1, pp. 268, 269; Chiswell Dabney–Mother, October 21, 1862, Saunders Family Papers, VHS.

13. Mitchell, ed., *Letters . . . Stuart*, p. 270; JEBS–My Darling One, October 1, 1862, Stuart Papers, VHS.

14. Lee, *Recollections*, pp. 250, 251; SHSP, v. 18, p. 390, 391; Johnson, *In the Footsteps*, p. 100.

15. R. Channing Price–Mother, October 15, 1862, Price Papers, UNC; Blackford, *War Years*, p. 162; Gallagher, ed., *Fighting For*, p. 140; James Longstreet–Louis T. Wigfall, October 9, 1862, Longstreet Papers, NC; OR, v. 19, pt. 1, p. 152.

16. OR, v. 19, pt. 2, p. 55.

17. Ibid., pp. 52, 57; JEBS–R. H. Chilton, October 14, 1862, Stuart Collection, MC; Julian Edwards–My dear Parents, October 15, 1862, Edwards Letter, VHS; T. J. Jackson–JEBS, n.d., Stuart Papers, VHS; Thompson, *Horses*, pp. 9, 10, 12.

18. R. Channing Price–Mother, October 15, 1862, Price Papers, UNC; McClellan, *I Rode*, p. 138; Julian Edwards–My dear Parents, October 15, 1862, Edwards Letter, VHS.

19. OR, v. 19, pt. 2, pp. 55–56.

20. Ibid., pp. 52, 57; R. Channing Price–Mother, October 15, 1862, Price Papers, UNC; Thompson, *Horses*, pp. 15, 20, 22; Conrad and Alexander, *When War Passed This Way*, p. 89.

21. OR, v. 19, pt. 2, pp. 52, 57; McClellan, *I Rode*, p. 139; Chiswell Dabney–Mother, October 21, 1862, Saunders Family Papers, VHS; Thompson, *Horses*, pp. 23, 25, 27, 30.

22. Chiswell Dabney–Mother, October 21, 1862, Saunders Family Papers, VHS; OR, v. 19, pt. 2, p. 56.

23. Thompson, *Horses*, p. 12; Blackford, *War Years*, p. 166; Richard H. Watkins–My Precious Mary, October 15, 1862, Watkins Papers, VHS.

24. Corson, *My Dear Jennie*, p. 96; Richard H. Watkins–My Precious Mary, October 15, 1862, Watkins Papers, VHS; Lafayette J. Carneal–Papa, October 15, 1862, Carneal Letters, VHS; Julian T. Edwards–My dear Parents, October 15, 1862, Edwards Letter, VHS.

25. Corson, *My Dear Jennie*, p. 97; Julian T. Edwards–My dear Parents, October 15, 1862, Edwards Letter, VHS.

26. Thompson, *Horses*, pp. 39, 41–45, 46, 47; Philadelphia *Weekly Times*, April 10, 1886; Julian T. Edwards–My dear Parents, October 15, 1862, Edwards Letter, VHS; Nanzig, *3rd Virginia Cavalry*, p. 23; Trout, *Galloping Thunder*, p. 117.

27. Thompson, *Horses*, pp. 49, 54, 55; Julian T. Edwards–My dear Parents, October 15, 1862, Edwards Letter, VHS; Hoke, *Historical Reminiscences*, p. 29; Account of General J. E. B. Stuart Capture, p. 1, USAMHI.

28. Account of General J. E. B. Stuart Capture, pp. 1, 2, 3, USAMHI; Chiswell Dabney–Mother, October 21, 1862, Saunders Family Papers, VHS; Hoke, *Historical Reminiscences*, pp. 30, 31; OR, v. 19, pt. 2, pp. 52, 57; Thompson, *Horses*, pp. 58–60.

29. Richard H. Watkins–My Precious Mary, October 15, 1862, Watkins Papers, VHS; Julian T. Edwards–My dear Parents, October 15, 1862, Edwards Letter, VHS; E. D. Cottrell–My Dear Grand Ma, October 16, 1862, Cottrell Family Papers, VHS; Chiswell Dabney–Mother, October 21, 1862, Saunders Family Papers, VHS; R. Channing Price–Mother, October 15, 1862, Price Papers, UNC; OR, v. 19, pt. 2, p. 52; Hoke, *Historical Reminiscences*, p. 31; Account of General J. E. B. Stuart Capture, p. 4, USAMHI.

30. Westhaeffer, *History*, pp. 12, 13, 15; Thompson, *Horses*, pp. 65, 66, 68; Bridges, *Fighting with JEB Stuart*, pp. 98, 329n.

31. OR, v. 19, pt. 2, p. 53; Thompson, *Horses*, pp. 70, 72; Conrad and Alexander, *When War Passed This Way*, p. 91; Brooks, *Butler*, p. 82; Heyser, Diary, KHS; Atkinson, Memoirs, p. 16, VATU; Account of General J. E. B. Stuart Capture, pp. 5, 6, USAMHI.

32. OR, v. 19, pt. 2, pp. 53, 55; Williams C. Wickham–H. B. McClellan, March 6, 1883, Wickham Family Papers, VHS; Blackford, *War Years*, p. 170.

33. OR, v. 19, pt. 1, p. 72; pt. 2, pp. 59, 61, 62, 65, 68; v. 51, pt. 1, pp. 878, 880, 881; Dispatch Book, Pleasonton Family Papers, UVA; William H. Lambert–Boys, October 21, 1862, Lambert Letters, USAMHI.

34. OR, v. 19, pt. 1, p. 73; pt. 2, pp. 65, 68; v. 51, pt. 1, pp. 878, 880, 881, 882; Dispatch Book, Pleasonton Family Papers, UVA.

35. Williams C. Wickham–H. B. McClellan, March 6, 1883, Wickham Family Papers, VHS; Trout, *Galloping Thunder*, p. 118; Thompson, *Horses*, pp. 74–77, 84; OR, v. 19, pt. 2, pp. 41, 42, 53.

36. Blackford, *War Years*, pp. 173, 174; E. D. Cottrell–My Dear Grand Ma, October 16, 1862, Cottrell Family Papers, VHS; JEBS–My Darling Wife, November 25, 1862, Stuart Papers, VHS; R. Channing Price–Mother, October 15, 1862, Price Papers, UNC; Freeman, *Lee's Lieutenants*, v. 2, pp. 290–92; JEBS–General, October 12, 1862, Stuart Letter . . . Lee, UVA; Thompson, *Horses*, pp. 85, 87.

37. R. Channing Price–Mother, October 15, 1862, Price Papers, UNC; *SHSP*, v. 8, p. 451; Blackford, *War Years*, p. 174; *OR*, v. 19, pt. 2, p. 53; Thompson, *Horses*, pp. 91, 92.

38. Richard H. Watkins–My Precious Mary, October 15, 1862, Watkins Papers, VHS; Williams C. Wickham–H. B. McClellan, March 6, 1883, Wickham Family Papers, VHS; *OR*, v. 19, pt. 1, pp. 73, 74; pt. 2, pp. 53, 58; Dispatch Book, Pleasonton Family Papers, UVA; Jerome B. Carr–Father, October 18, 1862, Carr Collection, NC.

39. *OR*, v. 19, pt. 2, pp. 53, 54; R. Channing Price–Mother, October 15, 1862, Price Papers, UNC; Nanzig, *3rd Virginia Cavalry*, p. 23; JEBS–General, October 12, 1862, Stuart Letter . . . Lee, UVA; Thompson, *Horses*, pp. 30, 98; Lafayette J. Carneal–Papa, October 15, 1862, Carneal Letters, VHS.

40. Gallagher, *Lee and His Army*, p. 18; Freeman, *Lee's Lieutenants*, v. 2, pp. 304, 305; R. E. Lee–Samuel Cooper, October 18, 1862, Lee Papers, VHS; *OR*, v. 19, pt. 2, p. 51.

41. Tower, ed., *Lee's Adjutant*, p. 48; Jones, *Rebel War Clerk's Diary*, v. 1, p. 172; William G. Deloney–My Dear Rosa, October 11, 1862, Deloney Family Papers, UGA; Hartley, *Stuart's Tarheels*, p. 157; *OR*, v. 19, pt. 2, p. 54.

42. Williams C. Wickham–H. B. McClellan, March 6, 1883, Wickham Family Papers, VHS; John O. Collins–Wife, October 20, 1862, Collins Papers, VHS; *SHSP*, v. 4, p. 57; Nanzig, *3rd Virginia Cavalry*, p. 23; Carter, *Sabres*, pp. 20, 22; Trout, *Galloping Thunder*, p. 121; JEBS–General, October 12, 1862, Stuart Letter . . . Lee, UVA.

43. R. Channing Price–Mother, October 15, 1862, Price Papers, UNC; Richard H. Watkins–My Precious Mary, October 15, 1862, Watkins Papers, VHS; Smith, *With Stonewall Jackson*, p. 21; Blackford, *War Years*, p. 128; Cozzens, ed., *B&L*, v. 5, p. 135.

44. R. Channing Price–Mother, October 15, 1862, Price Papers, UNC; Blackford, *War Years*, p. 180; Von Borcke, *Memoirs*, v. 1, pp. 309, 309n; Blackford, Annotations, UVA.

45. Telegram, October 16, 1862; JEBS–My Darling Wife, October 16, 1862, Stuart Papers, VHS.

46. *OR*, v. 19, pt. 2, pp. 85–88, 89, 91–93.

47. Return of the Cavalry, October 24, 1862, Stuart Collection, MC; JEBS–General, October 24, 1862, Stuart Papers, VHS; Blackford, *War Years*, p. 90.

48. Return of the Cavalry, Paper A, October 24, 1862, Stuart Collection, MC; JEBS–General, October 24, 1862, Stuart Papers, VHS.

49. JEBS–My Darling One, October 26, 1862; JEBS–General, October 24, 1862, Stuart Papers, VHS; Baylor, *Bull Run*, p. 150.

50. Robertson, *Stonewall Jackson*, p. 626; Warner, *Generals in Gray*, p. 167; McDonald, *History*, p. 105; Driver and Howard, *2nd Virginia Cavalry*, p. 63.

51. Return of the Cavalry, Paper B, October 24, 1862, Stuart Collection, MC; JEBS–General, October 24, 1862, Stuart Papers, VHS; *OR*, v. 21, p. 544; William G. Deloney–My Dear Rosa, December 6, 1862, Deloney Family Papers, UGA.

52. *OR*, v. 19, pt. 1, p. 143; pt. 2, pp. 618–19, 621, 633, 634, 639, 643, 660, 674; Gallagher, ed., *Fighting For*, p. 155; Wert, *General James Longstreet*, pp. 204–5.

53. Wert, *Sword of Lincoln*, pp. 175–76, 177, 178.

54. *OR*, v. 19, pt. 2, pp. 682–85.

55. Ibid., pp. 136, 141; JEBS–Colonel, February 27, 1864, Stuart Collection, MC.

56. *OR*, v. 19, pt. 2, pp. 125–26, 141–43; JEBS–Colonel, February 27, 1864, Stuart Collection, MC; Dispatch Book, Pleasonton Family Papers, UVA; Wise, *Long Arm*, pp. 349–50; Brennan, "Little Mac's Last Stand," *B&G*, v. 17, no. 2, pp. 16, 17, 19, 48.

57. *OR*, v. 19, pt. 2, p. 143; JEBS–Colonel, February 27, 1864, Stuart Collection, MC; Von Borcke, *Memoirs*, v. 2, pp. 34, 35.

58. Von Borcke, *Memoirs*, v. 2, p. 36; *OR*, v. 19, pt. 2, pp. 143–44, 693–94; JEBS–Colonel, February 27, 1864, Stuart Collection, MC; Brennan, "Notice Served," *N&S*, v. 2, no. 4, p. 21.

59. *OR*, v. 19, pt. 2, pp. 126, 144, 146; JEBS–Colonel, February 27, 1864, Stuart Collection, MC; Dispatch Book, Pleasonton Family Papers, UVA; Brennan, "Little Mac's Last Stand," *B&G*, v. 17, no. 2, pp. 50, 52, 53; Von Borcke, *Memoirs*, v. 2, pp. 45–48; Scheel, *Civil War in Fauquier County*, p. 45.

60. *OR*, v. 19, pt. 2, pp. 123, 127, 140, 144–45, 695, 703, 706, 707; JEBS–Colonel, February 27, 1864, Stuart Collection, MC; Robert E. Lee–JEBS, November 6, 7, 10, 1862, Stuart Papers, HL; Dispatch Book, Pleasonton Family Papers, UVA; Von Borcke, *Memoirs*, v. 2, pp. 51, 52.

61. Hubard, "Civil War Reminiscences," p. 60, UVA; *OR*, v. 19, pt. 2, pp. 145, 695.

62. Telegram, November [3], 1862; JEBS–My Darling Wife, November 2, 1862, Stuart Papers, VHS.

63. JEBS–My Darling Wife, November 2, 1862, Stuart Papers, VHS.

64. JEBS–My Dear, Dear Wife, November 6, 1862, Stuart Paper, VHS; Extract, Stuart Family Bible, Stuart Papers, VHS; Newspaper clipping, Stuart Papers, VHS; Cooke, *Wearing*, p. 16; Von Borcke, *Memoirs*, v. 2, pp. 48, 49; Diary, Cooke Papers, DU.

65. Extract, Stuart Family Bible, Stuart Papers, VHS; JEBS–My Dear, Dear Wife, November 6, 1862, Stuart Papers, VHS.

66. JEBS–My Dear Lily, November 16, 1862, Stuart Papers, DU.

67. R. Channing Price, et al–Mrs. Gen'l Stuart, November 9, 1862, Stuart Papers, HL.

68. Telegram, November 8, 1862, Stuart Papers, HL; Von Borcke, *Memoirs*, v. 2, pp. 62, 63; Thomason, *Jeb Stuart*, p. 335; JEBS–My Dear Lily, November 16, 1862, Stuart Papers, DU; William A. Stuart–Sister Flora, December 3, 1862, Stuart Papers, VHS; Perry, *Ascent*, p. 11.

69. Wert, *Sword of Lincoln*, pp. 174–78.

70. Ibid., pp. 174, 175, 180–83.

71. Ibid., pp. 184–86.

72. Robert E. Lee–JEBS, November 13, 1862, Stuart Papers, HL; *OR*, v. 21, pp. 1017, 1020; v. 51, pt. 2, p. 646; Mitchell, ed., *Letters . . . Mosby*, p. 26.

73. *OR*, v. 21, pp. 1026, 1027; Dowdey and Manarin, eds., *Wartime Papers*, pp. 339–41; Sutherland, *Seasons*, p. 198; Brennan, "Notice Served," *N&S*, v. 2, no. 4, p. 23; Longacre, *Gentlemen*, p. 117; John O. Collins–Wife, November 16, 1862, Collins Papers, VHS.

74. William G. Deloney–My Dear Rosa, November 21, 1862, Deloney Family Papers, UGA; Cisco, *Wade Hampton*, pp. 105–6.

75. *OR*, v. 19, pt. 2, pp. 709, 713, 1025; v. 51, pt. 2, pp. 652–53; Carter, *Sabres*, pp. 28, 29; Hubard, "Civil War Reminiscences," p. 61, UVA.

76. *OR*, v. 21, pp. 550, 551, 1027; Wert, *General James Longstreet*, p. 214; Chiswell Dabney–Mother, November 26, 1862, Saunders Family Papers, VHS.

Chapter 10: Winter War

1. R. Channing Price–Mother, November 30, 1862, Price Papers, UNC; Light, ed., *War at Our Doors*, p. 51.

2. Light, ed., *War at Our Doors*, pp. xvi, 48, 50; Von Borcke, *Memoirs*, v. 2, pp. 80–86; *OR*, v. 21, p. 564.

3. Light, ed., *War at Our Doors*, p. 52.

4. Ibid., pp. 53, 54; O'Reilly, *Fredericksburg Campaign*, p. 42.

5. O'Reilly, *Fredericksburg Campaign*, p. 42; Wert, *General James Longstreet*, pp. 216–18.

6. O'Reilly, *Fredericksburg Campaign*, pp. 51–52; R. Channing Price–Sister, December 4, 1862, Price Papers, UNC; McDonald, ed., *Make Me a Map*, p. 101; *OR*, v. 21, p. 28.

7. *OR*, v. 21, pp. 15, 690, 691; Freeman, *Lee's Lieutenants*, v. 2, pp. 398, 399; William G. Deloney–My Dear Rosa, December 6, 1862, Deloney Family Papers, UGA.

8. *OR*, v. 21, pp. 556, 1114.

9. Light, ed., *War at Our Doors*, p. 56; JEBS–My Dear *Dear* Lily, December

5, 1862, Stuart Papers, DU; Krick, *Staff Officers*, p. 87; A. Tinsley–JEBS, November 25, 1862, Stuart Papers, VHS.

10. JEBS–My Dear *Dear* Lily, December 5, 1862, Stuart Papers, DU; General Orders, No. 14, December 3, 1862, Stuart Papers, DU; Davis, *Jeb Stuart*, p. 249.

11. Wert, *Sword of Lincoln*, p. 188.

12. Ibid., pp. 189–90.

13. Ibid., p. 190.

14. Ibid., pp. 191–92; Mitchell, ed., *Letters . . . Stuart*, p. 285.

15. SOR, v. 3, p. 720; McDonald, ed., *Make Me a Map*, p. 99; JEBS–My Dear *Dear* Lily, December 5, 1862, Stuart Papers, DU; JEBS–My Darling Wife, December 10, 1862, Stuart Papers, VHS; Robertson, *Stonewall Jackson*, p. 653.

16. O'Reilly, *Fredericksburg Campaign*, pp. 102–5, 131; OR, v. 21, p. 547; R. Channing Price–Mother, December 17, 1862, Price Papers, UNC; Wert, *General James Longstreet*, p. 218.

17. O'Reilly, *Fredericksburg Campaign*, pp. 127, 142–44; Wert, *Sword of Lincoln*, pp. 194–95; Wise, *Long Arm*, p. 382; SHSP, v. 12, p. 468.

18. R. Channing Price–Mother, December 17, 1862, Price Papers, UNC; OR, v. 21, p. 553; O'Reilly, *Fredericksburg Campaign*, pp. 144–45; CV, v. 2, p. 74.

19. O'Reilly, *Fredericksburg Campaign*, pp. 146–47; Hassler, *Colonel John Pelham*, p. 146.

20. O'Reilly, *Fredericksburg Campaign*, pp. 147–48; Hassler, *Colonel John Pelham*, p. 148; Von Borcke, *Memoirs*, v. 2, p. 118; OR, v. 21, p. 547; R. Channing Price–Mother, December 17, 1862, Price Papers, UNC.

21. Wert, *Sword of Lincoln*, p. 195; Robertson, *Stonewall Jackson*, p. 654; Sorrel, *Recollections*, p. 131.

22. Wert, *Sword of Lincoln*, p. 196; OR, v. 21, p. 632; R. Channing Price–Mother, December 17, 1862, Price Papers, UNC; O'Reilly, *Fredericksburg Campaign*, pp. 168, 181.

23. Wert, *Sword of Lincoln*, pp. 196–97; O'Reilly, *Fredericksburg Campaign*, Chapters 7 and 8 are a detailed description.

24. Wert, *Sword of Lincoln*, pp. 197, 199.

25. Ibid., pp. 199–202.

26. Ibid., pp. 203–4.

27. Wert, *General James Longstreet*, p. 223; OR, v. 21, pp. 549–50.

28. OR, v. 21, p. 556; Mitchell, ed., *Letters . . . Stuart*, p. 284.

29. JEBS–Custis, December 18, 1862, Stuart Papers, DU; Thomas T. Munford–My dear Nannie, December 22, 1862, Munford Letter, USAMHI; Wert, *General James Longstreet*, p. 223.

30. Von Borcke, *Memoirs*, v. 2, p. 72; Thomason, *Jeb Stuart*, pp. 348, 349; R.

Channing Price–Mother, December 23, 1862, Price Papers, UNC; Hartley, *Stuart's Tarheels*, p. 179.

31. Smith, *With Stonewall Jackson*, pp. 35, 37; Douglas, *I Rode*, pp. 207, 209; Robertson, *Stonewall Jackson*, pp. 667, 669; Krick, *9th Virginia Cavalry*, p. 65.

32. Robertson, *Stonewall Jackson*, p. 669; Smith, *With Stonewall Jackson*, p. 38.

33. Richard H. Watkins–[Wife], December 20, 1862, Watkins Papers, VHS; Thomas T. Munford–My dear Nannie, December 22, 1862, Munford Letter, USAMHI; *OR*, v. 21, pp. 695–96.

34. *OR*, v. 21, p. 1067.

35. Ibid., p. 696; Longacre, *Gentleman*, p. 123.

36. *OR*, v. 21, pp. 695, 731; R. E. Lee–JEBS, December 23, 1862, Stuart Papers, HL; Cisco, *Wade Hampton*, p. 108.

37. *OR*, v. 21, pp. 731, 735; R. Channing Price–Sister, January 2, 1863, Price Papers, UNC.

38. *OR*, v. 21, pp. 731–32, 738, 742; R. Channing Price–Sister, January 2, 1863, Price Papers, UNC; McClellan, *I Rode*, p. 198.

39. *OR*, v. 21, pp. 732–33, 735; R. Channing Price–Sister, January 2, 1863, Price Papers, UNC; Freeman, *Lee's Lieutenants*, v. 2, pp. 401–2.

40. *OR*, v. 21, pp. 733, 737, 739; R. Channing Price–Sister, January 2, 1863, Price Papers, UNC; McClellan, *I Rode*, p. 200; Freeman, *Lee's Lieutenants*, v. 2, pp. 402–3.

41. *OR*, v. 21, pp. 733, 739; R. Channing Price–Sister, January 2, 1863, Price Papers, UNC; Carter, *Sabres*, pp. 35, 36.

42. *OR*, v. 21, pp. 733, 734, 739; R. Channing Price–Sister, January 2, 1863, Price Papers, UNC; Freeman, *Lee's Lieutenants*, v. 2, pp. 404, 405; Jones, *Rebel War Clerk's Diary*, v. 1, pp. 230, 233.

43. *OR*, v. 21, pp. 734, 739, 714, 717–18; R. Channing Price–Sister, January 2, 1863, Price Papers, UNC.

44. *OR*, v. 21, p. 734; Carter, *Sabres*, p. 37; Hubard, "Civil War Reminiscences," p. 64, UVA; John F. Milhollin–My Dear Wife, January 3, 1863, Milhollin Letters, USAMHI; Nanzig, ed., *Civil War Memoirs*, p. 73; R. Channing Price–Sister, January 2, 1863, Price Papers, UNC.

45. *OR*, v. 21, p. 734; R. Channing Price–Sister, January 2, 1863, Price Papers, UNC; Carter, *Sabres*, p. 37; Philadelphia *Weekly Times*, April 13, 1878; Wert, *Mosby's Rangers*, p. 31.

46. *OR*, v. 21, p. 734; Ramey and Gott, eds., *Years of Anguish*, p. 38; R. Channing Price–Sister, January 2, 1863, Price Papers, UNC; Carter, *Sabres*, p. 37; Hartley, *Stuart's Tarheels*, p. 180.

47. *OR*, v. 21, pp. 732, 734, 735, 966, 967; R. Channing Price–Sister, January 2, 1863, Price Papers, UNC: Hartley, *Stuart's Tarheels*, p. 180; Jones, *Rebel War Clerk's Diary*, v. 1, p. 230.

48. *OR*, v. 21, p. 734; Blackford, ed., *Letters*, p. 158; Trout, ed., *With Pen and Saber*, p. 158; R. Channing Price–Mother, January 28, 1863, Price Papers, UNC; Chiswell Dabney–Mother, February 4, 1863, Saunders Family Papers, VHS; JEBS–My Darling Wife, November 25, 1862, Stuart Papers, VHS.

49. *Annals*, p. 674; Greene, *Whatever You Resolve to Be*, p. 24; Smith, *With Stonewall Jackson*, p. 40.

50. *Annals*, p. 673; Diary, Cooke Papers, DU.

51. Hunter McGuire Narrative, Dabney Papers, UNC; Trout, *They Followed the Plume*, p. 39; Douglas, *I Rode*, p. 134; Autograph Book, Stuart Papers, VHS.

52. Adams, "Reminiscences," pp. 1, 3, VHS.

53. Thomason, *Jeb Stuart*, p. 131; William G. Deloney–My Dear Rosa, October 1, 1862, Deloney Family Papers, UGA; Blackford, ed., *Letters*, p. 115.

54. John W. Carlisle–Col. B. B. Foster, October 26, 1862, Carlisle Letter, copy in possession of Krick.

55. Diary, Cooke Papers, DU; *Annals*, p. 674; Bill, *Beleaguered City*, p. 159; Trout, ed., *With Pen and Saber*, p. 158.

56. Jedediah Hotchkiss–My Dearest One, January 11, 1863, Hotchkiss Papers, LC; R. Channing Price–Mother, March 25, 1863, Price Papers, UNC; Mitchell, ed., *Letters . . . Stuart*, p. 270; JEBS–My Darling One, October 26, 1862; JEBS–My Darling Wife, November 25, 1862, Stuart Papers, VHS.

57. Von Borcke, *Memoirs*, v. 1, p. 299; Autographs of Stuart and Staff, January 31, 1863, Lawrie Letters, USAMHI; Trout, *They Followed the Plume*, p. 118; JEBS–My Dear One, February 26, 1863; JEBS–My Darling One, March 4, 1863, Stuart Papers, VHS; R. Channing Price–Mother, March 2, 1863, Price Papers, UNC.

58. Krick, *Staff Officers*, pp. 132, 148, 166, 172, 247, 292; Reade, *In the Saddle*, pp. 21, 117; *CV*, v. 18, p. 291; *SHSP*, v. 37, p. 62; Trout, *They Followed the Plume*, pp. 123, 225; Chiswell Dabney–Mother, January 28, 1863, Saunders Family Papers, VHS.

59. JEBS–S. Cooper, November 11, 1862; JEBS–General, February 10, 1863, Stuart Papers, VHS.

60. McDonald, *History*, p. 196; Bushong and Bushong, *Fightin' Tom Rosser*, p. 2; Trout, *Galloping Thunder*, p. 160; JEBS–My Dear, Dear Wife, November 6, 1862; JEBS–General, [January 1863], Stuart Papers, VHS.

61. R. E. Lee–James A. Seddon, December 29, 1862, Lee Family Collection, MC; JEBS–General, January 13, 1863; JEBS–General, February 4, 1863, Stuart Papers, VHS; *OR*, v. 25, pt. 2, p. 604; Armstrong, *11th Virginia Cavalry*, pp. 8, 21, 22.

62. Trout, ed., *With Pen and Saber*, pp. 158, 159; Chiswell Dabney–Mother, February 28, 1863, Saunders Family Papers, VHS.

63. R. E. Lee–JEBS, February 15, 1863, Stuart Papers, VHS; *OR*, v. 25, pt. 2, p. 621; Jedediah Hotchkiss–My Dearest One, January 11, 1863, Hotchkiss Papers, LC; James Ellis Tucker–My dearest Mother, January 8, 1863, Bourn Family Papers, UCB; Smith, ed., "Watching Lee's Lieutenants," *CW*, v. 10. no. 4, p. 56.

64. Wert, *Sword of Lincoln*, pp. 214–17.

65. Sutherland, *Seasons*, p. 206; William G. Deloney–My Dear Rosa, January 4, 1863, Deloney Family Papers, UGA; Hartley, *Stuart's Tarheels*, p. 183; Cisco, *Wade Hampton*, pp. 108, 110, 111.

66. Driver, *5th Virginia Cavalry*, pp. 45, 46; Corson, *My Dear Jennie*, p. 100; Brennan, "Best Cavalry," *N&S*, v. 2, no. 2, p. 26; McWhiney, ed., *Lee's Dispatches*, p. 72.

67. "Jeff Davis Legion," Chapter 13, p. 2, Waring Papers, GHS; Driver, *10th Virginia Cavalry*, p. 31; John O. Collins–Wife, March 16, 1863, Collins Papers, VHS; Robert Brooke Jones–My Dear & Sweet Wife, n.d., Jones Family Papers, VHS; Noble J. Brooke–Father, January 12, 23, 1863, Brooke Papers, EU; Wittenberg, *Union Cavalry*, p. 62.

68. *OR*, v. 21, p. 1082; v. 25, pt. 2, p. 650.

69. Gerleman, "War Horses!," *N&S*, v. 2, no. 2, p. 57; Miller, "Southern Horse," *CWTI*, v. 45, no. 1, pp. 31, 34; Brennan, "Best Cavalry," *N&S*, v. 2, no. 2, p. 13; McClellan, *I Rode*, p. 257.

70. McClellan, *I Rode*, p. 258; Miller, "Southern Horse," *CWTI*, v. 45, no. 1, pp. 31, 32; Carter, *Sabres*, p. 48; Thomason, *Jeb Stuart*, p. 79.

71. Krick, *Staff Officers*, p. 206; McClellan, *I Rode*, pp. 257–58, 259; Redwood, "Horsemen in Gray," *CWTI*, v. 9, no. 3, p. 6.

72. McClellan, *I Rode*, p. 259; Redwood, "Horsemen in Gray," *CWTI*, v. 9, no. 3, p. 6; Nanzig, ed., *Civil War Memoirs*, p. 67; Thomason, *Jeb Stuart*, p. 69; Brennan, "Best Cavalry," *N&S*, v. 2, no. 2, p. 26.

73. McWhiney, ed., *Lee's Dispatches*, pp. 71, 72; "Jeff Davis Legion," Chapter 13, pp. 6, 7, Waring Papers, GHS; Von Borcke, *Memoirs*, v. 2, p. 179.

74. McWhiney, ed., *Lee's Dispatches*, p. 71; James Ellis Tucker–My Dearest, Dearest Mother, February 13, 1863, Bourn Family Papers, UCB; "Jeff Davis Legion," Chapter 13, p. 5, Waring Papers, GHS; *OR*, v. 25, pt. 1, pp. 25, 26.

75. James Ellis Tucker–My Dearest Mother, February 27, 1863, Bourn Family Papers, UCB; Richard H. Watkins–[Wife], February 27, 1863, Watkins Papers, VHS; Wittenberg, *Union Cavalry*, p. 48; Haden, *Reminiscences*, p. 22.

76. James Ellis Tucker–My Dearest Mother, February 27, 1863, Bourn Family Papers, UCB; Richard H. Watkins–[Wife], February 27, 1863, Watkins Papers, VHS; Wittenberg, *Union Cavalry*, pp. 40, 42, 49, 51, 55; McClellan, *I Rode*, p. 204; *OR*, v. 25, pt. 1, p. 25.

77. Bigelow, *Campaign*, p. 73.

78. *OR*, v. 25, pt. 1, p. 25; Richard H. Watkins–Wife, February 27, 1863, Watkins Papers, VHS; JEBS–My Dear One, February 26, 1863; JEBS–My Darling One, March 4, 1863; JEBS–My Darling Wife, March 15, 1863, Stuart Papers, VHS.

79. JEBS–My Darling Wife, March 13, 1863, Stuart Papers, VHS; Mitchell, ed., *Letters . . . Mosby*, p. 127; *OR*, v. 25, pt. 1, p. 6; Wert, *Mosby's Rangers*, p. 22.

80. Wert, *Mosby's Rangers*, pp. 17–22, 46; John S. Mosby–Joe, January 30, 1904, Bryan Papers, VHS.

81. John S. Mosby–Joe, January 30, 1904, Bryan Papers, VHS; JEBS–My Darling One, March 19, 1863, Stuart Papers, VHS; *OR*, v. 25, pt. 2, pp. 664, 856, 857; Wert, *Mosby's Rangers*, p. 46; Mitchell, ed., *Letters . . . Mosby*, p. 73.

82. JEBS–My Darling Wife, March 13, 19, 1863, Stuart Papers, VHS; Sutherland, *Seasons*, pp. 209, 217; Holland, *Pierce M. B. Young*, p. 71.

83. *OR*, v. 25, pt. 1, p. 47; Wert, *Sword of Lincoln*, pp. 223, 228.

84. *OR*, v. 25, pt. 1, pp. 47, 48; Coski, "Forgotten Warrior," *N&S*, v. 2, no. 7, p. 79; Carter, *Sabres*, p. 49; Bigelow, *Campaign*, p. 95; Wittenberg, *Union Cavalry*, pp. 71, 73, 79, 83.

85. *OR*, v. 25, pt. 1, pp. 48–52, 61–62; Carter, *Sabres*, pp. 49, 50; Jordan, Memoir, VATU; a fine recent account of the battle is Wittenberg, *Union Cavalry*, Chapter 3; Wert, *Sword of Lincoln*, p. 229.

86. *OR*, v. 25, pt. 1, p. 58; McClellan, *I Rode*, pp. 210, 211; Blackford, Annotations, UVA; Sears, *Chancellorsville*, p. 87; Wittenberg, *Union Cavalry*, p. 85; R. Channing Price–Mother, March 21, 1863, Price Papers, UNC.

87. R. Channing Price–Mother, March 21, 1863, Price Papers, UNC; *OR*, v. 25, pt. 1, pp. 50, 52; Jordan, Memoir, VATU; Fitzhugh, Memoirs, p. 20, MC; Wittenberg, *Union Cavalry*, p. 95.

88. *OR*, v. 25, pt. 1, p. 58; Wittenberg, *Union Cavalry*, pp. 98, 99, 102; Bigelow, *Campaign*, p. 101; Wert, *Sword of Lincoln*, p. 229.

89. R. Channing Price–Mother, March 21, 1863, Price Papers, UNC; Sutherland, *Seasons*, p. 220; Trout, *Galloping Thunder*, p. 180.

90. *OR*, v. 25, pt. 2, p. 858; Holland, *Pierce M. B. Young*, p. 71; H. Kyd Douglas–A. C. Hamlin, August 19, 1882, Hamlin Papers, HU; R. Channing Price–Mother, March 21, 30, 1863, Price Papers, UNC; Dowdey and Manarin, eds., *Wartime Papers*, p. 414.

91. Wise, *Long Arm*, pp. 302, 349; Mitchell, ed., *Letters . . . Stuart*, p. 299.

92. JEBS–My Dear Nannie, March 18, 1865, copy in possession of Krick; R. Channing Price–Major Moorman, March 25, 1863, Stuart Collection, MC; Mitchell, ed., *Letters . . . Stuart*, p. 299.

93. *OR*, v. 25, pt. 1, p. 60; R. Channing Price–Mother, March 30, 1863, Price Papers, UNC; JEBS–My Darling Flora, March 30, 1863, Stuart Papers, VHS.

94. JEBS–My Darling One, March 19, 1863; JEBS–My Dearest One, April 8, 1863, Stuart Papers, VHS.

95. JEBS–My Dear Sir, March 29, 1863, Stuart Letter, ADAH; Postscript, JEBS–[Flora], c. June 1863, Stuart Papers, VHS.

96. Blackford, *War Years*, p. 201.

Chapter 11: "Right Noble Did Stuart Do"

1. Scheibert, *Seven Months*, pp. ii, 42; Von Borcke, *Memoirs*, v. 2, p. 201.

2. Scheibert, *Seven Months*, pp. 39, 40.

3. JEBS–My Darling One, April 3, 1863, Stuart Papers, VHS; JEBS–Colonel, April 6, 1863, Stuart Papers, DU; Mitchell, ed., *Letters . . . Stuart*, p. 281; *Heritage Auction Galleries*, pp. 53, 57, 58.

4. *CV*, v. 33, pp. 93, 94.

5. Von Borcke, *Memoirs*, v. 2, p. 201; *OR*, v. 25, pt. 2, p. 858.

6. *OR*, v. 25, pt. 2, p. 858; Trout, *They Followed the Plume*, pp. 57, 59, 60; JEBS–General, March 26, 1863, Stuart Papers, VHS.

7. R. Channing Price–Mother, April 16, 1863, Price Papers, UNC; Taylor, Diary, WFU; *OR*, v. 25, pt. 2, p. 738; JEBS–General, April 20, 1863, Stuart Papers, HL.

8. *OR*, v. 25, pt. 2, pp. 740, 741; McSwain, ed., *Crumbling Defenses*, p. 18; Thomas T. Munford–E. A. Carman, December 10, 1894, Carman Papers, NYPL.

9. *OR*, v. 25, pt. 1, p. 85; R. Channing Price–Mother, April 16, 1863, Price Papers, UNC.

10. *OR*, v. 25, pt. 2, pp. 730, 731; Robert E. Lee–JEBS, April 21, 1863, Stuart Papers, HL.

11. Philadelphia *Weekly Times*, May 19, 1877; Conrad, *Rebel Scout*, p. 22.

12. Philadelphia *Weekly Times*, May 19, 1877; Leonard Williams–My Dear Anna, January 23, 1863, Williams, "Civil War Letters," USAMHI; Bigelow, *Campaign*, p. 60.

13. Conrad, *Rebel Scout*, p. 21; JEBS–Major, April 26, 1863, Stuart Papers, NC.

14. Scheibert, *Seven Months*, p. 44; McClellan, *I Rode*, pp. 225, 226.

15. General Orders, No. 14, April 23, 1863, Stuart Papers, HL; Hubbell, ed., "War Diary," *JSH*, v. 7, no. 4, p. 538; Thomason, *Jeb Stuart*, p. 10.

16. Davis, *Jeb Stuart*, p. 280; JEBS–My Darling One, April 19, 1863, Stuart Papers, VHS; Mitchell, ed., *Letters . . . Stuart*, pp. 306–7.

17. Wert, *Sword of Lincoln*, pp. 230, 232.

18. Ibid., pp. 230–32, quote on p. 230.

19. Ibid., p. 232.

20. Scheibert, *Seven Months*, pp. 44, 45, 55, 56; Robert E. Lee–JEBS, April 29, 1863, Stuart Papers, HL; OR, v. 25, pt. 1, p. 1046; pt. 2, p. 756; Bigelow, *Campaign*, p. 210.

21. Wert, *Sword of Lincoln*, pp. 232–33; OR, v. 25, pt. 2, pp. 756, 757.

22. Wert, *Sword of Lincoln*, p. 231.

23. Ibid., p. 233.

24. Reade, *In the Saddle*, p. 35; Scheibert, *Seven Months*, p. 57; Robert E. Lee–JEBS, 5:00 P.M., April 30, 1863, Stuart Papers, HL; OR, v. 25, pt. 1, pp. 1046–47; McClellan, *I Rode*, pp. 227, 229, 230.

25. OR, v. 25, pt. 1, p. 1047; Scheibert, *Seven Months*, p. 57; Von Borcke, *Memoirs*, v. 2, pp. 208–9.

26. OR, v. 25, pt. 1, p. 1047; Von Borcke, *Memoirs*, v. 2, pp. 210–16; Bigelow, *Campaign*, pp. 225–26; Wittenberg, *Union Cavalry*, pp. 146, 149, 150–56.

27. OR, v. 25, pt. 1, p. 1047; Von Borcke, *Memoirs*, v. 2, p. 216; Bigelow, *Campaign*, p. 227; Scheibert, *Seven Months*, p. 59; Wittenberg, *Union Cavalry*, pp. 156–58.

28. Thomas, *Robert E. Lee*, pp. 277, 278, 280, 281.

29. OR, v. 25, pt. 1, p. 797; Wert, *Sword of Lincoln*, p. 235.

30. Wert, *Sword of Lincoln*, pp. 235–36.

31. Ibid., pp. 236–37.

32. OR, v. 25, pt. 1, p. 1047; McClellan, *I Rode*, p. 231; Carter, *Sabres*, pp. 59, 60; Bigelow, *Campaign*, pp. 245, 246, 269.

33. OR, v. 25, pt. 1, pp. 866, 1049; Bigelow, *Campaign*, pp. 252, 253; Harrison, *Chancellorsville Battlefield Sites*, p. 57.

34. Bigelow, *Campaign*, p. 253; Robertson, *Stonewall Jackson*, p. 708; Columbus *Daily Sun*, May 19, 1863; Reade, *In the Saddle*, p. 38; Harrison, *Chancellorsville Battlefield Sites*, pp. 62, 63.

35. Trout, *They Followed the Plume*, p. 222; Reade, *In the Saddle*, p. 38; Scheibert, *Seven Months*, p. 63; General Orders, No. 15, May 10, 1863, Order Book, Hampton, USAMHI; Blackford, *War Years*, p. 91; Von Borcke, *Memoirs*, v. 2, p. 221.

36. Mitchell, ed., *Letters . . . Stuart*, pp. 317–18.

37. Scheibert, *Seven Months*, p. 63; Robertson, *Stonewall Jackson*, pp. 709, 710; Gallagher, ed., *Lee the Soldier*, p. 9.

38. Gallagher, ed., *Lee the Soldier*, p. 9; Robertson, *Stonewall Jackson*, p. 710.

39. Wert, *Sword of Lincoln*, p. 238; R. E. Lee–My dear Mrs. Jackson, January 25, 1866, Lee Letter, WLU; Robertson, *Stonewall Jackson*, p. 712.

40. McDonald, ed., *Make Me a Map*, p. 137; McClellan, *I Rode*, pp. 437n, 438n; Harrison, *Chancellorsville Battlefield Sites*, p. 63.

41. Krick, *Staff Officers*, p. 206; McClellan, *I Rode*, pp. v, vi, vii; CV, v. 30, p. 343; McClellan file, CSR, CSA Generals, NA; Fitz Lee–General, April 6, 1863; JEBS–My Dear Darling, April 6, 1863; JEBS–General, April 20, 1863, Stuart Papers, VHS.

42. McDonald, ed., *Make Me a Map*, p. 137; Robertson, *Stonewall Jackson*, pp. 712–14.

43. Wert, *Brotherhood*, p. 227; Robertson, *Stonewall Jackson*, p. 714; OR, v. 25, pt. 1, p. 798; Von Borcke, *Memoirs*, v. 2, p. 222.

44. OR, v. 25, pt. 1, p. 1047; Bigelow, *Campaign*, p. 274; William F. Graves–My Dear Gen, August 25, 1897; J. W. Watts–General, September 1, 1897, Munford–Ellis Family Papers, DU; Carter, *Sabres*, p. 60; Wert, *Brotherhood*, p. 227.

45. OR, v. 25, pt. 1, p. 1047; Wert, *Brotherhood*, p. 227; Chamberlaine, *Memoirs*, p. 58; Reade, *In the Saddle*, p. 40.

46. OR, v. 25, pt. 1, pp. 1047, 1049; JEBS–General, May 21, 1863, Stuart Papers, VHS; Wert, *Sword of Lincoln*, pp. 239, 240.

47. Wert, *Sword of Lincoln*, pp. 240–41.

48. OR, v. 25, pt. 1, p. 887; McClellan, *I Rode*, p. 235; Von Borcke, *Memoirs*, v. 2, p. 227; J. W. Watts–General, September 1, 1897, Munford–Ellis Papers, DU; Reade, *In the Saddle*, p. 42.

49. McClellan, *I Rode*, pp. 235, 247; OR, v. 25, pt. 1, pp. 885–86, 887; Reade, *In the Saddle*, pp. 42, 43; Taylor, Reminiscence, p. 8, USAMHI; Freeman, *Lee's Lieutenants*, v. 2, pp. 571, 582n; Krick, *Staff Officers*, p. 58; Von Borcke, *Memoirs*, v. 2, pp. 227, 228.

50. A thorough and excellent description of Jackson's reconnaissance and wounding is Krick, *Smoothbore Volley*, Chapter 1; CV, v. 4, p. 308.

51. Krick, *Smoothbore Volley*, pp. 17, 18, 20, 28, 29; Boswell, "Jackson's Boswell," *CWTI*, v. 15, no. 1, p. 37; Charlotte *Daily Observer*, March 7, 1897.

52. Krick, *Smoothbore Volley*, pp. 29, 30, 35–39; Randolph Barton–A. C. Hamlin, February 6, 1893, Hamlin Papers, HU; A. P. Hill–My dear Stuart, November 14, [1862], Stuart Papers, VHS; Taylor, Reminiscence, p. 8, USAMHI; Freeman, *Lee's Lieutenants*, v. 2, p. 571.

53. Undated fragment of a letter, "Confederate Letters & Notes on Battle of Chancellorsville," Hamlin Papers, HU; Randolph Barton–A. C. Hamlin, August 31, 1892, Hamlin Papers, HU; OR, v. 25, pt. 1, p. 942.

54. McClellan, *I Rode*, pp. 226, 247; Undated fragment of a letter, "Confederate Letters & Notes on Battle of Chancellorsville," Hamlin Papers, HU; Henry K. Douglas–A. C. Hamlin, April 21, 1893, Hamlin Papers, HU.

55. SHSP, v. 14, p. 157; Bigelow, *Campaign*, p. 340; E. P. Alexander–Father, May 11, 1863, Alexander Papers, NC; Gallagher, ed., *Fighting For*, p. 206; Jedediah Hotchkiss–My Dear Wife, May 20, 1863, Hotchkiss Papers, LC; Wise, *Long Arm*, p. 497.

56. Robertson, *Stonewall Jackson*, pp. 735, 737, 738.

57. SHSP, v. 14, p. 157; Hess, Field Armies, p. 185; Bigelow, Campaign, Map 23, Plan 3; Alexander, Military Memoirs, p. 342.

58. OR, v. 25, pt. 2, p. 769; SOR, v. 4, p. 518.

59. R. E. Lee–JEBS, 3:00 A.M. and 3:30 A.M., May 3, 1863, Stuart Papers, HL; copies in OR, v. 25, pt. 2, p. 769.

60. OR, v. 25, pt. 1, p. 890; Bigelow, Campaign, p. 342; Sears, Chancellorsville, p. 314; Hess, Field Armies, pp. 175, 180, 182, 312.

61. Hess, Field Armies, p. 182; Clark, ed., Histories, v. 1, p. 629.

62. Macon Telegraph, May 16, 1863; Clark, ed., Histories, v. 1, p. 669; Fox, Red Clay, p. 168.

63. OR, v. 25, pt. 1, pp. 887–88; CV, v. 1, p. 235; Clark, ed., Histories, v. 1, p. 377; Charlotte Western Democrat, May 19, June 9, 1863; George W. Koontz–Mattie, May 10, 1863, Koontz Papers, VMI; Blackford, Diary, USAMHI; Thomas Smiley–Sister, May 9, 1863, Smiley Correspondence, UVA; George R. Bedinger–My dear Virginia, May 4, 1863, Bedinger–Dandridge Family Papers, DU; Hess, Field Armies, p. 182.

64. Von Borcke, Memoirs, v. 2, p. 235; Poague, Gunner with Stonewall, p. 65; Cooke, Wearing, pp. 28, 29; Reade, In the Saddle, p. 48.

65. OR, v. 25, pt. 1, pp. 908, 911, 921, 968, 987, 996, 997, 1014, 1017, 1018; SHSP, v. 8, p. 491; John Garibaldi–Wife, May 11, 1863, Garibaldi Letters, VMI; Charlotte Daily Observer, March 17, 1895; Randolph Barton–A. C. Hamlin, August 31, 1892, Hamlin Papers, HU; Turner, ed., Ted Barclay, p. 78; Paxton, ed., Civil War Letters, p. 87; Joseph McMurran–Mr. Miller, May 4, 1863, McMurran Letter, copy in possession of Krick; Carmichael, "Reflections," ACW, v. 5, no. 6, pp. 41, 42; Cox, Memoirs, FSNMP.

66. Reade, In the Saddle, p. 48; Thomason, Jeb Stuart, p. 384; McClellan, I Rode, pp. 250–51; CV, v. 5, p. 289; v. 23, p. 457; Hassler, ed., General to His Lady, p. 235; Tumilty, "Filling Jackson's Shoes," CWTI, v. 42, no. 2, p. 31; Alexander, Military Memoirs, p. 347.

67. McDonald, History, p. 241; OR, v. 25, pt. 1, p. 1017; SHSP, v. 9, p. 468; Hassler, ed., General to His Lady, p. 235.

68. Wert, Sword of Lincoln, p. 244; E. P. Alexander–Father, May 11, 1863, Alexander Papers, NC; Hess, Field Armies, p. 185; Alexander, Military Memoirs, p. 347.

69. OR, v. 25, pt. 1, p. 930; Clark, ed., Histories, v. 1, pp. 146, 193; Sears, Chancellorsville, p. 364; Styple, ed., Generals in Bronze, p. 42; Wert, Sword of Lincoln, pp. 244–45.

70. Scheibert, Seven Months, p. 70; Fox, Red Clay, pp. 168, 169; Thomas, Robert E. Lee, pp. 285, 286.

71. Andrews, ed., Scraps of Paper, p. 114; Charlotte Western Democrat, May 19, 1863; Sears, Chancellorsville, p. 366; Hess, Field Armies, p. 182; Wert, Sword of Lincoln, p. 245.

72. McClellan, *I Rode*, p. 255; see modern evaluation of Stuart's performance in Sears, *Chancellorsville*, p. 325.

73. Wert, *Sword of Lincoln*, pp. 246–48; Sears, *Chancellorsville*, p. 403; OR, v. 51, pt. 2, p. 702.

74. R. E. Lee–Gen'l, 8:15 A.M., May 5, 1863, Stuart Papers, HL.

75. Ibid.; OR, v. 25, pt. 1, p. 802; Wert, *Sword of Lincoln*, pp. 249–52.

76. OR, v. 25, pt. 1, p. 802; pt. 2, p. 782; McDonald, ed., *Make Me a Map*, pp. 141, 142; Special Orders, May 6, 1863, Stuart file, CSR, CSA, NA; Robertson, *Stonewall Jackson*, p. 745.

77. Letter quoted in McClellan, *I Rode*, p. 256.

78. OR, v. 25, pt. 1, pp. 803, 886.

79. Wert, *Sword of Lincoln*, pp. 255–56; Driver, *10th Virginia Cavalry*, p. 34; JEBS–General, May 8, 1863, Stuart Collection, MC.

80. JEBS–General, May 8, 1863, Stuart Collection, MC.

81. R. E. Lee–JEBS, May 11, 1863, Stuart Papers, HL; copy in OR, v. 25, pt. 2, p. 792; Freeman, *Lee's Lieutenants*, v. 2, p. xxiv.

82. OR, v. 25, pt. 2, p. 792; Robertson, *Stonewall Jackson*, pp. 748–52, 753.

83. Thomason, *Jeb Stuart*, p. 412.

84. *Annals*, p. 674; Wert, *Brotherhood*, pp. 233–34; Armstrong, Diary, VHS; J. Kent Langhorne–Dear Mama, May 19, 1863, Langhorne Papers, VMI; Jedediah Hotchkiss–My Dear Wife, May 20, 1863, Hotchkiss Papers, LC.

85. Mrs. T. J. Jackson–My dear Sir, August 1, 1863, Stuart Papers, VHS.

Chapter 12: "The Hardest Cavalry Fight"

1. Jones, *Rebel War Clerk's Diary*, v. 1, p. 325; Wert, *General James Longstreet*, p. 247.

2. Wert, *General James Longstreet*, p. 247.

3. Ibid., p. 248; OR, v. 25, pt. 2, pp. 810, 811, 840.

4. JEBS–My Darling One, May 20, 1863, Stuart Papers, VHS; Hubbell, ed., "War Diary," *JSH*, v. 7, no. 4, p. 537.

5. Wert, *General James Longstreet*, pp. 248–49.

6. William G. Deloney–My Dear Rosa, May 12, 23, 1863, Deloney Family Papers, UGA; J. Kent Langhorne–Dear Mama, May 19, 1863, Langhorne Papers, VMI; "Jeff Davis Legion," Chapter 13, p. 8, Waring Papers, GHS; Nanzig, ed., *Civil War Memoirs*, p. 118.

7. OR, v. 25, pt. 2, pp. 782, 783, 828, 836; Coddington, *Gettysburg Campaign*, p. 16; R. E. Lee–JEBS, May 11, 1863; Petition of Texas Brigade Officers, June 12, 1863, Stuart Papers, HL.

8. OR, v. 25, pt. 2, pp. 820–21; SOR, v. 60, p. 108; Raiford, *4th North Carolina Cavalry*, p. 39; Coltrane, *Memoirs*, p. 11.

9. OR, v. 25, pt. 2, p. 789.

10. Ibid., p. 820; Coddington, *Gettysburg Campaign*, p. 15; William E. Jones–Sir, May 24, 1863, Letters Received . . . Confederate AIGO, NA.

11. Carter, *Sabres*, p. 64; "Jeff Davis Legion," Chapter 13, p. 17, Waring Papers, GHS; General Orders, No. 16, May 14, 1863, Order Book, Hampton, USAMHI.

12. Sutherland, *Seasons*, p. 233; Reade, *In the Saddle*, pp. 50, 51; Carter, *Sabres*, p. 64; Harrell, *2nd North Carolina*, p. 109; Montgomery *Daily Mail*, June 2, 1863; Watford, ed., *Civil War in North Carolina*, v. 1, p. 112.

13. JEBS–My Dearest One, May 26, 1863, Stuart Papers, VHS.

14. OR, v. 25, pt. 2, pp. 838, 846; Wise, *Long Army*, p. 578; Wert, *General James Longstreet*, p. 250; Dowdey and Manarin, ed., *Wartime Papers*, p. 490.

15. Blackford, *War Years*, p. 211; Von Borcke, *Memoirs*, v. 2, p. 264; Sears, *Gettysburg*, p. 62.

16. Von Borcke, *Memoirs*, v. 2, p. 265; Trout, *Galloping Thunder*, p. 217; Sutherland, *Seasons*, p. 239; Neese, *Three Years*, p. 167.

17. Hudgins and Kleese, eds., *Recollections*, p. 76; Bradshaw, ed., *Civil War Diary*, p. 9; Raiford, *4th North Carolina*, p. 40; "Diary," 12th Virginia Cavalry File, ANB; Clark, ed., *Histories*, v. 3, p. 460.

18. Trout, *Galloping Thunder*, p. 219; Bradshaw, ed., *Civil War Diary*, p. 10; Nanzig, *3rd Virginia Cavalry*, p. 35; Styple, ed., *Writing and Fighting*, pp. 226–27.

19. OR, v. 25, pt. 2, p. 844; Coltrane, *Memoirs*, p. 11; Neese, *Three Years*, p. 232; Henderson, *Road*, p. 95; Grimsley, *Battles*, p. 8.

20. West, *Texan*, p. 58; McCabe, *Grayjackets*, p. 175; Hunter, *Johnny Reb*, p. 163; Dyer, *Gallant Hood*, pp. 181, 182; "Jeff Davis Legion," Chapter 14, p. 2, Waring Papers, GHS.

21. OR, v. 27, pt. 3, p. 872; Grimsley, *Battles*, p. 8; Hall, "'Army Is Moving,'" *B&G*, v. 21, no. 3, pp. 17, 19; Sorrel, *Recollections*, p. 243; Reade, *In the Saddle*, p. 53.

22. Blackford, Annotations, UVA; Lee, *Recollections*, p. 96.

23. Wert, *General James Longstreet*, p. 250; Sears, *Gettysburg*, p. 64.

24. *Annals*, p. 395; Andrews, ed., *Scraps of Paper*, p. 125; Gallagher, "Brandy Station," *B&G*, v. 8, no. 1, p. 13.

25. Gallagher, "Brandy Station," *B&G*, v. 8, no. 1, p. 45; Brennan, "Thunder," *N&S*, v. 5, no. 3, p. 24; Hall, "'Army Is Moving,'" *B&G*, v. 21, no. 3, p. 17; Freeman, *Lee's Lieutenants*, v. 3, p. 5; McClellan, *I Rode*, p. 263.

26. OR, v. 27, pt. 2, p. 190; pt. 3, pp. 27–28; Wert, *Sword of Lincoln*, p. 260; Wittenberg, *Union Cavalry*, p. 251.

27. Wert, *Sword of Lincoln*, p. 256; Styple, ed., *Generals in Bronze*, pp. 116, 131, 132; Starr, *Union Cavalry*, v. 1, pp. 314, 314n.

28. Gallagher, ed., *Chancellorsville*, p. 66; *Annals*, p. 135.

29. OR, v. 27, pt. 1, p. 950; SOR, v. 5, p. 227; *Annals*, p. 448.

30. Cheney, Diary, p. 25, USAMHI; Wittenberg, *Union Cavalry*, p. 259; Coddington, *Gettysburg Campaign*, p. 56; *SOR*, v. 5, p. 372; Bradshaw, ed., *Civil War Diary*, p. 10; Bowmaster, "Confederate Cavalrymen," pp. 28, 29, USAMHI.

31. *OR*, v. 27, pt. 2, p. 680; Coddington, *Gettysburg Campaign*, p. 57; Brennan, "Thunder," *N&S*, v. 5, no. 3, p. 26; Philadelphia *Weekly Times*, June 26, 1880; Beale, *Lieutenant of Cavalry*, p. 84; Hopkins, *From Bull Run to Appomattox*, p. 91.

32. Chiswell Dabney–Father, June 14, 1863, Saunders Family Papers, VHS; Reade, *In the Saddle*, p. 56; *OR*, v. 27, pt. 2, pp. 680, 721.

33. Chiswell Dabney–Father, June 14, 1863, Saunders Family Papers, VHS; Reade, *In the Saddle*, p. 56; *OR*, v. 27, pt. 2, pp. 680, 721; McClellan, *I Rode*, pp. 268, 269.

34. Wittenberg, *Union Cavalry*, p. 261; Musick, *6th Virginia Cavalry*, p. 38; *Southern Bivouac*, v. 2, p. 357.

35. *OR*, v. 27, pt. 2, pp. 680, 721; *SOR*, v. 5, p. 228; Gallagher, "Brandy Station," *B&G*, v. 8, no. 1, p. 19; Clark, ed., *Histories*, v. 3, p. 90.

36. Cooke, *Wearing*, pp. 21, 23; Blackford, *War Years*, p. 90.

37. Wittenberg, *Union Cavalry*, p. xv.

38. Ibid., pp. 260–65; *OR*, v. 27, pt. 2, pp. 680, 721; *SOR*, v. 5, p. 228; James Z. McChesney–My Dear Sister, June 10, 1863, McChesney Papers, USAMHI; Gallagher, "Brandy Station," *B&G*, v. 8, no. 1, p. 19; Wise, *Long Arm*, pp. 594, 595.

39. *CV*, v. 32, p. 63; Neese, *Three Years*, p. 178; Styple, ed., *Writing and Fighting*, p. 232; *OR*, v. 27, pt. 2, pp. 749–50, 772; Cooke, *Wearing*, p. 18.

40. Philadelphia *Weekly Times*, June 26, 1880; *OR*, v. 27, pt. 2, p. 727; Freeman, *Lee's Lieutenants*, v. 3, pp. 8, 9; Myers, *Comanches*, p. 183.

41. Philadelphia *Weekly Times*, June 26, 1880; McClellan, *I Rode*, pp. 269, 270, 271; Reade, *In the Saddle*, p. 56.

42. *OR*, v. 27, pt. 1, p. 950.

43. Ibid., pt. 2, pp. 680, 733, 734, 736; Chiswell Dabney–Father, June 14, 1863, Saunders Family Papers, VHS; Brooks, *Butler*, p. 166.

44. Hunter, *Johnny Reb*, p. 385; *OR*, v. 27, pt. 2, pp. 681, 719, 735.

45. *OR*, v. 27, pt. 2, pp. 729–30, 744; Cadwallader J. Iredell–[Mattie], June 13, 1863, Iredell Papers, UNC; Brooks, *Butler*, p. 153; Wittenberg, *Union Cavalry*, pp. 296–303.

46. H. B. McClellan–My dear General, July 12, 1883, Wickham Family Papers, VHS; Chiswell Dabney–Father, June 14, 1863, Saunders Family Papers, VHS; Brooks, *Butler*, pp. 53, 155; Trout, *They Followed the Plume*, pp. 112, 113–14.

47. McClellan, *I Rode*, pp. 269, 271; Wittenberg, *Union Cavalry*, pp. 280, 281.

48. McClellan, *I Rode*, p. 271; *OR*, v. 27, pt. 2, p. 681; Wittenberg, *Union Cavalry*, pp. 281–82; Reade, *In the Saddle*, p. 57.

49. OR, v. 27, pt. 2, pp. 681, 749, 755; Wittenberg, *Union Cavalry*, p. 282; Frye, *12th Virginia Cavalry*, p. 38.

50. McClellan, *I Rode*, p. 272; Hall, "'Army Is Moving,'" *B&G*, v. 21, no. 3, p. 44.

51. OR, v. 27, pt. 2, pp. 681, 682, 722, 732; John S. Foster–Kate, June 13, 1863, Foster Collection, LSU; William G. Deloney–My Dear Rosa, June 10, 1863, Deloney Family Papers, UGA.

52. OR, v. 27, pt. 1, pp. 1024–25; pt. 2, p. 722; Augusta *Daily Constitutionalist*, June 20, 1863; Charlotte *Daily Bulletin*, June 18, 1863; Charlotte *Western Democrat*, June 30, 1863; McSwain, ed., *Crumbling Defenses*, p. 64; Baylor, *Bull Run*, p. 144; James Z. McChesney–My Dear Sister, June 10, 1863, McChesney Papers, USAMHI; History of the Bath Squadron, Gatewood Collection, USAMHI; John S. Foster–Kate, June 13, 1863, Foster Collection, LSU; Wittenberg, *Union Cavalry*, p. 287.

53. OR, v. 27, pt. 2, pp. 682–84, 771; SOR, v. 60, p. 59; Washington *Times*, June 8, 2002; James M. Scott, p. 10, Anderson War Record, VHS; Hillsborough *Recorder*, June 24, 1863; Gallagher, "Brandy Station," *B&G*, v. 8, no. 1, pp. 19, 20; Clark, ed., *Histories*, v. 2, pp. 91, 92, 93.

54. Beale, *Lieutenant of Cavalry*, p. 223; Thomas, *Robert E. Lee*, p. 305; Lippincott, "Lee-Sawyer Exchange," *CWTI*, v. 1, no. 3, pp. 39, 40.

55. OR, v. 27, pt. 1, pp. 950, 951; Wittenberg, *Union Cavalry*, pp. 302, 303.

56. Wittenberg, *Union Cavalry*, pp. 306, 308; "Civil War Union Soldier's 1863 Diary," USAMHI; Brumback, Diary, p. 4, Handley Library; Bradshaw, ed., *Civil War Diary*, pp. 12–13.

57. OR, v. 27, pt. 1, pp. 903, 904; pt. 3, p. 48; Starr, *Union Cavalry*, v. 1, p. 391.

58. O'Neill, *Cavalry Battles*, p. 20; McClellan, *I Rode*, p. 294; Blackford, *War Years*, p. 233.

59. Gallagher, "Brandy Station," *B&G*, v. 8, no. 1, p. 52; Tower, ed., *Lee's Adjutant*, p. 55; Styple, ed., *Writing and Fighting*, p. 232.

60. McDonald, ed., *Make Me a Map*, p. 150; OR, v. 27, pt. 2, p. 687; pt. 3, p. 876.

61. Wilkinson and Woodworth, *Scythe of Fire*, p. 216; Henry C. Burn–My Dear Father, June 11, 1863, Burn Collection, USC; John S. Foster–Kate, June 13, 1863, Foster Collection, LSU; Columbus *Weekly Enquirer*, June 23, 1863; Sutherland, *Seasons*, p. 257.

62. Anderson, Diary, copy in possession of Krick; Hamlin, "*Old Bald Head*," p. 133; Lafayette McLaws–My dear Emily, June 10, 1863, McLaws Papers, UNC; James Longstreet–My Dear General Wright, November 8, 1891, Munford–Ellis Family Papers, DU.

63. William G. Deloney–My Dear Rosa, June 15, 1863, Deloney Family Papers, UGA; Sears, *Gettysburg*, p. 73; Charleston *Mercury*, June 18, 30, 1863; Savannah *Republican*, June 17, 20, 1863.

64. Richmond *Examiner*, June 12, 1863; Richmond *Sentinel*, June 12, 1863; Richmond *Dispatch*, June 12, 1863.

65. "Jeff Davis Legion," Chapter 14, p. 9, Waring Papers, GHS; Sears, *Gettysburg*, p. 73; Younger, ed., *Inside*, p. 73; Jones, *Rebel War Clerk's Diary*, v. 1, p. 345; Richmond *Whig*, June 16, 1863.

66. JEBS–My Darling Wife, June 12, 1863, Stuart Papers, VHS.

67. JEBS–My Dear Flora, June 20, 1863, Stuart Letters, transcript copy in possession of Krick.

68. Ibid.; Richmond *Sentinel*, June 22, 1863, clipping, Stuart Papers, HL; James Longstreet–My Dear General Munford, November 8, 1891, Munford-Ellis Family Papers, DU.

69. *SHSP*, v. 8, p. 453; Douglas, *I Rode*, p. 280; "Jeff Davis Legion," Chapter 14, p. 9, Waring Papers, GHS.

70. Freeman, *Lee's Lieutenants*, v. 3, p. 18; Hall, "'Army Is Moving,'" *B&G*, v. 21, no. 3, p. 45; OR, v. 27, pt. 1, p. 41.

Chapter 13: To Gettysburg

1. Thomason, *Jeb Stuart*, p. 412.

2. Wert, *General James Longstreet*, p. 251.

3. OR, v. 27, pt. 2, pp. 687–88; O'Neill, *Cavalry Battles*, pp. 28, 29.

4. OR, v. 27, pt. 2, p. 688.

5. Wert, *Sword of Lincoln*, pp. 263–64.

6. OR, v. 27, pt. 2, pp. 688, 739–41; Brooke, Autobiography, p. 28, VHS; Robert Jones–My very dear & sweet Wife, July 15, 1863, Jones Family Papers, VHS; William F. Graves–My Dear Gen., August 25, 1897, Munford-Ellis Family Papers, DU; SOR, v. 5, pp. 471, 472; a fine, detailed description of the Aldie fight is in O'Neill, *Cavalry Battles*, Chapters 2 and 3.

7. Philadelphia *Weekly Times*, February 8, 1879; Wert, *Mosby's Rangers*, pp. 68–69; O'Neill, *Cavalry Battles*, p. 94.

8. OR, v. 27, pt. 2, p. 688; Philadelphia *Weekly Times*, February 8, 1879; Reade, *In the Saddle*, pp. 65, 67; Coltrane, *Memoirs*, pp. 12, 13; Von Borcke, *Memoirs*, v. 2, pp. 286, 287.

9. OR, v. 27, pt. 1, pp. 963–64; Coltrane, *Memoirs*, p. 13; Driver, *10th Virginia Cavalry*, p. 38; O'Neill, *Cavalry Battles*, pp. 72–74.

10. Glazier, *Three Years*, p. 230; OR, v. 27, pt. 2, p. 689; Chiswell Dabney–Father, June 20, 1863, Saunders Family Papers, VHS; O'Neill, *Cavalry Battles*, pp. 97, 98; Carter, *Sabres*, p. 70; Sears, *Gettysburg*, p. 104; Taylor, Diary, WFU.

11. OR, v. 27, pt. 2, p. 689; O'Neill, *Cavalry Battles*, pp. 101–9; Philadelphia *Weekly Times*, February 8, 1879; Blackford, Annotations, UVA; Scheibert, *Seven Months*, p. 105; Slivka, "Heros von Borcke's Home," *B&G*, v. 22, no. 4, p. 29.

12. Reade, *In the Saddle*, pp. 68, 69; Scheibert, *Seven Months*, p. 105; Blackford, *War Years*, p. 219; Slivka, "Heros von Borcke's Home," *B&G*, v. 22, no. 4, p. 29; Cleneay, "A Child's Recollection," UVA.

13. Blackford, *War Years*, p. 159; Scheibert, *Seven Months*, p. 42; Blackford, Annotations, UVA; Trout, *They Followed the Plume*, p. 280.

14. OR, v. 27, pt. 2, p. 690; Carter, *Sabres*, p. 20; O'Neill, *Cavalry Battles*, pp. 114, 117.

15. OR, v. 27, pt. 2, pp. 690–91; O'Neill, *Cavalry Battles*, pp. 120, 124, 126, 132, 147.

16. OR, v. 27, pt. 2, p. 691; McDonald, *History*, pp. 151–52; Bradshaw, ed., *Civil War Diary*, pp. 14, 15; Charlotte *Daily Bulletin*, July 7, 1863; Baylor, *Bull Run*, p. 149; "Jeff Davis Legion," Chapter 14, p. 15, Waring Papers, GHS; Coltrane, *Memoirs*, p. 14; Clark, ed., *Histories*, v. 3, pp. 533–34; Thomason, *Jeb Stuart*, pp. 424–25.

17. OR, v. 27, pt. 2, p. 691; pt. 3, p. 244; Clark, ed., *Histories*, v. 3, p. 566; Reade, *In the Saddle*, p. 72.

18. OR, v. 27, pt. 2, p. 315; Sorrel, *Recollections*, p. 243; O'Neill, *Cavalry Battles*, p. 168; "Jeff Davis Legion," Chapter 14, p. 16, Waring Papers, GHS.

19. Reade, *In the Saddle*, p. 72; H. B. McClellan–A. L. Long, March 14, 1887, Stuart Papers, VHS; Maurice, ed., *Aide-de-Camp of Lee*, p. 199; OR, v. 27, pt. 2, p. 316.

20. Freeman, *R. E. Lee*, v. 3, p. 41; OR, v. 27, pt. 3, pp. 913, 914, 915; R. E. Lee–JEBS, June 22, 1863, pp. 19–20, Lee Letterbook, VHS.

21. OR, v. 27, pt. 3, p. 915.

22. Ibid., pp. 915, 923.

23. R. E. Lee–JEBS, June 23, 1863, pp. 23–24, Lee Letterbook, VHS; Gallagher, ed., *First Day*, pp. 16, 145n; Trudeau, *Gettysburg*, p. 69n.

24. Gallagher, ed., *First Day*, pp. 17, 19; Maurice, ed., *Aide-de-Camp of Lee*, pp. 201, 207, 208n, 210; A. L. Long–H. B. McClellan, March 11, 1887, McClellan Papers, VHS.

25. OR, v. 27, pt. 2, p. 316; Gallagher, ed., *Lee the Soldier*, p. 14.

26. Sears, *Gettysburg*, p. 105; Gallagher, ed., *First Day*, pp. 14, 17, 20; Freeman, *Lee's Lieutenants*, v. 3, p. 57; Haines, "Confederate Command Failure," GM, no. 35, p. 17; SOR, v. 5, p. 83; Schildt, *Roads to Gettysburg*, pp. 147, 148, 196, 197; OR, v. 27, pt. 2, p. 297; Gallagher, ed., *Lee the Soldier*, p. 14.

27. Coddington, *Gettysburg Campaign*, p. 108; Thomas T. Munford–My dear Sir, January 21, 1898, Ropes Papers, BU; Sorrel, *Recollections*, p. 114; James Longstreet–My Dear General Munford, November 8, 1891, Munford-Ellis Family Papers, DU.

28. Sears, *Gettysburg*, p. 105; OR, v. 27, pt. 3, pp. 268, 272, 276, 281, 284, 285, 286, 295, 297, 307; James Longstreet–[H. B. McClellan], n.d., McClellan

Papers, VHS; Latrobe, Diary, VHS; *SOR*, v. 5, p. 83; Schildt, *Roads to Gettysburg*, pp. 180, 185, 190, 196, 197, 201, 203, 204; Haines, "Confederate Command Failure," GM, no. 35, p. 17; Gallagher, ed., *First Day*, p. 14.

29. A. L. Long–H. B. McClellan, March 11, 1887, McClellan Papers, VHS; *OR*, v. 27, pt. 2, p. 297; Alexander, *Military Memoirs*, p. 374.

30. *OR*, v. 27, pt. 3, p. 923; Freeman, *Lee's Lieutenants*, v. 3, p. 57; Callihan, "Jeb Stuart's Fateful Ride," GM, no. 24, pp. 10, 15; Philadelphia *Weekly Times*, February 8, 1879; Coddington, *Gettysburg Campaign*, p. 109; McClellan, *I Rode*, p. 315; Cozzens, ed., *B&L*, v. 6, p. 282.

31. Mitchell, ed., *Letters . . . Mosby*, p. 148; Cozzens, ed., *B&L*, v. 6, p. 282; *OR*, v. 27, pt. 3, p. 923.

32. McClellan, *I Rode*, pp. 316, 317.

33. Ibid., pp. 316, 317, 318.

34. Ibid., p. 317; *OR*, v. 27, pt. 2, p. 692; pt. 3, p. 923.

35. *OR*, v. 27, pt. 2, p. 923.

36. *OR*, v. 27, pt. 2, pp. 443, 464; pt. 3, p. 914; Nesbitt, *Saber*, pp. 65, 67; H. B. McClellan–A. L. Long, March 14, 1887, Stuart Papers, VHS.

37. McClellan, *I Rode*, p. 318; James Longstreet–My Dear General Munford, November 8, 1891, Munford-Ellis Family Papers, DU; *OR*, v. 27, pt. 2, p. 692.

38. McClellan, *I Rode*, p. 319.

39. *OR*, v. 27, pt. 3, p. 927.

40. Ibid.

41. *OR*, v. 27, pt. 2, p. 692; Carter, *Sabres*, p. 71; Richard H. Watkins–[Wife], July 18, 1863, Watkins Papers, VHS; Busey and Martin, *Regimental Strengths*, p. 244; Garnett, *J. E. B. Stuart*, p. 36.

42. *OR*, v. 27, pt. 2, p. 692; Thomason, *Jeb Stuart*, p. 427; Trudeau, *Gettysburg*, p. 67; Philadelphia *Weekly Times*, February 8, 1879; Beale, *Lieutenant of Cavalry*, p. 111.

43. *OR*, v. 27, pt. 2, p. 692; McClellan, *I Rode*, p. 321; Scott, Memoir, p. 16, VHS; Philadelphia *Weekly Times*, December 29, 1879; Carter, *Sabres*, p. 71; Schildt, *Roads to Gettysburg*, p. 210.

44. *OR*, v. 27, pt. 2, p. 692; Scott, John Z. H., Memoir, p. 16, VHS; Atkinson, Memoirs, p. 14, VATU.

45. McClellan, *I Rode*, p. 321; Powell, "Stuart's Ride," GM, no. 20, p. 35; Krolick, "Lee vs. Stuart," *Virginia Country's Civil War*, v. 2, pp. 28, 29; Philadelphia *Weekly Times*, December 29, 1879.

46. McClellan, *I Rode*, p. 321; *SHSP*, v. 4, p. 74; Sears, *Gettysburg*, p. 106; Callihan, "Jeb Stuart's Fateful Ride," GM, no. 24, p. 12.

47. Maurice, ed., *Aide-de-Camp of Lee*, pp. 222–23.

48. Scott, John Z. H., Memoir, pp. 16, 17, VHS.

49. *SHSP*, v. 4, p. 74; *OR*, v. 27, pt. 2, pp. 464–68, 707; Haines, "Jeb Stuart's Advance," GM, no. 29, pp. 55, 56.

50. Freeman, *Lee's Lieutenants*, v. 3, pp. xi, xxxii; Krolick, "Lee vs. Stuart," *Virginia Country's Civil War*, v. 2, p. 29; Brennan, "It Wasn't Stuart's Fault," *N&S*, v. 6, no. 5, pp. 35, 36.

51. Trout, ed., *Riding with Stuart*, p. 3; Philadelphia *Weekly Times*, February 8, 1879.

52. Philadelphia *Weekly Times*, December 29, 1879; Cozzens, ed., *B&L*, v. 6, p. 284; McClellan, *I Rode*, p. 315.

53. Cooke, *Wearing*, p. 231; *OR*, v. 27, pt. 2, p. 693; Carter, *Sabres*, pp. 71, 72; Whitehead, Campaigns, p. 74, UVA; Robinson, Reminiscences, p. 6, VHS; Wittenberg and Petruzzi, *Plenty of Blame*, p. 19.

54. *OR*, v. 27, pt. 2, p. 693; Philadelphia *Weekly Times*, February 8, 1879; Cadwallader J. Iredell–Shaw, July 9, 1863, Iredell Papers, UNC; Wittenberg and Petruzzi, *Plenty of Blame*, pp. 12–16.

55. Norman R. Fitzhugh–Sister, July 16, 1863, Corse Papers, UNC; Philadelphia *Weekly Times*, February 8, 1879; Jones, *Rebel War Clerk's Diary*, v. 1, p. 366.

56. Schildt, *Roads to Gettysburg*, pp. 214, 225, 256, 257, 281; Haines, "Confederate Command Failure," GM, no. 35, p. 18; Jones, *Rebel War Clerk's Diary*, v. 1, p. 366.

57. Beale, *Lieutenant of Cavalry*, p. 112; *OR*, v. 27, pt. 2, p. 693; Clark, ed., *Histories*, v. 5, p. 627; Wittenberg and Petruzzi, *Plenty of Blame*, pp. 25, 26; Gen. J. E. B. Stuart's Famous Raid in Maryland and Pennsylvania, Grinman Family Papers, VHS; Samuel S. Biddle–My dear Pa, July 16, 1863, Biddle Letters, DU.

58. *OR*, v. 27, pt. 2, p. 693; Trudeau, *Gettysburg*, p. 103; Armstrong, Memoirs, p. 15, USAMHI; Whitehead, Campaigns, p. 74, UVA; Philadelphia *Weekly Times*, February 8, 1879; McClellan, *I Rode*, p. 324.

59. *OR*, v. 27, pt. 2, p. 694; McClellan, *I Rode*, p. 324; Carter, *Sabres*, p. 72; Whitehead, Campaigns, p. 74, UVA; "Jeb Stuart in Maryland, June 1863," Keidel Papers, MDHS.

60. *OR*, v. 27, pt. 2, p. 694; CV, v. 9, p. 370; Johnson, *In the Footsteps*, p. 111; Carter, *Sabres*, p. 72; Reade, *In the Saddle*, p. 76.

61. *OR*, v. 27, pt. 2, p. 694; Wittenberg and Petruzzi, *Plenty of Blame*, pp. 34–35; Blackford, *War Years*, p. 225.

62. *OR*, v. 27, pt. 2, p. 694; CV, v. 31, p. 55; William H. F. Payne–Fitzhugh Lee, May 12, 1871, Payne Letter, GNMP; Samuel S. Biddle–My dear Pa, July 16, 1863, Biddle Letters, DU; Whitehead, Campaigns, p. 74, UVA; McClellan, *I Rode*, p. 325.

63. *OR*, v. 27, pt. 2, p. 694; Cooke, *Wearing*, p. 238; McClellan, *I Rode*, p. 326; Letter of Reverend W. Kent Boyle, June 29, 1863, Keidel Papers, MDHS.

64. Cooke, *Wearing*, p. 239; Callihan, "Jeb Stuart's Fateful Ride," GM, no. 24, pp. 12, 13; Coddington, *Gettysburg Campaign*, p. 206; Fitz Lee–W. C. Wickham, August 18, 1863, Virginia Cavalry 4th Regiment Papers, HL; Harrell, *2nd North Carolina Cavalry*, p. 154; "Jeff Davis Legion," Chapter 14, p. 21, Waring Papers, GHS; Carter, *Sabres*, p. 73.

65. *OR*, v. 27, pt. 2, p. 695; McClellan, *I Rode*, p. 326; Carter, *Sabres*, p. 73; Wittenberg and Petruzzi, *Plenty of Blame*, pp. 44–45; "Jeb Stuart in Maryland, June 1863," Keidel Papers, MDHS.

66. *OR*, v. 27, pt. 2, p. 695.

67. Ibid., p. 316; Cozzens, ed., *B&L*, v. 5, p. 369; Wert, *General James Longstreet*, p. 254; Smith, *With Stonewall Jackson*, p. 55; Maurice, ed., *Aide-de-Camp of Lee*, p. 218; Haines, "Jeb Stuart's Advance," GM, no. 29, p. 45.

68. Wert, *General James Longstreet*, pp. 254–55; *OR*, v. 27, pt. 2, p. 316; John Mosby–James Keith, January 27, 1906, Mosby Papers, NC.

69. Wert, *General James Longstreet*, p. 255.

70. Wert, *Sword of Lincoln*, pp. 265–66.

71. Ibid., pp. 266–68, 269.

72. Ibid., pp. 269, 270; Wert, *General James Longstreet*, p. 255.

73. *OR*, v. 27, pt. 2, p. 695; Diary of Mary Bostwick Shellman, Keidel Papers, MDHS; "Summary," Keidel Papers, MDHS; Klein, ed., *Just South*, pp. 43, 44; Wittenberg and Petruzzi, *Plenty of Blame*, pp. 48, 52.

74. *OR*, v. 27, pt. 2, p. 695; Diary of Mary Bostwick Shellman, Keidel Papers, MDHS; Klein, ed., *Just South*, pp. 52, 54, 79; Wittenberg and Petruzzi, *Plenty of Blame*, pp. 52–55; CV, v. 31, p. 55.

75. Klein, ed., *Just South*, p. 71; Diary of Mary Bostwick Shellman, Keidel Papers, MDHS; "Jeb Stuart in Maryland, June 1863," Keidel Papers, MDHS; Clark, ed., *Histories*, v. 2, p. 97; Wittenberg and Petruzzi, *Plenty of Blame*, p. 59.

76. Wittenberg and Petruzzi, *Plenty of Blame*, p. 59; Diary of Mary Bostwick Shellman, Keidel Papers, MDHS; Beale, *Lieutenant of Cavalry*, p. 113; Hubard, "Civil War Reminiscences," p. 93, UVA; Garnett, *Riding with Stuart*, p. 46.

77. Wittenberg and Petruzzi, *Plenty of Blame*, p. 60; CV, v. 31, p. 55.

78. Wittenberg and Petruzzi, *Plenty of Blame*, pp. 59, 61; Cooke, *Wearing*, p. 239; *OR*, v. 27, pt. 2, p. 695.

79. *OR*, v. 27, pt. 2, p. 695; S. C. Shriver–My dear Lizzie, June 30, 1863, Shriver Collection, LC; Klein, ed., *Just South*, pp. 179, 181, 183.

80. S. C. Shriver–My dear Lizzie, June 30, 1863, Shriver Collection, LC.

81. *OR*, v. 27, pt. 2, p. 695; William H. Shriver, "My Father Led General J. E. B.

Stuart to Gettysburg," Shriver Collection, LC; Andrew K. Shriver–My dearest Mother, August 11, 1863, Shriver Family Collection, UND.

82. McClellan, *I Rode*, p. 327.

83. OR, v. 27, pt. 2, p. 695; Krepps, "Before and After Hanover," *B&G*, v. 21, no. 1, pp. 47–49; William H. F. Payne–Fitzhugh Lee, May 12, 1871, Payne Letter, GNMP.

84. OR, v. 27, pt. 1, p. 992; pt. 2, p. 695; Wittenberg and Petruzzi, *Plenty of Blame*, pp. 80–86.

85. OR, v. 27, pt. 2, p. 695; Cooke, *Wearing*, p. 240.

86. OR, v. 27, pt. 1, p. 992; pt. 2, p. 695; 5th New York Cavalry, "Movements," USAMHI; Alexander, "Gettysburg," *B&G*, v. 6, no. 1, pp. 25, 27; Wittenberg and Petruzzi, *Plenty of Blame*, pp. 89–94.

87. Blackford, *War Years*, p. 226; Beale, *Lieutenant of Cavalry*, p. 133; McClure, *East of Gettysburg*, p. 91; William H. F. Payne–Fitzhugh Lee, May 12, 1871, Payne Letter, GNMP; OR, v. 27, pt. 2, p. 696; McClellan, *I Rode*, p. 328.

88. Blackford, *War Years*, p. 226; McClellan, *I Rode*, p. 328; Wittenberg and Petruzzi, *Plenty of Blame*, p. 97; OR, v. 27, pt. 2, p. 696.

89. OR, v. 27, pt. 2, p. 695; Ryan, "Kilpatrick," GM, no. 27, p. 26.

90. OR, v. 27, pt. 2, pp. 695–96; Wittenberg and Petruzzi, *Plenty of Blame*, Chapter 5; Krepps, "Before and After Hanover," *B&G*, v. 21, no. 1, p. 51; *Encounter*, pp. 49, 52, 55, 56; McClure, *East of Gettysburg*, p. 96.

91. OR, v. 27, pt. 2, p. 696.

92. Ibid., p. 696; Krepps, "Before and After Hanover," *B&G*, v. 21, no. 1, pp. 55–57; McClure, *East of Gettysburg*, p. 99; H. B. McClellan–Theo, July 19, 1898, Garnett Family Papers, UVA; McClellan, *I Rode*, pp. 329, 330; Halsey Wigfall–Louly, July 18, 1863, Wigfall Papers, LC; Thomas T. Munford–My dear Mrs. Hyde, July 25, 1915, Hyde Papers, UNC; Clark, ed., *Histories*, v. 2, p. 97.

93. Samuel S. Biddle–My dear Pa, July 16, 1863, Biddle Letters, DU; Richard H. Watkins–My Dear Dear Mary, July 5, 18, 1863, Watkins Papers, VHS; McClure, *East of Gettysburg*, pp. 97, 98; Watford, ed., *Civil War in North Carolina*, v. 1, p. 125; Driver, *10th Virginia Cavalry*, p. 44; Heath J. Christian–Father, July 13, 1863, Christian Papers, LVA; Halsey Wigfall–Louly, July 18, 1863, Wigfall Papers, LC; William H. Perry–Pa, July 11, 1863, Perry Papers, USC; Peck, *Reminiscences*, p. 32.

94. OR, v. 27, pt. 2, pp. 467–68, 696; McClellan, *I Rode*, p. 330; Carter, *Sabres*, p. 73; Thomas T. Munford–My dear Mrs. Hyde, July 24, 1915, Hyde Papers, UNC; Wittenberg and Petruzzi, *Plenty of Blame*, pp. 127, 128; Richmond *Times-Dispatch*, December 12, 1909.

95. OR, v. 27, pt. 2, p. 696; Carter, *Sabres*, p. 76; Beale, *Lieutenant of Cavalry*, p. 114; *Southern Bivouac*, v. 1, pp. 206, 207; Tousey, *Military History*, p. 234; Wittenberg and Petruzzi, *Plenty of Blame*, pp. 136, 137.

96. *OR*, v. 27, pt. 2, pp. 696–97; Tousey, *Military History*, p. 234; Warner, *Generals in Blue*, pp. 462–63; Wittenberg and Petruzzi, *Plenty of Blame*, p. 139.

97. Wittenberg and Petruzzi, *Plenty of Blame*, p. 141; *OR*, v. 27, pt. 2, p. 697; Norman R. FitzHugh–Sister, July 16, 1863, Corse Papers, UNC.

98. Tousey, *Military History*, p. 238; Carter, *Sabres*, p. 76; Trudeau, *Gettysburg*, p. 263; *SHSP*, v. 11, p. 323.

99. *OR*, v. 27, pt. 2, p. 697; Tousey, *Military History*, pp. 238, 242, 243; Cheek et al., *Draft*, p. 56; Reade, *In the Saddle*, p. 78.

100. Blackford, *War Years*, p. 228; *OR*, v. 27, pt. 2, pp. 308, 697.

101. Jones, ed., *Campbell Brown's Civil War*, pp. 204–5.

102. Ibid., p. 205, 329; Wittenberg and Petruzzi, *Plenty of Blame*, p. 266; *CV*, v. 30, p. 445; Scheibert, *Seven Months*, p. 113.

103. Jones, ed., *Campbell Brown's Civil War*, p. 206; Blackford, *War Years*, p. 228; *OR*, v. 27, pt. 2, p. 697; Ladd and Ladd, eds., *Bachelder Papers*, v. 2, p. 1204; Norman R. FitzHugh–Sister, July 16, 1863, Corse Papers, UNC.

104. Cooke, *Wearing*, pp. 245–46; *OR*, v. 27, pt. 2, p. 697; Freeman, *Lee's Lieutenants*, v. 3, p. 139; Shevchuk, "Lost Hours," GM, no. 4, p. 70.

105. *OR*, v. 27, pt. 2, pp. 470, 697; Jones, ed., *Campbell Brown's Civil War*, pp. 219, 220; *SHSP*, v. 11, p. 323; Norman R. FitzHugh–Sister, July 16, 1863, Corse Papers, UNC; Brooke, Autobiography, p. 31, VHS; Carter, *Sabres*, p. 77; William G. Deloney–My dear Rosa, July 4, [1863], Deloney Family Papers, UGA; "Jeff Davis Legion," Chapter 15, p. 1, Waring Papers, GHS.

106. Peck, *Reminiscences*, p. 33; Watford, ed., *Civil War in North Carolina*, v. 1, p. 125; James M. Pugh–My Dear Sallie, July 12, 1863, Pugh Papers, UNC; Thomas T. Munford–My dear Mrs. Hyde, July 24, 1915, Hyde Papers, UNC; Alexander, *Military Memoirs*, p. 376.

Chapter 14: "I Have Been Blessed with Great Success on This Campaign"

1. Wert, *Gettysburg—Day Three*, pp. 27, 30, 31, 32.

2. Ibid., pp. 26–27; *OR*, v. 27, pt. 2, p. 308.

3. Wert, *Gettysburg—Day Three*, pp. 28–29.

4. Ibid., pp. 29, 30.

5. *Annals*, p. 424; *OR*, v. 27, pt. 2, p. 320.

6. Thomason, *Jeb Stuart*, p. 441; *OR*, v. 27, pt. 2, pp. 697, 724.

7. Ladd and Ladd, eds., *Bachelder Papers*, v. 2, p. 1340; v. 3, p. 1441; "Jeff Davis Legion," Chapter 15, p. 3, Waring Papers, GHS; Hackley, *Little Fork Rangers*, p. 86; *OR*, v. 27, pt. 2, p. 322; Stephens C. Smith–Father & Mother, July 12, 1863, Smith Papers, DU; Miller, "Southern Horse," *CWTI*, v. 45, no. 1, p. 34; Busey and Martin, *Regimental Strengths*, pp. 315–17.

8. Wert, *Gettysburg—Day Three*, p. 260; Ladd and Ladd, eds., *Bachelder Papers*, v. 3, pp. 1439, 1440.

9. OR, v. 27, pt. 2, pp. 697, 698, 724; SOR, v. 5, p. 271; SHSP, v. 24, p. 345; Carter, *Sabres*, p. 77; Ladd and Ladd, eds., *Bachelder Papers*, pp. 1377, 1438.

10. OR, v. 27, pt. 2, p. 698; Ladd and Ladd, eds., *Bachelder Papers*, v. 1, p. 209; v. 2, p. 1290; Wert, *Gettysburg—Day Three*, p. 261.

11. Wert, *Gettysburg—Day Three*, pp. 257, 266.

12. Ibid., pp. 257, 258, 262; OR, v. 27, pt. 2, p. 697; Ladd and Ladd, eds., *Bachelder Papers*, v. 2, pp. 1206, 1219, 1287; v. 3, p. 1532.

13. OR, v. 27, pt. 2, pp. 697, 698; Ladd and Ladd, eds., *Bachelder Papers*, v. 3, p. 1438; V. A. Witcher–John W. Daniel, March 15, 1900, Daniel Papers, UVA; Styple, ed., *Generals in Bronze*, p. 259; McClellan, *I Rode*, p. 338.

14. Wert, *Gettysburg—Day Three*, pp. 257, 262–63; Busey and Martin, *Regimental Strengths*, pp. 109, 113, 114, 115.

15. Wert, *Gettysburg—Day Three*, pp. 263, 264, 265.

16. OR, v. 27, pt. 2, p. 698.

17. Ibid., pp. 698, 724; "Jeff Davis Legion," Chapter 15, p. 12, Waring Papers, GHS; Wert, *Gettysburg—Day Three*, pp. 266–67.

18. Wert, *Gettysburg—Day Three*, p. 267; OR, v. 27, pt. 2, pp. 698, 724, 725; Ladd and Ladd, eds., *Bachelder Papers*, v. 2, pp. 1207, 1230, 1257, 1266; "Jeff Davis Legion," Chapter 15, pp. 8, 12, Waring Papers, GHS.

19. OR, v. 27, pt. 2, pp. 698, 725; "Jeff Davis Legion," Chapter 15, pp. 12, 14, 15, Waring Papers, GHS; Wert, *Gettysburg—Day Three*, p. 268.

20. Wert, *Gettysburg—Day Three*, pp. 268–69; Carter, *Sabres*, p. 77; Compiled Records: Virginia Cavalry, NA; Troxler and Auciello, eds., *Dear Father*, p. 112; H. B. McClellan–My dear Sir, April 30, 1886, Fishburne Papers, UVA.

21. OR, v. 27, pt. 2, p. 725; Wert, *Gettysburg—Day Three*, pp. 269, 270; William G. Deloney–My Dear Rosa, July 4, 1863, Deloney Family Papers, UGA; Stephens C. Smith–Father & Mother, July 12, 1863, Smith Papers, DU; William H. Perry—Pa, July 11, 1863, Perry Papers, USC; Ladd and Ladd, eds., *Bachelder Papers*, v. 1, p. 210.

22. OR, v. 27, pt. 1, p. 957; pt. 2, p. 345; Wert, *Gettysburg—Day Three*, p. 270; Haden, *Reminiscences*, p. 25; Andrew Newton Buck–Brother & Sister, July 9, 1863, 7th Michigan Cavalry File, GNMP; Beale, *Lieutenant of Cavalry*, p. 116.

23. OR, v. 27, pt. 2, p. 699.

24. Wert, *Gettysburg—Day Three*, Chapter 5.

25. Ibid., Chapters 9–13, quote on p. 251.

26. Ibid., p. 290; OR, v. 27, pt. 2, pp. 309, 322.

27. OR, v. 27, pt. 2, pp. 291, 322; John Imboden–S. O. Downing, August 4, 1891, Imboden Letter, GNMP; James Longstreet–My Dear General Munford, November 8, 1891, Munford-Ellis Family Papers, DU.

28. *OR*, v. 27, pt. 3, pp. 927–28; Bowmaster, "Confederate Brig. Gen. B. H. Robertson," p. 80, VATU; John S. Mosby–H. B. McClellan, February 14, 1887, McClellan Papers, VHS; John S. Mosby–General, February 19, 1896, Coleman Papers, VHS.

29. Bowmaster, ed., "Confederate Brigadier General," GM, no. 20, pp. 19, 22; *SOR*, v. 60, p. 114; Bradshaw, ed., *Civil War Diary*, p. 17; Neese, *Three Years*, p. 184; Scheel, *Civil War in Fauquier County*, p. 60; James Longstreet–My Dear General Munford, November 8, 1891, Munford-Ellis Family Papers, DU.

30. Haines, "Confederate Command Failure," GM, no. 35, p. 11; John S. Mosby–H. B. McClellan, February 14, 1887, McClellan Papers, VHS.

31. *OR*, v. 27, pt. 2, pp. 309, 311.

32. Ibid., p. 311; Brown, *Retreat from Gettysburg*, pp. 64, 85.

33. *OR*, v. 27, pt. 2, pp. 311, 699; Brown, *Retreat from Gettysburg*, pp. 79, 80, 181.

34. *OR*, v. 27, pt. 2, pp. 309, 699–700.

35. Ibid., pt. 1, pp. 988, 994; Russell A. Alger–L. G. Estes, February 12, 1897, Alger Papers, UM; *National Tribune*, November 10, 1887; Brown, *Retreat from Gettysburg*, p. 143.

36. *OR*, v. 27, pt. 1, p. 994; Brown, *Retreat from Gettysburg*, pp. 179, 180.

37. *OR*, v. 27, pt. 1, p. 994; pt. 2, p. 700; Alexander, "Ten Days," *N&S*, v. 2, no. 6, p. 14; Brown, *Retreat from Gettysburg*, pp. 182–84.

38. *OR*, v. 27, pt. 1, p. 994; pt. 2, p. 700; Brown, *Retreat from Gettysburg*, pp. 182–84; Alexander, "Ten Days," *N&S*, v. 2, no. 6, p. 14.

39. *OR*, v. 27, pt. 2, pp. 700, 701.

40. Brown, *Retreat from Gettysburg*, pp. 212–13.

41. Ibid., p. 213; *OR*, v. 27, pt. 2, p. 701.

42. *OR*, v. 27, pt. 2, p. 701; Alexander, "Ten Days," *N&S*, v. 2, no. 6, pp. 16, 17.

43. *OR*, v. 27, pt. 2, p. 701; Brown, *Retreat from Gettysburg*, pp. 225–29; Alexander, "Ten Days," *N&S*, v. 2, no. 6, pp. 16, 17; Clark, ed., *Histories*, v. 3, p. 570.

44. *OR*, v. 27, pt. 1, p. 995; pt. 2, p. 702; Alexander, "Ten Days," *N&S*, v. 2, no. 6, pp. 17, 18; Brown, *Retreat from Gettysburg*, pp. 230–32.

45. *OR*, v. 27, pt. 1, pp. 928, 995, 999; pt. 2, p. 702; Brown, *Retreat from Gettysburg*, Chapter 10.

46. Alexander, "Ten Days," *N&S*, v. 2, no. 6, p. 14.

47. *OR*, v. 27, pt. 2, pp. 398, 702–3.

48. *OR*, v. 27, pt. 2, pp. 702–4; pt. 3, pp. 994, 998; Robert N. Pendleton–Papa, July 9, 1863, Pendleton Letters, Handley Library; Cheney, Diary, p. 34, USAMHI; Carter, *Sabres*, pp. 81–82; Bradshaw, ed., *Civil War Diary*, p. 19; R. T. Hubard, Jr.–My Dear Father, July 11, 1863, Hubard Family Papers,

UVA; General Orders, No. 13, July 20, 1863, Virginia Cavalry, 4th Regiment Papers, HL; William Ball–Father and Mother and brothers and sister, July 9, 1863, Ball Letters, WMU; Kidd, *Personal Recollections*, pp. 178–81.

49. OR, v. 27, pt. 2, pp. 703, 704; SOR, v. 5, p. 265; JEBS–My Dear *Dear* Wife, August 26, 1863, Stuart Papers, VHS; McClellan, *I Rode*, p. 364.

50. Shoemaker, *Shoemaker's Battery*, p. 47.

51. Lord, ed., *Fremantle Diary*, pp. 228–29.

52. Wert, *Sword of Lincoln*, pp. 306–7.

53. OR, v. 27, pt. 2, p. 705; pt. 3, p. 1001; Firebaugh, Diary, p. 62, USAMHI; Carter, *Sabres*, p. 82.

54. Reade, *In the Saddle*, p. 85; OR, v. 27, pt. 2, p. 705; Carter, *Sabres*, pp. 82, 83; Wert, *Sword of Lincoln*, pp. 307, 308.

55. Blackford, *War Years*, pp. 195, 235; OR, v. 27, pt. 2, pp. 705, 706; "Jeff Davis Legion," Chapter 16, p. 1, Waring Papers, GHS; Reade, *In the Saddle*, pp. 86, 87.

56. Robert Brooke Jones–My Very dear & Sweet Wife, July 15, 1863, Jones Family Papers, VHS; James Jeter, August 8, 1863, Jeter Letters, VHS; Stephens C. Smith–Father & Mother, July 12, 1863, Smith Papers, DU; Galloway, ed., *Dear Old Roswell*, p. 29; Driver and Howard, *2nd Virginia Cavalry*, p. 94.

57. McSwain, ed., *Crumbling Defenses*, p. 56; Thomas T. Munford–My dear Sir, January 21, 1898, Ropes Papers, BU.

58. "Jeff Davis Legion," pp. 1, 17–18, 19, Waring Papers, GHS.

59. JEBS–My Darling Wife, July 10, 1863; JEBS–My Dearest Wife, July 13, 1863, Stuart Papers, VHS.

60. Blackford, ed., *Letters*, p. 195.

61. Krick, *9th Virginia Cavalry*, p. 22; John S. Mosby–Judge James Keith, January 27, 1906, Wilson Collection, VMI; Cozzens, ed., *B&L*, v. 5, p. 367; Sorrel, *Recollections*, pp. 153, 154; Goldsborough, *Maryland Line*, p. 101; Thomas T. Munford–My dear Mrs. Hyde, July 24, 1915, Hyde Papers, UNC; Haskell, *Haskell Memoirs*, p. 57; Thomas, *Bold Dragoon*, p. 253.

62. Younger, ed., *Inside*, p. 84.

63. OR, v. 27, pt. 2, p. 307.

64. Ibid., p. 313; Maurice, ed., *Aide-de-Camp of Lee*, pp. 180, 181.

65. Reunion of Confederate officers . . . February 1887, McIntosh Collection, USAMHI.

66. OR, v. 27, pt. 2, pp. 316, 321.

67. Maurice, ed., *Aide-de-Camp of Lee*, pp. 214, 215; OR, v. 27, pt. 2, pp. 687–710; Coddington, *Gettysburg Campaign*, p. 202.

68. OR, v. 27, pt. 2, pp. 687, 707–9.

69. Ibid., p. 707; Coddington, *Gettysburg Campaign*, p. 205; McDonald, ed., *Make Me a Map*, p. 175; *Annals*, p. 667.

70. For some historians' assessments of Stuart's performance see Freeman, *R. E. Lee*, v. 3, p. 147; Coddington, *Gettysburg Campaign*, pp. 205, 208; Tucker, *Lee and Longstreet*, pp. 196, 197; Krick, *Smoothbore Volley*, p. 77; Sears, *Gettysburg*, p. 502; Powell, "Stuart's Ride," GM, no. 20, p. 43; Thomas, *Bold Dragoon*, p. 255; Gallagher, ed., *Fighting For*, p. 228; for Lee's view see Ross, *Cities and Camps*, p. 76; Lee, *Recollections*, p. 102; Cozzens, ed., *B&L*, v. 5, p. 367; Gallagher, ed., *Lee the Soldier*, pp. 13, 14, 18.

71. Alexander, "Ten Days," *N&S*, v. 2, no. 6, p. 32; Coddington, *Gettysburg Campaign*, p. 208; Royall, *Some Reminiscences*, p. 25.

72. Coddington, *Gettysburg Campaign*, p. 208.

Chapter 15: Corps Command

1. Charles E. Taylor–Sisters and Mother, August 6, 1863, Taylor Papers, UVA.

2. JEBS–My Darling Wife, July 30, August 2, 1863, Stuart Papers, VHS; Wert, *Sword of Lincoln*, pp. 310, 311.

3. Richmond *Dispatch*, August 19, 24, 1863; Richmond *Whig*, August 18, 1863; for the removal of Stuart see Mobile *Advertiser and Register*, July 7, 1863.

4. Younger, ed., *Inside*, pp. 90, 91.

5. JEBS–My Darling Wife, August 11, 12, 1863, Stuart Papers, VHS; JEBS–My Darling One, August 18, 1863, Stuart Letters to Flora Stuart, NYHS.

6. OR, v. 27, pt. 3, pp. 1006, 1007, 1075; Blackford, *War Years*, p. 229.

7. William E. Jones–R. H. Chilton, August 7, 1863; Special Orders, No. 196, August 10, 1863, Jones File, CSR, CSA Generals, NA: John S. Mosby–General, February 19, 1896, Coleman Papers, VHS; H. B. McClellan–George W. Davis, February 1, 1896, Stuart Papers, VHS.

8. McClellan, *I Rode*, p. 320; McDonald, *History*, p. 170.

9. H. B. McClellan–George W. Davis, February 1, 1896, Stuart Papers, VHS; General Orders, AIGO, October 8, 1863, Jones File, CSR, CSA Generals, NA.

10. OR, v. 29, pt. 2, pp. 771–72, 779.

11. OR, v. 27, pt. 2, p. 335; v. 29, pt. 2, p. 659; Robert Randolph–My dearest Bert, August 7, 1863, Minor Family Papers, VHS; Abraham Jones–Parents, August 21, 1863, Jones Papers, ECU; Jedediah Hotchkiss–My Darling, July 14, 1863, Hotchkiss Papers, LC; Savannah *Republican*, August 12, 1863; William G. Deloney–My Dear Rosa, August 17, 1863, Deloney Family Papers, UGA.

12. James M. Pugh–Salle, August 12, 1863, Pugh Papers, UNC; John O. Collins–Wife, August 11, 1863, Collins Papers, VHS; William H. Perry–Pa, July 30, 1863, Perry Papers, USC; Driver, *14th Virginia Cavalry*, p. 25; Corson, *My Dear Jennie*, p. 106.

13. John O. Collins–Wife, August 20, 1863, Collins Papers, VHS; Abraham G. Jones–Brother, September 4, 1863, Jones Papers, ECU; M. F. Magner–Madam, August 28, 1863, Magner Letters, USAMHI; General Orders, No. 25, July 29, 1863, Garnett Family Papers, UVA.

14. OR, v. 29, pt. 1, p. 932; Henderson, Road, pp. 20–23; Raleigh State Journal, August 26, 1863; JEBS–My Darling Wife, August 2, 1863, Stuart Papers, VHS.

15. OR, v. 27, p. 3, pp. 1068, 1069.

16. Ibid., p. 1069.

17. Ibid., v. 29, pt. 2, pp. 707–8, 788; Longacre, Lee's Cavalrymen, p. 254; Raiford, 4th North Carolina Cavalry, pp. 58, 60; Warner, Generals in Gray, p. 40.

18. Warner, Generals in Gray, pp. 110, 348; Hartley, Stuart's Tarheels, pp. 2, 264; CV, v. 6, p. 216; Atlanta Constitution, March 12, 1893; JEBS–General, November 25, 1862, Letters Received . . . Confederate AIGO, NA.

19. OR, v. 29, pt. 2, pp. 707–8; Warner, Generals in Gray, pp. 191, 336; JEBS–Colonel, April 6, 1863, Lomax Family Papers, VHS; Elijah S. Johnson Diary, Johnson Papers, VHS; Robert Brooke Jones–My dear Wife, September 18, 1863, Jones Family Papers, VHS; William Taylor–My Dear Mother, September 17, 1863, Taylor Letter, VHS; Richard H. Watkins–My darling Mary, September 13, 1863, Watkins Papers, VHS.

20. JEBS–General, September 10, 1863, Stuart Papers, VHS.

21. Fitzhugh, Memoirs, p. 21, MC; Thomas L. Rosser–My Dear Wife, August 31, September 22, 24, 26, 1863, Gordon and Rosser Family Papers, UVA; Mitchell, ed., Letters . . . Stuart, pp. 349, 350; Endorsements, October 3, 4, 1863, Letters Received . . . Confederate AIGO, NA; OR, v. 29, pt. 2, p. 788.

22. JEBS–My Darling One, September 4, 11, 1863, Stuart Papers, VHS.

23. Freeman, Lee's Lieutenants, v. 3, pp. 211, 212.

24. Sutherland, Seasons, p. 273; Robert Randolph–Sister and Brother, September 7, 1863, Minor Family Papers, VHS.

25. Wert, General James Longstreet, pp. 300, 301, 303.

26. Hudgin, Account, copy in possession of Krick; McClellan, I Rode, pp. 372, 373; New York Times, September 28, 1863.

27. OR, v. 29, pt. 1, pp. 112, 118; McClellan, I Rode, p. 373; Charles A. Legg–Parents, August 1, 1863, Legg Letters, USAMHI; Elizah S. Johnson Diary, Johnson Papers, VHS; McDonald, History, pp. 170–72; Henderson, Road, pp. 33, 35, 36, 38.

28. OR, v. 29, pt. 1, pp. 118, 124, 128; New York Times, September 17, 28, 1863; McDonald, History, pp. 172, 173; Henderson, Road, pp. 40, 41.

29. McDonald, History, p. 174; McClellan, I Rode, p. 374; Bradshaw, ed., Civil War Diary, p. 24; Cheney, Diary, p. 61, USAMHI; Henderson, Road, pp. 41, 42, 47.

30. Henderson, *Road*, p. 49; *SOR*, v. 60, p. 30; John F. Milhollin–My Dear James, September 30, 1863, Milhollin Letters, USAMHI; *OR*, v. 29, pt. 2, p. 742; Clark, ed., *Histories*, v. 1, p. 448; JEBS–My Darling Wife, September 26, 1863, Stuart Papers, VHS.

31. Galloway, ed., *Dear Old Roswell*, pp. 37, 38; McDonald, *History*, pp. 174, 175; Fortier, *15th Virginia Cavalry*, p. 46; Abraham G. Jones–Parents, September 24, 1863, Jones Papers, ECU; Baylor, *Bull Run*, p. 156.

32. Galloway, ed., *Dear Old Roswell*, p. 38; Cheney, Diary, p. 66; Leonard Williams–My Dear Anna, September 25, 1863, Williams, "Civil War Letters," USAMHI; Hartley, *Stuart's Tarheels*, p. 266.

33. Clark, *Histories*, v. 3, p. 573; McDonald, *History*, p. 175; Galloway, ed., *Dear Old Roswell*, p. 38; Coltrane, *Memoirs*, p. 20.

34. McDonald, *History*, p. 175; Baylor, *Bull Run*, pp. 156, 157; Clark, ed., *Histories*, v. 3, pp. 573, 574; Galloway, ed., *Dear Old Roswell*, p. 40; Abraham G. Jones–Parents, September 24, 1863, Jones Papers, ECU.

35. Abraham G. Jones–Parents, September 24, 1863, Jones Papers, ECU; JEBS–My Darling Wife, September 26, 1863, Stuart Papers, VHS.

36. JEBS–My Darling Wife, September 26, 1863, Stuart Papers, VHS; *OR*, v. 29, pt. 2, pp. 742, 743.

37. Blackford, *War Years*, p. 242; Mitchell, ed., *Letters . . . Stuart*, p. 343; JEBS–My Darling One, September 4, 17, 1863, Stuart Papers, VHS.

38. JEBS–My Darling One, September 17, 1863, Stuart Papers, VHS; Thomason, *Jeb Stuart*, p. 481.

39. Mitchell, ed., *Letters . . . Stuart*, pp. 343, 344.

40. *OR*, v. 29, pt. 2, p. 800; v. 51, pt. 2, p. 774; JEBS–General, September 30, 1863, Stuart Papers, VHS; H. B. McClellan–Col., October 3, 1863, Boteler Papers, DU.

41. Dowdey and Manarin, eds., *Wartime Papers*, pp. 589, 594; Wert, *Sword of Lincoln*, pp. 315, 316; *OR*, v. 29, pt. 2, pp. 639–40.

42. Wert, *Sword of Lincoln*, pp. 314, 315; *OR*, v. 29, pt. 1, p. 226; pt. 2, p. 764.

43. *OR*, v. 27, pt. 1, p. 410.

44. Ibid., pp. 439, 440, 458, 460; *SOR*, v. 5, p. 593; Richmond *Sentinel*, October 26, 1863.

45. *OR*, v. 29, pt. 1, pp. 9, 440, 441, 458, 460; Richmond *Sentinel*, October 26, 1863.

46. *OR*, v. 29, pt. 1, pp. 441, 463, 465; Corson, *My Dear Jennie*, pp. 111, 112; Carter, *Sabres*, p. 92; Richmond *Sentinel*, October 26, 1863.

47. *OR*, v. 29, pt. 1, pp. 390, 394, 443, 463, 465; Coltrane, *Memoirs*, p. 22; Henderson, *Road*, p. 96; Macombe, Diary, CMU; Carter, *Sabres*, p. 92; William H. F. Payne–Fitzhugh Lee, May 12, 1871, Payne Letter, GNMP.

48. *OR*, v. 29, pt. 2, pp. 443, 444, 463, 465; Corson, *My Dear Jennie*, p. 112;

Goldsborough, *Maryland Line*, p. 185; Elijah S. Johnson Diary, Johnson Papers, VHS; Ephraim Bowman Diary, Bowman Family Papers, UVA.

49. Thomas Smith–Brother, October 16, 1863, Smith Papers, NC; *OR*, v. 29, pt. 1, pp. 410, 445–47; Henderson, *Road*, p. 141.

50. *OR*, v. 29, pt. 1, p. 447.

51. Ibid.

52. Ibid.; Charlotte *Western Democrat*, November 10, 1863; Cadwallader J. Iredell–[Mattie], October 23, 1863, Iredell Papers, UNC; Bridges, *Fighting with JEB Stuart*, p. 190.

53. *OR*, v. 29, pt. 1, pp. 447, 448; Freeman, *Lee's Lieutenants*, v. 3, pp. 255, 256; Blue, *Hanging Rock Rebel*, p. 234; Ephraim Bowman Diary, Bowman Family Papers, UVA; Clark, *Histories*, v. 3, pp. 579–80; Coltrane, *Memoirs*, pp. 22–23, 24; Armstrong, *11th Virginia Cavalry*, p. 58.

54. *OR*, v. 29, pt. 1, p. 448; Henderson, *Road*, pp. 155, 156.

55. *OR*, v. 29, pt. 1, p. 448; *SOR*, v. 5, p. 594; Henderson, *Road*, pp. 154–56.

56. *OR*, v. 29, pt. 1, pp. 448, 461; McDonald, *History*, p. 193; Cadwallader J. Iredell–[Mattie], October 23, 1863, Iredell Papers, UNC; Charlotte *Western Democrat*, November 10, 1863.

57. *OR*, v. 29, pt. 1, pp. 448, 461; Clark, ed., *Histories*, v. 1, pp. 427, 456; v. 3, p. 581.

58. Richmond *Sentinel*, October 26, 1863.

59. *OR*, v. 29, pt. 1, pp. 410, 411, 449; Wert, *Sword of Lincoln*, p. 316.

60. Wert, *Sword of Lincoln*, pp. 316, 317; *OR*, v. 29, pt. 1, pp. 411, 449–50, 459, 463; Thomas Smith–Brother, October 16, 1863, Smith Papers, NC.

61. *OR*, v. 29, pt. 1, pp. 451, 463; v. 51, pt. 2, p. 778; Merington, ed., *Custer Story*, p. 68.

62. *OR*, v. 27, pt. 1, pp. 332, 387, 391; Merington, ed., *Custer Story*, p. 68; Wert, *Custer*, p. 119.

63. *OR*, v. 27, pt. 1, pp. 383, 387, 391, 392, 452; Cadwallader J. Iredell–[Mattie], October 23, 1863, Iredell Papers, UNC; Merington, ed., *Custer Story*, p. 68; Kidd, *Personal Recollections*, pp. 222–24; New York *Times*, October 22, 1863; Charles Chapin–Brother Wilbur, October 22, 1863, Chapin Letters, USAMHI.

64. *OR*, v. 29, pt. 1, p. 452; pt. 2, p. 794; Abraham E. Jones–Father, October 26, 1863, Jones Papers, ECU; Carter, *Sabres*, p. 97.

65. *OR*, v. 29, pt. 1, pp. 452, 454; Bradshaw, ed., *Civil War Diary*, p. 31; Wert, *Sword of Lincoln*, pp. 317, 319; Jedediah Hotchkiss–My dear Brother, October 25, 1863, Hotchkiss Papers, LC; Corson, *My Dear Jennie*, p. 113.

66. *OR*, v. 29, pt. 1, p. 454; J. A. Tompkins–Ma, October 18, 1863, Tompkins Family Papers, UVA; Carter, *Sabres*, p. 97.

67. Jedediah Hotchkiss–My dear Brother, October 25, 1863, Hotchkiss Papers, LC; *OR*, v. 29, pt. 1, p. 452.

68. *OR*, v. 29, pt. 1, p. 457; Dabney Ball–General, November 3, 1863, Stuart Papers, VHS.

69. James Longstreet–My Dear General, October 13, 1863, Stuart Papers, VHS.

70. Perry, *Ascent*, p. 4; JEBS–My dear Miss Ella, November 6, 1863, Grinnan, Bryan, Tucker Families Papers, UVA; Mitchell, ed., *Letters . . . Stuart*, p. 354.

71. SOR, v. 5, pp. 566, 567; Neese, *Three Years*, p. 233; Driver, *10th Virginia Cavalry*, p. 50; Carter, *Sabres*, p. 99; JEBS–My dear Miss Ella, November 6, 1863, Grinnan, Bryan, Tucker Families Papers, UVA.

72. Wert, *Sword of Lincoln*, pp. 318, 319.

73. Garnett, *Riding with Stuart*, pp. 15, 16, 27, 28, 32.

74. *OR*, v. 29, pt. 2, pp. 817, 828; McSwain, ed., *Crumbling Defenses*, pp. 18, 24; Thomas T. Munford–My dear Sir, January 21, 1898, Ropes Papers, BU; George C. Young–Sister, February 28, 1863, Young Civil War Correspondence, UVA.

75. Wert, *Sword of Lincoln*, p. 320.

76. Ibid., pp. 320, 321.

77. Ibid., pp. 321, 322.

78. Stuart's report on Mine Run is in *OR*, v. 29, pt. 1, pp. 898–901.

Chapter 16: "Grand Jeb Stuart"

1. JEBS–My Darling Wife, November 21, 1863, Stuart Papers, VHS.

2. *OR*, v. 29, pt. 2, p. 866.

3. Ibid.

4. Garnett, *Riding with Stuart*, p. 38; Nanzig, ed., *Civil War Memoirs*, p. 127; Duke, Recollections, v. 1, pp. 150, 151, UVA; Cadwallader, Diary, FSNBP; Carter, *Sabres*, pp. 104, 105, 110; Driver, *10th Virginia Cavalry*, pp. 51, 52; SOR, v. 81, p. 680; Neese, *Three Years*, pp. 244, 245.

5. Rosser, *Riding with Rosser*, pp. 13, 19; Joseph H. Trundle–My Darling Mother, November 24, 1863, Trundle Letters, USAMHI; JEBS–My Dear Cousin, December 18, 1863, Stuart, Alexander H. H. Papers, UVA.

6. Garnett, *Riding with Stuart*, pp. 25, 26, 38; *OR*, v. 29, pt. 2, pp. 862, 863; Coltrane, *Memoirs*, p. 27.

7. Blackford, *War Years*, p. 93; Ross, *Cities and Camps*, pp. 166, 167, 168.

8. Ross, *Cities and Camps*, pp. 168, 169; Trout, *They Followed the Plume*, p. 44; JEBS–My Dearest Wife, October 5, 1863, Stuart Papers, VHS.

9. Ross, *Cities and Camps*, pp. 174, 179, 181, 183; Virginia Pegram–Dearest Field, January 26, 1864, McIntosh Letter, VHS; JEBS–My Darling One, January 30, 1864, Stuart Papers, VHS; JEBS–My very Dear . . . Friend, [January 1864], Stuart Papers, VHS; CV, v. 20, p. 112; McClellan, *I Rode*, p. 445n.

10. Fleet and Fuller, eds., *Green Mount*, p. 299; Wiggins, ed., *Journals*, p. 91; Bill, *Beleaguered City*, p. 188; Chesnut, *Diary*, p. 357.

11. Furgurson, *Ashes*, p. 237; Dyer, *Gallant Hood*, p. 219; Davis, *Jeb Stuart*, p. 370.

12. JEBS–My Darling Wife, January 27, 30, 1864, Stuart Papers, VHS; Cooke, Diary, DU.

13. JEBS–My Dearest Flora, February 8, 1864, Stuart Papers, VHS.

14. Garnett, *Riding with Stuart*, p. 32; Cooke, Diary, DU.

15. R. E. Lee–Genl, February 6, 1864, West Papers, VHS; Garnett, *Riding with Stuart*, p. 38; H. B. McClellan–Gen'l, March 28, 1864, Virginia Cavalry, 4th Regiment Papers, HL; Scott, *History of Orange County*, pp. 115, 155; CV, v. 2, p. 12.

16. JEBS–My Darling One, October 3, 1863, January 30, 1864, Stuart Papers, VHS; JEBS–General, January 27, 1864, Stuart Papers, VHS; William W. Blackford–General, January 24, 1864, Stuart Papers, HL; Blackford, *War Years*, pp. 249, 250; JEBS–General, January 27, 1864, Garnett Family Papers, UVA; Garnett, *Riding with Stuart*, p. 31; Krick, *Staff Officers*, pp. 75, 136, 140.

17. JEBS–General, January 15, 1864, McClellan File, CSR, Confederate Generals, NA.

18. Krick, *Staff Officers*, p. 78; Trout, *They Followed the Plume*, pp. 69, 70; Statement of A. R. Boteler, November 4, 1863, Field Dispatch Book, copy in possession of Krick.

19. JEBS–My Dear Col., February 6, 1864, Boteler Papers, DU.

20. JEBS–Col., February 10, 1864, Boteler Papers, DU.

21. OR, v. 51, pt. 2, p. 821.

22. William H. Stiles, Jr.–Father, February 19, 1864, Stiles Papers, EU; Garnett, *Riding with Stuart*, pp. 16, 44; JEBS–My Darling One, April 24, 1864, Stuart Papers, VHS; Cooke, *Wearing*, pp. 9, 14.

23. *Heritage Auction Galleries*, p. 49.

24. Wert, *Custer*, pp. 139–42; Garnett, *Riding with Stuart*, pp. 40–42.

25. JEBS–My Dear General, March 16, 1864, Stuart Papers, VHS; Thomas, *Robert E. Lee*, p. 319.

26. JEBS–General, March 23, 1864, Stuart Papers, VHS.

27. Custis Lee–Beaut, March 2, 1864, Ibid.; Endorsement, March 23, 1864, Stuart Papers, VHS; Cisco, *Wade Hampton*, p. 131.

28. Cisco, *Wade Hampton*, p. 131; Chesnut, *Diary*, p. 395.

29. *OR*, v. 36, pt. 1, p. 1027; Cisco, *Wade Hampton*, pp. 131, 132; JEBS–Sir, May 2, 1864, Stuart Papers, VHS.

30. Trout, *Galloping Thunder*, p. 441; JEBS–General, March 24, 1864, Stuart Papers, VHS; Endorsement, April 21, 1864, Stuart Papers, VHS; Trout, *They Followed the Plume*, p. 80; Thomas Munford–Jedediah Hotchkiss, August 19, 1896, Hotchkiss Papers, LC; Neese, *Three Years*, p. 53; Shoemaker, *Shoemaker's Battery*, p. 69; *OR*, v. 36, pt. 1, p. 1027.

31. JEBS–My Dear Custis, April 9, 1864, Stuart Papers, VHS.

32. Ibid.

33. Ibid.

34. Ibid.; Richard H. Watkins–My own Dear Mary, April 4, 1864, Watkins Papers, VHS; Bryarly, "Notes," copy in possession of Krick; JEBS–General, April 4, 1864, Stuart Collection, MC; General Orders, No. 8, April 6, 1864, Stuart Collection, MC.

35. JEBS–Dear Dr., April 30, 1864, Stuart Collection, MC; Special Orders, No. 38, March 8, 1864, Virginia Cavalry, 4th Regiment Papers, HL; *OR*, v. 51, pt. 2, pp. 855, 878; Philadelphia *Weekly Times*, May 24, 1879; Trout, *They Followed the Plume*, pp. 294, 296–97.

36. Wert, *Sword of Lincoln*, pp. 329, 331.

37. Ibid., pp. 326, 327, 331.

38. Ibid., p. 330; Starr, *Union Cavalry*, v. 2, p. 74; Gallagher, ed., *Wilderness Campaign*, p. 111.

39. Wert, *Sword of Lincoln*, p. 335; Gallagher, ed., *Wilderness Campaign*, pp. 36, 44; *SOR*, v. 6, p. 270; Tower, ed., *Lee's Adjutant*, p. 148.

40. Scott, *History of Orange County*, p. 49; Koonce, ed., *Doctor*, p. 124.

41. Koonce, ed., *Doctor*, p. 124.

42. Wert, *General James Longstreet*, p. 378.

43. Boteler, Diary, LC; Philadelphia *Weekly Times*, May 24, 1879; Lee, "Report," MC; *OR*, v. 36, pt. 2, pp. 940, 941.

44. Lee, "Report," MC; Garnett, *Riding with Stuart*, p. 51; Philip H. Powers–[Wife], May 4, 1864, Powers Letters, FSNMP; Boteler, Diary, LC.

45. Boteler, Diary, LC.

46. Ibid.; Lee, "Report," MC; *OR*, v. 51, pt. 2, pp. 887, 888; Garnett, *Riding with Stuart*, p. 51; Rhea, *Battle of the Wilderness*, pp. 85, 89.

47. Boteler, Diary, LC; Garnett, *Riding with Stuart*, p. 51.

48. Boteler, Diary, LC.

49. Ibid.; JEBS–My Dearest One, April 16, 1864, Stuart Letters to Flora Stuart, NYHS.

50. JEBS–My Dearest One, April 16, 1864, Stuart Letters to Flora Stuart, NYHS.

51. *Annals*, p. 670.

Chapter 17: "I Had Rather Die, Than Be Whipped"

1. Savannah *Republican*, May 26, 1863; Scott, *History of Orange County*, p. 114.
2. Wert, *Sword of Lincoln*, pp. 335–38, quote on p. 336.
3. Boteler, Diary, LC.
4. Ibid.; Garnett, *Riding with Stuart*, pp. 52, 53; Rosser, *Riding with Rosser*, pp. 19–21; Lee, "Report," MC; Cadwallander, Diary, FSNMP; OR, v. 36, pt. 1, pp. 871, 876–77; Gallagher, ed., *Wilderness Campaign*, pp. 119–24.
5. Boteler, Diary, LC; Philip H. Powers–[Wife], May 6, 1864, Powers Letters, FSNMP; Rosser, *Riding with Rosser*, p. 21; JEBS–General, February 10, 1864, Gordon and Rosser Family Papers, UVA; JEBS–General, April 25, 1864, Stuart Papers, VHS.
6. McDonald, *History*, pp. 225, 229; Isaac I. White–Sister, April 9, 1864, White Letter, UND; Andrew Gatewood–My Dear Ma, April 29, 1864, Gatewood Collection, VMI.
7. Gallagher, ed., *Wilderness Campaign*, p. 128; Garnett, *Riding with Stuart*, pp. 53, 54; Rosser, *Riding with Rosser*, p. 21; OR, v. 36, pt. 2, p. 466; Wert, *Custer*, pp. 152, 153.
8. Rhea, *Battle of the Wilderness*, pp. 344–48; Kidd, *Personal Recollections*, pp. 264–70; Rosser, *Riding with Rosser*, p. 22; Garnett, *Riding with Stuart*, p. 54.
9. Bowmaster, ed., "Confederate Cavalryman," p. 42, USAMHI; Frank M. Myers–Home Folks, May 16, 1864, Myers Correspondence, USAMHI.
10. OR, v. 51, pt. 2, pp. 893–94; Lee, "Report," MC; Richmond *Sentinel*, May 21, 1864; Gallagher, ed., *Wilderness Campaign*, p. 129; R. E. Lee–Gen, May 6, 1864, Lee Papers, VHS.
11. Wert, *Sword of Lincoln*, pp. 340, 341, 342; Wert, *General James Longstreet*, pp. 383–87.
12. Wert, *Sword of Lincoln*, p. 342; Telegram, May 6, 1864, Stuart Papers, VHS; Philip H. Powers–[Wife], May 6, 1864, Powers Letters, FSNMP.
13. Wert, *Sword of Lincoln*, pp. 343, 344.
14. Ibid., p. 344; Lee, "Report," MC; Cadwallander, Diary, FSNBP; Richmond *Sentinel*, May 21, 1864; Rhea, *Battles for Spotsylvania*, p. 36.
15. Boteler, Diary, LC; OR, v. 36, pt. 2, pp. 969, 970; v. 51, pt. 2, pp. 897, 898; JEBS–Mrs. J. E. B. Stuart, May 7, 1864, Telegram, Stuart Letters . . . Wife, UVA.
16. Boteler, Diary, LC; Garnett, *Riding with Stuart*, pp. 57, 58; Rhea, *Battles for Spotsylvania*, pp. 28, 29.
17. Garnett, *Riding with Stuart*, p. 58; Lee, "Report," MC; CV, v. 29, p. 340; v.

38, p. 10; Cadwallander, Diary, FSNBP; Driver, *5th Virginia Cavalry*, p. 74; Richmond *Sentinel*, May 21, 1864; Rhea, *Battles for Spotsylvania*, pp. 45–49.

18. Mertz, "General Gouverneur K. Warren," *B&G*, v. 21, no. 4, p. 14; Milling, "Jim Milling," copy in possession of Krick; Lasswell, ed., *Rags and Hope*, p. 83.

19. CV, v. 38, p. 59; Mertz, "General Gouverneur K. Warren," *B&G*, v. 21, no. 4, p. 14; Rhea, *Battles for Spotsylvania*, p. 52.

20. Mertz, "General Gouverneur K. Warren," *B&G*, v. 21, no. 4, p. 14; Rhea, *Battles for Spotsylvania*, p. 52.

21. Rhea, *Battles for Spotsylvania*, pp. 53–59, quote on p. 57.

22. Ibid., pp. 57, 60, 69, 357n; Mertz, "General Gouverneur K. Warren," *B&G*, v. 21, no. 4, p. 16; SHSP, v. 7, p. 129.

23. Rhea, *Battles for Spotsylvania*, pp. 60–64, 65–66.

24. Ibid., pp. 60, 87, 89.

25. Ibid., p. 88; Garnett, *Riding with Stuart*, p. 58.

26. Boteler, Diary, LC; Garnett, *Riding with Stuart*, p. 59; OR, v. 51, pt. 2, pp. 905, 906.

27. Garnett, *Riding with Stuart*, p. 61.

28. Wert, *Sword of Lincoln*, p. 354.

29. Ibid.

30. Ibid., p. 355; Gallagher, ed., *Wilderness Campaign*, p. 111; OR, v. 36, pt. 1, p. 65.

31. Macomber, Diary, CMU; Kidd, *Personal Recollections*, pp. 288–92; Philadelphia *Weekly Times*, May 13, 1882; Joseph Jones–Father, May 18, 1864, Jones Papers, NC; Gallagher, ed., *Spotsylvania Campaign*, pp. 127, 128.

32. Lee, "Report," MC; Bryarly, "Notes," copy in possession of Krick; Gallagher, ed., *Spotsylvania Campaign*, pp. 129, 131.

33. Newspaper clipping, "Stuart's Last Battle," Redwood Collection, MC; Lee, "Report," MC; Gallagher, ed., *Spotsylvania Campaign*, p. 132.

34. Theodore S. Garnett–My dear Captain, February 13, 1868, Garnett Family Papers, UVA; Gallagher, ed., *Fighting For*, p. 374; Norman R. FitzHugh–My dear Mrs. Stuart, July 18, 1864, Stuart Papers, HL; Rhea, *Battles for Spotsylvania*, p. 119.

35. Theodore S. Garnett–My dear Captain, February 13, 1868, Garnett Family Papers, UVA; Lee, "Report," MC; Garnett, *Riding with Stuart*, p. 62; Rhea, *Battles for Spotsylvania*, p. 119.

36. Theodore S. Garnett–My dear Captain, February 13, 1868, Garnett Family Papers, UVA; Richmond *Times-Dispatch*, May 21, 1911; Lee, "Report," MC.

37. Lee, "Report," MC; Kidd, *Personal Recollections*, pp. 294, 295; Macomber, Diary, CMU; Gallagher, ed., *Spotsylvania Campaign*, p. 133.

38. Lee, "Report," MC; Garnett, *Riding with Stuart*, p. 63; OR, v. 51, pp. 911,

913; Notes in copy of Henry McClellan's memoir, Johnson, Marginalia Notes, copy in possession of Krick.

39. A. R. Venable–Governor, June 7, 1888, Venable Letter, VHS; JEBS–My very Dear . . . friend, [April 1864], Stuart Papers, VHS; Fleming, "Last Days," p. 1, FSNMP; *Old Homes*, p. 114.

40. Manarin, *Henrico County*, v. 2, p. 386; Fleming, "Last Days," p. 6, FSNMP; JEBS–My very dear . . . friend, [April 1864], Stuart Papers, VHS; A. R. Venable–Governor, June 7, 1888, Venable Letter, VHS.

41. A. R. Venable–Governor, June 7, 1888, Venable Letter, VHS; Theodore S. Garnett–My dear Captain, February 13, 1868, Garnett Family Papers, UVA; Lee, "Report," MC; Gallagher, ed., *Spotsylvania Campaign*, p. 134; *OR*, v. 51, pt. 2, p. 912.

42. Notes in a copy of Henry McClellan's book, Johnson, Marginalia Notes, copy in possession of Krick.

43. Kidd, *Personal Recollections*, p. 295; Gallagher, ed., *Spotsylvania Campaign*, p. 134; *OR*, v. 36, pt. 1, p. 777; v. 51, pt. 2, p. 916.

44. Lee, "Report," MC; Garnett, *Riding with Stuart*, p. 65; Richmond *Sentinel*, May 21, 1864; JEBS–Braxton Bragg, 6:30 A.M., May 11, 1864, Stuart Letter, RML.

45. Lee, "Report," MC; Richmond *Times-Dispatch*, May 21, 1911; Garnett, *Riding with Stuart*, p. 66; McClellan, *I Rode*, p. 411.

46. Richmond *Times-Dispatch*, May 21, 1911.

47. Gallagher, ed., *Spotsylvania Campaign*, p. 138; Manarin, *Henrico County*, v. 2, pp. 386, 387.

48. Manarin, *Henrico County*, v. 2, pp. 386, 387; Gallagher, ed., *Spotsylvania Campaign*, p. 141; H. B. McClellan–Mrs. Stuart, October 16, 1864, Stuart Papers, VHS.

49. Lee, "Report," MC; Garnett, *Riding with Stuart*, p. 66; Robinson, Reminiscences, pp. 11, 12, VHS; Rhea, *Battles for Spotsylvania*, pp. 201, 202; Starr, *Union Cavalry*, v. 2, pp. 103–5; Gallagher, ed., *Spotsylvania Campaign*, pp. 139, 140, 141.

50. Manarin, *Henrico County*, v. 2, p. 385; Trout, *Galloping Thunder*, p. 468; Garnett, *Riding with Stuart*, p. 68; *CV*, v. 7, p. 167; Robinson, Reminiscences, p. 11, VHS.

51. Gallagher, ed., *Spotsylvania Campaign*, p. 140; Rhea, *Battles for Spotsylvania*, pp. 203, 204, 206.

52. Garnett, *Riding with Stuart*, p. 66; Theodore S. Garnett–My dear Captain, February 13, 1868, Garnett Family Papers, UVA; Gallagher, ed., *Spotsylvania*, pp. 142, 143; Rhea, *Battles for Spotsylvania*, pp. 203, 204.

53. Garnett, *Riding with Stuart*, p. 67; Richmond *Examiner*, May 17, 1864; Gallagher, ed., *Spotsylvania Campaign*, p. 142.

54. Garnett, *Riding with Stuart*, p. 67; "Facts and events leading up to the death of . . . Stuart," Garnett Family Papers, UVA.

55. Lee, "Report," MC; Philadelphia *Weekly Times*, May 5, 13, 1882; Gallagher, ed., *Spotsylvania Campaign*, pp. 142, 143.

56. Lee, "Report," MC; Robinson, Reminiscences, pp. 11, 12, VHS; Driver, *5th Virginia Cavalry*, p. 77; Philadelphia *Weekly Times*, May 5, 13, 1882; Gallagher, ed., *Spotsylvania Campaign*, pp. 142–44.

57. Garnett, *Riding with Stuart*, p. 67; A. R. Venable–Governor, June 7, 1888, Venable Letter, VHS; Gallagher, ed., *Spotsylvania Campaign*, p. 144.

58. H. B. McClellan–Mrs. Stuart, October 16, 1864, Stuart Papers, VHS; Theodore S. Garnett–My dear Captain, February 13, 1868, Garnett Family Papers, UVA.

59. Gallagher, ed., *Spotsylvania Campaign*, pp. 135–37; Clark, ed., *Histories*, v. 1, pp. 465, 466.

60. "Facts and events leading up to the death of . . . Stuart," Garnett Family Papers, UVA; Shotwell, "War Reminiscences," *Greene County Magazine*, v. 7, pp. 6, 7; H. B. McClellan–Mrs. Stuart, October 16, 1864, Stuart Papers, VHS.

61. *SHSP*, v. 9, pp. 138–39.

62. Rhea, *Battles for Spotsylvania*, pp. 205–6; Gallagher, ed., *Spotsylvania Campaign*, p. 144; *OR*, v. 36, pt. 1, pp. 790, 813.

63. *OR*, v. 36, pt. 1, p. 818; Merington, ed., *Custer Story*, p. 94; Kidd, *Personal Recollections*, pp. 297, 300; Macomber, Diary, CMU; Philadelphia *Weekly Times*, May 13, 1882.

64. *OR*, v. 36, pt. 1, p. 818; Macomber, Diary, CMU; Kidd, *Historical Sketch*, n.p., no; Shotwell, "War Reminiscences," *Greene County Magazine*, v. 7, p. 8; Mark Holland–Papa, May 16, 1864, Holland Family Papers, UVA.

65. Gallagher, ed., *Spotsylvania Campaign*, p. 145; Boston *Evening Journal*, June 9, 1864.

66. Garnett, *Riding with Stuart*, p. 70; "Death of General J. E. B. Stuart as Told by G. W. Freed, His Orderly," Fishburne Papers, UVA; *CV*, v. 20, p. 120; Gallagher, ed., *Spotsylvania Campaign*, pp. 145–46; Rhea, *Battles for Spotsylvania*, pp. 207, 208.

67. *CV*, v. 39, p. 98; Garnett, *Riding with Stuart*, p. 29; Hopkins, *From Bull Run to Appomattox*, p. 269; H. B. McClellan–Mrs. Stuart, October 16, 1864, Stuart Papers, VHS.

68. *CV*, v. 19, p. 531; v. 20, p. 120; Driver, *1st Virginia Cavalry*, p. 83; H. B. McClellan–Mrs. Stuart, October 16, 1864, Stuart Papers, VHS; A. R. Venable–Governor, June 7, 1888, Venable Letter, VHS; *Southern Bivouac*, v. 3, p. 34; Johnson, *In the Footsteps*, p. 65; Richmond *Whig*, May 17, 1864.

69. CV, v. 17, p. 76; Driver and Howard, *2nd Virginia Cavalry*, p. 119; Hubard, "Civil War Reminiscences," p. 92, UVA; H. B. McClellan–Mrs. Stuart, October 16, 1864, Stuart Papers, VHS; in a postwar letter, Thomas T. Munford–My dear Sir, January 21, 1898, Ropes Papers, BU, the Confederate colonel stated, "*there* was no necessity for his [Stuart's] *life* being sacrificed as it was at Yellow Tavern."

70. OR, v. 36, pt. 1, p. 828; CV, v. 20, p. 120; Whitehead, Campaigns, p. 94, UVA; Gallagher, ed., *Spotsylvania Campaign*, pp. 164n–65n.

71. Manarin, *Henrico County*, v. 2, pp. 388, 390; Johnson, *In the Footsteps*, p. 66; CV, v. 17, p. 76; "Death of General J. E. B. Stuart as Told by G. W. Freed, His Orderly," Fishburne Papers, UVA; Richmond *Whig*, May 17, 1864; H. B. McClellan–Mrs. Stuart, October 16, 1864, Stuart Papers, VHS.

72. H. B. McClellan–Mrs. Stuart, October 16, 1864, Stuart Papers, VHS; CV, v. 19, p. 588; Staunton *Spectator and Vindicator*, November 13, 1903; Goldsborough, *Maryland Line*, p. 253; Richmond *Times-Dispatch*, September 22, 1907.

73. Newspaper clipping, "Stuart's Last Battle," Redwood Collection, MC: Richmond *Times-Dispatch*, September 22, 1907, May 21, 1911; H. B. McClellan–Mrs. Stuart, October 16, 1864, Stuart Papers, VHS.

74. A. R. Venable–Governor, June 7, 1888, Venable Letter, VHS; Lee, "Report," MC; Thomas, *Bold Dragoon*, p. 292; Longacre, *Fitz Lee*, p. 152.

75. A. R. Venable–Governor, June 7, 1888, Venable Letter, VHS; Theodore S. Garnett–My dear Captain, February 13, 1868, Garnett Family Papers, UVA; Rucker, Memoir, JML.

76. H. B. McClellan–Mrs. Stuart, October 16, 1864, Stuart Papers, VHS; A. R. Venable–Governor, June 7, 1888, Venable Letter, VHS; Theodore S. Garnett–My dear Captain, February 13, 1868, Garnett Family Papers, UVA; McClellan, *I Rode*, p. 415; SHSP, v. 37, p. 68; Richmond *Times-Dispatch*, May 21, 1911.

77. Gallagher, ed., *Spotsylvania Campaign*, p. 147; Bridges, *Fighting with JEB Stuart*, p. 237; H. B. McClellan–Mrs. Stuart, October 16, 1864, Stuart Papers, VHS.

78. Garnett, *Riding with Stuart*, p. 71; McClellan, *I Rode*, p. 415; Lee, "Report," MC; OR, v. 51, pt. 1, p. 250; Gallagher, ed., *Spotsylvania Campaign*, p. 148.

79. A. R. Venable–Governor, June 7, 1888, Venable Letter, VHS; Cooke, *Wearing*, p. 19; "Death of General J. E. B. Stuart as Told by G. W. Freed, His Orderly," Fishburne Papers, UVA; McClellan, *I Rode*, p. 415.

80. Theodore S. Garnett–My dear Captain, February 13, 1868, Garnett Family Papers, UVA; Richmond *Times-Dispatch*, May 21, 1911.

81. Richmond *Times-Dispatch*, May 21, 1911; Johnson, *In the Footsteps*, p. 66; Bill, *Beleaguered City*, p. 216; Envelope, Stuart Letters . . . Wife, UVA.

82. Garnett, *Riding with Stuart*, p. 72; Jones, *Rebel War Clerk's Diary*, v. 2, p. 206; Galloway, ed., *Dear Old Roswell*, p. 61; Richmond *Times-Dispatch*, May 21, 1911; Warner, *Generals in Gray*, p. 110.

83. Von Borcke, *Memoirs*, v. 2, pp. 312, 313; Garnett, *Riding with Stuart*, p. 72; Richmond *Times-Dispatch*, December 12, 1909; Slivka, "Heros Von Borcke's Home," *B&G*, v. 22, no. 4, p. 30.

84. H. B. McClellan–Mrs. Stuart, October 16, 1864, Stuart Papers, VHS; McClellan, *I Rode*, p. 416.

85. McClellan, *I Rode*, p. 416; Richmond *Times-Dispatch*, December 12, 1909; Bill, *Beleaguered City*, p. 302n; CV, v. 37, p. 198; SHSP, v. 8, p. 453; *Heritage Auction Galleries*, pp. 53, 55, 56.

86. H. B. McClellan–Mrs. Stuart, October 16, 1864, Stuart Papers, VHS; McClellan, *I Rode*, p. 416; Richmond *Whig*, May 17, 1864.

87. Johnson, *In the Footsteps*, p. 67; Blackford, Annotations, UVA; Fleming, "Last Days," pp. 1, 3, 5, FSNBP; Fisher, *History and Reminiscences*, p. 406.

88. Johnson, *In the Footsteps*, pp. 67, 68; Thomas, *Bold Dragoon*, p. 294.

89. Richmond *Whig*, May 17, 20, 1864; Von Borcke, *Memoirs*, v. 2, p. 313; McClellan, *I Rode*, p. 417; Thomason, *Jeb Stuart*, p. 501.

90. Richmond *Whig*, May 17, 1864; McClellan, *I Rode*, p. 417; Von Borcke, *Memoirs*, v. 2, p. 313; Furgurson, *Ashes*, p. 268.

91. Richmond *Whig*, May 17, 1864.

92. Ibid.

Chapter 18: "The Greatest Cavalry Officer Ever Foaled in America"

1. Richmond *Times-Dispatch*, May 21, 1911; Bill, *Beleaguered City*, p. 216; Patton, *Pattons*, p. 56; Richmond *Enquirer*, May 14, 1864.

2. Richmond *Enquirer*, May 14, 1864; Richmond *Whig*, May 17, 1864.

3. Richmond *Enquirer*, May 14, 1864; Richmond *Whig*, May 17, 1864; McCabe, *Grayjackets*, p. 503.

4. Richmond *Whig*, May 14, 1864; *Carolina Watchman Weekly*, May 23, 1864.

5. Richmond *Whig*, May 24, 30, June 3, 1864; McCabe, *Grayjackets*, pp. 282–83; CV, v. 33, p. 329; John Letcher–My Dear Sir, May 28, 1864, Stuart Papers, VHS.

6. Resolutions of the Richmond City Council, May 14, 1864, Stuart Collection, MC.

7. Endorsement, Resolutions of the Richmond City Council, May 14, 1864, Stuart Collection, MC.

8. Reunion of Confederate Officers . . . February 1887, McIntosh Collection, USAMHI; Lee, *Recollections*, p. 125.

9. Dowdey and Manarin, eds., *Wartime Papers*, p. 731; General Orders, No. 44, May 20, 1864, Lee Collection, MC.

10. Douglas, *I Rode*, p. 280; McDonald, ed., *Make Me a Map*, p. 205; Sorrel, *Recollections*, p. 243; Neese, *Three Years*, p. 282.

11. McClellan, *I Rode*, pp. 320–21; Thomas L. Rosser–My Dear Wife, May 17, 29, 30, 1864, Gordon and Rosser Family Papers, UVA.

12. General Orders, No. 6, May 14, 1864, McClellan Papers, VHS; Lee, "Report," MC.

13. Boteler, Diary, LC; Philip H. Powers–My Dear Wife, May 15, 1864, Powers Letters, USAMHI; Norman R. FitzHugh–My Dear Mrs. Stuart, July 18, 1864, Stuart Papers, HL.

14. H. B. McClellan–My dear Madam, September 23, 1864, Stuart Papers, VHS.

15. P. St. George Cooke–Mrs. J. E. B. Stuart, May 22, [1864], Stuart Papers, VHS.

16. Johnson, *In the Footsteps*, p. 62; Thomason, *Jeb Stuart*, p. 10.

17. Perry, *Stuart's Birthplace*, p. 169; Will of James E. B. Stuart, Stuart Papers, VHS.

18. JEBS–My Darling One, March 19, 1863, Stuart Papers, VHS.

19. Perry, *Stuart's Birthplace*, pp. 63, 169; Johnson, *In the Footsteps*, p. 62.

20. Perry, *Stuart's Birthplace*, p. 169; Mary Custis Lee–[Flora Stuart], [1864], Lee Family Papers, VHS.

21. Perry, *Stuart's Birthplace*, pp. 169, 170.

22. Ibid., p. 170; Flora Stuart–Sir, April 25, 1887, copy in possession of Krick.

23. Perry, *Stuart's Birthplace*, pp. 172, 174; Extract, Stuart Family Bible, Stuart Papers, VHS.

24. Perry, *Stuart's Birthplace*, pp. 169, 173; Johnson, *In the Footsteps*, p. 62; Extract, Stuart Family Bible, Stuart Papers, VHS.

25. Perry, *Stuart's Birthplace*, pp. 159, 171; CV, v. 31, p. 244; Estate of Mrs. Flora Stuart, Deceased, July 15, 1925, Stuart Papers, VHS.

26. Thomas, *Bold Dragoon*, p. 297; CV, v. 23, p. 194; SHSP, v. 20, p. 352; Thomas, "Wartime Richmond," *CWTI*, v. 16, no. 3, p. 42; Manarin, *Henrico County*, v. 2, p. 860.

27. CV, v. 8, p. 40; v. 11, pp. 27, 201; v. 18, p. 273; H. Ben Palmer–Sir, January 1, 1903, Veteran Cavalry Association Letter, USAMHI.

28. CV, v. 15, pp. 294, 348; v. 16, p. 17; Title page of prayer by Reverend Walter Q. Hullihen, copy in possession of author.

29. Philadelphia *Weekly Times*, October 5, 1878.

30. Thomas, *Bold Dragoon*, p. 299; Klein, "J. E. B. Stuart's Life," *CWTI*, v. 25, no. 5, p. 50.

31. *Annals*, p. 670.

32. Ibid., p. 670; Hubard, "Civil War Reminiscences," p. 93, UVA; Moses, Autobiography, p. 58, UNC.

33. Klein, "J. E. B. Stuart's Life," *CWTI*, v. 25, no. 5, p. 50; Vandiver, *Rebel Brass*, p. 104; Griffith, *Battle Tactics*, pp. 183, 184; McWhiney and Jamieson, *Attack and Die*, pp. 134, 139; Thomason, *Jeb Stuart*, pp. 79, 80; Nosworthy, *Bloody Crucible*, p. 291; Longacre, *Lee's Cavalrymen*, pp. 47, 48; Redwood, "Horsemen in Grey," *CWTI*, v. 9, no. 3, p. 8; General Orders, No. 26, July 30, 1863, Stuart Papers, HL; General Orders, No. 7, April 5, 1864, Stuart Collection, MC; Rhea, *Battles for Spotsylvania*, p. 211; Rhea, *Battle of the Wilderness*, p. 40.

34. Griffith, *Battle Tactics*, p. 181; Schaefer, "Tactical and Strategic Evolution," Ph.D. diss., p. 199; Sorrel, *Recollections*, p. 243; Hubard, "Civil War Reminiscences," p. 94, UVA; Freeman, *Lee's Lieutenants*, v. 3, p. xxxii; Nanzig, ed., *Civil War Memoirs*, p. 146.

35. Lee, "Report," MC.

36. Gallagher, ed., *Fighting For*, p. 374; Jones, ed., *Campbell Brown's Civil War*, p. 300; British newspaperman Francis Lawley shared Johnston's assessment of Stuart in comparison to Western cavalrymen, see Francis Lawley–My Dear General, November 21, 1863, Stuart Papers, VHS.

37. Crowinshield, *History*, pp. 21, 36; Freeman, *Lee's Lieutenants*, v. 3, p. 431.

Bibliography

Unpublished Sources

ALABAMA DEPARTMENT OF ARCHIVES AND HISTORY, MONTGOMERY, AL:
Stuart, J. E. B., Letter, March 29, 1863

ANTIETAM NATIONAL BATTLEFIELD, LIBRARY, SHARPSBURG, MD:
Bryce, John W., Jr., "The Battle of South Mountain"
"Diary Kept by Jacob H. Brumbeck of His Service During the Civil War," 12th
    Virginia Cavalry File

ATLANTA HISTORICAL SOCIETY, KENAN RESEARCH CENTER, ATLANTA, GA:
McBride, A. J., Papers

AUGUSTA COUNTY HISTORICAL SOCIETY, STAUNTON, VA:
Garber Family Papers

BABCOCK LIBRARY, ASHFORD, CT:
Whitaker, Edward, Civil War Letters, typescript

BOSTON UNIVERSITY, MASSACHUSETTS MILITARY HISTORICAL SOCIETY COLLECTION, HOWARD GOTLIEB ARCHIVAL RESEARCH CENTER, BOSTON, MA:
Ropes, John C., Papers

CENTRAL MICHIGAN UNIVERSITY, CLARKE HISTORICAL LIBRARY, MOUNT PLEASANT, MI:
Macomber, Dexter M., Diary, typescript

DUKE UNIVERSITY, RARE BOOK, MANUSCRIPT, AND SPECIAL COLLECTIONS LIBRARY, DURHAM, NC:
Boteler, Alexander, Papers
Cooke, John Esten, Papers
Fletcher, Lucy Muse (Walton), Diary

Peter Wilson Hairston Papers
Hooke, Robert W., Papers
Stuart, J. E. B., Papers
William R. Perkins Library:
      Bedinger-Dandridge Family Papers
      Biddle, Samuel Simpson, Letters
      Longstreet, James, Papers
      Munford-Ellis Family Papers
      Smith, Stephens Calhoun, Papers

EAST CAROLINA UNIVERSITY, EAST CAROLINA MANUSCRIPT COLLECTION, J. Y. JOYNER LIBRARY, GREENVILLE, NC:

Jones, Abraham G., Papers

EMORY UNIVERSITY, SPECIAL COLLECTIONS AND ARCHIVES, ROBERT W. WOODRUFF LIBRARY, ATLANTA, GA:

Brooke, Noble John, Papers
Mobley, Benjamin L., Papers
Shuler, Spartan McCain, Letters
Stiles, William Henry, Jr., Papers

ETOWAH VALLEY HISTORICAL SOCIETY, CARTERSVILLE, GA:

Young, P. M. B., Family Papers

FORT SUMTER NATIONAL MONUMENT, LIBRARY, CHARLESTON, SC:

Ferguson, Samuel Wragg, Memoir

FREDERICKSBURG-SPOTSYLVANIA NATIONAL MILITARY PARK, LIBRARY, FREDERICKSBURG, VA:

Cadwallander, James M., Diary
Cox, Leroy Wesley, Memoirs, Charlottesville Artillery File
Fleming, Vivian M., "The Last Days of General J. E. B. Stuart"
Powers, P. H., Letters
Slifer, George W., Letters

GEORGIA HISTORICAL SOCIETY, SAVANNAH, GA:

Waring, Joseph Frederick, II, Papers

GETTYSBURG NATIONAL MILITARY PARK, LIBRARY, GETTYSBURG, PA:

Imboden, John, Letter
McChesney, James Z., Letter
Payne, William H. F., Letter, transcript
Seventh Michigan Cavalry File

HANDLEY LIBRARY, ARCHIVES, WINCHESTER, VA:

Brumback, Jacob H., Diary, typescript

Chewning, Charles R., Journal, typescript, edited by Richard B. Armstrong
Miller, William, Quartermaster Reports
Pendleton, Robert Nelson, Letters, typescript, Eleanor Monahan Collection
Pierce, Hugh Ogilvy, "An Autobiography by an Old Man"

HARVARD UNIVERSITY, HOUGHTON LIBRARY, CAMBRIDGE, MA:
Hamlin, Augustus C., Papers, Mollus Collection

HAVEN, E. AMY, "IN THE STEPS OF A WOLVERINE: THE CIVIL
WAR LETTERS OF A MICHIGAN CAVALRYMAN," UNPUBLISHED
MANUSCRIPT

HENRY E. HUNTINGTON LIBRARY, SAN MARINO, CA:
Brock, Robert Alonzo, Collection:
    Virginia Cavalry, 4th Regiment Papers
Stuart, James Ewell Brown, Papers

JONES MEMORIAL LIBRARY, LYNCHBURG, VA:
Rucker, Samuel B., Memoir

KITTOCHTINNY HISTORICAL SOCIETY, CHAMBERSBURG, PA:
Heyser, William, Diary

KRICK, ROBERT K., FREDERICKSBURG, VA:
Copies in possession of:
    Anderson, George Thomas "Tige," Civil War Diary
    Bryarly, R. P., "Notes," photocopy
    Carlisle, John W., Letter, typescript
    Carter, Aida, "Works Progress Administration of Virginia Historical
        Inventory: Shepherd Farm," September 13, 1937
    Hudgin, Wescom, Account of Confederate Service, typescript
    Johnson, Bradley T., Marginalia Notes
    Jones, William E., Letter, transcript
    McMurran, Joseph, Letter, typescript
    Milling, James Alexander, "Jim Milling and the War, 1862–1865"
    Stancioff House, Description
    Stuart, J. E. B, General, Field Dispatch Book
    Stuart, J. E. B., Letters
    Stuart, J. E. B., Letter to Senator Thomas W. Bocock, transcript
    White, Edward, Memoir, typescript

LIBRARY OF CONGRESS, WASHINGTON, D.C.:
Boteler, Alexander R., Diary
Brooks, William Elizabeth, Collections
Carman, Ezra Ayers, Papers
Hotchkiss, Jedediah, Papers
Pleasonton, Alfred, Papers

Shriver, William, Collection
Wigfall, Louis T., Papers

LIBRARY OF VIRGINIA, RICHMOND, VA:
Christian, Heath Jones, Papers

LOUISIANA STATE UNIVERSITY, SPECIAL COLLECTIONS, HILL MEMORIAL LIBRARY, BATON, ROUGE, LA:
Boyd, David French, "Boyhood of General J. E. B. Stuart," David French Boyd Papers
Foster, James, Collection

MARYLAND HISTORICAL SOCIETY, BALTIMORE, MD:
Keidel, George C., Papers

MUSEUM OF THE CONFEDERACY, ELEANOR S. BROCKENBROUGH LIBRARY, RICHMOND, VA:
Fitzhugh, Thaddeus, Memoirs, CSA (Units) Collection: 5th Virginia Cavalry
Lee Family Collection
Lee, Fitzhugh, Papers
Lee, Fitzhugh, "Report of Major General Fitzhugh Lee of the Operations of His Cavalry Division A. N. V. from May 4th 1864 to September 19th 1864"
McClellan, H. B., Papers
Morning Report of the Surgeon of 1st Regiment of Cavalry, May–June 1861, McGuire Collection
Price, R. Channing, Papers
Redwood, Allen Christian, Collection
Smith, James Power, Correspondence
Stuart, J. E. B., Collection

NATIONAL ARCHIVES, WASHINGTON, D.C.:
Carman, Ezra Ayers, Collection, Antietam Studies, Record Group 94
Compiled Records Showing Service of Military Units in Confederate Organizations, M861, Roll 62, Virginia: First Cavalry Through Twelfth Cavalry (10th Virginia Cavalry)
Compiled Service Records of Confederate Generals and Staff Officers and Non-Regimental Enlisted Men, Record Group 94, M331
Compiled Service Records, Record Group 109
Letters Received by the Confederate Adjutant General and Inspector General, 1861–1865, Record Group 94
Letters Received by the Office of the Adjutant General, Main Series, 1822–1860, Record Group 94, M567
Returns from Regular Army Cavalry Regiments, 1833–1916: 4th Cavalry, March 1855–December 1863, Record Group 94, Microfilm 744, Roll 40

NAVARRO COLLEGE, PEARCE CIVIL WAR COLLECTION, CORSICANA, TX:

Alexander, E. Porter, Papers
Buford, John, Papers
Carr, Jerome B., Collection of Letters
Dibble, Oliver, Papers
Hill, Daniel H., Papers
Jones, Joseph, Papers
Lee, Robert E., Papers
Longstreet, James, Papers
Mosby, John S., Papers
Reamy, P. R., Papers
Smith, Thomas, Papers
Stuart, J. E. B., Papers
Taylor, John G., Papers

NEW-YORK HISTORICAL SOCIETY, GILDER LEHRMAN COLLECTION, NEW YORK, NY:

Johnston, Joseph E., Letter
Stuart, J. E. B., Letter to Archibald Stuart
Stuart, J. E. B., Letter to Fitz Lee
Stuart, J. E. B., Letters to Flora Stuart
Stuart, J. E. B., Letter to Robert E. Lee

NEW YORK PUBLIC LIBRARY, MANUSCRIPTS AND ARCHIVES DIVISION, NEW YORK, NY:

Carman, Ezra Ayers, Papers

RICHMOND NATIONAL BATTLEFIELD PARK, LIBRARY, RICHMOND, VA:

Forrester, Richard Hynson, Jr., Excerpts from Civil War Letters of Rawleigh W. Dunaway, Bound Volume No. 31
Timberlake, John H., Letters, Bound Volume No. 20

ROSENBACH MUSEUM AND LIBRARY, PHILADELPHIA, PA:

Stuart, J. E. B., Letter, No. AMS 532/14

SCHAEFER, JAMES ARTHUR, "THE TACTICAL AND STRATEGIC EVOLUTION OF CAVALRY DURING THE AMERICAN CIVIL WAR," PH.D. DISS., UNIVERSITY OF TOLEDO, OH, 1982

SMITH COLLEGE, SOPHIA SMITH COLLECTION, ALUMNAE GYMNASIUM, NORTHAMPTON, MA:

Garrison Family Papers

TREVILLIAN, CATHERINE N., LETTER TO AUTHOR, JANUARY 23, 2006, WYTHEVILLE, VA

UNITED STATES ARMY MILITARY HISTORY INSTITUTE, ARCHIVES, CARLISLE BARRACKS, PA:

Civil War Miscellaneous Collection:
> Blackford, Eugene, Diary
> Bowmaster, Patrick A., ed., "A Confederate Cavalryman at War: The Diary of Sergeant Jasper Hawse of the 14th Regiment Virginia Militia, the 17th Virginia Cavalry Battalion, and the 11th Virginia Cavalry," independent study project, Virginia Tech University, VA, December 1994
> Chapin, Charles, Letters
> "Civil War Union Soldier's 1863 Diary," typescript
> Firebaugh, Samuel Angus, Diary, typescript
> Lambert, William H., Letters
> McIntosh, David Gregg, Collection
> Wilkin, William Porter, "Civil War Letters of William Porter Wilkin"
> Williams, Leonard, "Civil War Letters of Captain Leonard Williams"

Civil War Times Illustrated Collection:
> Armstrong, John E., Memoirs
> Cheney, Jasper B., Diary
> Griffin, James, Letters
> Lawrie, W. C., Letters
> Milhollin, John F., Letters
> Myers, Frank M., Correspondence
> Taylor, M. F., Reminiscence of Service, 1861–1865

History of the Bath Squadron, Gatewood Collection

Lewis Leigh Collection:
> Account of General J. E. B. Stuart, Capture of Chambersburg, Pennsylvania, October 12, 1862
> Blackford, William W., Letter
> Byars, A. H., Letter
> 5th New York Cavalry, "Movements of Regiment"
> Legg, Charles A., Letters
> Magner, M. G., Letters
> Maine Cavalry—1st Regiment Letter
> McChesney, James Z., Papers
> Munford, Thomas T., Letter
> Order Book, Wade Hampton's Cavalry Brigade, May 18, 1863–June 15, 1863
> Powers, Philip H., Letters
> Trundle, Joseph H., Letters
> Veteran Cavalry Association: Army of Northern Virginia, Letter
> Young, Robert S., Letter

Long, Eli P., Papers

UNITED STATES MILITARY ACADEMY, WEST POINT, NY:
Archives:
    Register of Candidates
    Register of Delinquencies
    Register of Merit
Special Collections, Library:
    Stuart, James Ewell Brown, Papers

UNIVERSITY OF CALIFORNIA, BANCROFT LIBRARY, BERKELEY, CA:
Bourn, William B., Family Papers

UNIVERSITY OF GEORGIA, SPECIAL COLLECTIONS, HARGRETT RARE
BOOK AND MANUSCRIPT LIBRARY, ATHENS, GA:
Cobb, Thomas R. R., Papers
Deloney, William Gaston, Family Papers

UNIVERSITY OF MICHIGAN, ANN ARBOR, MI:
Bentley Historical Library:
    Kidd, James Harvey, Papers
    Stone Family Papers
William L. Clements Library:
    Alger, Russell A., Papers
    Hunt, George W., "Custer and His Red Necks: A Brief Sketch of Incidents of
        the Civil War of 61 & 65"

UNIVERSITY OF NORTH CAROLINA, WILSON LIBRARY, SOUTHERN
HISTORICAL COLLECTION, CHAPEL HILL, NC:
Alexander, Edward Porter, Papers
Allan, William, Papers
Blackford Family Papers
Corse, Montgomery D., Papers
Dabney, Charles William, Papers
Hairston, Peter Wilson, Papers
Hyde, Anne Bachman, Papers
Iredell, Cadwallader Jones, Papers
McLaws, Lafayette, Papers
Moses, Raphael J., Autobiography
Price, R. Channing, Papers
Pugh, James Thomas, Papers
Withers, Anita Dwyer, Diary

UNIVERSITY OF NOTRE DAME, DEPARTMENT OF SPECIAL
COLLECTIONS, HESBURGH LIBRARY, SOUTH BEND, IN:
Shriver Family Collection
White, Isaac Ira, Letter

UNIVERSITY OF SOUTH CAROLINA, MANUSCRIPT COLLECTIONS, SOUTH CAROLINIANA LIBRARY, COLUMBIA, SC:

Burn, Family Papers
Perry, William Hayne, Papers

UNIVERSITY OF SOUTHERN MISSISSIPPI, MCCAIN LIBRARY AND ARCHIVES, HATTIESBURG, MS:

Pitts, Jack E., "Stuart's Raid Around McClellan's Army," typescript

UNIVERSITY OF VIRGINIA, SPECIAL COLLECTIONS, UNIVERSITY OF VIRGINIA LIBRARY, CHARLOTTESVILLE, VA:

Additional Papers of the Randolph Family of Edgehill, No. 5533-d, Box 1
Bowman Family Papers, No. 6743
Cleneay, Bessie L., "A Child's Recollection of Baron Heros von Borcke," No. 9585
Duke, Richard Thomas Walker, Jr., Recollections, 5 volumes, Duke Family Papers, No. 9521
Fishburne, Elliott George, Papers, No. 6542
Garnett Family Papers, No. 38-45-b
Grinnan and related Bryan and Tucker Families, Papers, No 49, Box 4
Hubard Family Papers, No. 8039-a, b
Letters of Confederate Generals, No. 11576
Stuart, Alexander Hugh Holmes, Papers, No. 345
Stuart, J. E. B., Letter to Major Henry Hill, No. 38-442
Stuart, J. E. B., Letter to Robert E. Lee, No. 448
Stuart, J. E. B., Letters to his wife, Flora Cooke Stuart, No. 7442
Taylor, Charles Elisha, Papers, No. 3091, Box 1
Tompkins Family Papers, No. 705
Whitehead, Irvin P., The Campaigns of Munford and the 2nd Virginia Cavalry, No. 910
Young, George G., Civil War Correspondence, No. 3676
Alderman Library:
    Blackford Family Papers, No. 5088
    Blackford, W. W., Annotations, No. 5859
    Daniel, John W., Papers, No. 158
    Gordon and Rosser Family Papers, No. 1171
    Holland Family Papers, No. 902
    Hubard, Robert Thruston, Jr., "Civil War Reminiscences," No. 10,522
    Pleasonton Family Papers, No. 495
    Smiley, Thomas, Correspondence, No. 1807-A
    Stuart, J. E. B., Diary, 1860, No. 4015
    Venable, Charles S., "Personal Reminiscences of the Confederate War," McDowell Family Papers, No. 2969-A

UNIVERSITY OF WASHINGTON, SPECIAL COLLECTIONS, UNIVERSITY OF WASHINGTON LIBRARIES, SEATTLE, WA:

Crittenden Family Papers

VIRGINIA HISTORICAL SOCIETY, RICHMOND, VA:

Adams, Fannie Lewis Gwathmey, "Reminiscences of a Childhood Spent at 'Hay-field' Plantation Near Fredericksburg, Virginia During the Civil War"

Anderson, Sarah Travers Lewis, War Record of James McClure Scott, typescript

Armistead and Blanton Family Papers

Armstrong, Sally, Diary

Bates, Charles E., Letters

Baylor, Robert Payne, Letter

Brooke, St. George Tucker, Autobiography, typescript

Bryan, Joseph, Papers

Caperton Family Papers

Caperton, Lafette J., Letters

Carnel, Lafayette J., Letters

Coleman, Beverly Mosby, Papers

Collins, John Overton, Papers

Conrad, Holmes, Papers

Cooke Family Papers

Cottrell Family Papers

Cushwa, Daniel G., Papers

Downman Family Papers

Early Family Papers

Early, Jubal A., Papers

Edrington, John C., Papers

Edwards, Julian T., Letter

Freaner, George, Letter

Grinman Family Papers

Hunton Family Papers

Irving Family Papers

Jeter, James, Letters

Johnson, Elijah S., Papers

Jones Family Papers

Jones, Henry Francis, Letters, UDC transcripts, Volume 2, pp. 514–37

Kepner, John Price, Letters and Diary

Latrobe, Osman, Diary, typescript

Lee Family Papers

Lee, Robert E., Letterbook, 7 June 1863–12 October 1864, Army of Northern Virginia, CSA

Lee, Robert E., Papers

Lomax Family Papers

McClellan, Henry B., Papers

McIntosh, Virginia Johnson Pegram, Letter

Minor Family Papers

Mosby, John Singleton, Papers

Robinson, Leiper Moore, Reminiscences

Saunders Family Papers
Scott, Alfred Lewis, Memoir of Service in the Confederate Army
Scott, James McClure, Memoir
Scott, John Zachary Holladay, Memoir
Stuart, James Ewell Brown, Papers
Taylor, William, Letter
Venable, Andrew Reid, Letter
Watkins, Richard Henry, Papers
West, Georgia Callis, Papers
Wickham Family Papers
Wright, Gilbert J., Papers

VIRGINIA MILITARY INSTITUTE, ARCHIVES, PRESTON LIBRARY, LEXINGTON, VA:

Ervine, John H., Letter
Garibaldi, John, Letters
Gatewood, Andrew C. L., Papers
Koontz, George W., Papers
Langhorne, J. Kent, Papers
Wilson, Harry, Collection

VIRGINIA TECH UNIVERSITY, SPECIAL COLLECTIONS, BLACKSBURG, VA:

Atkinson, Archibald, Jr., Memoirs
Bowmaster, Patrick A., "Confederate Brig. Gen. B. H. Robertson and the 1863 Gettysburg Campaign," master's thesis
Cochran Family Papers
Garrett, Samuel Edwin, Papers
Jordan, Charles Francis, Memoir
Perry, Thomas David, Collection

WAKE FOREST UNIVERSITY, Z. SMITH REYNOLDS LIBRARY, WINSTON-SALEM, NC:

Taylor, Charles E., Diary

WASHINGTON AND LEE UNIVERSITY, SPECIAL COLLECTIONS, LEYBURN LIBRARY, LEXINGTON, VA:

Lee, Otho Scott, Reminiscences of Four Years Service in the Confederate Army
Lee, Robert E., Letter, January 25, 1866

WAYNESBORO PUBLIC LIBRARY, WAYNESBORO, PA:

Gallaher, William B., Letters

WERT, JEFFRY D, CENTRE HALL, PA:

Copies in possession of:
        Stuart, J. E. B., Letters

WESTERN MICHIGAN UNIVERSITY, REGIONAL HISTORY COLLECTION, KALAMAZOO, MI:

Ed Ridgeway Collection:
    Ball, William, Letters
Dr. Allen Giddings Collection:
    Harrington, George L., Diary

YALE UNIVERSITY, BEINECKE RARE BOOK AND MANUSCRIPT LIBRARY, NEW HAVEN, CT:

Stuart, James Ewell Brown, Journal of the March of Companies F, G, H, & K, 1st Cavalry . . . on an Expedition Against the Hostile Kiowas and Comanches, 1860

Newspapers

Atlanta *Constitution*
Augusta (Georgia) *Daily Constitutionalist*
Boston *Evening Journal*
Carolina Watchman Weekly (Salisbury, North Carolina)
Charleston *Mercury*
Charlotte (North Carolina) *Daily Bulletin*
Charlotte (North Carolina) *Daily Observer*
Charlotte (North Carolina) *Western Democrat*
Columbus (Georgia) *Daily Sun*
Columbus (Georgia) *Weekly Enquirer*
Greensboro (Alabama) *Beacon*
Hillsborough (North Carolina) *Recorder*
Laurensville (South Carolina) *Herald*
Macon (Georgia) *Telegraph*
Martinsburg (West Virginia) *Statesman*
Mobile *Advertiser and Register*
Montgomery (Alabama) *Daily Mail*
Natchez *Courier*
National Tribune
New York *Daily Tribune*
New York *Times*
New York *Tribune*
Philadelphia *Weekly Times*
Raleigh *State Journal*
Richmond *Dispatch*
Richmond *Enquirer*
Richmond *Examiner*
Richmond *Sentinel*
Richmond *Times-Dispatch*
Richmond *Whig*
Savannah (Georgia) *Daily Morning News*

Savannah (Georgia) *Republican*
Shepherdstown (West Virginia) *Register*
Staunton (Virginia) *Spectator and Vindicator*
Turnwold (Georgia) *Countryman*
Washington *Times*

Published Books and Articles

Ackinclose, Timothy R. *Sabres and Pistols: The Civil War Career of Colonel Harry Gilmore, C.S.A.* Gettysburg, PA: Stan Clark Military Books, 1997.

"Album of Historic Homes IX: The Bower." *Magazine of the Jefferson County Historical Society* 24 (December 1958).

Alexander, E. P. *Military Memoirs of a Confederate.* Reprint. Bloomington: Indiana University Press, 1962.

Alexander, Ted. "Gettysburg Cavalry Operations, June 27–July 3, 1863." *Blue & Gray Magazine* 6, no. 1 (October 1988).

———. "Ten Days in July: The Pursuit to the Potomac." *North & South* 2, no. 6 (August 1999).

Andrews, Marietta Minnigerode, ed. *Scraps of Paper.* New York: E. P. Dutton, 1929.

The Annals of the War Written by Leading Participants North and South. Reprint. Dayton, OH: Morningside House, 1988.

Armstrong, Richard L. *11th Virginia Cavalry.* Lynchburg, VA: H. E. Howard, 1989.

Auction Catalog. Bedford, NH: Scott J. Winslow Associates, March 2006.

Auction Catalog No. 41—Part I. Wells, ME: RWA, March 1997.

Autograph Catalog. Cos Cob, CT: Alexander Autographs, May 1998.

Autograph Catalog No. 37. Beverly Hills, CA: Profiles in History, December 2004.

Baird, Nancy Chappelear, ed. *Journals of Amanda Virginia Edmonds: Lass of the Mosby Confederacy, 1859–1867.* Stephens City, VA: Commercial Press, 1984.

Baylor, George. *Bull Run to Bull Run: Or, Four Years in the Army of Northern Virginia.* Reprint. Washington, D.C.: Zenger Publishing, 1983.

Beale, G. W. *A Lieutenant of Cavalry in Lee's Army.* Reprint. Baltimore: Butternut & Blue, 1994.

Beaudry, Louis N. *Historic Records of the Fifth New York Cavalry, First Ira Harris Guard.* Albany, NY: S. R. Gray, 1865.

Bigelow, John, Jr. *The Campaign of Chancellorsville: A Strategic and Tactical Study.* Reprint. Dayton, OH: Morningside House, 1985.

Bill, Alfred Hoyt. *The Beleaguered City: Richmond, 1861–1865.* New York: Alfred A. Knopf, 1946.

Billings, John Shaw. *A Report on Barracks and Hospitals with Descriptions of Military Posts.* Washington, D.C.: Government Printing Office, 1870.

Blackford, Charles Minor III, ed. *Letters from Lee's Army or Memoirs of Life in and out of the Army in Virginia During the War Between the States.* New York: Charles Scribner's Sons, 1947.

Blackford, W. W. *War Years with Jeb Stuart.* New York: Charles Scribner's Sons, 1946.

Blue, John. *Hanging Rock Rebel: Lt. John Blue's War in West Virginia and the Shenandoah Valley*. Edited by Dan Oates. Shippensburg, PA: Burd Street Press, 1994.

Bobrick, Benson. *Angel in the Whirlwind: The Triumph of the American Revolution*. New York: Simon & Schuster, 1997.

Boswell, James Keith. "Jackson's Boswell: The Diary of a Confederate Staff Officer." *Civil War Times Illustrated* 15, no. 1 (April 1976).

Bowmaster, Patrick A., ed. "Confederate Brig. Gen. B. H. 'Bev' Robertson Interviewed on the Gettysburg Campaign." *Gettysburg Magazine* 20 (January 1999).

Bradshaw, Ada Bruce Desper, ed. *Civil War Diary of Charles William McVicar*. Hampton, VA: n.p., 1977.

Brennan, Patrick. "The Best Cavalry in the World." *North & South* 2, no. 2 (January 1999).

———. "It Wasn't Stuart's Fault." *North & South* 6, no. 5 (July 2003).

———. "Little Mac's Last Stand: Autumn 1862 in Loudoun Valley, Virginia." *Blue & Gray* 17, no. 2 (December 1999).

———. "Notice Served." *North & South* 2, no. 4 (April 1999).

———. "Thunder on the Plains of Brandy." *North & South* 5, no. 3 (April 2002).

Bridges, David P. *Fighting with JEB Stuart: Major James Breathed and the Confederate Horse Artillery*. Arlington, VA: Breathed Bridges Best, 2006.

Bridges, Hal. *Lee's Maverick General: Daniel Harvey Hill*. New York: McGraw-Hill, 1961.

Brooks, U. R. *Butler and His Cavalry in the War of Secession, 1861–1865*. Reprint. Camden, SC: Gray Fox Books, n.d.

Brooksher, William R., and David K. Snider. "Stuart's Ride: The Great Circuit Around McClellan." *Civil War Times Illustrated* 12, no. 1 (April 1973).

Brown, Kent Masterson. *Retreat from Gettysburg: Lee, Logistics, and the Pennsylvania Campaign*. Chapel Hill: University of North Carolina Press, 2005.

Burdge, Edsel, Jr., and Samuel L. Horst. *Building on the Gospel Foundation: The Mennonites of Franklin County, Pennsylvania, and Washington County, Maryland, 1730–1790*. Scottdale, PA: Herald Press, 2004.

Busey, John W., and David G. Martin. *Regimental Strengths and Losses at Gettysburg*, 4th edition. Hightstown, NJ: Longstreet House, 2005.

Bushong, Millard Kessler, and Dean McKain Bushong. *Fightin' Tom Rosser, C.S.A.* Shippensburg, PA: Beidel Printing House, 1983.

Callihan, David L. "Jeb Stuart's Fateful Ride." *Gettysburg Magazine* 24 (January 2001).

Carmichael, Peter S. *The Last Generation: Young Virginians in Peace, War, and Reunion*. Chapel Hill: University of North Carolina Press, 2005.

———. "Reflections on Chancellorsville." *America's Civil War* 5, no 6 (May 2006).

Carpenter, John A. *Sword and Olive Branch: Oliver Otis Howard*. Pittsburgh, PA: University of Pittsburgh Press, 1964.

Carter, William R. *Sabres, Saddles, and Spurs*. Edited by Walbrook D. Swank. Shippensburg, PA: Burd Street Press, 1998.

Cashin, Joan E. "The Structure of Antebellum Planter Families: 'The Tie That Bound Us Was Strong.'" *Journal of Southern History* 56, no. 1 (February 1990).

Catalog No. 157. Chicago: Abraham Lincoln Book Shop, November 2005.

Chalfant, William Y. *Cheyennes and Horse Soldiers: The 1857 Expedition and the Battle of Solomon's Fork.* Norman: University of Oklahoma Press, 1989.

Chamberlaine, William W. *Memoirs of the Civil War.* Washington, D.C.: Press of Bryon S. Adams, n.d.

Chappell, Gordon. "The United States Dragoons, 1833–1861." *The Denver Westerners Roundup* 30, no. 2 (February 1974).

Cheek, Charles D., et al. *Draft: Carlisle Barracks Cumberland County, Pennsylvania Historic Preservation Plan.* West Chester, PA: John Milner Associates, 1990.

Chesnut, Mary Boykin. *A Diary from Dixie.* Edited by Ben Ames Williams. Boston: Houghton Mifflin, 1949.

Cisco, Walter Brian. *Wade Hampton: Confederate Warrior, Conservative Statesman.* Washington, D.C.: Brassey's, 2004.

Clark, Walter, ed. *Histories of the Several Regiments and Battalions from North Carolina in the Great War, 1861–'65.* 5 volumes. Reprint. Wilmington, NC: Broadfoot's Bookmark, 1982.

Coddington, Edwin B. *The Gettysburg Campaign: A Study in Command.* New York: Charles Scribner's Sons, 1968.

Colt, Margaretta Barton, ed. *Defend the Valley: A Shenandoah Family in the Civil War.* New York: Orion Books, 1994.

Coltrane, Daniel Branson. *The Memoirs of Daniel Branson Coltrane.* Raleigh, NC: Edwards & Broughton, 1956.

The Confederate Veteran Magazine. 40 volumes. Reprint. Wilmington, NC: Broadfoot Publishing, 1987–1988.

Conrad, Thomas Nelson. *The Rebel Scout: A Thrilling History of Scouting Life in the Southern Army.* Washington, D.C.: National Publishing, 1904.

Conrad, W. P., and Ted Alexander. *When War Passed This Way.* Shippensburg, PA: Beidel Printing House, 1982.

Cooke, John Esten. *Wearing of the Gray: Being Personal Portraits, Scenes and Adventures of the War.* Reprint. Gaithersburg, MD: Olde Soldier Books, 1988.

Copland, Mary Ruffin, ed. *Confederate History of Charles City County, Virginia.* West Point, VA: Tidewater Press, 1957.

Corson, William Clarke. *My Dear Jennie: A Collection of Love Letters from a Confederate Soldier to His Fiancee During the Period 1861–1865.* Edited by Blake W. Corson, Jr. Richmond, VA: Dietz Press, 1982.

Coski, John. "Forgotten Warrior: General William Henry Fitzhugh Payne." *North & South* 2, no. 7 (September 1999).

Cozzens, Peter, ed. *Battles and Leaders of the Civil War.* Volumes 5 and 6. Urbana: University of Illinois Press, 2002–2004.

Cozzens, Peter, and Robert I. Girardi, eds. *The New Annals of the Civil War.* Mechanicsburg, PA: Stackpole Books, 2004.

Crary, Catherine S., ed. *Dear Belle: Letters from a Cadet and Officer to His Sweetheart, 1858–1865*. Middletown, CT: Wesleyan University Press, 1965.

Crowninshield, Benjamin W. *A History of the First Regiment of Massachusetts Cavalry Volunteers*. Reprint. Baltimore: Butternut & Blue, 1995.

Cullum, George W. *Biographical Register of the Officers and Graduates of the U.S. Military Academy at West Point, N.Y.* Volume 2. Boston: Houghton Mifflin, 1891.

Davis, Burke. *Jeb Stuart: The Last Cavalier*. New York: Rinehart, 1957.

Davis, William C. *Jefferson Davis: The Man and His Hour*. New York: HarperCollins, 1991.

Douglas, Henry Kyd. *I Rode with Stonewall*. Chapel Hill: University of North Carolina Press, 1940.

Dowdey, Clifford, and Louis H. Manarin, eds. *The Wartime Papers of R. E. Lee*. Boston: Little, Brown, 1961.

Drake, Samuel Adams. "The Old Army in Kansas," *Civil War Papers Read Before the Commandery of the State of Massachusetts, Military Order of the Loyal Legion of the United States*. Volume I. Reprint. Wilmington, NC: Broadfoot Publishing, 1993.

Driver, Robert J., Jr. *5th Virginia Cavalry*. Lynchburg, VA: H. E. Howard, 1997.

———. *First and Second Maryland Cavalry C.S.A.* Charlottesville, VA: Rockbridge Publishing, 1999.

———. *1st Virginia Cavalry*. Lynchburg, VA: H. E. Howard, 1991.

———. *14th Virginia Cavalry*. Lynchburg, VA: H. E. Howard, 1988.

———. *10th Virginia Cavalry*. Lynchburg, VA: H. E. Howard, 1992.

Driver, Robert J., and H. E. Howard. *2nd Virginia Cavalry*. Lynchburg, VA: H. E. Howard, 1995.

Dubbs, Carol Kettenburg. *Defend This Old Town: Williamsburg During the Civil War*. Baton Rouge: Louisiana State University Press, 2002.

Duncan, Bingham, ed. *Letters of General J. E. B. Stuart to His Wife—1861*. Atlanta: Emory University Library, 1943.

DuPont, Henry A. *The Campaign of 1864 in the Valley of Virginia and the Expedition to Lynchburg*. New York: National Americana Society, 1925.

Dyer, John P. *The Gallant Hood*. Indianapolis: Bobbs-Merrill, 1950.

Eby, Cecil D., Jr., ed. *A Virginia Yankee in the Civil War: The Diaries of David Hunter Strother*. Chapel Hill: University of North Carolina Press, 1961.

Eckert, Edward K., and Nicholas J. Amato, eds. *Ten Years in the Saddle: The Memoir of William Woods Averell*. San Rafael, CA: Presidio Press, 1978.

Eggleston, George Cary. *A Rebel's Recollections*. Introduction by David Donald. Bloomington: Indiana University Press, 1959.

Encounter at Hanover: Prelude to Gettysburg. Reprint. Shippensburg, PA: White Mane Publishing, 1988.

Fisher, George D. *History and Reminiscences of the Monumental Church*. Richmond, VA: Whillet & Shepperdson, 1880.

Fleet, Betsy, and John D. P. Fuller, eds. *Green Mount: A Virginia Plantation Family*

During the Civil War: Being the Journal of Benjamin Robert Fleet and Letters of His Family. Lexington: University of Kentucky Press, 1962.

Fortier, John. *15th Virginia Cavalry*. Lynchburg, VA: H. E. Howard, 1993.

Fox, John J., III. *Red Clay to Richmond: Trail of the 35th Georgia Infantry Regiment, C.S.A.* Winchester, VA: Angle Valley Press, 2004.

Franklin, Pauline, and Mary V. Pruett, eds. *Civil War Letters of Dandridge William and Naomi Bush Cockrell, 1862–1863*. Lively, VA: Brandylane Publishers, 1991.

Freeman, Douglas Southall. *Lee's Lieutenants: A Study in Command*. 3 volumes. New York: Charles Scribner's Sons, 1942–1944.

———. *R. E. Lee: A Biography*. 4 volumes. New York: Charles Scribner's Sons, 1943.

Frye, Dennis E. *12th Virginia Cavalry*. Lynchburg, VA: H. E. Howard, 1988.

Furgurson, Ernest B. *Ashes of Glory: Richmond at War*. New York: Alfred A. Knopf, 1996.

Gallagher, Gary W., ed. *The Antietam Campaign*. Chapel Hill: University of North Carolina Press, 1999.

———. "Brandy Station: The Civil War's Bloodiest Arena of Mounted Combat." *Blue & Gray* 8, no. 1 (October 1990).

———, ed. *Chancellorsville: The Battle and Its Aftermath*. Chapel Hill: University of North Carolina Press, 1996.

———, ed. *Fighting for the Confederacy: The Personal Recollections of General Edward Porter Alexander*. Chapel Hill: University of North Carolina Press, 1989.

———, ed. *The First Day at Gettysburg: Essays on Confederate and Union Leadership*. Kent, OH: Kent State University Press, 1992.

———. *Lee and His Army in Confederate History*. Chapel Hill: University of North Carolina Press, 2001.

———, ed. *Lee the Soldier*. Lincoln: University of Nebraska Press, 1996.

———, ed. *The Richmond Campaign of 1862: The Peninsula and the Seven Days*. Chapel Hill: University of North Carolina Press, 2000.

———, ed. *The Spotsylvania Campaign*. Chapel Hill: University of North Carolina Press, 1998.

———, ed. *The Wilderness Campaign*. Chapel Hill: University of North Carolina Press, 1997.

Gallagher, Gary W., and Joseph T. Glatthaar, eds. *Leaders of the Lost Cause: New Perspectives on the Confederate High Command*. Mechanicsburg, PA: Stackpole Books, 2004.

Gallaher, DeWitt Clinton. *A Diary Depicting the Experiences of DeWitt Clinton Gallaher in the War Between the States While Serving in the Confederate Army*. N.p.: 1961.

Galloway, T. H., ed. *Dear Old Roswell: Civil War Letters of the King Family of Roswell, Georgia*. Macon, GA: Mercer University Press, 2003.

Garnett, Theodore S. *J. E. B. Stuart (Major-General): An Address Delivered at the Unveiling of the Equestrian Statue of General Stuart, at Richmond, Virginia, May 30, 1907*. New York: Neale Publishing, 1907.

———. *Riding with Stuart: Reminiscences of an Aide-de-Camp.* Edited by Robert J. Trout. Shippensburg, PA: White Mane publishing, 1994.

Gerleman, David J. "War Horses!: Union Cavalry Mounts, 1861–1865." *North & South* 2, no. 2 (January 1999).

Gimbel, Gary. "The End of Innocence: The Battle of Falling Waters." *Blue & Gray* 22, no. 4 (Fall 2005).

Glazier, Willard. *Three Years in the Federal Cavalry.* New York: R. H. Ferguson, 1874.

Goldsborough, W. W. *The Maryland Line in the Confederate Army, 1861–1865.* Reprint. Gaithersburg, MD: Butternut Press, 1983.

Goodwin, Doris Kearns. *Team of Rivals: The Political Genius of Abraham Lincoln.* New York: Simon & Schuster, 2005.

Greene, A. Wilson. *Whatever You Resolve to Be: Essays on Stonewall Jackson.* Baltimore: Butternut & Blue, 1992.

Griffith, Paddy. *Battle Tactics of the Civil War.* New Haven: Yale University Press, 1987.

Grimsley, Daniel A. *Battles in Culpeper County, Virginia, 1861–1865.* Reprint. Orange, VA: Green Publishers, 1967.

Hackley, Woodford B. *The Little Fork Rangers: A Sketch of Company "D" Fourth Virginia Cavalry.* Richmond, VA: Press of the Dietz Printing Co., 1927.

Haden, B. J. *Reminiscences of J. E. B. Stuart's Cavalry.* Charlottesville, VA: News, Book and Job Printing, n.d.

Haines, Douglas Craig. "Confederate Command Failure at the Blue Ridge." *Gettysburg Magazine* 35 (July 2006).

———. "Jeb Stuart's Advance to Gettysburg." *Gettysburg Magazine* 29 (July 2003).

Hairston, Peter W., ed. "J. E. B. Stuart's Letters to His Hairston Kin, 1850–1855." *North Carolina Historical Review* 51, no. 3 (July 1974).

Hall, Clark B. "'The Army Is Moving': Lee's March to the Potomac, 1863." *Blue & Gray* 21, no. 3 (Spring 2004).

Hamlin, Percy Gatlin. *"Old Bald Head" (General R. S. Ewell): The Portrait of a Soldier and the Making of a Soldier: Letters of General R. S. Ewell.* Reprint. Gaithersburg, MD: Ron R. Van Sickle Military Books, 1988.

Harrell, Roger H. *The 2nd North Carolina Cavalry.* Jefferson, NC: McFarland, 2004.

Harrison, Noel G. *Chancellorsville Battlefield Sites.* Lynchburg, VA: H. E. Howard, 1990.

———. *Fredericksburg Civil War Sites, December 1862–April 1865.* Volume 2. Lynchburg, VA: H. E. Howard, 1995.

Harsh, Joseph L. *Taken at the Flood: Robert E. Lee and Confederate Strategy in the Maryland Campaign of 1862.* Kent, OH: Kent State University Press, 1999.

Hartley, Chris J. *Stuart's Tarheels: James B. Gordon and His North Carolina Cavalry.* Baltimore: Butternut & Blue, 1996.

Haskell, John Cheves. *The Haskell Memoirs.* Edited by Gilbert E. Govan and James W. Livingood. New York: G. P. Putnam's Sons, 1960.

Hassler, William Woods. *Colonel John Pelham: Lee's Boy Artillerist.* Richmond, VA: Garrett & Massie, 1960.

———, ed. *The General to His Lady: The Civil War Letters of William Dorsey Pender to Fanny Pender*. Chapel Hill: University of North Carolina Press, 1965.

Helm, Lewis Marshall. *Black Horse Cavalry: Defend Our Beloved Country*. Falls Church, VA: Higher Education Publishers, 2004.

Henderson, William D. *The Road to Bristoe Station: Campaigning with Lee and Meade, August 1–October 20, 1863*. Lynchburg, VA: H. E. Howard, 1987.

Hennessy, John J. *Return to Bull Run: The Campaign and Battle of Second Manassas*. New York: Simon & Schuster, 1993.

———. "Thunder at Chantilly." *North & South* 3, no. 3 (March 2000).

Heritage Auction Galleries Inaugural Auction of Civil War History, Session Two, Catalog. Dallas: Heritage Auction, 2006.

Hess, Earl J. *Field Armies and Fortifications in the Civil War: The Eastern Campaigns, 1861–1864*. Chapel Hill: University of North Carolina Press, 2005.

Hoke, Jacob. *Historical Reminiscences of the War; Or Incidents Which Transpired in and About Chambersburg, During the War of the Rebellion*. Chambersburg, PA: M. A. Foltz, 1884.

Holland, Lynwood M. *Pierce M. B. Young: The Warwick of the South*. Athens: University of Georgia Press, 1964.

Hopkins, Luther W. *From Bull Run to Appomattox: A Boy's View*. Baltimore: Press of Fleet-McGinley Co., 1914.

Howard, McHenry. *Recollections of a Maryland Confederate Soldier and Staff Officer Under Johnston, Jackson, and Lee*. Reprint. Dayton, OH: Press of Morningside Bookshop, 1975.

Howard, Oliver Otis. *Autobiography of Oliver Otis Howard*. 2 volumes. New York: Baker & Taylor, 1907.

Howard, Wiley C. *Sketch of Cobb Legion Cavalry and Some Incidents and Scenes Remembered*. N.p.: 1901.

Hubbell, Jay B., ed. "The War Diary of John Esten Cooke." *Journal of Southern History* 7, no. 4 (November 1941).

Hubbs, G. Ward, ed. *Voices from Company D: Diaries by the Greensboro Guards, Fifth Alabama Infantry Regiment, Army of Northern Virginia*. Athens: University of Georgia Press, 2003.

Hudgins, Garland C., and Richard B. Kleese, eds. *Recollections of an Old Dominion Dragoon: The Civil War Experiences of Sgt. Robert S. Hudgins II Company B, 3rd Virginia Cavalry*. Orange, VA: Publisher's Press, 1993.

Hunter, Alexander. *Johnny Reb and Billy Yank*. New York: Neale Publishing, 1905.

Ide, Horace K. *History of the First Vermont Cavalry Volunteers in the War of the Great Rebellion*. Reprint. Baltimore: Butternut & Blue, 2000.

Johnson, Clint. *In the Footsteps of J. E. B. Stuart*. Winston-Salem, NC: John F. Blair, 2003.

Johnston, Joseph E. *Narrative of Military Operations Directed, During the Late War Between the States*. Reprint. Bloomington: Indiana University Press, 1959.

Jones, John B. *A Rebel War Clerk's Diary at the Confederate States Capital*. 2 volumes. Reprint. Alexandria, VA: Time-Life Books, 1982.

Jones, Terry L., ed. *Campbell Brown's Civil War: With Ewell and the Army of Northern Virginia*. Baton Rouge: Louisiana State University Press, 2001.

Joseph, John Mark. *War on the Rapidan*. Orange, VA: Moss Publications, 1988.

Keller, S. Roger. *Events of the Civil War in Washington County Maryland*. Shippensburg, PA: Burd Street Press, 1995.

Kesterson, Brian Stuart, ed. *The Last Survivor: The Memoirs of George William Watson*. Parsons, WV: McClain Printing, 1993.

Kidd, James H. *Historical Sketch of General Custer*. Reprint. Monroe, MI: Monroe County Library System, 1978.

———. *Personal Recollections of a Cavalryman with Custer's Michigan Cavalry Brigade in the Civil War*. Reprint. Alexandria, VA: Time-Life Books, 1983.

Klein, Frederic Shriver, ed. *Just South of Gettysburg: Carroll County, Maryland in the Civil War*. Westminster, MD: Newman Press, 1963.

Klein, Maury. "J. E. B. Stuart's Life: What Should We Think of the General?" *Civil War Times Illustrated* 25, no. 5 (September 1986).

Knapp, Ken R. *Confederate Saddles and Horse Equipment*. Orange, VA: Publisher's Press, 2001.

Koonce, Donald B., ed. *Doctor to the Front: The Civil War Journal of Thomas Fanning Wood, M.D., 1861–1865*. Greenville, SC: Spectrum Communications, 1997.

Krepps, John. "Before and After Hanover: Tracing Stuart's Cavalry Movements of June 30, 1863." *Blue & Gray* 21, no. 1 (Holiday 2003).

Krick, Robert E. L. *Staff Officers in Gray: A Biographical Register of the Staff Officers in the Army of Northern Virginia*. Chapel Hill: University of North Carolina Press, 2003.

Krick, Robert K. *9th Virginia Cavalry*. Lynchburg, VA: H. E. Howard, 1982.

———. *Parker's Virginia Battery C.S.A.* Berryville, VA: Virginia Book Company, 1975.

———. *The Smoothbore Volley That Doomed the Confederacy: The Death of Stonewall Jackson and Other Chapters on the Army of Northern Virginia*. Baton Rouge: Louisiana State University Press, 2002.

———. *Stonewall Jackson at Cedar Mountain*. Chapel Hill: University of North Carolina Press, 1990.

Krolick, Marshall D. "Lee vs. Stuart: The Gettysburg Altercation." *Virginia Country's Civil War* 2 (1984).

Ladd, David L., and Audrey J., Ladd, eds. *The Bachelder Papers: Gettysburg in Their Own Words*. 3 volumes. Dayton, OH: Morningside House, 1994–1995.

Lambert, Dobbie Edward. *Grumble: The W. E. Jones Brigade of 1863–1864*. Wahiawa, HI: Lambert Enterprises, 1992.

Lane, Mills, ed. *"Dear Mother: Don't Grieve About Me. If I Get Killed, I'll Only Be Dead": Letters from Georgia Soldiers in the Civil War*. Savannah, GA: Beehive Press, 1977.

Lasswell, Mary, ed. *Rags and Hope: The Recollections of Val C. Giles. Four Years with Hood's Brigade, Fourth Texas Infantry*. New York: Coward-McCann, 1961.

Lee, Robert E. *Recollections and Letters of General Robert E. Lee*. Garden City, NY: Garden City Publishing, 1924.

Light, Rebecca Campbell, ed. *War at Our Doors: The Civil War Diaries and Letters of the Bernard Sisters of Virginia*. Fredericksburg, VA: American History Company, 1998.

Lippincott, George E. "Lee-Sawyer Exchange." *Civil War Times Illustrated* 1, no. 3 (July 1962).

Lomax, Elizabeth. *Leaves from an Old Washington Diary*. Mount Vernon, NY: Books, Inc., 1943.

Longacre, Edward G. *Fitz Lee: A Military Biography of Major General Fitzhugh Lee, C.S.A.* New York: Da Capo, 2005.

———. *Gentleman and Soldier: A Biography of Wade Hampton III*. Nashville, TN: Rutledge Hill Press, 2003.

———. *Lee's Cavalrymen: A History of the Mounted Forces of the Army of Northern Virginia, 1861–1865*. Mechanicsburg, PA: Stackpole Books, 2002.

Lord, Walter, ed. *The Fremantle Diary: Being the Journal of Lieutenant Colonel James Arthur Lyon Fremantle, Coldstream Guards, on His Three Months in the Southern States*. Boston: Little, Brown, 1954.

"The Loss of the West." *Civil War Times Illustrated* 20, no. 3 (June 1981).

Low, Thomas. "Letters to Laura." *Civil War Times Illustrated* 32, no. 3 (July–August 1992).

Manarin, Louis H. *Henrico County—Field of Honor*. 2 volumes. Richmond, VA: Henrico County, 2004.

Mattes, Merrill J. *The Great Platte River Road: The Covered Wagon Mainline via Fort Kearny to Fort Laramie*. Lincoln: Nebraska State Historical Society, 1969.

Maurice, Frederick, ed. *An Aide-de-Camp of Lee: Being the Papers of Colonel Charles Marshall Sometime Aide-de-Camp, Military Secretary and Assistant Adjutant General on the Staff of Robert E. Lee, 1862–1865*. Boston: Little, Brown, 1927.

———. *Robert E. Lee the Soldier*. Boston: Houghton Mifflin, 1926.

Maury, Dabney Herndon. *Recollections of a Virginian in the Mexican, Indian, and Civil Wars*. New York: Charles Scribner's Sons, 1894.

McCabe, James D., Jr. *The Grayjackets: And How They Lived, Fought and Died for Dixie by a Confederate*. Richmond, VA: Jones Brothers, 1867.

McClellan, H. B. *I Rode with Jeb Stuart: The Life and Campaigns of Major General J. E. B. Stuart*. Introduction and Notes by Burke Davis. Reprint. Bloomington: Indiana University Press, 1958.

McClure, James. *East of Gettysburg: A Gray Shadow Crosses York County, Pa.* York, PA: York Daily Record/York County Heritage Trust, 2003.

McDonald, Archie P., ed. *Make Me a Map of the Valley: The Civil War Journal of Stonewall Jackson's Topographer*. Dallas: Southern Methodist University Press, 1973.

McDonald, William N. *A History of the Laurel Brigade Originally the Ashby Cavalry of the Army of Northern Virginia and Chew's Battery*. Reprint. Arlington, VA: R. W. Beatty, 1969.

McKale, William, and William D. Young, *Fort Riley: Citadel of the Frontier West.* Topeka: Kansas State Historical Society, 2000.

McSwain, Eleanor D., ed. *Crumbling Defenses or Memoirs and Reminiscences of John Logan Black Colonel C.S.A.* Macon, GA: Eleanor D. McSwain, 1960.

McWhiney, Grady, ed. *Lee's Dispatches: Unpublished Letters of General Robert E. Lee, C.S.A. to Jefferson Davis and the War Department of the Confederate States of America, 1862–1865.* New York: G. P. Putnam's Sons, 1957.

McWhiney Grady, and Perry D. Jamieson. *Attack and Die: Civil War Military Tactics and the Southern Heritage.* University: University of Alabama Press, 1982.

Merington, Marguerite, ed. *The Custer Story: The Life and Intimate Letters of General George A. Custer and His Wife Elizabeth.* New York: Devin-Adair, 1950.

Mertz, Gregory A. "General Gouverneur K. Warren and the Fighting at Laurel Hill During the Battle of Spotslyvania Court House, May 1864," *Blue & Gray* 21, no. 4 (Summer 2004).

Mewborn, Horace, ed. *"From Mosby's Command": Newspaper Letters and Articles by and About John S. Mosby and His Rangers.* Baltimore: Butternut & Blue, 2005.

———. "A Wonderful Exploit: Jeb Stuart's Ride Around the Army of the Potomac, June 12–15, 1862." *Blue & Gray* 15, no. 6 (July 1998).

Miller, Keith. "Southern Horse." *Civil War Times Illustrated* 45, no. 1 (February 2006).

Miller, William J., ed. *The Peninsula Campaign of 1862: Yorktown to the Seven Days.* 3 volumes. Campbell, CA: Savas Publishing, 1997.

Mitchell, Adele H., ed. *The Letters of John S. Mosby.* N.p.: Stuart-Mosby Historical Society, 1986.

———, ed. *The Letters of Major General James E. B. Stuart.* N.p.: Stuart-Mosby Historical Society, 1990.

Moore, Robert H., II. *Gibraltar of the Shenandoah: Civil War Sites and Stories of Staunton, Waynesboro, and Augusta County, Virginia.* Virginia Beach, VA: Donning Company Publishers, 2004.

Morrison, James L., Jr., ed. *The Memoirs of Henry Heth.* Westport, CT: Greenwood Press, 1974.

Mosby, John S. *Stuart's Cavalry in the Gettysburg Campaign.* New York: Moffatt, Yard, 1908.

Mosgrove, George Dallas. *Kentucky Cavaliers in Dixie: Reminiscences of a Confederate Cavalryman.* Edited by Bell Irvin Wiley. Reprint. Wilmington, NC: Broadfoot Publishing, 1987.

Murray, Elizabeth Dunbar. *My Mother Used to Say: A Natchez Belle of the Sixties.* Boston: Christopher Publishing House, 1959.

Musick, Michael P. *6th Virginia Cavalry.* Lynchburg, VA: H. E. Howard, 1990.

Myers, Frank M. *The Comanches: A History of White's Battalion, Virginia Cavalry, Laurel Brig., Hampton Div., A.N.V., C.S.A.* Reprint. Gaithersburg, MD: Butternut Press, 1987.

Nanzig, Thomas P., ed. *The Civil War Memoirs of a Virginia Cavalryman: Lt. Robert E. Hubard, Jr.* Tuscaloosa: University of Alabama Press, 2007.

————. *3rd Virginia Cavalry*. Lynchburg, VA: H. E. Howard, 1989.

Neese, George M. *Three Years in the Confederate Horse Artillery*. Reprint. Dayton, OH: Press of Morningside Bookshop, 1983.

Nesbitt, Mark. *Saber and Scapegoat: J. E. B. Stuart and the Gettysburg Controversy*. Mechanicsburg, PA: Stackpole Books, 1994.

Nevins, Allan, ed. *A Diary of Battle: The Personal Journals of Colonel Charles S. Wainwright, 1861–1865*. Reprint. Gettysburg, PA: Stan Clark Military Books, n.d.

Nisbet, James Cooper. *4 Years on the Firing Line*. Edited by Bell Irvin Wiley. Jackson, TN: McCowat-Mercer Press, 1963.

Nosworthy, Brent. *The Bloody Crucible of Courage: Fighting Methods and Combat Experience of the Civil War*. New York: Carroll & Graf, 2003.

Old Homes of Hanover County, Virginia. Hanover, VA: Hanover County Historical Society, 1984.

O'Neill, Robert F., Jr. *The Cavalry Battles of Aldie, Middleburg and Upperville: Small but Important Riots, June 10–27, 1863*. Lynchburg, VA: H. E. Howard, 1993.

————. "Cavalry on the Peninsula." *Blue & Gray* 19, no. 5 (June 2002).

Opie, John N. *A Rebel Cavalryman with Lee Stuart and Jackson*. Reprint. Dayton, OH: Press of Morningside Bookshop, 1972.

O'Reilly, Francis Augustin. *The Fredericksburg Campaign: Winter War on the Rappahannock*. Baton Rouge: Louisiana State University Press, 2003.

Outline Descriptions of the Posts and Stations of Troops in the Geographical Divisions and Departments of the United States. Washington, D.C.: Government Printing Office, 1872.

Patton, Robert K. *The Pattons: A Personal History of an American Family*. New York: Crown, 1994.

Paxton, John Gallatin, ed. *The Civil War Letters of General Frank "Bull" Paxton, CSA. A Lieutenant of Lee and Jackson*. Hillsboro, TX: Hill Junior College Press, 1978.

Pearce, T. H., ed. *Diary of Captain Henry A. Chambers*. Wendell, NC: Broadfoot's Bookmark, 1983.

Peck, R. H. *Reminiscences of a Confederate Soldier of Co. C., 2nd VA Cavalry*. N.p.: n.d.

Pedigo, Virginia G., and Lewis G. Pedigo. *History of Patrick and Henry Counties Virginia*. Reprint. Salem, MA: Higginson Book Company, 2005.

Perry, Thomas David. *Ascent to Glory: The Genealogy of J. E. B. Stuart*. Ararat, VA: Thomas David Perry, 2002.

————. *Stuart's Birthplace: The History of the Laurel Hill Farm*. Ararat, VA: Thomas David Perry, 2007.

Pfanz, Donald C. *Richard S. Ewell: A Soldier's Life*. Chapel Hill: University of North Carolina Press, 1998.

Poague, William Thomas. *Gunner with Stonewall: Reminiscences of William Thomas Poague*. Edited by Monroe F. Cockrell. Jackson, TN: McCowat-Mercer Press, 1957.

Powell, David. "Stuart's Ride: Lee, Stuart, and the Confederate Cavalry in the Gettysburg Campaign." *Gettysburg Magazine* 20 (January 1999).

Priest, John Michael, ed. *One Surgeon's Private War: Doctor William W. Potter of the 57th New York*. Shippensburg, PA: White Mane Publishing, 1996.

Proceedings of the General Court Martial, in the Case of Lieut. Col. H. Clay Pate, 5th Va. Cavalry. Richmond, VA: n.p., 1863.

Rable, George C. *Fredericksburg! Fredericksburg!* Chapel Hill: University of North Carolina Press, 2002.

Raiford, Neil Hunter. *The 4th North Carolina Cavalry in the Civil War: A History and Roster*. Jefferson, NC: McFarland, 2003.

Ramey, Emily G., and John K. Gott., eds. *The Years of Anguish: Fauquier County, Virginia, 1861–1865*. Annandale, VA: Bacon Race Books, 1965.

Reade, Frank Robertson. *In the Saddle with Stuart: The Story of Frank Smith Robertson of Jeb Stuart's Staff*. Edited by Robert J. Trout. Gettysburg, PA: Thomas Publications, 1998.

Redwood, Allen C. "The Horsemen in Gray," *Civil War Times Illustrated* 9, no. 3 (June 1970).

Reed, Germaine M. *David French Boyd: Founder of Louisiana State University*. Baton Rouge: Louisiana State University Press, 1977.

Reynolds, David S. *John Brown, Abolitionist*. New York: Alfred A. Knopf, 2005.

Rhea, Gordon C. *The Battle of the Wilderness, May 5–6, 1864*. Baton Rouge: Louisiana State University Press, 1994.

———. *The Battles for Spotsylvania Court House and the Road to Yellow Tavern, May 7–12, 1864*. Baton Rouge: Louisiana State University Press, 1997.

Robertson, Alexander F. *Alexander Hugh Holmes Stuart, 1807–1891: A Biography*. Richmond, VA: William Byrd Press, 1925.

Robertson, James I., Jr. *Stonewall Jackson: The Man, the Soldier, the Legend*. New York: Macmillan, 1997.

Rockwell, A. D. *Rambling Recollections: An Autobiography*. New York: Paul B. Hoeber, 1920.

Roland, Charles P. *Reflections on Lee: A Historian's Assessment*. Mechanicsburg, PA: Stackpole Books, 1995.

Root, George A., ed. "Extracts from Diary of Captain Lambert Bowman Wolf." *Kansas Historical Quarterly* 1, no. 3 (May 1932).

Roper, John Herbert, ed. *Repairing the "March of Mars": The Civil War Diaries of John Samuel Apperson, Hospital Steward in the Stonewall Brigade, 1861–1865*. Macon, GA: Mercer University Press, 2001.

Ross, Fitzgerald. *Cities and Camps of the Confederate States*. Edited by Richard Barksdale Harwell. Reprint. Urbana: University of Illinois Press, 1958.

Rosser, Thomas L. *Riding with Rosser*. Edited by S. Roger Keller. Shippensburg, PA: Burd Street Press, 1997.

Royall, William L. *Some Reminiscences*. New York: Neale Publishing, 1909.

Russell, Don. "Jeb Stuart on the Frontier." *Civil War Times Illustrated* 13, no. 1 (April 1974).

————. "Jeb Stuart's Other Indian Fight." *Civil War Times Illustrated* 12, no. 9 (January 1974).

Rust, Jeanne. "Portrait of Laura." *Virginia Cavalcade* 12, no. 3 (Winter 1962–1963).

Ryan, Thomas J. "Kilpatrick Bars Stuart's Route to Gettysburg." *Gettysburg Magazine* 27 (July 2002).

Scheel, Eugene M. *The Civil War in Fauquier County Virginia.* Warrenton, VA: Fauquier National Bank, 1985.

Scheibert, Justus. *Seven Months in the Rebel States During the North American War, 1863.* Translated by Joseph C. Hayes and edited by William Stanley Hoole. Tuscaloosa, AL. Confederate Publishing Company, 1958.

Schildt, John W. *Roads to Antietam.* Shippensburg, PA: Burd Street Press, 1997.

————. *Roads to Gettysburg.* Parsons, WV: McClain Printing Company, 1982.

Scott, Robert Garth, ed. *Forgotten Valor: The Memoirs, Journals, and Civil War Letters of Orlando B. Willcox.* Kent, OH: Kent State University Press, 1999.

Scott, W. W. *A History of Orange County Virginia.* Reprint. Baltimore: Regional Publishing Company, 1974.

————, ed. "Two Confederate Items." *Bulletin of the Virginia State Library* 16, nos. 2 and 3 (July 1927).

Sears, Stephen W. *Chancellorsville.* Boston: Houghton Mifflin, 1996.

————. *Gettysburg.* Boston: Houghton Mifflin, 2002.

Shepard, E. Lee. "Breaking into the Profession: Establishing a Law Practice in Antebellum Virginia." *Journal of Southern History* 48, no. 3 (August 1982).

"Sherman on West Point." *Civil War Times Illustrated* 10, no. 9 (January 1972).

Shevchuk, Paul M. "The Battle of Hunterstown, Pennsylvania, July 2, 1863." *Gettysburg: Historical Articles of Lasting Interest* 1 (July 1989).

————. "The Lost Hours of 'Jeb' Stuart." *Gettysburg Magazine* 4 (January 1991).

Shoemaker, John J. *Shoemaker's Battery Stuart Horse Artillery Pelham's Battalion Army of Northern Virginia.* Reprint. Gaithersburg, MD: Butternut Press, n.d.

Shotwell, Ellis Franklin. "War Reminiscences of Mr. E. F. Shotwell." *Greene County Magazine* 7 (1990).

Slivka, Stefan. "Heros von Borcke's Home and Grave in Poland." *Blue & Gray Magazine* 22, no. 4 (Fall 2005).

Smith, Everard, ed. "Watching Lee's Lieutenants." *Civil War: The Magazine of the Civil War Society.* 10, no. 4 (July–August 1992).

Smith, James Power. *With Stonewall Jackson in the Army of Northern Virginia.* Reprint. Gaithersburg, MD: Zullo & Van Sickle, 1982.

Sorrel, G. Moxley. *Recollections of a Confederate Staff Officer.* Edited by Bell I. Wiley. Reprint. Jackson, TN: McCowat-Mercer Press, 1958.

Southern Bivouac. 5 volumes. Reprint. Wilmington, NC: Broadfoot Publishing, 1992–1993.

Southern Historical Society Papers. 52 volumes. Reprint. Wilmington, NC: Broadfoot Publishing, 1990–1992.

Starr, Stephen Z. *The Union Cavalry in the Civil War.* 3 volumes. Baton Rouge: Louisiana State University Press, 1979–1985.

Stevenson, George J. *Increase in Excellence: A History of Emory and Henry College.* New York: Appleton-Century-Crofts, 1963.

Stiles, Kenneth. *4th Virginia Cavalry.* Lynchburg, VA: H. E. Howard, 1985.

Styple, William B., ed. *Generals in Bronze: Interviewing the Commanders of the Civil War.* Kearny, NJ: Belle Grove Publishing, 2005.

————, ed. *Writing and Fighting from the Army of Northern Virginia.* Kearny, NJ: Belle Grove Publishing, 2003.

Supplement to the Official Records of the Union and Confederate Armies. 100 Volumes. Wilmington, NC: Broadfoot Publishing, 1994–2001.

Sutherland, Daniel E. *Seasons of War: The Ordeal of a Confederate Community, 1861–1865.* New York: Free Press, 1995.

————. "Stars in Their Courses." *America's Civil War* 4, no. 4. (November 1991).

Symonds, Craig L. *Joseph E. Johnston: A Civil War Biography.* New York: W. W. Norton, 1992.

Taliaferro, William Booth. "Personal Reminiscences of 'Stonewall' Jackson." *Civil War Times Illustrated* 34, no. 2 (May–June 1995).

Taylor, Walter H. *Four Years with General Lee.* Reprint. Bloomington: Indiana University Press, 1962.

Teague, Chuck. "Leadership Impaired?: The Health of Robert E. Lee During the Gettysburg Campaign." *North & South* 6, no. 5 (July 2003).

Thomas, Emory M. *Bold Dragoon: The Life of J. E. B. Stuart.* New York: Harper & Row, 1986.

————. "'The Greatest Service I Rendered the State': J. E. B. Stuart's Account of the Capture of John Brown." *Virginia Magazine of History and Biography* 94, no. 3 (July 1986).

————. *Robert E. Lee: A Biography.* New York: W. W. Norton, 1995.

————. "Wartime Richmond." *Civil War Times Illustrated* 16, no. 3 (June 1977).

Thomason, John W., Jr. *Jeb Stuart.* New York: Charles Scribner's Sons, 1930.

Thompson, John W., IV. *Horses, Hostages, and Apple Cider: J. E. B. Stuart's 1862 Pennsylvania Raid.* Mercersburg, PA: Mercersburg Printing, 2002.

Tousey, Thomas G. *Military History of Carlisle and Carlisle Barracks.* Richmond, VA: Dietz Press, 1939.

Tower, R. Lockwood, ed. *Lee's Adjutant: The Wartime Letters of Colonel Walter Herron Taylor, 1862–1865.* Columbia: University of South Carolina Press, 1995.

Trout, Robert J. *Galloping Thunder: The Story of the Stuart Horse Artillery Battalion.* Mechanicsburg, PA: Stackpole Books, 2002.

————. *They Followed the Plume: The Story of J. E. B. Stuart and His Staff.* Mechanicsburg, PA: Stackpole Books, 1993.

————, ed. *With Pen and Saber: The Letters and Diaries of J. E. B. Stuart's Staff Officers.* Mechanicsburg, PA: Stackpole Books, 1995.

Troxler, Beverly Barrier, and Auciello Billy Daran Barrier, eds. *Dear Father: Confederate Letters Never Before Published.* Beverly Barrier Troxler and Billy Daran Barrier Auciello, 1989.

Trudeau, Noah Andre. *Gettysburg: A Testing of Courage.* New York: HarperCollins, 2002.

Tucker, Glenn. *Lee and Longstreet at Gettysburg.* Indianapolis: Bobbs-Merrill, 1968.

Tumilty, Victor. "Filling Jackson's Shoes." *Civil War Times Illustrated* 42, no. 2 (June 2003).

Turner, Charles W., ed. *My Dear Emma: War Letters of Col. James K. Edmondson, 1861–1865.* Verona, VA: McClure Printing Company, 1978.

———. *Old Zeus: Life and Letters (1860–62) of James J. White.* Verona, VA: McClure Printing Company, 1983.

———, ed. *Ted Barclay, Liberty Hall Volunteers: Letters from the Stonewall Brigade (1861–1864).* Natural Bridge Station, VA: Rockbridge Publishing, 1992.

Utley, Robert M. *Frontiersmen in Blue: The United States Army and the Indian, 1848–1865.* Lincoln: University of Nebraska Press, 1967.

Vandiver, Frank. *Rebel Brass: The Confederate Command System.* Baton Rouge: Louisiana State University Press, 1956.

Vogtsberger, Margaret Ann, ed. *The Dulanys of Welbourne: A Family in Mosby's Confederacy.* Berryville, VA: Rockbridge Publishing, 1995.

Von Borcke, Heros. *Memoirs of the Confederate War for Independence.* Two volumes in one. Reprint. Dayton, OH: Morningside House, 1985.

Warner, Ezra J. *Generals in Blue: Lives of the Union Commanders.* Baton Rouge: Louisiana State University Press, 1970.

———. *Generals in Gray: Lives of the Confederate Commanders.* Baton Rouge: Louisiana State University Press, 1970.

The War of the Rebellion: A Compilation of the Official Records of the Union and Confederate Armies. 128 Volumes. Washington, D.C.: Government Printing Office, 1880–1902.

Watford, Christopher M., ed. *The Civil War in North Carolina: Soldiers' and Civilians' Letters and Diaries, 1861–1865. Volume 1: The Piedmont.* Jefferson, NC: McFarland, 2003.

Waugh, John C. "Life at the Point." *Civil War Times Illustrated* 41, no. 2 (May 2002).

Wayland, John W. *Virginia Valley Records: Genealogical and Historical Materials of Rockingham County, Virginia and Related Regions (With Map).* Reprint. Baltimore: Genealogical Publishing Co., 1973.

Wells, Edward L. *Hampton and His Cavalry in '64.* Reprint. Camden, SC: Culler Printing, 1997.

Wert, Jeffry D. *A Brotherhood of Valor: The Common Soldiers of the Stonewall Brigade, C.S.A., and the Iron Brigade, U.S.A.* New York: Simon & Schuster, 1999.

———. *Custer: The Controversial Life of George Armstrong Custer.* New York: Simon & Schuster, 1996.

———. *General James Longstreet: The Confederacy's Most Controversial Soldier—A Biography.* New York: Simon & Schuster, 1993.

———. *Gettysburg, Day Three.* New York: Simon & Schuster, 2001.

———. "His Unhonored Service." *Civil War Times Illustrated* 24, no. 4 (June 1985).

———. *Mosby's Rangers.* New York: Simon & Schuster, 1990.

——. *The Sword of Lincoln: The Army of the Potomac*. New York: Simon & Schuster, 2005.

West, John C. *A Texan in Search of a Fight: Being the Diary and Letters of a Private Soldier in Hood's Texas Brigade*. Reprint. Waco, TX: Texian Press, 1969.

Westhaeffer, Paul J. *History of the Cumberland Valley Railroad, 1835–1919*. Washington, D.C.: National Railway Historical Society, 1979.

Wiggins, Sarah Woolfolk, ed. *The Journals of Josiah Gorgas, 1857–1878*. Tuscaloosa: University of Alabama Press, 1995.

Wilkinson, Warren, and Steven E. Woodworth. *A Scythe of Fire: A Civil War Story of the Eighth Georgia Infantry Regiment*. New York: William Morrow, 2002.

Wise, Jennings Cropper. *The Long Arm of Lee: The History of the Artillery of the Army of Northern Virginia*. Reprint. New York: Oxford University Press, 1959.

Wittenberg, Eric J. "The Cavalry Fight in Alsop's Field." *North & South* 6, no. 7 (November 2003).

——. *The Union Cavalry Comes of Age: Hartwood Church to Brandy Station, 1863*. Washington, D.C.: Brassey's, 2003.

Wittenberg Eric J., and J. David Petruzzi. *Plenty of Blame to Go Around: Jeb Stuart's Controversial Ride to Gettysburg*. New York: Savas Beatie, 2006.

Younger, Edward, ed. *Inside the Confederate Government: The Diary of Robert Garlick Hill Kean*. New York: Oxford University Press, 1957.

Index

Page numbers in *italics* refer to maps.